Kenneth Tynan

Kenneth Tynan: A Life

Dominic Shellard

Yale University Press
New Haven and London

For John, with all my love

For information about this and other Yale University Press publications, please contact:

U.S. Office: sales.press@yale.edu   yalebooks.com
Europe Office: sales@yaleup.co.uk   www.yaleup.co.uk

Set in Columbus and Officina by Northern Phototypesetting Co. Ltd, Bolton
Printed in Great Britain by Biddles Ltd, Guildford and Kings Lynn

Library of Congress Cataloging-in-Publication Data

Shellard, Dominic.
Kenneth Tynan: writing for posterity/by Dominic Shellard.
p. cm.
Includes bibliographical references.
ISBN 0-300-09919-3 (cloth: alk. paper)
1. Tynan, Kenneth, 1927-2. Authors, English—20th
century—Biography. 3. Theater critics—Great Britain—Biography. 4.
Theatrical producers and directors—Great Britain—Biography. 5.
Dramatic criticism—Great Britain—History—20th century. I. Title.
PR6070. Y6Z87 2003
822'.009—dc21   2003005830

A catalogue record for this book is available from the British Library.

10 9 8 7 6 5 4 3 2 1

Contents

Illustrations

Unless otherwise noted all photographs are © Roxana and Matthew Tynan

Introduction

I first became aware of someone – or something – called Kenneth Tynan when I was fourteen. My father was a heavy smoker and this caused all kinds of rows in our house about overflowing ashtrays that were rarely emptied, nicotine-induced car-sickness and yellowing walls. My sisters, Jess and Son, hated the parental rows, or, more often, silences, that were provoked by the 'cancer-sticks'. I longed for him to give up. Then, one day in 1980, he did. 'What's happened, Dad?' I asked. 'Kenneth Tynan's just died,' he said. I had no idea who Kenneth Tynan was, but he seemed a miracle worker to me. The more I subsequently learned about his contribution to British theatre, the more I discovered that this was quite an accurate description of him.

At school, I played a lot of sport, threw myself into all kinds of plays and sat my O Levels. One of my English teachers, Bob Jope ('the teacher you never forget', according to the Department for Education and Science's advertising campaign), recognising my left of centre sensibilities, suggested I read Kenneth Tynan's review of John Osborne's *Look Back in Anger*. I enjoyed it very much. It made me want to go to see the play. His indignation at what had gone before and the passion for this new direction had a very persuasive and muscular appeal – 'all scum and a mile wide', he had actually written – but it was sensitive, too. I liked the calculation of the silent minority of under-thirties, the claim that he could not love anyone who did not wish to see the play with him and his incisive, witty, wounding turn of phrase. Even though I had no idea about the context in which the review had been written, it all seemed to matter to him.

While I was at university, Dad bought me the collection of Tynan's reviews in *A View of the English Stage*. I read through the work. How rude he was about Loamshire plays. How convinced he was that they should be swept away. The writing seemed astonishingly fresh, even thirty-five years later. Ironically, my first book was to be about Tynan's great rival, Harold Hobson. Thrashing around for a Ph.D. topic, disconcerted that my original idea to write about the influence of Brecht on post-war British theatre (unwittingly influenced by Tynan) had been dreamed up by over a hundred students before me, I was relieved when my tutor, Francis Warner, suggested I go and see this ageing ex-critic, forgotten in his care home in Westhampnett, near Littlehampton. He was shrivelled and charming, and told me that his archive was currently being sold by the antiquarian book sellers, Quaritch's. If I hurried, I might be able to have a peek at it before it was sold.

This was the quest I had been looking for: sifting through archives (deeply unfashionable in academic circles in the early 1990s), differentiating between the paper bill and the letter from Pinter and trying to piece together a theatrical life long since forgotten. It was the detective work I had always hoped to conduct. As I was poring through Hobson's cutting books, I conducted my literature search for relevant material, as all good research students need to, and came across Kathleen Tynan's magnificent *A Life of Kenneth Tynan* (1988), which received rapturous reviews. I quickly read it. It was a wonderful evocation of her husband's life from the point of view of a second wife, who entered his world in 1962, but it was – perhaps inevitably – tilted to the National Theatre years. The part of his career that I wanted to learn about, his career as a theatre critic from 1952 to 1963 – the part which I have subsequently concluded encapsulates his brilliance – was curiously insubstantial.

No matter, I was writing about Hobson, but as I was about to turn my Ph.D. into my first book, *Harold Hobson: Witness and Judge*, Tynan intruded again. The *Evening Standard*, the first paper that employed him as a theatre critic, announced in their Diary column in 1995 that Kathleen Tynan had sold the Tynan archive to the British Library. Might there be any material in it relating to Hobson? I made a spec-ulative phone call to the Department of Manuscripts. The wonderful Sally Brown, the Curator of Modern Literary Manuscripts, who has since become a much-loved friend, patiently answered my inane questions. No, it was not possible to pull out any material relating to Hobson; No, the archive had not been catalogued yet, as it had only just been purchased, but, Yes, I could come and have a quick look.

Given my knowledge of Hobson and British theatre of this period, I was quickly able to establish that there was certain material that Kathleen Tynan had decided not to use for her book, and it was then that I conceived the initial idea for *Kenneth Tynan: A Life*. In 1994, Kathleen Tynan had published *Kenneth Tynan: Letters*, a metic-ulously researched volume of letters that Tynan had written. But I now knew that there were scores of letters written *to* him, that she had decided, perhaps for rea-sons of copyright or pressing deadlines (she was suffering from cancer by this stage) not to publish. I also felt that there would come a time when a work should be written that located Tynan firmly within the context of the development of post-war British theatre, to which he had contributed so much.

That time, I hope, is now, in 2003. Janet Munsil's stage depiction of Tynan's elegiac encounter with Louise Brooks, *Smoking with Lulu* (2000), necessarily focused attention in the new millennium on the last few years of his life – years of declining health, desperately failing self-confidence and personal self-loathing. The publication of the *Diaries* (2001) edited by John Lahr, Tynan's select (and selective) record of that period, unfortunately contributed to the sense that the pitiful last decade represented his whole career. Their explicit detailing of his sexual preference for spanking overshadowed everything, and reviewers wrote with a mixture of regret and titillation – not dissimilar to the reaction to *Oh, Calcutta!* in 1970. Even Elaine Dundy's autobiography, *Life Itself!* (2001), was considered notable not for its detailing of her life with Tynan between 1951 and 1963, but for the fact that he spanked her with a schoolmaster's cane and allegedly broke her nose in an ugly scene of wife-beating.

Michael Billington of the *Guardian*, whose prescience, style and gentle political commitment reminds me strongly of Tynan, made the following observation about *Smoking with Lulu* – and it could equally apply to the other two publications:

> What Munsil never captures . . . is the thing that makes Tynan really significant and that earns him a foothold in posterity: his combination of a voluptuous prose style with a crusading moral fervour. As a critic, he fought for a socially committed drama, a national theatre and an internationalist outlook with all the eloquence at his command. And he did this not in language of pseudo-academic earnestness, but in prose which clicks into place with the satisfying resonance of billiard balls struck by a perfectly aimed cue.[1]

For all the wisdom of this, such is the power of Tynan's salacious reputation that the article still appeared under the title (over which Billington presumably had no control) 'Spanks for the Memory'. This is precisely why, in my study of Kenneth Tynan's life, I have deliberately chosen to foreground his writing on the theatre, in the hope that this might introduce the twenty-first-century reader to the reviews of this brilliant man, who also just happened to be the first person to say 'fuck' on television, as well as explain why he played such a key role in the evolution of post-war British drama.

Harold Hobson, who launched Tynan on his career, and who bitterly regretted his early death in 1980, made the following observation on his younger rival's unique achievement: 'No one could manage with such superlative skill as Tynan the rapier that went through the heart of every charlatan or pretender to a talent he hadn't really got. He was sometimes considered supreme only in the art of destruction but this was entirely untrue. He recognised merit and praised it and reached heights of eloquence in doing so, often when it was hidden from everybody else.'[2] I hope that I have managed to capture the essence of this praise from Tynan's old sparring partner in the chapters that follow.

Acknowledgements

I would like to record my thanks to the following people:

Roxana and Matthew Tynan, for their support and encouragement of this project. John Walker, who has been so patient and supportive throughout this long process; Robert Baldock, editor *par excellence* at Yale, whose advice I always respect, Diana Yeh, Kevin Brown, Beth Humphries, Liz Smith, Douglas Matthews; Jessica Shellard, Sonya Shellard, Marcus Shellard, Christine Shellard; my great friend Sally Brown, Senior Curator, Modern Literary Manuscripts, British Library; the magnificent Kathryn Johnson, Curator of Drama, British Library; the staff in the Manuscripts Reading Room, British Library; Allan Hailstone; Gina Loveday, Anna Chester, John Haffenden, Miriam Handley, Bill McDonnell, Neil Roberts, the Arts and Humanities Research Board; Jacky Hodgson, Sheffield University Library; Michael Hannon, Director, Sheffield University Library, Vanessa Toulmin, Research Director of the National Fairground Archive; Beverley Hart, Theatre Museum; Steve Nicholson, Sarah-Jane Dickenson, Jack Reading; the staff at Durham University Library; the staff at the Brotherton Library, Leeds University; the staff at the Theatre Museum, Covent Garden; the staff at the Central Library, Leeds; Andy Ducker, QPR, David Lewis; Rosie Coughlan, Laura Priddle, Richard Eyre, Helen English, Helen Towers, the Sheffield University Research Fund; Sheffield University for granting me study leave to complete this book; Sally Shuttleworth; Rupert Rhymes, the Arts Council of England; Sue Powell, Rosy Runciman, Tracy Tynan and Elaine Dundy.

For permission to reprint extracts from copyright material the author and publishers gratefully acknowledge the following:

Roxana and Matthew Tynan, Tracy Tynan, Elaine Dundy, Jocelyn Herbert, Zoë Wanamaker, Helen Osborne, the Trustees of the Terence Rattigan Trust, Colin

Wilson, Christopher Logue, Alistair Cooke, the Comtesse Laurian d'Harcourt, the *Observer*, *The Sunday Times* and Bloomsbury Publishing Plc.

The extract from *The Sound of Two Hands Clapping* by Kenneth Tynan, published by Jonathan Cape is used by permission of the Random House Group Limited.

Extracts from Harold Hobson's reviews for *The Sunday Times* are © Times Newspapers Limited, London 1947–1976.

Extracts from Kenneth Tynan's published reviews are © Roxana and Matthew Tynan.

Every effort has been made to contact all copyright holders. The publishers will be glad to make good in any future editions any errors or omissions brought to their attention.

Chapter 1 *A Gift for Performance*

Sir Peter Peacock had a secret. From every Monday to Wednesday he was an astute businessman, successful politician and respected civic dignitary in the northern industrial town of Warrington. Nowadays the town is eager to proclaim itself as the birthplace of the film star Pete Postlethwaite and the former Beirut hostage Terry Waite, but at the dawn of the twentieth century it capitalised on its significance as a staging post from north to south by becoming an important manufacturing and trading centre on the River Mersey. Sir Peter's business empire centred on a series of shops that in the range of products and services they offered foreshadowed the modern supermarket. He was a well-known local councillor, having been elected in 1903 to represent the Liberal Party in Bewsey ward, and he enjoyed being a prominent local figure, first as a Justice of the Peace and – ultimately – as Mayor of the town in 1913. He had come a long way since leaving school in 1886 aged fourteen to go and work on the railways, and the mayoralty was an honour he was to hold on an impressive five further occasions, before being awarded the freedom of the Borough in 1918.

For the rest of the week Sir Peter Peacock lived as plain Peter Tynan eighty miles to the south of Warrington in the city of Birmingham as the unmarried partner – although to the eyes of their local community as the husband – of Letitia Rose Tynan. He had first come across Rose at a Warrington whist drive towards the end of the First World War. She was working for the Post Office, and the attraction was so strong for Peter that by 1921 he had decided to set up a separate home with the thirty-three-year-old Rose in Birmingham, well away from his wife, Maria, and his five children. Maria was actually Peter's second wife, having married him in 1893, three years after his first wife (Maria's sister Annie) had died in childbirth.

Peter immediately set about creating an elaborate double life. It was an incredible achievement, since he was possibly the most famous resident of Warrington. He played an energetic role in the war effort, by continually urging the men of the town to enlist, and was rewarded for his patriotism on 3 June 1918 with a knighthood. Rose accompanied him to Buckingham Palace for the investiture.[1] This prominence was no bar to taking the socially hazardous step of deserting his wife (now Lady Peacock) and choosing a distant city as his main residence. He joined forces with his brother, Albert, who was already established in Birmingham in a drapery business, and continued to develop his portfolio of land, housing and industrial firms. He possessed the wealth and confidence to be ferried by a chauffeur-driven Daimler or to take the train back to Warrington each week to look after his interests and, remarkably, he would maintain an active link with Warrington politics, as President of the local Liberal Party, until 1945. If people objected to his unusual domestic arrangement they kept their mutterings to themselves. Lady Peacock maintained a comfortable standard of living in Warrington, and her husband went to great lengths to ensure that the two parts of his complicated life never came into contact. He even possessed two ration cards during the Second World War. So began the exoticism tinged with sadness that was to become the pattern of his famous son's life.

It was into this strange environment that Kenneth Peacock Tynan was born on 2 April 1927 at the Hall Green nursing home, Birmingham. His father was fifty-four and his mother thirty-eight. Many of his Oxford contemporaries felt that his middle name was a suitable affectation for a flamboyant personality, but in reality it seems to be his father's one concession to his concealed antecedents. Although it is hard to credit that the 'secret' knowledge of his extended family in Warrington could have been hidden from the young boy, all the evidence points to the fact that Tynan only felt the full force of Peter's bizarre deception at the time of his father's death in 1948. From that moment on, he cut away from his Birmingham world as decisively as his father had sliced his own world in two.

A pronounced stammer prevented the much-doted-on boy from talking until the age of three. Although some, such as Eric Bentley, would wonder whether it was put on for show,[2] it was to impede his speech to varying degrees for the rest of his life, but the mellifluousness of his theatre criticism and the richness of his rhetoric would later compensate for any occasional inarticulacy, and from an early age he showed a prodigious interest in words and writing. At his first school in College Road, Birmingham, which he began attending in 1932, he started a journal at the precocious age of six, and at his second, the George Dixon Elementary School, he became a voracious reader of books and magazines. But it was at King Edward's, Birmingham, where he started as a Foundation Scholar in 1938, that his true precocity became apparent. Peter Tynan, concerned at the pampering he had received from his docile mother and wealthy father, had been minded to send his son to boarding school, but it seems that he bowed to his wife's desire to keep Kenneth in Birmingham, for fear of him discovering the family secret if he went elsewhere.[3] It was a decision that served their son well, for he flourished at the long-established grammar school. Academically gifted, he sailed through his schoolwork effortlessly, winning twelve school prizes along the way and receiving distinctions in several subjects. He became the secretary to the debating and literary societies, editor of the school magazine and a member of the 1st XI cricket team. A twice-weekly cinema-goer, he developed an early critical touchstone for assessing the quality of the films that he saw – could he remember if he had enjoyed them?[4] – and the touchstone film *par excellence* was *Citizen Kane*, which he saw five times when it came to Birmingham in March 1942. Fired by his mother's enthusiasm, he started to enjoy the music hall and theatre and was taken by her to see Donald Wolfit in *Macbeth* in 1938, a production that was to make a huge impression, and which he would see four times over the next six years; and an early sign of his predilection for hero worship emerged in his fastidious desire to collect signatures. Between 1939 and 1941 he had managed to obtain Winston Churchill's and the larger part of the war cabinet; and an aggrieved letter to the music hall comedian Arthur Askey, written in 1940, reveals the determination with which he set about his pursuit:

Dear Mr Askey,

This is the third time I have written to you, and on each of the previous occasions, I have been sent a photo with a PRINT of your autograph on it. Please, this time, could you oblige by sending me your personal autograph? I know you must get many requests for it, but couldn't you just do it this once, personally? I could not consider my collection complete without your autograph (personal!) in it. Third time lucky?

(Still) Your faithful 'fan',
(Master) Kenneth Tynan[5]

The twelve-year-old Master Tynan's persistence produced the desired result – Askey sent him a handwritten note – and Askey would not be the last person to succumb to his literary persuasiveness.

With academic success came intellectual confidence and an eagerness to make an impression on his contemporaries. One memorable way in which he achieved this was through a stylish and unorthodox dress sense. By the time Tynan was sixteen he was wearing a ladies' raincoat in black and white check, carrying an elegant black umbrella with a red silk ribbon wrapped around it and languidly smoking a Brazilian cigarette from a lengthy cigarette holder. Many of his most devoted admirers in the 1950s admired the louche, engaging way that he toyed with a cigarette. It seemed the epitome of style and cool – until emphysema killed him in 1980, providing the post-war generation with another iconic reminder of the dangers of smoking. His lifelong public celebration of sex began when he took part in a school debate and contested the motion that 'This House Thinks the Present Generation Has Lost the Ability to Entertain Itself' by eulogising the pleasures of masturbation, and he stood as an 'Independent Confucian' in a Civics Society election with an extremely progressive manifesto that included the repeal of the laws against abortion and homosexuality. In this, he was at least twenty years ahead of his time.

Apart from being evacuated with his class to Bournemouth Boys' School on the south coast for two terms on the declaration of war, the conflict seems to have impinged little on Tynan's life. By the winter of 1943 he was planning to make his first trip to London to see his great schoolfriend, Julian Holland. Julian, who was two years older than him, had just started a job with the BBC in the capital, having managed to avoid military service because of poor eyesight. Their correspondence, which began in September 1943, spawned well over a hundred letters and helps provide an insight into Tynan's thoughts during his last years at school and first years at university. At King Edward's they had collaborated on productions of *Alice* and *Hamlet* for the school drama society, and they were bound together by a love of theatre, movies and all things American. Holland would later become, amongst other things, a leader writer and jazz critic for the *Daily Mail*, a contributor to the ground-breaking satirical television show, *That Was The Week That Was*, the author of two books about Tottenham Hotspur Football Club and, principally, editor of the BBC *Today* programme on Radio 4 between 1981 and 1986, which he developed into the most important news programme on air. This varied and fruitful career mirrored the eclectic interests that he shared with Tynan.

Tynan's parents were at first opposed to his visit to the capital, as he confided to his friend in December 1943:

My parents have chosen to take my going to London as a matter for a vote of confidence. They say I have no right to go against their wishes at sixteen; and my mother has threatened (quite seriously) to disinherit me if I go. My father has become extremely traditional about it; he chooses to see a sinister design behind you taking a flat just before I arrive, and I think he thinks you are homosexual. My visiting aunts, uncles, and firemen have been enlisted to help her plead. I have had to insult them all, severally; to one weeping relation I actually said, 'Get the hell out of here, you bore me'. A family split is imminent; my mother feels the rest of the gang are laughing at her lack of control over me.

Their objections had apparently been precipitated by Holland's casual remark that the flat would be a fine brothel and Rose now viewed him as 'the incarnation of Carnal Temptation'. The suggested solution reveals as much about Tynan's attitude to his mother (which was as indifferent as it was indulgent), as it does about the two teenagers' plans for high jinks: 'What I want is for you to write to her, and explain how foolish her doubts and fears are. Be stolid, sober, and sincere, and she'll lap it up. Tell her what a good, restrained chap you are, and make her laugh at her qualms.'[6]

Holland was suitably emollient. Rose Tynan eventually relented and her son made his first trip to London, where he saw almost twenty plays and recorded his impressions as embryonic reviews. Many of these were incorporated in his first book, *He That Plays the King* (1950), which was so crucial in launching his professional career.

From now on Tynan's letters to Holland are peppered with anecdotes about his own immersion in theatre at King Edward's, such as deciding to play Shylock in a modern dress production of *The Merchant of Venice* as a 'young man, prematurely aged through persecution',[7] as well as his own observations about the plays that he witnessed at the Theatre Royal, Birmingham. As with so many of his contemporaries living in the regions, his imagination was particularly fired by Donald Wolfit. When he became a critic, Tynan was to tangle notoriously with this actor-manager, who viewed Tynan's reviews of him as brutal and vicious, but as a schoolboy he was fascinated by his energy and bravura. Wolfit's 1938 Macbeth, which he saw when he was eleven, stuck in his mind for several years and initially made heroic acting the virtue that he most enjoyed in the theatre. From an early twenty-first-century perspective, with the Arts Council of England eagerly supporting a long-overdue revival in the fortunes of regional theatre, it is salutary to be reminded that in 1944 Tynan's earliest sustained contact with live drama came about because of the willingness of Wolfit to eschew the theatre of London in favour of gruelling autumn and spring tours throughout the country. In spite of the London-centric approach of Tynan's later criticism, theatre in Britain has never been completely synonymous with theatre in London.

Wolfit's Hamlet at Stratford-upon-Avon in 1936 had elevated him to the ranks of the great performers of the day and the following year he formed the Donald Wolfit Shakespeare Company. Even at this early stage of his touring career, he was viewed by some as a more accomplished producer than actor, and most of his productions were initially a financial success. From 1938 to 1944 Wolfit cast himself in virtually all the major Shakespearian roles and during the Battle of Britain he earned great admiration for giving over a hundred lunchtime performances of Shakespearian scenes to help maintain morale. But it was his classic performance of King Lear in 1944 which finally earned him as much respect for his talent as his industriousness.

In 1943, his performance of the role had prompted James Agate of the *Sunday Times* to record that Wolfit must be 'relegated to the category of the immensely talented' since '*he does nothing which we cannot explain*'.[8] His face was too fleshy and round and he did not possess for the critic the aura of the tragedian. The following year, however, Wolfit bravely returned to the role. This time Agate was not alone in being bowled over, and he was happy to alter his judgement completely. Now there was nothing that could be explained, he wrote: 'Mr Wolfit had and was all the things we demand, and created the impression Lear calls for. I say deliberately that his performance on Wednesday was the greatest piece of Shakespearean acting I have ever seen since I have been privileged to write for the *Sunday Times*.'[9] Following this review, helpfully entitled 'Every Inch King Lear', the theatre was quickly sold out for the season, and Wolfit – albeit briefly – was the theatrical superstar of the nation.

In March 1944, Tynan's eyes and ears in London sent him a review of Wolfit's *Richard III* and his response to Holland reveals the embryonic critic: 'Agate always regarded this as one of his best: though, as Wolfit would be the first to admit, the moon-like face he possesses, shroud it though he may in whiskers and bedizen it with lines, is, like Garrick's, essentially a comic face, a comic mask, perhaps (witness his garrulous Bottom . . .).' There were some more serious flaws, though, and ones which established critics would progressively highlight – the poor supporting players of the company (which some would argue was a deliberate casting choice to show off the leading man in the very best light) and the laughably tasteless costumes. 'I agree with you about Wolfit's women players,' Tynan added; 'they succeeded in wrecking Lear. Agate's theory of the great actor dominating all rather falls through in practice, for even a Gielgud could not overawe such flimsy baggages as Wolfit is provided with.'[10] For now, though, Tynan concurred with Agate that the actor transcended the limitations of those around him.

Ten days later, he is recording for Holland with infectious enthusiasm the Wolfit performances he has witnessed: Macbeth (performed annually since 1937) was 'wild, rasping, and gory' (although the witches' scenes received 'their usual dreadful handling'). Lear (since 1942) was 'probably his best performance. Full of dignity, and with a grand entrance . . . Wolfit combines power with pathos to a remarkable degree.' *Twelfth Night* (since 1937) contained 'a nicely lugubrious Malvolio' and *A Midsummer Night's Dream* saw Wolfit play 'Bottom with great gusto' since 'he has a clown's mask'.[11]

The end of 1944 provided a week-long pre-Christmas feast of Wolfit for the Birmingham theatre-goers and Tynan, writing without capitals because his typewriter could only print them below the line, was there to record his impressions for his friend. Hazlitt would 'have loved' Wolfit's performance of Jonson's Volpone (added to his touring repertoire in 1942), for 'almost lovingly wolfit savoured every syllable; and in the colossal "milk of unicorns and panther's breath" speech the house was burdened with verbal perfume. how he impressed too with the hissing delivery of his triumphant "i am volpone, and thisssss my sssslave".' The young fan was hooked by Wolfit's mesmeric presence – 'the prowl which this great actor affects, the splayed-out hands and muscular solidity were terribly effective i bravoed at the last curtain – the first time i have ever done so. i would as happily see wolfit do this splendid comedy as see ellen terry in any of shakespeares' – and even if the rest of the company were not up to the occasion – 'joan greenwood was very bad' – it had been a thrilling event.

Wolfit's performance of Hamlet was equally impressive. The production 'spoke throughout of wonderfully accurate forethought' and his curtain call (a notable feature of every Wolfit show) was 'as ever, gorgeously theatrical', although the unfortunate Miss Greenwood was only 'tolerable'. But the *pièce de résistance* came, as always, with Wolfit's Macbeth, and in his evocation of the atmosphere of the occasion the seventeen-year-old fan gives an early hint of his unique talent for memorialising great performances: '. . . after much thought i find my ultimate opinion coincides with my original, spontaneous impression. this is the greatest piece of shakespearean acting i have ever seen.' The supreme moment came at the end:

> when macduff announces that he was 'untimely ripped', wolfit let fall his sword; and instantly the clang of battle ceased, and all became a pregnant hush. again, my heart all but stopped when wolfit bellowed at macduff: 'my names macbeeeeeettthh . . .' tomorrowandtomorrow i cannot imagine better spoken; what a violent, extravagant, peerless man of men! all must bow to him. his mastery of macbeth is absolute.[12]

In the same month Tynan learned that having sat the entrance exam for Oxford University and been interviewed by the critic and novelist C.S. Lewis, he had been rewarded for his academic prowess by being awarded a scholarship of £50 per year in Modern Subjects at Magdalen College, Oxford. It was the only one that they offered.

During his last year at school Tynan became involved with a local amateur theatre group called the New Dramatic Company (NDC). He proposed a typical trade-off: he would recruit several of his friends to play some of the minor male roles that the company could not fill, if they would allow him to play the part of Hamlet in a version that he and Julian Holland had been wrestling over for almost twelve months. Initially the committee of the company was unimpressed. After the decision was taken to make the first full-scale production of 1945 a light piece called *Berkeley Square*, Tynan reported his pessimism to his collaborator: 'I am doing my best to get into their good books; I even accepted a "bit" part in "B.S." to sweeten

them. But they all (the Committee, I mean) seem scared of *Hamlet*, especially since
they know next to nothing of the proposed protagonist. Still, we must hope. I am
myself feeling extremely downcast.'[13]

Things seemed more promising in the first month of 1945. Harry James, a member of the committee, had told him that the prospects for his proposed production
were now 'moderately bright' and this may have been in part due to a lecture that
Tynan had delivered to the school literary society, entitled 'Towards a New
Hamlet'. Having enlisted the help of Hugh Manning, a twenty-three-year-old NDC
actor (whom Tynan wanted to direct his *Hamlet*) to help read out extracts, the
determined tragedian delivered an impressively wide-ranging talk. He summarised
over twenty critical views of the play; discussed the great Hamlets of the British
stage (using the prompt copy of Kemble's Drury Lane *Hamlet*); took in several overseas productions; offered his main thesis that Shakespeare's strength was not as a
psychoanalyst but lay in his ability to achieve a 'willing suspension of disbelief';
and concluded by delivering some soliloquies and explaining how, if given the
chance, he would cut the play.[14] It was an audition piece *par excellence*.

With this characteristic mix of impudence and confidence, Tynan snared his
quarry. At the end of January the committee decided – 'by a narrow but perceptible
majority'[15] – that Tynan's *Hamlet* could take place with full financial support in late
May or June, and rehearsals quickly began. By March the young lead optimistically
believed that the 'theatrical circles in Birmingham are buzzing'[16] with the project.
The intensity of cutting lines, rewriting scenes and trying out new adaptations – not
to mention shouldering the responsibility of performing the lead in one of the most
demanding plays ever written – was increased by Tynan's flirtatious and transient
relationships with a number of women. Throughout his life he would experience a
cornucopia of tempestuous liaisons and these began in his adolescence. His initial
disappointment at the discovery that his Ophelia, Pauline Whittle, had a boyfriend
was tempered by the belief that she was 'very young [and] very impressionable', and
that she liked 'people who have preserved their poetic souls in the industrial heart
of the empire e.g. me'.[17] While he waited for his charm to work on her, he transferred his attention to another member of the company, only known by her first
name, Irene. She seemed quite prepared to sleep with him – 'I judged that she would
and could do it' – but it then emerged that she was 'too deeply entangled' and would
prefer to wait for his return from university.[18] Enid Julian, however, appeared much
more amenable, as he intimated in February to his confidant –

I am now within a pebble's flip of a sordid physical affair with petite, enigmatic,
intellectual 24 year old Enid . . . What gives me added zest is the fact that Enid
is also Lionel Dunn's mistress. Yes, Lionel is bisexual, with a slight preference for

the homo. What an imbroligo! Enid playing second fiddle to dozens of fiancés! I am taking her to the Molière play at the Rep (a new translation of *Le Malade imaginaire*). And (at last) she bites when she kisses. Hard. And I love it.[19]

– and two weeks later he finally lost his virginity with her, even if it was predictably and humorously problematic:

> . . . this is the big news, this week's psychological headline, this week's burn-this-immediately – I *have* slept in the same bed as Lionel Dunn. Last Wednesday. I went round to her flat, played around with her for awhile, and playfully desired her to undress. She did, instantly – stripped stark naked and leapt and lunged at me. God, what could I do? It was coitus interruptus at its juiciest. I have no illusions: she is a ruinous cobra, and a despicable hoyden; but she fascinates. I have not yet decided whether I am the fly and she the flypaper, or I the fly and she the ointment . . . Incidentally, I wrote a poem about my Enid experience. You see I had to try twice; the first time, vibrate as she might, I was impotent. It is a delightful poem and most subtly pornographic.[20]

In spite of his initial embarrassment – Tynan was nothing if not resilient – all appeared well and he asked Holland in March if Enid could accompany him to London on a planned visit to the capital. Two days later, however, he wrote again to announce that 'Enid is not coming to London. I can't stand her!'[21] He was now 'hysterically in love with Joy Matthews', with whom he had spent a weekend in Stratford. This whirligig of affairs came to a brutal end shortly after VE (Victory in Europe) night in May 1945, when he was stood up by his latest love. In an anguished, almost desperate letter, he revealed his humiliation and gave a hint of the introspection and depression that was to cloud much of his life, as well as his enviable ability to bounce back. During a night out with friends in Birmingham, he became aware that his new girlfriend had left his side:

> Then I noticed something. Joy, who would never let me kiss her in public, was kissing Bernard Owen all over the place in public. As on the previous night, she had arranged to meet me, and without a word disappeared with somebody else.
>
> At first I didn't mind. I told myself that, as before, everyone was kissing everyone else. I went around and kissed everyone else just to demonstrate the point to myself.
>
> Then we left the Union – about 100 strong – and made for Moseley, led by Hugh. The horrible rasping sore throat I had was getting rapidly worse. And so far as I could see the only two honourable girls in the party were Pat Evans and Pat Brewer. We walked along in a colossal line spread out across Bristol Road – all except Joy and Bernard, who walked ecstatically in front, embracing each

other every few yards. Then I got mad. I went completely berserk and walked bang into the headlights of a car approaching along Priory Rd. I was utterly, utterly despondent, and I ran wildly towards them. Hugh brought me down into the gutter by a flying tackle as the car passed. I dashed off after Joy, croaking in a reedy hoarse treble that I was taking her home and that I would slit both their throats if they didn't stop. Of course, they didn't. They stopped, *laughed at me* (O Christ) and proceeded to neck in front of me in the middle of the road.

It took eight of them to stop me strangling the filthy bitch and that low bastard.

Finally Hugh (who was perfectly *wonderful* to me all evening) suggested that we go to Moseley Park. Joy and Bernard had to go. I ran up to Joy and croaked goodnight. She laughed and walked on. I didn't see her again.

Desperate for consolation, Tynan explains how he invited another friend back home with him, and gives an insight into the awkward relationship he enjoyed with his mother, Rose:

That night I invited Pat Brewer to stop the night with me, as Hugh was running me home in the car anyway. She came. But mother *refused* to entertain her, and made her leave to walk 8 miles home. I was completely humiliated, and had to drag her back in tears. Mother was still nagging and shouting, and swearing not to give her any breakfast. I managed to smuggle her into a bed at about 3.30a.m., but she had gone by 7. Julian, I just cannot stand any more humiliation. I want to kill Joy, and to kill my mother. I write in the warm light of midmorning. This is not madness that I have uttered.[22]

His powers of recovery at the age of eighteen were swift, however. A few weeks later, at the beginning of June, he was announcing to Holland that the pursuit of the first object of his affections had paid off since he and Pauline Whittle, his Ophelia, were now intending to get engaged! After being stood up by her over a lunch date, he had bombarded her with phone calls and her resistance finally cracked when she made the confession that for the last six months she had 'been worshipping the ground' he walked on. Tynan knew that this information would come as a 'colossal surprise',[23] but this was trumped by the swiftly succeeding revelation that he had had a quick fling with an anonymous woman merely two days later. It might have been undertaken because he 'had a reputation as a libertine to keep up'[24] – but it did not bode well for the durability of the engagement. Tynan would always find it difficult to be monogamous.

The rest of his final summer as a schoolboy was less stressful. Buoyed by the discovery that the Minister for National Service, Ernest Bevin, had announced to the House of Commons that Oxbridge scholarship holders would be able to defer their military service to take up their places at university, Tynan was able to devote himself to the looming production of *Hamlet*. It opened in early June and its impresario and leading actor was thrilled by the attention that it brought him. '*Hamlet* was a great success,' he excitedly told Holland:

> Every seat at the Midland Institute was sold, and we had even to add an extra row of seats. This done, there were still people standing at the back of the hall. A very still and awed audience in every respect; the only centre of opposition being Lionel Dunn [Tynan's early rival], who, like the parasite he is, came on someone else's complimentary ticket. His only comment on the show was: 'Thanks, I had a very comfortable seat.' He showed his pedantic disapproval of the cuts by refraining from applauding and walking straight out, talking loudly, at the final curtain.

Of more significance was the view of outsiders:

> Kemp [the drama critic of the *Birmingham Post*] has begun to respect us. His crit . . . did us the signal honour of judging us by the standards of a professional company; that is, of assessing how much we fell short of the highest, & not by how much we excelled the lowest. He mentioned us as textual editors, and patently disapproved of the cutting of the advice to the players; and, in a moment of childish pedagoguery, put the word 'editors' in inverted commas.
>
> Of my performance, he said that I tended to argue too much, and that I should learn to appeal to the heart instead of to the head. He just did not like our reading of the Nunnery scene; he thinks it should be all rant; and he holds it fit that he should be the law on such matters of interpretation. He commends my forethought, but says uncompromisingly and flatly that my readings are 'often mistaken'. Nevertheless he insists that I always 'command attention'.[25]

It was an attribute that he would never lose.

Ignoring Kemp's critical slight on their editorial pretensions, Tynan, harking back to his days as an autograph collector, swiftly wrote to the hugely popular John Gielgud, to suggest that the cut version of *Hamlet* with which he was intending to tour Burma should be theirs. Gielgud seems to have been underwhelmed. 'He wrote back to say that he had already chosen the version he was going to use,' Tynan revealed, '& that he had done a Certain Amount of That Sort of Thing in his Time Before.'[26] Perhaps Tynan subconsciously recalled this peremptory response when – to general astonishment – he remorselessly mocked Gielgud's productions and performances in print during the mid-1950s.

Tynan enjoyed a more beneficial contact with a significant member of the theatre industry when he rounded off his career at King Edward's by organising a sixth-form conference. The events on offer were eclectic: a further performance by the New Dramatic Company of *Hamlet*, a recital of Mozart's Clarinet Concerto, a cricket match, a screening of *Citizen Kane*, for which he provided an introduction, and a talk by James Agate of the *Sunday Times*. At the end of the Second World War, the sixty-seven-year-old Agate was the pre-eminent theatre critic of his day. He had occupied the post since 1923, having begun to write for the *Manchester Guardian* in 1907, but in 1945 he was as well known for his *Ego* diaries (eventually totalling nine volumes, covering 1932 to 1948), as he was for his criticism. These diaries, which record his experience of London theatrical life in which we encounter the distinctive personalities of the time, are noteworthy for the style, wit and dynamism of the diarist. They reveal a critic aware of the literary tradition in which he is writing; one who is confident that his readers will trust his intuition in judging the theatrical temper of a piece; and one who is suspicious of too intellectual and theoretical an approach to criticism, preferring to refer to acknowledged models of theatrical excellence, such as Irving for acting (all traits that his successor, and Tynan's great critical rival, Harold Hobson, would inherit in varying degrees). They also demonstrate a Wildean delight in the pithy phrase or sentence that presents a point with clarity and brilliance whilst simultaneously highlighting the pertinacity of the raconteur. An example of this occurs in *Ego 8*, where Agate mentions his visit to King Edward's. On being asked after his talk to define the rules for good dramatic criticism, Agate replied that there were only two that mattered: 'One. Decide what the playwright was trying to do, and pronounce how well or ill he has done it. Two. Determine whether the well-done thing was worth doing at all.'[27]

Although this ostentatious clarity was sometimes compromised in his journalistic criticism by a predilection for the grandiloquent phrase which often said more about the observer than the observed, Agate cut a noteworthy figure in the 1930s and the 1940s. With his love of champagne and enormous cigars, flamboyant behaviour and devoted readership, he was someone whom the *Sunday Times* could be proud to count amongst its staff. There was one fact about Agate, though, of which the proprietor of the newspaper, the morally conservative Lord Kemsley, was, remarkably, unaware, given that it was an open secret throughout theatrical London – Agate was an energetic homosexual. Having met the distinguished speaker at Birmingham station in the middle of July, Tynan was made aware of this fact when, in the taxi on the journey back to the school, the elderly critic placed his hand on his knee and asked the President of the sixth-form conference if he was gay. It was a question that people would often want to ask of Tynan. 'I'm af-f-fraid not,' said the schoolboy. 'Ah well,' Agate replied, 'I thought we'd get that out of the way.'[28] All possibility of misunderstanding removed, Agate proceeded to give his talk, before watching a performance of *Hamlet*, in which Tynan sought to impress the critic. Agate returned to London with a copy of a prose poem, 'L'Art pour l'Art', that Tynan had written, and a brief exchange of correspondence resulted between the ambitious youngster and the formidable critic. Agate felt that Tynan was trying to cram too much into his poem and, in an interesting piece of self-analysis, Tynan agreed that his mistake was not 'of trying to say too much, but of seeming to know too much'.[29] It was a lesson he would put to good use in his theatre criticism.

Tynan's self-confidence had now returned, during the first summer of peace following the humiliation of VE Day. 'I believe in artifice for art's sake,' he told Agate at the end of July, but most of all he believed in himself 'quand même' (whatever the consequences).[30] It was a suitably cocksure attitude with which to be approaching university. Despite a final Birmingham letter telling Holland that Oxford was looking forward to his arrival with 'ill-concealed loathing',[31] he was taken there by his parents in early October in their chauffeur-driven Daimler with nervous expectation. Peter and Rose, proud and apprehensive, could scarcely have realised that this new adventure would bring about such a decisive change in their son's fortunes.

The self-fashioning that was to characterise so much of Tynan's professional career began in earnest at Oxford. The student body that collected at the start of the 1945 Michaelmas term bore testimony to the fact that the country had only recently emerged from six gruelling years of war. Battle-hardened soldiers returning to Oxford to take up or resume their academic careers gathered with fresh-faced eighteen-year-olds for whom the war had been a distant backdrop to more exciting domestic activities. The VE and VJ (Victory in Japan) celebrations had quickly given way to the more sober realisation that the post-war world would be every bit as complicated as the pre-war one. Stalin's obsession with reaching Berlin before the Allies had been a clear signal of that. But for those matriculating, their eyes were set on the future, even if it might prove to be as grey as the clothes that they were wearing.

The main thing that Tynan introduced to Oxford during the three years that he was there was colour – both in his lifestyle and in his dress. Given the utilitarian attitude of the country at large this was remarkable enough, but given his youth, provincial upbringing and lack of wartime experience it seemed outrageous. His purple doeskin suit, gold satin shirts, bottle-green suit and assortment of bow-ties (many of which are now in the Theatre Museum, London) remained in the minds of those who saw them long after they graduated. Together with his fellow undergraduate Alan Beesley, he revived the defunct newspaper, *Cherwell*, and succeeded in getting it banned for distributing a questionnaire on sex to 1,000 female undergraduates, and he gracefully taunted the heartier students with his carefully crafted effeteness to the point that they burned his effigy in public in a mock display of outrage. That this campaign of self-propagation made its mark was confirmed on his graduation, when the Oxford journal, *Isis*, was moved to publish a mock epitaph in his honour. It spoke of 'the Golden Age' being finished and wondered who now would be so fit 'to fill KEN TYNAN's place'.

Tynan's tutor at Magdalen was the Christian novelist C.S. Lewis, whom he liked from the very start. After one of his earliest tutorials, he told Julian Holland that he was 'terribly sound and sunny'[32] and as his first term progressed he became enraptured by Lewis's teaching of *Paradise Lost*, writing that he had 'discovered Milton hand in hand with C.S. Lewis' and that God was his 'co-pilot'.[33] Outside tutorials, Tynan began to investigate the Film Club, debates at the Oxford Union (which left him unimpressed) and the Experimental Theatre Club, where he entered an acting competition, and played Iago in a short extract from *Othello*. He also started to cultivate a number of female students, clearly unencumbered by his ongoing engagement to Pauline. Appropriately, his most significant contact with drama at university was as an observer. News had reached him of great events at the Old Vic and from November 1945 he began to plan a London visit to take in Olivier in *Oedipus Rex*, and Ralph Richardson in the two parts of *Henry IV*. After the trip he told Pauline that Olivier was 'unspeakably poignant' in *Oedipus Rex* but 'abominably careless' in *The Critic*[34]; the notes that he made after these performances would eventually find their way into *He That Plays the King*. But although from his second term he began to carve out a niche for himself as a drama critic for *Isis*, at this stage of his life he very much wanted to be an active participant in the theatre rather than a passive observer.

Intelligent and sharp, Tynan found that academic work came easy to him. His numerous extra-curricular interests nourished his essay writing, and his respect for Lewis continued to increase, as the tutor kindly offered to read out his essays for him when his stammer impeded the flow. As his confidence grew, however, merely being the centre of attention was no longer enough: he now needed to orchestrate events and to start to create. For this reason, he rejoined the New Dramatic Company to direct a summer production of Euripides' *Medea* (and played the Chorus himself in pink tights). In his private life, he was equally decisive. In an inevitable, if brutal, act he dispensed with his engagement to Pauline, having fallen in love with Jill Rowe-Dutton, who was reading medicine at St Anne's. Such was the intensity of their relationship that they quickly obtained the consent of Peter and Rose Tynan to marry, but it all ended in tears when Jill returned to her previous lover in the autumn of 1947. It was a 'cool, bloody, hateful, betrayal', in Tynan's eyes.[35]

Within the university, Tynan was becoming more widely known for his production work and as a director: his *Samson Agonistes* by Milton was notable for its shock tactics – an excessive amount of blood spewing from the mouth of the Messenger and an enormous crimson curtain that fell from the roof of St Mary's to the floor below to mark the fall of Gaza were among the highlights – whereas his *Winterset*, by Maxwell Anderson, demonstrated how his finger seemed to be on the pulse of all that was innovative and highlighted his love of all things American. It travelled to Paris for one performance, at the behest of two wealthy French students. As an actor he also provoked comment, not least when his performance of a literate Holofernes in *Love's Labour's Lost* appeared an extension of his own personality.

Outside Oxford, however, it was his writing that drew the eye. In September 1946 Tynan had sent James Agate a copy of a review he had composed of Frederick Valk's Othello played alongside Donald Wolfit's Iago. (This was published the following May in the first edition of *Oxford Viewpoint*[36] and reappeared in *He That Plays the King*.) Agate noted in his diary that here was 'a great dramatic critic in the making'.[37] Less approvingly, Harold Hobson, the newly installed critic of the *Sunday Times*, noted an attack on him by this precocious undergraduate in *Isis*.[38] Feeling that Tynan's presence in London might be dangerous, Hobson rather hoped that he did not take up theatre reviewing as a full-time profession.[39]

The frenetic pace of his university lifestyle caught up with Tynan in the middle of his final year. The stress of impending finals exacerbated the bronchitis and catarrh to which he was prone, and, following a series of chest X-rays, he requested that his final exams be postponed from May 1948 until the following December. The medical evidence was not particularly compelling, although he had missed several tutorials as a result of ill health, but Lewis managed to persuade the authorities that this was a justifiable request. Nobody knew at this point that Tynan suffered from an enzyme deficiency that would eventually result in emphysema, and irritating bouts of ill health would from now on be juxtaposed with his zest for life and his love of socialising. One lavish example of this occurred in April 1948, when he celebrated the occasion of his twenty-first birthday by hiring a river boat to sail through London on the Thames with over 200 party-goers.

With his time at Oxford drawing to a close, Tynan began to prepare for a second instalment of his great obsession, the First Quarto version of *Hamlet*, set in an eighteenth-century European kingdom. The cast included the future Royal Court and film director, Lindsay Anderson. Another pivotal Royal Court figure, Tony Richardson, was also beginning to direct at Oxford, illustrating the shared roots of the men who would help shatter the template of British theatre in the 1950s. Such was Tynan's confidence in the production that a tour was quickly planned and, in a sign of how Tynan's fame was beginning to spread, the opening night drew three significant Hamlets to the audience – Donald Wolfit, Paul Scofield and Robert Helpmann. Wolfit even contributed a short notice to the *Gloucestershire Echo*, commending its 'solid achievement' and praising Tynan's 'effective ghost, which would be even better if he'd discarded the modern craze for crediting Hamlet's father with sepulchral asthma'.[40] This small kindness was to become a bone of contention when the two later fell out so dramatically in the 1950s.

That the play opened at all was surprising, given the event that had occurred two weeks earlier. On 22 July 1948, while Tynan was resting in his hotel in Stratford, he learned that his seventy-six-year-old father, Sir Peter Peacock/Peter Tynan, had passed away that morning. He quickly returned to their Edgbaston home, where he was confronted with the stark image of his father's divided life. Tynan and Peacock families mingled freely together, and, although his relatives suspected that the student had been aware of his father's separate households all along, he was devastated by such a public confirmation. His daughter, Roxana, believes that the 'real damage to him was less the fact of illegitimacy, than the fact that it was kept such a secret'. During a brief foray into analysis in the 1960s, 'he began to reveal his deep insecurity on the subject, but then he dropped it. He wasn't one for introspection.'[41] To the embarrassment of those present, Tynan bitterly upbraided his mother for her deception in a painful confrontation, after having been given official confirmation of the Peacock 'secret' by the family solicitor and doctor. It must have been a crushing blow, not least because he had no control over the events that followed, nor the publicity that attended them.

As a significant politician and businessman, Sir Peter received several obituaries in both the local and the national press. His body was removed to Warrington and he was given an impressive funeral by the town to which he had contributed so much. Rose Tynan decided not to attend, and a bare two days later, his son was back with his *Hamlet* company.[42] Outwardly, he put a brave face on the public confirmation of his illegitimacy, but the scars were deep. He would find it difficult to trust again.

Sir Peter's will left a significant sum of money, over £120,000, to ten beneficiaries, and Tynan was well provided for, but this financial cushion did not alleviate the natural anxiety of a final-year student about his employment prospects – especially one who had just lost a parent in such confusing circumstances. He sincerely wanted to become a theatre director, but he knew that it was important to explore as many avenues as possible. One was his proficiency in writing, and he secured a lucky break when Harold Hobson, of all people, generously recommended him to his own publisher, Mark Longman, after Tynan had contacted him in the summer of 1948 about his desire to produce a collection of articles on the theatre.

Tynan's gift for performance helped him clear one further barrier to an immediate career: the threat of National Service. Attending his army medical examination, he drenched himself in Yardley scent, stammered continually and told the doctor that he could not have sex without the aid of spurs. The army felt that it could do without him. He was less successful in his finals, performing worse than expected on his language papers. The upper second that he emerged with was a keen disappointment, but Lewis consoled him with the perceptive observation that it signified 'comparatively little'.[43] Tynan's real achievements lay ahead.

On 25 February 1949, Tynan capitalised on Hobson's introduction by signing a contract with Longmans for a book on the theatre, for which he would receive £100 on publication. Time had not stood still, however. *Hamlet* had now transferred to the Rudolf Steiner Hall in London and Hobson had given it a notice in the *Sunday Times*. The play, he wrote, was

> under the direction of Ken Tynan of Magdalen, a long, lean, dialectically brilliant young man who seems to occupy in the contemporary University a position pretty similar to that of Harold Acton when I was up.
>
> In other words, Mr Tynan appears to be the mascot of, as well as the driving force behind, those cultural experiments of which Oxford, when at its best, is usually full. Undoubtedly he is a man of ideas, several of which he has crammed into his own production of *Hamlet* which, travestied as it is by its own text, he does not hesitate high-spiritedly to travesty still further by the lively pranks of his direction.[44]

These 'pranks' included an eighteenth-century setting, a king dressed in a coloured waistcoat and a queen wearing a green riding-cloak, and Hobson concluded that the evening, in which Tynan took the role of the Second Player, was 'memorable, irreverent and highly interesting' – a perfect description of Tynan's subsequent criticism. There was no thought of reviewing as a first-choice career just yet, though. Tynan had accepted an offer to run the David Garrick Theatre at Lichfield, Staffordshire. It was everything he had ever wanted.

The patron and financial backer of the Lichfield theatre was Joan Cowlishaw. Tynan's youthful energy, infectious confidence and ambitious plans had appealed to her and he was engaged to produce the familiar repertory diet of light entertainment and the occasional more serious work. But he quickly discovered – like so many recently graduated student thespians – that there was a great deal of difference between the cosseted world of the university and the financial grind of weekly rep. For a start, the turnover of plays was colossal – Tynan directed twenty-four in twenty-four weeks – and this inevitably put a limit to the amount of exciting experimentation that had initially fired him. In August 1949, having been at Lichfield for almost twenty weeks and having already directed *The Beaux' Stratagem*, *Anna Christie*, *Arsenic and Old Lace* and *Present Laughter*, he confided to Harry James, one of the founders of the NDC in Birmingham, that the experience had changed his artistic priorities:

The first thing one looks for in a weekly rep actor is his ability to learn lines quickly. That qualification romps away with the field: a photographic memory puts a man way ahead of his rivals: there is no photo-finish. My error has been engaging people who weren't accustomed to weekly; because I daren't admit to myself the over-riding importance of this knack: I now, with infinite regret and reluctance, turn away excellent players because they just cannot learn and remember – fine, flexible versatile people who won't and can't stuff a part down their throats in five or six rehearsals.[45]

It was a long way away from the languorous experimentation with the First Quarto of *Hamlet*.

One of Tynan's leading ladies in Lichfield was his old Birmingham friend and scourge of his mother, Pat Brewer, with whom he began a brief affair. It was a brief respite in an increasingly pressurised atmosphere. Productions of *Six Characters in Search of an Author*, *Pygmalion* and *Rookery Nook* tumbled out, but Joan Cowlishaw began to have doubts about the extremely young director's ability to temper his ambition with a necessary pragmatism. When he wanted to set Garrick's adaptation of *The Taming of the Shrew* in the deep south of America, her patience snapped, and he was brusquely dismissed.

Unbowed, Tynan relocated to London, leaving Pat Brewer behind in Lichfield. He declined an offer to direct a show for the Bromley Theatre in south-east London, because he would have no say in the choice of show; auditioned for a semi-nude revue at the Windmill Theatre, but was turned down by the owner, Vivian Van Damm, for being 'too queer';[46] and was finally engaged by the biggest theatre company in the West End, H.M. Tennent Ltd, to direct C.E. Webber's *A Citizen of the World* at the Lyric, Hammersmith. It was another step up the ladder and Hobson again gave the piece a favourable review. Tynan finally seemed to be inching closer to the theatrical big time.

Buoyed up by the experience of directing at the leading try-out venue in London and by the successful première of *A Citizen of the World* as a Sunday night production in the West End Phoenix Theatre, Tynan turned back to his nearly completed book. With his customary panache, he decided that he needed a theatre celebrity to make a contribution, and he managed to pull off the considerable coup of persuading Orson Welles, his boyhood hero, to write the preface to the work, which now largely focused on the current state of theatre criticism, heroic acting in Britain and the demands of tragedy in drama.

Welles had left the United States on a European odyssey in 1948 but was very much in the public eye following his enigmatic performance as Harry Lime in the magnificent film of *The Third Man*. Tynan had discovered, with the persistence of the born autograph hunter, that Welles's constant travelling in preparation for his film version of *Othello* (which was not completed until 1951) would bring him to Paris at Christmas, so he went out to the French capital to negotiate face to face. Welles had entered into a brief correspondence with Tynan in 1942, after the schoolboy had seen *Citizen Kane*, but the reality of his presence was far more disarming than he had expected. Impressed by his persistence and intrigued by the forceful opinions of one so young, Welles agreed to write the preface, but given his congenital embarrassment when confronted by admirers, he refused to discuss the manuscript or glance at the notes that Tynan thrust under his nose. The author was delighted and he returned to London with the valuable endorsement. It guaranteed the beginning of his publishing career and started a lifelong friendship with the actor.[47]

On his return to England, Tynan continued his dervish-like whirl around the theatrical world of London. In the spring of 1950 he decided to invest £2,000 of his inheritance (a very large sum for the time) in a new company at the Bedford Theatre, Camden and was given, in return, not the post of resident director which he craved, but several slots for his own productions. None of these were crowned with success. The most notable aspect of one of the shows, *The Bells*, was the burgundy dinner jacket which he wore to the first night. No matter, though, he was being noticed and talked about. A summer trip to a Harvard-sponsored seminar on American studies, at the invitation of William Becker, allowed him to perform in e.e. cummings's *him*, as well as attend lectures by Eric Bentley on Bertolt Brecht. Surprisingly, these made little impression, for, at that time, the most devoted supporter of epic theatre in the twentieth century was obsessed by one of the things that Brecht believed was blighting contemporary drama: heroic acting by theatrical superstars.

This became public knowledge when, shortly after he had directed a touring production of *Othello* for the embryonic Arts Council, *He That Plays the King* was published in October 1950. All of Tynan's adolescent precocity, undergraduate flair and delight in the irreverent were bundled into its 255 pages. Respect for age, achievement and tradition was still strong in post-war Britain, but Tynan's outspoken opinions signalled his hostility to unquestioning deference. As far as the theatre was concerned, he was going to tell it as he saw it. It was an astonishingly forthright and unashamedly personal analysis.

The opening section on 'The State of Dramatic Criticism' immediately set the tone. The critic's task, he argued, was to 'measure the impact of a personality upon him'[48] (a view that the dearth of good new plays would soon force him to modify), but contemporary reviewers were simply not up to the task. With impressive bravado, he attacked a succession of critics, barely attempting to disguise their identity by referring to their initials. 'H-H' (Harold Hobson), who had been so generous in his efforts to get the book published, received an unwelcome payback.

Tynan felt that he was 'whimsical and honest, better bred and more of a moralist than Agate, but lacking, fatally, his flair and savage gusto'.[49] 'I-B' (Ivor Brown), Hobson's rival at the *Observer*, fared even worse. He relied on 'many more semicolons than full stops, many more puns than points'[50] to fashion his column, but it was 'J.C.T.' (J.C. Trewin, the prolific journalist, who wrote for the *Illustrated London News*), who was most ruthlessly mocked. Aping this critic's erudite, polysyllabic and occasionally over-elaborate tone, Tynan observed that Trewin practised 'the coruscant-hyacinthine style, the silk-purse-out-of-a-sow's-ear tradition of Maxolatry [devotion to Max Beerbohm]',[51] discovering hidden gems where none were to be found. What was missing, he contested, was 'the breathless punch-drunk downrightness of James Agate'[52] and, as a consequence, the heroic actor was finding more and more that his treasures were 'swallowed up unnoticed'.[53] Tynan aimed to plug the gap.

The second chapter on 'Heroic Acting since 1944' formed the bulk of the book and comprised a large number of reviews that Tynan had composed himself between 1944 and 1948. The majority of these notices are positive, confirming the earlier claim that this was a book of 'enthusiasms',[54] with descriptions of memorable individual performances, such as Ralph Richardson in *Peer Gynt*, Paul Scofield in *Hamlet* and Frederick Valk as Solness in *The Master Builder*, coexisting with approbatory notices about individual productions, most notably Peter Brook's 1946 *Huis Clos* at the Arts Theatre, which was the best all-round production Tynan had seen up to that point. The writing is captivatingly atmospheric, with a freshness and certainty that comes from impetuous and spontaneous youth. It conveys the very essence of theatre, by highlighting its unpredictability, and manages to sound suitably euphoric without being gushing, when some of the real highs are reached. These tended to come most frequently when Tynan was watching Laurence Olivier, the epitome of the heroic actor. His description of Olivier's pain as Oedipus during the great wartime season at the New is one of the most convincing descriptions of a single moment in a theatre that has ever been written:

> I know that from the first I was waiting breathlessly for the time when the rack would move into the final notch, and the lyric cry would be released: but I never hoped for so vast an anguish. Olivier's final 'Oh! Oh!' when the full catalogue of his sins is unfolded must still be resounding in some high recess of the New Theatre's dome: some stick of wood must still, I feel, be throbbing from it.[55]

But despite the vast number of positive endorsements, it is Tynan's deliciously acidic descriptions – stylish, arch and wickedly enjoyable – that stick in the memory. Post-war theatre-goers were not used to this at all, and it added to the allure of the book. Vivien Leigh was a particular target and there now began the career-long argument that her lack of talent was imperilling the lustre of her husband, Laurence Olivier. In *Richard III*, he questioned her commitment:

> When Olivier revised this production in 1949 with a vastly inferior supporting company, the part of Lady Anne was given to Vivien Leigh, who quavered through the lines in a sort of rapt oriental chant. It was a bad performance, coldly kittenish, but it made the wooing credible, since this silly woman would probably have believed anything.[56]

In Thornton Wilder's *The Skin of Our Teeth*, where she played the part of Sabine, he objected to what he saw as her essential superficiality:

> Miss Leigh's particular brand of frail, unfelt *coquetterie* fits the part like an elbow-length glove . . . She passes the evening in a thigh-length caricature of a frilly housemaid's dress, flicking idly at non-existent mantel-pieces with a feather broom. She exceeds all the accepted repertoire of femininity – vapid eyelash fluttering, mock unconcern, plain silliness – with convulsive effect, and yet always with her brows slightly arched in boredom. She treats her lines as if she were going through a very fluent first reading, with little variation of pitch or tone; and the comparison with an adolescent Katherine Hepburn slightly bemused by drugs is irresistible . . . Miss Leigh is likewise sweet; but when you have said that half a dozen times, you have said everything.[57]

He even questioned her performance as Blanche Dubois in the acclaimed *A Streetcar Named Desire*, where she seemed to him to be 'a bored nymphomaniac with a frenziedly affected tremolo'.[58]

If anyone else had held these views, they had kept them to themselves. In the immediate aftermath of the war, people preferred to lock their private thoughts away in the deep recesses of their minds. Tynan's innovation was to break through the artificial restraints of *politesse* and to place them centre-stage. He was the arch-priest of the heretical, dedicated to stimulating debate and discussion, no matter what controversy was provoked.

The remaining chapters of *He That Plays the King* highlighted the strengths and weaknesses of his writing at the earliest stage of his career. The pen-portraits of 'Five Eccentrics' (Danny Kaye, Maurice Chevalier, Sid Field, Hermione Gingold and Stanley Parker) revealed his talent for profiles, which he would profitably exploit in later life. The diary of the 1948 Edinburgh Festival underlined his ability to distil significant moments from a production that would resonate throughout the theatre world. This occurred most memorably when he described the physicality of Jean-Louis Barrault's performance as Hamlet, which confirmed for many observers the over-reliance of the British actor on the voice ('they're dead from the neck down') at the expense of movement. And the chapter on directors (known at this point as producers) provided a further analysis of current practice, with Michael Benthall, Tyrone Guthrie and Peter Brook exuding international quality, as well as a personal prescription for the role of the director.

Less successful was the second part of the book, which was solely dedicated to tragedy. Over-elaborate, prone to flights of rich but unconvincing rhetoric and full of banal statements ('sad plays . . . must be about kings'),[59] it was the most undeveloped part of the work. It seemed tacked on, as if the author felt compelled to prove his intellectual prowess in the light of his upper second at Oxford, and possessed an overly portentous feel. Tynan's best writing would achieve a more spartan style and an insistent directness that avoided the type of purple prose that he had so condemned in Trewin, and he would soon learn how to précis his more extravagant paragraphs.

Shortly after the publication of this brilliant work ('witty, scholarly . . . and infuriating',[60] in the view of Michael Redgrave), a young American actress, Elaine Dundy, and her friend, Peter Martin, walked into the Buckstone Club, a basement behind the Haymarket Theatre. Dundy had recently arrived in London from Paris, where she had been attempting to carve out a career in the theatre, and was searching for some stability after a less than happy upbringing. On the face of it, Elaine had been blessed with a highly privileged background. Her maternal grandfather, Heyma Rosenberg, had undergone the classic rags-to-riches tale so beloved of American citizens. A refugee from Latvia, he had arrived in Manhattan in 1893 with barely a word of English, but he soon showed himself to be proficient in fixing small engineering problems, which saved his first employers, Curry's Sheet Metal Works, a great deal of money. He also began to produce various inventions and by 1900 he had entered into partnership with Dr Parker of Parker Sheet Metal Works. Their business quickly grew and his first major breakthrough came with the creation of an air cooling system that proved so efficient that it was installed in the New York Public Library, the Flatiron Building and the Metropolitan Museum of Art. Lesser men might have been satisfied with this lucrative discovery, but Heyma's restless mind continued to ponder new gadgets and it was the invention of a tiny screw with a hardened thread, capable of being screwed directly through sheet metal, which made him a multimillionaire. The Parker Kalon screw, as it became known, saved the construction industry an enormous amount of time and money, and it was soon used in Charles Lindbergh's *Spirit of St. Louis*, American military planes, and the Statue of Liberty, which required 64,000 to prevent it from disintegrating in 1938.

Heyma's daughter, Elaine's mother, married Samuel Brimberg, a Jewish businessman, in 1918. He, too, was extremely wealthy, having made his money through clothing manufacturing, and, although he suffered enormous losses in the Wall Street Crash of 1929, he managed to recover sufficiently to be able to buy in 1934 a major interest in the Universal Steel Equipment Corporation, from which he was to make his second fortune. Elaine's first eight years up to the Crash had been dominated by the luxury of their Park Avenue apartment, but 1929 brought personal trauma to her, as well. On the day of her eighth birthday she was knocked down by a car, resulting in a dislocated jaw, and she was then rendered gravely ill by a severe reaction to a tetanus jab. Of longer-term significance was the change in her father after he lost his fortune. He became, in her words, 'damaging' and 'destructive', prone to furious rages and unable to address her by her name: 'I was "you" when he was talking to me and "she" when he was talking about me in my presence to a third person.'[61] Like Tynan, this troubled relationship with her father was to dominate her early years. It was a bond that they shared.

After graduating from Mills College in Oakland, California (where she learned to enjoy avocados) and Sweet Briar in Virginia, Elaine went to work in 1943 at Arlington Hall, Virginia as a cryptographer. The war temporarily answered her need for stability and self-worth, but at its end she struggled to think of a career that would enable her to leave home for good. A chance encounter with the playwright Maxwell Anderson, the father of her friend Terry Anderson, helped make up her mind. The playwright asked her to read a part in his play *Truckline Café*, which he had given to an actress about whom he now harboured doubts. Although she declined Anderson's offer, he had boosted her confidence by believing in her and she decided to enrol at the Jarvis Theatre School, Washington.

Post-war Paris, newly liberated and fizzing with energy, held an enormous allure for young wealthy Americans. Having finished her training – and dissatisfied with the lack of job opportunities back in New York – Elaine decided to relocate to the French capital. She might find some work there, and it was the perfect way to escape her hostile father. For all his animosity, he still agreed to support her, and although the experience was no more rewarding in job terms than New York (she was mostly involved in dubbing French films), it was a more enjoyable time. It also provided a wealth of material for her eventual bestseller, *The Dud Avocado*.

By July 1950, Elaine was succumbing to 'wanderlust' again. She flew over to London for a short visit and was underwhelmed by the current critical hit, T.S. Eliot's *The Cocktail Party*, but was thrilled to find herself sitting one day on the same bus as the film star Wendy Hiller. This was egalitarian, austerity Britain in the flesh. A further three-week visit in August made her consider staying over for a while, and by the autumn she was beginning to spend time around the London theatrical scene.

The Buckstone Club was the latest place for upcoming thespians to be seen. Established only a year earlier, it was an unpretentious eating, drinking and, above all, meeting place, run by a portly actor called Gerry Campion, that served as a receiving house for all the latest gossip, contacts and news of auditions. Far removed from the elegant watering holes of the major West End players, generally associated with Binkie Beaumont's company, H.M. Tennent Ltd, its spartan surroundings gave it significant cachet for young theatre professionals. As Elaine walked into the club in October 1950, she was intrigued by the way that a confident young man was captivating a large crowd with great verve: 'He was holding court in a booth. That alone made it an incredible sight. Dozens of people squeezing in, some climbing in, some climbing out, some hanging over its edge. Peter Martin with whom I was lunching, said, "That's Ken Tynan. I think you should meet him. I don't know if it'll do you any good but it may. Let's go over."' Tynan invited her to sit down and she found herself 'looking at a thin man holding a cigarette between his third and fourth fingers and stammering out his bon mots to his mesmerised audience'. It was his persona that seemed so mesmerising: 'He wore a double-breasted camel's hair jacket, plum-colored trousers, yellow socks and black shoes and a Mickey Mouse wrist-watch. His long legs projected sideways from the booth, and his stammer was so violent it distorted his features so I could get no clear impression of them. After five minutes of reflected glory Peter and I were off.'[62]

On the recommendation of Peter Ustinov, Elaine read the latest fashionable work, *He That Plays the King*, and a week after finishing the book, she used it as a pretext to engage its author in conversation as he passed by her in the Buckstone. Never immune to a pretty face, Tynan duly invited her to lunch the next day, where they talked about Danny Kaye, before going to the Odeon in the Haymarket to see the double bill of *It's a Gift* with W.C. Fields and *A Day at the Races* starring the Marx Brothers. The afternoon held further surprises when, at the Rockingham drinking club, Peter Brook came and went, and Tynan made his customary proposal: 'I am the illegitimate son of the late Sir Peter Peacock. I have an annual income. I'm twenty-three and I will either die or kill myself when I reach thirty because by then I will have said everything I have to say. Will you marry me?' Elaine was hooked:

> He began to look just right for me . . . Tall and thin, fair English-pink complexion, high cheekbones dramatically dominating the outline of his elongated face. His forehead was high and bony, his pale beige-blond hair curved back from his brow like a wing, and his large well-shaped mouth gave him an attractive equine look. All this, together with his Mickey Mouse wristwatch, cast a spell over me.[63]

The couple quickly became besotted with each other. Elaine was amazed by his contacts – within two days they had had tea with Christopher Fry – as much as by his sexual magnetism: 'my eyes registered his cock, a beautiful cock, perfectly proportioned with his tall body'.[64] Within two weeks, she had moved into his flat at 19 Upper Berkeley Street, where she made tea and fry-ups and he set traps for the mice. It was so different from the prim environment of her parents' apartment and she loved the process of getting to know each other and of cherishing their trivia. She discovered that he did not stammer when he sang, that he had loved Indian food ever since regularly dining at the Taj Mahal in Oxford and that his curious (and later famous) way of holding his cigarette, between his middle and fourth fingers, was simply to avoid nicotine staining. His talent for success led her to call him one of 'Destiny's Tots',[65] whereas he gave her the pet-name 'Skippy'. His brilliant conversation startled those around him ('being with Ken meant never having to use a dictionary'[66]), and she quickly realised that their fractured childhoods gave them a strong affinity: 'Self-invented, divorced from our backgrounds, we had met and commingled to create something new, something we alone owned, a world with our own myths and traditions.'[67] They also shared a strong love of the theatre and quickly started to see shows together, their first being *Bartholomew Fair* at the Old Vic.

Tynan had always been impulsive, but their decision, taken on holiday in Elaine's beloved Paris over Christmas, to marry at the end of January seemed swift even by his standards. On 25 January 1951, accompanied by Elaine's maid of honour Tessa Prendergast and Tynan's best man Peter Wildeblood, an old Oxford debating rival, the couple were married at Marylebone Town Hall. Wildeblood's contacts as a journalist meant that several newspapers carried wedding pictures and the *Daily Mail* included a brief notice under a picture of a beaming Elaine:

> Roses for the dress. Feathers for the hair. Such were the accessories worn yesterday by Miss Elaine Dundy for her wedding to Mr Ken Tynan in London. The bride is an American actress. The bridegroom is a theatrical producer. They were introduced three months ago by Miss Tessa Prendergast, a 22 year-old Jamaican singer. After the wedding Miss Prendergast, over glasses of champagne, composed and sang a 'special' calypso to mark the occasion.[68]

Attention was also paid to the bridegroom's green carnation. The Tynan myth, with the deliberate echo of Oscar Wilde, was growing.

Elaine had not invited her parents to the wedding and was apprehensive about their reaction. She had sent a brief wire to New York, which baldly stated 'Have married Englishman. Letter follows.'[69] To her great relief, they were quickly reconciled to the idea and her father even agreed to raise her annual allowance. 'Ken and I were immensely grateful. It also shows how my attitude towards my father's money changed. I went from being determined to take as little as possible from him to thanking God he was rich and so what if I had to ask for it?'[70] How important Elaine's financial support would prove quickly became apparent after their wedding. Alec Clunes, who ran the Arts Theatre Club – a private theatre which, its prospectus claimed, existed to oppose 'the monotony of the leg-show and the dullness of the average West End drawing-room piece'[71] – had appointed Tynan to direct a translation of Cocteau's *Les Parents terribles*, entitled *Intimate Relations*. It promised to be a significant engagement, since the famous actress, Fay Compton, had been cast as the mother. This was a considerable coup for the venue, since Compton had already enjoyed a long and distinguished career, carving out key roles for Somerset Maugham in the 1920s, Dodie Smith in the 1930s and Coward in the 1940s, as well as playing Ophelia to Barrymore and Gielgud's Hamlets. On return from their honeymoon, Tynan set up a miniature theatre in his sitting room, around which he moved cut-outs of the performers for hours. He had very definite views about the role of the director, which he had explained in *He That Plays the King*. The director stood 'as *locum tenens* for the author: shaping, easing, smoothing, tightening, heightening, lining and polishing the thing made, the play'.[72] He was responsible for ensuring 'wholeness of conception, shape and completeness' and needed to be respected and obeyed. For an actress who believed in the innateness of her skill (a common belief at that time), this was difficult for Compton to swallow and there was a clash of personalities from the very beginning. Although he had undertaken detailed preparations, Tynan's decision to show a screening of Cocteau's film of the play to the cast proved disastrous, as many of them then felt that Tynan's innovations were actually derivative. Compton rose up and demanded that he be fired, or she would leave the show. Clunes was in an agony of indecision. As a supporter of progressive theatre, and well aware of Tynan's cachet following the publication of *He That Plays the King*, he was inclined to back his brash, opinionated director, but as an artistic director he knew the value of Compton to the box office. Reluctantly, he decided that Tynan had to go, but was so nervous about breaking the news that he asked the theatre's publicist, William Wordsworth, to do so. Wordsworth understandably did not feel that this was his job and, after tossing a coin, the unenviable task was handed to Brian Mellor, the Arts Manager. A new producer, Judith Furse, was then hurriedly drafted in to salvage the play.[73]

It was a great humiliation for Tynan, and another of his many crises. The damage to his confidence was such that he lost almost all his appetite for directing, not because of any lack of interest in the art, but through a crippling fear of rejection. The insecurity that he struggled to hide during his childhood, the fear of unexpected and unwelcome surprises, had now re-emerged and it was another trait that became a leitmotif in his life. What profession could Tynan now pursue? Ever the polymath, he had begun to write theatre criticism for the *Spectator* magazine, and his renown had been growing in literary circles, even if it was waning in drama ones. Here was a stark new dilemma: should he soldier on in his desire to create, or accept that, without a greater degree of resilience, it would be safer for him to explore his evident talent to observe? The retreat from the stage to the auditorium had begun.

Chapter 2 *The Necessary Side*

... criticism has taken a wrong turning into imperturbability and casualness: it has ceased to worry about communicating excitement or scorn: it is away and somewhere else; not vitally interested. (Kenneth Tynan, *He That Plays the King*)[1]

'Are you the new Garrick, Mr Tynan? Never mind, stay where your fellow actors really need you: on the other side of the footlights. On the necessary side.' (Orson Welles, in *He That Plays the King*)[2]

The colourlessness that Tynan ascribed to theatre criticism in his first book could equally be applied to Great Britain as a whole in 1951. Tynan's most influential criticism always reflected the world in which he was living. Although Britain was not under direct attack from an enemy aggressor, its inhabitants continued to feel under siege. The manifesto slogan of the victorious Labour Party in 1945 had been 'Let us face the future', but by 1951 many people were impatient with what they perceived to be the slow pace of the reconstruction work.

This had begun almost immediately after the election victory of Clement Attlee in July 1945. Although the dismissal from office of the wartime leader, Winston Churchill, was an enormous shock to international opinion and to Churchill himself – when his wife Clementine tried to console him by saying that the landslide defeat might well be a blessing in disguise, he could only reply that 'at the moment it's certainly very well disguised'[3] – there was a quiet logic to this surprise result. The Conservative Party was still viewed in many quarters as the party of social division, mass unemployment, and pre-war appeasement – Churchill himself had never truly been viewed as a Tory, given his Liberal past – and the wartime coalition government had allowed senior Labour politicians, such as Ernest Bevin, Herbert Morrison, Stafford Cripps and Attlee himself, to prove their competence. Churchill's infamous election broadcast, on 4 June 1945, in which he crassly argued that at the first sign of public discontent a 'socialist government . . . would have to fall back on some sort of Gestapo',[4] further alienated the electorate, and although voters greeted him with enormous enthusiasm whenever he appeared in public during the election campaign, they decided that he was not the man to build the peace. 'Never again' summed up the collective mood.

For the next eighteen months, Britain underwent, in the words of the eminent historian Kenneth O. Morgan, 'a massive transformation unique in her history'.[5] Domestically, the National Health Service Act and National Insurance Act of May 1946 introduced the principle of medical treatment free at the point of delivery and laid the foundations for the modern welfare state by enacting the recommendations of the Beveridge Report of 1942. Twenty per cent of the economy was quickly taken into public ownership, including the Bank of England, cable and wireless, railways, road transport, electricity and civil aviation; and the education system was transformed through the swift implementation of the 1944 Butler Education Act, which divided the secondary school system into grammars, for those who could pass the eleven-plus exam, secondary moderns for those who could not (the majority), and a small number of technical schools. In its bifurcation of the school population, this can hardly be viewed as the egalitarian initiative that it was seen to be at the time. Indeed, several mythical views of this period can now be dismissed from the vantage point of the twenty-first century. One of the most resistant is that the cross-party consensus of the war years continued after the cessation of hostilities. Attlee's foreign policy, which centred on providing a 'middle way' of democratic socialism that could provide a useful model for the country's colonies, was bitterly contested by Churchill, who resented any diminution of the Empire. But initially public opinion was supportive of retrenchment. When, in August 1947, two-thirds of the population of the Commonwealth, over 450 million people, were given their independence as Great Britain withdrew from India, the domestic population was unperturbed. It proved to be 'decolonization without trauma'.[6] It was only when the political mood began to change that withdrawal from areas such as Palestine in May 1948 came to be seen as a national humiliation. Unknown to the public, the government began a secret nuclear weapons programme in an attempt to maintain Britain's position as a central player on the world stage, while recognising that its economically straitened circumstances (the national debt in 1945 was four times what it was in 1939) meant that it could no longer support its imperial legacy.

With the help of a loan for £3.75 billion negotiated with the US on fairly stringent terms, the long journey to economic recovery began. But for the population at large, certain privations of the war continued. The reinstitution of bread rationing in July 1946 was a blow, as was the news that National Service was to be reintroduced in 1947 to provide a large body of men to protect the distant outposts of an increasingly disconsolate empire. Tynan was fortunate to avoid this chore. Yet up until the end of 1946, people were generally quiescent. Government posters urged communities to 'pull together' and the wartime ethos of 'fair shares' still applied. The dreadful winter of 1947 altered the public mood, however. Fuel and coal shortages brought into question the competence of Labour's economic planning. These in turn led to production difficulties in factories and caused a 25 per cent drop in exports. A balance of payments crisis resulted, and strict public spending cuts were needed in the summer to shore up the pound. No wonder the country turned to the escapism promised by the royal wedding of the future heir to the throne, Princess Elizabeth, to Philip Mountbatten.

Attlee's response to the worsening economic situation was to dig in. He appointed Sir Stafford Cripps, a strict vegetarian and teetotaller, in an era when such a combination was rare, to replace Hugh Dalton as Chancellor of the Exchequer in November 1947. As the man in control of the economy, Cripps seemed physically to embody the necessary but dispiriting thrift that the post-war rebuilding of the country required. Harold Macmillan observed that he was a 'strange monastic-looking man, emaciated and said to live off watercress grown on the blotting paper on his desk'.[7] As a committed Christian Socialist, Cripps saw the battle to rebuild the country's economy in moral as well as political terms. When he told the American Bar Association that 'Our only safety for the future lies in the positive and conscious exertion of spiritual control over material actions',[8] he merely reiterated his ethical approach to politics.

Although it was not immediately apparent, Cripps's medicine slowly began to work. His tight control of public spending, zealous battle against waste and devaluation of the pound in 1949 from $4.03 to $2.80 – which was at first seen as a national disgrace in the face of another economic crisis – helped create the conditions for the rising living standards which characterised the 1950s. Regrettably for the Attlee government, the electoral benefit that accrued from this was not to be theirs. The foundations of the welfare state had been put in place, but there was still a tremendous shortage of housing. The temporary box-shaped 'prefabs' made out of asbestos sheeting, which had provided shelter for so many bombed-out families, were unwittingly becoming permanent features. Unfilled bomb craters continued to scar the streets of many major cities. Problems with coal supplies disrupted the railways, steel shortages reduced the output of manufacturing industry, and food rationing, which still applied to meat, bacon, butter, cheese, tea, sugar and sweets, became even more severe in 1951, the year of Tynan's marriage. A trade dispute with Argentina reduced the meat ration from 1s. 6d. to a mere eightpence.

For some, Cripps's parsimonious approach to the country's finances epitomised the austerity that so debilitated the country. For others, he was administering necessary if painful medicine. For Tynan's generation, which had been too young to have served in the recent war, the continued impoverishment was stultifying and drab. Despite these varied perceptions, the early death of Cripps from cancer in 1951 was seen as another blow to the fragile self-confidence of the country. It certainly damaged the stature of the Labour government, which was increasingly seen as tired and worn out. Attlee, surprisingly, had called an election for February 1950 – if he had waited until the summer, the beneficial effects of the devaluation would have been more apparent – and the Conservatives decided to fight on the platform of a 'Tory ladder' against the 'Labour queue'. Labour's election slogan, at a time of greater public mobility and less esteem for age, was the misconceived 'Ask Your Dad', which encapsulated a rather backward-looking stance – and may have proved painfully ironic for Tynan. Labour's majority was whittled down to a mere six seats, and it was inevitable that the second Attlee administration was likely to be a short-lived one. A revitalised opposition, led by a re-energised Churchill, started a guerrilla war in the House of Commons. It forced a succession of late-night sessions that had a draining effect on the government by forcing Ministers to be on hand to stave off defeat in parliamentary votes. The new Chancellor, Hugh Gaitskell, then precipitated a damaging internal split in the Labour Party by choosing to levy small charges on dental and ophthalmic treatment, as a tiny contribution (£23 million p.a.) to the enormous arms budget (£4,700 million) that he felt was necessary in light of the international tension caused by the launch of the Korean war in the autumn of 1950. Nye Bevan, the founder of the NHS, resigned from the cabinet in April 1951, when Gaitskell refused to back down, and was supported by a significant number of his colleagues. The country was unimpressed by this bout of infighting.

At first the Korean war seemed to offer an opportunity for Attlee to play the world statesman to the credit of his country and his government. At a press conference on 30 November 1950, President Truman appeared to contemplate the use of atomic weapons, after General MacArthur's advance through North Korea was met by tens of thousands of Chinese 'volunteers' coming to the aid of that country. Attlee's dash to Washington was portrayed at home as a great diplomatic act, which resulted in clarification of Truman's words and a withdrawal of the threat (although subsequent analyses have questioned the degree to which Attlee influenced Truman's thinking). In any case, Churchill was the real beneficiary of the advent of this new Cold War. His chief obsession since 1945 had been the worsening international situation, and, although he was now aged seventy-seven, his previous experience was once more seen to have some validity.

In September 1951, Attlee sprung his second electoral surprise by seeking a third mandate from the country. The ageing leadership of the Prime Minister, Morrison, Dalton and Shinwell seemed exhausted and bereft of ideas. The wider public, too, 'now saw the uniformity and egalitarianism of earlier rhetoric as more drab than inspiring'.[9] As the memory of wartime sacrifice and victory faded, the national mood began to change. The electorate appeared to reject yet more consolidation, in favour of greater consumer choice, more individual liberty and the aspirational ending of rationing. Churchill's pledge to 'set the people free' had a strong appeal.

Even more people voted Labour than Conservative in October 1951, with Attlee's party receiving the highest number of votes ever recorded up to that point (almost 14 million, 48.8 per cent of the vote). The vagaries of the electoral system, however, handed the keys of Downing Street to Churchill for the second time, with a majority of seventeen; but for many – not least Tynan – one shade of grey had been replaced by another.

To escape from this greyness, Britons went to the cinema, music hall and theatre – and read newspapers in vast numbers. In 1950, the three London evening newspapers alone (the *Evening News*, the *Star* and the *Evening Standard*) had a combined circulation of almost 4 million readers.[10] The nation-wide *Sunday Times* and the *Observer* catered for the intellectual end of the market, faithfully sustaining an interest in the arts, current affairs and political developments. Their status as the pre-eminent Sunday papers allowed them to pronounce in an authoritative fashion on matters of the day, and, for many of their readers, they were the only contact they had with new developments in the theatre. It was not uncommon for certain households to buy copies of each publication to compare and contrast their different perspectives, since the *Sunday Times* generally adopted a right of centre perspective and the *Observer* a left of centre one. Jimmy Porter at the beginning of *Look Back in Anger* reflected the bitter-sweet taste of their highbrow approach, when he mocked the 'posh papers' and observed to his friend Cliff, 'I've just read three whole columns on the English Novel. Half of it's in French. Do the Sunday newspapers make you feel ignorant?' For all the subsequent (and arguable) claims of innovation for *Look Back in Anger*, its famous protagonist begins the play engaged in the quintessentially British activity of lounging about with the Sundays.

Papers such as the *News of the World*, the *Daily Sketch* and the *Evening Standard* catered for the mass market, and had a significantly greater reach. They filled their pages with respectful stories about the royal family, exposés of sexual misbehaviour, profiles of key movers and shakers, envious allusions to the vibrancy of America and a liberal dose of showbiz gossip. This was a period of full-blown hero worship, with stars afforded a degree of unquestioning respect that seems distinctly quaint today.

The supreme stars were the two daughters of King George VI, Princess Elizabeth and Princess Margaret, with public interest in the heir to the throne carefully nurtured by the press. Since the end of the war much of the population had been fascinated by Princess Elizabeth. She was a favourite subject for popular magazines eager to emphasise her beauty, shy smile and eligibility, and when American magazines, less reticent than their British cousins, began to hint at an engagement with Philip Mountbatten, public interest increased still further. The four-month royal tour to southern Africa in early 1947 was seen in some quarters (probably mistakenly) as an attempt by her parents to separate the young Princess from her lover, since Philip had faced difficulty in securing his naturalisation as a British citizen, given his Greek and German connections, so there was a mixture of joy and relief when their engagement was finally confirmed in June 1947.

The royal wedding the following November was described as the 'carnival of the decade'.[11] It was the first opportunity for post-war Britain to indulge in the pageantry so beloved of the British. Every detail of the preparations was pored over, with most interest focusing on the dress and the cake. Norman Hartnell's creation, rumoured to be adorned with 10,000 pearls, drew enormous crowds when it was put on public display, and children up and down the country were mesmerised by the news that at a time when sugar rationing still existed there were no fewer than twelve cakes. The quick birth first of Prince Charles (November 1948) and then of Princess Anne (August 1950) confirmed Elizabeth's reputation for 'wholesomeness'[12] and provided a newsworthy contrast with her sister's growing delight in the arts, and the creation of her own 'set'.

The sisters' youthfulness and smiling dignity – never too vigorous and never too closely scrutinised – were seen by editors as a useful palliative for the pervading monochrome. They did nothing more spectacular than travel to Ascot and wear large hats, or make a long overseas trip to a country that few people could imagine. They never gave interviews and were always quoted making the most anodyne statements (even when Elizabeth addressed a Mothers' Union rally in 1949 and declared that divorce and separation were responsible for 'some of the darkest evils in our society'),[13] but their polite, enigmatic smiles made them very photogenic and allowed them to be depicted as a symbol of stability and hope for a country currently lacking in self-confidence. Their vitality also provided a contrast to the less welcome (but again highly newsworthy) ailing health of their father, the King, whose decline since undergoing major lung surgery in March 1949 was charted with meticulous concern.

This reverential approach extended to the world of the arts. The theatrical royalty were the husband and wife pairing of Laurence Olivier and Vivien Leigh, who since 1944 had occupied their demi-palace at Notley Abbey (near Thane,

Buckinghamshire). Appearance and reality merged in April 1949 when Princess Elizabeth celebrated her twenty-third birthday by going to see *The School for Scandal* at the New Theatre, before returning to the fashionable Café de Paris restaurant with the two actors. Olivier and Leigh, too, symbolised glamour, success and (deceptively) harmonious marital union. Film idols, such as Burt Lancaster, flitted in and out of the centre pages, and music hall stars like Danny Kaye (another social companion of Elizabeth) were paid a degree of attention that is inconceivable today. Above all, these celebrities were given a respect that often ignored less than accomplished performances. It was considered bad form to be anything other than hagiographically blind to their more obvious faults.

In *He That Plays the King*, Tynan had written that criticism had lapsed into 'imperturbability and casualness' at the expense of 'excitement and scorn'. How accurate a diagnosis was this in 1951? The leading critics of this period were W.A. Darlington (*Daily Telegraph*), Alan Dent (*News Chronicle*), Philip Hope-Wallace (*Manchester Guardian*), J.C. Trewin (*Illustrated London News*), T.C. Worsley (*New Statesman*), Ivor Brown (*Observer*) and Harold Hobson (*Sunday Times*). Invited by Christopher Fry, the playwright, to record their approach to criticism for a short volume about their profession, their responses reveal how many of them believed that theatre criticism was a reactive art rather than a didactic one. W.A. Darlington, who wrote for the *Daily Telegraph* from 1920 until 1969, believed that

> Almost always, the 'opinion' which a critic is called upon to express is not a reasoned judgement alterable by argument. It is a report on an emotional reaction subconsciously experienced during the play, and is not susceptible to argument at all. The daily-paper critic acquires a knack of getting swiftly in touch with his sub-conscious mind, and knows his opinion at, or shortly after, the end of the play.[14]

As the *Daily Telegraph* required its copy within thirty minutes of the final curtain, Darlington's detractors felt that it was significant that his reviews normally only included details about the beginning and the middle of the plays he had witnessed. Some believed that on his retirement after over half a century as a critic, he had never seen the end of *Hamlet*.[15]

Alan Dent of the *News Chronicle*, who had been bitterly disappointed not to have succeeded James Agate after his death in 1947 at the *Sunday Times*, preferred to emphasise a lofty belief in justice and impartiality:

> A good critic has no business to be consciously kind or consciously unkind: it is his sole business to be just and nothing but just, whether to plays or producers or performers. When I explain this in exactly these terms to stage-folk who

thank me for having been 'kind', they stare, and their gaze is as cold and uncomprehending as the moon's.[16]

J.C. Trewin (*Illustrated London News*), who was to become a prolific author of books on theatrical matters, often in partnership with his wife, Wendy, was eager to stress his desire to seek out the good rather than scrutinise the bad:

> I am a dramatic critic because I love the theatre. I prefer to approach it as a friend, seeking the best, [rather] than as an enemy with the phrase that withers: another Young Marcius preparing to mammock the gilded butterfly. Few things in journalism (and a critic is a journalist) are simpler than condemnation. 'Let the world thump 'eee with great thumps!' said a preacher in my native village. Often young men begin by thumping; they grow out of it, learn to realise that nothing is more ingenuous than extreme sophistication.[17]

(Did Trewin have Tynan in mind here?) Ivor Brown (*Observer*), too, explained that he was suspicious of a disrespectful tone. Preferring to accentuate the positive, he felt that his loyalty was to the performers – neatly highlighting the chasm between his approach and Tynan's, to whom he would reluctantly pass the baton at the *Observer* in 1954:

> I believe that the ideal critic is an enthusiastic introducer. True, he must dismiss the shoddy as such. But his primary function is not to go slamming about the place and showing what a bright boy he is, but to act as a persuasive, not a dictatorial, guide. He can dismiss his dislikes briefly; his admirations he should communicate as fully as possible in these days of scanty space ... It is the primary business of a critic to be readable. He owes that to his editor, to the buyers of the paper, and above all to the artists. What is the use of powerful approbation if nobody can wade through it? The theatre is not helped by chunks of what is known in newspaper office as 'basic slag'.

But readability must not mean the sacrifice of manners:

> On the other hand, the effort to be readable should not involve cheap scores at the author's or artist's expense. It is easy to approach a play with a sour quip on its title and a few ready-made jokes. Nor do I favour cutting remarks, even though justified, about the personal appearance of the players. That a player is too old or insufficiently handsome for a part can be sufficiently intimated without having to lacerate the feelings of the artist. The public may titter over some 'crack' of this kind, but it is a poor way of being readable. The critic can be mannerly without being misleading. He ought to know and love the history of the theatre if he is to serve its present and promote its future. Above all, he ought to

realise that a slight sentence may do cruel harm to a number of people, in self-respect as well as in finance and employment. This is not to say that he should never censure; but his damns must follow deliberation and his curse [be] tempered by courtesy.[18]

There was only one critic in 1951 who made notorious personal comments. In a profile for the *Daily Sketch* in October, for example, Tynan had described Orson Welles as 'hunching his blubber shoulders in laughter. The shoulders rise like boiling milk, and he chokes over his own good humour, fuming like an awakened volcano.'[19] Brown disapproved of this type of impertinence – particularly when it was hailed as fresh and dynamic – and he would grow to loathe this upstart.

Philip Hope-Wallace (*Manchester Guardian*) and T.C. Worsley (*New Statesman*) both felt less constricted by a sense of decorum, possibly due to their comparative youth. Hope-Wallace, a relative newcomer to theatre criticism having begun writing in 1945, was conscious of the need to retain a greater sense of detachment to the profession than some of his critical colleagues –

A critic is concerned with the end product, not with the means of manufacture. You don't have to be an egg to make an omelette; nor a cook to know a good omelette from a bad one; above all, not a personal friend of the cook and in difficulty in tasting his omelette because you know his wife is deceiving him and that the kitchen caught fire earlier in the day[20]

– and Worsley, who enjoyed a large following among young intellectuals attracted by his willingness to challenge sacred cows, was explicit about his mission to expose, and probably closest to Tynan in critical temperament:

The age-long cry of the artist and the child [is] 'Love me. Understand me. Praise me.' But the good parent must sometimes harden her heart against her child and refuse. If she didn't, the child would never grow up. As to understanding, it is the business of the writer to make himself understood and, if he doesn't – in the theatre above all places – it is the business of the critic to tell him so. Of course, he may write off the critics as nit-wits and comfort himself with the belief that posterity will understand. Well, I cheerfully give him posterity. But you notice that he isn't content with that. Most of our modern playwrights share something else with the child – the insistence of having it both ways. They want the seventy thousand a year and the chorus of adulation while they live, and the dinners, few but choice, when they are dead as well.[21]

The most intriguing critic of this period, though, and the one who along with Tynan would electrify theatre criticism in the second half of the decade was Harold Hobson.

The story of Hobson's accession to the post of theatre critic of the *Sunday Times* in 1947 is one of incredible triumph over adversity. His tenure lasted until 1976, but it was his weekly duels with Tynan between 1954 and 1958 and 1960 and 1963 that both facilitated and recorded the excitement of this period of enormous theatrical upheaval. Born on 4 August 1904 at Thorpe Hesley, Rotherham, Hobson was struck by polio when he was seven years old and paralysed on his right side from his hip down. A succession of doctors were unable to offer his parents any hope for Harold's recovery and one, Dr Birks, told them that he would be bedridden for the rest of his life and unable to earn a living.[22] Desperate to help their son, his parents scoured South Yorkshire in the hope of a cure until one day in 1912, his father, Jacob Hobson, discovered a Christian Science Reading Room in Sheffield. Attracted to the Christian Scientist belief that, since man was created in God's image, sin and sickness are included within a range of mortal errors to be corrected and overcome by a scientific understanding of God, his parents left the Church of England to join this growing religion. Although no dramatic physical improvement occurred in Hobson's condition, he always felt that he owed much to the discovery of this new spirituality, claiming that 'had not my parents discovered Christian Science . . . my life would have been ruined'.[23] A Christian Science practitioner, Stanley Sydenham, came to talk to Hobson about the 'unreality' of the disease and each week asked him to learn a text from the religion's key book, *Science and Health* (1875), written by the Church's founder, Mary Baker Eddy. Gradually, Hobson became stronger and within a month of Dr Birks giving up on the patient, the young boy was able to get out of bed. Friends rallied round. The son of his father's boss, Mr Gibson, came to entertain him by impersonating the melodramatic actor, John Martin Harvey, whom he had seen performing the roles of Oedipus and Sydney Carton in London. This made a great impression on the fragile child. When he was ten, Clara Richardson, an elementary-school teacher who attended their local Christian Science church, started to teach him for an hour on Saturdays, encouraging him to read Walter Scott; and a few months later the big breakthrough occurred when Harold passed the test set by the Local Education Authority that permitted him to attend a special school in Sheffield. He succeeded by explaining the meaning of the word 'vehemently' and for the next few years the family lived in the centre of the city to permit his attendance.

Hobson's immersion in Christian Science during his early teens was to have a profound influence on his later criticism. He developed a taste for rich and profound oratory ('the reading of the Bible in the Authorised Version has been one of the formative influences of my taste')[24] and he discovered, through the lessons of Arthur Allen, a touchstone that he would employ in his later critical writing and that would set him apart from Tynan:

When he read Paul's admonition, 'If there be any virtue, and if there be any praise, think on these things', he taught me the central lesson of criticism, a lesson appreciated by Balzac, and by me never forgotten. It is a good lesson, for what matters in a creative artist is not what he does wrong, but what he does right.[25]

But the intellectual stimulation that the services provided also emphasised the cosseted and over-protected environment that he had been compelled to endure on account of his disability, and so at the age of fifteen he left the house on crutches on his own for the first time to ask the headmaster of the Pupil Teaching Centre (which later became Sheffield Grammar School), Joseph Batey, whether he might attend his much-respected institution. Batey, clearly impressed by Hobson's intellectual capacity and mental fortitude, accepted him as a student, and instructed the school doctor only to examine Hobson's chest, thereby permitting him to satisfy the health requirements of the school. Hobson's delayed educational career had now begun in earnest. In 1923, aged eighteen, he sat for the Northern Universities Board matriculation, obtaining the necessary credits in English, History, Latin and French, and then proceeded to win a scholarship to Sheffield University. But a chance reading of Matthew Arnold's 'The Scholar-Gipsy' turned his thoughts towards Oxford, and he wrote to the Provost of Oriel College, Lancelot Ridley Phelps, to ask whether there might be a place for him, even though he was lame and had only £20 a year to live on. The reply was encouraging. Although the College was full for entry in 1923, Phelps encouraged Hobson to apply for 1924, and, to the great pride of his parents, he was awarded a place the following year to read History.

Even in 1990 Hobson was as eager as ever to recognise the formative influence of his historical training:

My theory of theatre criticism was that on each visit to the theatre . . . something happens to the critic's mind and heart and the thing becomes a sort of historical event. Therefore any criticisms, I should say, are records of how I feel at a particular evening, at a particular play, they are the foundation of a historical record more than the passing of a judgement. They're the narration of something that happened to me in the theatre rather than a judgement passed on the merits of the thing that I was seeing . . . I regarded what was happening to me in the theatre as the basis for a historic record.[26]

The remarkably confident conviction that there would be a readership for his own passions and prejudices – and that his weekly bulletin on the condition of London theatre would constitute a historical record for future generations – meant that during the 1950s Tynan would have an equally egocentric rival who believed that he, too, was writing for posterity. It created a weekly dramatic spectacle that complemented the most riveting action on stage.

Hobson's career at the *Sunday Times* was the result of another lucky break. He had married his first wife, Elizabeth, a teacher, in 1935 and soon afterwards been taken on to the permanent staff of the *Christian Science Monitor* at a salary of £400 p.a. Their joint income allowed them to set up home together in a London suburb, Wanstead – the first time that Hobson had been able to live away from his parents – and Elizabeth gave birth to a daughter, Margaret, in April 1936. As the decade drew to an end and the international situation worsened, Hobson became concerned about the possibility of Elizabeth being evacuated with her school. In April 1939 he telephoned the Board of Education and was astounded to be informed by a civil servant not only of their destination, but of the general plans for evacuation – in theory, a highly classified piece of information. Realising that this was a scoop of the first order, Hobson wrote up the information and submitted the article in May 1939 to one of the two most significant Sunday newspapers, the *Sunday Times*. The story, entitled 'Families Who Will Make Their Own Evacuation Plans',[27] duly appeared on the front page the following Sunday and Hobson's fifty-year connection with the newspaper had begun.

Although Hobson continued to be the drama critic of the *Christian Science Monitor*, supplying informative descriptions of the condition of the wartime London stage, the *Sunday Times* became his main employer from 1943. He was largely occupied with writing editorials and book reviews, but these were considered to be of high enough quality for him to be chosen to deputise for the film critic, Dilys Powell, when she fell ill in September 1943. In 1944 he was promoted to the position of assistant literary editor, published a plodding pot-boiler about cricket called *The Devil in Woodford Wells* in 1946 and became the television critic of the *Listener* in May 1947.

Hobson's eventual accession to the post of theatre critic was always described by him as 'an irrelevant accident of social morality',[28] but in reality it illustrated the precarious position of the homosexual in London at that time. A few days after Agate had returned from attending Tynan's sixth-form conference in July 1945, he became embroiled in an embarrassing scrape that had disastrous consequences for the Scotsman Alan 'Jock' Dent, and unexpected ones for Hobson. Dent had been the critic of the *Manchester Guardian* between 1935 and 1943, as well as Agate's secretary from 1926 to 1941. For many years he was considered to be Agate's prospective successor at the *Sunday Times*, and it was a view to which Agate had certainly subscribed.[29] Hobson himself alluded to this somewhat indiscreetly in an article he wrote for the *Christian Science Monitor* in 1948 about Dent's screenplay for Olivier's version of *Hamlet*. He observed that the prize that he had gained had been the goal that Dent failed to achieve, since for years 'he was the secretary to James Agate, who never ceased to regard him as his proper successor'.[30]

This was certainly Agate's view in the final week of July 1945 – and it was a view that damaged Dent's chances irreparably. Hobson relates the circumstances:

> . . . one day, as I was walking down the corridor of the *Sunday Times*, the editor W.W. Hadley . . . came very perturbed out of his room and said to me 'You've written reviews for the *Christian Science Monitor* about the theatre. Well, you write instead of Agate on Sunday because Jimmy is ill'. He continued, 'Jimmy has written to me saying that he had asked Alan Dent to write his article . . . I've told him that he can have time off because he's ill, but *I* shall choose who shall substitute.' Now, he had never done this before, but I didn't ask him why he said this, I just wrote the article. I substituted for Agate.[31]

The reason for Hadley's agitation was that shortly before this meeting, Agate had had to escape from a male brothel in his nightshirt. It was something that Lord Kemsley had found so shocking that, when he was informed, he wanted to sack the critic on the spot.[32] Hadley, however, had pointed out that this would attract a considerable amount of bad publicity and Kemsley reluctantly backed down. Nevertheless, Dent was banned from the paper on account of his intimacy with Agate and then cruelly disowned by the critic, who, possibly in a vain attempt to rescue his reputation with Lord Kemsley, wrote to his friend Sydney Carroll – an influential adviser to the magnate – to recommend that he be succeeded by Hobson.[33] Thwarted in his cherished ambition, Dent became the drama critic of the *News Chronicle* in 1945, where he laboured until 1960.

Relations between Agate and Hobson, who from now on was regarded as his permanent substitute, were strained. Although Hobson records that, having recovered, Agate was always very polite to him (perhaps out of a misplaced fear of blackmail) and that they were to lunch every week at the Ivy restaurant, agreeing to pay for each other's drinks – 'I paid for his bottle of champagne, he paid for my bottle of lemonade'[34] – Agate was unhappy with the state of affairs over the next two years. This did not, however, prevent him from regaling the younger man with stories about his testicles, which he alleged had, over recent years, become as large as billiard balls and a brilliant orange colour, or from continually expressing his ardent desire to become the first theatre critic to be awarded a knighthood (an honour that, ironically, was to fall to Hobson).[35]

Agate died, while correcting some of his proofs, of a heart attack on 6 June 1947. After the embarrassment of Agate's sexual proclivities, the prejudiced Lord Kemsley wanted to ensure that there was no similar 'mistake' in the appointment of the new critic. In the 1970s, when he was engaged on research for *The Pearl of Days*, a book about the history of the *Sunday Times*, Hobson discovered that Kemsley had told Hadley: 'Hobson's all right. Hobson has a daughter. Let's have Hobson.'[36] This discovery caused some pain, as he told me in 1991: 'I thought I'd been asked to deputise and to be their drama critic because of my brilliance as a craftsman, but I found out the real reason . . . well, I always say that my life has been full of accidents – but that was the genuine, humiliating reason.'[37]

Hobson's accession to the post of drama critic in July 1947 coincided with the first decline in London theatre attendance for several years. Whilst popular, lavishly staged musicals such as *Oklahoma!*, *Annie Get Your Gun* and *Bless the Bride* retained their appeal, many new works seemed derivative. *Now Barabbas* and *Boys in Brown* were both about prison regimes; *Miranda* and *A Fish in the Family* told the adventures of mermaids; *Dark Emmanuel* and *Calcutta in the Morning* investigated nuclear destruction; and *Birthmark* and *Spanish Incident* continued the fashion for plays about Nazis. For inspiration, Hobson turned to the French. It was a crucial career decision. He found Jean-Louis Barrault's performance as Hamlet at the second Edinburgh Festival in 1948 as electrifying as Tynan had and began to hail imports such as Jean-Paul Sartre's *Crime passionel* (1948) as useful models for British writers to emulate. The play, he wrote, in a column given the Latin title 'Sartre Resartus', 'goes further towards justifying Sartre's position as the most important – certainly the most publicised – force in the contemporary drama than any of his works we have seen in London'.[38] The only home-bred playwright from whom Hobson expected much was Christopher Fry, who had demonstrated in *The Lady's Not For Burning* (1948) that he was 'bemused with the glory of words, who scorneth tea-cups, and is not interested in little misdemeanours on drawing room sofas'.[39] He had as high hopes for Christian Verse Drama as he had for all things French.

At the beginning of 1949, Hobson first encountered the young man who was to become his chief professional rival during the next decade when he saw the OUDS First Quarto *Hamlet* at the Rudolf Steiner Hall. For all their sense of competition, their personal relationship was always to remain cordial and generous. (Writing in May 1980 to inform Tynan of the death of his wife, Hobson observed: 'The great days when you and I did weekly battle over new plays – generally, indeed almost always ending in your victory – now seem a part of some legendary Homeric past'.[40])

A few months later their paths crossed again. In the autumn of 1949, the publishers of *He That Plays the King* sent Hobson – who had recommended Tynan to Longmans – a proof copy to read. An endorsement from the *Sunday Times* critic would be something worth having, especially as he was now earning praise for his atmospheric description of great acting performances (Olivier's Lear and Richard III); his passionate support for what he was later to term the 'foreign revelation'[41] – foreign plays on the London stage that might help stimulate a much-needed revival in British writing (such as Tennessee Williams's *A Streetcar Named Desire* which he vigorously defended in October 1949);[42] and his deft sense of irony. This was famously displayed in a 1949 review of Camus's *Caligula*:

> Caligula throttled his mistress, rammed poison down the throat of an old man who shot round the stage like a terrified mouse, seduced a middle-aged lady before the eyes of her husband and the guests at a dinner party, and still yelled and shrieked for fresh experiences. Caligula yearned, I yawned, the more fortunate among us went to sleep, and a few brave souls left the theatre. The evening went on and on, until at the end of three hours the stage lights were lowered while a band of singularly leisurely conspirators stabbed Caligula to death in the darkness. After this, there came a moment of supreme horror, for the lights went up, and Caligula was seen clinging, with bleeding mouth, to a mirror from which the glass had been thoughtfully removed. He then uttered the electrifying threat, 'I'm still alive', and I dare say that not a man in the audience did not turn pale, fearing that there was more to come. The alarm proved groundless, but I doubt if my nerves will ever be the same again.[43]

Hobson's response to the book was better than the publishers could have dared hope, particularly given the young man's less than flattering reference to him personally, and he replied directly to the author:

[*Sunday Times*, Kemsley House, London WC1   23 December 1949]

My dear Ken Tynan,

Mark Longman tells me that he would very much like to get that brilliant player and director Orson Welles to write a preface for your book. This would, of course, be a tremendous honour, but I honestly believe that it would not be a greater honour than the book deserves.

I personally have long been an admirer of Welles, ever since that tremendous film 'Citizen Kane' showed that a new and titanic genius had burst into the cinema. If he allows his name to be associated with your book, he would be joining something that, in my opinion, is of very high value.

Of all branches of dramatic criticism, the evocation of acting is the most difficult, and in this you are an absolute master. Much though I disagree with some of your individual judgements, your book seems to be the most dazzling thing written upon theatre during my lifetime.

Yours ever,

Harold Hobson[44]

They would soon continue to dispute their individual judgements in their weekly Sunday columns – to the delight of the theatre-going public.

It was another disastrous immersion in a drama production that hastened Tynan's entry into full-time theatre reviewing. Alec Guinness, buoyed by the success of his Ealing comedies, *Kind Hearts and Coronets* and *The Lavender Hill Mob*, decided to direct and star in a modern-dress production of *Hamlet* for the government-sponsored Festival of Britain in the summer of 1951. The Festival had been conceived as a centenary celebration of the Great Exhibition of 1851 to illustrate the best of the country's talent in art and design. With more than half an eye on improving public morale, an incredible £11 million had been allocated to the celebrations to create what the organiser, Gerald Barry, called 'fun, fantasy and colour' as 'a tonic to the nation'.[45] Hundreds of thousands of Britons on specially chartered trains travelled to the South Bank of the Thames to marvel at the 'Dome of Discovery', which showcased exhibits pointing to the future. They went on rides at the Funfair at Battersea Park, enjoyed the sculptures, murals and mobiles by Moore, Piper, Epstein and Sutherland, which had been assembled by the design team under Hugh Casson and Misha Black, and scratched their heads about the cigar-shaped symbol of the Festival, the 'Skylon'. It was a rare opportunity to celebrate the past and look forward to the future in the arts and in science.

Confident of what he did not want to do – either a Victorian piece of stylisation or a modern interpretation leaning on Freud – but with no clear perception of what he actually wanted to achieve, Guinness cast Tynan as the Player King. He had seen the Rudolf Steiner Hall production and felt that Tynan's distinctive approach and appearance would complement this innovative production. Mistake compounded mistake, however. A second director, Frank Hauser, a BBC radio producer with no experience of the stage, was engaged to offer further insight – but simply ended up confusing the cast with contradictory directions. The costumes, in 'authentic' Elizabethan style, were so heavy that they creaked and the absence of a pre-West End run meant that there was no opportunity to smooth out the problems of the lighting plot. The result, when the production opened on 17 May, was one of the great first-night catastrophes and the event was subsequently referred to by Guinness as 'my notoriously disastrous *Hamlet*'.[46] Elaine Dundy, who went along with Harold Clurman, recalled the difficulties:

> Something went wrong from the very start. It was the lighting plot, which was several cues off. This became blindingly apparent when the scene with the ghost was flooded with light and subsequent scenes were plunged into darkness. And it continued for a very long time, the lights brightening and darkening incomprehensibly as they skipped along their unchecked lunatic way . . . the lighting man was the villain, not Claudius.[47]

As the curtain fell, the gallery booed, but this was nothing compared to the derision of the critics. For Harold Hobson, the failure was complete: 'Dickens had his *Hard Times*, Shakespeare his *Titus Andronicus*, Napoleon his Waterloo, Wellington his premiership, and now Mr Alec Guinness has acted Hamlet. It is the custom of genius to do things in a big way, and the cropper that Mr Guinness came on Thursday night was truly monumental.'[48]

Numerous things had laughably gone awry. Guinness's attempt to 'portray the dark underside of the Prince's mind' was confusing, Rosencrantz's black eye-patch was comically distracting and there was a very poor level of supporting acting. Hobson was not alone in his dismay. T.C. Worsley felt that the whole thing had been a 'complete misfire',[49] Ivor Brown described it as a 'lullaby performance'[50] and Anthony Cookman in the *Tatler* discreetly termed it 'very odd'.[51] Only W.A. Darlington recognised Guinness's performance as 'intelligent and sardonic',[52] if marred by production problems.

The theatre critic and Conservative MP Beverley Baxter chose a slightly different approach in the *Evening Standard*. Pulling no punches in 'The Worst *Hamlet* I Have Ever Seen', he swooped on the performance of one particular actor. 'I am a man of a kindly nature who takes no joy in hurting those who are without defence,' he trilled, 'but Mr Ken Tynan . . . would not get a chance in a village hall unless he were related to the vicar. His performance was quite dreadful.'[53] (Baxter had mistakenly believed that an anonymous survey of theatre critics in the journal *Panorama*, which derided his own 'merciless volubility',[54] had been written by the drama critic of that publication – Kenneth Tynan – and he wanted his revenge. It had, in fact, been written by Gavin Lambert.[55]) Given the battering that he had received as a consequence of his involvement with the practical side of drama in 1951, the ironic fact of his lifelong sensitivity to adverse comment, and the necessity of still having to appear in the castigated play, Tynan's response was elegantly restrained. Writing to the *Evening Standard* four days later, he denied the thrust of Baxter's criticism and plaintively observed: 'I am quite a good enough critic to know that my performance in *Hamlet* is not "quite dreadful"; it is, in fact, only slightly less than mediocre. I do not actually exit through scenery or wave at friends in the audience.'[56]

Coincidentally, Charles Curran, the features editor of the paper, and a growing fan of the newsworthy Tynan, had dined with him at the Savoy on the very day of the opening of *Hamlet*. He had been attempting to engage Tynan for the *Evening Standard* for some months now, and wanted to suggest a series of freelance articles. Tynan's public profile, youthful insouciance and the public spat with Baxter merely increased his allure, and the editor, Percy Elland, wrote to Lord Beaverbrook the following day, confirming the series and adding that, 'I think his sharp pen may do well in the *Standard*'.[57]

In mid-June Hobson revisited the New Theatre and wrote a second notice, slightly ashamed that because of an urgent engagement in Scotland he had broken his usual practice and written his first piece three hours after the curtain fell. He was also aware that the adverse reviews had meant that the production was being withdrawn at the end of June, losing the producer, Henry Sherek, an astronomical £15,000. 'Hamlet Revisited' notes the damage that the first wave of reviews had caused and regards the early closure as 'regrettable'. It acknowledges that the faults of the first night constituted a distraction and states that these have now been ironed out – the supporting cast 'proves itself worthy of its leading actor', the lighting has improved and Guinness has dispensed with his comical beard. Guinness's own performance, highlighting the weakness and indecision of the Prince, appears more comprehensible and the overall production is now 'memorable in its originality, integrity, courage and pathos'. Hobson completes his retraction by urging the reader to make a visit – 'If the New Theatre is not thronged at every one of the last sixteen performances I shall lose all hope of the British public'[58] – and although this must have infuriated the company, bitterly aware that the damage had already been done, it provides a useful reminder that performances can improve.

Offered the opportunity to contribute a series of theatre profiles while still performing in Hamlet, Tynan sought to administer an antidote to lazy deference and to carve out his own distinctive critical style. His chosen approach was elegant irreverence – anathema to early 1950s society – and it was an approach that was to both underpin his subsequent theatre criticism and help facilitate the reorientation of British drama that would soon make the country the centre of the theatrical world. Under the provocative title, 'Is He Great? I Say No', Tynan's first profile, published on 29 May 1951, featured a subject from He That Plays the King, Danny Kaye. Its concluding paragraph refused to pull its punches:

His attributes add up to a highly specialised and energetic skill: and all highly specialised talents carry two concomitant perils – narrowness and the inability to develop. The narrowness is already perceptible, for Kaye is very ordinary without his wife [Sylvia Fine]'s brilliant lyrics. On the other matter, we will suspend judgement.[59]

For a fan of the star, Teresa N. Coghlan of Chippenham, this was too much and she wrote to the paper two days later to express her indignation – 'jealousy is a terrible thing! Danny has something the writer of that slanderous and unkind article will never have . . . charity towards his fellows, the inability to do an unkind act, or think an unkind thought.'[60] Barbara Aarons of Cannon Hill, Hampstead, however, was excited by Tynan's boldness, even if she phrased this in an alarming manner:

Congratulations to Mr Kenneth Tynan on his courage in trying to restore a sense of balance in our attitude to Danny Kaye. It seems one can openly criticise royalty and politicians, but never film stars – the public revolts. Violent Danny Kaye fans will probably write Mr Tynan threatening letters, some even suggesting murder.[61]

Beneath these two antithetical views, Tynan was allowed to add: 'Without forgetting the immense exhilaration he has so often given me, I want to rescue Kaye from these idolaters who have told him it adds up to "greatness".'[62] The attention that he sought had been aroused – and it was good journalism, too.

The following week, Charles Laughton, the great Old Vic character actor of the 1930s, whose successful film career took him away from the stage in the 1940s, was the target. Tynan's ability to encapsulate the physical mannerisms of a performer in an arresting simile was apparent, when he linked Laughton's stage presence to his appearance at their interview:

Laughton arrives at his characterisations panting, having picked up a hundred assorted oddments on the way: and the result is always a fascinating and unique mosaic . . . He walks top-heavily, like a salmon standing on its tail. Laughton invests his simplest exit with an atmosphere of furtive flamboyance; he left the hotel for all the world like an absconding banker. He took leave of me in the manner of a butler begging an afternoon off. As a friend of mine once commented: 'Considering he's a great man, Charles makes his voice do an awful lot of bowing and scraping.'[63]

It was the third piece that was the dynamite, however. Vivien Leigh had just enjoyed a monumental success starring in a double bill opposite her husband in Shakespeare's *Antony and Cleopatra* and Shaw's *Caesar and Cleopatra*. Opening on 10 and 11 May at the St James's Theatre, the productions were an integral part of the Festival of Britain. Hardly any of the 8 million people who had visited the Festival by the end of the summer would have seen Leigh and Olivier perform together, but their much-reported triumph contributed to the general feeling of well-being. Ivor Brown summed up the sense of national pride in one of his most famous and enthusiastic reviews:

In two nights of glory at the St. James's Theatre, the English theatre has given Festival performances of a quality which I do not believe could have been equalled elsewhere in the world . . . the challenge is to Cleopatra and Vivien Leigh takes it not only with the necessary beauty, which was certain anyway, but with a technical skill, power of voice, and an emotional power that are a revelation of developed artistry. She moved me almost beyond endurance . . . Here is the seemingly unattainable, the 'lass unparalleled'![64]

In his third theatre profile for the *Evening Standard* ('How Great Is Vivien Leigh?', published on 9 July 1951), the twenty-four-year-old Tynan chose to dissent from the majority view. In his obituary of Tynan in 1980, Hobson accurately stated that 'like Latimer and Ridley [he] would have been proud to be called a heretic'[65] and his determination to stand out from the crowd is nowhere better illustrated than in this attack on a member of the theatrical monarchy that is as memorable as it was cutting. In his opening remarks he professes the desire – evident in the Danny Kaye profile – to rescue the actress from her idolaters and to undertake a sober reconsideration:

> Overpraise in the end, is the most damaging kind of praise, especially if you are an actress, approaching forty, who has already reached the height of her powers . . . fondly we recall her recent peak; when, in 1945, she held together the shaky structure of Thornton Wilder's play, *The Skin of Our Teeth*. She used her soul in this display; and was sweet.

No critics in 1951 would dare argue that Leigh had peaked over six years ago, least of all highlight her age in such a blatant fashion – but Tynan was prepared to be more audacious yet:

> She remains sweet. In all her gentle motions there is no hint of that attack and upheaval, that inner uproar which we, mutely admiring, call greatness; no breath of the tumultuous obsession which, against our will, consumes us. In *Caesar and Cleopatra* she keeps a firm grip on the narrow ledge which is indisputably hers; the level on which she can be pert, sly and spankable, and fill out a small personality . . . *Antony and Cleopatra* is another world . . . 'You were a boggler ever' says Antony at one point to his idle doxy, and one can feel Miss Leigh's imagination boggling at the thought of playing Cleopatra. Taking a deep breath and resolutely focusing her pert, winkle charm, she launches another of her careful readings: ably and passionately she picks her way among its great challenges, presenting a glibly mown lawn where her author had imagined a jungle . . .

One feeling consumed Tynan as he watched Leigh's performance unfold – but not the feeling of rapture that united critical opinion; rather

> the feeling Mr Bennet in *Pride and Prejudice* was experiencing when he dissuaded his daughter from further pianoforte recital by murmuring that she 'had delighted us long enough'. Though at times, transported by Shakespeare, she becomes almost wild, there is in Miss Leigh's Cleopatra an arresting streak of Jane Austen. She picks at the part with the daintiness of a debutante called upon to dismember a stag; and her manners are first rate . . .

As if this was not shocking enough, the true heresy came in the final paragraphs. The consequences of the actress's deficiencies were more serious than for other performers, Tynan wrote, because

> Miss Leigh's limitations have wider repercussions than those of most actresses. Sir Laurence, with that curious chivalry which, some time or other, blights the progress of every great actor, gives me the impression that he subdues his blow-lamp ebullience to match her. Blunting his iron precision, levelling away his towering authority, he meets her half-way. Antony climbs down: and Cleopatra pats him on the head. A cat, in fact, can do more than look at a king: she can hypnotise him.[66]

Readers of British newspapers were unused to such demolitions, and critical letters swiftly flooded in to the *Evening Standard*. David Merrian, of the York Buildings, Adelphi, summed up their outrage when he stormed that

> I think Mr Tynan's article on Vivien Leigh is disgraceful. Miss Leigh is a highly competent actress and there are few indeed who could have done as well as she in the Cleopatras. She undertook a unique and tremendous task and has earned high praise from our best critics.[67]

But that was the point for Tynan. The unquestioning eulogising of the theatrical stars was a part of the pre-war stasis and a symptom of the country's post-war malaise. Young people of his generation did not feel bound by the fetters of respect and duty that had brought their parents together. Not having fought in the Second World War, and given the changed perspective of the Cold War, they did not see the point of National Service. Bowed down by the class system and with little disposable income, they had few forms of rebellion as yet, but Tynan's dissection of the London stage – so long the bastion of conservative values, upper-middle-class sensibilities and resolutely escapist entertainment – was a liberating form of dissent that gave the briefest glimpse of a shift of power. Elaine Dundy neatly summarised her husband's general appeal by observing that:

> When Ken began work in his permanent role as the *Standard*'s drama critic, with his vastly expanded audience, he made history. I was not the only one experiencing the euphoria of his performances. For what he induced in what must be called his 'audience' (rather than use a word so essentially passive as his 'readership') was the happy contagion its spectators shared with each other. It was as if they were watching him perform live. His reviews were seductive, alluring, appealing, erudite, outrageous and funny, funny, funny. The apt quotations with which he sprinkled his writing were bonuses, ones you'd never come across

before so you were learning at the same time that you were laughing. These pieces changed one's mood.[68]

Was this piece, though, simply further evidence of Tynan's own version of star worship? On this, Dundy is equally revealing:

From then on [*Antony and Cleopatra*] Ken's worship of Olivier's performances on stage was unabashed and unconditional. Many people would see these public displays as embarrassing personal confessions of love. I saw them differently. From the first I saw Ken not as a man surrendering himself body and soul to his idol but as a man cannily campaigning for a big job with his idol. Ever since I'd known him he was as determined that England have a National Theatre as he was determined to be part of it.[69]

Throughout his career, Tynan was much more calculating and manipulative than his admirers might like to concede.

Ever the canny operator, Tynan moved swiftly to capitalise on the notoriety that this piece brought. Having been invited to dine with the famous proprietor of the *Evening Standard*, Lord Beaverbrook, six days after publication of the Leigh profile, he wrote a note of thanks for 'a fine evening', at which he had been 'duly tongue-tied', and enclosed a copy of *He That Plays the King*. A touch impudently – but in a manner guaranteed to leave an impression – he concluded: 'I still like parts of it; and the rest is, at worst, *characteristically* bad.'[70]

Hamlet closed in July, and the married couple of six months decided to take a second honeymoon in Spain. The subsequent trip to Valencia developed a new interest for Tynan: bullfighting. Elaine, who had been amused by her husband's meticulous preparations for the trip, flicking through travel guides, phrase books and Hemingway's *Death in the Afternoon* (all mirroring the detailed research he undertook for his writing), was unsure what to expect. At their first *feria*, they were initially indifferent to the spectacle, but during the final fight, involving the ageing Rafael Ortega, who employed the dangerous technique of charging towards the bull, the couple were swept up by the crowd's enthusiasm:

We left on a cloud. Immediately Ken took out a subscription to *El Ruedo*, the bullfight magazine, and back home he read everything he could find out about the *corrida*, undaunted that most of it was in Spanish. A *feria* he liked the sound of – a week's worth of bullfighting at the end of July – was taking place in Valencia. The newest sensation, Litri, a young matador dubbed El Atomico, whose pictures and write-ups intrigued Ken, would be fighting there. Ken decided we must go. He had decided to write about bullfighting.[71]

The immediate result of this new, breathless enthusiasm was an article for the *Evening Standard*. In *He That Plays the King* Tynan had argued that a bullfight was a 'dirty and disorganised version upon the high tragic theme',[72] and he now chose to emphasise in 'Matador' the nobility of the spectacle. The current star of the ring was the twenty-year-old Litri, whom Tynan managed to interview in his hotel after Litri had been gored by a bull. The young matador seemed, in spite of his enormous popularity, to be an appealingly modest figure, brushing off his injury as bad luck and his fame as the work of others: 'I am only a judge of bulls. The public is the "judge of fighters".' At the end of the article Tynan strikes a delicately elegiac note when he speculates that 'I have a conviction that Litri's perfect fight, the one that most truly satisfies him, will be the one that ends in his death',[73] and his interest in the conjunction of death and finesse would eventually result in the highly atmospheric and beautifully crafted account of three weeks of bullfighting during July 1952, which was published as *Bull Fever* by Longmans in 1955.

On his return to England, Tynan had other occupations: gentler profiles of the photographer Cecil Beaton – with whom he was shortly to collaborate on a book about the great cultural personalities of the day – and the historian G.M. Trevelyan;[74] a month covering the August holiday of the paper's film critic, Milton Shulman; and the odd column deputising for Beverley Baxter, who was increasingly distracted by his parliamentary duties harrying Attlee's weary government. The repulsively titled 'Citizen Coon', in October, on Orson Welles's *Othello* reminded both the readership and his employers of his compelling bravado. Whilst praising Welles's conception as the director, he lambasted his performance as an actor – 'what we saw was a tightly limited acting performance on a bound-bursting production'[75] – and there was no false gratitude for the introduction to *He That Plays the King*:

> No doubt about it, Orson Welles has the courage of his restrictions. In last night's boldly staged *Othello* at the St James's he gave a performance brave and glorious to the eye; but it was the performance of the magnificent amateur.
>
> I say this carefully, for I am young enough to have been brought up on rumour of his name, and I sat in my stall conscious that, in a sense, a whole generation was on trial.
>
> If Welles was wrong, if a contemporary approach to Shakespeare in his thunderbolt hands failed, then we were all wrong.

Fortunately, the attempt to modernise the play was a success, but it was at the cost of the director's own magnetism in performance:

> Welles's own performance was a huge shrug. He was grand and gross, and wore some garish costumes superbly. His close-cropped head was starkly military, and

he never looked in need of a banjo. But his voice, a musical instrument in one bass octave, lacked range: he toyed moodily with every inflection.

His face expressed wryness and strangulation, but little else. And his bodily relaxation frequently verged on sloth. Above all, he never built to a vocal climax, he positively waded through the great speeches, pausing before the stronger words like a landing craft breasting a swell. (When dead, his chest went on heaving like the North Sea).

Welles's Othello is the lordly and mannered performance we saw in *Citizen Kane*, slightly adapted to read Citizen Coon.

The playful impudence of this review was remarkable. Welles had been invited by Olivier and Leigh, who managed the St James's Theatre, to occupy the venue while they were touring in America. He had snatched at the opportunity and, to great press interest, had spent the summer with the Oliviers at Notley Abbey, preparing for the production and working on a novel. Tynan had no time for reputations – or even past favours – though. The production appeared to demonstrate that Welles's mind was preoccupied by other projects (including *The Black Museum*, a radio series about gruesome crimes from the files of Scotland Yard, and the protracted film version of *Othello*)[76] and Tynan chose to give his honest and forthright opinion. Regrettably, in his search for the eye-catching epithet, he also reflected the insensitivity of the 1950s as to matters of race and ethnicity.

Although he was not to realise it at the time, the budding theatre director produced his final piece of live theatre in November 1951. Along with Ellen Pollock, he mounted an abridged version of *Titus Andronicus* at the tiny Irving theatre in Leicester Square, and in its wallowing in the gruesome aspects of the plot (Lavinia has her tongue cut out and her hands cut off), it recalled the undergraduate excess of *Samson Agonistes*. Tynan took great delight in the fact that the Lord Chamberlain, who administered theatre censorship in Britain until 1968, insisted on two St John Ambulance men being present at every show. Each performance duly provoked the predicted audience fainting.[77]

Tynan's life at this time was exciting, uncertain and action-packed. In December he sailed with his now pregnant wife to New York on the ocean liner *Liberté*. It was the first time he had visited the country that he had loved since a child, and it did not disappoint. Elaine's parents put them up for their fortnight's stay at the Essex House on 59th Street, giving them 'a floor high enough to see the whole vista of Manhattan from Central Park and east and west up to the Bronx'.[78] They threw a party for her sisters and relatives, and began to get acquainted with their son-in-law's green suits, notoriety and inhibiting stammer. News of Tynan's youth, impetuosity and brilliant writing had filtered across the Atlantic, and he and Elaine began to receive a welter of celebrity invitations. They were given the best tables at Sardis and 21; socialised with Hermione Gingold, Harold Clurman and Joshua Logans; and took in one of the finest shows of the period, *Guys and Dolls*. Tynan thought it a masterpiece.

Towards the end of their stay, he made himself known to the wider New York public by writing an article for the *New York Times*. It surveyed the current Broadway scene and managed to produce some complimentary words about what was generally agreed to be a rather poor season. He praised the country's leading playwrights for creating worthwhile roles for women under thirty, something which set it apart from the London stage,[79] and he developed this theme in the *Spectator* on his return.[80] Further projects began to evolve from his fertile mind. He began to think about a short monograph on Alec Guinness and a series of celebrity profiles with the photographer, Cecil Beaton (eventually realised in 1953 as *Persona Grata*). Articles for *Panorama* on Noël Coward and monthly profiles for *Harper's Bazaar* on Guinness, Gielgud and Carol Reed all tumbled from his pen, and the expectant couple also found time to move into a new flat at 29 Hyde Park Gardens to secure more space for their new arrival. Tynan found it smart, warm and huge, loving the view over the park and describing it to Beaton as 'pure House and Gardens and mobiles and statics and pitchpine and pile'.[81] Elaine, somewhat to her surprise, enjoyed the unfamiliar task of furnishing a new property and she was particularly proud of Tynan's study, which, on his suggestion, she had had covered with photographs from the Spanish bullfighting magazine, *El Ruedo*. The domestic requirements of the new flat and the level of hospitality were not cheap, so Elaine's inheritance of $10,000 from her grandfather in February was a welcome addition to her allowance and Tynan's freelance earnings. Although he could command up to £90 for an American magazine article, it was apparent that a permanent post would need to be secured in the not too distant future.

In early 1952, Beaverbrook's patience with Baxter's absences in the House of Commons began to wane. For several weeks over Christmas and the new year, Ronald Duncan was invited to submit a covering column, but his analysis of contemporary theatrical events was insipid in comparison to Tynan's and on Friday, 16 May 1952, almost a year since the Danny Kaye profile, Tynan was taken on as the permanent critic. Tynan's year-long tenure as the critic of the *Evening Standard* has been too easily dismissed as a necessary but routine apprenticeship for his position at the *Observer*. Indeed, it has been tempting to view his role as Literary Manager at the National Theatre from 1963 to 1974 as the most important part of his career (the opinion not least of Kathleen Tynan). But the simple truth is that, without diminishing his achievements at the National, it is his ten years as a theatre critic between 1952 and 1962 that constitutes his most significant contribution to the evolution of post-war British theatre. Of all the voices in Britain at that time, it was his that reached out to the largest number of new, young, potential audience members, who would demand the reorientation of the British stage that made its products the envy of the world. As Elaine Dundy records:

> Ken and the fifties were a perfect match. The explosion of post-war theatre needed a pre-eminent illuminator and memorializer, and there was Ken, able to illuminate, memorialize, celebrate and excoriate like no other critic. Like Beerbohm and Shaw before him, he was as much a star as those performing on the stage. Moreover, for the delectation of first-night audiences among whom he sat, he would appear in eye-catching outfits, such as a suit of dove gray with a velvet collar, enlivened by pastel-colored shirts in primrose, ashes of rose or apple green.[82]

Fresh from directing his first (and only) television play, Jean-Jacques Bernard's *Martine* in May 1952, and now the proud father of a daughter, Tracy, who was born on 12 May, Tynan set to work at a time of critical complacency about the London theatre. Mesmerised by the glamour of H.M. Tennent Ltd, reassured by the regularity of productions by star playwrights such as Rattigan and continually deluded that the glut of Shakespearian productions obviated the need for new, indigenous plays, almost all the critics believed that drama was in a generally robust state of health. Only Harold Hobson chose to sound some alarm bells. In spite of his love of all things French, he had lamented in the autumn of 1951 that Jean Anouilh, with *Traveller without Luggage*, his seventh play on the London stage in the last four years (after *Ardèle*, *Ring Round the Moon*, *Point of Departure*, *Antigone*, *Fading Mansions* and *Thieves' Carnival*) was now the 'most popular British dramatist'.[83] In December 1951 he repeated his belief in 'Perpetual Rebel' that foreign works should show British plays the way forward in a time of sterility – not replace them[84] – and a further trip to Paris in the spring of 1952 – always a cathartic experience – finally convinced Hobson that he needed to speak out in protest at the vacuous nature of the British theatre. The resulting article, 'London Survey', was another example of Hobson's unpredictability and meant that Tynan was not alone in experiencing dissatisfaction at what he was being asked to review.

On his return from Paris, Hobson had noticed marked differences between the two capitals. The most striking aspect of the London stage was 'its extraordinary detachment' and its 'indifference' to the world in which it was living. The remoteness appeared deliberate and unremitting. 'I came back to a country whose newspapers are mainly filled with tidings of war, insurrection, industrial unrest, political controversy, and parliamentary misbehaviour; and to a theatre from which it seems to me, in the first shock of re-acquaintance, that all echo of these things is shut off as by sound-proof walls.' The increasing tension over West Germany, the imminent atom bomb test in Nevada, the strikes that had crippled coal production in Wales and the ongoing discussions about closer European ties made no impact on the London theatre at all.

The list of entertainments to which he had been invited that week – comedians at the Palladium, 'a persuasively restful' production of *Uncle Vanya*, a dramatisation of Jane Austen's *Lady Susan* and another revival of the Stratford *Tempest* – verifies this impression. It draws forth a surprising conclusion:

> That the human race is passionate, pathological, physical, poetic, paradoxical, and even philosophical is recognised in the West End: the first in *The Deep Blue Sea*; the second in *Third Person, The Same Sky* and *Women of Twilight*; the third in *Bet Your Life* and *The Vortex*; the fourth in *Much Ado About Nothing*, though scarcely in the Old Vic's *King Lear*, a doubly staggering production that astonishes no less than it totters; the fifth in *White Sheep of the Family*; and the sixth in *Nightmare Abbey* and *The Love of Four Colonels*, both extremely diverting. But, except in the way of fantasy in the last-named play, that the human race is also political the contemporary English theatre by implication and neglect absolutely denies.

Hobson goes on to add that, while much in contemporary politics is worth ignoring and French drama does possess the advantage of being able to utilise such searing topics as collaboration, the treatment of broader issues might be rewarding in Britain, too.

This is a seam that Tynan was to mine so richly when he joined the *Observer* in September 1954 – and one that Hobson would examine only sporadically over the coming decade. The article usefully counters the myth that Tynan was a lone voice in the 1950s in his insistence that British theatre would continue to stagnate if it persisted in talking to itself. It also puts Tynan's first two years as a full-time critic into context. Although undeniably the most cutting and effective voice, his tenure at the *Evening Standard* is marked less by describing a new agenda for theatre to follow than by pricking the bubble of complacency that had enveloped his critical colleagues, with the exception of Hobson. Tynan's reviews during the summer of 1952 are a case in point. Theatre Workshop's polemical *Uranium 235*, for example, was merely 'a bold attempt to prove that the experimental theatre, on which so many playwrights either cut or broke their teeth in the twenties, is stone dead'.[85] Similarly, Rodney Ackland's *The Pink Room*, another experimental work that attempted to break the tyranny of the drawing room by being set in a bohemian drinking club on the eve of the 1945 general election – and deliberately challenged the prevailing belief that the war had been an exercise in unparalleled heroism – was surprisingly damned with faint praise. Dismissing it as 'broken-backed', Tynan lazily opined that 'it takes, I am afraid, a heart larger than his to write about the small sins of small people without sentimentalism or shallow moralising. Chekhov could do it, and in his hands *The Pink Room* might have been a minor masterpiece.'[86] What really interested him in the summer of 1952 – following in the vein of the Kaye and Leigh articles – was the success or otherwise of the stars. It was his emphatic views on their performances – so different from the sculptured opinions of Hobson's – that heightened his public profile.

John Gielgud's Stratford production of *Macbeth* with Sir Ralph Richardson in the role of the Scottish usurper was one of those theatrical combinations that ought to have presaged a thrilling success. At the end of 1948, Olivier and Richardson had been foolishly let go by the governors of the Old Vic, who feared that their extended absences caused by their enormous overseas success and film commitments would harm the long-term project to create a National Theatre. Since that period Olivier had established a company at the St James's Theatre, but Richardson had trod water somewhat. He joined Anthony Quayle's Shakespeare Memorial Company at Stratford-upon-Avon in 1952 with a view to remind the public how short-sighted the Old Vic governors had been. Although he had never performed *Macbeth* before, he took some false reassurance from a critically acclaimed wireless production that he had undertaken during the war. He would have been wiser, however, to have acknowledged the cooling relationship between himself and Gielgud, who continued to feel excluded from Richardson's wartime collaboration with Olivier and who felt unnerved by Richardson's obvious disapproval of his homosexuality.[87] The production, which opened in June 1952, was a supreme disaster – worse even than Guinness's *Hamlet* – and it was Tynan who wrote the most castigating account. Under the withering headline 'Sir Ralph does it all by numbers', he pointed the finger at the director:

Last Tuesday night at the Stratford Memorial Theatre Macbeth walked the plank, leaving me, I am afraid, unmoved to the point of paralysis.

It was John Gielgud, never let us forget, who did this cryptic thing: Gielgud as producer, who seems to have imagined that Ralph Richardson, with his comic, Robeyesque cheese-face was equipped to play Macbeth: Gielgud who surrounded the play's fuliginous cruelties with settings of total black, which is about as subtle as setting *Saint Joan* in total white; Gielgud who commanded dirty tatters for Macbeth's army and brisk, clean tunics for Malcolm's, just to indicate in advance who was going to win.

The production assumed, or so I took it, that the audience was either moronic or asleep: it read us a heavily italicised lecture on the play and left nothing to our own small powers of discovery.

When, in the banquet scene, a real table and some real chairs, chalices and candelabra were brought on, life intervened for a moment: but once the furniture had gone, we were back in the engulfing, the platitudinous void, with its single message: 'Background of evil, get it?'

Gielgud's direction shredded, Tynan now turned to the acting:

> In the Banquet Scene, spurred perhaps by the clever handling of Banquo's ghost, which vanished dazzlingly in one swirl of a coat, Richardson came to life for a few consecutive sentences and I could not help recalling a line he had uttered earlier in the evening: 'My dull brain was wrought with things forgotten'.
>
> Up to this point he had appeared a robot player, a man long past feeling, who had been stumping across the broad stage as if in need of a compass to find the exit. Now, momentarily, he smouldered, and made us recall his excelling past, littered with fine things encompassed and performed. And then, and ever after, Sir Ralph's numbness, his apparent mental deafness returned to chill me: Macbeth became once more a sad facsimile of the Cowardly Lion in *The Wizard of Oz.*

As if this was not enough, the bravado of the critic increases, to complete the dissection:

> At the height of the battle, you remember, Macbeth contemplates suicide, rejecting the thought in the words: 'Why should I play the Roman fool, and die on my own sword?' Sir Ralph, at this juncture, gripped his blade by the sharp end with both hands, and practised putts with it: it was as if the Roman fool had been the local pro.
>
> His feathery, yeasty voice with its single springheeled inflection starved the part of its richness: he moved dully, as if by numbers, and such charm as he possessed was merely a sort of unfocused bluffness, like a teddy-bear snapped in a bed light by a child holding its first camera.
>
> Sir Ralph, who seems to me to have become the glass eye in the forehead of English acting, has now bumped into something quite immovable. His Macbeth is slovenly; and to go further into it would be as frustrating as trying to write with a pencil whose point has long since worn down into the wood.[88]

Richardson's reaction was understandably one of humiliation. Waiting for the reviews to appear in the Green Room, he asked if anyone had seen his talent. 'It's not a very big one, but I seem to have mislaid it.' During the subsequent run of *Volpone* – another ill-conceived production – Richardson made a comment to a fellow actor that has now passed into theatrical folklore. 'Give me five pounds,' he demanded. 'Why?' the puzzled actor asked. 'If you don't give me five pounds I'll have it put about that you were in my *Macbeth*.'[89] It is a testament to Richardson's famous amiability that he later granted Tynan an interview in 1979 for an article that was eventually to appear in his collection of theatre profiles, *Show People*.

Tracy Tynan had one particularly impressive godparent at her christening, Katharine Hepburn, whom Tynan had reviewed two weeks after his hatchet job on both Richardson and Gielgud. Although disliking the Shaw play – *The Millionairess* – in which she had starred, Tynan demonstrated that he was equally able to capture a scintillating theatrical performance as to dissect a tortuous one:

> The part is nearly unactable: yet Miss Hepburn took it, acted it, and found a triumph in it. She glittered like a bracelet thrown up at the sun; she was metallic, yet reminded us that metals shine and can also melt. Epifania clove to her, and she bestowed on the role a riotous elegance and a gift of tears not of the author's making.
>
> Her first entrance was as if she had just emerged from the sea, and were tossing the spray from her eyes; and it was not one entrance but two, for she had swept in, out and then in again before I could blink. She used her mink wrap as Hitler is said to have used the Chancellery carpet, hurling it to the floor and falling upon it, pounding her fists in tearful vituperation . . . Miss Hepburn is not versatile, she is simply unique.

This mixture of unorthodox imagery, eye-catching phrases and an idiom that people could relate to from everyday life (and not from some French salon) was already hardening into Tynan's call sign. He told Harold Clurman that his new job was causing him to 'simplify his style' since he could no longer display 'the full panoply of his mandarin vocabulary'.[90] Secretly he knew that the discipline required to write a weekly column was no bad thing. The same month the producer, Henry Sherek, highlighted the intellectual appeal of the critic's fresh approach, in a letter that is as complimentary as it is ingratiating. 'I thought your review in the *Spectator* of *Winter Journey* was quite brilliant,' he wrote. 'It was not as flattering as some others, but I found it a model of theatre criticism, and because my vocabulary is very much smaller than yours, it cost me money, as I had to buy an Oxford Dictionary – the pocket edition, of course . . .'[91]

Another producer, the combative Emile Littler, was less impressed by Tynan's directness, and – perhaps aware of the commercial impact of the critic's views – wrote to dispute his negative view of British musicals expressed in an article published in August:

> Do you really think it is possible to compare 'South Pacific', 'Oklahoma' and 'No, No Nanette' with 'Blue for a Boy' or 'Zip Goes A Million'? True, all are Musical Shows, but then salmon, chop suey and fish and chips are all classed as

foods, but they are for different tastes . . . A New York Producer friend of mine who saw 'Blue for a Boy' came back to London the following summer and found it still packing Her Majesty's Theatre, and he said to me quite seriously: 'You know, Emile, I would love to do this show of yours in New York, and there would be a big public for it, but there's one thing which will stop getting a production over there. The critics would tear the show up on the first night, and you wouldn't be able to survive it'. You, Mr Tynan, will probably say: 'Quite right, the critics should tear it up', but in doing so you are denying a very large audience of the Living Theatre from seeing the type of show they wish to see. In the cinema we have Laurel and Hardy, and why can't we have sheer lunatic fun also on the stage? . . . The next time you go pioneering, I hope you will go out and see one of my provincial shows. I don't think you will find canvas flapping off the flats, or the band playing old fashioned orchestrations, and I sincerely hope that 'Probably' won't be the verdict for 'Love from Judy'.⁹²

This correspondence continued into September, with Littler now questioning whether Tynan's heartfelt views precluded him from writing on the subject: 'I am not sure in my own mind whether a critic who does not like musical farcical comedy, has any moral right to accept the job of sitting in the stalls and criticising it . . . Some time we must meet and have a long argument.'⁹³ Intriguingly, when Tynan finally came to see *Love from Judy* at the end of September, he afforded it a sympathetic reception, calling it 'the neatest show of its kind I can remember' and concluding that 'most of *Love from Judy* is well worth loving'.⁹⁴ The director, Eric Maschwitz, who had written the screenplay for *Goodbye Mr Chips*, was as thrilled as Littler. 'On behalf of Judy Abbott let me thank you most warmly for the charming notice you awarded to *Love From Judy*,' he wrote. 'I doubt if anything could have thrilled a young actress more. And as for Impresario Littler, he was so bowled over that he immediately booked front page space in your newspaper for a reprint of the notice – on Tuesday next, I believe.' Had the plaintive correspondence had an effect? Not even Tynan seemed immune to some gentle lobbying.

It was not just producers and directors who now began to be wary of Tynan. Even the leading playwright of the day, Terence Rattigan, felt the need to issue a gentle pre-emptive strike after an interview he undertook with the critic. Such was Tynan's charm – and venomous potential – that Rattigan thought it wise to ask for a chance to see the proofs before permission to print could be given:

The reason why I wanted to see your article before it was published is that I like to make a distinction between a serious interview and the ordinary day to day newspaper stuff. When talking to somebody like yourself I think it's such a cracking bore to apply the rule that one applies naturally to some such character as

Harold Conway [another journalist/critic], to wit, that everything one says can be used in evidence against one. It isn't that I don't have every confidence in your tact and discretion regarding myself, but I may have said things about other people which, if published, could give annoyance. That would be no fault of yours, after all you can't know much about my own personal relationships.[95]

Although the *Evening Standard* was published every day except Sunday, Tynan had slightly more leisure to compile his column than other daily reviewers. The paper's film column, written by Milton Shulman, appeared on a Thursday and the theatre column followed it on a Friday. This gave Tynan a little more opportunity to reflect on the earliest responses to work that he had seen during the week, for if a première had occurred on a Tuesday, he was able to digest diverging views and react to them if he chose. The privilege of having the final word was granted to the Sunday critics – hence their elevated status – and it was a privilege that Tynan, in particular, would soon take advantage of. At the moment, however, he was writing urgent, white-hot responses that were beginning to electrify readers more used to the arid pontifications of Beverley Baxter.

Tynan's creative routine, as observed by Elaine, remained fairly consistent for the next decade as a critic. Starting at ten in the morning, and clad in a beige woollen bathrobe (replaced by a yellow silk dressing gown trimmed in blue by the end of the 1950s), he began by scanning several weekly magazines, such as the *Spectator*, the *New Statesman*, *Punch*, *Picture Post*, *Time* and *Newsweek*. The last two helped give him a foreign perspective on the world that would draw his focus away from an entirely London-centric one. When these had been devoured, he relocated to the study, to begin the task of writing. Several packets of Three Castles cigarettes, a bottle of German Riesling, Gewürztrammer, Alasatian Traminer or Sylvaner, cans of chilli, corned beef hash or mulligatawny soup were needed to stimulate his creative juices, and Elaine would make sure that these were always on tap. By eleven at night she would go to bed to the sound of hesitant taps on the typewriter, which would increase in speed if things were going well, and she would be awoken by Tynan when the purgatory was over to see the final creation. The whole business might have taken eighteen hours. It was clearly a demanding process –

In the first year I noticed two bumps like incipient horns standing out on his forehead between his eyebrows: eye strain – eventually he would have to wear glasses. He would take off his dressing gown, and in his pajamas with the wine and smoke smell clinging to them, fall into bed like a log, plunging instantly to sleep[96]

– and runs counter to the diffident public image of easy creativity, so carefully cultivated by Tynan himself. Initially, Elaine would take the copy by taxi to the newspaper's office herself, but eventually she passed it over to a trusty cabbie, usually in its 'third draft, single-spaced with a few penned corrections in the margin inserted in a small but highly legible hand'.[97]

A change of scene, particularly a trip to a foreign country, also helped his writing. For their summer holiday in 1952, Tynan and Elaine went to Pamplona for the bullfights to write an article for *Harper's Bazaar* with Henri Cartier-Bresson and from this visit emerged the fascinating book *Bull Fever*, with its loving descriptions of the atmosphere, technique and danger of the sport. The book is a testimony to Tynan's powers of description, his delight in the exotic and his conviction that the most perfectly executed duels between matador and bull represented some of the finest theatre in the world.

The preface tackles the morality of the blood sport head-on. Acknowledging that it is strange that somebody opposed to capital punishment, enthralled by mimetic stage deaths and repulsed by English country sports, should be a fan of the Spanish bullfight, Tynan explains that he became an addict from the time of his first *corrida* in 1950. The bullfight now seems to him to be 'a logical extension of all the impulses my temperament holds – love of grace and valour, of poise and pride; and beyond these, the capacity to be exhilarated by mastery of technique'.[98] But *Bull Fever* is no piece of polemic. Tynan concedes that there is a strong argument in favour of describing the practice as barbaric, and later on in the book accepts that many are repulsed by the bullfight, but he himself has never been shocked in the way that a retired brigadier was shocked, when, having read one of his articles about bullfighting, he demanded that the editor ensure that people who so misuse their passport should be sent to prison for a month. Tynan prefers to see such ritualised aggression as a safety valve, and couches this in a generational manner which would soon pervade his criticism: 'Like many other members of the first adult generation since the war, I look on violence as part of my condition, and would rather have it in a bullring, ordered and codified, than on a battlefield. With those who cannot sympathise, I do not argue. Where the bulls are concerned there is no point in preaching except to the converted.'[99]

The pressure to justify his passion removed, the book proceeds to take on the feel of a travel guide, encompassing a dozen bullfights witnessed over three weeks in various towns and cities on the Iberian peninsula.[100] First stop is the festival at Pamplona. Images and experiences tumble over one another in a riot of colour and confusion. Elaine eating rice as live pigeons are shot all around her ('the Spanish will hunt anything, boar, or bull or eagle, relishing the skill and the risk of it').[101] The famous, frenetic and frightening early morning bull run through the streets. The six-year-old child begging a cigarette and then hawking a painting. The middle-aged Englishman, bawling at the patient clerk, who understood his request to hire a car perfectly, and the varied group of American 'left-bankers', who ever since Hemingway's *The Sun Also Rises* had followed the *corridas* across Spain. Tynan summed up their respective national differences in a customary aphorism: 'The English, in general, come to Spain looking as if at any moment it were going to offend them; the Americans, in general, as if they were going to offend it.'[102]

The action begins with a detailed description of a fight involving the bright new star, Antonio Ordonez. Although modestly proclaiming his inexperience, Tynan clearly possesses a great deal of knowledge about the technical nature of bullfighting. Even today, *aficionados* rate the intelligence of his writing highly. But he wears his learning lightly. The general reader, for whom the practice is likely to be a complete mystery, is shown that it is not enough simply to kill the bull. True success comes for the matador by performing his *faena* – a solo series of passes with his *muleta* (the crimson cape and stick) and the *espada* (the sword) – in a graceful, daring, often balletic manner. A crude kill can earn the matador hoots of derision from the passionate crowd, but a courageous and artistic one can earn him a series of trophies awarded by the President. 'The fight is a romantic spectacle, but its practice is science,'[103] Tynan teaches. The prizes range in ascending order from an ear through two ears, two ears and a tail, to the ultimate two ears, a tail and the hoof.

Tynan, quoting directly from his diary, describes a series of uneven fights. Ordonez has an inauspicious début – there is a suspicion that the horn of the bull he encounters has been shaved, thereby reducing the animal's ability to judge distances – but, like the greatest performers, he is able to recover in his next bout to give a glimpse of his genius with 'a breathless series of linked passes'.[104] Tynan was characteristically pleased to note that, for all the *olés* of the crowd, the young matador was not entirely happy with this recovery as he left the ring. He wanted to strive for more, and this was a demonstration of true greatness. Tynan's elation was momentarily punctured, however, when he asked Mme Cartier-Bresson, the wife of the photographer, whose pictures illuminate the book, how she had enjoyed the event:

I could have bitten my tongue immediately afterwards; I had forgotten that she is a Hindu, for whom the bull is the object of ultimate reverence. She looked at me impassively, pursing her lips. At length, quite lightly, she said: 'I think I understand. This is your revenge. Western Europe revenging itself on the East. Very well. Man kills bull – so Shiva creates the atom bomb.' She was not angry: it was merely that her profoundest suspicions about the occident had been confirmed. She added that, of course, she would never again enter a bullring, and that she proposed to light a candle every afternoon in the cathedral for each bull that was marked down for slaughter. I believe she will, too.

The next stop was Madrid, *en route* to the great *corrida* in Valencia. Tynan had hoped to be able to compare at Pamplona the performance of Ordonez with the legendary Litri – enigmatic, hugely successful, highly unorthodox but possibly in decline. It was to Litri in 1950 that Tynan had owed his infatuation with bullfighting, and he had followed his career ever since. But Pamplona failed to deliver the required satisfaction. Litri performed badly, confirming the predictions of his detractors, whereas Ordonez was accomplished, but unspectacular. The true gladiatorial struggle, where they demonstrated the height of their skills, would have to wait until they reached the South of France.

At various points in the book, Tynan's profession insinuates itself into the narrative. The Madrid interlude affords him an opportunity to compare the distinctive styles of the matadors with actors he had witnessed in London. The courageous, energetic Sevillian fighter called to mind Jean-Louis Barrault, 'a brilliant mime, tumbler and talker'. His temperamental opposite, the *rondeño* fighter – 'imaginative and classical' – evoked John Gielgud, 'whose style is surgical in its detachment, nobly removed from the tumult'.[105] He also speculates on the overt sexuality of bullfighting, and here his private desires intrude, in the same way that he had seen Vivien Leigh as 'spankable'. Whilst dismissing the notion that 'algolagnia, sexual pleasure in the infliction of pain, plays any part in the ritual', he believes that 'in the more precise sense of the word, it is sublimely, even exultantly sadistic':

> Mr Geoffrey Gorer has defined de Sade's general philosophy as one of 'pleasure in the ego's modification of the external world'. This pleasure can – and in de Sade's case did – lead to indulgence in pyromania and kindred fantasies: but it is present, less anti-socially, in most of us. And nothing satisfies it better than a man demonstrating his mastery over a force as objective and uncompromising as a bull. Some of us, finding nobility in the spectacle, can accordingly cite as our text: 'The admiration of the noble draws us upwards.' Others, finding nothing there but self-indulgence, turn away in horror and all efforts to convert them are wasted. The question of bullfighting probes spots so sore that for the aficionado Jowett's advice is perhaps the best. Never apologise, never explain.[106]

Was this perhaps a very public appeal to Elaine, who was now beginning to become uncomfortable with his desire for sado-masochistic sex, to have a greater understanding of the elemental nature of his demands as he saw them?

The climax of the book takes place in Valencia, where Ordonez and Litri would be pitting themselves against the bulls and each other in the fifth and last *corrida* of the fair. In one of the earlier fights, Litri enjoyed what seemed to be a resurrection of his talent. Tynan's rapturous description of his solo passes echoes his richest descriptions of Olivier's achievements:

His faena was of an intelligence and complexity beyond all my hopes, and icono-clastic into the bargain, a Vázquez turned inside out. As always, he led off with the garnishings instead of the meat: who but Litri would initiate a faena with eight manoletinas in the centre of the ring? As the bull passed, he tipped his flinty little face backwards, for all the world like a child successfully imitating his father at a party. A bizarre sequence of passes next took shape – afarolado, derechazo, afarolado, molinete, afarolado, chest-pass – all with unbroken rhythm, and all twenty yards from the nearest auxiliary. They succeeded each other like images in a symbolist poem, a series of shocks which coalesced into meaning only at the end of the sequence. This was the *montage* technique applied to bullfighting.[107]

But, as with all potential tragedy, there then followed a moment of peripeteia (the reversal of fortune), as he tripped in his next fight, lost his *muleta* and was slow-handclapped by the crowd. How would he perform when placed side by side with Ordonez in the final bullfight?

Devoting a breathless, awestruck chapter to their competition, Tynan provides an early justification not just for his presence as a witness but for his function as a dramatic critic: 'Interpretative artists, such as actors and bullfighters, stand in espe-cial need of observers to immortalise them.' Citing Olivier's Oedipus as a bench-mark, he adds, 'the critic-artist is naturally drawn to those players who achieve what seems to be accidental and unpremeditated beauty, needing the refinement of art to attain its fullest expression'.[108] Under a louring sky, with the bullring becoming slip-pery after a succession of downpours, Litri defied both the animal and a storm, in a manner that demonstrated the nature of his genius:

Anxiety was hardening into determination; the insect was really roused. Some of the passes left feet of air between him and the horns, but it was fantastic, in this cloudburst, to be passing the bull at all. The band struck up in his honour, a whip cracking pasodoble. Litri stamped his thin foot, citing for a seventh manoletina, passed the bull beneath his right arm and, as he turned, took the horn straight in his left buttock. The bull had slipped and veered too quickly. Litri fell between the forelegs and slumped, covering his face with his arms until a peon's cape took the bull away; and then, scratched and livid with pride, bounded to his feet, stretched upon tiptoe, and ripped in with the sword. He leaned nervelessly across the horns, knowing as we knew that the estocada was perfect, and sprang back to watch the bull tilt and topple. As it did so, every fuse in the world blew: a river of forked lightning flowed across the sky. It was a moment of operatic hallucination. Litri was given the bull's ears for the kind of courage which is his speciality: courage in circumstances where classical bullfighting is an impossibility and grace an implausible accident. His faena was tauromachy stripped to the skin.[109]

Ordonez could not hope to match this excitement, even though his performance was deemed sufficiently adept by the President to be awarded the ears and the tail. The flawed genius had proved that he was still capable of rising to the occasion and this was what most electrified Tynan during the whole of the three weeks. This 'critic-artist' would apply a similar standard to theatrical performances.

Back home, Rose Tynan, an intermittent visitor and a tolerated rather than loved figure, had been left to baby-sit the young Tracy. After Rose's death, Tynan was to rebuke himself for his peremptory dealings with his mother and their lack of sustained contact, but at this point in his life she continued to prove the embarrassment she had been during his adolescence. When she arrived in London from Birmingham, she shocked the home-help, Mary, by talking about the 'terrible' Jews who had packed the train and had kept trying to trip her up. This anti-Semitism was not a new feature. Shortly after their marriage, the Tynans had travelled north for Elaine to meet her. On learning that she was an actress, Rose had confusingly told her that she had just been watching an American play, *Counselor at Law*, on television and that Elaine could have been in it. 'Of course, they were all Jews,' she muttered unpleasantly, indifferent to the fact that Elaine was Jewish herself. How her son must have squirmed.

On his return, the new London season contained glimpses of better things ahead. There were renewed signs that a younger generation of actors was emerging that might in time challenge the dominance of Gielgud, Wolfit, Richardson and Edith Evans. Charles Morgan's *The River Line* (1952) was part of a genre of works that centred on crises of conscience suffered by ex-combatants after the war had ended. Three allies, a young American, a naval commander and his wife, meet for dinner after the war and reminisce about how they first encountered each other on the 'River Line' – an escape route for Allied prisoners of war through France to Spain. The dark side to their story, though, is their killing, on suspicion of treachery, of a major called 'Heron'. This has haunted them ever since. Tynan was characteristically impatient, as he was with all backward-looking Second World War dramas – 'its construction looks like the Tay Bridge after the disaster'[110] – but there was one saving grace: the appearance of Paul Scofield. Hailed by Hobson in 1947 as 'one of the most promising of our younger players'[111] after playing Tybalt in *Romeo and Juliet*, Scofield (together with Richard Burton) embodied the hope that a less mannered, more instinctive type of acting might be on the horizon. Tynan, a committed fan of this young performer, felt that Scofield, as the earnest, scholarly GI, gave a performance worthy of a masterpiece: 'He is miscast, of course, but like a good many star performers he thrives on miscasting . . . whatever he plays, Mr Scofield has a habit of going beyond the province of pure acting into something else – the projection of his own unique and highly eccentric personality, on which I dote.'

Tynan's enthusiasm was similarly roused by another one of the imports that he enjoyed so much – the American musical. *Porgy and Bess* arrived in London in October 1952, in the wake of *Oklahoma!*, *Annie Get your Gun*, *Pal Joey*, *Kiss Me Kate* and *Call Me Madam*, and offered a rare counterpoint to the greyness of Britain. Tynan's excitement is almost palpable: 'Off our gramophone records it came, at last in the flesh, a breast-beating, heart-pounding show: and though its simple warmth sometimes approaches simple-mindedness, it remains the fullest exploration of the Negro mind any white man has ever made.' And, in a phrase that would be adapted so memorably to hail the likely youthful audience for *Look Back in Anger* three years later, he adds: 'I would not respect anyone who loved all of it, but I will tolerate no one who does not travel miles to see it.'[112] Such vibrancy on the stage was rare – and it merely served to highlight the meagre nature of other theatrical fare. He was far more likely to be called upon to review a French import, a mannered detective story or a further interminable revival of Shakespeare. By the end of 1952, irked by the docility of his colleagues – but acutely aware that this was what gave him his opportunity – he decided to take a stand. With the arrival in *Sweet Peril* (a thin piece by Mary Orr and Reginald Denham) of Michael Denison and Dulcie Gray (the respected married couple who since *Rain on the Just* in 1948 had frequently appeared on stage together), he found his target – and penned his most polemical article so far.

The rudeness of the review – entitled 'Hardly the People for This Lordly Address' – is still evident fifty years later. Even now, a guilty pleasure attaches itself to a reading. What must it have felt like to have encountered it at Christmas in 1952? This was still a supremely deferential era, with men opening doors for women, children giving up seats for adults, and women expected to have tea on the table at six. Yet behind the frisson of excitement lay an important change of emphasis in Tynan's approach. He was now deepening his range by adding to his desire to scrutinise the 'stars' more realistically, a need to highlight the paucity of new writing that touched on the contemporary world in any authentic way. Escapism had its place in theatre, but its dominance was stifling creative life, and *Sweet Peril* epitomised for Tynan the worst of this tendency:

> The pre-Christmas lull in the theatre, which has now lasted since the spring equinox, subsided to a new level of inertia with the arrival of *Sweet Peril* at the St James's – a drama of raw passions played out in a Cornish cottage.
>
> 'Played out' are the exact words, but 'raw' may be an overstatement: 'under-done'

would be more precise, since the principal characters, a frustrated writer and his staunch little wife, behave with all the desperate restraint of Michael Denison and Dulcie Gray, who have chosen, appropriately enough, to play them.

Apart from certain details of the plot, which could have been procured from a garrulous usherette in the form of a pirated synopsis, I could have reviewed the play without clapping an eye on it.

This is a new tack for the critic, who now has the formulaic nature of British plays in his sights:

It was a safe bet that Mr Denison would be idealistic and stiffly tormented, and a glance at Miss Gray, or her career, is enough to indicate that her speciality is patient endurance. I might even have guessed that they would be mutually enclasped for the final curtain, though I could hardly have hoped for a tableau as eloquent as the one I got: she reclining against his breast, he taking the strain and both staring in profile out to sea. This came well down to expectations.

John Gielgud memorably summed up the feelings of many in the acting profession when he argued that Tynan's waspish observations were 'wonderful-when-it-isn't-you'[113] and here is an early case in point. There could be no brief dismissal of the married couple's performances or a benign indifference to the anaemic state of the play, such was the enervating dominance of this type of drama, and in its focus on the brooding ex-soldier, Tynan argued that it demonstrated the same limitations as *The River Line*, since its narrow canvas excluded the interest of the young:

What had gone before (I cannot resist the language of the magazine serial) contained the germs of an honest and provocative playlet; but the authors Mary Orr and Reginald Denham too often called to mind a pair of nervous swimmers prodding each other to take the plunge and then settling for a romp round the dunes instead.

The scene is a medium-sized cave dwelling, about ten seconds vertically from the sea. Here Mr Denison gnaws his quill, while his wife, off-stage, writes her memoirs.

She is battling to keep him off the bottle, for he belongs to a lost generation, the lad of good family, blighted by the war, and now a permanent hostage to apathy and despair. His nostalgia for the thirties is as violent as that of the thirties for the twenties: or that of London dramatic critics for the Old Vic season of 1945–6.

The climax of the first scene is the ritual opening of two packages of canned goods from America. The groceries herald the approach of an ex-mistress of Mr Denison's, accompanied by her husband, a New York publisher. The reunion is an uncomely flop.

The publisher buys the American rights of Miss Gray's autobiography, thereby wounding Mr Denison's pride and imperilling him to make a rather grim pass at his old bed-fellow. She rejects him pitilessly; the scene is the tautest in the play. He retires with a bottle instead, whereupon Miss Gray tosses her head and walks out on him.

The repulsively false reconciliation between the Denisons in the last act cannot even be said to be trumped up, because the authors hold no trumps in their hand. Miss Gray returns, feigning pregnancy, and Mr Denison is instantly reformed. A race to the cottage door ensues, resulting in the above mentioned heroic tableau.

Everything about this review rebukes the backward-looking nature of London theatre, as Tynan now saw it. The reliance on conventional stars who have seen better days; the hankering for a golden pre-war idyll that never existed; the depiction of 'good families' and 'acceptable backgrounds'; the nostalgia of the critics for long-memorialised classical performances; and the formulaic construction of so many new pieces. He ends his tirade by neatly expressing his dismay that his great idol had not, so far, managed to break this cycle:

> A revival of the highest traditions of actor-management was what we all predicted when Laurence Olivier took over the St James's. *Sweet Peril* is the second cliff-cottage melodrama in succession at this lordly address, and, in order to forestall what threatens to become an institution, I am now hacking into shape a one-act tragedy, based on coastal erosion, in which the cottage falls into the sea immediately on the rise of the curtain.[114]

Other critics were much more benign. Ivor Brown felt that the play had 'more amusing lines than usually occur in such tales of love'[115] and the anonymous reviewer for the *Times* stated that the examination of marriage was conducted 'very shrewdly, often amusingly, and with what may strike the spectator as a happy regard for character'.[116]

By the autumn of 1952, Tynan was clearly conscious of his growing stature. In a letter to Christopher Fry, written in October, he magisterially upbraided the playwright for the rumours he was hearing about his treatment in Fry's survey of contemporary reviewers, *An Experience of Critics*, that would be published just before Christmas. What particularly irked him was his inclusion by Fry's editor, Kaye Webb, in the list of critics whose 'judgments are often subjected to sub-editors with a passion for headlines, or managements who have a Policy'.[117] Firstly, he demanded the correction in any subsequent edition of the erroneous claim that Harold Conway was the official critic of the *Evening Standard*. 'I have been the official critic

. . . since July, and Harold Conway has remained what he always was, the overnight reporter and columnist,' he seethed. More serious was the imputation of editorial interference:

> A playwright's idea of how a critic works is, I now see, almost as uninformed as the public's. You are our raw materials, and we sculpt you as best we can; but we are merely your scapegoats. I am astonished that you should imagine that any word of mine has been censored, inspired, or any way amended by the chieftains of the Beaverbrook press. As a matter of course I avoid obscenities and outré allusions, both of which are thankfully reprintable later, but otherwise what I write is uninterruptedly mine.[118]

The mild-mannered playwright's emollient reply, in which he claimed that he had not seen the book until it had been published, calmed Tynan down. Slightly chastened, he wrote a second letter five days later regretting his tone: 'What happened was that, like you, I didn't see the book until after I wrote the letter – a too-solicitous friend read the relevant bits over the phone to me, and I assumed that Kaye[Webb]'s note was by you. I don't want to blow my top again, so why don't you forward my letter to you on to them?'

Having now seen the book, though, Tynan remained steadfastly unimpressed:

> . . . I can't help feeling it's going to stimulate the worst enthusiasms and emphasises the wrongest antitheses. So many definitions of the critic and the artist, so little common ground . . . I wish someone had said, early on, that the real distinction is that the playwright writes words that are speakable, the critic words that are readable.[119]

He would never lose this combative streak.

Professionally, Tynan began 1953 in an enviable position. Now established as a full-time critic, his coruscating analyses and denunciations of the past six months had provided a colour that was missing elsewhere. He had told a Foyles literary luncheon in November 1952 that the role of the critic was to 'write for posterity' and he was now beginning to live up to this self-imposed job description. Lord Beaverbrook was intrigued by this young *ingénu*, and invited both Tynan and Elaine to his residence at Chertly Court for dinner. Surrounded by pliant Labour politicians, the Tory press baron was very taken by Elaine, somewhat to her husband's annoyance. Believing that Beaverbrook was treating her as if she were the power behind the throne, he tackled his wife after the meal. 'I'm American,' she told her husband. 'He thinks I'm Wallis Simpson.'[120] Either way, Beaverbrook's attention was helpful. Permission was given for the young couple to visit New York in January, with Iain Hamilton deputising in their absence, and Tynan felt secure enough to take on the mighty Tennent empire in his penultimate column before he sailed for America. It was as if he wanted to demonstrate that, having highlighted the paucity of new plays of quality, he would focus on one of the reasons why the current set-up was so unconducive to innovation.

John Gielgud was the acting jewel in the crown of the Tennent empire, and the first six months of 1953 would see him appear in three separate productions. His style was laconic, eschewing energetic physical movement for mellifluous vocal delivery, and the productions he directed himself were renowned for their sumptuousness, precision and star-studded quality. The days were long gone when a teenager would place his picture on her pillow (as in Dodie Smith's *Call it a Day*, 1935), but he was still the gold standard of the British theatre. Tynan was the first to question the value of the precious metal.

The first production, *Richard II*, reflected another theatrical facet of the coronation year – the disproportionate number of Shakespearian productions that were performed. This revealed less an over-reverence of the dramatist's work, than the lack of good-quality scripts of a more recent origin to perform. The sense of national pride that the Festival of Britain had sought to engender was also responsible for this glut, and when the torrent showed no signs of abating by the summer, Tynan was not alone in protesting vigorously. Under the headline, 'Shakespeare Enslaved', the critic argued that the playwright 'would benefit from a little neglect':

> We have seen him denuded, overdressed, mangled, racked and upended, we have stood by as scholars sampled his blood and pronounced him Catholic, Lutheran, pagan and Bacon; and yesterday I received from the Middle East a typewritten monograph appealingly headed: 'Was Shylock a Jew?'[121]

This epitomised the retrospective attitude that Tynan was coming to despise.

Gielgud's *Richard II* at the Lyric, Hammersmith kicked off the Bard-fest in January. With Paul Scofield as the lead, the reviews were ecstatic, yet Tynan not only disliked the tragedy, describing the deposed King as a 'Hamlet without a conscience, a mission or a sense of humour', but felt that the production was symptomatic of everything that the theatre-going public complacently appreciated about a Tennent's production. It was time to demand more:

> What did amaze me was the extraordinary inadequacy, in nearly every department, of John Gielgud's production. Shakespeare having dug Richard's grave, Mr Gielgud, zealously misguided, has embalmed him.
>
> Everything we associate with 'style' in the theatre has been packed on to the Hammersmith boards: vocal resonance and purity, assiduous cultivation of word-music, pictorial elegance, gestures few and weighty.

Only one thing is lacking: a single portrait, accurately observed and honestly felt, of a human being

In this, we can see further gropings towards a more realistic form of theatre, which Tynan would later come to argue could be learned from Brecht. In the meantime, what defined Gielgud's approach was its studious unreality:

The stage is filled by a throng of good actors, none of them (or so it struck me) acting, none of them behaving as people, even 14th century people, ever behaved, none of them showing any real awareness that Richard II might be of more intimate emotional significance than the illuminated manuscript it has been dressed to resemble.

Mr Gielgud's production is a triumph of 'style' over humanity, and it is a costly victory, involving the martyrdom of some first-rate performers.

How often one longed to interrupt them and say: 'For just a moment there, by some oversight, you relaxed a little and made contact with life. Please, in the betrayed name of William Shakespeare, do it again; forget about being stylish, abandon all canting theories about the virtues of conventionalised acting – and above all stop listening to the echoes of your admirable voices.'

Renowned French actors, such as Jean-Louis Barrault (the Gallic Laurence Olivier) had often caustically remarked on the preference for fastidious articulation over physical movement on the part of many British and this was borne out for Tynan by the production at the Lyric, Hammersmith:

I felt this (though compressed into a muffled oath) throughout the evening: Eric Porter as Bolingbroke, Brewster Mason, Paul Daneman, Richard Wordsworth – all of them kept taunting me with glimpses of the actor's real craft.

But as I blinked, they would be off again intoning away, devoutly addressing an audience which no longer exists. In many ways, the entire production is an essay, on Mr Gielgud's part, in mass ventriloquism.[122]

In a private letter to Cecil Beaton, he went even further: the whole production was 'as cold and clammy as the estuary of the Ob' with 'everyone sleepwalking: even Scofield'.[123] This would not be the last time that Gielgud's emphasis on the vocal would be derided by Tynan.

By the mid-point of 1953 the fearless young critic was riding high in public esteem. Such was the attention that Tynan was now garnering that from mid-May his column was adorned with his picture and a short biography. Eager to capitalise on his youth, the literary editor of the *Evening Standard*, Charles Curran, wrote the following description: 'Aged 26. At Oxford he was editor of the Cherwell, President of the Experimental Theatre Club and Secretary of the Union. Became *Evening Standard* critic in August 1952.'[124]

Tynan's assessment of Gielgud was mild compared to his treatment of Donald Wolfit. Wolfit was as prolific as Gielgud in 1953 but his every appearance attracted a venomous response from the critic. Ever since Wofit's wartime Lear, he had intermittently been mentioned as a potential director of the National Theatre, with the *Daily Telegraph* acting as principal cheer-leader. It was a prospect that filled Tynan with horror, and, contrary to the pervading view of theatre historians, it was therefore Wolfit, and not Vivien Leigh, who suffered most at the hands of Tynan. Tynan's reaction to Wolfit's revived *King Lear* in February – once such a favourite – set the tone:

> Mr Wolfit's present supporting company explores new horizons of inadequacy. Only Richard Goolden, a macabre Fool with a senile stoop and a child's skipping legs was of much assistance to the play. Extricate Mr Wolfit's Lear from the preposterous production, and you have a great flawed piece of masonry, making up in weight what it lacks in delicacy: a tribal chieftain, rather than a hereditary monarch.
>
> Mr Wolfit scorns the trick (known to many lesser actors) of flicking speeches exquisitely to leg; he prefers to bash them towards mid-off and run like a stag. In the mad scenes this impatience with finesse is a weakness; the insanity looks too much like tipsiness.[125]

His Macbeth received the briefest of withering lines – 'at the King's Head, Donald Wolfit has revived that mighty display of castle-storming (barn-storming is too light a phrase) called Macbeth. His supporting company offers only token resistance'[126] – and *The Taming of the Shrew*, whilst 'no directorial effort has been spared to bring out the full flavour of the old play's essential charmlessness', needs 'the most delicate fantastication, which Mr Wolfit is unable to provide'.[127] But the real nadir was *The Wandering Jew*, an example of a play that Tynan hoped would be banished from the stage in the post-war era, interpreted by an actor whose blustering persona struck the critic as overbearing and selfish.

'To the Flames! – and No Wonder' (appearing on 10 April 1953) is the lip-smacking title of Tynan's most pungent attack since *Sweet Peril*. In its subject matter, direction and performance it was the clearest anachronism Tynan could imagine:

> The revival of E. Temple Thurston's *The Wandering Jew* . . . is one of the most reassuring theatrical experiences in years.
>
> Have we really progressed so far? In 1920 the play survived 390 performances; to-day not a line of it but rings flat and false. Only in village pageants, and in *The Glorious Days*, do traces of its style persist.

But it was the performance of Wolfit that provoked the most derision:

> In the first scene Mr Wolfit wears a burnous, a shiny red wig, and his usual make-up, a thick white line down the bridge of the nose. As ever, he delivers each line as a challenge, flung in the teeth of invisible foes; his voice roars like gravel at the bottom of a barrel; and when he swirled off, girding his rude bathrobe about him, to spit at his saviour, I fell to wondering exactly where his ponderous vibrato methods belong.
>
> Not in the little club theatres, I decided; nor in the larger West End houses, where they would soon grow oppressive. Nor yet at the Old Vic: I picture Mr Wolfit erupting at the very thought. Where, then, is his spiritual home?
>
> My answer is nowhere in particular: he is a nomad, part of the great (albeit dead) tradition of the strolling player, who would erect his stage in a tavern yard, and unravel his rhetoric to the winds. Mr Wolfit is not an indoor actor at all. Theatres cramp him. He would be happiest, I feel, in a large field.

In a clear echo of his review of *Sweet Peril* Tynan concluded with the mock-threat of his own play:

> After *The Wandering Jew* I evolved the idea of a wandering playwright, condemned to write plays through eternity for having once cheapened the name of dramatic art. He thrives in every age, always with the same sentimentalism and poverty of imagination. He is by now skilful enough to avoid gross errors of technique: his beacon-light is mediocrity.[128]

This was too much for Wolfit, who was famous for declaring war on critics who had given him a bad notice, and he sued both the *Evening Standard* and the critic for libel. Much to Tynan's irritation, the paper decided to settle out of court. It was a sign of future vulnerability that he chose not to see.

Theatre reviewing occupied only a portion of Tynan's time during the spring of 1953. Ever teeming with creative ideas, he tried to interest Alec Guinness in appearing in a television production of an Orwell novel that he was planning. In March they arranged to meet up to discuss the book, and Guinness indicated that he was eager to explore the new medium:

> . . . I've just finished *1984*. I have been HORRIFIED by it – quite in the first class of nightmares. But I *did* find it fearfully formless and consequently often monotonous and repetitious. I shall be fascinated to see what you do with it as a script. I'm v. anxious to do a really good T.V. – I've never appeared in bright blue in the Oxford Street stores – so do let me read it when it is ready.[129]

Acting commitments, and Guinness's own doubts, prevented this plan coming to fruition, but no matter, Tynan was also working on a slim study of the actor's stage and screen performances, which was published later in the year by Rockliff. Handsomely illustrated with a large number of stills from various Guinness productions, the book was a brisk canter through the star's prodigious career so far. Although Tynan argues early on that the actor is 'a prodigy, belonging to no tradition', this is no lazy hagiography. Tynan admires the fact that he embodies 'a modern-dress manner of acting, neither classic nor romantic, into which the doubt, the indecision, and even the cynicism of the twentieth century have all been craftily assimilated'.[130] But he is also frank about the wrong turns that the actor has taken – his over-dependence on Gielgud's offers of work in the mid-1930s ('from which, psychologically, he later found it hard to escape');[131] his alternating roles in productions for Gielgud ('the actor's actor') and Tyrone Guthrie ('the producer's producer')[132] in the second half of that decade; and the disastrously misconceived *Hamlet* in 1951, in which he cast Tynan as the Player King. There is something cathartic about the author's reflections on his only professional stage appearance. The production was 'a failure born of indecision', and, fostered by the cancer of Guinness's 'humility', this led to a 'fatal ambiguity, both in the production and his own performance'.[133] By eschewing both the hackneyed trappings of earlier *Hamlet*s – the heroic strutting, the excessive declamation and the portentous scenery – as well as the more modern approach, that, like Olivier's film version, had embraced Freudian readings, Guinness fell between two stools. Having rejected so much, he needed a conception to fill the vacuum, but none was forthcoming. He seemed to Tynan from his insider's vantage point to be 'a highly intelligent, extremely self-conscious man who, thinking too precisely on the event, refuses to commit himself to ridicule'.[134]

But ridicule is what followed. The casting was eccentric (with Tynan confessing alarm at the prospect of playing 'a robust and bearded tragedian' at the age of twenty-four); there was no clear-cut direction because this was shared between Guinness and Frank Hauser to the frustration of all concerned; inventive touches discovered early on in the rehearsal process were watered down as the first night approached; the customary pre-London tour was dispensed with, allowing no time to iron out any flaws; and the stage business was ill-thought-out and invited mockery. Tynan was involved in the most humiliating example of this:

[Guinness's] visual sense is not his strongest point, and it was at its most erratic in the climax of the play-scene, when he suddenly decided to indulge in a little expressionism. This took place just after I had taken leave of the Player Queen and dropped off to sleep. As the murderer crept up to slip me the potion, there was a slow black-out, except for a single spot-light on Claudius' face. Phospho-rescent paint had been applied to the crown, the vial of poison and a great plastic left ear which I wore over my own: these glowed in the darkness, and the tableau as poison was poured took on the aspect of an advertisement for a proprietary brand of rum. As an idea, provocative; but in execution, comic. It was cut out after the first performance. I remember handing the ear over to the stage manager and feeling, for a moment, remarkably like Van Gogh.[135]

Generously, Guinness took the blame for the fiasco, telling the company that he had given up after the first night, but it was clearly a bruising experience for all concerned. The production closed after fifty-two performances.

The authenticity of Tynan's first-hand relation of the infamous *Hamlet*, and the honesty of his report, lends credibility to his more complimentary descriptions. The root of Guinness's appeal for the critic lies in his versatility and anonymity. His ability to transform his appearance is evident from the well-chosen photographs that accompany the text. Whether he appears as the white-faced Fool in Olivier's *King Lear*, a hirsute Fagin in *Oliver Twist*, the juvenile Herbert Pocket in *Great Expectations* or the urbane Sir Henry Harcourt-Reilly in *The Cocktail Party*, Guinness demonstrates the chameleon capability more generally ascribed to Olivier. Guinness's anonymity was first apparent to Tynan when he observed him as Drugger in the Old Vic's 1947 production of *The Alchemist*. Recalling this performance, Tynan now wrote that 'He can seem unobserved: he can make every member of the audience an eavesdropper on a private ceremonial. His art is the art of public solitude.'[136] In this he differs from Oliviers who

ransacks the vaults of a part with blow-lamp, crowbar and gunpowder: he is the best of Bill Sikeses. Guinness, on the other hand, is the nocturnal burglar, the humble Houdini who knows the combination and therefore makes no noise. He does everything by stealth. The technique is his patent, which in part explains why it will leave no descendants . . . The conclusion is inescapable: a big performance from him must concentrate on the interior, not the exterior of the character he is playing. His territory is the man within.[137]

This patient, atmospheric evocation of Guinness's talent is emblematic of the volume as a whole. Neatly paced and entertainingly written, it set a new standard for the short study of the performer. Guinness recognised its fair-mindedness and its endorsement of his talent when he complimented the author after publication: 'Thank you for writing such a delightful, amusing, worthwhile and, as far as I can see, honest book about me. It is *very* readable. For me it's like a lovely long session with a fortune teller – a real basking for the ego . . .'[138]

The year 1953 was proving a prolific one for Tynan, as he also undertook a second book – *Persona Grata* – a collaboration with the famous photographer, Cecil Beaton. Its eventual foreword betrays the confidence approaching hubris that was consuming Tynan at this time:

This book is an alphabetical anthology of unique human beings; a portrait gallery in words and photographs of a hundred living people whom we, its self-appointed curators, both admire . . . Honesty dictated that our bias be towards actors, actresses, writers, painters, dancers and clowns. One politician has slipped in; so has a horse; but these are the exceptions.

We sought, as we made our choice, certain qualities; chief among them were craftsmanship, energy, elegance, wit, and a dash of the unpredictable. Those who possess any of them in a high degree can hardly help enlivening the times in which they live. They are welcome people: *personae*, in fact, *gratae*.[139]

Was the *enfant terrible* riding for a fall?

It would be a mistake to argue that there was nothing of which Tynan approved during this period. Graham Greene's *The Living Room* (April 1953) proved the novelist 'a potentially great dramatist' and launched 'a potentially great actress', Dorothy Tutin. Greene had given her 'a chance which has been withheld from young English actresses for nearly thirty years: the chance of playing a long, serious part in an important new play . . . Miss Tutin's performance is masterly: the very nakedness of acting. In her greatest sorrow, she blasts like a diamond in a mine.'[140]

Interestingly, Tynan had met Tutin during the pre-West End run in Brighton. Such was his growing status – particularly amongst the young in the profession, who saw him as a kindred spirit – that his advice was eagerly sought. Wisely, he declined to give any, fearing that it might compromise his critical integrity, but Tutin's response made clear her disappointment: 'I was so sorry that you said you'd only criticise from the safe distance of your paper because I'd value your criticism and can imagine your writing "Miss Tutin must learn to etc etc". And it would seem a waste not to say something now when I can do something about it!'[141] She would certainly have been appeased by his printed assessment.

Tynan's verdicts were being taken increasingly seriously now, and his archive reveals a growing amount of correspondence from those he referred to in print. Some professionals, such as Paul Scofield, wrote to thank him for his approbation and to praise the quality of his writing – perhaps motivated partially by genuine gratitude and partially by a desire to take out an insurance policy against future maulings.[142] Others, such as the director Theodore Komisarjevsky, seethed with indignation at what they perceived to be his temerity:

[Mr Theodore Komisarjevsky, Darien, Connecticut, USA   10 July 1953]

As to your reference to myself as a 'recluse' – see the *Evening Standard* of June 30th, 1953 – I'd like to mention that, since my arrival in this country and up to this day, I've been Professor of Drama at Yale University; I've directed seven great operas in New York and a few plays, including John Gielgud's *Crime and Punish-*

ment in N.Y. and on the road; I've produced Verdi's *Aida* at the Montreal Stadium and *Cymbeline*; I've written quite a few articles in magazines, opened a 'Drama Studio' etc etc . . .

Theodore Komisarjevsky PhD[143]

His employers were delighted with his notoriety. Whether in his dismissal of the old guard or his embracing of new trends, such as the American musical, he was attracting a younger audience for his columns. They loved his eye-catching, beautifully phrased lamentations – one especially notable elegy was for Ralph Richardson's first appearance since his disastrous Stratford season in R.C. Sherriff's *The White Carnation*:

> Over the last few years, the resemblance between Sir Ralph's demeanour on stage and that of a human being has been getting progressively more tenuous. He has taken to ambling across our stages in a spectral, shell-shocked manner, choosing odd moments to jump and frisk, like a man through whom an electric current was being intermittently passed: behaving, in short, as if insulated against reality.[144]

And they rose to his energetic enthusiasm for all things across the Atlantic, which he often couched in the latest American idiom. The apotheosis of this approach came at the end of May:

> *Guys and Dolls* . . . at which I am privileged to take a peek last evening, is a 100 per cent American musical caper, cooked up out of a story called *The Idyll of Miss Sarah Brown*, by the late Damon Runyon, who is such a scribe as delights to give the English language a nice kick in the pants.

Tynan had seen the Broadway version on his visit the previous January, and was vibrantly unconcerned about any teething problems the show might have:

> The Coliseum is no rabbit hutch, and maybe a show as quick and smart as this *Guys and Dolls* will go better in such a theatre as the Cambridge Theatre. Personally, I found myself laughing ha-ha last night more often than any guy in the critical dodge has any right to.
>
> And I am ready to up and drop on my knees before Frank Loesser, who writes the music and the lyrics. In fact, this Loesser is maybe the best light composer in the world. In fact, the chances are that *Guys and Dolls* is not only a young masterpiece, but the *Beggar's Opera* of Broadway.[145]

How different this tone was from the prim, censoriousness of Harold Hobson, who maintained a lifelong disapproval of musicals, partly owing to the loathing of them by his wife, Bessie. Where Tynan saw light, fresh air, exciting nonconformism and rebellion in the young, Hobson saw cynicism, doubt, immaturity and pointless disrespect:

> Is America really peopled with brutalised half-wits, as this picturisation of Damon Runyon's stories implies? Is it really witty to bring a Salvation Army girl to the edge of fornication by the not very original trick of putting intoxicants into her milk-shake? Is it clever to quote words of Jesus in the melancholy hope of raising a laugh? Let me make it clear that I am not protesting against irreverence or impropriety as such. I only ask that they should attain a certain level of intelligence. I see no reason why religion should not be attacked or even traduced in the theatre. It is, I am sure, quite strong enough to defend itself. But let the attack have some intellectual basis. Otherwise it becomes a bore. That, alas, is what *Guys and Dolls* is, despite its numerous striking incidental merits; an interminable, an overwhelming, and in the end intolerable bore.[146]

Even T.C. Worsley wrote that 'One reaches the interval . . . bludgeoned with boredom'.[147] Twenty-six years younger than Hobson, and at least fifteen years younger than any of his other critical rivals, Tynan truly belonged to the avant-garde.

The *Evening Standard* rather strangely decided to capitalise on their new asset by running a publicity campaign inviting their readers to compare the merits of their previous critic – the ageing Baxter – and their current one. The idea was prompted by a critical letter that they published in May from Kay Chiles of Sussex Lodge, Hyde Park, in which she asked 'When, oh when can we have Mr Baxter back as your dramatic critic? I can no longer stomach Mr Tynan's impertinences.' In addition to finding him 'irritating' and 'boring', she was particularly incensed by Tynan's treatment of Anna Neagle, who she felt was one of the country's 'greatest actresses'. Her conclusion was pointed: 'Surely dramatic criticism should be a little more constructive, and less an expression of animosity that leaves the reader with the feeling that the critic is suffering from some personal grievance?'[148] The paper was inundated with responses, and it printed a selection of them the following week. Devoting a quarter of a page to 'Who's for Baxter?' and 'Who's for Tynan?', the younger man undoubtedly came off the worse. Only one letter was thoroughly positive ('Tynan will be remembered as one of the outstanding personalities of the Elizabethan age'), and the only others to defend him were unhelpfully ambiguous. (One contended that 'Never has anyone, even a dramatic critic, written nonsense so readably', and the other accepted that he was irritating, but argued that a good critic needed to be.) Baxter's supporters seemed to have the better lines. 'He is always adult and objective and often amusing . . . Tynan's tricks have become tiresome. They no longer interest anyone but himself. He has become the worst of all people – a ham!' moaned G. Beresford of St Pancras.

F. A. Hamilton of Islington plunged the knife in further by berating Tynan for expending 'too much frantic effort to be brittle, cynical and worldly-wise' and Jonathan Wren, another Islington resident, was repulsed by his 'boorish near-witticisms'.[149] If the paper had left off here, the result might not have been so disastrous. In its defence, it was probably aiming to stimulate sales by highlighting the qualities of two of its prize columnists – Baxter had recently been writing profiles of artists such as Graham Sutherland – and it had also invited some pithy discussion of its film critic, Milton Shulman, earlier in the month, but it myopically chose not to prevent the controversy from escalating, and continued to publish a large number of letters. On 25 May, a second round of antithetical views appeared. 'Heaven (and Lord Beaverbrook) protect writers and players of talent and experience from [Tynan's] ignorant, immature sarcasm,' thundered Bryan Mattheson of Paddington. Herbert Buckmaster of New Bond Street felt that Baxter was 'the greatest dramatic critic on either side of the Atlantic', whilst Henry Rayner of St John's Wood believed that Harold Conway (the second string critic) was better than either of them.[150] It was hard not to believe that the protagonists' relatives were now writing in to advance their cause.

In spite of stating that this would be the last word on the subject, further letters appeared following a brief respite for the coronation. An especially personal one from James MacKinlay of Hampstead was printed on 3 July. Incensed by Tynan's treatment of Gielgud, he aimed for the critic's Achilles' heel and parodied one of his most famously dismissive lines: 'A word about Tynan himself. One can forgive him (with some difficulty) the downright inadequacy of his Player King in Guinness's *Hamlet*, but may one just say about his subsequent career, "He possesses every attribute of the potentially great critic of the theatre, except humility and a sense of proportion."'[151] But it was a letter sent in by, of all people, Alan Dent, that broke the camel's back. With a high level of *schadenfreude*, the critic remarked that his rival possessed 'true wit, keen perception and a vivid pen', but that that was not enough. 'Young though he is, he is probably now too old to acquire other desirable, if not indispensable, attributes of the craft such as tact, good taste, good manners, the sense of fair play, and the subtler kinds of sensibility.'[152] Understandably outraged at what he perceived to be the disloyalty of his employers for publishing such a negative letter from a fellow critic, Tynan wrote to the editor, Percy Elland, to inform him that if the paper printed another critical letter he would be compelled to sue for slander and libel. It was an act of impetuosity that underlined his lack of experience and, perhaps, hubris, but he had every reason to be aggrieved. Surprised by the forcefulness of Tynan's threat, Elland took him seriously and promptly dispensed with his services. Given the level of hostility directed against him, this may have been what the paper had been angling for all along.

Yet this had not been the outcome that Tynan was expecting. It was a rerun of the painful expulsion from *Les Parents terribles* in 1951 and his new-found sense of invulnerability – masking a brittle self-confidence – was shattered again. He tried to retract his original letter, by telling Elland that he had written in haste. He asked Elaine, who had a good relationship with the paper's famous publisher, to write to Lord Beaverbrook, but the paper stood firm. Even Charles Curran's interventions were to no avail, as his good friend reported at the end of July:

[9 Stone Buildings, Lincoln's Inn, WC2   26 July 1953]

PERSONAL

My dear Ken,

I am tremendously sorry. I have done everything I could; but unfortunately there is no going behind your letter. I can well understand your feelings in writing it, but I wish you had posted it in the fire. If you want to have a row with someone do it by word of mouth; never, never, never in writing.

I wish I could have helped, for I feel this is a personal loss. I tried unsuccessfully to bring you on the paper in 1950, and I was delighted to push you again later. If it were a matter for me then I would not let you go. I regard you as the most brilliant arrival in Fleet Street since the war, someone with a magnificent future.

This is not a disaster, and you must not imagine that it is. These last 12 months have put you on the map, and made you the most discussed theatre critic in London. No other critic – not Agate or Shaw or Walkley or Archer or Beerbohm – has ever established himself at so early an age. You are entitled to feel satisfied with yourself, and I hope you do.

All this hubbub will not do you the slightest harm. On the contrary; it will simply emphasise your position as a commanding and controversial personality. I advise you to let other people do the talking about it, and to say as little as possible yourself. Say only that there was a disagreement, and behave as though you didn't care a damn. There is no reason why you should either. This is just a piece of anecdotage, material for one chapter of autobiography.

I have no doubt that in 1960 you will look back on all this with amusement. I have no doubt either that long before then you will be recognised on both sides of the Atlantic as the most gifted and the most influential theatre critic now living.

With all good wishes (and tell Elaine not to worry, because it doesn't matter and there is no harm done)

Yours ever

Charles Curran[153]

This sagacious advice spurred Tynan into action. Harold Clurman, too, reassured him that he would soon have a more important post,[154] so whilst Elaine lapsed into a bout of heavy drinking,[155] something to which she had become increasingly prone after their marriage, Tynan contacted the editor of the *Observer*, David Astor, with a rather unexpected enquiry.

Astor had been the editor since 1948. The son of Viscount Astor, one of the richest men in the world, and Nancy Astor, the first female MP, he had turned the *Observer* – the oldest Sunday newspaper in the world, with the slogan 'Unbiased by prejudice, uninfluenced by party' – into an influential highbrow political and cultural broadsheet, which cherished its non-partisan stance and was respected by both the left and the right. The author, Anthony Sampson, joined the paper in 1955 as Astor's assistant at a time when the paper was at the zenith of its existence. He felt at the hub of the civilised world: 'Its sixteen pages every Sunday seemed to be at the centre of all serious debates, discussed at dinner parties and setting agendas for politicians. It was original and unpredictable, linked to neither major political party, and defying conventional wisdom. Coming from South Africa I felt I had joined a topsy-turvy world where black was white, and left was right.'[156] Astor supported Labour Party policy on hanging, censorship, human rights and anti-colonialism, but was closer to Conservative sentiment on taxation, nationalisation and trade union reform. He demanded a similarly questioning and independent attitude from all his journalists.

Above all, Astor cherished good writing. Stimulated by his friendship with George Orwell, he recruited Arthur Koestler, Philip Toynbee and Harold Nicolson to the paper. Vita Sackville-West began a column on gardening, John Davy tapped into the growing interest in science and Terence Kilmartin's literary pages were admired for their unstinting quality. The paper was also distinguished by its physical appearance. Having cleared classified advertisements off the front page and introduced a fresher typography, he was the first editor to hire a picture editor, Mechtild Nawiasky, and the paper quickly pioneered the use of quality images by photographers such as Jane Bown. This mixture of the visual and the literary received the ultimate accolade when it began to be copied by its arch rival, the *Sunday Times*. Lord Kemsley's paper was much more conservative, commercially driven and establishment-orientated than the *Observer*, and was given to printing reverential editorials about the royal family in italics. Their fierce rivalry led to a boom in sales of broadsheet Sunday newspapers in the 1950s, and by 1956, much to Kemsley's dismay, the *Observer* had edged ahead in the circulation battle.

Unknown to Tynan, Astor was also very keen on the theatre. Many of his journalists detected the air of the impresario in him, and Sampson remembers his employees calling him the last great actor-manager. Astor regarded his journalists as 'temperamental actors',[157] in need of direction, praise and reassurance, and he had even briefly run a troupe of players touring Yorkshire seaside resorts during the war. This mutual interest in the dramatic did not immediately produce a beneficial result, however. Complying with the fiction dreamed up by the *Evening Standard*, that his departure was mutually agreed, Tynan asked whether he might act as second or third string to the resident critic, Ivor Brown.[158] Astor was unsure about this. Tynan seemed to lack the gravitas for a position on this serious Sunday broadsheet, and he viewed him as 'all flash but no substance'.[159] On learning of his concerns through a mutual friend, Elaine, the great facilitator, took it upon herself to send Astor a copy of *He That Plays the King*. Astor melted a little, and he agreed to meet Tynan in September. The promise of a meeting would not be sufficient to earn him a living wage, however, and when the *Daily Sketch* approached him about becoming their theatre critic, Tynan reluctantly decided to accept.

Tynan's connection with the *Daily Sketch* was brief, but it further confirmed his reputation for outspoken, irreverent notices. It also coincided with the publication of *Persona Grata* and his study of Alec Guinness, thereby enhancing his standing in the eyes of Astor. Tynan's persona was a shock to the regular journalists on the tabloid, and provoked mixed reactions. Responding to a letter that the dying Tynan had placed in the *Listener* in 1980 requesting memories about his early career for his projected autobiography, Olga Franklin recalled that some of them felt that he had been sent to save the ailing newspaper like some gift from the gods. Others, however, were more equivocal. There was a legitimate feeling that he was not committed to the paper and was loath to write too frequently. Franklin remembered that her boss, Walter Hayes, did not much care for Tynan but that he was most likely to have been jealous: 'I think we all resented you a bit because you were good looking and spoilt but mostly because you never did much.' She was struck, however, by Elaine – 'The thing I admired most about you in those days was your first wife. She was super. Wish I could write like her. I'd never have to worry about inflation, redundancy money or whatever . . .'[160] At that time, they were a very striking couple.

Appearing on a Friday, Tynan's first column, on 2 October 1953, was accorded banner headlines and a welcoming fanfare: '*Introducing Kenneth Tynan – the liveliest writer of the day*'. His opening sentence alone provided the sensational tone that his new employers required – 'This week in the theatre has been so painfully drugless that I feel I can only obliterate it from my mind by reviewing, instead of the things I saw, the things I would *like* to have seen' – and he proceeded to itemise his current wish-list. His main desire was to see Laurence Olivier, who had 'dawdled disturbingly' since the Old Vic season, as Macbeth, and (in a further swipe at Vivien Leigh) with 'a more challenging Lady Macbeth than his charming wife'. His other hopes provide a handy check-list of his current interests. He wanted to witness Fry's 'long incubated' new play; a 'single English actor (apart from Olivier) capable of taking the stage in the company of the best continentals'; the announcement that Tennent's had bought the Arts Theatre; the British première of *Pal Joey*; and, in a hint as to how the focus of his criticism might eventually move away from performers to playwrights, 'A marital farce in which an outraged husband does not round on his wife and bellow: "Don't change the subject"'; and 'An audience which can accept a kiss, a reference to virginity or a heroic gesture on stage without nudging itself and shifting in its seat'.[161]

Over the next three months, Tynan began to broaden his repertoire. He wrote a profile of Michael Hordern that took in his work in the theatre, film and television.[162] Significantly, he began to speculate on why it was 'the worst theatrical season anyone could remember'.[163] One reason he advanced, harking back to *Sweet Peril*, was the number of couples that were appearing in the West End, including the Clements (John Selby Clements and Kay Hammond), Oliviers, Wolfits and Riordans (Jack and Diana).[164] More convincing was his emerging belief that the plays on offer reflected an unusually narrow view of life. Having hailed Wynyard Browne's work, *A Question of Fact*, as a 'landmark' amongst the dross, he offered a numerical analysis that foreshadowed some of his most powerful *Observer* polemic: 'For the benefit of the statisticians: there are now 26 straight plays running in the West End. *A Question of Fact* ranks high in the group of 21 which are wholly concerned with life in the upper and middle classes of society.'[165]

Fans of his new style of cutting notice (and there were many) were treated to several choice offerings. The imported musical, *The King and I*, which he had seen eighteen months earlier on Broadway, was 'like one of those Oriental dinners, meaty and cloying by turns, which leave you sagging at the stomach for a good half hour, after which you feel unaccountably peckish again'.[166] N.C. Hunter's star-laden work, *A Day by the Sea*, was dismissed as 'an evening of unexampled triviality . . . Mr Hunter's pseudo-Chekhov is as about as close to the real thing as an aspidistra to a woodland fern . . . To say that the cast rise above their material is an understatement: except by collapsing flat on their faces they could scarcely fall below it'(the fact that Gielgud, Thorndike and Richardson were all appearing together cut no ice);[167] and the producer Emile Littler's decision to close the gallery for the first performance of *Thirteen for Dinner* for fear of organised booing was derided. It was 'no more than a confession of insecurity' and a just reward for putting on such 'a febrile, frantic and foolish bagatelle . . . Certain plays should never open at all.'[168]

His most notorious *Daily Sketch* review occurred when his dislike of the formulaic upper-middle-class offering coincided with his recurrent conviction that Olivier's frequent appearances with his wife were squandering his talent. '*But Oh*

What a Wicked *Fairy'* was just the type of review that had his fans curling their toes with pleasure, as one anonymous admirer wrote to him,[169] and establishment figures frothing at his impertinence. Written with an irony bordering on sarcasm, it attacked Rattigan's whimsical *The Sleeping Prince*, the docility of the London audience in the face of such candyfloss and the limitations of Vivien Leigh as an actress. The opening was brutal:

> Once upon a time there was an actor called gruff Laurence Olivier, whose wife was an actress called pert Vivien Leigh, and a playwright called clever Terence Rattigan wrote a play for them, called *The Sleeping Prince*, with a gruff part for him and a pert part for her, and to nobody's surprise it ran happily ever after, with twice-weekly matinées.

It had only opened the night before, but Tynan knew that Rattigan's success was guaranteed since he was a master of serving up to the playgoer exactly what s/he had been conditioned to enjoy:

> This is a quilted cushion of a play. You become embedded in it rather than caught up by it . . . It is a living monument to Mr Rattigan's views on his craft, as set down in the preface to his collected plays, shortly to be published by Hamish Hamilton. In this document he firmly declares that the theatre is no place for ideas: and he admits that his best audience is an imaginary Aunt Edna in West Kensington, and he defines what he calls the 'experimental' element in his comedies as consisting in their cunning avoidance of verbal wit.
>
> *The Sleeping Prince* demonstrates, once and for all, that he means what he says. Aunt Edna will dote on it, and so will her cousin, Aunt Sadie in Manhattan . . . There is also Miss Leigh, looking (I must say) very well indeed in a white dress and a strawberry-blonde wig. Admirers of her art will recognise this as her 'American type' performance, complete with sing-song accent à la Katharine Hepburn. I found her beautiful without being attractive, technically competent without being emotionally convincing. It is a strangely bloodless display.[170]

Tynan's book with Cecil Beaton, *Persona Grata*, was published in the same month as this review and offered an interesting reminder that he had not always been so hostile to those, such as Gielgud, Rattigan and Binkie Beaumont, who were connected with H.M. Tennent. Beaumont, in a portrait that pleased him, was described as a master manipulator, and Tynan did not, at this point, consider that his influence was necessarily malign:

> His basic gift repels definition. If questioned how he manages to bring the right men and the right moment into such unfailing theatrical collaboration, he raises

an eyebrow, smiles a small, arcane smile, and says: 'I hear curious drums beating
. . .' Apart from a tendency to revive and overdress bad Victorian plays at the drop
of a box-office receipt, he has been righter, on a higher level, than anyone else
in the theatre of his time.[171]

Gielgud, too, was a significant figure, even if he comes off second best to Olivier:

He is the guarantee, rather than the product; the seal and the signature, rather
than the proclamation. It is as patron, not merely as participant, that he lends what
dignity it possesses to the ramshackle business of stage pretence . . . When Olivier
enters, lions pounce into the ring, and the stage becomes an arena. Gielgud, on
the other hand, appears: he does not 'make an entrance'; and he looks like one
who has an appointment with the brush of Gainsborough or Reynolds. The
face is reposeful, save when emotion convulses it, and then it twitches, suddenly
constricted, working intensely, as if a bowl of ammonia had been thrust beneath
its nostrils.[172]

It was Christopher Fry who interestingly represented the greatest threat to progress,
with the writing of verse plays being 'like speaking Latin, an enjoyable intellectual
exercise for a minority',[173] whilst Olivier, as always, remained the performer that
everybody else had to strive to emulate:

Between good and great acting is fixed an inexorable gulf, which may be crossed
only by the elect, whose visas are in order. Gielgud, seizing a parasol, crosses by
tight-rope; Redgrave, with lunatic obstinacy, plunges into the torrent, usually
sinking within yards of the opposite shore: Laurence Olivier polevaults over,
hair-raisingly, in a single, animal leap. Great acting comes more easily to him than
to any of his colleagues: he need do no more than lift his head, neigh, and extend
a gauntletted hand to usher us into the presence of tragic matters. One wonders
what will become of him now.[174]

Looking back from 2001, Dundy observed that 'To this day, whenever some stage
or screen personality in the book dies, Ken's words about them find their way into
print again',[175] but care needs to be taken with selective quotation from *Persona Grata*.
This interregnum period between the *Evening Standard* and the *Observer* displayed a
shift in his critical views and priorities. His early love of grandeur and heroic acting
was being supplanted by a concern for relevance and more realistic theatre, and some
of the views expressed on the personalities in *Persona Grata* were quietly dropped
over the coming years. The book itself was well received by his contemporaries.
Reviewers marvelled at the quality of his prose – Leo Lerman in the *New York Times*
called him the 'bad boy of English dramatic criticism' and compared him to George

Jean Nathan in the 1920s;[176] frequent reference was made to the fact that he was only twenty-six; and those being profiled were thrilled by the attention. Alastair Cooke, who had been gently rebuked for being dishevelled, told him that he had 'already taken [his] hands out of [his] pockets and [I] hope to appal you less with my sprucer surface'[177] and Maurice Chevalier, brimming with glee, spoke of him in the highest terms: 'you are yourself a phenomenon arrived – so young – with such a large culture and coming like arrows – those blows of good sense . . .'[178] Astor was beginning to come round to this view himself. The pungency of Tynan's reviews, the style of *Persona Grata*, not to mention the insight of his study of Alec Guinness began to convince him that here was a very talented young man indeed.

Tynan had begun to submit a few freelance articles following his September meeting with Astor, and the editor now gave serious thought to employing him permanently. Having secured the agreement of the resident critic, Ivor Brown, to retire, Astor opened negotiations with Tynan. It was a risk, since Tynan had already gained some serious enemies (not least the Society of West End Theatre Managers, who disliked his savaging), but it was a risk that Astor now wanted to take. In spite of a change of mind by Brown about his desire to retire and a campaign conducted by his wife, the theatre producer Irene Hentschel, to persuade the *Observer*'s chairman, Dingle Foot, that Tynan was not the type of writer who should be associated with the paper, negotiations were concluded in December. Tynan was offered a three-year contract at £1,500 per annum to begin in September 1954. 'Now I'm just a critic,' he told his wife,[179] but, although it was not the resident directorship that he had always wanted, it was a most prestigous appointment. The press brouhaha was as loud as it was predictable. He was mocked for his clothes, precocity and stammer. Critical rivals, such as W.A. Darlington of the *Daily Telegraph*, sent nervous congratulations[180] and loyal friends, such as Charles Curran, sent genuine expressions of delight. In his letter, Curran alluded to the numerous derisive references to him as the new Shaw made by envious competitors: 'As the author of the comparison with Shaw I want to say that I stand by every word of it. I believe that you are the most talented theatre critic to enter Fleet Street since Shaw arrived in the eighties; and I believe also that in a very few years from now this will be recognised by everyone . . .'[181]

His move to the *Observer* in nine months' time arranged, Tynan quickly gave his notice to the *Daily Sketch*. Although he was employed until March, Tynan's columns became more erratic, but he did give some signs of new interests that might be developed at the *Observer* in his review of the previous year. 'Lots of accomplishment, little progress: such was London theatre in 1953,' was his verdict, and, '1954 finds us in desperate need of new producers and new playwrights; and if that prayer is vain, at least let's have some new translators, who can bring to us some of the mass of fine European plays unseen in this country.' The coronation had been the 'most opulent' drama and Tennent's had acted 'on their well-known assumption that a play is a coat-hanger'.[182]

Just at the point when Tynan was establishing some professional stability, his relationship with Elaine began to show its first signs of stress. From her perspective, his increasing interest in S&M sex began to threaten the marriage, particularly as it drew unhappy parallels with the childhood that she had been so keen to escape. 'Now I had to face the bitterest irony of all,' she recalled. 'I'd married a man who in one fatally important aspect *was* like my father. Both men were violent towards women.'[183] Tynan's sexual taste, according to Elaine, was to 'cane a woman on her bare buttocks, to hurt and humiliate her', and 'his weapon of choice' was a head-master's cane.[184] He tried to interest her in role-play by showing her pornographic photographs from his private collection and lending her some books to read about the subject, but their sexual incompatibility was never to be resolved, and would lead to each of them engaging in a litany of brief affairs. Tynan also began to indulge in 'ledge-standing', going out on to the ledge of their flat and threatening to jump if he did not get his way, a tendency to cry wolf that extended into his second marriage. But it was clear that Elaine faced difficulties, too. She had resumed her drinking with all the concomitant erratic behaviour and, looking back, was quite willing to concede that he had plenty to be angry about with her as well.[185]

The period between March 1954 and the start of Tynan's *Observer* contract gave the couple an opportunity to engage in their favourite mutual pastime: going abroad. In March they travelled to Hollywood, in May to Rome and then to Madrid for the summer, where Tynan conducted more research on bullfighting. But the happiness of their first year of marriage was dissolving rapidly. When Marlene Dietrich made a personal appearance at the Café de Paris in London, Tynan became obsessed with her. She, too, was interested in the author of such an intriguing portrait in *Persona Grata* and they spent hours in each other's company. Hugely irritated by what was likely to have been a platonic affair, Elaine retaliated by having a brief fling with another *Persona Grata* celebrity, the novelist Henry Green. It was a chain of events that would recur repeatedly during the period that was to seal Tynan's greatness – his first tenure as theatre critic of the *Observer*.

Chapter 3 *1954–56: Loamshire*

Little had happened in Britain at large between Tynan's first theatre criticism for the *Evening Standard* in 1951 and his appointment as the *Observer*'s theatre critic in 1954 to challenge that notion that Britain had become a 'haven for the elderly'.[1] The defeat of Attlee's weary government at the October general election of 1951 ushered in the second term of office for Winston Churchill, who, although still revered for his achievement as the wartime leader, was already seventy-seven himself when he moved into Downing Street for a second time. His biographer, Roy Jenkins, has little doubt about the new PM's limitations –

> It is impossible to re-read details of Churchill's life as Prime Minister of this second government without feeling that he was gloriously unfit for office . . . With the exception of one issue which increasingly dominated his mind, the saving of the world from destruction in a reciprocal holocaust of H-Bombs, his struggle to prolong his life in office became more important than any policy issue.[2]

– and Churchill became notorious within cabinet circles for getting up late, paying very limited attention to cabinet papers and obsessively playing bezique. None of this filtered through to the country at large, however, given a largely deferential media and the absence of televisual scrutiny. Indeed, the public face of Churchill's administration deviated little from his intention, announced in his first House of Commons speech after the election and successfully delivered over the four years of his leadership, to give the country 'several years of quiet steady administration'.[3] Through a combination of pragmatism, consensus and luck, living standards rose sharply during this period. The early decision to cut back on the previous administration's enormous rearmament budget and focus instead on the 'massive retaliation' of a nuclear programme (publicly admitted in 1952 with the testing of atomic rockets at Woomera in northern Australia, and re-emphasised in the Defence White Paper of 1954) produced a large financial windfall. The conclusion of the Korean war also boosted the country's balance sheet and permitted the lifting of rationing of sugar, sweets, eggs, bacon, margarine, butter, cheese and meat (the 'red meat' that Churchill had promised the country during the election);[4] and the highly successful rebuilding programme resulted in the Minister of Housing, Harold Macmillan, handing over the key to the 300,000th house built in 1953 on 31 December, thereby fulfilling a manifesto pledge that many had felt would be impossible to implement. Indeed 300,000 new houses were built each year for the next five years.

By accepting the broad parameters of the welfare state and embarking on the most limited policy of denationialisation, industrial conflict with the trade unions was avoided, and the stability that this created, coupled with a large fall in the cost of imports in 1953, helped the government achieve full employment (where unemployment is 1 per cent of the total working population) by 1955. It also allowed commentators to observe that a policy of consensus between the two main political parties seemed to have been inadvertently hatched. Churchill was now continuing the job of transforming a war-weary country that had been begun by Attlee, with little deviation – and it was difficult to see the joins. The *Economist* in 1954 coined the term 'Butskellism' – eliding the names of Butler, the Chancellor of the Exchequer and Gaitskell, his predecessor and current shadow – to describe a so-called (but exaggerated) continuity of policy at the Treasury. Originally devised as a satirical observation, it quickly became more widely used to describe, in tones of quiet approval, a sensible, gentlemanly co-operation for the good of the country. By its nature, however, consensus is unexciting. For the undeferential young, maturing rapidly in the post-war period with spending power to match, party politics seemed to be operated by dull, archaic and distant men, who mostly belonged to the pre-war period. Any social and political protest that they might wish to make would need to find different outlets.

The accession of Princess Elizabeth to the throne on 6 February 1952 underlined the paradoxical nature of this period. Whilst appearing young, vivacious and an embodiment of future hope – there was much fevered talk of the arrival of 'a new Elizabethan age' – her very position at the apex of an establishment that depended on the rigidities of a class system suggested that she would not herself be the initiator of fundamental change for the post-war generation. Detached from the wartime urgings for self-sacrifice, she was dismissive of the dreariness of post-war consensus, however virtuous.

Political and generational change was thwarted too, since the death of George VI reinvigorated Churchill's appetite for power. His cabinet colleagues had believed that he would resign a year or so into the life of the government to allow the Foreign Secretary, Anthony Eden, to succeed, but there now began a process of perpetual postponement on Churchill's part worthy of the play that was shortly to be staged for the first time in Paris, *Waiting for Godot*. Not even a severe stroke in June 1953 could shift Churchill's tenacious grip on power. A cover-up of enormous proportions was quickly co-ordinated by his close family and the media barons Lord Camrose and Lord Beaverbrook. With Eden himself incapacitated by a botched abdominal operation the previous April (an event which in itself illustrated the sickly nature of the political elite), there was no obvious successor, so a decision was taken to play for time. Churchill's doctors, Lord Moran and Sir Russell Brain, issued the blandest of public statements – 'The PM has had no respite for a long time from his very arduous duties and is in need of complete rest. We have therefore advised him to abandon his journey to Bermuda and to lighten his duties for at least a month'[5] – and Churchill was spirited away, extremely ill, to his country retreat of Chartwell. The press submitted to its gagging – an event that would have been impossible even three years later – but nevertheless, it is hard not to agree with Roy Jenkins's assessment that the maintenance of 'the veil of secrecy about the nature and severity of his illness was [a] near miracle'.[6] No public mention was made of the dread word 'stroke' until it was uttered by Churchill himself in the House of Commons a year later.[7]

Remarkably, Churchill struggled to regain his health. He chaired his first cabinet – much to the distress of some of his colleagues – on 18 August and managed to deliver a low-key conference speech – his first major public appearance – to the Conservative Party faithful in October. Even more remarkable, however, was the acquiescence of the political class in this deception of the public. No one was prepared to tell him to his face to go, even when he gave private indications of his desire to be relieved of the burdens of office. R.A. Butler, who acted as *de facto* Prime Minister throughout the second half of 1953 and during the period of Tynan's brief tenure at the *Daily Sketch*, remembered Churchill telling him over dinner that 'I feel like an aeroplane at the end of its flight, in the dusk, with the petrol running out, in search of a safe landing'.[8]

By the first months of 1954, the deferential attitude of the media to what was becoming known as 'the Churchill retirement problem' was beginning to crack. A parliamentary débâcle in April 1954, where Churchill became rambling and occasionally incoherent during a speech on nuclear proliferation – the one issue for which it could just conceivably be argued he should stay, because of his status as a war leader – led to comments which, by the quiescent standards of the early 1950s, could be described as savage. The *Times* observed that 'his sense of occasion [had] sadly deserted him', the *Manchester Guardian* felt that 'he had blundered' and the

Daily Mirror believed that the country was witnessing the 'twilight of a giant'.[9] The magazine *Punch* went further by publishing a cartoon depicting a total wreck of a man[10] – which alarmed Churchill greatly, given its widespread presence in doctors' waiting rooms – and Eden, the increasingly frustrated heir apparent, commented privately, 'This simply can't go on; he is gaga; he cannot finish his sentences.'[11]

But go on he did. In the absence of anybody of sufficient stature to force him to stand down, Churchill, following private urgings on the part of Macmillan and Eden to retire gracefully, finally fixed the date for 20 September 1954, yet postponed his departure once again when it looked as if there might be the possibility of a three-way summit between the USA, the UK and the USSR. It was against this background of stasis, obstinacy and disproportionate (to say nothing of dangerous) respect for the elderly that Tynan became the youngest national theatre critic in the country. A disdain for this sclerotic attitude to government, which was reflected in the arts, and, in particular, the theatre, was to suffuse his writing for the next four years – writing which helped encourage the repositioning of British theatre from being the most insular in Europe to being the most dynamic in the space of ten years, and allowed the younger generation to see that not every aspect of British life need be governed by the outdated concept of automatic respect.

Before we consider Tynan's dramatic first period as the critic of the *Observer* between 1954 and 1958, there are several myths that cling tenaciously to this period of theatre history that need dispelling. The first – and most pervasive – is that the reorientation of British theatre that was to lead to a glorious period of drama on the London stage began with the first night of *Look Back in Anger* on 8 May 1956. As we shall see, this is only part of the story. For a start, this undeniably important event was preceded by the equally seminal British première of *Waiting for Godot* in 1955. The introduction at the Arts Theatre of the Absurdist theatre of Beckett and Ionesco by the young director Peter Hall caused critical consternation and great excitement. Here was a form of drama that so questioned the linear structure of all that had gone before that the old certainties of post-war theatre – the need for a star performer, a sumptuous set and a series of decisive curtain falls – were quickly placed under scrutiny. From the perspective of the twenty-first century, it is possible to identify a political dimension to this work that has been repeatedly under-emphasised to maintain a false binary divide between the theatre of Brecht ('epic theatre') on the one hand and the theatre of Beckett, Ionesco and the early Pinter, on the other.

Secondly, *Look Back in Anger* did not quite arrive in the theatrical desert that conventional theatre history describes. In the mid-1950s, Britain could boast an intriguing mix of world-class performers – Olivier, Gielgud, Richardson, Redgrave, Ashcroft and Evans, for example – and young, innovative directors, such as Peter Hall and Peter Brook. Some green shoots of recovery were already emerging in the form of Theatre Workshop and established playwrights, such as Rattigan and Philip King, who were seeking to redefine their work from within. In his first season as the *Observer* critic from September 1954 to July 1955 Tynan was to witness three thinly veiled plays about homosexuality – Rattigan's *Separate Tables*, Gide's *The Immoralist* and King's *Serious Charge*; a refreshingly unorthodox approach to *Richard II* by Theatre Workshop and a bold, if ultimately unsuccessful, performance by Joan Littlewood of a controversial German text that would later have a profound influence on European drama, *Mother Courage*. Add to these the British première of Ionesco's *The Lesson* and celebrated productions of *Twelfth Night* starring Gielgud and *Macbeth* featuring Olivier, and one might not feel that this was such a poor season compared to, say, certain periods in the 1980s.

What was missing, however, was vibrant contemporary plays by indigenous playwrights that broke out of the upper-middle-class mindset that had gripped British theatre since the end of the Second World War. George Devine and the Royal Court may have been the most visible – and celebrated – protagonists in the dismantling of the old Binkie Beaumont legacy, but the ground for their success had been prepared for them by similar feelings of dissatisfaction by many of the companies and playwrights mentioned above and, crucially, by the brilliant, insistent, much-debated weekly dispatches from the battleground filed by Tynan. Without his compelling diagnoses of the failings of mid-1950s theatres – reaching far beyond the theatre world of London and thrilling politically minded young people up and down the country – the theatrical revolution of the late 1950s and early 1960s would have been less sure of victory.

A final myth to challenge is that Tynan was the only critic who exhibited dissatisfaction with the lack of innovative work that was being served up to him before the break points of 1955 and 1956. Ivor Brown's valedictory piece for the *Observer* at the end of August 1954 is prescient and provides a useful reminder that much of his work – particularly his crusade against the iniquities of entertainment tax – was more forward-looking than is generally remembered. 'It is high time,' he urged,

> for a renewal of interest in new writing; reviving the classics with star-clustered casts can be a menace to our theatre as well as a service of tradition . . . The question of 'Who wrote it?' should be just as urgent as the query of 'Who's in it?' . . . The alteration needed is not of the over-weening actor, but of the over-timid audience, which tempts managers to cautious massing of the stars in 'safe, box-office propositions'.[12]

Harold Hobson, too, felt that by the early summer of 1955 the London stage was in danger of being atrophied –

Aesthetically the weakness of the London theater is that it still tends to reflect the secure, well-bred world of the pre-war period. It has devised no new techniques to deal with the insecurity and desperate searching for safety of contemporary mankind[13]

– although as a critic who preferred to accentuate the positive and saw as his prime aim the celebration of the actor's craft, he was only intermittently to return to this theme. Tynan, then, was not alone in feeling that something was very wrong, but he was the only critic capable of widening his disaffection with British drama to embrace the castigation of insipid British attitudes – most notably social, cultural and political conservatism – in language that was fresh, incisive and thrillingly provocative.

What should have been a triumphant moment for Tynan, the start of his eagerly anticipated reign as *Observer* critic, was blighted by a high degree of private turmoil. The year 1954 had been a grim one for his marriage, with a great deal of friction being caused both by Elaine's drinking and by his desire to engage in S&M practices. This humiliating situation – humiliating for both parties – highlighted their incompatibility. Dundy acknowledges now that there was fault on both sides: 'If I had plenty to be angry about Ken, he had plenty to be angry about me. I mean my drinking. If Ken didn't say enough about his sexual problems, before we married, I'd said nothing about my drinking problems – even after I saw they weren't going away.'[14] Behind the couple's public bravado and vibrant social life was much private pain.

Dundy's unwillingness to satisfy her husband's particular sexual needs was used by him to justify what was to become a regular series of affairs, but they now both engaged in infidelity. After Elaine had embarked upon her brief relationship with Henry Green, Tynan flirted with Carol Saroyan, whom he had met in Los Angeles in March 1954, and Marlene Dietrich, whom he had eulogised in *Persona Grata* and who was appearing at the Café de Paris from June 1954. A brief truce was arranged for the married couple's pilgrimage to Spain in August, but this was broken when Tynan made an unsuccessful play during their holiday for a young American woman they had befriended, Margot Scadron. A fourth liaison is hinted at in a letter to Tynan from Betsy Holland, written on 10 September 1954, only five days after Tynan's first drama column for his new employers: 'You sound awfully Chekhovian in your gloom,' she wrote. 'I remain, [however], naively perhaps, joyful and belief-ful . . . You don't mention Elaine or your marriage, but I assume they are the boats you have to burn – or CONSIDER burning – before you are ready for the "fulltime emotional . . . years" with me . . .'[15]

During the autumn of 1954, Tynan and Holland, another young American with theatre in her blood, started to collaborate on adapting S.J. Perelman's story, *All-Girl*

Elephant Hunt, into a piece of musical theatre. Even on the eve of his full-time position, Tynan was reluctant to accept that he would no longer be directly involved in practical theatre, but this project evaporated when Perelman refused to give his permission in early 1955, along with Holland's expectation that Tynan would leave his wife.

This private emotional turmoil explains the rather flaccid start to his *Observer* career, since his first two columns can be described, at best, as settling-in pieces. Harold Hobson took some quiet satisfaction from this, prematurely believing that his new competitor would prove no rival.[16] 'Ins and Outs', the first article, published on 15 September 1954, pays a double-edged compliment to Tynan's aggrieved predecessor, describing Brown as 'a man of roots in a rootless time'; Tynan celebrates his own unpredictability by commenting that he has 'little or no idea where [he is] going'. The metaphor that he chooses to describe his attitude to criticism is as contrived as his later writing is fresh and spontaneous, but it immediately flags up one of his most passionate critical beliefs – that the theatre and not the cinema should act as the site of intellectual debate:

> Critics in the past have seen themselves variously as torch-bearers, pall-bearers and lighthouses shining over unmapped seas; I see myself predominantly as a lock. If the key, which is the work of art, fits snugly into my mechanism of bias and preference, I click and rejoice; if not, I am helpless, and can only offer the artist the address of a better locksmith. Sometimes, unforeseen a masterpiece seizes the knocker, batters down the door and enters unopposed; and when that happens, I am a willing casualty. I cave in *con amore.* But mostly I am at a loss. It is a sombre truth that nowadays our intellectuals go to the cinema and shun the theatre. Their assistance is sadly missed; but their defection is my opportunity.[17]

His second review, 'Purple Hedda', reminds his new readership – intelligent, middle-class and attracted to the paper's free-thinking liberalism – of the absence of intellectual input in the contemporary scene, but it does so in a rather tired manner. Tynan wryly observes that Warren Chetham-Strode's *The Pet Shop* is about whether an unmarried mother should adopt her child in order to conceal its illegitimacy – 'The *scène à faire*, in which [twenty years later the child] discovers her bastardy, is conceived as if the information to be imparted were that she had a touch of leprosy'. But the prose does not flow.

Further pressure was added by the fact that Tynan was being observed expectantly by those who had viewed his rapier style at the *Evening Standard* and the *Daily Sketch* as a breath of fresh air, whose every word had to be devoured, and with hostility by those who saw him as an attention-seeking upstart, dangerously threatening to upset the cosy status quo. Alan Brien's October article for the weekly magazine *Truth*, ambiguously entitled 'The Boy Wonder', embraced both views. In an intriguing and dubious manner, Brien chose to highlight the paradox as he saw it between the eloquence of Tynan's written voice and the impediment that occasionally afflicted his spoken one. With some relish, he luridly described Tynan's stutter, which starts 'as a nervous spasm in the solar plexus and leaps to the jaw muscles' before he makes 'four or five snapping sounds like a man taking quick bites from an apple and produces a long balanced sentence in which pun cannons into pun in a verbal break at billiards'.[18] There was also a questioning of his sexuality, with a thinly veiled reference to effeminacy. The following week Tynan responded with a letter published in the magazine. He took direct issue with the allusion – 'I must . . . congratulate you on the detailed physiological description of my stammer, which delighted my young daughter: and I would appreciate a clarification of the inference that I am effeminate, which I was cowardly enough to withhold from her'[19] – and provided a warning that he would from now on return published attacks with interest.

By the middle of September and his third review Tynan finally began to get into his stride. Recognising that people expected him to be provocative, he sought to fulfil expectations with his first withering diagnosis. Gifted the opportunity by Leonard Huizinga's drab *No News from Father*, he let rip under the headline 'The Second Rate', arguing that the current sterility was the responsibility of practitioners and spectators alike:

> The results of our culpable indulgence surround us. No playwright rises above his audience's expectations for very long; why should he do his best work when *Dry Rot* and *The Love Match* are delighting the public with their worthlessness? Nobody wants to see the secondary theatre abolished, but it is imperative that it should be judged by higher critical standards. Twenty seven West End theatres are at present offering light comedies and musical shows of which perhaps a dozen are good of their kind. The number of new plays with a claim to serious discussion is three: *A Day by the Sea, The Dark is Light Enough* and *I am a Camera*. One need not be a purist to be ashamed by the discrepancy. Our garden is beset with weeds, and 'the coulter rusts that should deracinate such savagery'. The secondary theatre must put forth better shoots, and fewer; it is so easy, as the elder Dumas said, not to write plays.

No News from Father at the Cambridge was a case in point:

> A robustly eccentric ethnologist comes home after ten years in the Arctic to find his daughter contemplating marriage and his wife rather more than contemplating an affair with her solicitor. A meaningless imposture, by which the hero

pretends to be somebody else, is despairingly invoked to keep things going for three acts. Thankfully, Mr Bernard Braden, miscast in the central role, is unable to achieve its full, foghorn repellence. The character is a monster of rodomontade, who loses his trousers and bawls Eskimo; Mr Braden, a born miniaturist, behaves as if he were telling an anecdote about the man rather than attempting to play him. Were I running a school for prospective comedians, I should make this part the test-piece; anyone getting more than six laughs out of it would be summarily dismissed on grounds of insensitivity . . . The director is Mr Warren Jenkins, who must not be blamed for having failed to turn a strip of coconut matting into a magic carpet. If the play takes, it will be a triumph for the secondary theatre, which has its headquarters at the Garrick and the Whitehall, and fifth columns in Shaftesbury Avenue, at the Saville and the Lyric. We are, meanwhile, directing operations from Hammersmith, and praying that our retreat is only temporary and tactical.[20]

This piece ushered in a series of articles published in the 1954/5 season that offered a general, withering survey of the inadequacies of British theatre. In its use of simple memorable phrases ('Our garden is beset by weeds'), scientific appeal to reason (only three out of twenty-seven theatres are producing new serious plays of any merit), acidic précis of an absurd plot (a 'robustly eccentric ethnologist comes home after ten years in the Arctic . . .') and cod military metaphor (he is praying that the 'retreat is only temporary and tactical'), this piece demonstrates all the call signs of Tynan's finest theatre articles. Unambiguous in its attack on the H.M. Tennent empire, which was based in Shaftesbury Avenue; scathing about the low standards that British theatre set for itself; and, above all, astounded by the utter irrelevance of such works to the condition of early 1950s Britain, Tynan was bearing early witness to how theatre and the wider arts would offer one outlet for social protest in the absence of meaningful party politics in the years ahead. Nor is he afraid to highlight the culpability of London audiences. The economic success of these works, which is the basis for their stranglehold on the West End, is guaranteed by the unquestioning consumption of them by quiescent theatre-goers. Sights would have to be raised much higher.

Four weeks later one of the most memorable articles of Tynan's entire career was published. 'West End Apathy', of which 'The Second Rate' had clearly been the precursor, was the type of denunciation that David Astor had employed Tynan to produce. It begins in mid-conversation and initially adopts a cosy, reassuring, authentic tone, as if a group of friends were having a drink in the pub and mulling over recent developments in the arts. By conveying a sense of the normality of discussing such topics – and in its underlying reference to youth – the piece immediately divests the discussion of culture of a class-bound context. The arts, and that includes the limping theatre, too, should be for everyone. It is necessary to quote it in its entirety, to feel its full effect:

'And how,' ask my friends, having debated the opera, the ballet, politics and Italian cinema, 'how is the theatre getting along?' The very set of their features, so patiently quizzical, tells me I am being indulged; after the serious business of conversation, they are permitting themselves a lapse into idleness. I shrug cheerily, like a martyr to rheumatism. A wan, tingling silence ensues. Then: 'De Sica's new film is superb,' says somebody, and talk begins again, happy and devout. I stew, meanwhile, in what Zelda Fitzgerald once called 'the boiling oil of sour grapes.'

The bare fact is, that apart from revivals and imports, there is nothing in the London theatre that one dares discuss with an intelligent man for more than five minutes. Since the great Ibsen challenge of the nineties, the English intellectuals have been drifting away from drama. Synge, Pirandello, and O'Casey briefly recaptured them, and they will still perk up at the mention of Giraudoux. But – cowards – they know Eliot and Fry only in the study; and of a native prose play-wright who might set the boards smouldering they see no sign at all. Last week I welcomed a young Frenchwoman engaged in writing a thesis on contemporary English drama. We talked hopefully of John Whiting: but before long embarrass-ment moved me to ask why she had not chosen her own theatre as a subject for study. She smiled wryly. 'Paris is in decline', she said. 'Apart from Sartre, Anouilh, Camus, Cocteau, Aymé, Claudel, Beckett and Salacrou, we have almost nobody.'

If you seek a tombstone, look about you; survey the peculiar nullity of our drama's prevalent *genre*, the Loamshire play. Its setting is a country house in what used to be called Loamshire but is now, as a heroic tribute to realism, sometimes called Berkshire. Except when someone must sneeze, or be murdered, the sun invariably shines. The inhabitants belong to a social class derived partly from romantic novels and partly from the playwright's vision of the leisured life he will lead after the play is a success – this being the only effort of imagination he is called on to make. Joys and sorrows are giggles and whimpers: the crash of denunciation dwindles into 'Oh, stuff, Mummy!' and 'Oh, really, Daddy!' And so grim is the continuity of these things that the foregoing paragraph might have been written at any time during the last thirty years.

Loamshire is a glibly codified fairy-tale world, of no more use to the student of life than a doll's house would be to a student of town planning. Its vice is to have engulfed the theatre, thereby expelling better minds. Never believe that there is a shortage of playwrights; there are more than we have ever known; but they are all writing the same play. Nor is there a dearth of English actors; the land is alive with them; but they are all playing the same part. Should they wish to test themselves beyond Loamshire's simple major thirds, they must find employment in revivals, foreign plays, or films. Perhaps Loamshire's greatest triumph is the crippling of creative talent in English directors and designers. After all, how many ways are there of directing a tea-party? And how may a designer spread his wings in a mews flat or 'The living-room at "Binsgate", Vyvyan Bulstrode's country house near Dynsdyke'? Assume the miracle: assume the advent of a masterpiece. There it crouches, a pink-eyed, many muscled, salivating monster. Who shall harness it? We have a handful of directors fit to tame something less malleable than a mouse and a few designers still capable of dressing something less submissive than a clothes-horse. But they are the end, not the beginning, of a tradition.

Some of us need no miracles to keep our faith; we feed it on memories and imaginings. But many more – people of passionate intellectual appetites – are losing heart, falling away, joining the queues outside the Curzon Cinema. To lure them home, the theatre must widen its scope, broaden its horizon so that Loamshire appears merely as the play-pen, not the whole palace of drama. We need plays about cabmen and demi-gods, plays about warriors, politicians, and grocers – I care not, so Loamshire be invaded and subdued. I counsel aggression because, as a critic, I had rather be a war correspondent than necrologist.[21]

Such is the brilliance of the writing (nobody has demonstrated such mastery of the 800-word review) and the ingenuity of the conceit that 'West End Apathy' resonates across the decades. British theatre criticism had never before – even with the young Shaw – experienced anything so gently and appropriately cutting, and 'Loamshire' immediately became a handy term of dismissal for those dissatisfied with the anaemic fare of the West End stage. People were simply not used in the early 1950s to reading such devastatingly frank critiques – it went against the general consensus and was considered bad taste to be too frank – and Tynan's skill lay in recognising that there was a body of opinion yearning for the old, rigid rules of *politesse* to be demolished. Indeed, the whole article can be seen as a satirical attack on the ossification of Great Britain. As Tynan was composing this article, the newspapers were beginning to make mention of the celebratory dinner that the new Queen Elizabeth II would be having to mark the eightieth birthday of her Prime Minister, Winston Churchill, on 30 November. The dislocation between the old and the young had never been so apparent and it is no coincidence that Tynan couches his embarrassment at being a theatre-lover in the company of energetic cinema-goers in terms of geriatric illness: 'I shrug cheerily, like a martyr to rheumatism.'

The second paragraph brutally highlights the stasis that has gripped English theatre – and by extension England as a whole – over the previous fifty years. There
is nothing worth discussing with an intelligent man for 'more than five minutes';
the great plays of this period have been written by the Irish, only to be appropri-
ated by the English in typical colonial mode; the latest 'smart' playwrights, Eliot
and Fry, the leading members of the Christian Verse Drama movement, are known
by reputation alone (and are, Tynan prophetically hints, not up to much theatrically); prose is considered too brutal and contemporary to use to write drama in
this new 'Elizabethan' age; hope for the future is absurdly invested in one playwright alone, John Whiting; and such is the reverence of the French for drama – a
nation, incidentally, occupied during the Second World War and surely in no position to have rebuilt its cultural life so quickly – that a visiting student is dissatisfied
that there are 'only' eight indigenous dramatists of note working in Paris.

Tynan then delivers his *coup de grâce* with the famous Loamshire conceit. The
most popular English plays since the 1920s have all been of the same ilk. Resolutely
upper middle class, devoid of true realism, formulaic in their construction, all
embracing and 'crippling of creative talent', the Loamshire play embodies attitudes
that Tynan from now on makes it his business to expose and harry. His humour is
lacerating – 'Joys and sorrows are giggles and whimpers: the crash of denunciation
dwindles into "Oh, stuff, Mummy!" and "Oh, really, Daddy!"' – but Loamshire's
legacy is deadly serious: 'Its vice is to have engulfed the theatre, thereby expelling
better minds.'

A concerted effort is needed to rescue theatre from its clutches, a military campaign even, that reaches out to 'people of passionate intellectual appetites'. Tynan's
conclusion becomes a critical manifesto for his time at the *Observer* – 'We need plays
about cabmen and demi-gods, plays about warriors, politicians, and grocers – I care
not, so Loamshire be invaded and subdued. I counsel aggression because, as a critic,
I had rather be a war correspondent than necrologist' – and there is a hint in this
that he was already planning the new front against Loamshire, which he would
launch in early 1955, the crusade for Brecht. The days when heroic acting was in
the middle of his telescopic sights were long gone.

Tynan has skilfully incorporated into 'West End Apathy' issues that were current
in Britain in 1954 – the emerging gulf between the generations, the desire for a genuine cause to fight for on the part of the young, the decline in Britain's imperial
status, the envy at the swift reconstruction of France and Germany and, above all,
the demarcation barriers of class – but they are also issues that have transcended
the immediate context from which the article sprang. The freshness of the writing
and the irreverence of the approach are among the reasons why the piece still holds
such a powerful appeal for young people in the twenty-first century, but it is also

instructive that in 2003 the dislocation of the young from the political process, an insular mistrust of our European partners and repeated insecurity about Britain's status in the world (brought to the fore by the wars in Afghanistan and Iraq and the 'war against terrorism') are still prominent concerns. Back in October 1954, things were crystal clear for Tynan. He had now discovered the 'good, brave cause' worth fighting for that Jimmy Porter would soon doubt had ever existed: the salvation of post-war British theatre.

Tynan's tenure as a war correspondent began with this article, since at its very end is his opening barrage against a specific 'Loamshire' play:

Anyone curious to see how the Loamshire vogue began should visit the New Theatre, Bromley, where *The Second Mrs Tanqueray* is opulently revived with that iron tigress, Miss Catherine Lacey, in the name part. 'Highercoombe, near Willowmere, Surrey', is the *milieu*, wherein you may watch Pinero softening an Ibsenite clash of wills into an Ibsenite clash of class. With this piece the rot set in; but like all fruits of first decay, it can still tickle the palate.

Tynan was shrewd enough to recognise that the 'Loamshire' work is not without a certain dangerous allure and it is important to recognise that his newly launched campaign was against the way the enervating Loamshire attitude that militated against progressive experimentation had suffused every aspect of the theatre, as much as against the deficiencies of certain works. In his first three months at the *Observer* his targets are, therefore, varied. For most British critics, the dominant English playwright of the previous thirty years had been Shaw. For Tynan, Shaw's *Saint Joan* was 'the first of his plays into which Shaw's senility creeps. The jokes misfire; the debates languish; and Shaw's passion for penal reform obtrudes to the detriment of the end'[22] – although he enjoyed Kenneth Williams's 'brilliantly fussy dauphin'.

For Harold Hobson, Christopher Fry was the greatest hope the English theatre possessed. Ever since *The Lady's Not for Burning* opened in 1948, Hobson had championed Fry with insistent passion, believing him to be 'bemused with the glory of words', eager to see an ethical (and Christian) dimension reintroduced into drama and writing works that were 'not interested in little misdemeanours on drawing room sofas'.[23] For Tynan, however, Fry's medieval poetic fantastications offered little hope of loosening the grip of Loamshire, and in many ways, their celebrated unreality offered a variation on the same theme. It was also tactically useful for Tynan to dissent so publicly from his rival's cherished belief and he did so in the provocatively titled 'Dead Language':

. . . the brute fact is that no Englishman since the third decade of the seventeenth century has written an acknowledged dramatic masterpiece . . . Mr Christopher

Fry has produced prodigies of artificial respiration, the words are there, and richly he deploys them; but do they not resemble the bright, life-stimulating dyes which American morticians apply to the faces of the dead? To gain admission to drama, words must be used: they must put on flesh, throng the streets and bellow through the buses.[24]

The dull, unadventurous, overly reverent attitude to Shakespeare is criticised for squeezing the life out of the playwright –

Actors employed in minor Elizabethan plays, such as *Love's Labour's Lost* (Old Vic) tend to emerge masters of two completely arid skills: that of making bad verse sound poetic, and that of making dead puns sound funny. One depends on passing before archaic epithets, so that they seem fire-new instead of text-cold. The other consists in delivering moribund quips as if the speaker alone thought them comic[25]

– and the ritualistic attitude to theatre-going, be it in the trotting out of pantomimes at Christmas or the playing of the National Anthem before the rising of the curtain, became a popular target:

The National Anthem, through which all playgoers stand while imaginary generals pin imaginary medals to their breasts, has never struck me as a particularly invigorating piece of work: but by contrast with the scores I have heard in the past week its riches seem positively Wagnerian.[26]

By Christmas 1954, Tynan was finding his range.

There was no clearer symbol of the conservatism of British theatre in 1954 than the figure of the Lord Chamberlain, the censor of British drama. It is customary to consider the institution of censorship in relation to the 1960s, when successive playwrights and theatres became increasingly strident in their stand against the Lord Chamberlain. This stridency ultimately led to the abolition of his powers to censor in 1968. However, a consideration of the Lord Chamberlain's papers, deposited in the 1990s at the British Library, suggests that it is instructive to consider the effects of censorship from the beginning of the post-war period rather than merely from the end. As far as Tynan was concerned, state control of theatrical subject matter was a debilitating strait-jacket that needed throwing off.

The most recent guidelines that the first post-war Lord Chamberlain, Lord Clarendon, could call upon were those issued by the Parliamentary Joint Select Committee in 1909, under the heading 'Proposals with respect to the Licensing of Plays'. These decreed that the Lord Chamberlain, the most senior member of the

Royal Household, whose main duties involved organising the monarch's official ceremonials, should license a play, unless he considered that it might be reasonably held:

(a) to be indecent
(b) to contain offensive personalities
(c) to represent in an invidious manner a living person, or a person recently dead
(d) to do violence to the sentiment of religious reverence
(e) to be calculated to conduce to crime or vice
(f) to be calculated to impair friendly relations with a Foreign Power
(g) to be calculated to cause a breach of the peace.

In addition to these catch-all provisions, successive Lord Chamberlains and their readers from 1945 onwards referred to both past precedent and personal whim to reach their decisions.

If a theatre manager in the immediate post-war period wished to produce a play on a public stage, he first had to apply for a licence from the office of the Lord Chamberlain – the granting of a licence being a legal requirement for a public performance (and hence a handy way of periphrastically asserting that the Lord Chamberlain never suppressed drama, since he merely withheld a licence). On the payment of a fee of one guinea for a one-act play, or two guineas for a play of two acts or more, the submitted script would be vetted by the Lord Chamberlain's readers – mostly ex-military men – at Stable Yard, St James's Palace. They would write a summary of the work and recommend to the Lord Chamberlain whether a licence should be awarded. The script was then either returned unamended with a licence attached, returned with a request for modifications before a licence could be granted, or, on occasion, returned with the message (after either some or no correspondence with the managers) that a licence could in no circumstances be granted. The only way to stage a work that had been refused a licence was to take advantage of a legal loophole and produce it in an invariably small and financially constrained club theatre, which could perform shows only to its members.

In 1945 the number of plays that were banned from public performance was four, in 1946 five, in 1947 two, in 1948 three, in 1949 one, in 1950 eight, in 1951 seven, in 1952 three, in 1953 six and in 1954 three – 42 plays in ten years, with 27 in the first half of the 1950s alone – a significantly higher number than is normally realised, since the general perception has been that the Lord Chamberlain and respective managers usually managed to reach some form of compromise. This view has been partly formed by the regular discreet meetings and exchange of elegant letters between the supreme producer of the period, Binkie Beaumont, and the Lord Chamberlain. Up until the mid-1950s, the type of work that he wished to stage was not likely to breach any of the censor's guidelines on taste or subject matter.

The reasons given for outright suppression – and the deliberate creation of a whole generation of lost plays – are both familiar and surprising. Of the forty-two banned works, eighteen were refused a licence on account of alleged sexual impropriety; fourteen because of their treatment of what the Lord Chamberlain was to refer to in his handwritten note to the Reader's Report on Reginald Beckwith's *No Retreat* in 1957 as 'the forbidden subject', homosexuality; four because they included representations of Queen Victoria, who could only be portrayed 'in strictly accurate historical plays',[27] and not in those, such as *My Good Brown* (1951), which gently alluded to the fact that she might have had a liaison with her gamekeeper; three for referring to living people; two because of political objections; and one for being deemed offensive to Christianity. As a former director, Tynan was well aware of the strictures of the Lord Chamberlain's office, and his first season of reviewing for the *Observer* provided him with the opportunity to open up a new flank in the 'Loamshire' campaign, by attacking the mealy-mouthed approach to homosexuality that censorship obliged playwrights to adopt, if they wished to see their works performed.

In September 1954, Terence Rattigan's *Separate Tables* was premièred at the St James's Theatre. Although Britain's most popular living playwright, Rattigan was in some need of a success, after the anaemic offering of *The Sleeping Prince* in November 1953. Written as a light fantasy to celebrate the coronation and to provide a suitable vehicle for the return to the stage of Olivier and Leigh after a two-year absence, it had failed on both counts. By the end of 1953, people had grown rather weary of coronation-inspired occasions, and the script was deemed too thin to support the weight of the Oliviers. 'It seems a pity that in these spare times so much talent should have gone into so little,'[28] observed Milton Shulman, Tynan's successor at the *Evening Standard*, and whilst the play had a respectable run of 274 performances, with people lured to the Phoenix Theatre by the Oliviers' fame, it seemed that Rattigan was now in the middle of a variable run of productions. Only *The Deep Blue Sea* (1952) in the last four years had been judged a work of quality.

Rattigan had compounded his own misfortune with the invention of what he had intended to be a light-hearted character, but who would turn out to be a personal nightmare: Aunt Edna. To coincide with the première of *The Sleeping Prince*, Hamish Hamilton had published two volumes of Rattigan's Collected Plays in November 1953. In the preface to the second one, Rattigan introduced a nice, respectable, middle-class, middle-aged, unmarried lady, with time on her hands and money to spend, whom playwrights ignored at their peril. This 'typical' playgoer, who lived in a West Kensington hotel and bore a strong resemblance to Rattigan's own mother,

Vera, was culturally (and, by implication, politically) conservative. She was suspicious of Kafka, disconcerted by Picasso and baffled by Walton, but although 'a hopeless lowbrow', the weight of her recommendation to her matinée-going friends meant that she possessed enormous power in the economics of the theatre.

Somewhat contentiously, Rattigan argued that Aunt Edna had been a permanent fixture throughout the history of drama. Nowadays, she was prepared to be teased a little, but she should never be crossed; and she had been both a blessing and a boon to Rattigan himself. He had tried to put some distance between them by striving not to write too deliberately to please his audience, but he was continually aware of her influence. 'A play does not fail because it is too good,' he claimed. It fails because it is 'not good enough'.

Rattigan had not meant this preface to be a serious analysis of the reception of theatre, but critics immediately latched on to what they saw as a foolish admission that he wrote to the lowest common denominator. John Barber of the *Daily Express* told Rattigan to 'come off it'. His claim that he did not pander to Aunt Edna was scarcely believable. 'To be so prosperous, so gifted – and so spoiled' was a terrible waste, and Rattigan was only edgy because his recent comedies had received such a variable reaction.[29] From now on, Rattigan's work would be coloured by the misfire of Aunt Edna, even when, like *Separate Tables*, it contained a depth and sensitivity that went far beyond her simple major thirds. It was a grievous error.

Separate Tables consists of two pieces, *Table by the Window*, a play in three scenes, and *Table Number Seven*,[30] a play in two, which take place in the same setting, the Beauregard Private Hotel, near Bournemouth, an English seaside resort on the south coast that was notable for its large number of elderly residents. The very name of the hotel intimates the concern with appearances that so pervaded 1950s Britain. The plays are set within eighteen months of each other and, with quintessential Rattigan efficiency, nine of the characters in the first play appear in the second one. The whole atmosphere is one of stasis, with the outside world a disconcerting presence for the majority of residents, to be mediated through the television, gossip in the dining room or prejudice in the residents' lounge.

The cordially respectful relationship that Tynan had struck up in the occasional letter with Rattigan in 1952 had by this time become more wary. Rattigan was aware that Tynan could bite; and Tynan was aware that Rattigan, as a private homosexual in an era of repression, longed to break out of the code that he was forced to adopt. This appears to have intrigued Tynan greatly in the second piece, in which Major Pollock is revealed to have been convicted for the faintly ludicrous 'crime' of nudging women in a cinema. The matriarch of establishment, the formidable socialist-hating Lady Railton-Bell, attempts to rally her fellow residents in a cruel attempt to evict him from their midst, but the support of the owner of the hotel, Miss Cooper, and, crucially, the lonely, sexually and socially inhibited daughter of Lady Railton-Bell, Sybil, proves vital in giving him the strength to dispense with the lies that he has told about his past – he concedes that he has never been a 'Major', for example – and to decide to remain in the hotel.

In many ways, the play counters the notion of Rattigan as the epitome of the Loamshire trend. It challenges the necessity of 'keeping up appearances'; the vigorous Tory sentiments of Lady Railton-Bell seem overstated and anachronistic; the world that the residents inhabit, cocooned and looking back to the war, is unappealing and divorced from reality; and audiences immediately recognised that the Major's true 'offence', which could not possibly be directly spoken about on the stage, was that of soliciting men (something Rattigan confirmed to the American producer of the play in 1956). It was this reticence, partly personal, partly brought about by the external constraints of censorship, that drew Tynan's attention and 'Mixed Double', his review of the two plays, provides a brilliant pastiche of the work through an imagined dialogue between Tynan's alter ego, the young protagonist, and Aunt Edna, Rattigan's ideal playgoer. It is another review whose craft requires savouring in its entirety:

(The scene is the dining-room of a Kensington hotel, not unlike the Bournemouth hotel in which *Separate Tables*, Terence Rattigan's new double bill, takes place. A Young Perfectionist is dining; beside him, Aunt Edna, whom Mr Rattigan has described as the 'universal and immortal' middle-class playgoer.)

AUNT EDNA: Excuse me, young man, but have you seen Mr Rattigan's latest?

YOUNG PERFECTIONIST: I have indeed.

A.E.: And what is it about?

Y.P.: It is two plays about four people who are driven by loneliness into a state of desperation.

A.E. (*sighing*): Is there not enough morbidity in the world . . . ?

Y.P.: One of them is a drunken Left-wing journalist who has been imprisoned for wife-beating. Another is his ex-wife, who takes drugs to palliate the loss of her looks. She revives his masochistic love for her, and by the curtain-fall they are gingerly reunited.

A.E. (*quailing*): Does Mr Rattigan analyse these creatures?

Y.P.: He does, in great detail.

A.E.: How very unwholesome! Pray go on.

Y.P.: In the second play the central character is a bogus major who has lately been convicted of assaulting women in a cinema.

A.E.: Ouf!

Y.P.: His fellow guests hold conclave to decide whether he should be expelled from the hotel. Each contributes to a symposium on sexual deviation . . .

A.E.: In pity's name, stop.

Y.P.: The major reveals that his foible is the result of fear, which has made him a hermit, a liar and a pervert. This revelation kindles sympathy in the heart of the fourth misfit, a broken spinster, who befriends him in his despair.

A.E.: (*aghast*) I *knew* I was wrong when I applauded *The Deep Blue Sea*. And what conclusion does Mr Rattigan draw from these squalid anecdotes?

Y.P.: From the first, that love unbridled is a destroyer. From the second, that love bridled is a destroyer. You will enjoy yourself.

A.E.: But I go to the theatre to be taken out of myself!

Y.P.: Mr Rattigan will take you into an intricately charted world of suspense. By withholding vital information, he will tantalise you; by disclosing it unexpectedly, he will astound you.

A.E.: But what information! Sex and frustration.

Y.P.: I agree that the principal characters, especially the journalist and the major, are original and disturbing characters. But there is also a tactful omniscient *hotelière*, beautifully played by Beryl Measor. And what do you say to a comic Cockney maid?

A.E.: Ah!

Y.P.: Or to Aubrey Mather as a whimsical dominie? Or to a pair of opinionated medical students? Or to a tyrannical matriarch – no less than Phyllis Neilson-Terry?

A.E.: *That* sounds more like it. You console me.

Y.P.: I thought you would feel at home. And Peter Glenville, the director, has craftily engaged for these parts actors subtle enough to disguise their flatness.

A.E.: (*clouding over*) But what about those difficult leading roles?

Y.P.: Margaret Leighton plays two of them, rather externally. Her beauty annihilates the pathos of the ex-wife, who should be oppressed with crow's-feet. And her mousy spinster, dim and pink-knuckled, verges on caricature. It is Eric Portman who commands the stage, volcanic as the journalist, but even better as the major, speaking in nervous spasms and walking stiff-legged with his shoulders protectively hunched. He has the mask of the true mime, the *comédien* as opposed to the *acteur*.

A.E.: Yet you sound a trifle peaky. Is something biting you?

Y.P.: Since you ask, I regretted that the major's crime was not something more cathartic than mere cinema flirtation. Yet I suppose the play is as good a handling of sexual abnormality as English playgoers will tolerate.

A.E.: For my part, I am glad it is no better.

Y.P.: I guessed you would be; and so did Mr Rattigan. Will you accompany me on a second visit tomorrow?

A.E.: With great pleasure. Clearly, there is something here for both of us.

Y.P.: Yes. But not quite enough for either of us.

Although Tynan makes hay from the figure of Aunt Edna, he prefers at this stage to adopt a more benign attitude to Rattigan's drama than other critics. Rattigan's circumscribed approach to adult issues, such as adultery and homosexuality, was as much the result of convention and the Lord Chamberlain as his own timidity, and he was to be given some credit for being willing to allude to them at all. Tynan would be less charitable in the future.

Nevertheless, an intriguing letter lies in the Tynan archive at the British Library that suggests there was soon a falling out between the new Sunday critic and the supreme West End playwright of the period. Sent from Rattigan's home in Eaton Square, London, on 13 January 1955, it reveals that Rattigan, hiding behind the figure of his mother (who sounds alarmingly like Aunt Edna), was wary of Tynan's power:

> I can't possibly think why we shouldn't be speaking. As I remember you weren't rude about *Separate Tables*; only perhaps a little equivocal. But I gathered – I hope not wrongly – that you quite liked it.
>
> On the other hand my mother, whose voice on the telephone has just inter-rupted this letter, tells me that *she* is definitely *not* speaking to you. She seems to have read some article of yours, while I was in Paris, that stated that the only successful plays on in London were farces and light comedies. Is this, she asks, a fair description of the two plays at the St. James Theatre, or is it possible, she also asks, that you have failed to notice the queues round that building?
>
> Anyway this is *her* quarrel with you and not mine. You must make your peace with her as you may.[31]

As Rattigan's detractors, armed with the stick of Aunt Edna, became ever more vociferous in their denigration of him with the arrival of the angry young men, Tynan and the playwright's correspondence become frostier. Rattigan saw Tynan as part-author of his demise, but as 'Mixed Double' implies, Tynan was quite prepared to concede the quality of Rattigan's work. It was simply his ambiguity that he resisted.

Philip King's *Serious Charge*, which appeared in February 1955, was another play that skirted around the 'forbidden subject', but Tynan recognised that the play-wright had little leeway. The consequences of censorship for good, authentic drama – so desperately needed – were serious, however:

Its subject is small town gossip, aimed at that most vulnerable target, the English male virgin – in this case a young clergyman living with his mother (Miss Olga Lindo). The first act hedges and dallies: Mr King loves suspense, and sixty minutes pass before he tells us where his play is going, during which time we have the sensation of flying blind through a heavy mist. Are we to focus on the frumpish spinster (avidly played by Miss Victoria Hopper) who seeks the vicar's heart? Or on the pregnant village girl who gets run over? Mr King says nothing, and says it in English small-talk, which, being so much smaller than the talk of other nations, has effectively aborted the emergence of many a fine English dramatist.

The second act lifts us into the world of cause and effect. The vicar denounces the girl's seducer, a repulsive blond spiv, who responds by crying for help and alleging indecent assault: the village, already predisposed to think the vicar a homosexual, credits the accusation: and so ends an admirable act, bitterly exciting and extremely well-played by Messrs Anthony Wager and Patrick McGoohan. But English censorship will not bear so perfect a trap. To avoid a miscarriage of justice, the villain must confess, which involves a scene of melodramatic falsification wherein he behaves like a certifiable lunatic. The promise of the middle act is dissolved in untruth. A master dramatist, rewriting *Serious Charge*, would have given the hero suppressed homosexual tendencies of which he is made suddenly and poignantly aware; that would have been the forging of a tragedy as honest as Miss Lillian Hellman's *The Children's Hour*. But Miss Hellman's play is banned in this country, and so would Mr King's have been had he ventured so far. Perhaps the idea occurred to him; and with it the certain knowledge that the Lord Chamberlain would have crushed it on sight. One cannot blame him for playing safe.[32]

There had been no such reticence in the treatment of homosexuality in the adaptation of Gide's *The Immoralist* in November 1954, even if it was still a long way from an honest, open depiction of the issues. No retarding embarrassment on the part of the author, and hence no possibility of the Lord Chamberlain issuing a licence. The price for public exposure was relegation to the tiny Arts Theatre, where only members could see the show. It was a situation that Tynan found ridiculous, particularly given the play's recent exposure on Broadway:

> . . . *The Immoralist* is the frankest, most detached play about homosexuality our theatre has yet seen, as free from sentimentality as it is from sensationalism . . . Plays like this are always accused of naïveté: we scoff nervously, forgetting that censorship has so brusquely retarded the theatrical treatment of sex that it is still, to our shame, in its infancy. *The Immoralist* is a stumble towards maturity . . . In America *The Immoralist* ran for ninety-six performances; here the ex-Governor of Bombay has celebrated his second anniversary as Lord Chamberlain by refusing

it a licence. The rules governing his curious office lay down the following reasons for suppressing a play: profanity, improper language, indecency of dress, offensive representation of living persons, and anything likely to provoke a riot. Nothing in *The Immoralist* comes under any of these headings. As when *Oedipus* was banned forty-five years ago, the Lord Chamberlain seems to have over-stepped his brief. The granting of a conditional licence, forbidding twice-nightly exploitation while permitting serious managements to stage the play, would be an excellent face-saver.[33]

Lord Scarborough, a former Tory MP and the ex-Governor of Bombay in question, had succeeded Lord Clarendon as Lord Chamberlain in 1952. Tynan was putting him on notice for the battles to come.

After a slow start, Tynan had found his voice in the autumn of 1954 and he could depart for Paris at Christmas with some satisfaction. Elaine, who was beginning to find that her husband's fame was inhibiting her chances of being cast in plays, was initially reluctant to go. She had auditioned in November for a part in *The Ghost-writers*, a work that investigated blacklisted American writers, to be directed by Bernard Braden at the same progressive Arts Theatre, and wanted to remain in England to see if she had secured the part. Tynan, however, had caused a scene – 'another ledge standing'[34] – and she eventually relented. When she returned to England, however, she discovered a telegram from the company, saying that because they had been unable to get hold of her they had reluctantly decided to offer the role to another actress. Elaine was devastated, and this appears to have made her realise that acting was going to be a difficult profession to pursue. If she wanted to establish her own independence within her marriage, she would need to find something else to do.

While in Paris, the couple, having left Tracy with her nanny, saw numerous plays and went frequently to the Crazy Horse Saloon, a popular cabaret of scantily clad women. Elaine believes that it was this establishment that gave Tynan the idea for a 'sexy sophisticated nude revue' that later became *Oh, Calcutta!*[35] The visit was sig-nificant in another way, too. Having targeted 'Loamshire' plays and the power of the Lord Chamberlain, Tynan now needed something to champion in his critical manifesto. Paris gave him his first proper introduction to Bertolt Brecht.

Since settling in East Berlin in 1948, and founding the Berliner Ensemble with his wife, the formidable actress Helene Weigel, Brecht had steadily built up the international stature of his Epic theatre. His theory of drama differed radically from the Stanislavskian approach, which encouraged total immersion in a role, and which was having, through the Actors' Studio in New York, a profound impact on Method acting in America. Brecht wanted his plays – and, in particular, the performers in them – to remind the audience that they were watching a piece of artifice, set up not simply for their delectation, but for their scrutiny. Detachment was crucial on the part of the spectator *and* the performer. Having observed in Berlin in the 1920s how audiences came to plays to escape from their everyday concerns, Brecht sought to create drama that confronted the audience with these everyday concerns and might consequently arouse in them a capacity to act on what they saw. In that way, for example, audiences were left to resolve the dilemma of Shen Te in *The Good Person of Sezuan* (1943), whose poverty prevents her from being 'good' and forces her to resort to prostitution. At the end of the play, the actor playing the waterseller, Wang, the choric commentator of the piece, steps out of character and challenges the audience to find a better ending when they leave the theatre. In *The Life of Galileo* (1943), the protagonist's apprentice, Andrea, is disgusted by Galileo's recantation of what he knows to be right (that the earth is not the centre of the universe). He had been tortured by the Catholic Church, whose power was threatened by such a claim, since it could lead to the dismantling of the feudal society upon which its power depended. 'Unhappy the land that has no heroes,' Andrea laments. 'No, unhappy the land where heroes are necessary,' Galileo replies, and the burden of judgement is again passed back to the audience. Through this typical piece of verbal dialectic, Brecht contends that the issues raised in a didactic work cannot be neatly resolved before the play ends. The audience needs to wrestle with them for some time after. And at the end of *Mother Courage* (1941), when Courage, having lost her two sons to the war, takes up the reins of her cart once again, any feelings of admiration for her courage and stoicism should be replaced by dismay at her refusal to learn from her experience. It is small-time traders such as herself who sustain military conflict, Brecht is saying, as much as the generals who make the key decisions.

This belief in the immediacy and relevance of theatre was bound to appeal to Tynan. Brecht's emphasis on the importance of process – 'eyes on the course, not on the finishing line' was one of his favourite phrases – offered a direct challenge to the linear structure of the well-made play. His insistence on making reference to issues of contemporary concern – war, poverty, politics – was the very antithesis of the 'Loamshire' approach, and his self-confessed Marxism – Brecht lived in East Germany, a country not even recognised by the United Kingdom at that time – made him an appealing, anti-authoritarian figure. The Lord Chamberlain, the theatre and the political establishment were not going to like him.

When Tynan started at the *Observer* rumours of Brecht's significance in continental Europe were beginning to reach England. By December 1954, Tynan, remembering his 1950 seminar with Eric Bentley on the playwright, felt sufficiently intrigued to attempt a summary of the two dramatic approaches that were causing such excitement elsewhere. In a column entitled 'Indirections' he chose to use a review of a book by the director of the Old Vic, Hugh Hunt, *The Director in the Theatre*, to give his readers a flavour of the new approach:

> Two schools of thought dispute the field of Western acting. One, derived from the deep-burrowing naturalism of Stanislavsky, is practised in America by directors like Mr. Elia Kazan and actors like Mr. Marlon Brando; the other, based in East Berlin, is the 'Epic Theatre' of Bert Brecht. Stanislavsky, emphasising illusion, taught his actors to immerse themselves in their parts; Brecht, rejecting illusion, teaches detachment, employing a sort of stylised shorthand whereby the actor makes no pretence to be a real 'character' expressing 'emotion', but declares himself instead a professional performer illustrating a general theme. 'You are in a drawing room,' says Stanislavsky to his audience, 'witnessing life.' 'You are in a theatre,' says Brecht, 'witnessing actors.'
>
> That, roughly, is the conflict. We in London hear the distant thunder of the guns, but how shall we judge of the outcome? We know Stanislavsky only in genteel, dramatic school dilution, and of Brecht, whose plays have captured central Europe, we know nothing at all. We are like those complacent anglers who, as A.B. Walkley said, 'continued to fish for gudgeon under the Pont-Neuf while the Revolution raged overhead.' ... Let us, by all means, dismiss Stanislavsky and Brecht; but let us first engage a few foreign directors to give our actors instruction. Then perhaps we shall know what we are dismissing.[36]

As always, he felt, Britain was being left behind. The momentous action was happening elsewhere.

His Paris trip in December 1954 gave him an opportunity to experience Brecht for himself for the first time. His euphoric dispatch in early January was brief but to the point. *Mother Courage* was 'a glorious performance [by the Théâtre Nationale Populaire] of a contemporary classic which has been acclaimed everywhere in Europe save in London'. But at this stage his grasp of Epic theory was still shaky, because he seems to betray an empathetic admiration of Courage:

> Into this ribald epic of the Thirty Years War, the squalor of all wars is compressed. Does Germaine Montero, as the sleazy, irresistible heroine nag where she should dominate? Yes: but the play carries her. Never before have I seen a thousand people rise cheering and weeping in their seats.[37]

No matter, though. Such was the spectacle of the event that he was bowled over, and he converted to Marxism instantly. Elaine memorably records the epiphany:

By the time I arrived back at our hotel room, his views were in place. 'I have become a Marxist', he announced. He went on to describe the extraordinary experience he had just been part of . . . In a magnificent performance of this epic of the Thirty Years War, Brecht had compressed the squalor of all wars.[38]

Of course, there was something incongruous about a man who enjoyed his luxuries and who was, according to Elaine, living off her father's investments,[39] so brazenly renouncing capitalism. But his embracing of Brecht was, in part, motivated by his belief that all drama was political, and he had at last found a playwright who was wholeheartedly endorsing that view. At a time of Cold War tension, it was also something spectacularly controversial to do – East Germany was a pariah state – and it fitted in perfectly with his desire to provoke as much as scrutinise. Although Tynan's conversion to Eastern Bloc socialism was never more than skin deep, it also conveniently put clearer water between him and the conservative Christianity of Hobson, whose detestation of Brecht would soon become apparent.

It would take a second trip to Paris, this time in June 1955, for Tynan to offer his readers a more detailed appraisal of Epic theatre. At the second Paris Drama Festival, the Berliner Ensemble presented *The Caucasian Chalk Circle* and Tynan, who admitted that he had recently 'read a great deal about Brecht's theory of acting, the famous *Verfremdungseffekt*', was enthralled: 'Bertolt Brecht's "Epic Theatre" borrows heavily from the Chinese: the emphasis is on how the events happen, not on the emotions of the people they happen to. Once in a generation the world discovers a new way of telling a story; this generation's pathfinder is Brecht, both as playwright and as director of the Berliner Ensemble.' Even though he was not as enthusiastic about *The Caucasian Chalk Circle* as he was about *Mother Courage* it was the model that Brecht was offering to world drama that Tynan found so invigorating:

> . . . if I was unmoved by what Brecht had to say, I was overwhelmed by the way in which he said it. It is as shocking and revolutionary as a cold shower. In the British theatre everything is sacrificed to obtain sympathy for the leading characters. *Chez* Brecht, sympathy is nowhere; everything is sacrificed for clarity of narrative . . . No time is wasted on emotional climaxes. Situations which our playwrights would regard as cues for sentimental tirades are drowned by the clatter of horses' hooves or cut off by the whirr of the closing curtain

Tynan concludes with one of his compelling overstatements for effect:

> One sees why Brecht feels that our method is as different as driving a carriage and four is from driving a car. Unless we learn it soon, a familiar process will take place. Thirty years from now, Brecht will be introduced to the English critics, who will

at once decry him for being thirty years out of date. The ideal way of staging *Henry IV, Tamburlaine, Peer Gynt* and a hundred plays yet unwritten will have been ignored; and the future of the theatre my have been strangled in its cot.[40]

Happily, and in no small part due to Tynan's insistent championing, that did not happen.

One can imagine the convert's excitement on his return to England to be able to travel down to the Devon Arts Festival at Barnstaple to witness the British première of *Mother Courage* by Theatre Workshop. This company had come to Tynan's attention several times since September 1954. Their production of Hašek's *The Good Soldier Schweik*, and in particular the stage presence of Harry Corbett, had caught his attention in November, and he felt that 'with half a dozen replacements, Theatre Workshop might take London by storm'. By January 1955, he was questioning the aptness of Corbett's portrayal of an effeminate Richard II, but complimenting the company for making up in 'barn-storming what it lacks in finesse'.[41] It came off well against the much more lavishly resourced Old Vic production that also opened in the same week. And in March, Theatre Workshop's willingness to experiment and refusal to be over-reverent was refreshingly apparent in *Volpone*:

> The new production by Theatre Workshop, modern-dress and naturalistic, rightly refuses to impose the 'Shakespeare voice' on Jonson's versified prose. Deprived of tights, ruffs and declamation, the actors have to act; and how keenly the present cast accepts the challenge! Mr Howard Goorney's Corbaccio, walnut-wrinkled in beret and wheelchair, could not be bettered. Mr Harry Corbett, wrestling with submarine fishing gear, makes Sir Politick Would-be wickedly recognisable; and Mr Maxwell Shaw, a sly, spear-collared gigolo, is by far the most convincing Mosca I have seen.
>
> This cruelly diverting entertainment needs two things to make it really memorable: a Volpone of greater amplitude, and at least twice as much vocal projection from everyone in the cast. Even so, it stimulated me much more than *As You Like It* (Old Vic), a plain, pastel production directed by Mr Robert Helpmann in accordance with Mr Glen Byam Shaw's discovery that the play begins in winter and ends in spring.

It is salutary to be reminded of the degree of experimentation that Theatre Workshop was undertaking in very straitened circumstances at the Theatre Royal Stratford East, well over a year before George Devine's English Stage Company (ESC) was born. Their role in changing theatrical attitudes in the 1950s has been unfairly overshadowed by the activities of the ESC, and this needs redressing.

Tynan's expectations for Joan Littlewood's *Mother Courage* the following summer were cruelly dashed, however. That he devotes two-thirds of his review to the text of the work cannot disguise his disappointment at the production. This was meant to be the great clarion call, the proof of the pudding, the literal demonstration of what he had been arguing for six months. Instead, Joan Littlewood herself was under-rehearsed, barely audible and clearly ill at ease as a director with the requirements of Epic theatre. The cast of fourteen was too small for the work's epic nature and 'Theatre Workshop . . . was dismally unequal to the strain', Tynan lamented. Littlewood was a 'lifeless mumble', some of her directorial blunders were made out of 'sheer perverseness' and the result was 'a production in which discourtesy to a masterpiece borders on an insult'.[42]

If Tynan was downcast, Harold Hobson was more equivocal – at least in his *Sunday Times* column:

Brecht wants Mother Courage to appeal, not to our emotions, but to our understanding; this is why the actress must put us at a distance. She must never raise the question, 'Do we like Mother Courage or despise her', but only the questions 'How did Mother Courage happen? What were the social conditions that produced her?' We must comprehend the social process, not pity or condemn the individual. It is in loyally trying to convey this that Miss Littlewood comes a cropper, and one has for her a certain sympathy. Brecht requires the actress to do the almost impossible, and the simple truth is that Miss Littlewood has not come near it.[43]

Hobson also wrote a weekly article for the American *Christian Science Monitor* and in this analysis of the same play for a readership much more hostile to Communism, he was more strident:

The essence of Brecht's play is that we cannot say of any human being or any human action that it is good or bad until we know what is the process that has produced it. These things are not to be judged by the canons of humanity, Christianity, fair play, generosity, love, or any criteria like these; but only by whether they aid or hinder a certain social development. In judging events, we must beware pity or contempt; and the massacre of political opponents is justified if it helps the establishment of the classless society, even though these opponents may be individually good and kindly men. This is the meaning of Brecht's theory. The western world will, of course, recoil from it in horror, and it is right to do so, for it is the negation of everything that is most valuable in humanity. But in its recoil the western world would do well not to be too self-righteous, for, in time of war at least, it is ready enough to adopt this doctrine itself. Between 1939 and 1945 all the western countries were ready to sacrifice, in mass bombing raids, the lives of worthy people, because this sacrifice contributed to a certain social process, the winning of the war. Brecht extends this principle to times of peace; he regards the setting up of a classless society as equally important as a military victory. It is a terrible theory.[44]

This was the flavour that Hobson would give his British readers from 1956. Battle would be joined with Tynan over this when the Berliner Ensemble visited England themselves in August of that year.

By the spring of Tynan's first *Observer* season he had established three critical themes that he would return to continually over the next four years: the insularity of the 'Loamshire' mindset, the dead hand of the Lord Chamberlain and, more positively, the example that Brecht's Epic theatre offered for revitalising theatre. All three of these themes reflected his general belief that British theatre was too insular and, whilst boasting several wonderful performers, needed new plays fast. At the end of January, he submitted a second survey piece to follow up 'West End Apathy'. In its focus on health and frailty, it drew subtle comparisons with the fragility of the eighty-year-old Churchill, who was now in danger of seriously harming his reputation by his public – and more widely reported – gaffes. The most famous of these occurred just prior to his eightieth birthday celebrations in November 1954, when the ailing Prime Minister had made a speech in his Woodford constituency, in which he appeared to allude to an order he had given to Field Marshal Montgomery at the very end of the war instructing him to collect the weapons of the Germans so that they could be reissued to German soldiers if the Soviet advance continued too far westwards. At a time when Churchill was still vainly hoping to bring Eisenhower and Malenkov together in a three-way summit to discuss the need to tackle nuclear proliferation, this seemed a bizarre thing to say at the very least. Montgomery quietly questioned the veracity of the statement, the leader column in the *Times* posed the question, 'What on earth made him say it?' and the general consensus was that this was a figment of the imagination of a declining man. Churchill's most severe detractors felt that it reinforced his image as an 'instinctive warmonger'[45] and even his supporters felt it was now finally time for him to retire. Despite having admitted to his doctor, Lord Moran, that 'I made a goose of myself at Woodford,'[46] though, Churchill seemed incapable of letting go. R.A. Butler records that between November 1954 and April 1955 he had 'eight gargantuan dinners with [him] alone; the dinners being followed by libations of brandy so ample that I felt it prudent on more than one occasion to tip the liquid into the side of my shoe. The subjects discussed were always the same: his retirement and the succession, the fag-end government syndrome, a Russian summit and, strange to relate, space travel . . .'[47] Churchill's limpet-like clinging to power when he was clearly no longer able to devote the necessary energy to the position became a symbol for many of the inert nature of mid-1950s Britain. In March 1955, Tynan drew on this feeling to convey his belief in the importance of context for drama and his newly affirmed sense that all drama is political, in another magnificent column – tellingly entitled 'Convalescence' – which concluded that there were some superficial signs of life in the decrepit body of West End theatre:

Night nurses at the bedside of good drama, we critics keep a holy vigil. Black circles rim our eyes as we pray for the survival of our pet patient, starved and wracked, the theatre of passion and ideas. We pump in our printed transfusions – 'honest and forthright', 'rooted in a closely observed reality' – but so avidly do we seize on signs of relapse that we fail to observe that, for the moment at least, the cripple is out of bed and almost convalescent. He can claim, this season, three successes! *Hedda Gabler*, *Time Remembered* and *The Rules of the Game*: and he had a vestigial hand in *Separate Tables* – Mr Rattigan is the Formosa of the contemporary theatre, occupied by the old guard, but geographically inclined towards the progressives. Further tonics lie ahead, among them a Giraudoux and another Anouilh before spring is out. Implausible as it may sound, good drama may be able to walk unaided within a year or so.

But what of bad drama, the kind which repudiates art and scoffs at depth, which thrives on reviewers who state themselves 'shocked, but I rocked with laughter'? We assume that it is healthy; in fact, it looks extremely frail. Many a frankly 'commercial' play has come smiling to town in recent months and walked into an upper-cut from both critics and public . . . One begins to suspect that the English have lost the art of writing a bad successful play. Perhaps some sort of competition should be organised: the rules, after all, are simple enough. At no point may the plot or characters make more than superficial contact with reality. Characters earning less than £1,000 a year should be restricted to small parts or exaggerated into types so patently farcical that no member of the audience could possibly identify himself with such absurd esurience. Rhythm in dialogue is achieved by means either of vocatives ('That, my dear Hilary, is a moot point') or qualifying clauses ('What, if you'll pardon the interruption, is going on here?'); and irony is confined to having an irate male character shout: 'I am perfectly calm!'

All plays should contain parts to be turned down by Miss Gladys Cooper, Miss Coral Browne, Mr Hugh Williams and Mr Robert Flemyng. Apart from hysterical adolescents, nobody may weep; apart from triumphant protagonists, nobody may laugh; anyone, needless to say, may smile. European place-names (Positano and Ischia) are romantic: English place-names (Herne Bay and Bognor Regis) are comic. Women who help themselves unasked to cigarettes must be either frantic careerists or lustful opportunists. The latter should declare themselves by running the palm of one hand up their victim's lapel and saying, when it reaches the neck: 'Let's face it, Arnold, you're not exactly indifferent to me.' The use of 'Let's face it' in modern drama deserves in itself a special study. It means that something true is about to be uttered, and should strike the audience with the same shock as the blast of the whistle, before the train plunges into the tunnel . . .

But I falter. I cannot convince myself that these rules, archaic already, will assure success. For bad plays, dependent on what is topical and ephemeral in mankind, are much harder to write than good ones, for which the rules are permanent and unchanging. The commercial writer must blind himself to history, close his eyes, stop his ears, shutter his mind to the onslaught of reality; he must ignore all the promptings which instinct tells him to be valid, about unity of action and the necessity of reducing one or more of his characters to a logical crisis of desperation; he must live the life of a spiritual hermit. Such self-abnegation is seldom found. The great age of the thoroughly bad play seems to be over, and it behoves the critic to sing a requiem.[48]

Of course for 'commercial' writer we should read 'Loamshire' writer and it would take the breakthrough at the Royal Court to produce playwrights who no longer wish to close their eyes and stop their ears to contemporary reality. For now, contact with the best of foreign drama – Harold Hobson's prescription for revival, too – was the way out of the morass. At times, it feels as if Tynan believes that anywhere has more dynamic theatre than England. Giraudoux's *Tiger at the Gates*, a piece that dealt, like *Mother Courage*, with the vagaries of war, is described as 'a masterpiece' that represents 'the highest peak in the mountain-range of the modern French theatre'.[49] In February, he turned eastwards to Sweden, wryly listing the 'four Strindbergs, four Shakespeares, three Chekhovs, three Pirandellos, two Molières, two Shaws, two Ibsens, two Giraudoux, and one each from Vanbrugh, Wycherley, Lorca, Kafka, Brecht, Ugo Betti, Arthur Miller, Anouilh, Eliot, Bernanos and Samuel Beckett – not to mention the *Oresteia* of Aeschylus' that had been on offer there in the previous season,[50] and in March he flew west with Elaine to experience the New York scene. It was to prove a cathartic experience.

The intermittently warring, occasionally loving couple stayed at the Buckingham Hotel and flung themselves into a social and theatrical whirl. Their friend

Johnny Marquand Junior organised a party to mark their arrival and there was barely a minute when they were not exchanging celebrity gossip or attending Broadway shows. Tynan was only able to remain for two weeks, but Elaine, perhaps relishing the chance to be back in her home city, stayed on longer. Tynan recorded his appreciation of the seriousness with which New Yorkers treated their theatre – 'in New York, as in London, it is a social necessity to go to the theatre: to be going, or lately to have gone. First nights are matters of instant and urgent debate, whether they take place in the two dozen major theatres around Times Square or in the smaller "off Broadway" houses, where Ibsen and O'Casey reward the pious' – and he was delighted to find himself in the middle of a debate about the theoretical and practical approaches to drama. Here was the intellectual cut and thrust that seemed so painfully absent in London:

In New York one is always conscious of the theatrical revolution wrought by 'the method' – the holy word of Stanislavsky, handed down by the Group theatre in the thirties and now enshrined in Elia Kazan's Actors' Studio. Beside the 'method actors,' most American players over forty-five (and most English players of any age) are breaths of stale air; the young inhabit a tradition of realism as radical and lively as any on earth. Some accuse them of acting too exclusively with their nerves, like the restless actress at whom a director hissed: 'Don't just *do* something, *stand* there!' Others, such as the brilliant television writer Paddy Chayevsky, assert that 'method actors' frequently lack talent refined enough to play what their intelligence has uncovered.

A perfect answer to these criticisms lies in the performance I have mentioned. The actress, Eileen Heckart, plays a bereaved mother, tipsy and listless, with such total identification that one of the rarest things in all theatre takes place: the audience is allowed to form its own opinion of the character. Most players would have implied a moral judgement on the part; would have made it either pathetic or hateful, would have invited either love or loathing: for actors love to 'editorialise.' Miss Heckart leaves that to us. Simply the thing she is shall make her live; and live she does, abundantly, tactfully and in depth. Another triumph for 'the method' is recorded in William Inge's play, *Bus Stop*. The situation yawns with familiarity: a group of loveless, disparate people thrown together by an act of God, in this case passengers on a bus halted overnight by a snowstorm. What might have been hopelessly stereotyped is made palatably so by the sheer force of method-infected acting.[51]

The highlight of the feast of playgoing was a visit to the enormous hit, Tennessee Williams's *Cat on a Hot Tin Roof.* Williams was another of Tynan's celebrity correspondents. He had written to Tynan from Key West, Florida the previous November, giving him an indication of the problems he was having in agreeing with Elia Kazan on a suitable ending. The letter illustrates how Tynan engaged with the key players of the time behind the scenes while becoming a personality in his own right. He was clearly somebody to court.

Williams began by recalling that during the previous summer – he was not sure whether it had been in July or August – he had been given the edition of *Encounter* in which Tynan had written about Williams and Arthur Miller. He had meant to express his thanks immediately, since it had been particularly gratifying, but a summer full of numerous distractions had arrested his best intentions, and he was no longer sure whether he had actually got round to writing or whether he had simply forgotten to post the letter.

He was making up for lost time now, however, given that he was currently resident in Key West, where certain scenes from the film version of *Rose Tattoo*, with the stars Anna Magnani and Burt Lancaster, had been shot. Now that the crew had departed for Hollywood, he was free to pursue a new project, a play with the title *Cat on a Hot Tin Roof*. It was proving quite a tricky business, as Elia Kazan, who wanted to stage it as soon as possible, felt that the ending was too dismal, and this had irked the playwright to the point that if they were unable to resolve their difference of opinion, he would be tempted to stage it himself.

This is where Tynan came in. Did he know a producer who might help him stage one of his works in London the following spring? Because of the need for an authentic flavour of the American south, it was important, Williams felt, that he had a personal say in the direction, and he was strongly attracted to returning to England, a country that he liked, but from which he had been absent for quite a while.[52]

One can imagine Tynan salivating at this prospect, which clearly never materialised. Unfortunately no record of his reply exists.

Cat on a Hot Tin Roof opened on 24 March 1955 and the following Sunday, Williams held a party at the St Regis hotel for his mother. It was a star-studded occasion, buoyed up by a rapturous critical reception that had united Brooks Atkinson of the *New York Times* and Walter Kerr of the *New York Herald Tribune* (the Hobson and Tynan of Broadway) in affirming that Williams was the playwright who came 'closest to hurling the actual blood and bone of life onto the stage'.[53] Marilyn Monroe, Gore Vidal and Carson McCullers all made an appearance, with Monroe's entrance so captivating that 'everybody stopped what they were doing, freeze-framed with their drinks, hors d'oeuvres or cigarettes halfway to their mouths.' Elaine was as bowled over as anyone, recording that the star 'was more astonishingly beautiful than on celluloid and we all stared silently in reverence'.[54]

Perhaps inevitably, Tynan dissented somewhat from the dominant critical reaction to the work in New York in a thoughtful and considered report for his British readers in April:

> . . . there is no avoiding it: the most august, turbulent and alarming play in New York is Tennessee Williams' *Cat on a Hot Tin Roof*. Several alien strands must be disentangled before this formidable piece can be analysed. One is Kazan's over-powering direction, which conceals the play's weaknesses in a series of violent artificial climaxes. Another is Jo Mielziner's setting, a wall-less room giving on to eternity, with pillars of taut ropes soaring up to the sky; all of which is awe-inspiring but wrong, since it gives the drama a portentousness that the author never intended. The third distraction is Williams's free use of bad language and sexual images, which will surely forbid the play a London showing . . . The play is an operating theatre in which each character is cut to the bone, and the bone's marrow pours out, a cherished falsehood. Big Daddy, a self-made Southern millionaire (played with ventripotent grossness by Burl Ives) is sustained by the lie that he is not dying of cancer. The first act is a duologue between his younger son, a homosexual drunkard, and the boy's frustrated wife. The second act deepens the feud in a long exchange between father and son, which painfully unveils the son's real reason for drinking; his pathos is unmasked as a soiled, gigantic lie. The last act orchestrates the theme to include the entire family. Elder son vies with younger for Big Daddy's money, and a peak of mendacity is reached when the alcoholic's wife (Barbara Bel Geddes, successfully cast against type) announces that she is pregnant. Her husband acquiesces in this falsehood, and now must sleep with her to support it.

If we dismiss the characters as 'despicable', we must first consider Williams's remark, in another context, that the theatre is a place where we have time for people whom we would kick downstairs if they came to us for a job. It might more soundly be urged that the play's focus is uncertain: we are never sure whether the action centres on father, son or wife. It is also true that so much anti-feminism verges at times on neurosis: the women are either all gold-diggers or fools. Discussing the incidence of genius, Somerset Maugham once said: 'The lesson of anatomy applies: there is nothing so rare as the normal.' What we get from Williams is a partial, abnormal view of life prone to hysteria and limited in its sympathies. His play is flawed: it sees a vast subject through a special squint. But this is the price we have to pay for its kind of overheated genius. If *Cat on a Hot Tin Roof* fails, it fails on a level to which only Anouilh and Arthur Miller, of living playwrights, have any access at all.

On re-reading the play in August, Tynan recanted his earlier judgement, blaming the original deficiencies on the director, Kazan, and citing the work as the best American play since *Death of a Salesman*. Needless to say, there was no chance of the play being staged in London because of the constraints of censorship:

> ... the fact is that no London management has submitted it to the Lord Chamberlain. The key to Brick's secret, I should have mentioned, is guilt left over from a passionate friendship with a man who killed himself, a friendship 'too rare to be normal, any true thing between two people is too rare to be normal.' No management would be stupid enough to imagine for a moment that the ex-Governor of Bombay would tolerate such filth on our stages. And so we may talk about the play, as I have done, and we may read it aloud in our homes, but unless a club theatre chooses to mount it, we shall not see it on the boards for which it was written, and which it so ripely and deeply illuminates.[55]

Tynan's initial American verdict troubled Williams, but did not impair their friendship, and the two men continued to correspond throughout the summer. Williams's letters are personal, searching and confessional, and often seem to labour under the misapprehension that Tynan had greater power than he did to have plays produced. This may have been an impression that Tynan, ever the frustrated impresario, wanted to convey. In June a run-down Williams, writing from Italy, reflected on the appearance of *Cat on a Hot Tin Roof* in New York. Temporarily based in the Via Corsini, in Trastevere, Williams began by apologising for not having contacted him earlier. This had been quite simply because after a particularly draining year his nerves were frayed and he had felt unwell. Life was now more peaceful, however. The apartment was congenial, and this was just as well since his first ever consultations with an analyst in New York, whom he visited twice just prior to his departure, had proved very disturbing.

There seems to be some evidence that Tynan had wanted to meet the playwright in Rome, but the changes in their relative travel arrangements – Tynan could no longer get to Italy, and Williams had decided to visit Greece and Turkey – meant that they would now have to meet up in Spain.

Williams then becomes more conrfessional. He was undertaking a film collaboration with Kazan, although this seemed to be more out of a sense of duty than pleasure. He looked forward to teaming up with the critic in Spain, although even this was double-edged as he had been rather alarmed by his review of *Cat on a Hot Tin Roof*. Revealingly, he went on to observe that he was still discomforted by the play himself and, despite the pleasure he gained from the second and third acts, remained unconvinced by the writing of the first.

Finally, Williams returned to the old enquiry. Was there any chance of a production in London? Who might take the role of Maggie? He favoured Margaret Leighton, but hoped that this was not disloyal to Vivien Leigh, who was a dear friend. How Tynan must have swallowed at this point.[56]

In early July he reflects on their mutual love of bullfighting, gives an insight into how widely read and influential Tynan's columns were becoming and suggests arrangements for their planned summer holiday. Following a tip-off from Tynan, Williams had booked a flight from Barcelona to Valencia to enjoy a whole week of bull-fighting. He had become obsessed with bulls shortly after reading Hemingway's book on the subject, he confessed. His mood now was lighter, particularly following the reassurance offered by his correspondent that he had enjoyed *Cat on a Hot Tin Roof,* after all.

More holiday reminiscences were proffered: Greece had been great fun, even though he had felt isolated. Turkey, however, had been loathsome. Of greatest interest to Tynan, though, would have been the fact that 'Tenn', as the writer now signed himself, had been so struck by the critic's enthusiasm for Brecht, that he requested a copy of *Mother Courage* to see for himself what all the fuss was about. This was some recommendation.

But in a remarkably confessional letter at the end of July, Williams gives numerous intimate reasons to explain why he is apprehensive about a long profile that Tynan wished to write. The opening conveys both his nervousness and the essentially epistolary nature of their relationship. Williams had had to get drunk and down some secconal too inform his friend of his reluctance to be scrutinised. Despite being flattered by the suggestion, the more he thought about it, the more apprehensive he became. They may now know each other reasonably well, he wrote – in spite of having spent little actual time in each other's company – but Tynan could reveal things that would harm his career in the US, where he still had professional ambitions. In particular, he highlighted the danger posed to him by *Time* magazine.[58]

The difficulty of recognising where the critic ends and the friend begins is at the bottom of Williams's concern. That said, the main body of the letter, which runs to over 2,000 words, is remarkably forthright. It gives his true date of birth (1911); an insight into why his father called him 'Miss Nancy' ; and three long, detailed pages about his illness and hospitalisation with peritonitis in 1946. All in all, a remarkably open self-analysis.

On Tynan's return from New York, he suffered his own bout of ill health when he was struck down with hepatitis. Elaine's return from the US was eagerly awaited and she quickly became a dutiful nurse, permitting him only to drink champagne and ensuring he received sufficient bed rest by renting a projector and watching films with him. Elaine herself, though, was becoming increasingly restless. Her life lacked direction, her marriage was turbulent, her husband had sexual needs that she could not reciprocate and his growing notoriety meant that her pursuit of an acting career was becoming impossible. He was also prone to bouts of depression and had begun a course of therapy with the analyst John Pratt in January 1955. This consisted of twice-weekly visits and lasted two months: his consumption of the popular amphetamine Dexamyl, prescribed by his doctor and taken to give him 'enough confidence to start work', was a more permanent fixture.[59] This pattern of private emotional upheaval, which counterpointed the highs and lows of his public career, was already the dominant motif of his life.

Elaine decided that her life needed a new direction. Her husband suggested that she write a novel – 'The letters I'd written him during my stay in New York showed him I could write a very good novel' – and she began in the summer of 1955 to draft what was eventually to become *The Dud Avocado*. Tynan resumed his writing, too, and in his first column after a newspaper strike in mid-April, he incorporated the political event that Britain had been expecting for months into his analysis of John Gielgud's eagerly awaited Stratford production of *Twelfth Night*.

The brilliance of this review, 'Arrivals and Departures', lies in Tynan's skilful linking of the eventual resignation of Churchill as Prime Minister with the growing sense that the era of the star actor, who directs, performs and controls a production through the force of his own personality, was also coming to an end. Since his conviction for cottaging in 1953, John Gielgud had inevitably faced a crisis of confidence. He had, after all, been convicted of an offence to which the Lord Chamberlain would allow absolutely no reference on stage. At the time of his arrest, he was beginning the pre-London tour of N.C. Hunter's *A Day by the Sea*, which he directed and in which he played the part of Julian Anson. Although the play was a welcome success, the onstage rapport between Gielgud and Ralph Richardson was not matched by backstage harmony. Richardson had been disconcerted by Gielgud's conviction, and this may have led to Gielgud proffering some of the most famous bad advice in the history of theatre. A new playwright, Samuel Beckett, had sent Richardson a script of a work called *Waiting for Godot*, in the hope of persuading him to play one of the tramps alongside Alec Guinness and under Peter Glenville's direction. Richardson was perplexed by the work and found – inevitably – differing views amongst the company about its merits. Irene Worth encouraged him to have a stab, but Gielgud told him not to touch it with a bargepole. The rest, to Richardson's great regret, is history.[60]

The following two productions in which Gielgud was involved in 1954 – *Charley's Aunt* at the New Theatre (February) and *The Cherry Orchard* at the Lyric, Hammersmith (May) – saw him shun the stage and receive slightly less exposure as the director. His belief that he had let his friends down and his sense of humiliation continued to mount, however. An unhappy experience playing the minor role of the Duke of Clarence in Olivier's film of *Richard III*, which seemed to confirm Olivier's professional hostility to him, further lowered his spirits and he underwent a minor breakdown at the end of 1954. His self-imposed medicine was not complete rest but, after a short time to recuperate, renewed immersion in his work. In the circumstances, it did not seem wise that he should agree to make his first engagement the directing of *Twelfth Night* as the first production of the new Stratford season – with Olivier as Malvolio and Vivien Leigh as Viola.

In the run-up to rehearsals, Olivier was undergoing a crisis, too. His marriage to Leigh was, by now, a terrible strain. He had tried to separate his wife from her lover Peter Finch during the filming of *Elephant Walk*, but this had simply increased her mental instability. Having been replaced by Elizabeth Taylor, she submitted to several brutal electric-shock treatments in an attempt to regain some stability, but her erratic behaviour continued. As rehearsals began, Leigh would leave their rented house to spend nights in a local hotel with Finch. Olivier, exhausted from filming *Richard III*, felt there was little he could do.[61]

The rehearsal process was a complete disaster. Gielgud and Olivier had not worked in the theatre together for twenty years, since the traumatic experience of their pre-war *Romeo and Juliet* in which they had alternated the roles of Romeo and Mercutio, and a fractious Olivier now refused to submit to the nervous and pernickety direction of Gielgud. Sheridan Morley, Gielgud's official biographer, gives a flavour of the atmosphere:

> At one point during rehearsals relations between Olivier and John reached such a crisis that Olivier turned to his director saying, 'Darling John, please go for a long walk by the river and let us just get on with it.' John, brooding on the problem of Olivier's Malvolio, and unable to sleep, rang his old rival at two the next morning. As Olivier sleepily answered the phone, John said, 'I've got it, darling boy, just play him very, very Jewish.' Olivier uttered a stream of invective about the time of night and the general idiocy of the suggestion, at the end of which John just said, 'Oh, all right then, play him very, very not Jewish.'[62]

As it was, Olivier's Malvolio appeared at times to be a parody of high camp, which Gielgud took as a personal slight. His confidence had been all but shattered.

None of this backstage turmoil filtered through to the public and demand for tickets was enormous. The announcement in February 1955 of a season that included *Twelfth Night*, Olivier and Leigh in *Macbeth* and Gielgud as Lear jammed the Stratford phone lines and resulted in a complete sell-out by March. This was fortunate, because a newspaper strike broke out at the end of March, keeping papers off the streets until the middle of April. Was this the reason, perhaps, that Winston Churchill finally chose the end of March to summon R.A. Butler and his nominated successor, Anthony Eden, into the cabinet room? Butler recalls that 'Winston made a slip by asking me to sit on the right, but then corrected himself and beckoned to Anthony. We all gazed out over Horse Guards Parade. Then Winston said very shortly "I am going and Anthony will succeed me. We can discuss details later".'[63] It was a bathetic end to a historic career.

In his first review for a month, Tynan makes clear that the revitalisation that Churchill's departure might presage on the political front seems a long way off on the theatrical. His travels had reminded him once again of the parochial condition of British drama:

Of all the events which passed unpublicised through the newspaper strike . . . one in particular struck home to those, who in Sir Desmond MacCarthy's phrase, watch the hour hand as well as the minute hand of history. This was the formal resignation of British drama, which handed over its seals of box-office to Paris and New York, thereby making official what had long been an open secret, and ending months of anxious speculation. Of the shows which came to the West End while the critics were 'resting', three were American, one was French, and one (the direst) was British. Of those which are announced for arrival between now and the end of May, five are French, three are American, and none is British.

British drama, the Old Pretender, coeval with Pinero and du Maurier, has tip-toed home; let us wish it a fruitful retirement, designing the costumes which are its special joy; and let us hope that its successors, the exuberant youth of France and America (twin volcanoes beside which we are as Pompeii), refrain from scoffing too brutally at its weaknesses, while it is still, technically, alive.

The eagerly awaited *Twelfth Night* encapsulated the other-worldly nature of a British theatre trapped in a time warp of pre-war *politesse*. Gielgud was its finest exemplar and Vivien Leigh, for whom Tynan had lost none of his venom, a technically limited clothes-horse:

At Stratford-upon-Avon Sir John Gielgud's production of *Twelfth Night* (Memorial Theatre) trod softly but sternly on the dream that Shakespearean comedy was a world of gaiety and refreshment. An astringent frost nipped the play, leaving bleakness behind it and an impression for which the polite word would be 'formal' and the exact word 'mechanical'. A frigid charm was sought and achieved, in pursuance of which Sir John muted the clowns, so that we got no more than a whisper of Maria from Miss Angela Baddeley, and from Mr Alan Webb no Sir Toby at all. The comics were clearly warned to be on their best behaviour, on pain of expulsion from the soirée. Carousing is frowned upon; and the warmth normally generated by even the worst performance of the play is shunned as a corrupting plague.

In applying his novocaine injections Sir John finds an ideal accomplice in Miss Vivien Leigh, who buries her stock-in-trade, brittle vivacity, beneath a dazzling vocal monotony, unchanging in pace, pitch, tone or emphasis. This Viola does not, as she promises, speak 'in many sorts of music'; she commands but one sort. A music recognisable to sheltering wayfarers as that of steady rain on corrugated tin roofing. No trace of ardour disturbs this small tranquillity.

Laurence Olivier, in a self-evidently sub-standard performance, was, as always, pardoned by Tynan. Other critics, though, such as John Barber in the *Daily Express*, were beginning to question how much longer this forty-eight-year-old could pretend to be the matinée idol of earlier years. The fault for Tynan here lay both in the vehicle and the direction – although interestingly, Gielgud's suggestion of Jewishness does appear to have been evident to Tynan:

Remain Sir Laurence Olivier, whose sun peeped through the chintz curtains of the production and might, with any help, have blazed. Hints abounded of a wholly original Malvolio, a self-made snob, aspiring to consonance with the quality but ever betrayed by vowels from Golders Green; Malvolio was seen from his own point of view instead of (unusually) Sir Toby's. Yet the sketch remained an outline; a diverting exercise, but scarcely the substance of Sir Laurence's vocation.[64]

Twelfth Night was a turning point. In the face of a rapidly changing world – Churchill's resignation had been preceded by the announcement on 1 March that Britain intended to manufacture an H-bomb – its star-laden vision of a pastoral idyll was becoming anachronistic. Tynan, who is commonly thought to be a critic who worshipped stars, was now extremely conscious that the finest performers had little worth performing in and this became the new front in his attack on the 'Loamshire' brand. Occasionally, the scarcity of quality new plays did not matter, as with the Old Vic production of the two parts of *Henry IV* in May[65] and the second Stratford production in June 1955, in which Olivier starred as Macbeth. His performance has gone down as one of the great post-war achievements, Tynan believing that Olivier 'shook hands with greatness' and Hobson, in a rare and significant moment of consensus, writing of Olivier's 'terrible grandeur'. What impressed both critics was the way that Olivier disproved the commonly held view that the play dies away towards the end. Indeed, Hobson chose a typically idiosyncratic simile (which his adherents loved and detractors – generally Tynan readers – scorned) to illustrate the scale of Olivier's achievement:

> His performance reminds one of the insolent magnificence of that Sunderland football 'team of all talents' which, in the season before the first world war, stayed at the bottom of the League all through September, and the following April finished at the top with a record number of points. For, it must be admitted, the opening scenes of Sir Laurence's Macbeth are bad; bad with the confident badness of the master who knows that he has miracles to come.[66]

The only performer who was deficient for Tynan was, yet again, Olivier's wife – 'Miss Vivien Leigh's Lady Macbeth is more niminy-piminy than thundery-blundery, more viper than anaconda, but still quite competent in its small way'.[67] People were now beginning to see Tynan at the end of his first season as a national critic as a writer who, rather than wielding hatchets in the demolition of his pet hates, chose the rapier as his weapon of attack. His supportive comments, on the other hand, earned immense gratitude, perhaps because of his increasing power and readership. Orson Welles was particularly pleased with Tynan's June notice of the widely slated *Moby Dick*, which he described as 'dazzling',[68] and he threw a wine and cheese party for Tynan.

[Telegram   15? July 1955]

DEAR KEN YOUR REVIEW MORE THAN APPRECIATED COULD YOU LOOK IN ON THE SHOW BEFORE WE CLOSE VERY MUCH WANT YOUR OPINION AND ADVISE [*sic*] ON MY OWN PERFORMANCE WHICH WAS ENTIRELY MISSING ON OPENING NIGHT BUT NOW IN WORK WARMEST REGARDS ORSON[69]

Welles's own performance was not the only thing that had gone awry. In spite of an eclectic cast that included Joan Plowright and Kenneth Williams, erratic lighting cues, back-to-front scenes and a false nose that gradually fell off Welles's face left most other critics wholly unimpressed.[70] It was typical of the perfectionist in Welles that he still sought out Tynan's advice. It also signalled the changing relationship between the falling star, whom Tynan had always seen as father-figure, and the rising critic.

Those on the receiving end, however, were now more inclined to fight back – a testament to his growing influence. A scathing review of Sam Wanamaker in *The Lovers* started vituperative private correspondence; his description of Danny Kaye as an entertainer who had dwindled into a 'charmer'[71] caused private mutterings; and J.B. Priestley took issue with Tynan's succinct dismissal of his drama. Priestley had been a household name during the war, but he now appeared a slightly faded figure, lamenting the thwarted ambitions of the Labour government, and struggling to write plays of the quality of *An Inspector Calls* (1946). Having finally sorted out the tangled web of his private life by divorcing his wife Jane and marrying his secret lover Jacquetta in 1952, he had since dedicated himself to reviving his theatrical career. Tynan saw him as a worthy figure from a bygone era, but the prolific novelist, critic and dramatist was having none of it. In June 1955, he particularly objected to a dismissive reference that Tynan had made to him in the *Journal of the National Book League*:

... you really must not lump me in with Galsworthy, Morgan, Greene as a novelist who occasionally writes for the Theatre. This is to accept the Shaftesbury Avenue idea of me. It is by no means the view of the World Theatre with which you would prefer to be associated. I am a dramatist – and apart from Shaw, no dramatist writing in English has been played in more foreign theatres than I have i.e. during the last 20 years. Moreover, I have made more experiments in the theatre than any other living dramatist I know about. For various reasons I have been out of the Theatre here for some years, but hope to return to it shortly. A new piece of mine, *Take The Fool Away* is to have a world premiere at the Burgtheater, Vienna, (which moves back into its old playhouse, now re-built, this autumn) sometime late this year. What tends to defeat me here is the star system. Before the war, I used to make stars.

His own defence mounted, Priestley proceeded to query Tynan's own enthusiasms in the manner of the grand old man of letters.

I don't pretend to be well acquainted with Brecht's work, but from the little I do know I think you and Bentley (not a good critic) overestimate him. I saw his Mutter Courage in Zurich years ago, and was not greatly impressed. The 'epic' method dodges the dramatist's main problem – concentration – and loses force. Films do this better.

This is meant as a friendly remonstrance. As I told you when we met briefly at Moura Budberg's, I like the way you write. By the way, you could have paid a tribute to your predecessor, for Ivor Brown's early dramatic criticism, in volume form, had some very good pieces in it. Incidentally, I have always felt strongly that the dramatic critic should either refrain from general comment on the Theatre, or (what would be much better) explain to his readers exactly why

present conditions are so unfavourable for the serious dramatist, with some reference to the whole economics of theatrical production here and on Broadway.[72]

There was more chance of Tynan writing a Loamshire play than refraining
from making 'general comment on the Theatre', and he was already beginning to
question the economic premise of London theatre. As Priestley's fortunes in
the theatre dwindled – only one more of his plays was a West End success, his
adaptation of Iris Murdoch's *A Severed Head* (1963) – Tynan's were growing.

As always, Tynan travelled to Spain for his summer holiday in 1955. *Bull Fever* had
been published to some acclaim in April and he had never felt more comfortable
amongst the *aficionados*. Thomas Dozier of the *New York Times* was particularly
taken by the work and demonstrated the *élan* with which Tynan was now viewed
Stateside with a rapturous review. *Bull Fever* was, he told his readers,

> a short, sparkling book by a prodigious Englishman, Kenneth Tynan . . . Mr
> Tynan crams into 221 pages more facts, wit and incisive understanding of the
> *fiesta* and its participants than most writers could handle in 500. *Bull Fever* is by
> far the most intellectually stimulating work of its kind yet published. And it is
> extraordinarily well-written. This reviewer, for one, would award Mr Tynan both
> ears and the tail for his compact first chapter in which the progression and shape
> of the fight is fully explained in only four pages, ending with 'We shall drop Ital-
> ics now, except when introducing new words.' *OLE!*[73]

Alec Guinness, too, privately testified to its appeal for non-devotees when he wrote
to Tynan in mid-May that 'I have never been to a bull fight, but having just read your
book I feel not only that I am very familiar with the ring but, more important to me,
that I have had a glorious sunny and exotic holiday. It's a fascinating and charming
book.'[74] Elaine was equally impressed and touched by the inscription at the front.
Some time after publication, she thanked him again for dedicating *Bull Fever* to
her, but was stunned by the response. 'Why shouldn't I have?' her husband replied.
'You paid for it.' Although he earned a reasonable salary at the *Observer*, their lifestyle
was sustained by the wealth of Elaine's father. This, coupled with their turbulent
relationship, was proving difficult for the recently converted Marxist to bear.

On 16 July Tynan met up with Tennessee Williams in Barcelona and then
travelled south for the *feria* in Valencia, where he was joined by Elaine and Peter
Wildeblood. The highly strung playwright departed early, however, unsettled by
power cuts, problems with the water supply and wild rumours of disease plaguing
the dock area.[75] The rest of the holiday was uneventful and Tynan returned to
London in early August, unaware that two days later he would witness the dawn of
a new theatrical era.

It is hard to overstate the incomprehension that greeted the British première of *Waiting for Godot* on 3 August 1955. One audience member, Jack Reading, was aware that something of great significance had occurred:

> *Waiting for Godot* left the members of the audience who sat it out to the end completely *stunned*. We knew we had seen things on stage that could not be related to anything theatrical previously experienced. It was almost beyond discussion or rational appraisal. It had been an entirely new experience: a play (for want of a better word) that had taken its audience into a new extension of imagination.[76]

Few critics were to be so prophetic. The daily critics barely sought to conceal their loathing. Milton Shulman in the *Evening Standard* claimed that 'the excellent work of the cast cannot obscure many deadly dull and pretentious passages;[77] David Lewin in the *Daily Express*, under the evocative title, 'Nothing Happens, It's Awful, (It's Life)', agreed that the play was well acted, but hated the 'passages when no one could carry the thought through' and he, too, 'became weary of waiting for Godot . . . who never comes';[78] and W.A. Darlington, the critic of the *Daily Telegraph* who was notable for his love of plays that had a beginning, a middle and an end, observed that Beckett was the Head Boy of 'a school of dramatists at present whose pupils love obscurity for obscurity's sake'.[79] There was one Sunday newspaper critic, however, already attuned to the nuances of Absurdist theatre, for whom the arrival of *Waiting for Godot* was most opportune.

In the reactionary *Sunday Times* in 1955, Harold Hobson's civilised, considered style did not appeal to every theatre-goer, and certainly not to the young and recently educated, yearning for the overthrow of conservative values. Hobson was unable and unwilling to match the crisp political vignettes that Tynan could produce. As a deeply religious fifty-one-year-old he could not have had a more different outlook than the twenty-eight-year-old atheist. He preferred subjective impressions to Tynan's rational deductions, shafts of perception to insistent campaigning. He tried to look ahead by refusing to be tied to the significance of contemporary events – one of Tynan's critical touchstones – firmly believing that in criticism 'the player who is going to make a lasting reputation is one who will fit the taste of many tomorrows';[80] and, above all, he offered an intuitive reaction to what he witnessed which was sometimes wrong, more often right and rarely uninteresting.

Hobson's attention had been drawn to the potential of Absurdist drama five months earlier. Having seen Ionesco's *The Lesson* in Paris in 1951 and urged a London director to bring it to the capital, he was delighted when the young Peter Hall duly did so in March 1955. After seeing the first night at the Arts Theatre, Hobson was eager to celebrate the worth of this highly disturbing vision of existence, in

terms that were anathema to Tynan. The play's very illogicality was worth savouring, he felt – it dealt with an impossible lesson in arithmetic that a professor gives
an eighteen-year-old girl – for the 'theatre is not a school of logic' but 'a place of
passion, feeling, excitement, terror and exaltation. It has similarities to a madhouse,
but none at all to Euclid.'[81] In this review, Hobson was deliberately differentiating
between his approach and Tynan's and the demarcation line was to become ever
more entrenched from now on.

The title chosen for Hobson's *Sunday Times* review of *Waiting for Godot* was simply 'Tomorrow'. In the first half of the review he adopts the highly unconventional
(and dramatic) approach of listing the apparent deficiencies of the play, because he
wishes to convey to the reader the importance of approaching a play of this type
with a mind unshackled by previous habits of theatre-going:

> The objections to Mr Samuel Beckett's play as a theatrical entertainment are
> many and obvious. Anyone keen sighted enough to see a church at noonday can
> perceive what they are. *Waiting for Godot* has nothing to seduce the senses. Its
> drab, bare scene is dominated by a withered tree and a garbage can, and for a
> large part of the evening this lugubrious setting, which makes the worst of both
> town and country, is inhabited only by a couple of tramps, verminous, decayed,
> their hats broken and their clothes soiled, with sweaty feet, inconstant bladders,
> and boils on the backside.
>
> This is not all. In the course of the play, nothing happens. Such dramatic
> progress as there is, is not towards a climax, but towards a perpetual postpone-
> ment. Vladimir and Estragon are waiting for Godot, but this gentleman's appear-
> ance (*if* he is a gentleman, and not something of another species) is not prepared
> with any recognisable theatrical tension, for the audience knows well enough
> from the very beginning that Godot will never come. The dialogue is studded
> with words that have no meaning for normal ears; repeatedly the play announces
> that it has come to a stop, and will have to start again; never does it reconcile
> itself with reason.

The play appears, then, to follow none of the conventional rules of the theatre: it
has no development, some of the dialogue is incomprehensible and the work
frequently displays a consciousness of its own artifice. Hobson is skilfully leading
the reader to the precipice of incomprehensibility before swiftly pulling him back
from the edge. Only such shock treatment will permit an acceptance of the play on
its own terms. The third paragraph now slyly addresses the suspicion that the
description thus far will have aroused, by paralleling this with the scorn of the first
night audience:

It is hardly surprising that, English audiences notoriously disliking anything not immediately understandable, certain early lines in the play, such as 'I have had better entertainment elsewhere,' were received on the first night with ironical laughter; or that when one of the characters yawned, the yawn was echoed and amplified by a humorist in the stalls. Yet at the end the play was warmly applauded. There were even a few calls for 'Author!' But these were rather shame-faced cries, as if those who uttered them doubted whether it were seemly to make too much noise whilst turning their coats.

The fourth paragraph of 'Tomorrow' begins to prepare the reader for the crux of the criticism, with a consideration much discussed by Hobson of late, namely that of meaning in a play. Oddly, the critic claims to have identified one in *Waiting for Godot*:

> Strange as the play is, and curious as are its processes of thought, it has a mean-ing; and this meaning is untrue. To attempt to put this meaning into a paragraph is like trying to catch Leviathan in a butterfly net, but nevertheless the attempt must be made. The upshot of *Waiting for Godot* is that the two tramps are always waiting for the future, their ruinous consolation being that there is always tomor-row; they never realise that today is today. In this, says Mr Beckett, they are like all humanity, which dawdles and drivels its life, postponing action, eschewing enjoyment, waiting only for some far-off, divine event, the millennium, the Day of Judgement.
>
> Mr Beckett has, of course, got it all wrong. Humanity worries very little over the Day of Judgement. It is far too busy hire-purchasing television sets, popping into three star restaurants, planting itself vineyards, building helicopters. *But he has got it wrong in a tremendous way.* And this is what matters. There is no need at all for a dramatist to philosophise rightly; he can leave that to the philosophers. But it is essential that if he philosophises wrongly, he should do so with swagger. Mr Beckett has any amount of swagger. A dusty, coarse, irreverent, pessimistic, violent swagger? Possibly. But the genuine thing, the real McCoy.

The moment of peripeteia, indicated by my italics, is all the more effective because the reader can now see that she has been coaxed up to this point to consider Hobson's verdict in a way that relies not on the reader's past experience of the theatre, but on her future expectation of ground-breaking developments. The lack of contemporary theatrical accoutrements – a lavish, naturalistic set, well-bred, recog-nisable characters, a linear development of plot and the reassurance of a comprehen-sible meaning – is the very basis of the appeal of this new type of play. Hobson now seeks to secure the play's reputation by stressing its universal relevance:

Vladimir and Estragon have each a kind of universality. They wear their rags with a difference. Vladimir is eternally hopeful; if Godot does not come this evening then he will certainly come tomorrow, or at the very least the day after. Estragon, much troubled by his boots, is less confident. He thinks the game is not worth playing, and is ready to hang himself. Or so he says. But he does nothing. Like Vladimir he only talks. They both idly spin away the great top of their life in the vain expectation that some master whip will one day give it eternal vitality. Meanwhile their conversation often has the simplicity, in this case the delusive simplicity, of music hall cross-talk, now and again pierced with a shaft that seems for a second or so to touch the edge of truth's garment. It is bewildering. It is exasperating. It is insidiously exciting.

Hobson's conclusion to this review emphasises his desire to create an audience for Absurdist drama. It also manages to trump the memorable claim that the play is 'insidiously exciting' by combining an enthusiastic adjuration to visit the Arts Theatre with a colourful and original lyricism:

> Go and see *Waiting for Godot*. At the worst you will discover a curiosity, a four-leaved clover, a black tulip; at the best, something that will securely lodge in a corner of your mind for as long as you live.[82]

It is the passionate nature of Hobson's advocacy, the deeply felt conviction that *Waiting for Godot* represented a new way forward for drama and must be defended from its exaggeratedly hostile detractors, and the literary skill with which he advances his argument that make this review so famous – and so compelling. The sentiments are clearly overstated, but Hobson's achievement is that he recognised that, in certain circumstances, arguments need to be overstated in order to gain an audience. A grateful Beckett read the criticism with emotion and considered it to be courageous and touching.[83]

Whenever devotees of the British theatre think back to the gladiatorial struggle that was waged between Tynan and Hobson, a struggle that made London theatre seem so vibrant and vital, they remember the significance and rarity of these two critical titans agreeing. Sunday, 7 August 1955 was one such occasion. Tynan independently came to the same conclusion as Hobson – that this was a unique work:

> A special virtue attaches to plays which remind the drama of how much it can do without and still exist. By all the known criteria, Samuel Beckett's *Waiting for Godot* is a dramatic vacuum. Pity the critic who seeks a chink in its armour, for it is all chink. It has no plot, no climax, no *dénouement*, no beginning, no middle, and no end. Unavoidably, it has situation, and it might be

accused of having suspense, since it deals with the impatience of two tramps, waiting beneath a tree for a cryptic Mr Godot to keep his appointment with them; but the situation is never developed, and a glance at the programme shows that Mr Godot is not going to arrive. *Waiting for Godot* frankly jettisons everything by which we recognise theatre. It arrives at the custom-house, as it were, with no luggage, no passport, and nothing to declare; yet it gets through, as might a pilgrim from Mars. It does this, I believe, by appealing to a definition of drama much more fundamental than any in the books. A play, it asserts and proves, is basically a means of spending two hours in the dark without being bored.

It was essentially a one-off:

The play sees the human condition in terms of baggy pants and red noses. Hastily labelling their disquiet disgust, many of the first-night audience found it pretentious. But what, exactly, are its pretensions? To state that mankind is waiting for a sign that is late in coming is a platitude which none but an illiterate would interpret as making claims to profundity. What vexed the play's enemies was, I suspect, the opposite: it was not pretentious enough to enable them to deride it. I care little for its enormous success in Europe over the past three years, but much for the way in which it pricked and stimulated my own nervous system. It summoned the music hall and the parable to present a view of life which banished the sentimentality of the music hall and the parable's fulsome uplift. It forced me to re-examine the rules which have hitherto governed the drama; and having done so, to pronounce them not elastic enough. It is validly new, and hence I declare myself, as the Spanish would say, *godoista*.

Tynan was happy to welcome its uniqueness in a notice that drew the following lawdotory response from Harold Clurman: 'Congratulations on your *admirable* review of *Godot* (*Godot* an affectionate French diminution for God: I mean anglo-French?) Your holiday seems to have been very useful to you. The writing is delightful, the argument tight, the statement and the thinking terse . . .'[84]

What differentiated Hobson's attitude from Tynan's was that Hobson recognised the play as the latest example of European Absurdist drama and that he was determined to champion it with a passionate intensity that verged upon magnificent obsession. He enjoyed the allusive nature of drama that deliberately avoided closure and gained a similar thrill from the unexpected use of language that he had celebrated in the works of Fry and Eliot. In its freshness and innovation, he believed Absurdist theatre to be the potential catalyst for the revitalisation of English theatre – and saw as its spiritual home his favourite foreign country, France. This inevitably sharpened the divide between him and Tynan. Although the latter had declared himself a *Godoista*, it was a specific play that he was endorsing, not a dramatic philosophy, and over the next few years Tynan would distance himself from an approach which he felt militated against an engagement with real life issues. He preferred more didactic, recognisably contemporaneous works. The seeds of his own disagreement with Absurdism – which would develop into a full-blown spat with Eugène Ionesco in 1958 – had ironically been sown in March 1955, by the same première of Ionesco's *The Lesson* at the Arts that had enthralled Hobson. Tynan's review chose to locate the work in the context of 'Dadaist shock tactics and Artaud's "theatre of cruelty"'and in a damning conclusion he argued that although it was theatrically thrilling it was 'humanly nothing'.[85] Given that Tynan wanted, above all, realistic drama that dealt with human concerns, this was a grave failing. From the autumn of 1955 onwards, he would set the didacticism of Epic theatre against the allusiveness of Absurdism. It had been a very exciting start to his second season as the *Observer* critic.

Looking back at this extraordinary season that was to change the face of British theatre, Tynan observed the following July how it had been a period of theatrical extremes. Unexpected riches from the spring of 1956 onwards – 'I forgot that the finest blooms often flower late'[86] – presaged a new direction, but they had been preceded from August to May 1955 by a period of sterility almost unparalleled in post-war history. The fault lay, in Tynan's view, with elderly playwrights, insular producers, timid audiences, an obtuse Lord Chamberlain and the savage entertainment tax. This was an issue on which Tynan's predecessor, Ivor Brown, had campaigned vigorously, and Tynan now drew attention to its stifling of creativity. Introduced as a 'temporary tax' in 1916,[87] threatened by an (unfulfilled) Labour Party pledge to abolish it in 1924 and widely vilified by West End producers in the 1940s, entertainment tax had become a durable fixture. It was a huge financial burden for the theatre and by 1948 had risen to 10 per cent of gross profits, which represented over a quarter of the price of a ticket by 1948.[88] With such a large sum to recoup from ticket sales, it was little wonder that producers were unwilling to take the risk on new works. Star-studded classics were much less risky commercial ventures.

Until recently there had been one way in which the burden of entertainment tax could be lifted. To encourage straitened producers at the end of the First World War to produce more plays without jeopardising this welcome source of revenue for the Treasury, the wartime government had stated that plays that could be classed as educational or 'cultural' would be exempt from the tax. After 1945, the Arts Council appointed three officials, generally known as the 'three blind mice', to rule on whether plays claiming exemption could be classed as educational,[89] but the furore that surrounded the first London production of Tennessee Williams's *A Streetcar Named Desire* in 1949 closed off this loophole. To offset the high production costs of over £10,000, Binkie Beaumont's management company, Tennent Productions, had turned itself into a non-profit-making registered charity. This was Tennent's fortieth such venture, and powerful voices were now heard criticising this piece of creative accountancy. Ivor Brown had frequently condemned this practice, commenting as early as 1947, in a thinly veiled reference to Binkie Beaumont, that 'the distinction between non-profit and profit-making theatre companies has become altogether shadowy when profit makers create "non-profit" subsidiaries with the same offices and largely similar directorates'.[90] The address of both the parent company, H.M. Tennent Ltd, and the tax-avoiding subsidiary, Tennent Productions Ltd, was tellingly the same: the Apollo Theatre, Shaftesbury Avenue.

On this occasion, however, Tennent's action was challenged by MPs in the House of Commons. Public anticipation for *A Streetcar Named Desire* at the Aldwych had been enormous. The theatre had received over 10,000 postal applications[91] to witness the appearance of Vivien Leigh in a modern American play directed (for the enormous salary of £500 per week)[92] by her husband, Laurence Olivier. The fights which had broken out amongst eager members of the first night queue brought welcome publicity for this spectacular event. After the opening performance, though, the reaction was sharply – and antagonistically – divided. Some critics were attracted to the poignancy of Leigh as the abused Blanche; the *Times*, for example, described her performance as 'impressive . . . for its delicately insistent suggestion of a mind with a slowly loosening hold on reason'.[93] Others, however, were outraged by what they chose to see as an indecent, lavatorial work. Baroness Ravensdale of the Public Morality Council spluttered that the 'play is thoroughly indecent and we should be ashamed that children and servants are allowed to sit in the theatre and see it';[94] Princess Alice cancelled a visit, stating that it was not the 'kind of entertainment she would enjoy';[95] and the parish notes of the Reverend Colin Cuttell, priest-Vicar of Southwark, rebuked the indolence of the censor: 'Is there no statesman in high places who will speak out from other than political and economic motives and tell the United States to keep the sewage? A pathological obsession with sex is a mark of this age, as it has been the mark of any dying civilisation from Babylon to Rome. Peradventure the Lord Chamberlain (the chief licensee of all theatres) is on a journey or sleepeth . . .'[96]

His clarion cry was quickly taken up by a variety of MPs. When the Financial Secretary, Glenvil Hall, sought to explain that it was perfectly in order for the management to claim exemption on educational grounds, the Conservative MP for Brighton, A. Marlowe, asked whether the Minister was aware 'that this particular play is only educational to those who are ignorant of the facts of life?'[97] It was a myopic response to a poignant and powerful work, but the furore brought into focus the anachronistic nature of the 'educational' exemption. The play was to run at the Aldwych for 333 performances, but an investigation was launched in 1950 by a Select Committee into the practice of managements forming non-profit distributing subsidiaries in the light of the controversy provoked by the play, and the loophole was closed. This was a considerable blow to Tennent's and made them liable for income tax backdated to 1945. But it was, in reality, an even greater blow to West End theatre as a whole, since, for all its convoluted implications, the loophole did provide commercial organisations with a safety net to experiment. In his retrospect of July 1956, Tynan was in no doubt about the diminishing effect of this tax: 'Behind impenetrable walls of Entertainment Tax, the native drama languished in prison, guarded by its kindly Shadbolt, the Lord Chamberlain.'[98]

There was an echo of Vivien Leigh's momentous performance of Blanche Dubois in the first great classical production of the 1955/6 season. It was another Stratford extravaganza, with Brook directing Olivier in the title role of *Titus Andronicus*, and Leigh as his brutalised daughter, Lavinia. The play, as always, was much criticised for its alleged implausibilities (Titus cuts off his own hand in a failed attempt to save his son; Lavinia has her hands cut off and tongue ripped out after being raped by two brothers; and Titus kills the two rapists and bakes them in a pie which he feeds to their mother). A subsequent letter to the *Observer* protested that Shakespeare's earliest tragedy was 'thoroughly revolting to modern taste'.[99] Tynan partially agreed and chose an analogy which revealed that his mind was half on his recent holiday – 'it's the casualness of the killing that grows tiresome, as a bad bullfight. With acknowledgement to Lady Bracknell, to lose one son may be accounted a misfortune: to lose twenty-four, as Titus does, looks like carelessness'[100] – before launching into his ritual denigration of Leigh and eulogy of Olivier. Tynan's attack on Leigh was as brief and incisive as it was consistent – 'As Lavinia, Miss Vivien Leigh receives the news that she is about to be ravished on her husband's corpse with little more than the mild annoyance of one who would have preferred foam rubber' – whereas his encomia on Olivier continued to grow more lavish:

Sir Laurence Olivier's Titus, even with one hand gone, is a five-finger exercise transformed into an unforgettable concerto of grief. This is a performance which ushers us into the presence of one who is, pound for pound, the greatest actor alive. As usual, he raises one's hair with the risks he takes: Titus enters not as a beaming hero but as a battered veteran, stubborn and shambling, long past caring about the people's cheers. A hundred campaigners have tanned his heart to the leather, and from the cracking of the heart there issues a terrible music, not untinged by madness. One hears great cries, which, like all of this actor's best effects, seem to have been dredged up from an ocean-bed of fatigue. One recognised, though one has never heard it before, the noise made in its last extremity by the cornered human soul. We knew from his Hotspur and his Richard III that Sir Laurence could explode: now we know that he can suffer as well. All the grand unplayable parts, after this, are open to him – Skelton's Magnificence, Ibsen's Brand and Goethe's Faust – anything, so long as we can see those lion eyes search for solace, that great jaw sag.

In his appreciation of the artistry of the actor, Tynan was writing – exceptionally – in the vein of Harold Hobson. As long ago as 1933, Hobson had written in the *Christian Science Monitor* that for him the performer was the most important member of the theatrical triumvirate of director, actor and playwright:

> Where the actor is confined to embodying merely the ideas of the author, there is something lost to the world, namely, the ideas and vision of the actor himself. But in a theater, where the actor is allowed and indeed expected to use the written drama purely as a kind of musical instrument on which he plays any sort of tune that best harmonises with his own outlook, the world loses nothing.[101]

Only when he came to write about Olivier did Tynan convey this same belief – after joining the *Observer* it was almost always the playwright who held the key to vibrant drama. This makes it all the more remarkable then, that with this production there was a complete role reversal, with Hobson choosing to stress the contemporary relevance of *Titus Andronicus*. The horrors of the play would not be wasted, he argued, 'if they wake up the British stage to a sense of reality', and it is significant, given his interest in the linguistic dexterity of Beckett and Ionesco, that it is the language and modern sense of the play that he finds most striking:

> There is absolutely nothing in the bleeding barbarity of *Titus Andronicus* which would have astonished anyone at Buchenwald . . . Even in its moments of curious verbal delicacy *Titus Andronicus* parallels exactly our own age. The dismemberment of Lavinia is described as 'trimming', as one might talk of decorating a hat; just as today we speak of torment and torture by a hygienic term like 'brain washing', as though it were something similar to sending clothes to a laundry. The

audience which thinks that its sensationalism makes *Titus Andronicus* unreal and absurd is probably weak in the stomach; it is undoubtedly weak in the head.

But this does not mean that the piece is an effective play, because 'something more than a vigorous picture of objective reality is needed to make great drama. Theatre must be a consistent point of view.' This implicit side-swipe at Brecht (misunderstanding Epic theatre, it must be said) is made explicit when he concludes: 'It is well known that Shakespeare was never quite sure how to write his own name. I should not be surprised if, about the time he was thinking of *Titus Andronicus*, he thought the proper spelling was Brecht.'[102]

In the absence of worthwhile distractions on the West End stage, people began to turn their attention to this battle of the critics. For the next few months Hobson and Tynan would take selective pots at each other's particular enthusiasms, and it became common for those with an interest in the theatre to buy both the *Observer* and the *Sunday Times* to compare their theatre columns. Their distinctive literary styles – Tynan's pithy, incisive and epigrammatic, Hobson's lyrical, romantic and dignified – produced distinctive and compelling reading. They were a marketing department's dream. A young, unknown playwright, whose first work would soon transform the stage, alluded to their growing status in the theatre world at the beginning of *Look Back in Anger*. Although Jimmy Porter mocks the pretentious excesses of what are clearly the *Sunday Times* and the *Observer* – 'I've just read three whole columns on the English Novel. Half of it's in French. Do the Sunday newspapers make you feel ignorant?'[103] – both he and Cliff are first seen 'sprawled way out beyond the newspapers which hide the rest of them from sight', and Jimmy evidently recognises the social implications of adhering to the religious ritual of working one's way through the Sunday papers:

JIMMY: Haven't you read the other posh paper yet?
CLIFF: Which?
JIMMY: Well, there are only two posh papers on a Sunday – the one you're reading, and this one

To read Tynan and Hobson was to find some of the excitement that was missing from the stage.

The two critics soon demonstrated their different tastes when one of France's finest performers, Edwige Feuillère, arrived in London in September to play Marguérite Gautier in Dumas's *La Dame aux camélias* at the Duke of York's. She had played the part since 1940; together with the role of Ysé in Claudel's *Partage de midi*, which she had first performed for the Barrault-Renaud company in 1948, it was considered to be one of the finest female interpretations in Europe at the time. Hobson's reaction to her performance revealed the stark contrast between his critical style and Tynan's. Passages of evocative, romantic prose – 'Her performance is not made up of discrete notes, like a firework piece on a piano. It has rather the unbroken beauty of a violin' – are interrupted by moments of rhapsodic praise – 'her death scene is . . . miraculously moving'; breathless, emotional reactions are listed alongside moments of revelatory insight gleaned from the tiniest gestures (a feature of Hobson's reviews), such as the force of a 'jamais' uttered by Feuillère; phrases in French are quoted to give an indication (to those familiar with the language) of the magnificence of touch; and Hobson freely acknowledges his deliberately impressionistic approach by concluding that: 'to detail the beauties of Mme Feuillère's performance is to give the wrong impression'.[104] Removed from the event, Hobson's praise seems excessive (particularly given the deficiencies of his own spoken French), but the scorn that this form of criticism provoked had more to do with the appetite for a different theatrical taste, the rejection of the Romantic in the desire for the Augustan, than any intrinsic failing on Hobson's part. It seemed incredibly detached from the wider world, where there was renewed superpower tension over Moscow's refusal to release German prisoners of war, over ten years after their capture. Stephen Bagnall, in a letter to the *Sunday Times* the following week, spoke for many when he objected to the critic's other-worldliness and, in particular, his 'incomprehensible francomania'[105] – and this was the furrow that Tynan chose to plough.

Whereas Hobson reviewed *La Dame aux camélias* on 11 September, Tynan held back his notice until the 18th. This allowed him to reflect upon Hobson's views, and, unusually, he chose to make a direct reference to his rival's column:

> It is the opinion of one of my colleagues that Mme Feuillère is the greatest actress on earth. Lucky the man who can make such a claim! And as lucky he who, in another journal, confidently challenged it with his own contender, Dame Edith Evans! For here, surely, are critical eyes that have scanned the field, and shrewdly concluded that where Mmes Maria Casères, Katina Paxinou, Helene Weigel, Anna Magnani and Inga Tidblad (to name but five) won't do, Dame Edith Evans and Mme Edwige Feuillère will. Herein lies my embarrassment, and with it my envy, for I have seen only four of these seven ladies on the stage.

That said (completely tongue in cheek), he asserts that Feuillère is peerless in her gracefulness – 'Every ripple of her voice, every line of her body is alive with the beauty of transience: her performance glows in the mind like a sunset'; she is the best '*romantic* actress' he has ever seen; but, crucially, she lacks a 'capacity to frighten' or 'to compel awe', which happens to be the basis of Olivier's talent.[106]

Although restrained by professional courtesy to a colleague, and perhaps mindful of the debt he owed to Hobson for his support of *He That Plays the King*, Tynan's mocking of Hobson's portentousness is apparent. He deliberately notes their age gap and suggests that Hobson's critical faculties have become befuddled by one mesmerising performance. There is even a cheeky hint at early dotage. The title of his review, 'Passion's Slave', could thus be seen as ambiguous – is it referring to Feuillère or to Hobson?

The following week Hobson replied to Bagnall's overt and Tynan's implied charge of Francomania with a vigorous defence of his love of the French. The critical opprobrium that had greeted *Waiting for Godot* had merely reinforced his passion:

> It is this complacent inability to recognise the highest when they see it, this apparently natural enmity towards exultation of the spirit, which for a moment checks one's heart. It is this attitude that is the reason why Olivier and Gielgud are playing Shakespeare, why Redgrave is playing Giraudoux, and Wolfit Hochwälder. It is the reason why some of us are Francomaniacs. It has left *them* nothing else to do. It has left *us* little else to be.[107]

It is also evident that although the two critics disagreed on the cure for the sickly state of British theatre, they did agree on a diagnosis of its ailments – no good British plays to occupy British acting talent. It was a theme that was always profitable for Tynan. Needing a cause to arouse him, he was now, after the space of a year, regarded as the most didactic critic in London, conscious of the world around him, capable of the finest writing and dismayed that the West End theatre in its insularity simply reflected the country as a whole. A year after the seminal 'West End Apathy' and the launch of the 'Loamshire' campaign, Tynan issued a further rallying call in September 1955, provocatively entitled 'Post Mortem'. He chose to raise the alarm by suggesting that the battle had already been lost:

> In an empty week, I have been dismaying myself with a few statistics. In the past year, my diary records, I have seen more than a hundred plays in and around London. About ninety of them were imports or revivals: nineteen were both new and British. Of the nineteen, all but six were pot-boilers; of the six, three had a certain distinction of utterance; but only one – Mr Rattigan's *Separate Tables* – combined technical assurance with serious purpose. And it would be the glibbest chauvinism were I to number *Separate Tables* among the best half-dozen evenings of my twelve month.

The blame now, he now feels, has shifted. It cannot be solely laid at the feet of the playwright:

It is notorious that the British playgoer has a ravenous appetite for comedies about country-house families coping with the economic problems of living in country houses and the social problems of living in the twentieth century at all. Successful British plays about people who cannot afford London seasons for their daughters are as rare as people who *can* afford them. One knows the conventions by heart: no youngest daughter is ever ugly, no mamma ever other than sporty, and all servants are loyal clowns. In sustaining these fictions, this masquerade of hieroglyphs, our playwrights are satisfying a national taste, and cannot be condemned for that.

Their inability to offer any other fare also stems from their restricted view of life, ensconced in their country residences in Loamshire:

Every British dramatist is subject to the recurrent delusion that he knows how the lower-income groups speak. This delusion is usually based on conversations held through panes of glass with London taxi-drivers, most of whom discovered long ago that the more closely they conform to their clients' picture of them as Dickensian drolls, the higher their tips are likely to be. On the whole, then, though one blames the public for the specific atrophy of the playwright's mind, one must blame the playwright for the specific atrophy of his own ears. I seriously doubt whether our knowledge of the ways in which the English use their tongues has been perceptibly broadened by any native dramatist since Galsworthy. In writing plays the ear is paramount: when that withers, everything withers.

As if this was not gloomy enough, he swiftly rejects the notion that technical changes could lead to greater innovation. Stephen Joseph's first London introduction of the 'theatre-in-the-round' is given short shrift:

The individual spectator in a normal theatre sees a group of players in depth to exactly the same extent, without the handicaps of a) staring half the time at their backs and b) seeing beyond them rows of total strangers staring fixedly in the opposite direction. 'Theatre in the Round' is unquestionably well-meaning: but then, as Saki said, 'impertinence often is.'

This conservative view was unusual for Tynan, but it stemmed from his conviction that only the writer with a keen sense of reality could break the log jam: 'The answer to our dramatic impasse lies not in the director's power to make us look, but in the playwright's power to make us listen.'[108] In this lay the first seeds of his prophetic review of *Look Back in Anger*.

Tynan's sense of the proletarian in his writing was not always reflected in his personal life. In October he, Elaine and Tracy moved into a flat in the heart of London's richest district, Mayfair. Number 120 Mount Street, a large eight-room second-floor flat, was close to Park Lane, the Curzon Hotel and the West End theatre land. Refurbished by the architect Peter Miller and stocked with furniture from Elaine's parents' flat in New York, which they were vacating, it became an ideal base for Tynan to write up his reviews and Elaine to continue with her novel. It also offered a more spacious home to entertain guests from the theatre and arts world, since it had 'sky high ceilings' and two enormous reception rooms,[109] and was full of conversation pieces: a blow-up of Hieronymus Bosch's *Garden of Pleasure*, a library painted jet black, and an image of the cleft of the buttocks of La Goulue (which Tynan invited guests to identify). Sunday evenings were often devoted to entertaining and impressing guests – early ones included Christopher Isherwood and his partner, Don Bachardy – and the rest of the week was geared to 'composition day', the hell of Fridays, which saw Tynan retire to his study with several bottles of white wine to write, write and write again his Sunday copy.[110] He was receiving more and more private letters urging him on. One, from the music critic Neville Cardus, encapsulated the excitement that many felt at the freshness of his writing:

> For several years I have been waiting for a critic of the theatre in London with a less than provincial view – a writer of wit, sensibility and the courage of his intuitions. In a word, I've been waiting for somebody to follow in the track of Shaw, Walkley, Montague and Agate. For my own part I hail you a true successor of these; and as I have once upon a time, worked as a colleague of Montague, I think I can smell the blood Royal . . .[111]

To Tynan, the move to Mount Street felt like the confirmation of his stature as a critic of distinction. The one room that was rarely used was the kitchen. Elaine preferred not to cook, and her husband's favourite meal-time was to drop into the cocktail lounge at the Connaught Hotel and then dine out in a local curry house.

Tynan's developing social conscience, which was manifesting itself in his reviews, was in firm evidence at home. He subscribed to the *Guardian* and the *Daily Express*, the right-wing vehicle for Lord Beaverbrook's views, which never failed to provoke his ire. 'Sometimes even a headline in the *Daily Express* was enough to raise his indignation to the level where it literally shot him out of bed,'[112] Elaine remembers. This was particularly true during the Suez crisis, when Beaverbrook unstintingly supported the government. They would debate the issues of the day together before getting up, with Elaine increasingly dedicating herself to her novel. Now that she had this task to focus on, her drinking reduced and the autumn of 1955 became a period of domestic calm.

Looking back on this time from the summer of 1956, Tynan was convinced that it was one of the most poverty-stricken periods for British theatre:

> . . . there was a point at which the very survival of British theatre seemed doubtful. The great winter drought, when for four months between October and February not a single new British play opened in London, scared the critics to death; they recall it with horror, as the Irish recall the potato famines. Professional reviewers met in furtive conclave to frame joint protests against the day, surely imminent, of their dismissal; some tried to insure against the risk of redundancy; and one or two even contemplated going out in the daytime and learning about life.[113]

Paradoxically, there was a great deal of life to write about in the autumn of 1955. Internationally, the Russians exploded the largest H-bomb ever made in November, and their assurance that it would never be used offensively was subject to nervous debate in the media. Further evidence of the power of class, deference and the notion of duty in Britain (all anathema to Tynan) was provided in the same month when Princess Margaret was made to renounce her boyfriend, Peter Townsend. This alliance had convulsed the British press since rumours about the affair of the Queen's younger sister with the dashing and divorced Group Captain began to surface in the American press in June 1953. The British reporter Audrey Whiting, of the *Daily Mirror*, had actually first spotted the couple together on Coronation Day (2 June 1953), but the paper's editor had refused to print the story, saying that they could not 'upset the ladies' day . . .'

As stories began to circulate, Buckingham Palace quickly moved to limit the damage. The Princess was only twenty-three and, under the eighteenth-century Royal Marriages Act, which George III had devised to rein in the wayward George IV, she was not free to marry without the Queen's consent until she was twenty-five. Incredibly, the Palace then sent Townsend to Brussels to see out the remaining period, unduly terrified that a royal marriage to a divorcee would spark a constitutional crisis similar to the one that had occurred in the 1930s.

Townsend returned to Britain in August 1954. Media interest in the romance continued to flourish and cameras began to follow him around. In the popular press Townsend and Margaret were viewed as doomed lovers and a debate began over whether it was the Princess's duty to give up personal happiness for the good of the monarchy. The shadow cast by Mrs Simpson was a long one. In October 1955, matters came to a head. On 26 October, the editor of the *Times*, Sir William Hayley, opined that the royal family was a national symbol of family life and that if the Queen's sister married a divorced man, it would damage the monarchy. The *Daily Mirror* took the opposite view: it would be cruel for the Palace to force Margaret to adopt Hayley's advice by choosing between love and status. On 31 October it printed a story urging Margaret to hurry up and decide about her lover, under the headline: 'Come on Margaret!' In early November, a statement was issued from Buckingham Palace by Margaret. Under pressure from the Queen Mother and the Prime Minister, Sir Anthony Eden, she had decided not to marry Townsend. 'Mindful of the church's teaching that Christian marriage is indissoluble and conscious of my duty to the Commonwealth, I have resolved to put these considerations before any others', she announced – hardly the spontaneous words of a lively twenty-five year-old, known for her love of theatre (she had appeared in pantomimes at Windsor and was often photographed mixing with stars such as Noël Coward, Danny Kaye and Douglas Fairbanks), and enjoyment of socialising with her bohemian friends, known as 'Margaret's set'. The establishment had triumphed but there was a pervasive sense of hypocrisy. The Church of England had been founded on a royal divorce; hasty wartime marriages had led to numerous separations in the post-war period, even though the Church of England refused to sanction them; and the new Prime Minister Eden and three of his ministers had been divorced themselves, with Eden quickly remarrying. After the Princess's death in 2002, she was frequently described as the royal rebel. In reality, she was the ultimate conformist, but to the young in 1955 her fate confirmed again that the country, in spite of Churchill's resignation and growing signs of affluence, was still in the grip of the old guard.

During this furore, Tynan was away in Moscow, following Peter Brook's production of *Hamlet*, which confirmed his earlier view[114] of the enormous potential of Paul Scofield as Olivier's 'natural heir', once he had mastered 'realistic acting'.[115] He made no direct comment on Margaret's renunciation of Townsend but in his reiteration of the need for drama about reality, empathised with the sentiments of those who felt that Margaret's treatment was as anachronistic as it was unnecessary. Moscow was an eye-opener. Actors had permanent job security, theatre critics were required to go to shows on three successive nights before they could file a notice and there was an enormous choice of over 160 shows for the theatre-goer. However, the choice, he felt, was illusory, since Soviet theatre could not conceive of tragedy, because the concept did not exist in a socialist utopia. Tynan's ideal, therefore, was 'a Western theatre organised on Russian lines, but without Russian ideology'.[116] His Marxism would always be that of Brecht, who had an empathy with the working class, a conviction that man could be changed for the better, a love of Cuban cigars, and the reassurance of a Swiss bank account and an Austrian passport.

Tynan chose the new year to open a new front in his crusade. January 1, 1956 fell on a Sunday and, rather than fall back on reviewing pantomimes, he wrote his first full-length piece on a topic that was to change his life in the 1960s: the National Theatre. David Garrick had called for the creation of such an institution in the eighteenth century, but the idea did not receive general support until 1848, when Effingham Wilson, the Radical bookseller, proposed in a couple of pamphlets that a publicly owned 'house for Shakespeare' be established where the works of the 'world's greatest moral teacher' would be constantly performed.[117] Little was done to advance this suggestion until the publication in 1907 of *The National Theatre: A Scheme and Estimates* co-authored by the critic William Archer and the director and playwright Harley Granville-Barker. This blueprint included detailed plans for the embryonic institution. The company was to number 66 (44 men and 22 women), seats would be priced between an affordable 1 shilling and 7s. 6d. and the total start-up costs would amount to a third of a million pounds.[118] Such was the interest that the Shakespeare Memorial National Theatre Committee (SMNTC) was formed in 1908 and a private member's bill to establish a National Theatre passed with a small majority in 1913. A site was then purchased in Bloomsbury and it looked as if the opening date of 23 April 1916, the alleged tercentenary of Shakespeare's death, might prove feasible, until the First World War dealt a severe blow to the project's prospects and all plans were shelved.

During the inter-war years, the plan was held back by the open hostility of the supporters of Lilian Baylis's Old Vic (who saw their own theatre as the prototype national institution), the economic depression and the inability to raise private funds. Although Granville-Barker issued a new edition of the proposals in 1930, in which he advocated having two theatres under the same roof, the original site in Bloomsbury was sold. The campaign did not cease, however, and by 1937 the SMNTC was able to purchase a new site opposite the Victoria and Albert Museum in Kensington.

Again war intervened, but this time the outbreak of hostilities was to prove less detrimental to the campaign. The Council for the Encouragement of Music and the Arts (CEMA) opened up the prospect of state support for the project. Equally encouraging was the reconciliation between the Old Vic and the SMNTC which led to the creation of a *de facto* National Theatre at the Old Vic in 1944; the memorable Olivier/Richardson collaborations; and the passing of a new parliamentary bill committing £1 million to the project in January 1949. But the worsening state of the British economy delayed allocation of the money, and although Queen Elizabeth, the Queen Mother, laid a third foundation stone in 1951 (this time on the South Bank), interminable, possibly fatal delay once again threatened. Indeed, as the specific location of the new building frequently changed during the 1950s, the Queen Mother was reported to have suggested that the foundation stone should be put on castors.[119] It was at this point that a clearly exasperated Tynan chose to speak out.

'Payment Deferred' lamented the stalling of the project and, after a brief résumé of the sorry history of the plan, Tynan offered his first shot:

Must it again be urged that Britain is the only European country with a living theatrical tradition which lacks a national theatre; and that the public money which gave us a visual library, the National Gallery, is needed just as vitally to provide (in Benn Levy's phrase) a 'living library' of plays? . . . The general impotence of our theatre, as opposed to the individual excellence of our actors, is the laughing-stock of the Continent; and it is unthinkable that anyone nowadays would sink to the crassness of saying, as a daily paper did in 1938: 'To have no National Theatre is a tribute to our liberty

As Tynan well knew, there were powerful voices who spoke against the whole idea. Harold Hobson was one. He would later express his fear that a national theatre would become obsessed with Shakespeare and old classics, and would militate against new writing, given its link to the establishment. He had already argued as long ago as 1949 that it was unlikely that a national theatre would be able to secure sufficient star names to ensure that it gained 'a national repute' and that it might threaten the viability of the Old Vic.[120] Tynan considered this attitude pusillanimous:

. . . what, the die-hards may ask, will the National Theatre give us that Stratford and the Old Vic do not? Firstly, a modern theatre, comparable with those abroad and capable of staging the widest variety of plays. Secondly, not a cast of underpaid second-stringers like the Old Vic, nor yet, a starry, short-term band, like Stratford; but a large, experienced, permanent company drawn from our finest talent and paid accordingly. Of the six objects prescribed for the National Theatre, Stratford and the Old Vic fulfil but one, that of presenting Shakespeare. The others (those of reviving the rest of our classical drama, presenting new plays and the best of foreign drama, and preventing recent plays of merit from rusting in oblivion) have no roof at all over their heads. At the X Theatre the play is good; at the Y, the acting; and the décor at the Z is magnificent. But there is nowhere we can send our guests, confidently saying: 'This is our theatre's best. On this we stand.'

Having set out his philosophy (from which he was to deviate little as the National Theatre's first Literary Manager), he even ventured to suggest the job description and some possibilities for the post of Artistic Director. He – no thought of it being a woman – needed to be a 'captain for the rocket-ship. He should be a man like Brecht in Berlin or Khedrov in Moscow: a combination of sage and ball of fire. The type is rare in our theatre, though Granville-Barker could have (and Gordon Craig might have) developed into it. Even so, a few names spring to mind; and two of them, in spite of the drawbacks involved, are the names of actors – Quayle and Olivier.'[121]

The elderly Gordon Craig was highly delighted by this reference – 'so much you say of theatre seems to me so much better than what the others say,' he wrote to

Tynan[122] – but Elaine was convinced that this was a further staging post on a journey that had begun with her husband's effusive reviews of Olivier. They, she felt, had had but one goal in mind: 'It took no feat of intelligence to figure out that if glorious circumstance came to pass, Sir Laurence Olivier, premier English actor *and* premier actor-manager, would be running it.'[123] Time would tell.

The winter and early spring of 1956 was an arid time for West End theatre, and Tynan used it to continue to mount his campaign for committed, honest, contemporary writing. When several of his colleagues berated Sartre's *Nekrassov* in January for being too propagandistic, he regretted that it was not more so:

> All I seek to establish is that propaganda has a place in the hierarchy. Brecht once drew an analogy which I think worth quoting. Some surgeons, he said, are content to supply merely a diagnosis: others feel it their duty to recommend a cure. Most propaganda plays, admittedly offer quack remedies. The danger is that our hatred of quacks may lead us to despise the true healers.[124]

He rejected the elitism he chose to see in the versification of Eliot and Fry – they were like 'a pair of energetic swimming instructors giving lessons in an empty pool'[125] – and urged writers to follow the example of Tennessee Williams, who wrote prose 'fuelled with human speech, taking off and soaring with a warm jet-driven roar'.[126] The Arts Theatre should put on *Cat on a Hot Tin Roof* as soon as possible; it was outlawed because of the intransigence of the Lord Chamberlain. Sam Wanamaker's *The Threepenny Opera*, whilst not the best example of Brecht's Epic theatre, at least established a bridgehead for the playwright at the Royal Court in February. Tynan was pleased (though not elated: the true glory was *Mother Courage*) and he was moved to define a 'Brechtian' as 'one who believes that low drama with high principles is better than high principles with no audience; that the worst plays are those which depend wholly on suspense and the illusion of reality; and that the drama of the future will be a wedding of song and narrative in which neither partner marries beneath itself.'[127]

Theatre Workshop's *The Good Soldier Schweik*, a 'comic defence of pacifism'[128] which transferred to the West End in March, was the only home-front offering that approached the Berliner Ensemble's example. For, as ever, the twin weights of the Lord Chamberlain and 'Loamshire' exerted their retarding influence. Rumours began to spread around the theatre world in early spring that the Lord Chamberlain, 'who creates his own precedents, and is accountable to no one',[129] had now refused a licence for a second contemporary American work, Miller's *A View from the Bridge*. Tynan attempted to ascertain the grounds for this decision, but he simply received the customary, infuriating, stonewalling response from St James's Palace:

Dear Sir,

I am directed by the Lord Chamberlain to acknowledge your letter of 15th March [1956], and to inform you that all correspondence between the presenter of a play and his Lordship is considered to be confidential. No comment can, therefore, be made upon the question you ask.

What information the presenter of a play chooses to impart to those enquiring about it is, of course, entirely a matter for him to decide.

Yours faithfully,
Anthony Haw
Assistant Comptroller[130]

Deprived of a 'social playwright' from the west, there was now an even more pressing need, Tynan argued in early April, for someone to bring Brecht's company over to London from the east.[131] There was no other way that he could see to wean both audiences and playwrights alike from the mother's milk of 'Loamshire'.

In mid-March, a prime specimen of the genre, *Tabitha*, provoked another brilliantly witty denunciation. Drawing on all his talent for wry, ironic humour, he sparked across the sky once again, with 'The Gentle Art of Padding':

There is a kind of Englishman who regards all drama that is powerfully exciting as a gross invasion of his privacy; who likes his plays eked out with long stretches of eventless time in which he can meditate undisturbed on the nature of his destiny. For such playgoers *Tabitha* (Duchess) might have been written. At discreet intervals, a 'plot point' is made: between points, the characters brew tea, drink whisky and chat quietly among themselves. During these interludes, I submit, it would be a courtesy on the part of the management to turn on the house lights and serve tea and whisky to the audience, but I suppose one cannot have everything.

With the plot I shall not long detain you. It rears its head only intermittently, signalling for attention like the hamburger stands that enliven one's journey across the baking plains of Arizona. Three impoverished gentlewomen (well played by Janet Barrow, Christine Silver and Marjorie Fielding, though Miss Fielding's aloofness suggested at times that she had not been formally introduced to the rest of the cast) consider murdering their landlady, who has lately poisoned their pet cat, Tabitha. Should she continue to pilfer their liquor, they decide she will find it lethally laced. Squeamishly, they abandon the plan; and yet the landlady is poisoned. How? The answer, like the hamburger stand, is visible far off, so that the last scene is about as suspenseful as the Coronation ceremony.

Anne Leon zestfully plays an *ingénue* of the breed which American columnists are wont to describe as 'veddy veddy British.' The authors, Arnold Ridley and Mary Cathcart Borer (I will repeat that), show an interesting ineptness in the management of entrances and exits, but by these technical matters only specialists are likely to be absorbed. For the most part, the audience is left to its own devices.[132]

This review – provocative, scornful, compelling – is quintessential Tynan. No wonder his readership, young, frustrated and intellectually inquisitive, loved him.

At times in this period, it seemed as if Tynan was a lonely voice. He was certainly the most visible, effective and consistent critic in articulating a sense of protest, but away from the front line significant plans for change were afoot. Following his resignation from the Old Vic Theatre School in May 1951 – a potential but ultimately aborted force for revitalisation – George Devine, the actor and director, had gone freelance, directing five operas at Sadler's Wells and five plays for the Stratford Memorial Theatre between 1951 and 1955. In 1952 he met Tony Richardson, then a young television director, who persuaded Devine to appear in a production of Chekhov's *Curtain Down*.[133] It soon became apparent as their friendship grew that the two men shared a desire to create a programme of intelligent work for a committed public in a way that had only been sporadically possible in the West End up until then because of the conditions of commercial production. Accordingly, they devised a nine-page memorandum that lamented the lack of an outlet for the 'modern movement', and in the fourth draft of 'The Royal Court Theatre Scheme' (dated 13 August 1953), they objected to contemporary drama's status as the poor relation:

Although the major classics are now well catered for by the Old Vic, the Shakespeare Memorial Theatre, Sir John Gielgud's productions, etc, there is no theatre in England which consistently presents the whole range of contemporary drama. Modern movements in music, sculpture, painting, literature, cinema and ballet all have reasonable circulation, but the comparable body of work in the theatre has no outlet . . . [134]

The dynamism of continental cinema was a consistent leitmotif in Tynan's laments. Intriguing innovations were also being introduced in ballet at Covent Garden, and experimental approaches in opera – most noticeably in the hugely controversial avant-garde *Gloriana* written for the coronation by Benjamin Britten, which moved a long way away from the hagiographic 1950s attitude to royalty.

Modern literature was also seen to be developing in a stimulating manner. Stephen Spender, the poet and literary editor of *Encounter*, had noticed in its second edition published in December 1953 a growing resentment of the powers of the 'Establishment' – a 1950s term first used to describe a metropolitan cultural elite: 'There are a good many signs in literary England today of what might be called a rebellion of the Lower Middlebrows . . . It is an uprising against the intellectual trends of Oxford, Cambridge and London, and the influence on literary figures of Paris and Berlin.'[135] John Wain's *Hurry on Down* (1953) and Kingsley Amis's *Lucky Jim* (1954), with their criticisms of the old guard, confirmed this trend, and they were joined by writers such as Philip Larkin, Donald Davies, Robert Conquest, Elizabeth Jennings and D.J. Enright. Although 'The Movement' (a term devised by J.D. Scott in 1954) began to be disavowed by its alleged members in 1957, A. Alvarez's introduction to his 1962 anthology of 1950s poetry – tellingly entitled 'The New Poetry, or Beyond the Gentility Principle'[136] – points out how the anti-romantic, witty, sardonic and occasionally satirical (all words that could be applied to Tynan) tone of Movement poetry quickly set it apart from its immediate poetic predecessors. Whereas T.S. Eliot described himself as 'Anglo-Catholic in religion, royalist in politics and classicist in literature',[137] Alvarez identified the 'pre-dominantly lower middle-class, or Labour, ideal of the Movement'.[138] Long-held values were beginning to be questioned, class assumptions challenged and the cultural consensus brought about by increasing affluence subverted.

In addition to a manifesto for modern theatre, Devine and Richardson's memorandum contained a detailed budget, a proposed repertory, a list of twenty-one neglected writers (with only two being British, emphasising the task of these visionaries) and plans for the formation of a small, permanent company, training courses for actors and writers and a suggested first ten productions. The need for a permanent base was paramount and with this in mind Devine began to negotiate with Alfred Esdaile, a retired music-hall entertainer, who managed the lease for the Royal Court Theatre, located in Sloane Square at the top of the King's Road. Devine wanted a three-year tenancy for the venue, which had seen three brilliant years of activity between 1904 and 1907 when Harley Granville-Barker had helped establish the reputation of Shaw, but negotiations were protracted. A series of developments soon convinced Esdaile that the market value of the theatre could be very high. The Arts Council approved Devine's plan (which lent status rather than money); Devine convinced Anthony Quayle that the Royal Court could become an innovative, contemporary and non-Shakespearian base for the Shakespeare Memorial Theatre (vital if Stratford were to fend off the Old Vic as a possible site for a new National Theatre); and the current production at the Royal Court, Laurier Lister's revue, *Airs on a Shoestring*, proved to be unexpectedly long-running and profitable. Consequently, in the autumn of 1953, Esdaile demanded £70,000 for the tenancy – an impossible sum and a 'bitter blow'[139] to Devine.

The whole project might have foundered there, were it not for the fact that a wholly separate group of people had also been attempting to challenge the West End hegemony. The poet and playwright Ronald Duncan had launched the Taw and Torridge Festival in Devon in 1953, together with the composer Benjamin Britten, J.E. Blacksell and Lord Harewood, with the modest aim of enabling some of its productions to tour other arts festivals and perhaps stop off briefly in London. Duncan's main interest was verse drama, which he saw as the prime catalyst for revitalisation, and this would cause tension within the English Stage Company (ESC) later.

Funding, as ever, was the problem, and Blacksell suggested that a Manchester businessman, Neville Blond, be asked to become the chairman of the newly formed ESC. Blond, a shrewd negotiator, agreed in November 1954 with the proviso that a permanent London base be sought, and he immediately approached Esdaile and persuaded him to grant the ESC the tenancy of another one of his theatres, the Kingsway.

At this point, the ten-man board required an Artistic Director, and Oscar Lewenstein, Esdaile's General Manager and a former member of the Unity Movement, recalled Devine's 1953 project. After a meeting between Duncan and Devine, it was agreed in March 1955 to offer the post to Devine at a salary of £1,500 per annum. To gauge the scale of this, Tynan was shortly to be offered the post of script editor for the declining Ealing Studios – a position he held in addition to his *Observer* post until 1958 – at £2,000 per annum. Devine, content with the proposed salary, only had one stipulation: that Richardson be made his associate director.

The turnaround in Devine's hopes for the project had been as swift as it was unexpected, and the helter-skelter pace continued. It quickly became apparent that the Kingsway was unsuitable, given the cost of repairing the damage to it caused by the Blitz and the difficulty of obtaining planning permission for the work. Ironically, the ESC turned back to the Royal Court, a move facilitated by Esdaile's membership of the board, and Devine was able to hold preliminary auditions in August 1955 for the new company.

The ethos that Devine imbued in the ESC was simple: he believed in the supremacy of the writer; wanted to reposition London theatre away from the West End's disengagement from important contemporary issues; and advocated a clean break with the past in design as well as subject matter. In his 'Thoughts on the Construction of a New Theatre', written in January 1955, he was quite explicit about this latter point – 'What is needed . . . is not adaptability, or a synthesis of the past but for the theatre to create a new milieu in modern terms which will be a completely fresh restatement of the old traditions . . . The stage must have space and air and freedom from the trappings which are used to pretend that it is something which it is not'[140] – and, looking back, he observed that there was no shortage of new issues to complement this new, pared-down form: 'There had been drastic political and social changes all around us; the new Prosperity State was more than suspect, both political parties looked the same. No man or woman of feeling who was not wearing blinkers could not but feel profoundly disturbed.'[141]

Given these sentiments, he was bound to find such an active and effective champion in Tynan, who had independently (and unwittingly) been preparing the ground for the ESC's reception since 1953. Devine's beliefs were further reinforced on the tour of Noguchi's *Lear* between September and December 1955, when he visited the Hebbel Theater in Berlin and met Bertolt Brecht and Helene Weigel. Not only did he secure permission to stage *The Good Person of Sezuan* for his new company, but he was able to gauge the extent to which the Berliner Ensemble had created a 'people's theatre', observing that 'Brecht's theatre is above all a theatre of its time, of its place, and of its nation. This is its exemplary value.'[142] These were views that Tynan could fully endorse.

It would be fallacious to state that subsequent Royal Court practice under Devine was deeply indebted to the Brechtian model (many of Devine's early ideas had been formulated before his contact with Brecht), but in its desire to challenge and disrupt conventional expectations, its determination to question the contemporary cultural hegemony and its artistic and technical innovation, the ESC shared Brecht's aspirations.

In the creation of the company and the formulation of the first season, Devine displayed his renowned pragmatism. By proposing to open with a work by a novelist (very much in vogue in the spring of 1956) – Angus Wilson's *The Mulberry Bush* – and choosing to deploy the commercially risky new work *Look Back in Anger* as the third production (the rights for which he had paid £325), he was able to reassure the more timid members of his board, whilst remaining true to his own hopes for the company. The twenty-two performers that he gathered together for the first season were chosen wth surprisingly little bias towards the Old Vic Theatre School (only Joan Plowright and Sheila Ballantine had served that apprenticeship) because Richardson felt the style of such graduates to be unsuited to realistic theatre.[143] The group was young and vibrant, however, and included Robert Stephens, Kenneth Haigh, Mary Ure and Alan Bates, in addition to Plowright and Ballantine. Devine also strove hard to dissolve the age-old barriers between artistic and technical staff – still very much apparent in the hierarchy of H.M. Tennent Ltd – leading actors into the workshops for parties, when time permitted, or arranging picnics at which company members could mix together.

One further unorthodox (and, of course, prudent) policy was the payment of wages that at their highest represented barely half the West End average. Although star performers were sometimes brought in (Peggy Ashcroft as Shen Te in *The Good Person of Sezuan*, for example), many performers were to speak of the invaluable nature of the Royal Court experience as compensation for the low financial reward, and it is testimony to this process that so many performers were repeatedly drawn back to the ESC. Comparable circumstances had necessitated a similar policy for Lilian Baylis at the Old Vic before the war, with equally beneficial results.

The gulf between the financial scale of a Royal Court production and a blockbuster West End one is apparent when one examines the first year production costs of the H.M. Tennent musical, Leonard Bernstein's *West Side Story*, which opened on 12 December 1958. Whereas the ESC could spare at most £25 per week for its highest paid actors, *West Side Story* devoured £10,755 for scenery, £5,302 for costumes, £5,881 for hotel accommodation and £8,050 in 'Rehearsal Expenses' in its first year alone.[144] Such lavish expenditure on a musical simply seemed to generate more money, however – the profit for the fourth year of the Drury Lane run of *My Fair Lady* (April 1961 to March 1962) was £138,381. How would the ESC be able to compete?

Contrary to received opinion, the story of the company's first season at the Royal Court is not one of instantaneous commercial and popular success following the première of *Look Back in Anger* on 8 May 1956. The début work, Angus Wilson's *The Mulberry Bush*, reflected Ronald Duncan's belief that adaptations of modern novels could stimulate a theatrical revival, but it attracted several disappointing notices following the opening on 2 April. Philip Hope-Wallace of the *Manchester Guardian* spoke of a 'rather diffident start'[145] to the Royal Court project and the *Illustrated London News* echoed many by observing that the play seemed untheatrical and 'was better as a novel'.[146] Tynan's column was dominated by a long, not terribly enthusiastic notice for another adaptation, this time of Graham Greene's *The Power and the Glory*. A much-heralded production, it offered another opportunity for Tynan's favourite young actor, Paul Scofield, to shine but contained a Catholic message that he found difficult to swallow. About *The Mulberry Bush*, the critic was even less enthusiastic. The acting was 'insecure' and 'crepuscular', the plot confusing and even though the play had been improved by rewriting since its previous incarnation in Bristol, it carried little conviction. Tynan was almost elegiac in his final paragraph: 'The English Stage Company embark with this production on a repertory season of new plays. I wish their enterprise too well to embarrass it with further criticism.'[147]

The collective weight of the reviews had a marked effect on the box office and seemed an inauspicious omen. Although the second work to enter the repertory a week later, Arthur Miller's *The Crucible*, was a much finer play and received slightly better notices, ticket sales were equally patchy. To compound the financial difficulties, Devine had been forced during the rehearsal period to reinstate a character he had cut – that of Giles Corey – at the instigation of Miller, who had threatened to have the play withdrawn if his wishes were not followed. Limited funds, expedient casting decisions, simple, inexpensive sets and unpredictable performances by complete newcomers – the *Sunday Express* hailed 'the splendid performance'[148] of Joan Plowright in *The Crucible* – this atmosphere of living on the edge was to permeate the company's first season at the Court.

The play, inspired by the anti-Communist witch-hunts of Senator McCarthy in the early 1950s, had also previously been seen in Bristol (in 1954), and was felt by some to take as a point of reference a political controversy whose time had passed (McCarthy had been thoroughly discredited by 1956). Tynan's second glimpse of the ESC produced an equally brief notice. The play had 'gained in emotional power' now that its political significance had receded, and he had left the theatre 'convinced and impressed'; but the ESC seemed to share the same failings that he had perceived in early productions by Theatre Workshop – erratic performances by members of the company in minor roles. The production was 'spattered with supporting performances of an atrocious debility'[149] and it is easy to imagine the demoralising effect such a phrase would have.

The Crucible played to 45 per cent houses and was thoroughly overshadowed, as were all other productions in the second week of April, by a quintessential H.M. Tennent production, Enid Bagnold's *The Chalk Garden*, which had already proved a big Broadway hit in October 1956. Elaine had been accompanying her husband less and less often to first nights as she concentrated fully on her novel – 'I could not put down my writing and concentrate on other things that now presented themselves as annoying interruptions.'[150] It may have been also that she wanted to draw away a little from a profession that had been so unwelcoming to her. But the first night of *The Chalk Garden*, directed by John Gielgud and starring Edith Evans and Peggy Ashcroft in a Broadway success by the author of the novel *National Velvet*, was an occasion that 'wild horses wouldn't have made [her] miss'.[151]

Star-laden, sumptuously dressed and resolutely unreal (it centred on the hiring of a governess who turns out to have recently served a sentence for murder), it was a celebration of the *ancien régime* and the apotheosis of 'Loamshire'. It unashamedly offered an intimate portrait of an upper-class world and Khrushchev's concurrent visit to London – the first visit of a Soviet leader to Britain – neatly highlighted the dichotomy between a Tennent show and the outside world. Even at a time of growing East–West tension, however, there were moments of comedy from a Binkie Beaumont-inspired light farce. On a visit to Oxford, Khrushchev, having watched the choir singing on Magdalen tower, was perplexed as to its purpose; Epstein's sculpture of Lazarus in New College Chapel was dismissed as 'decadent rubbish'; and when Bevan and George Brown rebuked him for the treatment of political dissidents in the Soviet Union he observed that 'if these are your socialists, I am for the Conservatives'.[152]

Tynan's 'Glorious Sunset' struck an appropriately retrospective tone, celebrating a glorious moment but predicting that its era was over:

> On Wednesday night a wonder happened: the West End theatre justified its existence. One had thought it an anachronism, wilfully preserving a formal, patrician acting style for which the modern drama had no use, a style as remote from reality as a troop of cavalry in an age of turbo-jets. One was shamefully wrong. On Wednesday night, superbly caparisoned, the cavalry went into action and gave a display of theatrical equitation which silenced all the grumblers. This engagement completed, the brigade may have to be disbanded. But at least it went out with a flourish, its banners resplendent in the last rays of the sun.

The play was a triumph – it 'may well be the finest artificial comedy to have flowed from an English (as opposed to an Irish) pen since the death of Congreve' – and the ensemble acting, suavely directed by Gielgud, achieved what only English actors can do, namely reproducing 'in the theatre the spirited elegance of a Mozart quintet'.[153] The playwright was ecstatic at this unexpected endorsement – 'I wish I could make you feel the sense of glory you communicated to me. All the hard work, the long years (six now) were suddenly marshalled, stood in a row and crowned. "On Wednesday night a wonder happened." What could one think, dream . . . of such an opening . . . Pierre came galloping out here bringing me the Observer on Saturday evening. The pleasure on reading was so violent it has taken me days to get every corner out of it'.[154] The Tynans subsequently spent a weekend at Bagnold's house in Rottingdean, near Brighton. Supporters of the young ESC, however, were mortified at the indifference of the critic most likely to champion their cause to their own exertions, even if they privately acknowledged that *The Mulberry Bush* reflected very different dramatic priorities from those which Devine truly wished to advance. In a sign of the significance with which the young guard viewed Tynan's powers of advocacy, Lindsay Anderson, the documentary film director, who from 1957 would become a key member of Devine's team, swiftly wrote to Tynan at the end of April to register his dismay:

> On Friday evening I disregarded your advice and went to see *The Mulberry Bush* at the Court . . . I was somehow so moved by the evening, given a ray of hope in our present theatrical desert, not exactly by the *achievement* of it but by the endeavour of it, that I felt I just had to write to you, and take the risk of seeming impossibly self-righteous and interfering, and reproach you for wanting to

put me off, by your notice, supporting this venture. I don't think I'm personally biased *towards* it any more than I can believe that you are personally biased *against* it: my opinion of George Devine is not very high, and I thought his *Lear* quite monstrous . . . But there is something here, and a young company of (I should have thought) promise, and a quite extraordinary sense of purpose, and it seems to me nothing less than criminal to dwarf their debut with long pieces of approbation for presentations by H.M. Tennent Ltd.

Anderson has clearly missed the irony of 'Glorious Sunset', but there is an understandable element of bitter disappointment in his rebuke. The final, dismissive paragraph of *The Mulberry Bush* review had really riled him, and he believed that such was the power of Tynan's pen that it threatened to stifle the company's chances at birth. His passionate defence of the ESC is infectious:

I am sure you absolutely *cannot* have intended it – but such remarks as 'I wish this company too well to embarrass it with further criticism' can only give a hypothetical impression of someone who does not wish well to a company at all. It's the sort of thing you may think to yourself, in not further criticising them, but if you say it, it merely gives the impression of nameless horrors in store for anyone rash enough to visit the Royal Court. But what will they really find?

At the least a play which rashly sets out, inexperienced and even at times dramatically inept, to tackle a subject of social and moral and human significance, with relevance to contemporary life, and which never cheapens or seeks to evade, and which uses grown-up language, and which has in it all the time a transparently sincere belief in the importance of human beings. And this gives it (to me) a dignity very strange in the London theatre, and there is *no one* I would discourage from seeing it . . . Perhaps you will say that the English Stage Company seems to you so bad that the sooner it's finished off the better . . . But I would find this difficult to square with your statement that you wish it well, or indeed with the position which you have so finely taken and maintained all the time you have been occupying your present influential position . . . Let me say no more that as an enthusiastic reader and supporter of yours I was shocked by the *meanness*, above all by the spiteful edge with which you have discouraged support for this season.

Perhaps mindful of the fact that there were more plays to come at which the *Observer* critic would doubtless be present, Anderson's concluding comments are more conciliatory and almost shamefaced at the effusiveness of his views: 'Well, I won't go on. Excuse me for writing so much anyway. Take it as a tribute to the esteem in which I hold you; and also because I found that evening at the Court so moving – and so vulnerable that I would have felt some sort of a traitor if I hadn't raised a supporting arm.'[155] Did the passion of his commitment and the veracity of his analysis influence Tynan in any way when he came to write his famous review of the ailing company's third offering in May?

A brief interlude in New York followed this spat, and from across the Atlantic, *The Chalk Garden*'s gilt edges – it was to run for one month short of two years – seemed unable to disguise the continuing thinness of the London season. American audiences enjoyed 'seeing themselves dramatised' whereas the British were content with witnessing 'aliens and antiques'.[156] Musicals in New York showed how this genre could thrive, whereas in Britain it was stunted. With half the number of theatres of London, Broadway managed to cover a broader range of plays, and 'when it borrows from Europe, it often improves what it borrows'.[157] *My Fair Lady*, *The Diary of Anne Frank* ('clever, right-thinking but somehow obscene') and a *Waiting for Godot* with the lion from *The Wizard of Oz*, Bert Lahr, testified to the diversity of productions on offer. The US was now surpassing Germany as Tynan's model for vibrancy. Would Britain ever be able to keep up?

The third play to enter the repertory of the ailing ESC was to be directed by Tony Richardson and needed to be a success. In August 1955, Devine had placed an advert in the *Stage*, the house newspaper for the theatre profession, stating that the ESC had been formed with the object of producing new plays, and particularly new plays by new writers. John Osborne, an intermittently employed actor then living on a houseboat tied up on the River Thames near Chiswick, had in June completed the script of a play (variously titled 'Farewell to Anger', 'Angry Man', 'Man in a Rage', 'Bargain from Strength', 'Close the Cage Behind You' and 'My Blood is a Mile High'),[158] which he had tried so far unsuccessfully to place with several agents. Kitty Black, for example, then the principal play reader for the literary agents Curtis Brown and, significantly, a previous reader for Tennent's, prefaced her rejection with the comment that 'I feel like the headmistress of a large school in which I have to tell its most promising pupil that he must think again.'[159] *Look Back in Anger*, however promising, simply did not fit the Tennent formula.

Within days of sending the script in response to the advert, Osborne received a letter from the ESC offering £25 to secure an option on the play and suggesting a meeting on the houseboat between Devine and the playwright. Over 750 scripts had been sent to Devine and Richardson, but Osborne's was the only one that intrigued both the directors: '[George] read three pages and then brought it upstairs. "Look at this", he said. "This might be interesting".'[160]

In an era in which it was considered slightly daring to use garlic, travel abroad or wear a duffel coat, it was not surprising that many of *Look Back in Anger*'s unorthodoxies, which admittedly can appear tame, jejune and even sexist fifty years on, pro-

voked equal measures of admiration and disapproval. The opening curtain rose on
an unfamiliar scene of cramped, suburban shabbiness (gone was the uncluttered stage
of the first two productions), with Alison Porter performing the most mundane of
tasks – the ironing. One contemporary witness, Bernice Coupe, remembered that the
first shock of the evening was the depressing nature of the Porters' flat, and she was
particularly disconcerted by the sight of the ironing-board to which Alison seemed
chained – an object which belonged in the home and certainly not the theatre.[161]

Another early surprise was the fact that the actors were not articulating in
politely strangulated accents, but speaking in a variety of regional tones that had
previously been the preserve of maids, bobbies and artisans. A recording of Richard
Burton playing the film role of Jimmy Porter still has the power to shock with the
violent intensity of the delivery, the un-mellifluous rasp of the accusations and the
unpredictability of his frequent outbursts. For many people in the 1950s, when a
well formulated diction was proof positive of intelligence, Jimmy Porter's combination of volubility, accent and intellectual prowess was very hard to accept, and
this challenge to contemporary assumptions was compounded by the sheer irreverence of many of Jimmy's attacks. Whether the target was J.B. Priestley, likened to
Alison's Daddy, 'still casting well-fed glances back to the Edwardian twilight from
his comfortable, disenfranchised wilderness',[162] or senseless, upper-class ambition,
symbolised by Alison's brother, variously described as 'the straight-backed, chin-
less wonder from Sandhurst' and 'the platitude from Outer Space',[163] it was difficult to perceive which aspect of Jimmy's critique should be construed as the more
unorthodox: the passionately and implicitly left-wing nature of the attack, or the
confident and riveting new idiom in which it was formulated. To many, in particular the young and university-educated, this depiction of a reinvigorated, eloquent
liberal conscience at work was the revelation they had been waiting for. Frustrated
by the mental atrophy that they discerned in British society, they were thrilled by
Jimmy Porter's clarion call to rebellion, be it in his exasperation at British docility
('Nobody thinks, nobody cares. No beliefs, no convictions and no enthusiasm'),[164]
his dangerously radical toying with taboos –

> I've just about had enough of this 'expense of spirit' lark, as far as women are
> concerned. Honestly, it's enough to make you become a scoutmaster or some-
> thing, isn't it? Sometimes I almost envy old Gide and the Greek Chorus boys.
> Oh, I'm not saying that it mustn't be hell for them a lot of the time. But, at least,
> they do seem to have a cause[165]

– or his central complaint, that intelligent people such as himself had no opportunity to contribute to society:

There aren't any good, brave causes left. If the big bang does come, and we all get killed off, it won't be in aid of the old-fashioned, grand design. It'll just be for the Brave-New-nothing-very-much-thank-you. About as pointless and inglorious as stepping in front of a bus. No, there's nothing left for it, me boy, but to let yourself be butchered by the women.[166]

The hyperbole of the last sentence is typical of Osborne's technique: a serious point is pricked by exaggeration, raising the question as to whether there is more to the work than a passionate denunciation of society's failings. This fine linguistic distinction was lost by many in the critical reaction that greeted a play that broke with the timidity of the recent British theatrical past. The journalist Edward Pearce, then a young student, remembers how disappointing the reality of post-war life had proved to be with the onset of 1950s affluence and consensus, compared to the excitement of the pre-war causes he had read about in his textbooks. Everything had 'settled down into a blancmange-like existence of common sense, tolerance and half-a-grain change'; he, too, longed for a good, brave cause 'preferably not to die for, but to get paid for' – as well as the therapy of conflict.[167] *Look Back in Anger* was significant because it represented such a break from the past and suggested that the old world was now over. Even Rattigan, in yet another personally disastrous comment, inadvertently recognised this. Confronted by a reporter from the *Daily Express* during the interval of the first night, he claimed that Osborne was saying 'Look, Ma, I'm not Terence Rattigan'[168] (although he wrote to Devine the following day to point out that his 'rather feeble wisecrack' had simply been intended to point out that Osborne 'was being a little self-conscious about his modernism').[169] The conventionality of the play's form merely accentuated the revolutionary nature of its content – the speaking from the heart, the escape from emotional inhibition – and it was the generational conflict that the work seemed to incite that attracted most interest after its première on 8 May 1956.

The first-night reaction to *Look Back in Anger* contained in the daily newspapers was mixed. Patrick Gibbs of the *Daily Telegraph* claimed that Jimmy Porter was 'a character who should have gone to a psychiatrist rather than have come to a dramatist',[170] whereas John Barber of the *Daily Express* was attracted to the work because the hero was 'like thousands of young Londoners today': the play itself was 'intense, angry, feverish, undisciplined. It is even crazy. But it is young, young, young.'[171] Colin Wilson voiced a common view when he wrote in the *Daily Mail* that Osborne was a good dramatist who had somehow written the wrong play,[172] and even Milton Shulman of the *Evening Standard*, who was unable to share John Barber's enthusiasm, feeling that the work was a 'self-pitying snivel' and a failure because of 'its inability to be coherent about its despair', conceded that 'When he stops being angry – or when he lets us in on what he is angry about – he may write a very good play.'[173] Good try, better luck next time, seemed to be the general consensus. Reviews such as these, which considered the work to be significant, but not quite complete, were not good 'box office'.

There is a pertinent irony to the 'desultory talk of being "saved by the Sundays"'[174] which, Osborne relates in the second volume of his autobiography, *Almost a Gentleman*, was passing around the ESC after the appearance of the daily reviews, since the play itself in the opening scene presented the Sunday newspapers as symptoms of the prevailing intellectual paralysis. Osborne recalls that at the time he considered both the *Sunday Times* and the *Observer* to equally obsessed with anything French (clearly alluding to Hobson's Francomania):

> For as long as I could remember the literary and academic classes seemed to have been tyrannised by the French. The 'posh papers' every Sunday blubbered with self-abasement in the face of the bombast of the French language and its absurd posture as the torch-bearer of Logic, which apparently was something to which no one in these islands had access. Certain writers gave the impression that it was downright indelicate to write in English at all, which is why the *Sunday Times* and the *Observer* were peppered with italics until they sometimes looked like linguistic lace curtains.[175]

With this dim view of the intellectual judgement of the 'posh papers', it was a rather desperate exercise in keeping the company's hopes up to have expected the salvation of so contemporary a play from such devotees of the French, although as successive commentators have pointed out, there is a latent streak of respect for certain English institutions and an element of nostalgia running through this ostensibly revolutionary work. Osborne himself, for all his deprecation of these two papers, was certainly interested in their views when he made his way to a newsagent in Mortlake the following Sunday and sat reading their verdicts on 'a corporation bench in the bright May early morning sunshine'.[176] He was convinced before he had read them that the previous evening's performance of *Look Back in Anger* was destined to be its last.

'It is the best young play of its decade' (Kenneth Tynan, 'The Voice of the Young', *Observer*, 13 May 1956); 'he is a writer of outstanding promise' (Harold Hobson, 'A New Author', *Sunday Times*, 13 May 1956). Cheerfully brushing aside Jimmy Porter's opening critique of their respective publications – Hobson perceptively wrote that the hero possesses 'a sort of admiring hatred' of the 'posh papers' – the two most influential theatre critics in Britain were united in their admiration for this third production of the ESC. It was a momentous event. Tynan's joy at discovering a work that was the antithesis of the much-loathed Loamshire play was unconfined, and – fired by the realisation that here was a work that embodied many of the attitudes that he had been expressing himself throughout his career as a critic – he created in 'The Voice of the Young' one of the most famous theatre reviews in history:

'They are scum,' says Mr Maugham's famous verdict on the class of State-aided university students to which Kingsley Amis's 'Lucky Jim' belongs: and since Mr Maugham seldom says anything controversial or uncertain of wide acceptance, his opinion must clearly be that of many. Those who share it had better stay well away from John Osborne's *Look Back in Anger* (Royal Court), which is all scum and a mile wide.

Its hero, a provincial graduate who runs a sweet-stall, has already been summed-up in print as 'a young pup' and it's not hard to see why. What with his flair for introspection, his gift for ribald parody, his excoriating candour, his contempt for 'phoneyness', his weakness for soliloquy and his desperate conviction that the time is out of joint, Jimmy Porter is the completest young pup in our literature since Hamlet, Prince of Denmark. His wife, whose Anglo-Indian parents resent him, is persuaded by an actress friend to leave him: Jimmy's prompt response is to go to bed with the actress. Mr Osborne's picture of a certain kind of modern marriage is hilariously accurate: he shows two attractive young animals engaged in competitive martyrdom, each with its teeth sunk deep in the other's neck, and each reluctant to break the clinch for fear of bleeding to death.

The fact that he writes with charity has led many critics into the trap of supposing Mr Osborne's sympathies are wholly with Jimmy. Nothing could be more false. Jimmy is simply and abundantly alive; that rarest of dramatic phenomena, the act of original creation, has taken place; and those who carp were better silent. Is Jimmy's anger justified? Why doesn't he *do* something? These questions might be relevant if the character had failed to come to life: in the presence of such evident and blazing vitality, I marvel at the pedantry that could ask them. Why don't Chekhov's people *do* something? Is the sun justified in scorching us? There will be time enough to debate Mr Osborne's moral position when he has written a few more plays. In the present one he certainly goes off the deep end, but I cannot regard this as a vice in a theatre that seldom ventures more than a toe in the water.

Look Back in Anger presents post-war youth as it really is, with special emphasis on the non-U intelligentsia who live in bed-sitters and divide the Sunday papers into two groups, 'posh' and 'wet'. To have done this at all would be a signal achievement; to have done it in a first play is a minor miracle. All the qualities are there; qualities one had despaired of ever seeing on the stage – the drift towards anarchy, the instinctive leftishness, the automatic rejection of 'official' attitudes, the surrealist sense of humour (Jimmy describes a pansy friend of his as 'a female Emily Brontë'), the casual promiscuity, the sense of lacking a crusade worth fighting for and, underlying all these, the determination that no one who dies shall go unmourned.

One cannot imagine Jimmy Porter listening with a straight face to speeches about our inalienable right to flog Cypriot schoolboys. You could never mobilise him and his kind into a lynching mob, since the art he lives for, jazz, was invented by Negroes; and if you gave him a razor, he would do nothing with it but shave. The Porters of our time deplore the tyranny of 'good taste' and refuse to accept 'emotional' as a term of abuse; they are classless and they are also leaderless. Mr Osborne is their first spokesman in the London theatre. He has been lucky in his sponsors (the English Stage Company), his director (Tony Richardson), and his interpreters: Mary Ure, Helena Hughes and Alan Bates give fresh and unforced performances, and in the taxing central role Kenneth Haigh never puts a foot wrong.

That the play needs changes I do not deny: it is twenty minutes too long, and not even Mr Haigh's bravura could blind me to the painful whimsy of the final reconciliation scene. I agree that *Look Back in Anger* is likely to remain a minority taste. What matters, however, is the size of the minority. I estimate it at roughly 6,733,000, which is the number of people in this country between the ages of twenty and thirty. And this figure will doubtless be swelled by refugees from other age-groups who are curious to know precisely what the contemporary young pup is thinking and feeling. I doubt if I could love anyone who did not wish to see *Look Back in Anger*. It is the best young play of its decade.[177]

Hugely intelligent, and continually searching for satisfying outlets for his creativity; repulsed by the 'phoneyness' of society and the insularity of Britain; instinctively left-wing, but alienated from party politics by the flabby drive for consensus; desperate to question the sacred cows of morality, tradition and class; locked in a stressful marriage, but unsure whether to leave; treated with suspicion by his wife's parents who fail to understand him; confined by the dictates of monogamy and possibly unfulfilled in his sexual needs – Jimmy Porter is in many ways the mirror image of Kenneth Tynan. The traditional analysis of this review centres on the brilliance of the gripping, provocative opening and the heart on sleeve endorsement at the end. But there is a powerful biographical thread running through the notice. *Look Back in Anger* was the breakthrough play for Tynan, offering a vibrant alternative model for British play-writing that had not been seen before, but his appreciation was stirred by his personal empathy with its main protagonist.

The notice also demonstrated how Tynan had finally discovered the philosophy behind his critical approach. Gone was the laboured conceit of the key fitting the lock of his first *Observer* review in September 1954; he now realised that as a crusader for change he had a role that transcended the present. At the end of this momentous season, he put this philosophy into words:

What counts [about critics] is not their opinion, but the art with which it is expressed. They differ from the novelist only in that they take as their subject-matter life rehearsed, instead of life unrehearsed. The subtlest and best-informed of men will still be a bad critic if his style is bad. It is irrelevant whether his opinion is 'right' or 'wrong': I learn far more from G.B.S. when he is wrong than from Clement Scott when he is right. The true critic cares little for here and now. The last thing he bothers about is the man who will read him first. His real rendezvous is with posterity. His review is better addressed to the future; to people thirty years hence who may wonder exactly what it felt like to be in a certain playhouse on a certain distant night. The critic is their eye-witness; and he has done his job if he evokes, precisely and with all his prejudices clearly charted, the state of his mind after the performance has impinged on it. It matters little if he leans towards 'absolutism' or 'relativism', towards G.B.S. or Hazlitt. He will find readers if, and only if, he writes clearly and gaily and truly; if he regards himself as a specially treated mirror recording a unique and unrepeatable event.[178]

Harold Hobson had always felt that, as a trained historian, he had the dual function of being both a witness and a judge in the theatre. The former was by far the more important role. Tynan, too, believed that he should be 'writing for posterity'. That he had helped create theatre history with the brilliance of this review would only emerge later.

Hobson, the Romantic critic, interested in theatricality and emotional power, naturally took a different line from Tynan. 'A New Author' begins with a characteristic piece of Hobson rhetoric, mixing apparent dismissal with vivid exaggeration and then enthusiastic encouragement: 'Mr John Osborne, the author of *Look Back in Anger*, is a writer who at present does not know what he is doing. He seems to think that he is crashing through the world with deadly right uppercuts, whereas all the time it is his unguarded left that is doing the damage. Though the blinkers still obscure his vision, he is a writer of outstanding promise, and the English Stage Company are to be congratulated on having discovered him.' Although Hobson is not as enraptured as Tynan by the depiction of young talent frustrated by conservative attitudes, he locates the promise of Osborne in the depiction of the relationship between Jimmy and Alison, which 'is controlled by a fine and sympathetic imagination, and is superbly played, in long passages of pain and silence, by Mary Ure'. He continues:

Alison Porter is a subsidiary in *Look Back in Anger*; it is not she, but her husband, who throws into the past a maleficent gaze. But it is her endurance, futile endeavour to escape, and her final breakdown which are the truly moving part. The dramatist that is in Mr Osborne comes in the end to feel this himself, and it is to Alison, when at last she makes her heart-broken, grovelling, yet peace-securing submission, to whom the final big speech is given.

Hobson considers this attempt at marital reconciliation the fundamental moment in the play: 'Here is in its way a kind of victory; and because it is a kind of victory, it releases instead of depressing the spirit. To know when to give up the struggle, to realise when the battle no longer counts, this also is a sort of triumph.' This con-centration on a single moment of emotional power, the preference for insidious feel-ing as opposed to overt didacticism, and the delight in the portrayal of marital tenderness (no matter how oblique) is archetypal Hobson. It also explains why his appeal lay with the over-thirties, and Tynan's with the under – and, as he memorably put it, 'refugees from other age-groups'.

The *Look Back in Anger* phenomenon derived momentum from many sources. Firstly, there was the almost instantaneous identification by the media of a group of young, committed writers dedicated to challenging the status quo, handily (and somewhat artificially) gathered together under the title 'Angry Young Men' (brilliantly coined by a Royal Court publicist after Leslie Allen Paul's 1951 auto-biography, *Angry Young Man*). The public aggressiveness of this group, either energetically berating journalists or denigrating previously unsullied icons, as when Osborne likened the royal family to a gold tooth in a mouthful of decay,[179] helped keep the group in the public eye. Allied to this was the utilisation of other cultural movements by young people as ways of disrupting consensus and challenging notions of respect (with all its class and generational implications). The most impor-tant of these was rock and roll (with its anthem, Bill Haley's 'Rock around the Clock', leading to riots in cinemas on its release in May 1955), followed by fashion (teddy boys appropriating the formerly sedate Edwardian jacket as their call-sign and adding drainpipe trousers as a visible statement of independence) and alterna-tive, irreverent comedy (typified by the television shows of Tony Hancock, which explored suburban angst, a topic previously considered too mundane for mirth). Literary culture, too, soon became, in the words of Stephen Lacey, 'imbued with a sense of loss, of disillusion with the immediate past and a loathing of the material priorities of a newly affluent Britain',[180] emotions that *Look Back in Anger* was per-ceived to have unleashed. And political engagement – outside of the party struc-ture – soon became appealing again with the fiasco of Suez and the growth of the Campaign for Nuclear Disarmament. There was now also the possibility that a new, untapped audience might decide to turn to drama, and a relief that, at last, an indigenous playwright had written something that might start to challenge the notion that only continental Europeans and the Americans could write stimulating works on contemporary dilemmas.

The phenomenon was not instantaneous. Tynan's review was tremendous publicity, but it was not until the BBC televised an extract on 16 October 1956, viewed by an estimated 5 million people, that box-office takings dramatically increased from £900 to £1,700 per week.[181] On 28 November, the play was televised at peak viewing by ITV, helping to cement its notoriety and giving the widest possible publicity to the *raison d'être* of the ESC.

From this moment on, the theatre scene began to look up as far as Tynan was concerned. The very next week he was able to announce with some satisfaction that the producer Peter Daubeny would be bringing the Berliner Ensemble to London in August. 'So ends a long battle,' he wrote, 'and for a while we can all relax'.[182] The last thing he did personally was relax, however. Firstly, he took up the post of script-editor for Ealing Studios at the princely salary of £2,000 per annum. The offer had come about after Sir Michael Balcon, who ran the organisation, had read 'Tight Little Studio', an article Tynan had written for *Harper's* magazine about the organisation the previous August. Ealing was famous for its realistic post-war films, such as *Dance Hall*, as well as comedies such as *Passport to Pimlico* and *The Ladykillers*, but since the growth in popularity of television, stimulated by the transmission of the coronation, it had been struggling. Tynan's appointment was part of a wider strategy to refocus its output on dramas with a documentary background and comedies about ordinary people.

The job involved 'vetting scripts, giving advice, and having ideas',[183] and Tynan assured his editor, David Astor, that it would not interfere with his first priority – writing for the *Observer* – and would stimulate him considerably. Astor agreed. Alas, it was not to prove a mutually beneficial liaison. In the two years that he remained in post only one of his projects was seen through to completion – *Nowhere to Go* – and his brush with cinema production was as unsatisfying as his contact with theatre directing. Ealing Studios ceased production entirely in 1957.

Secondly, his private life continued to become ever more complicated. While Elaine was away in the States in the early summer, Tynan began a brief relationship with the novelist Elizabeth Jane Howard, whose popular work, *The Long View*, had just been published. It was a physical affair that ended when Elaine returned, but Howard, in an interview with Kathleen Tynan, revealed that she had found Tynan extremely attractive, resolutely living in the present, with no time for reflection and sexually insecure.[184] This probably meant his continual, but frequently repressed, need for sado-masochism, rather than a desire to experiment with partners of his own sex. In a diary entry in 1976, Tynan confided that he regarded it 'as a gap in me that I've never been turned on by the sight, touch or thought of a man'.[185]

And thirdly, he moved swiftly to help consolidate the gains achieved by *Look Back in Anger*'s appearance and after-life. Theatre Workshop's presentation of Brendan Behan's *The Quare Fellow* was another piece of social realism (which took up the progressive cause of the abolition of capital punishment) that provided particular satisfaction. Tynan passed on overheard conversation from the audience (a tactic he would use several times over the next two years):

> 'Bloody sparklin' dialogue,' said a pensive Irishman during the first interval of *The Quare Fellow* (Theatre Royal, Stratford East) and sparkle, by any standards, it amazingly did. The English hoard words like misers; the Irish spend them like sailors; and, in Brendan Behan's tremendous new play language is out on a spree, ribald, dauntless and spoiling for a fight . . .

He expressed admiration for the structure of the play (as much the result of Joan Littlewood's work as of Brendan Behan's):

> . . . far from trying to gain sympathy for the condemned man, an axe-murderer known as 'the quare fellow,' Mr Behan keeps him off-stage throughout the action. All he shows us is the effect on the prison population of the knowledge that one of their number is about to be ritually strangled.
>
> There are no tears in the story, no complaints, no visible agonies; nor is there even suspense, since we know from the outset that there will be no reprieve. Mr Behan's only weapon is a gay, fatalistic gallows-humour, and he wields it with the mastery of Ned Kelly, the Australian bandit, whose last words, as the noose encircled his neck, were: 'Such is life' . . . The tension is intolerable, but it is we who feel it, not the people in the play. We are moved precisely in the degree that they are not. With superb dramatic tact, the tragedy is concealed beneath layer after layer of rough comedy . . .

And he offered the opinion that – the inaudibility of the cast notwithstanding – the play's deliberate alignment with the MP Sydney Silverman's long campaign to abolish hanging (not finally successful until 1965) would help ensure its longevity:

> The curtain falls but not before we have heard the swing and jerk of the drop. I left the theatre feeling overwhelmed and thanking all the powers that be for Sydney Silverman . . . Miss Littlewood's cast knows perfectly what it is doing. She must now devote a few rehearsals to making sure that we can understand precisely what it is saying. That done, *The Quare Fellow* will belong not only in such transient records as this, but in theatrical history.[186]

Of particular pleasure was the failure of a revival of a play written by that high priest of upper-middle-class taste and dogged elitism, T.S. Eliot. Tynan had always loathed what he considered to be his sterile versification that throttled the life out of drama. Despite the appearance of the much-appreciated Paul Scofield in *The Family Reunion*, the old guard appeared to be faltering just at the point when the new wave was beginning to come to life. Tynan administered a crushing *coup de grâce*:

> The play contains two splendid jokes (in prose), and many passages of bony analytic precision. It also demonstrates Mr Eliot's gift for imposing a sudden chill, as ghosts are said to do when they enter a room. Images of vague nursery dread insistently recur: the attraction of the dark passage, the noxious smell untraceable in the drain, the evil in the dark closet (which was really, as Dylan Thomas used impiously to say, the school boot-cupboard), the cerebral acne in the monastery garden, the agony in the dark, the agony in the curtained bedroom, the chilly pretences in the silent bedroom (one of these phrases is out of place. Entries by Ash Wednesday). But though Mr Eliot can always lower the dramatic temperature, he can never raise it; and this is why the theatre, an impure assembly that longs for strong emotions, must ultimately reject him. He is glacial, a theatrical Jack Frost: at the first breath of warmth, he melts and vanishes.[187]

Such was Tynan's optimism that his customary end of season report, this year entitled 'Hindsight View', showed unusual energy:

> . . . My usual practice, at the end of a theatre season, is to write a jeremiad, auction off all the unused complimentary tickets on my desk, and then depart for the south, there to brood about Bert Brecht. This year I feel I owe the season an apology . . . for the first time I can remember, there are more good new-fangled plays running than bad-fangled plays . . . Suddenly in the second week of April, the spring offensive began with Enid Bagnold's hand-made, fully-fashioned high comedy, *The Chalk Garden* . . . and the Royal Court's new management gave us Arthur Miller's *The Crucible* and then provoked an historic fissure of critical opinion by staging John Osborne's *Look Back in Anger* . . . We cannot yet speak of anything as cohesive as a 'movement'. But we can at least establish what these new plays are *not*. None of them is a tragedy; none is a farce; none is a 'mood' play; and none (except by implication Mr Behan's) is propaganda. What Messrs. Osborne, Dennis, Hastings and Behan have in common – widely disparate as they are in style and background – is an attitude towards life. They see through it; they detest its shams; and they express what they see with a candour at once wry and savage. Their mistrust of authority is coupled with a passionate respect for the sanctity of the individual. Their sense of humour is too strong to permit them to

Chapter 4 *1956–58: Writing for Posterity*

Tynan's good fortune was that he was writing at a time when British theatre was undergoing its greatest renaissance since the 1600s. British theatre's good fortune was that Tynan was a critic skilful, perceptive and young enough to act as a witness, cheerleader and judge. For many, he became synonymous with the new wave that he had spent the last three years advocating, and he was now uniquely placed to interpret the diversity that suddenly flourished on the London stage. The final two seasons of his first stint at the *Observer* – 1956/7 and 1957/8 – were two of the most exciting in the history of theatre and Tynan's achievement is that he made them live for a contemporary readership, only a tiny proportion of whom could have experienced at first hand the events he was describing. His reviews have also served to delight subsequent generations eager to sense the vibrancy of this period.

In 1956, the Tynans' summer holiday in Spain was its ritual mixture of celebrity encounters, bullfights and marital unhappiness. This time they stayed at first with their New York friends, John and Sue Marquand, who had a villa near Barcelona, and a mordant Tynan speculated quite openly that he might leave home and make a clean break of things.[1] Nobody believed that he had the willpower to do anything so decisive, however, least of all Elaine, who felt that her emotions were 'a battleground between "Now I can love him" and "Now I must hate him"'.[2] At the Hotel Colon in Barcelona they met up with Tennessee Williams, who took them twice to the ballet, where they saw a South American company dance an all-male *Swan Lake*. Elaine realised that a party of overwhelmingly male guests and a beach in San Sebastian, where virtually no women were present, represented the playwright's attempt to introduce them to the region's gay community.[3] Moving south, they stopped off at Málaga and called in at the house of two wealthy Americans, Bill and Anne Davis, where Cyril Connolly was chief house-guest. Although he despised bullfighting, and preferred to lounge around the pool 'wearing an unbe-coming fake leopard-skin bathing suit',[4] the author of *The Unquiet Grave*, chief book reviewer of the *Sunday Times* and 1950s 'thinker' quickly struck up a friendship with his two fellow writers – a friendship that Elaine and he would take further over the coming months.

While they were in Spain, two pieces of news came through that were to have a significant impact. The first was the death of Brecht; the second was the nationalisa-tion of the Suez Canal by the Egyptian government on 25 July. Both developments were to have far-reaching consequences for British theatre. The British government had been expecting a crisis to develop in Egypt for several months. Ever since Eden, as Foreign Secretary, had had a disastrous meeting with President Nasser in 1955 (at which Eden had spent much of the time recalling his days at Christ Church, Oxford where he read Oriental languages), he had viewed the Egyptian leader as a quasi-Hitler. Believing that Nasser had expansionist ambitions in the region, Prime Minis-ter Eden was now obsessed with his belief that Nasser intended to flirt with Communism. In October 1955, he told the ambassador in Cairo, Sir Humphrey Trevelyan, that 'Russia has put us on notice that she intends to open a third front in the Cold War, this time in the Middle East',[5] and from early 1956 the British govern-ment began a covert operation to destabilise the Egyptian leader. Friendly relations with Egypt were 'no longer possible', Eden told his cabinet and he urged the US to join forces with Britain and withdraw financial support for the construction of the Aswan dam. On 19 July the US Secretary of State, John Foster Dulles, authorised the cessation of aid (further forcing the Egyptians to look East for support) and, in retaliation, Nasser announced on 25 July the nationalisation of the Suez Canal – the symbolic umbilical cord between Britain and its Empire.

Eden was apoplectic, but in a bind. Under international law, it would be difficult to argue that this was an illegal action, so the initial public spin was that an inter-national asset was at grave risk from an incompetent administration not fit to run such a vital waterway. Privately, the government was bent on military action. On 27 July, the Chiefs of Staff were asked to begin preparations for a landing; Britain's fleet was put on war alert; and the temperature was raised further when the Labour leader, Hugh Gaitskell, alluded in the House of Commons to the appeasement of dictators in the 1930s – a matter of acute sensitivity to Conservatives.

During August secret military preparations were undertaken for an intervention by 15 September, whilst publicly a conference of 'Canal Users' was convened by Eden and Dulles in London. But it was apparent by early September that any mil-itary action was likely to have severe ramifications both at home and abroad. Doubts began to be heard within government about the advisability of including the French in any proposed action – militarily essential, but politically problematic, given the hostility in the Arab world to their actions in Algeria. Cabinet ministers, such as Monckton and Salisbury, a newly invigorated Labour Party, and large sections of the press believed that any action should be taken under the auspices of the United Nations. And, most critically of all, dissent came from the highest quarters in the US. With a Presidential election looming, Dulles (who loathed British colonialism) and Eisenhower (who felt that any conflict would be destabilising) were implacably opposed to a military campaign. As if all of this was not bad enough, there were immense logistical challenges involved in invading Egypt from bases in Cyprus 300 miles away. September was a jittery month for the country at large, as the government's options were energetically discussed.

It was against this unpropitious background that the Berliner Ensemble made its first London appearance. A theatre group from the rabidly Communist East Germany was going to have a difficult reception at the best of times: with talk about possible Soviet expansion in the Middle East on everybody's lips, there was little prospect of a hearty welcome from the press. The British government had even considered refusing to grant the group entry visas, since it had no diplomatic relations with East Germany, but decided at the last minute that it was better to allow them exposure to the superior Western way of life. The group arrived without the messiah that Tynan had long heralded. Brecht had been ill for several months. A combination of overwork in the rehearsal room, continual rewriting and repeated bouts of influenza had greatly weakened him. During the summer of 1956, he was engaged on an intriguing project – an adaptation of Beckett's *Waiting for Godot* – but a further decline in his health meant that he only reached page 33 of the German translation. (The main change he made was to transform the Pozzo–Lucky sequence into a dream of Vladimir's). Helene Weigel persuaded her husband to spend the second half of August and early September in a private sanatorium in Munich, but as he was leaving a morning rehearsal on the day of his departure, 14 August, it was discovered that he had suffered a heart attack three days previously. He lapsed into unconsciousness at 6 p.m. and died just before midnight at the premature age of fifty-eight.

It was a huge blow to all those – but especially Tynan – who saw Epic theatre as the catalyst for change. George Devine, currently planning to bring *The Good Person of Sezuan* (retitled *The Good Woman of Sezuan*) to the Royal Court, shared his disappointment with Eric Bentley, but, perhaps conscious of the international situation, worried more about the exploitation of his legacy: 'What a blow about Brecht's death. Far too young and far too disturbing to be allowed to disappear. I fear his posthumous reputation and his supporters as much as I admire what he has actually done.'[6]

During the rehearsals for the London début at the end of August, an ailing Brecht had revealed how important he considered preparation for the coming tour to be and had pinned to the company's noticeboard a memorandum detailing his thoughts. On his return from holiday, and the day before *Mother Courage* opened at the Palace Theatre on 27 August, Tynan reproduced this note in his column, in an attempt to show that there was a continuity to Brecht's work that would survive the death of the 'maestro'. It was crucial to stress that Epic Theatre was not dependent on the presence of one individual alone:

> For our London season we need to bear two things in mind. First: we shall be offering most of the audience a pure pantomime, a kind of silent film on stage, for they know no German . . . Second: there is in England a long-standing fear that German art (literature, painting, music) must be terribly heavy, slow, laborious and pedestrian.
>
> Hence our playing needs to be quick, light, strong. This is not a question of hurry, but of speed; not simply of quick playing, but of quick thinking. We must keep the tempo of a 'run through' and infect it with quiet strength, with our own amusement. In the dialogue the exchanges must not be offered reluctantly, as when offering somebody one's last pair of boots, but must be tossed like so many balls. The audience must see that here are a number of artists working together as a collective ensemble to convey stories, ideas, bits of art to the spectator, by a common effort.

Tynan rounded off this advice with a valedictory observation for his readers: 'There speaks the practical Brecht, whom actors loved. The playwright-poet speaks tomorrow. Full synopses in English will be provided with every play. Don't walk, in fact: *run*.'[7]

It is often forgotten that the three productions performed by the Berliner Ensemble – *The Caucasian Chalk Circle*, *Mother Courage* and *Trumpets and Drums* – were performed in a language that the vast majority of the London audience would not have understood, synopses notwithstanding. It is little surprise, then, that the majority of the reviews focused on the visual and aural dimensions of the plays, and that they were marked by an unacknowledged defensiveness about their lack of German. Even Tynan, who had read the works in translation, studied their genesis and seen two of them before in Paris, followed this pattern by defying 'anyone to forget Brecht's stage pictures':

> Brecht's actors do not behave like Western actors; they neither bludgeon us with personality nor woo us with charm; they look shockingly like people, real potato-faced people such as one might meet in a bus-queue. Humanity itself, not the exceptional eccentric, is what their theatre exists to explore. In their lighting, an impartial snow-white glow, and their grouping, which is as panoramic as

Breughel's, life is spread out before you. It does not leap at your throat and yell secrets in your ear . . .

The physical ordinariness of the actress playing the key role in *The Caucasian Chalk Circle* drew comment – 'Angelika Hurwicz is a lumpy girl with a face as round as an apple: our theatre would cast her, if at all, as a fat comic maid. Brecht makes her the heroine, the servant who saves the governor's child when its mother flees from a palace revolution' – and he called upon a chance remark from a member of the audience to illustrate Brecht's essential philosophy:

As Eric Bentley said, 'Brecht does not believe in an inner reality, a higher reality or a deeper reality, but simply in reality.' It is something for which we have lost the taste: raised on a diet of gin and goulash, we call Brecht naïve when he gives us bread and wine. He wrote morality plays and directed them as such: and if we of the West End and Broadway find them as tiresome as religion, we are in a shrinking minority. There is a world elsewhere. 'I was bored to death,' said a bright Chelsea girl after *Mother Courage.* 'Bored to life' would have been apter . . .

Intriguingly, the rearrangement of a statutory part of the London theatre-going experience – which has nothing to do with the play at all – is harnessed to illustrate the much-discussed concept of *Verfremdung* ('Alienation', or the making strange of the familiar to provoke fresh insight) –

. . . the clearest illustration of the 'A-effect' comes in the national anthem, which the Berliner-Ensemble have so arranged that it produces instead of patriotic ardour, laughter. The melody is backed by a trumpet *obbligato* so feeble and pompous that it suggests a boy bugler on a rapidly sinking ship. The orchestration is a criticism of the lyrics, and a double flavour results, the ironic flavour which is 'A-effect' . . .

– but there is a defensiveness to the whole review which alludes to the international situation and a consciousness that his previously hyperbolic endorsement of the playwright made him a very lone voice. His final comments represent a moderation of his previous views. Brecht, in his commitment and call to action, offers some signposts for theatrical change but not a definitive map:

Is it mere decadence that makes us want more of this, more attack, more abandon? I think not. Brecht's rejection of false emotions sometimes means that the baby is poured out with the bath-water: the tight-wire of tension slackens so much that the actors fall off: and instead of single-mindedness, we have half-heartedness. Yet as a corrective he is invaluable. He brings the wide canvas and the eagle's eye-view back to a theatre hypnotised by keyhole impressionism and worm's-eye foreshortening. It is possible to enter the Palace theatre wearing the familiar British smile of so-unsophisticated-my-dear-and-after-all-we've-rather-*had*-Expressionism (what *do* such people think expressionism was?); and it is possible to leave with the same faint smile intact. It is possible: but not pleasant to contemplate.[8]

The key point here is the notion that Brecht and Epic theatre could act as a corrective – a view that few of his critical colleagues were prepared to endorse. Crucially, however, Tynan's editor, David Astor, was pleased that Tynan had placed the *Observer* so publicly behind this movement. 'I went to see *Mother Courage* and was thrilled,' he wrote in a card to his young employee:

> It was everything you had led one to expect. Was incidentally terribly proud that you had associated the paper with Brecht so prominently.
>
> Won't start writing a long account of my impressions, but things I specially liked were the absence of bright colours (strange that one *should* like that), the solidity of what few props there were and absence of plaster (unlike in *Godot*), the simplicity and directness of the language (as far as I could get it) and of course their 'God save the Queen'.[9]

This was a significant vote of confidence at a time of some uncertainty. Tynan had very publicly championed Brecht, but would the playwright prove to be a damp squib in Britain? It was only at the turn of the decade and in the early 1960s that the true impact of the Berliner Ensemble's visit on the evolution of post-war British theatre could be assessed. One of the principal directors at the new National Theatre, William Gaskill, had been astonished by what he had seen: 'For me the visit in '56 was the most striking and influential theatrical experience I shall ever have. *Courage* really shattered me, it was extraordinary. Everything suddenly clarified and came into focus.'[10] Gaskill's production of *The Recruiting Officer* at the National, the RSC's 1962 version of *The Caucasian Chalk Circle* and new writers such as John Arden (*Serjeant Musgrave's Dance*, 1959), Arnold Wesker (*Chips with Everything*, 1963) and Edward Bond (*Saved*, 1965) all demonstrated evidence of Epic techniques. The true impact that the 1956 visit had – either directly or indirectly – was on practitioners, a fact that made an older Tynan feel proud and vindicated.

At the end of September, Tynan made his first trip to Berlin, 'The Dramatic Capital of Europe', according to the *Observer*. Its rival, the *Sunday Times*, felt that this was Paris, and George Devine wished that it was London. Again Tynan drew away from his previous breathy enthusiasm, in a desire to offer the Ensemble as a catalyst and not as a cure. Some of the plays he saw at the home of the Ensemble, the Theater am Schiffbauerdamm, were dreary propaganda – 'one, written by the Minister of

Culture, yawningly chronicles the Nazi defeat outside Moscow; sad stuff, redeemed only by Brechtian stagecraft and settings'.[11] What Berlin could offer London, though, was lessons on ensemble acting, the shunning of the 'star system' and a regime of funding that allowed drama to breathe: 'Germany long ago outgrew the folly of trying to make plays pay; beside Berlin's broad canvas the London theatre resembles a pygmy boudoir vignette. We call our system democratic because it submits every new production to the test of popular opinion; in fact it is a dictatorship, ruled by economic pressure. In the West End all plays are equal, but farces and melodramas are more equal than others.'[12]

Devine's ESC was dedicated to loosening the stranglehold of such works, and in October Brecht's *The Good Woman of Sezuan* opened at the Royal Court as part of this campaign. The director, drawing on his wide contacts, had secured Peggy Ashcroft, one of the few leading Shakespearian actresses who could hold her own with Olivier and Gielgud, to play the split role of Shen Te and Shui Ta. Whilst Ashcroft was touring Berlin in the Gielgud production of *Much Ado About Nothing* in September 1955, she and Devine had called on Brecht and Weigel to begin negotiations about the London première. Determined to create an authentic 'Epic' performance, they agreed to employ one of Brecht's designers, Teo Otto and the composer, Paul Dessau, and once rehearsals started the following year, Helene Weigel herself came along to the Court to offer advice. From the start, however, the production was flawed. At the end of the play, in the 'epilogue', the actor playing the waterseller, Wang, steps out of character, comes to the front of the stage and challenges the audience to find a better ending to the one that they have just witnessed. This emphasises the didactic nature of the piece and makes sense of the bizarre disappearance of Shen Te into the heavens on a pink cloud. It is a critical part of the work, reminding the audience of their responsibility to act on what they have seen and right inequality, but, foolishly, it was omitted. The translation by Eric Bentley, as well, sounded forced and too Americanised. The supporting actors seemed hesitant and uncertain of their lines. Peggy Ashcroft herself appeared to be searching for the appropriate style and lacked the earthiness required of the prostitute, who 'cannot say no', and the brutal invasion of Hungary that preceded the production's run led to widespread anti-Soviet feeling that had a depressing effect on the box-office. The associate director, Tony Richardson, felt that, all in all, they had only managed to create a 'drab, hopeless copy of an Ensemble production'.[13]

Tynan struggled to keep the flag flying in the face of taunting 'I told you so' daily reviews gleefully claiming that Brecht was the emperor with no clothes. The *Times* spoke for many when it objected to Brecht's fondness for stating the obvious in a 'forbiddingly portentous' manner.[14] 'More and more', Tynan riposted, continuing the theme of the paradox of Epic theatre, 'one sees Brecht as a man whose feelings were so violent that he needed a theory to curb them. Human sympathy, time and again, smashes his self-imposed dyke.' The problem with the evening was not one of the script but one of the production: 'Mr Devine forgets that the Brechtian method works only with team actors of great technical maturity. With greener players it looks like casual dawdling'; he is not helped by 'Eric Bentley's clumsy translation' and Peggy Ashcroft's indecision. The 'only complete performance is that of Mr Devine himself, as a doting barber'. Nevertheless, it was important to keep faith: 'the production must not be missed by anyone interested in hearing the fundamental problems of human (as opposed to Western European) existence discussed in the theatre. In the context of our present prosperity, these problems may appear irrelevant. They are still cruelly relevant to more than half of the inhabited world.'[15]

Harold Hobson saw no reason to be charitable. Having seen the Berliner Ensemble in August, he had found the central desire of Epic theatre to provoke new thinking to run too directly against his love of the implicit, the suggestive and the revelatory moment to accept it as theatrically effective: 'To claim that the theatre, where hundreds of people are crowded together in conditions of more or less discomfort, subject to all the influences of mass suggestion, is a suitable place for clear thinking seems to me childish . . . The audience which thinks that it is thinking at these performances flatters and deceives itself.'[16] Now that he had seen *A Good Woman of Sezuan* he went for the jugular:

> An audience which goes to the Court Theatre and plays the game properly, which throws away its sophistication, abandons its irritation at being told the same thing over and over again, leaves its intelligence in the cloakroom, and is willing to introduce the mentality of six into the bodies of sixteen, twenty-six or sixty will have a tolerable time.

However, he was most concerned by the after-life of the productions, and their potentially negative influence:

> There is an alarming rumour . . . that John Osborne, who appears in *The Good Person of Sezuan* (not to much advantage, by the way), is likely to be influenced by Brecht in the new play he is writing to follow up the striking *Look Back in Anger* . . . I earnestly hope that this is not so, though Mr Osborne himself does not deny it. Mr Osborne has a decided theatrical talent for representing young people as morbid, cowardly, self-pitying, complaining and weak-willed. It is in this that his genius lies, not in devising techniques to suit the sort of people who failed at eleven-plus. It will be a desolating day for his own future, and, in a small way, for the future of the English theatre, if anyone persuades him the case is otherwise.[17]

It is in this elitist concern that the impact of Brecht's legacy can best be gauged.

One of Hobson's favourite performers was Ralph Richardson, a biography of whom he would write in 1958. The week after Tynan's review of the Berliner Ensemble, two events offered him a reason to remind his readers that the battle against the old guard was far from over: Richardson's performance as Timon of Athens and a variation on the Loamshire theme. After the disappointing reception of his favourite overseas company, the *Observer* critic demonstrated that he was at his strongest when on the attack. *Look Back in Anger*, *The Quare Fellow* and Brecht were still but initial skirmishes:

> I should like to say that *Timon of Athens* (Old Vic) and *A River Breeze* (Phoenix) represent the worst that London can offer: in fact, and tragically, they are the ghastly norm . . . To the role of the scoutmaster Sir Ralph Richardson brings his familiar attributes: a vagrant eye, gestures so eccentric that their true significance could be revealed only by extensive trepanning and a mode of speech that democratically regards all syllables as equal . . . *A River Breeze*, by Roland Culver, is a theatrical coelacanth: a thing we had long thought extinct, now surfacing unexpectedly in semi-fossilised form. It is a Loamshire comedy. The heroine's head, shaved because of ringworm, reveals a birthmark (the nine of diamonds) which proves that she was switched in the cradle with another tot. This is lucky, since she has fallen in love with the boy she thought to be her brother. Incest and vermin keep the plot spinning, and there is a long and irrelevant pause in which a kitchen accessory known as the 'Kenwood Chef' is interminably demonstrated. Mr Culver himself, squinting irascibly so as to hold in each eye a monocle of wrinkles, plays a comic colonel who is not comic. In fact, the drink-tabled, French-windowed, dead-ended farce, which we had thought banished is impudently back. I invite all theatre-lovers to blockade it by sending troops in force to the Berliner Ensemble, a hundred yards away at Cambridge-circus. No action, of course, is contemplated: a simple show of force should suffice.[18]

The metaphor about the blockade sprang directly from speculation as to whether Britain would attempt to lay siege to the Suez Canal. Tynan always had his eye on events beyond the stage, and a national crisis was looming.

A few weeks before hostilities broke out, a surprising conflagration erupted in the West End, initiated by some of the keenest adherents of conservatism. Binkie Beaumont, his fellow producer, Donald Albery, Stephen Arlen (a director of Covent Garden) and Ian Hunter (an ex-director of the Edinburgh Festival) announced their intention of reviving the New Watergate Theatre Club. By taking advantage of the loophole in the law which permitted private performances of unlicensed plays to paid-up members of a theatre club, they wanted to present three banned works

– *A View from the Bridge, Cat on a Hot Tin Roof* and *Tea and Sympathy*. All three had been deprived of licences by the Lord Chamberlain for touching on homosexuality. Although the producers stated that their intention was not to circumvent the law, but to offer 'interesting plays to minority audiences', this was seen as a flimsy ruse. For a start, every one of the plays had been a huge Broadway success, and there was little commercial risk. Instead of going to the usual little theatre, the Arts Theatre, they transformed the much larger Comedy Theatre into the club venue to maximise their profits. Tynan was riled by this necessary chicanery:

> I am in little doubt that the true creator of the new venture, the catalyst to whom our thanks are due, is that anachronistic bogey, the Lord Chamberlain.
>
> Forbear, if you can, to smile at the mighty machinery of evasion that had to be constructed before London might see, properly produced, three plays which have been staged with no trouble at all on Broadway and almost everywhere in Western Europe. Do not mistake me: I applaud the new enterprise: but I wish it had taken a firmer stand against the mischievous anomaly of a censorship which Walpole invented for his own political use, which licensed Ibsen only because it thought his characters 'too absurd to do any harm,' and which is implicitly to blame for the fact that the whole panorama of British theatre contains only a handful of plays dealing at all controversially with sex, politics, the law, the Church, the Armed Forces, and the Crown . . .

He quite correctly pointed out that it was the theatre profession's acquiescence in this state of affairs which was as much to blame as the censor:

> The obstacle to reform can be simply stated: most theatre managers approve of the Lord Chamberlain. He is their guarantee of safety: once blessed with his licence, they are immune from legal action. This attitude is likely to persist as long as our theatre skulks inside the nursery, irresponsibly refusing to claim the right which, long ago, the film industry demanded and won: that of censoring itself. The Lord Chamberlain should be replaced by an advisory panel, drawn from and elected by the theatre itself. To this body all scripts would be submitted; but its veto (unlike that of the film censors) would not be absolute; the management concerned would retain the right to go ahead and run the risk of prosecution under the existing laws relating to blasphemy, sedition and obscenity.[19]

People flocked to *A View from the Bridge*, encouraged by the whiff of controversy, the Broadway pedigree and a clutch of admiring notices. Tynan felt that Eddie Carbone's lack of self-knowledge led to the play falling 'just short of being a masterpiece' but he counselled that the Lord Chamberlain should be made an honorary member of the club to be confronted by 'a spectacle that he has pronounced unfit for human consumption'.[20] His exasperation was exacerbated by the presentation of Lillian Hellman's *The Children's Hour* at the Arts Theatre. This time he argued that the work, banned over twenty years previously for its reference to lesbianism, was being performed to a liberal audience which least needed to be confronted by the work's progressiveness. Utilising Nancy Mitford's social division of people into Us and Them, he wryly observed that 'to present it to Arts theatre audiences who are predominantly Us, is like sending oil to Texas. And to present it to Them, for whom it was originally written and to whom it would still appeal, is legally prohibited'.[21] How limited a victory the Watergate exercise proved to be was revealed when Beaumont and Albery, emboldened by the commercial success of *A View from the Bridge*, went to Lord Scarbrough to explain that they intended to open a second club theatre to stage *Tea and Sympathy*. This was swiftly met with the threat of legal action and they immediately backed down.

Part of the hype that surrounded the Miller play centred on the persona of his wife, Marilyn Monroe. She had been shooting *The Prince and the Showgirl* with Olivier prior to the opening of *A View from the Bridge*, and was the object of enormous fascination. Photographers trailed her every move, the public marvelled at her figure, enhanced by the red dresses into which she was sewn and, for the moment at least, her marriage to Arthur Miller appeared a glamorous American version of the Olivier/Leigh axis. At the suggestion of Marilyn's acting coach, Paula Strasberg, who had a decisive hold on her,[22] the Tynans decided to host a dinner party for the famous couple. Monroe had just finished her final scenes for *The Prince and the Showgirl* and Miller had been overseeing a run of *A View from the Bridge*. There were to be ten guests in addition to the Tynans, Miller and Monroe. Those invited included John Osborne and Mary Ure (Alison Porter in *Look Back in Anger*), Peter Hall and his wife Leslie Caron, Maria St Just (Britneva at the time) and Cyril Connolly. Elaine decided to get in outside caterers (the Tynans scarcely cooked for themselves, let alone others) and a simple, mouth-watering feast was prepared for serving in the largest Mount Street room: rich pâté, pheasant, crème brulée and a cheeseboard. An hour before the starting time, Miller phoned Tynan. Monroe was indisposed, but he would be coming along. A quarter of an hour later, the plan changed: they would both be coming. Five minutes later, the final message: neither would be coming. 'My wife,' Miller told Tynan 'is hysterical.' 'So is mine,' replied Tynan.[23] Miller offered his apologies the following day:

Dear Kenneth Tynan

I beg your forgiveness for not having come to your party. Marilyn is only now getting back on the road to her normal energies and as that evening approached it didn't seem wise to go out. As you know, the movie production hours of work are cruel and she has been doing this almost without a break since last January when she started *Bus Stop* . . .

My best regards

Arthur Miller[24]

The hosts contemplated cancelling but, given the imminent arrival of the other guests, decided to proceed. It was the right decision. The remaining guests were in the vanguard of new, contemporary theatre and Connolly, whose *Sunday Times* book reviews had an avid following, was considered a significant 1950s intellect following the publication of *Enemies of Promise* (1938) and *The Unquiet Grave* (1944), a pot-pourri of critical commentaries, quotations and aphorisms. Tynan greatly admired his work, despite Connolly's mordant morality, and Elaine found herself increasingly attracted to him. Shortly after this evening she embarked upon an affair with the man whom she memorably described as 'the most gluttonous, envious, lustful and slothful man I have ever liked',[25] which lasted for the next twelve months. In the context of the emotional turmoil of their respective marriages, it seemed an inevitable thing to do.

Context is everything for theatre. The Suez crisis of November 1956, when the political old guard miscalculated, changed the mindset of the nation and increased the receptiveness of theatre audiences to the type of plays that Tynan wished to see produced. It was an event that temporarily split the country. In the absence of a mandate from the United Nations, Eden spent October secretly searching for a pretext to attack Nasser's Egypt. At a private meeting with General Maurice Challe on 14 October, an idea began to emerge that involved drawing in Israel. Israel was currently threatening to attack its neighbour, Jordan. If the Israeli Prime Minister, David Ben-Gurion, could be persuaded to attack Egypt instead, Britain and France would not come to Egypt's aid. Furthermore, the Europeans would then urge both countries to stop hostilities and withdraw ten miles from the Canal. In the inevitable event that Egypt refused this ultimatum, the Anglo-French forces could then attack and occupy the Canal Zone. On 24 October, an agreement was transacted in Paris; Eden then had the document destroyed.

The Israelis launched their attack on 30 October, and the Anglo-French ultimatum duly followed. As predicted, the Egyptians refused to withdraw and an air attack on Cairo and Port Said began. Tension gripped the British cabinet, with signs of concern about the wisdom of the secret collusion. The doubts were fuelled by the surprisingly hostile response of a section of the media and the Sunday newspapers. The *Observer* in its editorial of 4 November was the most implacably opposed to the British invasion:

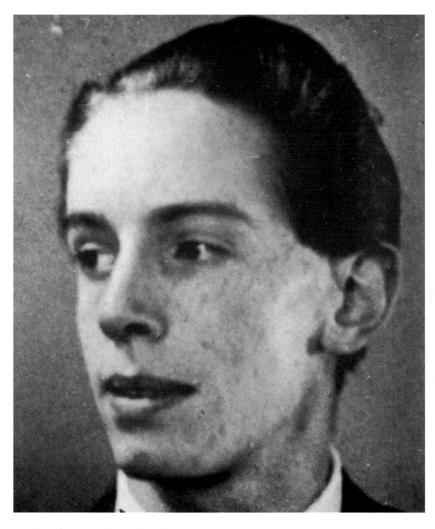

1. Ken, the precocious schoolboy

2. Ken's twenty-first birthday party, on the River Thames, 2 April 1948

3. A birthday salute by Westminster Bridge

4. The student bon viveur

5. Ken 'abroad'

6. Ken directing at Oxford

7. Ken and Elaine in Spain

8. Ken, the coruscating critic. A portrait by Cecil Beaton

10. Ken and Elaine at Mount Street

9. (*facing page*) Ken, Elaine and Tracy at home in Mount Street

11. Ken on the set of 'Tempo', with Lord Harewood

12. Ken, the dramaturg of the National Theatre

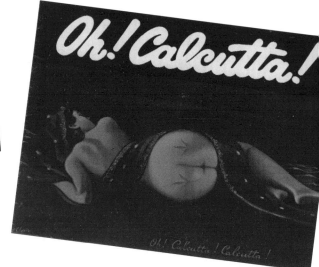

13 and 14. Programme covers for *Soldiers* and *Oh! Calcutta!*

15. Scene from *Oh! Calcutta!*, 1970

16. Ken and Kathleen

17. Ken and Matthew

18. Ken after the National Theatre

19. Ken and Laurence Olivier, 1975

. . . this action has endangered the American alliance and NATO, split the Commonwealth, flouted the United Nations, shocked the overwhelming majority of world opinion and dishonoured the name of Britain. The diversion of world attention from what is now happening in Hungary is perhaps its most evil effect.[26]

In a full page analysis Astor turned his attention to the Prime Minister:

We had not realised our government was capable of such folly and such crookedness. In the eyes of the world, the British and the French Governments have acted, not as policemen, but as gangsters. It will never be possible for the present Government to convince the peoples of the Middle East and of all Asia and Africa that it has not been actively associated with France in an endeavour to re-impose nineteenth-century imperialism of the crudest kind. In our view there is one essential. Sir Anthony Eden must go. His removal from the Premiership is scarcely less vital to the prospects of this country than was that of Mr. Neville Chamberlain in May 1940.

It was one of the defining leader columns of the twentieth century. Published the day before British troops were about to be dispatched, it provoked a furious reaction from the paper's more conservative readers and howls of treachery from the *Observer*'s gleeful rivals, who believed that Astor's passion for Africa, anti-colonialism and the American alliance had led him into disastrous speculation about British collusion with France. Three of the *Observer*'s seven trustees resigned. Older readers deserted the paper in droves – just when it had inched ahead in the circulation war with the *Sunday Times* – and advertisers began to look elsewhere. In the short term, a whole new generation of younger readers were drawn to the paper. In the long term, the *Observer*'s underlying financial health was enormously damaged, but Astor's courage was undeniably vindicated.

The cabinet met on that Sunday evening and Eden was forced to call a vote on whether the planned airborne landing should proceed. The vote was 12–6 in favour, hardly overwhelming, but not close enough to stop the action. British forces therefore occupied Port Fuad and a part of the Canal Zone the following day, and proceeded to bomb Cairo on 5 and 6 November, causing up to 1,000 casualties.

Global reaction was outrage and, in the words of the historian Kenneth Morgan, 'the next few days shook the world'.[27] A furious Eisenhower ordered Eden to withdraw the British troops, pointing out the effect this cack-handed action would have on third world and Arab opinion. It could only increase the allure of the Soviet Union. Eden did his cause no good at all by clumsily trying to deceive the President about the extent of the collusion with Israel, but Eisenhower was not fooled. To turn the screw – and to emphasise the seriousness with which Eisenhower viewed Eden's breach of trust – the US began to encourage a run on the pound, which threatened a sterling crisis of even greater gravity than that of 1947. At the UN, Britain was condemned as an international aggressor by 64 votes to 5, and country after country queued up to express their anger that attention had been diverted from the Soviet invasion of Hungary. At home there was an outpouring of furious indignation. Two ministers, Nutting and Boyle, Economic Secretary to the Treasury and, perhaps most damagingly, Eden's spokesperson, resigned. The Labour Party, under a passionate Gaitskell, headed up a 'Law not War' campaign. A public meeting at Trafalgar Square on 4 November (a dramatic day) resulted in clashes between the police and angry students, and up and down the country people discussed the implications for a nation that was quite clearly no longer the world power that it had hoped to be. 'It is long since opinion in Britain has been so keenly and deeply divided as it has been throughout the Suez Canal crisis,'[28] Astor observed the following Sunday.

Within days, the run on the pound forced Eden to reconsider and on Thursday, 8 November he was humiliatingly forced to declare a cease-fire. (By the end of November over £300 million of gold and dollar reserves had left the country – an enormous figure.) The instant analysis of the fiasco was withering and it was again Astor and the *Observer* – which came of age as a political paper during the Suez crisis – who led the condemnation. 'The events of the last three weeks', the paper argued on 11 November, 'have not only shaken the foundations of Russia's East European empire. They have not only broken the precarious peace of the Middle East and jeopardised Britain's moral position in the world. They seem also to have shattered the East–West *détente* of the last three years – with incalculable consequences.'[29]

The immediate crisis was over, but Britain still had to extricate its troops from Egypt and its reputation from the mire. Eden was forced to agree to a withdrawal in favour of a multinational force, even though he was unable to secure agreement that the Canal would remain unblocked. The symbol of his failure quickly became the fact that clear passage of the Canal – the main aim of the collusion with Israel – had not been achieved, since it was now totally blocked by ships that the Egyptians had deliberately sunk! Eden, who had waited so long to succeed Churchill, and who had retained the public's popularity ever since his resignation in protest against appeasement in the 1930s, was the biggest political casualty. On 23 November he informed his colleagues that on his doctor's advice he needed an immediate vacation (he had suffered from poor health for some time), and swiftly departed for the West Indies. This departure was mercilessly caricatured in some quarters as an evasion of duty, with Eden seen as akin to those who had left the country during the darkest days of the war and had 'gone with the wind up'.

The fallout continued during Eden's absence. The British and French argued about their respective culpability; their international reputations sank further, with claims of flagrant breaches of international law and accusations of outright lying; and logistical difficulties meant it was not until 22 December that the last British troops were withdrawn. Eden did not return to Britain until the New Year and promptly resigned on 9 January 1957, a disgraced man. The wily Harold Macmillan, who had been positioning himself to succeed during Eden's absence, duly became Prime Minister.

The legacy of Suez was profound. The nature of the 'special relationship' between the US and Britain was called into question and the latter became a pariah state at the UN for a time. Suez proved that Britain was no longer able to exert itself as an imperial power, and hastened the process of decolonisation. It introduced passion into political debate and radicalised middle-class opinion in a way that had not seemed possible even three months previously. And it led to a practical outpouring of the emotion that allegedly motivated the 'Angry Young Men' of the new wave of British theatre. It is important to note that this was primarily a middle-class reaction. The population at large did not punish the Conservatives at the general election of 1959, because they were generally happy with the unprecedented level of affluence that had swept the country. It was university students, middle-class liberals, readers of the *Observer* – all the people who were likely to go to the theatre to see a more realistic form of drama – who were galvanised by Suez. This fiasco caused by the establishment was to give crucial impetus to Tynan's crusade.

In the midst of the crisis, as British planes rained bombs on Cairo, one of British theatre's most successful playwrights opened his new play, *Nude with Violin*. In November 1956, Noël Coward was at the height of his press unpopularity. This was less to do with his drama than with his status as a tax exile, which reportedly saved him an astronomical £30,000 per year.[30] The Beaverbrook press in particular remorselessly portrayed him as a bogus patriot living abroad, and the decision of the Inland Revenue to grant him an extra ten days' tax exemption so that he could witness the opening of his new play in London added fuel to their fire. The play took a dismissive, sneering view of modern art. It encapsulated the elitist, patronising attitude to creativity that Tynan loathed and it provoked, in 'The Rake's Regress', one of his suavest parodies:

When Sir John Gielgud appears in modern dress on the London stage for only the second time since 1940, selecting as his vehicle Noël Coward's *Nude with Violin* (Globe), one's expectations are naturally low. Sir John never acts seriously in modern dress; it is the lounging attire in which he relaxes between classical bookings; and his present performance as a simpering valet is an act of boyish mischief, carried out with extreme elegance and the general aspect of a tight, smart, walking umbrella.

The play of his choice is at once brief, and interminable. Its tone underlines Mr Connolly's famous maxim: 'Tory satire, directed at people on a moving staircase from a stationary one, is doomed to ultimate peevishness.' The target is modern art. The three celebrated 'periods' of a great modern painter, recently dead, are exposed as the work of three untalented hirelings – a mad Russian princess, a tipsy chorus-girl and (culminating joke) a Negro. Kathleen Harrison's Cockney chorine is game, and Patience Collier's rambling Russian is game, set and match: but the rest of the cast resemble a cocktail party at which the gin has run out. The conclusion recalls those triumphant Letters to the Editor which end: 'What has this so-called "Picasso" got that my six year-old daughter hasn't?'

When not boggling, my imagination went in for speculation. Mr Coward's career can also be divided into three periods. The first began in the twenties: it introduced his revolutionary technique of 'Persiflage', the pasting of thin strips of banter on cardboard. In the early thirties we encounter his second or 'Kiplingesque' period, in which he obtained startling effects by the method now known as 'kippling' – i.e. the pasting of patriotic posters on to strips of banter pasted on cardboard. (The masterpieces of this period, *Cavalcade* and *In Which We Serve* have been lost. The damp got at the cardboard).

In 1945 a social holocaust destroyed all but a few shreds of the banter. In this third and final phase, a new hand is discernible. *Is it Mr Coward's?* The question must be faced. Where Mr Coward was concise, the newcomer brandishes flabby polysyllables: and the clumsiness of his stagecraft was described by one expert last week as a 'dead give-away'. An American student of the last three 'Coward' plays has declared that they must have been written by Rip Van Winkle. The new work, on the other hand, with its jocular references to at least thirty place-names, both homely and exotic, tends to support the theory that the new crypto-Coward is in reality a Departures Announcer at London Airport. I take no sides. On this last, decisive period I reserve judgement. We are too close to it. Much, much too close.[31]

Nude with Violin received uniformly hostile reviews, but it proved surprisingly durable and ran for twelve months on the strength of the pairing of John Gielgud and a Noël Coward work.

By the end of November, the implications of Suez were becoming apparent and Tynan became ever more impatient with preciousness and unreality. Jean-Louis Barrault, one of Hobson's favourite French performers, came to London to star in the French-language production of *Christophe Colombe*. It was a world of revelation for Hobson; a world of artifice that, in the light of Suez, was a complete anachronism for Tynan:

One's summing up of M. Barrault's theatre must be that it is balletic, comedic, mimetic, Dionysiac even; but essentially out of touch with life. Art preserve me from insisting that theatre should always be life-like: that would be to fall into the old puritan error of condemning poetry on the grounds that it is all lies and feigning. My quarrel with M. Barrault is that he feigns too much and too exclusively; he has uprooted himself from the soil that should nourish him. He has lost contact with his base.[32]

The hesitancy apparent over Brecht, the momentary loss of confidence in the light of political objections, had gone. Suez had reiterated the importance of clear, committed opinions. Tynan's third viewing of *The Diary of Anne Frank* at the beginning of December now made him conclude that the play was 'a superb piece of theatrical journalism . . . Berlin was too close to the problem. New York was too remote. The half-way English, neither too involved nor too removed, have come off best.'[33] The need to champion new writing led him to announce in the same column the first *Observer* play competition, more details of which would be given in the new year. And the English Stage Company's first classical production – of Wycherley's *The Country Wife* – displayed new acting talent, regional accents (Joan Plowright was a 'gorgeous little goof, with a knowing slyness that perfectly matches her Rochdale accent') and a sensible avoidance of lavish, over-complicated sets. Devine later enjoyed the irony of the fact that 'the contemporary theatre was saved by a classic revival',[34] since *The Country Wife* played to 95 per cent box office and saved the ESC from closure following the box-office disaster of *The Good Woman of Sezuan*. Tynan particularly applauded Devine for the avoidance 'of tushery, rogueypoguery and sentimental good cheer'.[35]

The degree to which Tynan had been reinvigorated by Suez can be gauged by his end of year report. For the first time since becoming a critic he had witnessed the green shoots of recovery. 1956 had been full of good theatrical auguries. How would these shoots grow? He chose to be cautious:

> In spite of everything, about four good native plays will be performed and supported. None of them, however, is likely to deal with Suez, Cyprus, Kenya, the United Nations, the law, the armed forces, Parliament, the Press, medicine, jazz, the City, English cities outside of London, or London postal districts outside the S.W. and N.W. areas. Two thousand wish-fulfilling plays will be written about life after the next war. Ten will be staged. One will be good.[36]

He would willingly be proved wrong.

The New Year saw Elaine working hard on her novel. Bent over her portable typewriter, she was such a determined writer that she began to develop back problems, which were temporarily relieved by twice-weekly visits to the Turkish baths at the Dorchester Hotel, 'close by and surprisingly inexpensive'.[37] Whilst at dinner one evening with Sandy Wilson (author of the phenomenally successful *The Boyfriend*, which had opened in January 1954 and was to run for 2,084 performances), she remarked on the impressive avocado plants that they had grown. Her own attempts in a yoghurt bottle had always been unsuccessful. 'What you have is a dud avocado,' Tynan observed, before adding 'That's a good title for a book.'[38] Elaine duly wove the appropriate reference into her text, as the overall structure began to take shape.

Tynan chose the first two months of 1957 to make similarly creative suggestions for British theatre. It may be tempting to conclude that *Look Back in Anger* changed the nature of drama overnight, but to observers on the ground, change was slow and barely discernible. Tynan wondered in February whether the establishment of the London Studio, as a British version of the Actors' Studio in New York devoted to the 'Method', might disrupt the 'status quo':

> Among senior theatricals, mistrust of 'Method' acting verges on hysteria. Actors, they boast, are born, not made: beyond a certain stage, training is both useless and undesirable, as futile as trying to educate the Baritsu. The intensity of this feeling, particularly strong along the Coward–Gielgud axis, hints at a disquiet that has recently spread throughout the derrière garde of the profession. Young actors are abroad, of appalling seriousness and assurance, speaking an impenetrable alien language with every appearance of understanding it. Reports filter through of acting classes, held (if you please) in the morning, and attended, incredibly, by actors who are not out of work . . .

The total immersion in a role, the importance of research and the distrust of artifice that underpinned 'Method' acting might provoke a reassessment of theatre's relationship with the contemporary world, he believed:

> . . . The production of plays has too long been regarded as a furtive magical rite, to be carried out in secret behind locked doors; something too fragile to be opened to public inspection. This merely encourages the feeble heresy that actors are unaccountably different from other people, that they shrivel outside a specially protective environment, and wince and blink in daylight. The London Studio brings acting out into the open. It may thus dispel the self-consciousness, the reluctance to make a fool of oneself, the desperate clinging to inhibitions, that account for the non-committal tentativeness of so much English acting.[39]

Directing, too, needed an overhaul. There were promising new directors throughout the West End – Peter Hall and Peter Brook were the most obvious examples – but the economic structure of West End theatre meant that their scope for experimentation was severely restricted. With half an eye on his own bitter experiences at Lichfield when he was fired, it was time to give them more freedom, he contended:

> The English director is like an interior decorator employed by a householder to execute a scheme of design on which the householder has already decided. He is a tolerated stranger, engaged *ad hoc* and invited only for a strictly limited period. The manager, having chosen the play, casts the director. Ideally, the director should choose the play and then cast the actors . . . At present we are rich in directors, but our directors are not rich enough; they lack the cash to buy theatre leases.[40]

And English writing, still devoid of relevance, could do worse than look east again. In January, Tynan had travelled to Berlin to watch the first production of the Berliner Ensemble since the death of Brecht. There was much speculation as to whether the East German authorities, increasingly repressive and intolerant of dissident thought, would permit a production of *The Life of Galileo*, a play, in Tynan's words, 'whose main purpose is to show the demoralising effect of conformity'. To his relief, the production went ahead and he picked out the recantation scene as evidence of Brecht's ability to pinpoint the political context of moral dilemmas. Provocative, intelligent and controversial, the scene made English writing seem like candyfloss, and, with an eye to the growing number of people who were insinuating that the death of Brecht meant the death of Epic theatre, he argued that the production had also provided 'reassuring evidence of continuity, and a proof of Brecht's abiding maxim that no man is indispensable – and if he is, he is up to no good'.[41]

On his return to a Britain wrangling about the fallout from Suez, Tynan decided that he had a practical role to play in stimulating a renaissance by actively championing the *Observer* play competition, that had been briefly mentioned before Christmas. Ever since his disastrous tenure at Lichfield he had bristled at suggestions that he had been a failure in practical theatre. What better way to rebut this than to help facilitate the discovery of new scripts that would achieve successful commercial runs? There would be a first prize of £500, and two smaller ones of £200 and £100, with the winning entry guaranteed a run at the Arts Theatre, 'if it reaches a high enough standard'. The judges were impressively high-powered – Alec Guinness, Peter Ustinov, Michael Barry, Head of BBC Television Drama, Peter Hall and Tynan himself – and there was the possibility of publication by Heinemann and the receipt of royalties. His eagerness to demonstrate a practical way of stemming the malaise may in part have been stimulated by Hobson's new role from 1956 as an adjudicator at the National Union of Students Festival in Scarborough. It would not do to have Hobson so prominently associated with youth – the very constituency that Tynan was making his own – while he sat idly by.

Tynan again announced this intention in his column of 3 February, written under the appropriate byline, 'A Matter of Life'. The deadline for entries was, after all, only three months away, on 14 April. The French magazine *France Observateur* had recently published a 'curt and devastating survey of the English theatrical scene', he warned:

> Admiration for our actors, pained astonishment at our plays: such is the typical reaction. A sampling of intelligent foreign opinion would almost certainly reveal that in the eyes of the world the English theatre is little more than a bewilderingly elaborate joke. There might be some dispute over what should be done about it, one group favouring vivisection and another euthanasia; but otherwise I should expect the verdict to be unanimous.

Swift action was needed –

> It is in an effort to reverse it or at least to wangle a stay of execution that this paper has launched a Play Competition, notably gambling £800 on the results. In a similar spirit of all-hands-to-the-oars, the Arts Theatre has offered to stage the winning entries, should the judges deem them worthy of production. These sizeable inducements are intended to attract not only unknown writers but people who have already made their mark in other literary fields – novelists, philosophers, poets, historians, reporters, columnists, essayists, advertising copy-writers and even critics . . .

– and he illustrated the seriousness of this task with one of his most brilliant contemporary and withering conceits:

> English drama is like the Suez Canal, a means of communication, made hazardous by a myriad sunken wrecks. There, scarcely visible above the ooze is the mighty hulk that was Pinero:[42] and there, stranded on a sand-bar the flimsy outrigger Stephen Phillips.[43] Salvage work is being carried out on the doughty tanker Priestley but it remains a peril to navigation; and a whole stretch of waterway has been declared unsafe because of the presence, just on the surface, of the first aluminium leviathan, the captain has not yet abandoned his ship, on whose prow may be read the legend: 'Noël Coward: Teddington'. The lighthouse at Shaw's corner is out of action, and traffic at any point is likely to be menaced by the sudden appearance of the deserted Esther McCracken, whose crew are thought to have jumped overboard in the middle of tea, which is laid in every cabin: a veritable mystery of the sea. And the ghost-frigate Eliot still provokes the superstitious to chant: –

> But why drives on that ship so fast,
>   Without or wave or wind?

The air is cut away before,
And closes from behind

The fledgling pilot has many such dangers to avoid. Yet there is – there must be
– a way through. I am sure our competitors will find it.

When the competition had been trailed before Christmas, its first condition of entry
had been that the action in all scripts submitted must take place 'in the period since
the last war'. T.C. Worsley, the critic of the *New Statesman*, had scoffed at this, arguing that that would have ruled out an entry by Shakespeare – and even Brecht.
Tynan was adamant on this point, however. The exceptions of these two great playwrights could not cause him to ignore the poverty of writing about contemporary
matters: 'Evidence of a living vernacular is what we seek and need; evidence, too,
that playwrights are not ignoring the contemporary environment that has helped
to shape them. Escape into the past is a familiar evasion that has produced a
hundred bad plays for every good one.'[44] The subsequent deluge of scripts proved
that there was indeed a desire to write about this period.

The constructive nature of the project was matched by Tynan's increasing desire
in the spring of 1957 to scorn moments in the theatre that he felt were regressive.
When this was applied to people it teetered on the boundary of the destructive;
when plays were the object, it seemed more amusing and palatable. Three performers came into his orbit in February and March about whom he was scathing.
One, Donald Wolfit, was an old adversary, and the actor-manager issued instructions that Tynan was to be denied a ticket for the opening night of Henri de Montherlant's *The Master of Santiago*. Tynan makes liberal reference to this in his column
and chooses the sarcastic approach: 'A critic less engaged than I might have judged
Mr Wolfit's performance too bluntly combative, too emphatic in its humility: might
have suspected that he liked to play saints because saints do not need to make intimate contact with other human beings, including actors. I prefer to felicitate him
on his restraint: he is as still as a rock.'[45]

A month later, Wolfit opened another de Montherlant play, *Malatesta*, and took
the lead role. His long-term detractor could scarcely contain his disdain: 'Mr Wolfit
himself bullies the action along at a great pace, sometimes spitting in his enthusiasm, but he is not really the actor for Malatesta, whose kaleidoscopic mind he
reduces to a few, primary colours.'[46] Wolfit, a much-reduced figure, had less grounds
for redress than in 1953, as he had been overtaken by the shift in taste away from
big bravura performances. Hobson's great favourite, Edwige Feuillère, was dispatched in an equally peremptory manner, for her performance in *Phèdre*: 'The plain
truth is that [Feuillère] is wanting in the majestic attack that should compel awe . . .
Her performance is an immensely graceful apology for Phèdre, a sort of obituary

notice composed by a well-wishing friend: but it is never a life, nakedly lived before our eyes.'[47] But, surprisingly, it is Sam Wanamaker, a left-leaning actor and director who had left the United States to escape the McCarthy purges, who provoked the most venom.

Sam Wanamaker's first job in theatre was acting in Shakespeare in 1936, ironically in a mock-up Globe Theatre, which was one of the main attractions of the Great Lakes' World Fair in Cleveland, Ohio. Although he is best known in Britain now as the original and persistent visionary who brought about the construction of the New Globe, on the South Bank of the River Thames, he enjoyed a long career as an actor and director of both stage and screen productions. After a spell in the army in the South Pacific during the Second World War, Wanamaker returned to the US, where he received his 'big break' on Broadway at the age of twenty-seven playing opposite Ingrid Bergman in *Joan of Lorraine*. Within two weeks he took over direction of the play and became a huge success. After producing, directing and acting in several Broadway plays, he moved to Hollywood where he directed and acted in a clutch of films. In 1949 Sam Wanamaker paid his first visit to the UK to star in the film *Give Us This Day*. He returned in 1951 for another film and stayed to produce, direct and star in Clifford Odets's *Winter Journey* with Sir Michael Redgrave. He decided to remain in Britain, on account of the hearings into Un-American Activities, and soon took over the Shakespeare Theatre in Liverpool, where he formed his own company. This evolved into an early arts and performance centre. He also continued his acting career, performing as Iago with the Royal Shakespeare Memorial Theatre in *Othello* opposite Paul Robeson,[48] although, having seen *A Hatful of Rain*, which arrived in London in March, Tynan wished that he had not. Another overheard conversation gave the critic a way in – 'Not a spark of intelligent conversation in the whole pack of them,' said Miss Wimbledon, enthroned behind me' – but for once, Tynan could endorse the views of this forerunner of the Chelsea Girl. The play itself, dealing with drug addiction in New York's East Side, at least had the virtue of 'clarity'. Bonar Colleano, the original Stanley in the 1949 London première of *A Streetcar Named Desire*, produced 'a frighteningly good piece of acting' as the addict, but one significant piece of grit in the oyster spoiled the piece for Tynan:

> There remains Sam Wanamaker, who both directs and appears in the play. As director, he has wrought marvels with Miss Howes and Mr Colleano, but I should like to hear his defence of George Coulouris as Papa, who gives a nervous, blustering performance, as distinct from a performance of a nervous, blustering man: and, though medical science may accept the snail's pace at which the drug spree in the last act is taken, theatre audiences will not. As well as staging

whole scenes behind a layer of gauze opaquely ribbed with planks, Mr Wanamaker has indulged in such time-wasting fripperies as electric drills, crying babies, passing trains and zooming planes. His culminating gaffe is to have cast himself as Polo. The balance of the play demands that Polo should be a well meaning simpleton: Mr Wanamaker, who is nothing if not complex, makes him every bit as neurotic as his junkie brother, and appears, what with his battery of anguished smiles, exasperated shrugs and despairing cries, to be acting out the part to a group of exceptionally dense children. He is one of those maddening actors who can hold an audience while at the same time wrecking a play. You watch him with fascination, yet sigh with relief when he leaves. Without him, the play might never have reached London. With him, it has arrived with its faults as sharply underlined as its strengths.[49]

This excessive panning provoked an unusual, spirited and courageous response from Wanamaker. Perhaps accustomed to being under attack for his politics in Hollywood, he chose to fight back in a manner that British performers seldom chose, since, apart from Donald Wolfit, they generally subscribed to the unwritten law that dialogue with reviewers was futile. He wrote directly to the critic, and his previously unpublished letters, held in the Tynan archive, express the full fury of his reaction:

[31, Abbey Lodge, Park Road, NW8   12 March 1957]

Ken,

I've come to the conclusion that you *are* deliberately vicious and destructive. I've also come to the conclusion that you ought to be told. No doubt you've been told this before, by men or women whom you respect more, nevertheless, I will not quietly accept and will fight against your almost psychopathic desire to denigrate me and my work.

I believe you are a brilliant but adolescent mind who by sheer gall has attained a position of tremendous power in the theatre and you've wielded that power like a bludgeon, wilfully like a spoiled brat who knows he can get away with it. . . . You must know, as you peck viciously over a deliciously destructive (ah, but so clever) phrase, that its end result is not only to prevent people from going to the theatre to see the play, but will in future remind them not to support any theatrical activity of the subject of your spleen.

Above all, I write because you are a hypocrite, because you have no real convictions except those of an avant-guard opportunist – the object is to be first – ahead of the others. As a critic – you will last only so long as you can deceive the public of your honesty and integrity and so long as others are willing to hold their tongues – out of fear of your position to destroy them. Well, not me. I will fight – when my home and family are attacked I will fight . . . I write this in passion, but if O'Casey can answer critics back, surely there is room for a few others. Answer not as brilliantly but with equal indignation at injustice and dishonesty.[50]

Over the next two weeks a written dialogue ensued, but Tynan's response only inflamed the impassioned director. On 21 March 1957, Wanamaker sent a four-page letter in tight blue typescript from the Prince's Theatre:

Dear Ken,
Private fight: round four.

I maintain that your criticism of my work in general and of my acting in particular has been vicious, destructive and vindictive – not only in this, but in everything I've done here.

You defend your review as analytic and constructive, yet you make no attempt to probe into *why* I used the sound effects and the music . . . Apart from committing 'gaffes' all over the place the 'culminating one' was to cast myself as Polo, you say. In your letter you say I am a mannered actor, difficult to cast properly. Yet I seem to recall your rhapsodic ecstasies over such other mannered actors as Scofield, Gielgud, Harry Corbett, Edith Evans, Peggy Ashcroft and others. The only unmannered actors are the bad ones or those who lay smokescreens between the audience and their latent homosexuality, like Redgrave and Guinness . . . Your analysis is superficial – and from my observation of the body of your work in relation to those plays that I have seen, you are invariably influenced by outside elements and prejudgements and conceptions . . . You seize upon the quick response and reaction in yourself – you never seem to question your judgement, to admit doubt or uncertainty, to probe deeply, to be objective about your prejudices – all these are signs of immaturity and neuroticism. In short, you are a fraud as a critic and will never grow into an honest or a great one (which potential you have) until you develop humility and respect for honest work, integrity and sincerity . . . You may have gathered by now that I do not agree that Polo is a stumbling well-meaning simpleton. Nor do I agree that he is a neurotic – or complex – or that I play him that way. What you chose to see as neurotic is the attempt to portray and reveal layers of character and two or three major personal conflicts. Remembering you as an actor in that celebrated performance of 'Hamlet', how would you have dealt with Polo's love–hate for his father; his love for his brother's wife; his love for his brother; his guilt for loving his brother's wife (who is also pregnant); his hate for his brother for further alienating him from his father because of the money . . . And much more.

At this point in the letter, Tynan makes the following annotation in pen – '*he is aware but audience not*'. Wanamaker was now warming to his theme of Tynan as someone who was obsessively bent against him:

> . . . You write a full column about the necessity to develop and train actors in this country in the 'Actor's Studio' style – yet when I, an exponent of that way of working (and a fairly good one, if not the only example around at the moment) present a serious piece of work – you ridicule and insult it on what you must finally admit to be a personal bias of such magnitude as to 'shake loose the very roots of reason'. The 'personal animosity' must be deeply rooted, and *because* it has *no* basis makes it all the more suspect.

Tynan's annotation here is '*anti-Semite*'. In other words, he saw this as Wanamaker claiming he was motivated by racism:

> Your comment that in fact by my acting I am wrecking the play is the most vitriolic piece of critical groin kicking I have ever come across . . . In general your criticism of the production was flippant, superficial and as always with your work on the theme of 'look-at-me-and-see-how-clever-I-am!!' Perhaps I did not suc-ceed in what I attempted, but you as a critic had a responsibility to examine *what* I attempted and where I failed. To dismiss with the wave of a cheap phrase like 'time wasting fripperies' is not adult or intelligent criticism . . . In conclusion, you may wish to know why I have, against the anxious advice of one or two people, written to you in this way and at great length. I believe the readers of the 'Observer' are the most intelligent and progressive members of the British population. They support the theatre. What you write (and because of your real talent) carries a good deal of weight with them. You have a great responsibility insofar as you can shape and mould and change the course of British theatre through what you believe in and how you write about it. For any other critic to have written what you have about me would have meant very little to me personally, except insofar as it affected business at the box-office. Because I recognise your position, and because of the uniqueness of your readership, I feel it is necessary to force you to recognise your weakness and attack you sharply from time to time before you get too important to criticise.
> Sam
>
> p.s. I shall be delighted to accept your invitation for a drink, at such time in the future when you demonstrate sufficiently that you have warranted my renewed respect[51]

Wanamaker's implied charge of anti-Semitism, whilst understandable, is unfounded. After all, Tynan's wife was Jewish and he appeared on several anti-racist stages during his tenure at the National Theatre. What was more wounding for Tynan was the suggestion that he lacked the professional expertise to judge (a charge that goes with the territory of being a critic) and the reference to the disastrous *Hamlet* production of 1951. The accusation that he was a critic whose philosophy was 'look-at-me-and-see-how-clever-I-am' was one that would be used by his detractors in the future. But it ironically confirmed the importance of his opinions, a view that Wanamaker accepted when he concedes that Tynan had the power to 'shape and mould and change the course of British theatre through what you believe in and how you write about it.' Even those who disliked him with a passion now recognised the power of his pen.

Wanamaker's private remonstrations notwithstanding, Tynan showed no signing of moderating his views. 'Theatre historians, in particular,' he urged in his column while this correspondence was raging, 'should grasp their chance of bagging the last goggle-eyed, Lawks-mum parlour-maid the London stage will ever see,'[52] in William Douglas Home's *The Iron Duchess*, and he positively loathed Samuel Beckett's *Fin de partie* at the Royal Court, since he now believed that the playwright saw man as a 'pygmy who connives at his own inevitable degradation'. For the putative Marxist this pessimism was incongruent with the belief that man could fashion his own destiny and Tynan remained immune to the considerable publicity that surrounded the week-long run of performances. The final verdict on his experience was unequivocal: the 'production, portentously styled, piled on the agony until I thought my skull would split'.[53] When he returned to the Royal Court the following week, however, the tectonic plates of British theatre had shifted once more.

Laurence Olivier had initially loathed John Osborne's *Look Back in Anger*, viewing it as a 'travesty on England',[54] but a second visit to the play in July 1956 with Arthur Miller altered his perspective. Surprised by Miller's enthusiasm, Olivier posed the following question to Osborne after the performance: 'Do you suppose you could write something for me?'[55] The result was *The Entertainer*.

At this point Olivier's career was in a state of flux. In spite of outstanding Shakespearian performances, including his recent Titus which had reawakened a discussion about the 'modernity' of Shakespeare, Olivier was clearly conscious that he was in danger of becoming an anachronism. Looking back thirty years later he was to observe that

> I had reached a stage in my life that I was getting profoundly sick of – not just tired – sick. Consequently the public were, likely enough, beginning to agree with me. My rhythm of work had become a bit deadly: a classical or semi-classical film; a play or two at Stratford, or a nine-month run in the West End . . .

I was going mad, desperately searching for something suddenly fresh and thrillingly exciting. What I felt to be my image was boring me to death. I really felt that death might be quite exciting, compared with the amorphous purgatorial *nothing* that was my existence.[56]

That Olivier, the most versatile actor of the post-war period, should reinvent himself by playing the role of the washed-up music-hall comedian, Archie Rice, the protagonist in a play that links the passing of the age of the music hall to Britain's transient grip on its empire, is supremely fitting. It was also one of the most adroit and significant career moves that an actor has ever made, since it not only relaunched Olivier's career at the same time as he met his future wife, the young ESC actress Joan Plowright, but it possessed a remarkable symbolic value for theatre. Given the status of Olivier, the West End could no longer resist the coming new drama as something peripheral or irritating. It also left him well positioned to be considered for the post of director of the future National Theatre, which he told Tynan in 1958 he wanted to run.

Focusing on three generations of the Rice family, *The Entertainer* exhibits many of the thematic concerns of the 'new wave'. Written in thirteen numbers, with an overture and two intermissions, the structure of the play (possibly influenced by Epic theatre, in spite of Hobson's warnings) replicates that of a music-hall production, but the weariness and cynicism of the Rice family, ossifying in a small flat in a coastal resort, is meant to signify both the dying nature of this form of entertainment and the depersonalised character of a country that is finding it difficult to come to terms with its reduced importance on the world stage. The Suez crisis of November 1956 and its aftermath overhang the play. In the first few months of 1957 currency restrictions, cuts in spending on social security and the reintroduction of petrol rationing, which limited car mileage to 200 miles per month, all offered visible reminders to the British population of the direct price to be paid for the ill-judged intervention. The granting of independence to Ghana in March 1957 also emphasised the accelerating pace of decolonisation. This filters through into the play. One of Archie's sons, Mick, has been captured while fighting abroad and, after false hope has been raised, is reported as having been killed. His daughter, Jean, has been on a march in Trafalgar Square protesting about the conflict, but although she rejects the middle-class comfort offered by her conventional solicitor boyfriend, she cannot embrace the political activism that is sweeping through the young. Archie's second wife, Phoebe, is similarly governed by inertia – humiliated by Archie's philandering, she cannot leave him and has to seek refuge in alcohol; and Archie's father, Billy, is one of Osborne's familiar characters who personifies (as a respected music-hall performer in his own right) a lost age and induces ambivalent feelings of nostalgia and pity.

The enervating stasis of the family, the emotional confusion of its members and, above all, the desperate stoical cheerfulness of Archie – cracking risqué jokes, seeming to relish his perennial evasion of the taxman but revealingly described as 'dead behind the eyes'[57] – act as a powerful metaphor for a country that on the one hand was enjoying strong economic growth but on the other had alienated many of its inhabitants through class barriers, a collective sense of disenfranchisement and an unacknowledged international impotence. Archie's speech to Jean (initially Dorothy Tutin, but then Joan Plowright on the play's transfer to the West End six weeks later) at the end of the first half is one of the few moments of genuine emotion on his part. Delivered in a slow laconic drawl by Olivier, it was a thrilling moment in this first production and encapsulated the overarching theme of illusory security sought behind emotional deception:

> Well, Mick wouldn't want us to cut the celebration short. We'll drink to Mick, and let's hope to God he manages. Old Nick and the income tax man. With you it's Prime Ministers, with me it's dogs. Nuns, clergymen and dogs. Did I ever tell you the greatest compliment I had paid to me – the greatest compliment I always treasure? I was walking along the front somewhere – I think it was here actually – one day, o, it must be twenty-five years ago, I was quite a young man. Well, I was there walking along the front, to meet what I think we used to call a piece of crackling. Or perhaps it was a bit of fluff. No that was earlier. Anyway, I know I enjoyed it afterwards. But the point is I was walking along the front, all on my own, minding my own business, (*pause*) and two nuns came towards me – (*pause*) two nuns – (*He trails off, looking very tired and old. He looks across at Jean and pushes the bottle at her*) Talk to me.[58]

The critics did not know whether to marvel most at an unexpectedly great performance by Olivier; Osborne's achievement at writing a second success within twelve months; or George Devine's entrepreneurship at staging the work at the Royal Court just seven days after the coup of *Fin de partie*. It certainly cemented the reputation of the ESC, and provided the crucial financial lifeline that was to ensure the viability of the company over the next two years of experimentation. Tynan was of the view that whilst Tony Richardson's direction was lax, the supporting cast under-utilised (a familiar complaint of his against the ESC) and even the didacticism too ambitious ('Mr Osborne has planned a gigantic mural and carried it out in a colour range too narrow for the job'), the play's form of a vaudeville show was a 'stunningly original device' and the playwright had created 'one of the great acting parts of our age'. His admiration for Olivier's performance of 'miracles' was untrammelled, and he was deeply affected by the ending: 'The crown, perhaps, of this great performance is Archie's jocular, venomous farewell to the audience: "Let

me know where you're working tomorrow night – and I'll come and see *you*.'"
Harold Hobson agreed: 'You will not see more magnificent acting than this anywhere in the world.'[59] No wonder Tynan felt able to begin his review with the claim
that 'This has been the most varied, nourishing and provocative week that the London theatre has known since the war.'[60]

When *The Entertainer* transferred to the Palace in September, for a lucrative run in
a commercial West End theatre, Tynan revised several key aspects of his earlier enthusiasm for Osborne. What struck him now was that the writing of this Angry Young
Man contained less of the revolutionary and more of the retrospective. Osborne's
objective in the play, he wrote, was to show 'a single wrecked family and to suggest
that the clue to its disintegration lies in the breakdown of solid Edwardian values' and
that 'in spite of his skin-deep modernity, Mr Osborne's heart belongs to reminiscence'.[61] His use of a contemporary idiom and creation of bravura roles had been
ground-breaking, but he no longer inspired any certainty in Tynan that he might
become the British Brecht. Indeed, it was apparent that the adherents of the 'Angry'
movement, such as it was, had little in common other than a sense of frustration at
atrophy and a collective middle-class sensibility. Although the publication of *Declaration*, a collection of essays by 'Angry' writers, in April was hailed as a manifesto for
the disgruntled contributors – and the controversy surrounding Osborne's famous
comment that the royal family was the gold tooth in a mouthful of decay resulted in
the cancellation by the Royal Court's Council of the launch party at the theatre[62] –
the disparate nature of their essays highlighted their very different preoccupations.
Colin Wilson, the author of *The Outsider*, for example, wanted writers and artists to
adopt a 'common credo' in the light of the fact that the 'Church has failed civilisation'.[63] John Wain, who had written another 'new wave' novel, *Hurry On Down*, felt
that contemporary life had been ruined by excessive industrialisation, resulting in 'all
our thinking becoming mechanistic'.[64] John Osborne preferred to focus on the irrelevance of the monarchy, remarking that nobody could 'seriously pretend that the royal
round of gracious boredom, the protocol of ancient festivity, is politically useful or
morally stimulating',[65] and Tynan himself, in a rather flaccid chapter, revealingly
reminded his readers of his insistent desire to practise rather than observe. He had one
specific plan for the future: 'If I can forget for a few months how insuperably difficult
it is to write one, [I want to write] a play.'[66] They might yearn for anger and action,
but the general mood of the country was tranquil and compliant. Protest at this time
would centre around minority middle-class concerns.

It was perhaps for this reason that Tynan's short visit to New York at the end of
May should strike him as so refreshing. American theatre practitioners seemed so
passionate about their work. Audiences flocked to coffee bars and restaurants to
dissect what they had seen. American newspapers contained a much broader

analysis of the latest theatrical trends. Literary prizes, such as the prestigious
Pulitzer, could be awarded to pieces of drama, the latest being *Long Day's Journey
Into Night* – 'a work of implacable majesty', in Tynan's view[67] – and there was a
cause that people were now battling over. Lee Strasberg had stated just before
Tynan's arrival that the 'Method' had made the American theatre 'the most vital
theater in the world',[68] and having witnessed several shows, Tynan felt compelled
to observe that 'New York theatre is more often and more urgently in touch with
the life around it than any other in the world.' It was during this visit that the seeds
of a plan to take a sabbatical in New York began to take root.

A change of scene might be just what his tempestuous marriage needed to make
it more bearable for both parties, too. Elaine completed her novel in June and sent
it to the publisher of *Lucky Jim*, Victor Gollancz. He was deeply impressed, and only
had two stipulations: retain your married name and make the title sound less like a
cookery book. Elaine was indignant at the suggestions and refused, and the publisher reluctantly backed down, allowing her to sign the contract in July. Her
husband was equally positive. Having read the manuscript in one go, he said that it
was 'going to be a colossal best-seller'[69] and made some helpful observations about
the characterisation of the protagonist, Sally Jay. His endorsement and their collaboration hinted at the bonds that kept them together, but, as always, their differing
sexual needs drove a wedge between them. On his return from the US, Tynan told
his wife that he intended to go to Spain that summer with Carol Saroyan, whom
he had met on an earlier visit to Los Angeles, and with whom he claimed he was
sexually compatible. Elaine, still continuing her affair with Cyril Connolly, was not
placated by a beautiful black cocktail dress that he had bought for her from the Cal-
ifornian boutique, Jax, where Marilyn Monroe was known to shop, and threatened
to divorce him if he went through with this. On 20 July Tynan departed for the *feria*,
but not before he had left messages on scraps of paper taped all around the flat with
varying pleas: 'Oh Skip stay with me please', 'You are everything beautiful', 'I have
nothing to do any more without you my darling' or 'My life turns on you only my
love.'[70] Up until the final decade of his life, he always seemed to believe that he could
get away with it – whatever 'it' was.

Elaine was unmoved. She threw a party two days after his departure to celebrate
both her contract and her impending divorce, and she hired a lawyer to help her
secure evidence of her husband's adultery. Without proof that she was the 'injured
party', English law would not grant her a divorce, even if both parties consented to
the agreement. Soon enough, a distraught Tynan phoned. He had been surprised in
bed with Carol Saroyan in their hotel room by a detective and would be flying home
the next day. He was mortified, penitent and desperate to try and patch things up. He
suggested a trip away to help their reconciliation and Elaine initially agreed – until

she heard the detective's report of two people perfectly content in each other's company. Her husband implored her to give him a second chance and she finally relented, agreeing to give up the divorce and to spend the summer at the house of Anne and Bill Davis, friends of Cyril Connolly, near Málaga. But it was a useless compromise. Their frequent rows threatened the tranquil atmosphere and Tynan's insistence that they return to his S&M sex practices – 'He hadn't come back to me to be deprived of those, he said'[71] – led to an almost irrevocable split. Elaine endured this for a week before precipitating an enormous row at dinner in front of their hosts. They left the next morning, but not before Elaine had explained to a sympathetic Anne Davis the reason for her fury. The fact that Elaine's book was due for publication in early 1958 seemed to be one of the few threads that were now keeping them together, although they were destined to spend another seven years as husband and wife.

Given the tremendous emotional strain that the unhappy couple were under, it seems remarkable that they were able to function, let alone finish a novel or compile a theatre column that was the envy of the profession. Regular visitors to Mount Street became familiar with Elaine's bouts of drinking, Tynan's solicitous concern for her when she was inebriated, her messages written in lipstick on the bathroom mirror and his snarling rows and wounding comments. They could neither live together nor live apart. Friends were also struck by their ability to break off and go and write and, of course, it was their respective artistic talents that kept them going for now. Incredibly, in the midst of this trying period of domestic mayhem, Tynan penned one of his funniest columns, in which he created a calling card for the two directorial wunderkinds, Peter Hall and Peter Brook, who were developing a reputation for being able to create hits out of the most unpromising material:

Hall & Brook Ltd., the Home of Lost Theatrical Causes. Collapsing plays shored up, unspeakable lines glossed over, unactable scenes made bearable. Wrecks salvaged, ruins refurbished: unpopular plays at popular prices. Masterpieces dealt with only if neglected. Shakespearean juvenilia and senilia our speciality: if it can walk, we'll make it run. Bad last acts no obstacle: if it peters out, call Peter in. Don't be fobbed off with Glenvilles, Woods or Zadeks: look for the trademark – Hall & Brook.[72]

Domestic turbulence, far from stifling Tynan's creativity, seemed to spur it. And his personal charisma meant that he was never short of company. The thirty-year-old critic – the age at which he had earlier predicted he would die – was never short of company. When Elaine was either unable or unwilling to attend the theatre with him, Tynan referred to the list of about twenty women in the back of his diary for 1957, whom he could call up to accompany him to a first night.

One piece of welcome news arrived in August, when David Astor, well aware of the star status of his theatre critic, offered him a new three-year contract. His writing had given 'a great brilliance and integrity to the paper',[73] he told him, and Tynan, never immune to praise from his superiors, was delighted and gratified: 'I can't tell you how much your letter cheered me. In the past three years I have often felt as if I were walking on egg-shells. It's wonderfully encouraging to discover that in spite of my fears none got broken. Thank you for giving me the opportunity.'[74]

For the past few years, Tynan had wanted to shed the tag of being a failed director and the *Observer* play competition had been conceived partly as a way of proving that he could facilitate change as well as observe it. When it had first been announced at the end of 1956, he had expected around 500 entries. As it was, the paper was swamped with over 2,000 scripts. A small minority of these belonged to a new category of plays that were the successors to 'Loamshire' works – 'dodo-dramas' – that 'begin with the telephone ringing in the library of a brigadier's country house in Lower Nattering', but most adhered to the requirement for freshness and relevance. 'We wanted eyes that were focused, ears that were bent, on the world around us', Tynan proudly announced in 'The Play Competition' in August 1957, and such was the quality of the submissions that the judges decided to award four extra prizes, in addition to those already announced.

He divided the entries into five main categories. Unsurprisingly, the aggression of the Soviet Union against Hungary led to theatrical consideration of this event. 'Many competitors wrote about Livaria, a People's Republic menaced by Dragonja, its gigantic neighbour: and there tended to be lines like: "Has Chava brought the Vagchicks from Drifkop?"' Tynan had hoped for 'a more documentary approach'. On a related subject, the Cold War and the arms race gave rise to numerous plays that dealt with the bomb. Shortly after the deadline for scripts, the government's defence White Paper of April 1957 stated that the country's future military strategy would be based on the concept of 'massive retaliation'. The detonation of Britain's first H-bomb on Christmas Island in May 1957 was met by increasingly vocal protests, and the Campaign for Nuclear Disarmament was formed in the following year. This was Anger made real. But the submitted plays on the topic were generally ineffective, and Tynan complained that: 'as with Hungary, hot blood produced bad drama'. An equally prolific, but ultimately disappointing, theme was that of the frustrated lower-middle-class intellectual. It was inevitable that *Look Back in Anger* should spawn numerous copies, but none matched, in the judges' eyes, the incisiveness of the original.

This left two more promising groups. Firstly, several works focused on the colour bar and race relations in general, and secondly a large entry from Australian playwrights, a previously unnoticed cohort until the arrival of *The Summer of the Seventeenth Doll*. The prizes were awarded as follows: 1st prize – Errol John's *Moon on a Rainbow Shawl*; 2nd – Gurney Campbell and Daphne Atlas's *Sit on the Earth*, 3rd equal

– Ann Jellicoe's *The Sport of My Mad Mother*, N.F. Simpson's *A Resounding Tinkle* and Richard Beynon's *The Shifting Heart*. Only three would resonate – albeit faintly – beyond 1957, but the competition had placed the *Observer* at the heart of the drive for new theatre. Tynan himself was as pleased that they had received only one script in poetic form, as he was at the final verdict. 'Prose has decisively counter-rebelled,'[75] he cried.

Not everybody was as pleased as Tynan at the advance (however slow) of social realism. John Whiting had first come to prominence in 1951 with his light-hearted comedy set at the time of the Napoleonic wars, *A Penny for a Song*. Critically popular but a commercial failure, his next work, *Saint's Day* – a challenging poetic fantasy produced at the Arts Theatre – bewildered the critics, but was championed by John Gielgud, Tyrone Guthrie and Peggy Ashcroft. There then followed successive struggles to get his work staged, and by 1957 he was beginning to tire of being described as an interesting and challenging member of the 'avant-garde' who could not find a theatre to stage his work. An 'artist-aristocrat',[76] in the words of his biographer, Eric Salmon, Whiting decided to fight back with a lecture at the Old Vic on 'The Art of the Dramatist'. For Tynan, this was 'Romanticism's last stand':

> Everything, we swiftly gathered, militated against Mr Whiting's concept of pure drama. All we were offered in the modern English theatre were plays of 'social significance', plays set in concentration camps, plays made up of 'the idiot mumblings of the half-wit who lives down the lane.' Instead of looking within themselves for their own unique modes of utterance, playwrights were content to reproduce the 'direct unornamented speech' of everyday life. Austerity was no longer prized: instead, fashionable authors (Mr Whiting did not actually name John Osborne) allowed their characters to indulge in long, dishevelled, emotional outbursts. Three years, he reminded us without rancour, had passed since one of his plays had been seen in London; even so, he found himself as convinced as ever that it was no part of the author's job to surrender to his audience by approaching it on its own terms. A play, he said, 'has nothing to do with an audience.'

This sounded dangerously like T.S. Eliot's conception of the superiority of the artist. The poet was famous for his assertion in the Preface to *For Lancelot Andrewes* (1928) that he was 'classical in literature, royalist in politics and Anglo-Catholic in religion' and, like Whiting, had publicly lamented the decline in literary standards since 1945. Nothing was more guaranteed to provoke Tynan than this:

> It was hereabouts that I began to wonder whether we were talking about poetry or the novel, private arts intended to be sampled by one person at a time? Had we not somehow strayed from the drama, a public art which must

be addressed to hundreds of people at the same time? Somewhere in Mr Whiting's imagination there glows a vision of an ideal theatre where the playwright is freed from the necessity of attracting customers, where his fastidious cadences are not tainted by the exposure to rank plebeian breath. It is a theatre without an audience. And it exists – again in Mr Whiting's imagination – as a gesture of defiance against those other, equally mythical London theatres whose socially significant plays about concentration camps are constantly being staged to the vociferous approval of 'the masses'. (Anyone not a playwright belongs, in Mr Whiting's mind, to the masses – who belied, by the way, their imputed stupidity by turning up in force to hear his lecture, and by asking at the end a number of surprisingly literate questions). On the whole I find Mr Whiting's dream world extremely seductive. He says it exists, and wishes it didn't. I know it doesn't, but rather wish it did. There would be few complaints from me if the West End were full of contemporary plays enthusiastically acclaimed by mass audiences.

The conclusion was as brutal as the heading of the column, 'Out of Touch':

> At one point in his lecture, to illustrate the deadness of naturalism, Mr Whiting read out an invented snatch of dialogue such as one might hear in a bus-queue. How repetitive! he implied: how drab and dull! It was in fact infectiously and rivetingly alive. One longed to hear more. I realised then, with a sense of wild frustration, that Mr Whiting was a born playwright determined at all costs not to be a playwright at all.[77]

If audiences were beginning to develop a taste for contemporary plays, they were doing so in a small number of venues. It was now apparent that the Royal Court and Theatre Workshop were two dazzling beacons, whose success was achieved despite, and not because of, state funding. By October, Tynan was urging that the Arts Council be given a much larger slice of government support (only £1 million was given for the whole of the arts) and that the penury that weighed down Joan Littlewood's company be removed. Whereas George Devine had just been able to secure one of the very first commercial sponsorship arrangements, when Schweppes offered 'commercial patronage' to sponsor *The Sport of My Mad Mother*, its poorer counterpart in the East End had been offered £1,000 in grant aid only if they could raise a further £2,000 themselves. The foolishness of this was apparent to anyone who went to see Joan Littlewood's latest production, *You Won't Always Be on Top*, at Stratford East in October. The set alone demonstrated the degree to which she wanted to banish artifice from the theatre and Tynan was staggered. It was 'performed against and upon the most spectacular and elaborate setting I have ever seen

... John Bury has reproduced a three-storey building in course of construction, complete with scaffolding, cement-mixer, workmen's hut and no-man's land of plank-transversed mire. It is an astonishing achievement.'[78]

By the end of 1957, there was finally some evidence that the consolidation promised by *Look Back in Anger*, but only intermittently apparent in the rest of 1956, was beginning to emerge. The commercial West End was producing works such as *Flowering Cherry* by Robert Bolt, which seemed to have been influenced by the new mood. Jim Cherry had worked for a city insurance firm for twenty years and longed to escape by buying an orchard in Somerset. Writing with half an eye on Brecht, Bolt depicts the disintegration of Cherry's marriage and the collapse of his dream in a powerful scene where he seizes an iron poker – an obvious symbol of his sexual fragility – and attempts to bend it behind his neck. In spite of the poker yielding a little, the exertion proves too much and Jim collapses to the floor with a heart attack. As he lies dying, an image of the orchard is projected on to the back-cloth, powerfully challenging the audience – many of whom might have shared this 1950s desire for a rural idyll (examined in Wesker's *I'm Talking about Jerusalem*) – to consider how Jim might have avoided his fate. Its portrait of a middle-class family was 'vivid' and 'complex' in Tynan's eyes and something to get genuinely excited about. He even managed to be reasonably nice to Ralph Richardson: 'No actor in England is more interesting to watch ... Sir Ralph is a genius. What I seriously doubt is whether this is a part for a genius.'[79] Harold Hobson was the play's greatest champion, reviewing it on three separate occasions.

Theatre outside London was showing signs of a renaissance and was beginning to rebel against its historic role as a try-out for West End shows. Sam Wanamaker's Northern Arts Centre in Liverpool was commended to the Merseysiders – 'If Liverpool does not support its visitors, it might just as well jump in the Mersey'[80] – and Wanamaker himself avoided criticism, having played the choric lawyer in *A View from the Bridge* with 'exemplary calm'. The next show, the musical *Finian's Rainbow*, was given a favourable notice, too, although there is again some evidence of the undercurrent that existed between the critic and the director: 'Sam Wana-maker, whom we associate with the drama of clenched fists and beetle brows, has relaxed for Christmas by producing one of the blithest and best of the post-war Broadway musicals'.[81] And one of the prizewinners in the *Observer* competition received its début on no less a stage than the Royal Court. Tynan considered *A Resounding Tinkle* 'a revolutionary funny piece of work',[82] although subsequent gen-erations have appeared more immune to its charm.

The Royal Court was now a robust institution, reliant on Osborne as its 'financial keystone', but unlikely to wither away. Younger actors, such as Scofield, Albert Finney of Birmingham Rep, Peter O'Toole of Bristol Old Vic, Mary Ure, Jill Bennett,

Barbara Jefford and Dorothy Tutin were changing the atmosphere of acting; and theatre could once again begin to challenge film as a topic for discussion. In his retrospect for 1957, therefore – safe in these gains – Tynan announced a new campaign, and one which would have dramatic implications for him personally:

> What the Royal Court has achieved is in fact exactly what the second house of the National Theatre ought to be achieving, that smaller affiliated auditorium envisaged by Archer as the home of off-beat moderns and neglected classics. Here, of course, we reach the gap that still aches and gapes, the lack of a National Theatre. But even in this stagnant quarter things are cheering up: public controversy on the subject has lately been revived. Sir Donald Wolfit has been writing some commendably heated letters; and as long as we take care to reward him for his efforts with a peerage instead of the directorship of the theatre, nothing but good will have been done.[83]

Behind the scenes he took a much less benign attitude to the news of Wolfit's interest in the project. Clearly convinced that Wolfit's involvement would be disastrous, and desiring to play a formative role in any new institution, he contacted Anthony Quayle, the director of the Stratford Memorial Theatre, to sound out this plausible candidate for the directorship of the national company. The fact that it was not in his gift and that no post yet existed was immaterial. Quayle's response is enlightening. At this stage, Tynan's relationship with Olivier was evidently not strong enough to prevent him from attempting to hook his star to that of a rival:

> My dear Ken,
>
> I don't know which frightens me more – the idea of Donald Wolfit as the leader of the National Theatre Movement or that of myself! Both thoughts, in their different ways, fill me with horror.
>
> Your friendly warning is greatly appreciated and I am truly flattered that you should think me capable of the job. My feelings haven't changed since we had lunch in New York: I don't think I could possibly face up to the job if it were to materialise in the next year or two – I simply haven't the heart to throw myself into such an intolerable headache. But who knows what changes of head and heart may take place as the years roll by?
>
> When Christmas is over, could we not meet and have another word about it?
>
> Yours ever
> Tony[84]

Tynan's manoeuvring for the NT post was just beginning, and he kept himself publicly associated with the project later on in the year when he staged the mock laying of another foundation stone, complete with undertaker's garb, on the South Bank to protest at its perpetual postponement.

The year 1958 began with a crisis in the theatre, but this time, to Tynan's great satisfaction, it was a crisis in French theatre. His usual New Year trip abroad this year took him to Paris, and there is a delicious sense of irony when he begins his bulletin with the mock-weary 'There's always the acting . . .' The previous year he had been discomforted by the general tone of disappointment that greeted a Brechtian work. Now it was Harold Hobson's turn to feel uncomfortable. 'Consumed by a sick mingling of xenophobia and self-disgust, of chauvinism and cynicism, the average French audience seems to me in grave danger of becoming an audience of neurotic simpletons',[85] Tynan noted, with scarcely concealed pleasure.

Tynan was now without doubt a man of influence and a focus of interest. Only just turned thirty, he was approached by Robert Knittel of Jonathan Cape to write his autobiography – the suggested title was 'One Score and Ten' – but he could not find the time to get down to the project.[86] Members of the public and the profession wrote to him asking for his help in advancing either themselves or a relative in the profession. One extraordinary example came when the eminent Dame Sybil Thorndike, away touring in Australia, contacted him from the Theatre Royal, Sydney:

Dear Kenneth Tynan,

This letter needs no answer – but I wondered if, in your theatre-seeking, you touch Dublin. They are doing at Lord Longford's Gate Theatre a production of *The Tempest* (my son is producing, Christopher Casson) that's why I am specially interested – from what I've heard, from what Christopher has written me it seems a very significant production . . .

Yours very sincerely,

Sybil Thorndike Casson[87]

With his public persona becoming as important as his literary one, Tynan's actions were scrutinised carefully by friends and foes alike. One particularly disgruntled audience member the previous October had written to Astor to remonstrate about his theatre critic's very public irreverence:

Several people wondered last night at the Old Vic (First Night of *Henry VI, Part 3*), whether it is in keeping with your paper's policy that your dramatic critic Kenneth Tynan should go on reading a book whilst the National Anthem was being played. If he shares the anti-royal attitude of some of the other 'Angry Young Men' he might at least ponder to think which paper he represents when visiting a theatre as a critic on that paper's behalf.

Yours faithfully,
E Barr[88]

Tynan clearly did share their indifference to the reverence of royalty and made this explicit in his list of the 'Hazards of Playgoing'. These included the difficulty of finding out which theatre is showing which play; the cramped nature of cloak-rooms; 'the scandal of London theatre programmes'; the difficulty of getting to the bar at the interval, 'where warm gin is dispensed by surly, glaring, female teeto-tallers'; and the pre-eminent hazard, 'the playing of the National Anthem, during which we stand to attention, while gloves, scarves and programmes fall unregarded to the floor'. To the indignation of royalists, he commended Theatre Workshop, whose programme disingenuously stated that the National Anthem would be played only in the presence of royalty or heads of state.[89] An unlikely occurrence at Stratford East.

Any illusion of pre-eminence in his own marriage was challenged somewhat by the publication of Elaine's book *The Dud Avocado* on 12 January. The following Sunday it received excellent reviews, not least from the *Sunday Times*, where John Metcalfe found it 'As delightful and delicate an examination of how it is to be twenty and in love in Paris as I've read . . .'[90] The book quickly became a huge success, with Penguin publishing it in paperback, a competition for the movie rights and numerous compliments from friends who had been connected with the husband in the first instance ('I was so pleased to read Elaine's notices. Please give her my love and congratulations', John Osborne cabled Tynan in early February).[91] This attention further complicated their relationship. Tynan, not used to being upstaged in his own home, took the ribbing of his colleagues on the *Observer* badly, and Elaine reports his warning that if she ever wrote another book, he would divorce her. 'That did it. Early next morning I sat down and started a new novel.'[92] She also embarked on another affair, with Mark Culme-Seymour.

'There were happy times with Elaine',[93] Tynan told his diary a quarter of a century later, but they were not apparent in 1958. Tracy Tynan recalls constant rows, distressing scenes revolving around her father's sado-masochism and the abuse of drugs, such as Dexamyl, a stimulant and antidepressant then known as the 'house-wife's helper'.[94]

Publicly, Tynan betrayed no sign of this private distress. The couple had an amazing capacity to be resilient and to soldier on. Instead, he redoubled his hostility towards anything resembling the dododramas he had identified from the play competition. N.C. Hunter's *A Touch of the Sun* (February 1958) was an archetype of the genre and Tynan loathed 'the vacuity of the author's attitude towards life':

The hero, God help us all, is an intellectual. Being a Socialist and a teacher of backward children, he is, of course, priggish, humourless, inhibited, unable to dance and (he admits it to himself) 'twisted with envy'. This penurious swot takes his family to stay with rich in-laws near Cannes. His wife and children relish the *luxe* of it all, to his mounting fury; and after an ugly scene he whisks them back to the squalid austerity of Leatherhead. Mr Hunter's message, delivered with what is either stupefying naïveté or brazen impertinence, seems to be that the rich man's life is not only different from but qualitatively better than the schoolmaster's.[95]

As something of a champagne socialist, Tynan was doubtless irked by the common charge that socialists relished the wearing of hair shirts. He also completed another one of his famous parodies to lambast the Catholic superstition of Graham Greene's *The Potting Shed*. A young psychiatrist interviews a failed drama critic (ten years hence) who has lost his faith in theatre, having seen this play. 'Tell me about the play. Force yourself back into that theatre. Slump now as you slumped then in D16,' the psychiatrist urges. *The Potting Shed*, by refusing to see the theatre as a place where human problems could be stated in human terms, had shot drama back into the Dark Ages, the critic sobs and departs 'to perform in a spirit of obedient humility the offices laid down for him by the Society of West End Theatre Managers'.[96] This production saw the end of the 1950s vogue for novelists to write plays, and dealt a fatal blow to Christian drama, Verse or otherwise.

In February, Peter Brook and his wife, the actress Natasha Parry, invited the Tynans to a dinner party. Unknown to them, the other guests were Laurence Olivier and Vivien Leigh. Given Tynan's acid comments about Leigh this created a potentially awkward situation, but it proved a surprisingly harmonious evening, with Elaine impressed by the vivacity and beauty of Leigh. The two women quickly struck up a friendship and started to lunch together. Leigh was preparing for rehearsals of Giraudoux's *Duel of Angels*, in a version by Christopher Fry to open in April, and told Elaine that she had insisted that the producer, Binkie Beaumont, dress the production in costumes by Christian Dior. It was not the type of approach that would appeal to her husband. After the production closed for a short while to allow Leigh a break, she invited Elaine to the famous mansion, Notley Abbey, which was synonymous with the grand lifestyle of the Oliviers. Elaine was unsure whether she should allow her husband to accompany her: Leigh was in fragile health and might be provoked by his presence. The invitation had been for her alone. Their recent meeting had passed without difficulty, however, and Tynan was eager to go. Elaine relented and they travelled down together.

It was a bizarre stay. Moments of tranquillity – a picnic by the river – were interspersed with moments of nervous tension. Leigh was rendered almost hysterical by a distracting wasp, and had a fierce row with her mother (who with her father and the household retainer, Bill, were the only other occupants, Olivier being away in Spain). Leigh claimed that her mother had never wanted her to play Blanche du Bois in *A Streetcar Named Desire*. Such was the pain of this scene that Bill contacted Olivier, who told him he would fly back the following day.

After this outburst, the Tynans retired to their room for a nap and Elaine awoke to see her husband draped in chainmail armour. It had been worn by Sybil Thorndike in her production of Shaw's *Saint Joan*, he explained.[97] Leigh had asked him to put it on. Tynan's diary recollection twenty years later was more graphic. There were single beds in their room and he had been awoken from his siesta by a naked Leigh manipulating his genitals. Initially responsive, he froze when he thought of the situation and disentangled himself. According to him, it had been after dinner that Leigh had suggested he dress up in the chain mail.[98]

Olivier returned earlier than expected and a frigid meal at an enormous dining table ensued. After dinner, whilst Elaine and Leigh retired to listen to records, their husbands began to discuss the topic closest to both their hearts, the imminent National Theatre. Tynan was thrilled to learn that Olivier wanted to be its head and had been making discreet plans and enquiries. It seemed almost too good to be true that the actor whom he idolised above all others was willing to be involved in the project that he cherished the most. The elation quickly subsided, however, when Olivier asked Tynan to leave Notley, on account of the destabilising effect he was having on his wife. How he must have regretted those *Evening Standard* articles at that instant.

The private stand-off at Notley that February was mirrored by a public stand-off between the government and the supporters of nuclear disarmament. Ever since the publication of the Duncan Sandys White Paper on Defence the previous April, indignation had been rising about the dangers of nuclear arms and nuclear energy. The detonation of the first British H-bomb in May 1957 had been followed by a serious nuclear accident at the Windscale establishment in October. Full details of this potentially disastrous incident were hushed up by the government, but sufficient information emerged to give momentum to the broad constituency of protesters who were now coalescing around this issue. For many, this protest movement was a vehicle for expressing wider cultural dissent and the first meeting of the Campaign for Nuclear Disarmament (CND), at the Conway Hall on 17 February 1958, drew many political, literary, cultural and religious figures. These included Joan Littlewood, J.B. Priestley, the philosopher Bertrand Russell, the historian A.J.P. Taylor, Christian representatives such as Father Trevor Huddleston and politicians including Michael Foot and Tom Driberg. Here was the protest movement yearned for since 1956, promised after Suez but never delivered. The inaugural meeting was a significant gathering – if largely ignored by the press – and CND, with its distinctive symbol of a droopy cross within a circle, became an immediate badge of honour for middle-class dissenters. Although not present at Conway Hall, Tynan quickly wrote to the left-wing newspaper *Tribune* to express his support for CND's aspirations. On account of the government's commitment to a nuclear deterrent, 'we have volunteered for annihilation', he said. 'We shall go to our graves in quiet heart, secure in the knowledge that by our sacrifice we shall have made our island uninhabitable to the invading hordes, or for that matter anybody else.' Continuing the irony – and in a deliberate allusion to the 'Red Flag' – he expressed mock-concern for the possible fate of the monarchy in the face of nuclear oblivion:

> To expose the Royal Family to radiation would be to risk the most dynastic consequences. Both patriotism and common sense lead inescapably to the conclusion I have respectfully suggested.
>
> The Royal Family should take up residence, with all convenient speed, in some distant dependency. Let cowards flinch and traitors glare: we'll keep the old flag flying there.[99]

In his swipe at the monarchy Tynan hints at the hope of many at the time that this movement might transcend its single-issue origins. Certainly the initial success of CND was impressive. On Good Friday, in poor weather, several thousand protesters began a march from Trafalgar Square to the atomic weapons research establishment Aldermaston, fifty miles away. Tynan turned up at the start, but did not make the journey to Berkshire. The following Monday, in rather better weather, he characteristically took a taxi down to Aldermaston to join the head of the march behind its banner. CND attracted exactly the type of reader that enjoyed Tynan's denunciations of 'dododramas'. It sought to radicalise those who were already likely to be in the vanguard of the radicals, but in its moral display of defiance in the face of overwhelming odds it provided a model of civil defiance that had previously been unthinkable in conventional British politics.

Tynan's preferred form of direct action was with the pen and he used it to brilliant effect in the spring of 1958. With the Royal Court now a beacon of hope, it was all the more important to secure its gains. One third-prize winner in the *Observer* play competition, Ann Jellicoe's *The Sport of My Mad Mother*, received its première at the theatre – and was accorded lavish praise: '. . . for all its faults, this is a play of spectacular promise and inspiring imperfection. It is inimitable both at its best and its worst; and nothing of which that can be said should be shunned by enquiring playgoers'.[100] It is now recognised as the first truly experimental work at the Court and, although the generally poor reviews from critics other than Tynan resulted in a run of only fourteen performances, it marked a significant moment in the ESC's development.[101]

The Royal Court as a cultural institution was hailed on the second anniversary of its opening production in April. 'Two years ago last Tuesday there was no English Stage Company,' Tynan began his celebratory piece. 'What a dull theatre we must have had! And what on earth did we playgoers find to argue about?' The catalyst for change had been John Osborne, 'the Fulham flame-thrower', and it was now hard to remember what life was like before the Royal Court's inception: 'We quarrelled among ourselves over Brecht and the future of poetic drama: in debates with foreign visitors we crossed our fingers, swallowed hard and talked of Terence Rattigan; but if we were critics, we must quite often have felt that we were practising our art in a vacuum.' The great virtue of George Devine's operation was that it had made drama 'a matter of public controversy' and even 'the theatrical establishment has bowed to it', as seen by Olivier's appearance in *The Entertainer*. The personal effect on Tynan himself had been huge, and his gratitude was immense: '. . . it has given my mind a whetstone, and my job a meaning, that the English theatre of five years ago showed few signs of providing. If (and the if is crucial) it can hold its present nucleus of talent together, it may well change the whole course of drama.'[102] This was another one of Tynan's discerning predictions that was to come true.

There was no room for complacency, though, as an extraordinary event in March had proved. Tynan always needed to crusade, and the great sadness of his final decade was the absence of causes – in the manner of Jimmy Porter – that he felt were worth fighting for. After the première of a Christian work of abnegation, on the stage of the home of social realism, a literal fight took place. Tynan was now becoming as intolerant of works that portrayed man as fallen without the redemption promised by Christianity, as he was of Loamshire or dododramas that portrayed man as inevitably bound by the chains of class. In the summer of 1958, this would boil over into a very public spat with Eugène Ionesco, but Stuart Holroyd's *The Tenth Chance* touched an equally raw nerve:

> *The Tenth Chance* (Royal Court, last Sunday night), a short play by Stuart Holroyd, began by showing us three men incarcerated in a Norwegian Gestapo prison during the war. One was a priest (i.e. soul), another a blustering sex-mad prole (i.e. body), and the third an agnostic journalist (i.e. mind) with a 'crying need' for faith. At once I applied, for purposes of verification, one of Tynan's laws of Middlebrow Drama, which is that characters who boast of being agnostic in Act One invariably join the Church in Act Three. (The reverse, in English plays at least, never applies). So far the play had reached a fair high-school level and roused in me nothing more than a mild bewilderment that the Royal Court had even considered it for public performance. I calmed myself by summoning from the recesses of my memory dusty and tolerant criteria I had used to assess,

at the age of fifteen, those early war-time quickies in which refugee German directors were apt to turn up as actors, playing Überleutnant Schmierkäse, the beast of Bergen-op-Zoom.

The second half of Mr Holroyd's playlet, however, was offensive as well as childish. The agnostic, covered in ketchup, declared that he had found God through torture; and in a phantasmagoria of choral music and beloved pain he presented what appeared to be clinching proof that Nazi oppression was the way to salvation. It was a sick, misguided spectacle, and I would worry about any Christian who endorsed it, for Christianity as I understand it is not entirely dependent on the celebration of physical agony . . .

. . . A friend of mine who reads all the daily papers tells me that I was described in one of them as having called Mr Holroyd's play 'sadistic rubbish'. This is a blatant and understandable aural error. What I said was 'sadistic spinach' . . .[103]

Light was shed on the aftermath of this bizarre performance twenty years later, when Christopher Logue reminded Tynan of the events that surrounded the pre-mière:

I remember it like this: Elaine, yourself and I went to the Court from Mount St. The theatre was full and you sat nearer to the stage than Elaine and I, whose stalls were in the middle of a row.

We had not discussed [*The Tenth Chance*] before going; indeed, though Colin Wilson was at the height of his fame, Michael Hastings and Bill Hopkins beginning to loom, Stuart Holroyd I had never met, and, perhaps, never heard of.

The play was didactic and boring. Its final minutes consisted of a sort of chant ('Receive him into the Kingdom of Light' according to John Barber in the *Express*, 10.3.58) by some members of the cast uttered as they paced around the hero (Robert Shaw?) who was tied to a chair, and the thought this tableau expressed had something to do with the equation of pain felt by those the Gestapo (or SS) had tortured, with the suffering induced by unrequited love, or, requited but adulterous love (wrong: apparently the play featured a man who is converted to Christianity through torture. It was (so Holroyd, via Barber, said) based on the diary of a Roman Catholic lorry driver from Oslo).

The noise, plus the wrong-headed pretentiousness of the scene, got my goat, and as much to my own surprise as anyone else's, I stood up and bellowed 'rubbish!'

The action and the chanting stopped, and, in the silence, the voice of Anne Hastings (Michael Hastings' first wife) rose up from the front stalls, saying 'Christopher Logue, get out of this theatre'. Which earned a good laugh from the audience and revealed the play's absurdity far more than my interruption.

When the laugh died away and Shaw had led the cast back into the text,

Elaine said: 'Let's get out of here'. And so we did, obliging those seated to our left to stand up, and thereafter making our way to the pub via the Court's emergency exit whose fire doors closed behind us with a large clang.

Once in the pub nervousness overcame me and Elaine bought us both large brandies.

I suppose the play had ten or fifteen minutes to run. Anyway, by the time it was over we were feeling rather pleased with ourselves and waiting, a little apprehensively for yourself, when the door of the pub burst inwards and Anne Hastings, followed by [Colin] Wilson, Hastings and Holroyd charged towards our table. Crying: 'I'll crush you with my Daimler!', Mrs Hastings launched herself at me and overturned my chair. We finished up on the floor, Mrs H on top, me with my arms around her.

By the time I got to my feet, Wilson and co had surrounded me, with yourself, Lindsay, John Osborne, Colin Wilson, and quite a large crowd standing behind them. It looked as if there was going to be a punch-up. Elaine, in an action which won my love, took off her shoe and said: 'Don't worry about the women, Christopher – I'll deal with them'.

Tynan: (to Colin Wilson) 'It was sadistic rubbish'
Wilson: 'We'll stamp you out'
Tynan: 'Get out of my life'

And I suppose he did.

Afterwards a number of us returned to Mount St. We were eating and drinking when a journalist arrived. Invited to sit down he chose a stool that collapsed underneath him.

My step-sister kept a few press reports. One of these says that punches were thrown – but I doubt it. By the time I got to my feet the barmen were on the scene, policing it, so to speak.[104]

Colin Wilson, famous for sleeping rough on Hampstead Heath whilst writing *The Outsider* by day in the British Museum and for hating *Look Back in Anger*, which he described as 'self-pitying verbiage',[105] protested to the *Observer* the following week that the review had been 'violently unfair' and motivated by personal considerations. Tynan eagerly refuted this – 'if to disagree is to be "unfair" then I plead guilty'[106] – but Wilson, whose star was waning somewhat by 1958 after the universal savaging of his second book, *Religion and the Rebel* (1957), and who had been called a 'Scrambled Egghead' by *Time* magazine, was soothed by an exchange of private correspondence and was able to write: 'Many thanks for your extremely fair and good tempered letter. It verifies the suspicion I'd had that you're not the

irritable and trigger happy writer that many of my friends have assured me you are!'
He also asked Tynan to pass his regards on to Elaine and hoped that 'I shall be
reading her next book soon.'[107]

The summer saw an increase in the exchange of private letters between the critic
and playwrights. An old adversary, Terence Rattigan, re-emerged after a silence of
four years with *Variation on a Theme*. Tynan's beef with Rattigan had always been that
as a skilful writer he ought to be more honest and write realistically about the themes
that appeared to be submerged beneath the surface of his upper-middle-class
dramas. Tynan continued to believe that his treatment of homosexuality in both
Separate Tables and *Variation on a Theme* was pusillanimous. His review, 'Musing Out
Loud' – an imagined discussion with Rattigan's neglected muse – was as cutting as
it was amusing:

Let us suppose that Terence Rattigan's Muse, a brisk, tweedy travelling repre-
sentative of Thalia-Melpomene Co-Productions Ltd, has just returned home after
four years' absence. We find her reading the reviews of Mr Rattigan's *Variation
on a Theme* (Globe). After a while she flings them impatiently down. Her tone, as
she addresses us, is querulous: –

MUSE: This would never have happened if I'd been here. We get *Separate Tables*
launched, I go off on a world cruise, and as soon as my back's turned, what happens? He tries to write a play on his own. Oh, he's threatened to do that before
now, but I've always scared him out of it. 'Look what happened to Noël Coward,' I'd say. 'Inspiration doesn't grow on trees, you know.' But Master Terence
Slyboots knows better. Thinks you can write plays just like that, haha. The
minute I heard what he was up to I came beetling back, but they were already
in rehearsal.

'What's the meaning of this?' I said, and I can tell you I was blazing. 'Well,
darling,' he said, 'four years is a long time, and –' 'Don't you darling me,' I
said. 'I'm a busy Muse. I've got my other clients to consider. You're not the only
pebble on the Non-Controversial Western Playwright's beach, you know. Now
let's get down to cases. What's this play about?' 'Well,' he said, 'the central
character, who's rich and bored and lives in a villa near Cannes, gets desperately
fond of a cocky young boy from the local ballet company, and –' 'Hold your
horses,' I said. 'We've never had a play banned yet, and by George we're not
starting now. Make it a cocky young *girl*.' 'The central character,' he said, very
hoity-toity, 'is a *woman*.'

Black mark to me, I must admit. But once I'd grabbed hold of the script and
taken a good dekko at it, my worst fears were confirmed. About the best you
could say about it was that it wouldn't be banned. This heroine (he calls her Rose

Fish and then, if you please, makes jokes about whether or not she has gills) started out as a typist in Birmingham. She's married four men for money before she meets this ballet-boy. He's been keeping company with a male choreographer, but give the devil his due, Master Terence knows his Lord Chamberlain well enough to keep *that* relationship platonic.

Egged on by the choreographer, Rose gives the lad up for the good of his career. He reforms overnight, but returns to her just as she's in the last throes of succumbing to a wonky lung. And in case you haven't cottoned on to the fact that it's Marguerite Gautier all over again, Rose has a daughter whose pet author is Dumas *fils*. Master Terence makes no bones about his sources. Trouble is, he makes no flesh either. That's where I should have come in. Honestly, I could slap the scamp.

'Interesting subject, don't you think?' he said when I gave the script back to him. 'No', I said, 'but you've made a real Camille of it, haven't you?' He ignored my barbed word-play. Ruthlessly I pressed on. 'Whatever became,' I asked 'of that subtle theatrical technique of yours we hear so much about? T.B., indeed, in this day and age. And making the boy symbolically sprain his ankle. And having Rose leave her farewell message to him on tape-recorder. And giving her a *confidante* I'd have been ashamed to wish on Pinero. And what about that Sherman lover of hers who is talking the so comic English? If you'd written the play, well, it would have been bad enough. As it is –' 'I thought the theme would carry it,' he said, 'a young boy living off an older woman.' That made me plain ratty. 'You're not Colette,' I said, 'and don't you think it.'

I lectured him about the need for honesty and true, fresh feeling, which is my province as a Muse. I told him how sloppy, second-hand ideas invariably expressed themselves in sloppy, second-hand technique. Then I saw the production, by Sir John Gielgud, in which Michael Goodliffe, George Pravda and Jeremy Brett gave the sort of vague, general, superficially convincing performances that are provoked by plays like this. Even the Birmingham accents were phoney. As far as I could see the star of the show was Norman Hartnell, from whose contributions —a white diamanté sack, a shocking pink cocktail dress in pleated chiffon, a casual ensemble of blouse and pedal-pushing slacks, and a two-tiered ball-gown in navy-blue pebble-crêpe – the lean extremities of Margaret Leighton nervously protruded. Miss Leighton, traipsing about looking wry and motherly, knocking back brandies and making rueful little *noués* of despair, modelled the clothes splendidly. I didn't spot much real acting going on, but then there wasn't much reality to begin with.

Anyway, I've told Mr Terence that from now on he can whistle for his Muse. I'm not going to come crawling back to him. He thinks the play will succeed in spite of me, in spite of its lack of inspiration. He thinks it's what the public wants. But that reminds me of Groucho Marx's comment when 3,000 people turned up at the funeral of a commercially successful but universally detested Hollywood mogul. 'You see what I mean?' he said, 'Give the public what they want, and they'll come to see it.' I hope Master Terence heeds the warning. I can get along without him, thank you very much. But he can't get along without me.[108]

A weary Rattigan, away in Beverley Hills, California, during the filming of *Separate Tables* by the Hecht–Lancaster studio, was eager to contest the general principles of Tynan's critical philosophy. In a reasoned and rather poignant communication, he mounted a defence of his own position, which he did not want to be used in the press:

Let's leave our public disagreement where it is, and let the various 'disgusteds' and 'constant theatregoers' have a go. I hope they do. It should be fun . . . The point I wanted to make in my letter . . . is that you are perfectly in order in having a weekly bash at the deplorable state of the British theatre, but you are instantly out of order when you use the New York or Paris theatre as yardsticks. I have been going to NY yearly (except for the war) for nearly 25 years, and theatregoing in Paris for even longer. Their theatres, *in general*, are just as fussy as ours, and in many ways (such as direction in Paris, or character acting in NY) a good deal worse. Of course they have their Tennessees and their Anouilhs. We have our Christopher Frys (if only he'd bloody well write) and our Osbornes and our Whitings.

Commercialism? Broadway is far worse in that respect than Shaftesbury Avenue.

Nothing new to see? How often, in Paris in the summer, have you been maddened by that one word 'Relache' (which I once took to be the title of a play so evidently fascinating that it was playing in about twenty theatres at the same time).

The same week (I think) that we had our tour you reviewed a play by Montherlant and another by Obey. How could you do that in New York? Well, I suppose you might, off Broadway, but you'd be bloody lucky with your week's theatregoing.

Does it fuss you that those two plays were by Frenchmen . . . Two years ago, or possibly three, I had great trouble in getting *The Deep Blue Sea* on in Paris because the French critics were outraged at the spate there had recently been of British and American plays. Il y avaient un Emlyn Williams, et un Noël Coward et un Tennessee Williams et un J.B. Priestley et un Arthur Miller, et maintenant un Terence Rattigan – c'était trop fort.

Heureusement, they were fairly kind. But look at the current Paris list (I confess I haven't) and I'd bet you'd find a pretty high proportion of foreign plays, as well as the usual crop of 'Paris Tout Nu' stuff, which as a rule outnumbers the Anouilhs and the Sartres by quite a bit.

I've written at length, because on this subject I feel strongly. New York had one brief period in the thirties (Group Theater, Odets etc) when it was better than ours. Paris had one brief period, just after the war (early Existentialist school) when it certainly *seemed* better – but perhaps just because we hadn't seen it for 5 years. Anyway I'd give it to you, as a point, if you want it.

But now – with your angry young playwrights popping up all over the place (who's as young as Osborne in Paris or New York?) with Stratford and the Old Vic flourishing (not always good, but certainly flourishing) with your Arts theatre and your Royal Court, and your Comedy (Queer Plays Ltd) Theatre, surely it's not as really terrible as you, weekly, have it.

Well maybe it is, but not, which is my point, in comparison with any other theatre, except perhaps East Berlin – which I have never visited.

Regards. I should like to hear from you – not necessarily at this length. You probably haven't the time. At the moment I have. We're changing directors, and I have nothing to do.[109]

It is hard to escape the impression that Rattigan was an unnecessary casualty of the Royal Court revolution. As the revival of his works in the 1990s demonstrated, the understated nature of his drama, which seemed so insipid to Tynan in the late 1950s, now appears to have a more didactic side than was apparent in an era when allusion was treated suspiciously. Tynan had little time in 1958 for implied criticism and emotional catharsis, but this did not necessarily render works which demonstrated those traits either unstageable or indefensible.

This is most obvious in his dismissal of Harold Pinter's famous first run of *The Birthday Party* at the Lyric, Hammersmith. True, the play was staged in the same week in May as the eagerly awaited performance of the visiting Moscow Art Theatre's *Uncle Vanya* (an important sign of détente in the Cold War climate), but the grounds of his dismissal are revealing: 'the theme is that of the individualist who is forced out of his shell to come to terms with the world at large, an experience which in all such plays is seen as castratingly tragic . . . the notion that society enslaves the individual can hardly be unfamiliar to any student of the cinema or the realistic theatre. That is why Mr Pinter sounds frivolous, even when he is being serious.'[110] Harold Hobson was famously to disagree. He had first encountered Pinter in Bristol when the Old Vic Theatre School and the University Drama Department had staged *The Room* at the NUS drama festival the previous January. Its 'nightmare world of insecurity and uncertainty' had been a 'revelation'[111] and although the daily reviews were vituperative and the show was to end after five days, he travelled to the Thursday matinée of *The Birthday Party* with a sense of expectation. His experience has gone down in theatre history. At the interval, one of the actors was heard by the feeble audience of just sixteen people to say that this was the most awful rubbish he had ever appeared in. Hobson, mortified by this outburst and convinced that it was an act of betrayal, went on to pen the bravest review of his life, with one of the most notable opening paragraphs:

> One of the actors in Harold Pinter's *The Birthday Party* at the Lyric, Hammersmith, announces in the programme that he read history at Oxford, and took his degree with Fourth Class Honours. Now I am well aware that Mr Pinter's play received extremely bad notices last Tuesday morning. At the moment I write these lines it is uncertain whether the play will still be in the bill by the time they appear, though it is probable it will soon be elsewhere. Deliberately, I am willing to stake whatever reputation I have as a judge of plays by saying that *The Birthday Party* is not a Fourth, not even a Second, but a First; and that Mr Pinter, on the evidence of this work, possesses the most original, disturbing, and arresting talent in theatrical London.

It was an extraordinary lone opinion. No other critic began to approach this view and Hobson was risking ridicule by being so emphatic. However, the events of the 1960s, when Pinter teamed up with Peter Hall at the RSC, proved him right, and, if his words did not manage to save *The Birthday Party*, they did at least lodge in the mind of the producer, Michael Codron, when he was approached with a script of a new work called *The Caretaker* in 1960.

Interestingly, part of Hobson's appreciation lay in the play's relevance to the Cold War:

> Mr Pinter has got hold of a primary fact of existence. We live on the verge of disaster. One sunny afternoon, whilst Peter May is making a century at Lords against Middlesex, and the shadows are creeping about the grass, and the old men are dozing in the Long Room, a hydrogen bomb may explode. That is one sort of threat. But Mr Pinter's is a subtler sort. It breathes in the air. It cannot be seen, but it enters the room every time the door is opened. There is something in your past – it does not matter what – which will catch up with you. Though you go to the uttermost parts of the earth, and hide yourself in the most obscure lodgings in the least popular of towns, one day there is the possibility that two men will appear. They will be looking for you, and you cannot get away. And someone will be looking for *them*, too. There is terror everywhere. Meanwhile, it is best to make jokes (Mr Pinter's jokes are very good), and play blind man's buff, and to bang on a toy drum, anything to forget the slow approach of doom. *The Birthday Party* is a Grand Guignol of susceptibilities.[112]

This first enthusiastic review – which Hobson would refer to again and again up to his retirement in 1976 – rather belies the general notion that Pinter is an integral member of the Theatre of the Absurd. Tynan's indifference was a surprising blind-spot.

One unexpected consequence of *Variation on a Theme* was the appearance of a play which might have a claim to being *the* truly ground-breaking work of the 1950s – *A Taste of Honey* (1958). According to theatrical lore, Shelagh Delaney, a teenager from Salford, had been so incensed by the mealy-mouthed depiction of homosexual issues in Rattigan's work in a pre-London production at the Opera House, Manchester, that she swiftly reached for her pen and wrote a counter-blast. The script was sent to Joan Littlewood and Theatre Workshop, and, after much reworking, it was premièred at the end of May. In the character of Geoffrey, Jo's caring friend, there appeared the first, uncensored openly gay character of the post-war period. How had the Lord Chamberlain allowed such a visible representation of 'the forbidden subject' to pass? The answer was the open discussion that surrounded the controversial Wolfenden Report.

The 1950s had been a period of persecution for the gay man in Britain. The publication in 1948 of Alfred Kinsey's *Sexual Behaviour in the Human Male*, stating that 37 per cent of American men had had at least one homosexual experience to the point of orgasm since adolescence was swiftly glossed over and the defection in 1951 to Moscow of the two British spies Guy Burgess and Donald Maclean, both homosexual, provided a scarcely needed pretext for a clampdown on 'deviants'. The American security agencies (still enmeshed in the McCarthy purges) pressured the British to weed out known or suspected homosexuals from government to prevent further security lapses, and this resulted in liaison between the FBI and Scotland Yard, where the new Commissioner of Police, Sir John Nott-Bower, instituted a full-scale persecution.

In 1952 Alan Turing, OBE, the mathematician who cracked the Enigma code during the Second World War, was compelled to undergo hormone therapy. He grew breasts as a result of the enforced treatment, and subsequently committed suicide in 1954. Brave figures, such as Gordon Westwood, published works such as *Society and the Homosexual* (1952), which deprecated the law, but the annual figure for 'indecency between males' offences began to rise. In 1952 it reached 1,686 (compared to 299 for the period 1935–9). A series of high-profile court cases were salaciously reported by the tabloid press. The MP William Field was charged in January 1953 with persistently importuning men for an immoral purpose in Piccadilly Circus. Although protesting his innocence, he was found guilty on one of two counts, and fined £15 with costs of 20 guineas. Lord Montagu of Beaulieu and film director Kenneth Hume were charged in October 1953 with 'serious offences' involving two Boy Scouts, and in the same month, as we have seen, Sir John Gielgud pleaded guilty to persistently importuning for an immoral purpose in a public lavatory, and was fined £10. These cases led in December 1953 to Desmond Donnelly (Labour) and Sir Robert Boothby (Conservative) calling in the House of Commons for the government to set up a Royal Commission to investigate the law relating to homo-sexual offences.

The Montagu/Hume Case reached the Winchester Assizes just before Christmas. On the August Bank Holiday weekend in 1953 Edward Montagu and Kenneth Hume had taken two Boy Scouts to a beach hut at Beaulieu for a bathe. Edward Montagu had reported the loss of a camera to the police and the purpose of the visit to the beach hut had originally been to look for the camera. When the police arrived the Boy Scouts said that they had been indecently assaulted in the hut.

Edward Montagu was charged with committing an 'unnatural offence' and inde-cent assault. He was acquitted on the former, more serious charge but the jury dis-agreed on the lesser charge. The Director of Public Prosecutions decided that Montagu and Hume should be tried again on the charge of indecent assault. The case generated new levels of hysteria when on 9 January 1954 Lord Montagu, his cousin Michael Pitt-Rivers and Peter Wildeblood, the best man at Tynan's wedding, were arrested three weeks after the end of the first Montagu/Hume trial. (Tynan unhesitatingly agreed to stand bail for his friend and travelled to Lymington police station to hand over the surety.)[113] Their premises were searched without a warrant and they were charged with several specific indecency charges with two RAF men, Edward McNally and John Reynolds, at the beach hut near Beaulieu and also at the Pitt-Rivers estate in Dorset. They were also accused of conspiring with Edward Montagu to commit these offences. This would inevitably prejudice the chances of Edward Montagu's acquittal at his retrial.

In March 1954 the trial, which attracted huge media interest, began in the hall of Winchester Castle. Peter Wildeblood had borrowed the beach hut for a holiday in 1952, and there had been a party on the first night attended by Edward Montagu and some of his house-guests from Beaulieu. The prosecution tried to suggest that this developed into a revolting bacchanalian orgy. The principal witnesses against the three defendants were two airmen who had been shown to have been involved in twenty-four other homosexual affairs. Edward McNally also had a friend called Gerry, a male nurse, whom he described as 'my husband'. The Director of Public Prosecutions gave his assurance that Reynolds and McNally would not be prosecuted in any circumstances, no matter how many offences they admitted to. It was clear to many that the Crown was determined to have a show trial and put Edward Montagu behind bars. It was the UK's closest experience to McCarthyism.

The trial lasted eight days and all three defendants were convicted. Michael Pitt-Rivers and Peter Wildeblood were sentenced to 18 months in prison, and Edward Montagu was given 12 months. In its persecution of men for a 'victimless' crime, it repulsed many and after the end of the trial the *Sunday Times* devoted an entire lead-ing article to the subject entitled 'Law and Hypocrisy'.[114] This was followed by an article in the *New Statesman* entitled 'The Police and the Montagu Case'.[115] While the charges had been pending, an interim report was issued for private circulation by a group of Anglican clergy and doctors through the Church of England Moral Welfare Council, which made a plea for a change in the law. The Moral Welfare Council even went so far as to suggest that there should be an equal age of consent. Against this, an April 1954 analysis in the medical journal the *Practitioner* noted that in 'over 100 cases of castration of sexual perversion and homosexuality [sic] . . . [there were] gratifying results in all but one case'. By the end of 1954 the annual figure for 'indecency between males' offences had climbed to 2,034.

On 28 April 1954, a month after sentences had been passed, the Home Secretary and the Secretary of State for Scotland agreed to the appointment of a departmental committee to examine and report on the law of homosexual offences and also on the law relating to prostitution. The composition of the Wolfenden Committee was officially announced in August. It was chaired by John Wolfenden (1906–85), who had previously been headmaster of Uppingham and Shrewsbury schools and had become the Vice-Chancellor of Reading University in 1950. Later on he was appointed Director of the British Museum. Other members of the committee included a consultant psychiatrist, the chairman of Uxbridge magistrates' court, the vice-president of the City of Glasgow Girl Guides, a Scottish Presbyterian minister, a professor of moral theology, a High Court judge, a Foreign Office minister, and the Conservative MP for Putney. There were all in all fifteen men and one woman.

The committee met for the first time on 15 September 1954, in a room provided by the Home Office – room 101. Its members deliberated over a period of three years, during which time they met in private on 62 days, 32 of which were used for interviewing witnesses. The Home Office civil servants, reflecting the repressive nature of the time, were concerned about the sensibilities of the secretarial staff when dealing with the material and in internal memoranda they referred to homosexuals and prostitutes as 'huntleys' and 'palmers'. (Huntley and Palmers was a well known firm of biscuit makers.)

While the committee was sitting, further events highlighted the inequities of the current repressive law. In November 1955 Peter Wildeblood published his autobiography, explaining the horror of his arrest and imprisonment and his emergence from the ordeal as a stronger and more honest person who was not ashamed to announce to the world, 'I am homosexual'. He later gave the following evidence to the Wolfenden Committee: 'The right which I claim for myself, and for all those like me, is the right to choose the person whom I love.' Nevertheless, the persecution continued: the 1955 annual figure for 'indecency between males' offences peaked at 2,322, with 1,065 men gaoled.

On 4 September 1957 the Wolfenden *Report on Homosexual Offences and Prostitution* was published. Its remit had been 'to consider . . . the law and practice relating to homosexual offences and the treatment of persons convicted of such offences by the courts' and to review offences related to prostitution, and it made the startling (and welcome) recommendation that homosexual behaviour in private between consenting adults (defined as those over twenty-one), should be decriminalised; but that curbs on prostitution should be tightened.

Twelve of the thirteen members of the committee who had served for the full three years recommended that homosexual behaviour between consenting adults in private should no longer be a criminal offence. The words 'consent' and 'in private' were not defined but were to be interpreted as they would be in relation to heterosexual conduct. Contrary to the evidence provided by nearly all the psychiatric and psychoanalytic witnesses, the committee found that 'homosexuality cannot legitimately be regarded as a disease, because in many cases it is the only symptom and is compatible with full mental health in other respects'.

Publication of the report produced a storm of debate in the press and filled the front pages of the newspapers. The lumping together of the issues relating to homosexuality and prostitution allowed some newspapers to refer to it in headlines as the 'VICE REPORT'. Beaverbrook's *Daily Express* was particularly virulent, wondering in its editorial column why the government had ever sponsored 'this cumbersome nonsense' and relieved that Tory MPs, nervous about an electoral backlash, were likely to scupper plans for legislation.[116] However, in October 1957 the Archbishop of Canterbury, Dr Fisher, surprisingly voiced his support for the Wolfenden Report, arguing that there was 'a sacred realm of privacy . . . into which the law, generally speaking, must not intrude' and the recommendations were also endorsed by the British Medical Association, the Howard League for Penal Reform, and the National Association of Probation Officers.

The first parliamentary debate was initiated on 4 December 1957 by Frank Pakenham (later Lord Longford). He had already become recognised as a social reformer and prison visitor, and as a result of the Montagu case came to know Peter Wildeblood and C.H. Rolph, who was to become the chair of the Homosexual Reform Society. Of the seventeen peers who spoke in the debate, eight broadly supported the recommendations in the Wolfenden Report.

The Home Secretary, Sir David Maxwell-Fyfe, spoke for the government. He expressed doubt that the general population would support the recommendations and stated that further research was required. The report was, quite simply, 'ahead of its time'. This seemed to the liberal sections of the press to be prevarication of the worst kind. After the Home Office asked the sociologist Richard Hauser in 1958 to undertake a survey of homosexuality in Great Britain, there was an outcry. A.E. Dyson and the Reverend Hallidie-Smith founded the Homosexual Law Reform Society in May 1958, as a pressure group dedicated to persuading Parliament of the strength of support for law reform by public figures, and of refuting the claim that the recommendations were 'in advance of public opinion'. In June 1958, the *Daily Telegraph, Observer* and *Daily Mirror* all called for an end to the Home Secretary's shameful prevarication in implementing the Wolfenden recommendations – but it would be another ten years before homosexuality was decriminalised in Britain.[117]

It was against this background that *A Taste of Honey* was staged. The Lord Chamberlain, ever mindful of public opinion, was sensitive to the increasing debate about reform of the law, and quietly decided that the portrayal of Geoffrey as an openly gay character, but one who was unthreatening and not proselytising, could stand. More significantly, in November 1958 he lifted his absolute ban on plays with homosexual themes, although with some significant caveats. In a secret memorandum to his readers he explained his change of heart:

> I have decided to make a change in the policy of the censorship, and I think it desirable to place on record as clearly as possible the nature of the change so that all concerned may be fully aware of it.
>
> First, the reason behind this change. For some time the subject of homosexuality has been so widely debated, written about and talked about, that it is no longer justifiable to continue the strict exclusion of this subject from the Stage. I do not regret the policy of strict exclusion which has been continued up to now, and I think it has been to the public good. Nevertheless, now that it has become a topic of almost everyday conversation, its exclusion from the Stage can no longer be regarded as a reasonable course, even when account is taken of the more effective persuasion which the living Stage can exercise as compared with the written word. I therefore propose to allow plays which make a serious and sincere attempt to deal with the subject. It will follow also that references in other plays will be allowed to the subject which appear necessary to the dialogue or the plot, and which are not salacious or offensive. Licences will continue to be refused for plays which are exploitations of the subject rather than contributions to the problem; and similarly references to the subject which are unnecessary or have merely an exploitation value will be disallowed.

For possibly the only time in his existence, the Lord Chamberlain was actually running ahead of government opinion and social legislation, although he was hardly a bastion of progressive thought, as his stipulations revealed.[118]

For Tynan, *A Taste of Honey* was further confirmation that a more mature, accurate and affirmatory mood was sweeping through British theatre. The play was the epitome of realism, as far as he was concerned, and all the more welcome for being so:

Miss Delaney brings real people on to her stage, joking and flaring and scuffling and eventually, out of the zest for life she gives them, surviving. Suffering, she seems to say, need not be tragic; anguish need not be neurotic; we are all, especially if we come from Lancashire, indestructible. If I tell you that the heroine was born of a haystack encounter between her mother and a mental defective; that a Negro sailor gets her pregnant and deserts her; and that she sets up house, when her mother marries a drunk, with a homosexual student – when I tell you this, you may legitimately suspect that a tearful inferno of a play awaits you at Stratford, E. Not a bit of it.

The first half is broad comedy (comedy, perhaps, is merely tragedy in which people don't give in); almost too breezily so; and Joan Littlewood's direction tilts into farce by making Avis Bunnage, as the girl's brassy mother, address herself directly to the audience, music-hall fashion. The second half is both comic and heroic. Rather than be lonely, the gutsy young mother-to-be shares her room (though not her bed) with a skinny painter who enjoys mothering her and about whose sexual whims ('What d'you do? Go on – what d'you do') she is uproariously curious. Together they have what amounts to an idyll, which is interrupted by mother's return with her puffy bridegroom, who likes older women and wears an eyepatch: this brings him, as he points out, at least half way to Oedipus. By the end of the evening he has left and so, without rancour, has the queer. A child is coming: as in many plays of this kind, life goes on. But not despondently: here it goes on bravely and self-reliantly, with a boisterous appetite for tomorrow.

Miss Delaney owes a great deal to Frances Cuka, her ribald young heroine, who embraces the part with a shock-haired careless passion that suggests an embryonic Anna Magnani. This is an actress with a lot of love to give. There are plenty of crudities in Miss Delaney's play: there is also, more importantly, the smell of living. When the theatre presents poor people as good, we call it 'sentimental'. When it presents them as wicked, we sniff and cry 'squalid'. Happily, Miss Delaney does not yet know about us and our squeamishness, which we think moral but is really social. She is too busy recording the wonder of life as she lives it. There is plenty of time for her to worry over words like 'form', which mean something, and concepts like 'vulgarity' which don't. She is nineteen years old: and a portent.[119]

How positive this seemed in comparison to the enervating and dangerous glumness of French Absurdism. By now, Tynan had come to view the work of Ionesco and Beckett as grave threats to realism and, on seeing *The Chairs* and *The Lesson* in an ESC double bill at the Royal Court, he wrote a stunning denunciation. It was his apotheosis as a social realist. With scarcely concealed glee, he begins 'Ionesco: Man

of Destiny?' with the news that 'French audiences are drifting away from the theatre because they feel the theatre is drifting away from them. They are frankly bored
with it.' The Ionesco double bill confirms the 'versatility' of Joan Plowright, but,
for Tynan, showed misplaced signs of hero worship. 'Ever since the Fry–Eliot
"poetic revival" caved in on them, the ostriches of our theatrical intelligentsia have
been seeking another faith', and the new 'messiah' of their incipient cult is Eugène
Ionesco, in Tynan's words, the 'founder and headmaster of l'école du strip-tease
intellectuel, moral et social'. His drama has no 'traceable roots in life' and he is a
'self-proclaimed advocate of *anti-théâtre*: explicitly anti-realist, and by implication
anti-reality as well'. He is a 'writer ready to declare that words were meaningless
and that all communication between human beings was impossible'. Worse, his
world is full of 'isolated robots, conversing in cartoon-strip balloons of dialogue
that are sometimes hilarious, sometimes evocative, and quite often neither, on which
occasions they become profoundly tiresome'. Aspects of his plays might remain
'pungent and exciting' but they are poor models for committed writing. The cult
needs to be arrested: 'The peril arises when it is held up for general emulation as
the gateway to the theatre of the future, that bleak new world from which the
humanist heresies of faith in logic and belief in man will forever be banished.'[120]

This statement of Tynan's only critical creed caused Ionesco, to his editor's
delight, to fight back. The type of writers Tynan supported, he argued in his position statement, 'The Playwright's Role' the following week, were simply 'representatives of a left-wing conformism, which is just as lamentable as the right-wing
sort'.[121] This was the new hegemony, he argued. How swiftly things had changed
in two years. 'A work of art is the expression of an incommunicable reality that one
tries to communicate – and which sometimes can be communicated,' Ionesco concluded, but Tynan was unconvinced. Their dialogue spilled over into one more
week. All theatre was political, the critic countered and 'whether M. Ionesco admits
it or not, every play worth serious consideration is a statement'.[122] A flourishing
debate ensued in the letters pages of the *Observer* – exactly as Tynan, the conscious
self-publicist, had hoped. 'I enjoy *testing* people,' he confided his diary in 1976.[123]
It was his strongest trait.

By the time the summer holidays came, Tynan could look back with enormous
satisfaction at the changing theatrical scene. If 1956 had been the year of breakthrough and 1957 a year of tentative hope, 1958 had proved the year of real achievement. Original new plays were becoming the norm. Arnold Wesker's panoramic
Chicken Soup with Barley, which Tynan had found 'fair, accurate and intensely exciting',[124] was a late summer offering from the ESC and no longer seemed at odds in
its contemporaneity with other works in London. It celebrated political engagement
in its depiction of the Kahn family, and made reference to recognisable events from

the very recent past, not least the squandering of Attlee's legacy. T.S. Eliot's *The Elder Statesman* at the Edinburgh Festival conversely provided an evening that offered 'little more than the mild pleasures of hearing ancient verities tepidly restated',[125] and seemed to confirm that the old guard was in headlong retreat. 'The Elder Staggers', Tynan's column screamed. His wishes were being fulfilled.

It was against this background of success that he received a phone call that was to change his life. Back in December 1956, Tynan had heard a rumour that the distinguished critic of the *New Yorker*, Wolcott Gibbs, might be about to retire. He had contacted his New York agent, Edith Haggard, to see if there was any opening for him, but although she made some discreet enquiries the picture was uncertain. Tynan had never made a secret of his love for New York and American theatre and would jump at the chance of a new direction. In August 1958, Gibbs unexpectedly died. Staying with Elaine at the George Hotel in Edinburgh for the Festival, Tynan was summoned to the phone. It was the editor of the *New Yorker*, William Shawn. Would Tynan fly over to see them? After discussing the wisdom of such a move with Elaine – she was naturally not averse to the idea of returning to her home town – Tynan flew to New York on 9 September, and entered into negotiations with the formidable editor. He had already discussed the situation with his *Observer* editor, David Astor, with whom he had only the previous year signed a new contract. Astor was unwilling to lose his star critic, but generously recognised the opportunity that this represented for him. He suggested a compromise: Tynan should go for a probationary three months, and then decide if he wanted to stay on for a whole season. Tynan returned to London on 11 September and informed Astor that Shawn had agreed to this as, in any event, he only wished to employ him as a guest critic for a maximum of two years. It was a deal that Astor could live with, as long as Tynan continued to submit a monthly piece on culture to the *Observer*.[126]

For Tynan, it was the perfect arrangement. It represented a new challenge and an essential change of scene for him and Elaine. It gave him added kudos and allowed him a lucrative salary of $1,540 per month in the heart of 'the most vital theatre in the world'. It also left him well positioned if the English National Theatre was finally born around the turn of the decade. The only drawback was that he had to start as soon as possible, and by November at the latest. Astor reluctantly acquiesced.

There was one personal fly in the ointment – the deteriorating health of his mother. His contact with Rose had been intermittent since the death of his father in 1948. She had moved to a more manageable property in Great Barr and enjoyed a reasonably comfortable lifestyle, having been granted £1,800 p.a. in Sir Peter's will, but she seemed to live a lonely existence, sustained by a reawakened faith and quiet attendance at a local Methodist church. Tynan disliked returning to

Birmingham, so mother and son generally met when she travelled to London to care for Tracy whenever the couple dashed off on a foreign journey. From 1955, her health began to decline and in the spring of 1958 she was discovered on the platform of a Yorkshire station, confused and dishevelled, carrying a case with a sign saying 'I don't know where I'm going, but I'm going to those that love me.'[127] She was initially admitted to a small mental home in Birmingham, before Tynan, racked with guilt, placed her in October in a well-respected psychiatric hospital near Northampton. It was an experience that haunted him for the rest of his life, as the following poignant entry in his diary testifies:

> I suppose there is no doubt that I hastened the death of my mother. By leaving her to live alone in Birmingham and visiting her rarely while I lived in London, I condemned her to the isolation that eventually – combined with the anaemia that dried up the blood supply to the brain – led to her inability to live without constant supervision. If she had come to London and lived with me in the fifties, she could have been sustained by human contact: but I never invited her, and, lacking it, she degenerated until there was no alternative but to consign her to the palatial but heartless home in Northampton wherein, appallingly emaciated, she died. I could have postponed her death at the expense of my own absorption in self-advancement: I chose not to.[128]

In October, the news of Tynan's imminent departure across the Atlantic was confirmed. One might have expected Hobson to greet the departure of his great rival with silent satisfaction, but he paid a very public and gracious tribute to Tynan's skill in the aptly titled 'London's Loss and New York's Gain':

> . . . he is harsh about the theater only because he is passionately devoted to it. He cannot bear to see it doing anything less than its best. The slack conventionalities of bourgeois comedy and drama drive him to ecstasies of impatience.
>
> He is a man who has brought excitement and emotion into English drama criticism. He writes about the theater as if it were a vital part of life and not merely a means of passing the evening only one degree less boring than looking at the television . . . He kicks the theater hard and accurately, but its well-being matters to him profoundly.[129]

Just how profoundly it mattered to him was apparent in one of his last reviews, when he hailed the arrival of Brendan Behan's *The Hostage*. The boundaries of drama had shifted so radically so recently that it would be unwise of him to term this a play. 'I use the word advisedly', he wrote, 'and have since sacked my advisers: for conventional terminology is totally inept to describe the uses to which Mr Behan and his director, Joan Littlewood, are trying to put the theatre'. Whereas when he first became a critic, he was witnessing a collapsing drama, he was now observing a 'collapsing vocabulary'. This work, about the capture of a British soldier by Irish Nationalists, was a 'communal achievement based on Miss Littlewood's idea of theatre as a place where people talk to people, not actors to audiences. As with Brecht, actors step in and out of character so readily that phrases like "dramatic unity" are ruled out of court: we are simply watching a group of human beings who have come together to tell a lively story in speech and song.' Above all, the production supplied 'a boisterous premonition of something we all want – a biting popular drama that does not depend on hit songs, star names, spa sophistication or the more melodramatic aspects of homosexuality'.[130]

The London scene had shifted sufficiently since 1954 for it now to be safe for him to take his sabbatical, and on 1 November, having let Mount Street for two years to Melvin Lasky, an editor of *Encounter*, the Tynan family boarded the same French liner, *Liberté*, which had taken them to New York for the first time.

Chapter 5 *Dissent*

William Shawn and Kenneth Tynan shared several similarities. They enjoyed an equally tangled private life; they were renowned for their meticulous approach to copy; and their contemporaries felt that their promise might be better fulfilled beyond their current occupations. Indeed, it was during his sabbatical in the United States at the *New Yorker* that Tynan showed the strongest signs yet that he wanted to play a more direct role in shaping the future of British theatre. The approaching National Theatre seemed an ever more appealing project.

Shawn had joined the staff of the *New Yorker* in 1933 as an unnamed reporter for the 'Talk of the Town' section on a meagre salary of $2 an inch, thus beginning a fifty-four-year connection with the magazine. Initially, he had aspirations to be a writer, but these were to remain largely unfulfilled throughout his life: he published only one signed piece during his career, a brief fictional work about a meteor striking New York. Instead, it was his efficiency and organisational skills that began to be noticed around the office. In 1935, he turned his hand to editing and this, together with the accomplished piano playing which enlivened many staff parties, soon drew him to the attention of the senior management team. The Second World War broke out and the managing editor who was responsible for non-fiction, St Clair McKelway, was called up to join the armed forces. Shawn was proposed as his successor and the *New Yorker*'s founding editor, Harold Ross, agreed.

It was during the war years – and with Shawn's gentle prompting – that the magazine began its slow journey away from being a parochial listings sheet for upper-middle-class New Yorkers to a journal that had a broader, more analytical view of the world and a taste for good literary writing. According to John Leonard, a book critic at the *New York Times*, 'Shawn changed the *New Yorker* from a smarty-pants parish tip sheet into a journal that altered our experience instead of just posturing in front of it.'[1] It was a process that he initiated in collaboration with Ross. In 1945, he persuaded his editor to devote a whole issue to John Hersey's article about the destruction of Hiroshima by the atomic bomb and the lasting effect that this would have on its inhabitants. It was a sharp departure from its usual format of levity, cartoons and caustic observations and was an enormous success.

Harold Ross's health began to fail in 1951 and, after he had indicated his wish that Shawn succeed him, the baton was passed over in 1952. Often referred to as a benevolent dictator, Shawn quickly established his reputation as a perfectionist – 'Falling short of perfection is a process that just never stops',[2] he once famously remarked – and he became renowned for the amount of time he devoted to each of his writers, frequently taking them into his office to pore over every syntactical query. He thought nothing of putting in eighteen-hour days and, above all, he insisted that the world was rapidly changing in the 1950s and that his writers needed to reflect this. His approach to Tynan at the 1958 Edinburgh Festival had been a synthesis of his cherished beliefs in precise writing, a sharp perspective on the world and an elegant style.

On the surface, Shawn and Tynan's personalities were a world apart. Shawn's idea of a working lunch was orange juice and cereal in the Rose Room at the Algonquin Hotel, whereas Tynan's was a glass of champagne at W.H. Auden's fiftieth birthday party in his flat in St Mark's Place in the East Village. 'Is it true the *New Yorker* proofreads your poems and even suggests grammatical changes?' Tynan asked the famous exile. 'Oh yes,' replied the poet. When Tynan asked if he minded, Auden was surprisingly unperturbed: 'Not at all, at least it shows they *care*.'[3] For the only time in his career, Tynan submitted to this internal scrutiny of his writing.

Shawn was distressed by crowds, heights, fast driving, blood, air conditioning and self-service elevators. (When the elevators at the *New Yorker* were automated, a single manual one was left *in situ* to accommodate his whim.) He so disliked disorder that he typed out his order for lunch every day (cream cheese on date-nut bread and a coffee) to preserve a semblance of control in the world beyond the office. Tynan, on the other hand, loved the frenetic bustle of New York, which at the end of the 1950s was undergoing another burst of construction frenzy. There was so much to fit in that he often did not have time to eat. (His appetite was reduced anyway by the three packets of cigarettes that he would smoke a day. A suicidal pursuit, but a sign of great virility in the 1950s. It was at this time that his nightly coughing began).[4] He relished socialising with newly made friends such as Norman Mailer, George Plimpton, James Baldwin and Allen Ginsberg and was able to maintain his spirits in spite of the habitual spats with Elaine, which continued unabated on a new continent. One of the many problems in their marriage was her drinking, which she now confessed really did make her an alcoholic.[5] The following summer they both

embarked on another round of affairs and it was this that was the hidden point of
contact between Shawn and his theatre critic. Six years after Shawn's death in 1992,
his secret partner of over forty years, Lillian Ross, published her memoirs. In *Here But
Not Here* she describes how he conducted an affair with her with fastidious precision, whilst simultaneously remaining with the wife he had married in 1928. The
two women lived a few blocks from each other and he installed a separate phone at
his marital home so that Ross could call him. Such was his ability to keep his two
lives separate that he even managed to raise an adopted child with her. It was all very
reminiscent of Sir Peter Peacock, even if the link remained quietly unacknowledged.
There was to be no clear-cut separation of private spheres for Tynan, though. The
strain of marital disharmony was enormous for both partners and would erupt into
trauma again the following summer.

For all Shawn's alleged suspicion of commercialism, the pages of the *New Yorker*
that Tynan joined in November 1958 reflected the affluent lifestyle which its readers – 75 per cent of whom had first encountered the magazine in their college days[6]
– either enjoyed or aspired to. 'Scaasi's dramatic extravagance for Ben Kahn in
Empress Chinchilla – the precious fur for a precious few' was a typical slogan above
a glamorous model exhibiting the coat and leaning decorously on a silver-topped
cane. It certainly provided a stark contrast with the rather tired looking typeface of
the *Observer* and the spartan use of advertisements (until the advent of its weekly
review section the following year). Shawn was reportedly concerned about Tynan's
potential use of indecorous language and his controversial political stance (what did
he expect?)[7] and after his first review was submitted – of Robert Dhéry's *La Plume
de ma tante* – there was a discussion about whether the word 'pissoir' could remain.
The editor won out and it was replaced by 'a circular kerbside construction'.[8]

Tynan quickly became aware of how apolitical the Broadway stage of 1958/9
actually was. Whereas the Off-Broadway scene was much more eclectic (Bernard
Kops's *Hamlet of Stepney Green* opened in the same week as *La Plume de ma tante*), the
strict rules of engagement at the *New Yorker* meant that this more fertile territory
was surveyed by Donald Malcolm. This hierarchical division was meant to preserve
the prestige of the senior drama critic, but in reality it consigned Tynan to a less
rewarding experience. Working in the bedroom of the furnished flat at 56 East 89th
Street, he meticulously constructed his weekly report. If this meant working
through the night in search of inspiration, Elaine slept on the sofa. During the
day he shifted to the living room with the secretary provided by the magazine.[9]
Occasionally he was late with his copy, which Shawn once collected personally
during a snowstorm.[10]

During the few weeks that remained before Christmas, he settled down to survey the scene. Early signs were not encouraging, since hardly any shows exhibited

a realistic engagement with a complex modern world. The influence of the Actors' Studio, now not quite so venerated, produced a 'bloated, leaden and interminable' performance of O'Casey's *Shadow of a Gunman* in early December. The best he could say was that the production quashed the fallacy that Method actors could only mumble and not project: 'not to mumble is not enough,'[11] however. Elmer Rice's *Cue for Passion* took the familiar nature over nurture approach and merely accentuated the deficiency of this attitude – 'Nobody since Arthur Miller wrote *Death of a Salesman* seems to have looked out of the window and tried to analyze the society from whose soil sprung the diseased domestic bloom'[12] – and the prevailing trend appeared to be for autobiographical plays or inferior British imports. In this former category Tynan included *The Glass Menagerie, Long Day's Journey into Night, The Dark at the Top of the Stairs* (William Inge) and *The Cold Wind and the Warm* (S.N. Behrman). 'We have been lashed by storms, and dampened by drizzles, of autobiographical emotion, recollected sometimes in tranquillity and sometimes, one suspects, with the aid of tranquillizers,'[13] he wrote. To the latter category belonged John Gielgud's triumphant declamation of Shakespearian scenes, *Ages of Man,* and a tour of *Hamlet* and *Twelfth Night* by the Old Vic. Gielgud's performance was admirable, because 'I have always felt (and once wrote) that Sir John Gielgud is the finest actor on earth from the neck up.' *Ages of Man* was 'one of the most satisfactory things he has ever done', because in motion he is 'constricted, hesitant and jerky'.[14] Tynan was less enamoured by the touring Old Vic, because New Yorkers mistakenly believed that this was, in the fact, the British National Theatre company. It was essential for him to correct this error, because Tynan clearly saw the new National Theatre as a company created from fresh with its own distinctive ideology. The Old Vic company, he argued, was 'in no sense the official home of British drama'; it was overshadowed by Stratford; and it suffered because younger players wanted to perform in contemporary and not Shakespearian works. As if to force this home, he alluded to the disappointing performances of *Hamlet* and *Twelfth Night* 'by a group of not very exciting young (and youngish) players who were short of "emotional firepower"'.[15] The only aspect of the *Hamlet* he commended was the choice of the First Quarto text, doubtless because this was the one that he had used in 1945.

Tynan's reputation for an acerbic pen was confirmed for New Yorkers when he lacerated the moral certainty of Archibald Macleish's work based on the biblical Book of Job, *J.B.*, and the vapid exoticism of the latest Rodgers and Hammerstein musical, *Flower Drum Song. J.B.* exhibited all the traits of the much-despised Christian Verse Drama and provoked the withering 'Long before the final curtain, I was bored to exasperation by the lack of any recognisable human response to calamity.'[16] *Flower Drum Song* was simply facile:

The authors' attitude toward exotic peoples in general seems to have changed hardly at all since they wrote *South Pacific* and *The King and I*. If friendly, the natives have a simple, primitive, childlike sweetness. If girls, they do not know how to kiss, but once they have been taught they are wild about it. They also beg to inquire, please, just what it is that is said with flowers. In their conversation, as you may have gleaned, there is more than a smidgin of pidgin, and I should not have been surprised in the least if the heroine of the present work, which is elsewhere full of self-plagiarism, had at some point embarked on a lyric beginning, 'Baby talk, keep talking baby talk'.[17]

He had made quite a start.

In spite of their constant rows, the Tynans were a much sought after couple. *The Dud Avocado* had been published in the US the previous July and had reached the top of the bestseller list the following month. Elaine was valued as much for her talent as her success. Tynan was willing to discuss the problems of the US from a political perspective in a way that was seen as fresh and daring, and people actively wanted to be seen in their company. 'We went to parties non-stop,' Elaine recalls. They met Stravinsky at Lennie and Felicia Bernstein's; Hollywood stars and important publishers at George and Joan Axelrod's; and the latest 'in' writers at the *Paris Review* bashes.[18] It was a whirl of social activity. In January 1959, Tynan took off with the original Jimmy Porter, Kenneth Haigh, and his current partner Jean Marsh for Mexico City. In between visits to nightclubs, exotic bars and the local architectural sights Tynan languidly attempted to persuade Marsh to go to bed with him. She refused, and his efforts were curtailed by the arrival from New York of Elaine.[19] Following the trip, Elaine wrote a short story entitled 'The Sound of a Marriage', which was published in *Queen* magazine in April 1960. There seemed to be a strong autobiographical dimension to the final line, uttered by the narrator: 'The sound of a marriage was not the sound that we would ever make.'[20] Even their precocious daughter Tracy, now six, and seen by many of the Tynans' acquaintances as the last remaining tie between them, was aware of the dysfunctional nature of her family. 'We're not a real family,' she told her mother. 'Real families have meals together.'[21] Elaine tried to explain that this was because of the requirements of theatre performances, but the implication was clear.

A common misconception about Tynan's writing is that it was always carried by the quality of the work that he was reviewing. It was his good fortune, some have argued, that he was around at the birth of the new wave in the UK, and he could hardly fail to shine. We have already seen that this facile observation ignores the dearth of interesting work between 1952 and 1956, as well as the disappointments of 1957, and his writing at the *New Yorker*, coinciding with a dreadful couple of

Broadway seasons, also refutes this claim. The quality of his work was as high as ever. Readers quickly came to enjoy his witty vignettes of famous performers. Gertrude Berg, the personification of the 'Jewish mother', earned one of the most memorable for her role in Leonard Spielgass's *A Majority of One*:

> She sails through the play like the Queen Elizabeth, all graciousness and ocean-going aplomb. In her presence, the stage takes on that lived-in look, and the theatre becomes a sort of vast parlor in which Mrs Berg is at home with her friends. Her relaxation is total and euphoric. From time to time she touches up her hair with the back of her hand, but otherwise she needs few gestures to make her point.[22]

She also earned the Tony Award for best actress.

The spring of 1959 might have served up a succession of turkeys – most notably musical versions of *Pride and Prejudice* and *Juno and the Paycock*, a religious piece called *God and Kate Murphy* (for whom the 'curtain fell, looking more than usually like a guillotine')[23] and a delightfully silly musical called *Redhead*, 'a sort of timeless Edwardia' which 'delves into a foggy, nocturnal London half-world where dancers are garrotted with purple scarves and one almost expects Basil Rathbone to lounge out of the shadows, making cryptic remarks about the behaviour of dogs'[24] – but Tynan was as eager to offer prescriptions as well as diagnoses. With echoes of his early *Observer* themes from 1954, he felt compelled to state in February that the 'legitimate theatre of today deals mostly in domestic anecdote. Devoted to the manufacture of imaginary storms in domestic teacups, it demands of its audience no mental effort more exacting than that involved in reading the tea leaves.'[25] He rebuked *Tall Story* for fitting into 'the prevalent Broadway mold of satire that ends up by endorsing what it sets out to satirize'. In this comedy a humourless Professor of Ethics, who is depicted as a 'figure of fun, hopelessly idealistic and so puritanical that he disapproves of toy guns for children', refuses to allow a student who flunks all his exams to remain at college even though he is a brilliantly talented basketball player. Gradually he is convinced of the college's need for this sportsman, and, to great approval, he recants his earlier decision and learns to love 'Big Fraternity Brother'. Tynan's conclusion, deliberately imputing suggestions of totalitarianism to the American obsession with sport, is stark: 'I am sure that Herman Shumlin, who directed the play, would be astonished to hear that sobersides like myself were reading into it such sinister implications. So would the audiences that laugh at it. In a way, that is what worries me.'[26] And he lectured Tennessee Williams in a most forthright manner about his new play, *Sweet Bird of Youth*, which opened in March:

> . . . almost everything . . . dismayed and alarmed me. The staging, by Elia Kazan, is operatic and hysterical; so is the writing; and both seem somehow unreplen-

ished, as if they had long been out of touch with observable reality . . . For my part, I recognized nothing but a special, rarefied situation that had been carried to extremes of cruelty with a total disregard for probability, human relevance, and the laws of dramatic structure. My brain was buzzing with questions . . . I suspect that *Sweet Bird of Youth* will be of more interest to Mr Williams' biographers than to lovers of theater . . . none of Mr Williams' other plays has contained so much rot. It is as if the author were hypnotized by his subject, like a rabbit by a snake, or a Puritan by sin.[27]

The *New York Times* called *Sweet Bird of Youth* one of Williams's 'finest dramas',[28] but Tynan now belonged to the body of opinion that saw Kazan as a dictatorial director who manipulated the playwright's true intentions and Williams as a timid writer happy to go along with this if it guaranteed a lucrative run. The play ran for a healthy 375 performances, but Tynan felt that there were disturbing similarities with the much-maligned Rattigan, who was also unable to integrate the appropriate amount of the autobiographical.

Tynan's first three months had seen him witness a 'distressingly tame' Broadway season, he told his British readers in his March bulletin for the *Observer*. Astor spotted an opportunity to lure him back earlier than expected. 'You are tremendously missed,' he wrote, 'and the paper is not the same without you – are you coming back in the autumn?',[29] but Tynan needed to remain out of Britain until April 1960 for tax reasons, although he promised to return after that. Astor was delighted: 'I had become slightly depressed by the search for a convincing substitute.'[30] Tynan shrewdly kept his profile high back in London by writing an account of the plans for the Lincoln Center for the Performing Arts, established to foster drama, dance and music, neatly reminding people of his enduring interest in a British National Theatre. The chairman of the project, Robert Whitehead, had proposed a programme of drama that avoided the classical repertory and focused instead on contemporary American writing. This was the model to emulate, Tynan argued, clearly concerned at the growing head of steam building back home to transform the current Old Vic company into the new National ensemble. He was eager to spike this if at all possible.

The depth of his support for works that challenged the contemporary mindset can be gauged by his April review of a Broadway work that had closed by the time his article was published, after only seven performances. *Desert Incident* by Pearl Buck, an active member of the American Civil Rights Movement and the winner of the Nobel Prize for Literature in 1938, had an unusual subject for a Broadway play. It centred on a group of scientists in an American desert who were working on an experimental project which would either give the US a decisive advantage in the highly topical issue of the race for supremacy in thermonuclear weapons or could be used to benefit the world as a whole in a peaceful fashion. The jigsaw cannot be completed without the help of a young English physicist, who is flown out to help them, but as the play progresses a familiar debate about the morality of the scientists' action ensues. After a series of complicated sub-plots, the play ends with the scientists attempting to rouse their colleagues to protest. Although Tynan applauded Buck's assertion that 'the human race must go on existing, at any cost' – a heretical view for many in the Eisenhower administration – he would not have lingered over the play's 'clumsy' writing were it not for a subsequent discussion he had had with a senior newspaper executive. During lunch, his companion had implied that he would rather be 'Dead than Red' and he fully expected a nuclear war. 'My wife and children know what to expect, and they've accepted it,' he said. 'I've told them that there'll probably be an exchange of hydrogen bombs before the end of June, and I've explained to them that it will probably mean the death of all of us.'

There had undoubtedly been a rise in East–West tension since Tynan had been in the US. The launching of Sputnik 1 and Sputnik 2 in October and November 1957 had come as an enormous shock to the American people. It seemed inconceivable that the backward Soviet Union could have gained such a technological advantage over their own country. The inferior weight of America's first satellite, Explorer – 30 pounds to Sputnik 2's 1,120 – increased their indignation, and US military chiefs finally had proof that Khrushchev's boast that the USSR now possessed intercontinental ballistic missiles (ICBMs) had not been an idle one. A missile that could launch satellites could also send nuclear warheads to American cities.

Public opinion and Democrat politicians called for a rapid response to this threat. Although Eisenhower was aware through secret U-2 surveillance that the Soviets had not actually deployed ICBMs and that there was no Soviet superiority, the so-called military-industrial complex was launched to speed up the arms race. Khrushchev's boast had ironically backfired. To reassure its NATO allies that its commitment to the defence of Western Europe remained strong, the US announced in early 1958 its intention of siting intermediate-range missiles in several countries, including West Germany. The Soviets, alarmed at the prospect of missiles so close to their border, countered in March 1958 by supporting the proposal of the Polish government for a nuclear-free zone in Central Europe. The West swiftly rejected this plan and in November 1958, in a further attempt to prevent the siting of nuclear weapons in West Germany, Khrushchev began to turn the screw on Berlin. He proposed a demilitarised 'free city' with guaranteed access to the Western sectors, but that if no solution was reached within six months, the USSR would transfer all access routes to East Germany and thereby cut off Berlin from the rest of the world. In the early months of 1959, there seemed a very real threat of a nuclear conflict over this issue.[31]

The journalist that Tynan was dining with was happy to 'sacrifice mankind itself' to preserve the freedom of mankind, but it was a logic that horrified the critic. His revulsion was explicit:

> I do not know how many there are of him scattered across the countries of the world. There may be only a few, but even a few would be enough to carry out that deadly dream of June and make this our farewell summer. I realize that considerations like these are not supposed to affect the judgement of a theatre critic. All the same, as long as there are men like my host at luncheon, I cannot imagine myself pouring scorn on any play that challenged their opinions, however cloudily and with whatever disregard for *Realpolitik*. Mrs Buck botched her attempt, partly out of inexperience (this was her first work for the theatre) and partly because her cast, except for Shepperd Strudwick and Cameron Prud'homme, was frankly amateurish and in some instances embarrassing. Yet she chose the most important subject in the world, and though she handled it vaguely and emotionally, she came down on the side of life, while the detached, historical viewpoint of my smiling friend led him to espouse the cause of death. Because of her choice, and for her commitment, I am prepared to forgive Mrs Buck a great deal.[32]

For Tynan, in theatre context was everything. This was 'The Biggest Question', the title of the review, and just the type of writing that Shawn had hired him to produce. Scores of letters flooded in to the *New Yorker*, praising Tynan for being, in the words of one correspondent, 'a human being on the side of life',[33] and asking him to publish the name of the sinister journalist. Less welcome was the attention of the FBI and the Senate Internal Security Subcommittee, a sister body of the infamous House Un-American Activities Committee, that the article attracted.

In April 1959, Tynan offered further evidence that he was not unduly concerned by the opinions of the American establishment, when he travelled to Cuba to write an article for *Holiday* magazine about the recent seizure of power by Fidel Castro. For the previous thirty-four years, Cuba had been run by the brutal dictator Fulgencio Batista, who had allowed vast US business interests to flourish in the production of oil and sugar, whilst doing little to alleviate the chronic poverty that afflicted the majority of the islanders. Forty-six per cent of Cuba's land was owned by 1.5 per cent of the landowners,[34] unemployment was high and disease rife: the majority of the inhabitants were therefore receptive to the revolutionary programme of housing, medical and agrarian reform that Castro promised on his accession on 1 January 1959. The Eisenhower administration, though, was hostile to the coup from the very beginning. Although not yet a supporter of Communism, Castro posed a clear threat to US business interests, and he pressed ahead with his land-reform plans, dismantling large estates, redistributing property to the poor and signalling that big international concerns could leave Cuba forthwith. He quickly became a folk hero for his willingness to stand firm in the face of US disapproval. Some of his allure began to slip, however, when it became clear in the first four months of his tenure that his enlightened economic views were not matched by a similar respect for human rights. Show trials and summary executions of Batista's supporters were multiplying by the time Tynan flew to Havana, creating a complicated picture of economic emancipation and political oppression. Tension was further raised when Castro chose to visit the US in the same month but was refused a meeting with Eisenhower.

The highlight of Tynan's stay on the island was his humorous meeting with Ernest Hemingway and Tennessee Williams, which he captured in an article for *Playboy* magazine in 1964. He found Havana 'bursting with libertarian fervour' and was caught up 'in the midst of a genuine, do-it-yourself revolution'. Intoxicated by its atmosphere, he set out to meet Hemingway for drinks on his Floridita estate in the suburb of San Francisco de Paula. The meeting passed pleasantly, Hemingway appearing a 'gruff, gigantic boy, shy and reticent in manner despite the heroic head and white, Michaelangelo curls', and they arranged to meet for lunch the following day. Back in his hotel that evening, Tynan noticed Williams in the bar. Remembering his scathing review of *Sweet Bird of Youth*, he approached nervously, but Williams appeared to bear him no ill will, and they started to drink together. The playwright, who was waiting for 'a banana millionairess', then asked if Tynan would care to lunch the following day, but Tynan explained that he already had an arrangement with Hemingway. 'Why not come along?' he asked – but Williams was hesitant. 'They tell me that Hemingway usually kicks people like me in the crotch.' Tynan went away to phone the novelist, and came back to put his mind at rest. Hemingway would be happy to meet him.

The first ever meeting of these literary giants is related by Tynan with an exemplary eye for the humour of a situation. Williams, extremely nervous and sweating profusely, opened the conversation. 'What I've always admired about your work, Mr Hemingway . . . is that you care about honour amongst men. And there is no quest more desperate than that.' 'What kind of men, Mr Williams, did you have in mind?' Hemingway replied, ominously. 'People who have honour never talk about it. They have it, and they confer immortality on each other.' 'That seemed to take care of *that*,' Tynan confided to his readers.

Unabashed, Williams tried another gambit by launching into a story about how a great bullfighter had shown him his 'cogidas' on the beach last summer. 'He showed you his *what?*' Hemingway exploded, unaware that 'cogidas' meant scars, but the tension and misunderstandings of the early part of the meeting were soon dissolved by liberal supplies of cocktails and strong liquor, and just before Tynan left for an afternoon meeting with Castro, the two writers clicked while discussing their health. 'You can survive on one kidney,' Hemingway thundered, 'but if your liver goes, you're through.'[35] Williams accompanied Tynan to see the Cuban leader, who made a distinct impression on the Englishman. Writing to Terence Kilmartin shortly after their encounter, he said that he had found Castro 'excellent, ebullient and a real radical', but that he feared for his survival. 'Alas, I desperately feel that the rich Americans who supported him, thinking he'd never really stick to the programme he promised, are now about to pull out, which may mean both the collapse of his regime and his imminent assassination.'[36] It was one of his less accurate predictions.

Tynan himself was immortalised in print during this trip. Alec Guinness was in Cuba at the same time to complete the filming of *Our Man in Havana*. He came across Tynan in a bar, who proceeded to 'take his breath away', as Guinness related in his autobiography:

> Sipping elegantly at his daiquiri and drawing deeply on a cigarette he looked pale and urgent. His speech impediment became very pronounced when he said to me, 'I have t-two t-tickets for the fort tonight. One o'clock. Care to join me?'
> 'What's on?' I asked.
> 'They are shooting a couple of sixteen year olds. A boy and a girl. I thought you might like to see it. One should see everything, if one's an actor.' I declined. Ken, usually so liberal-minded, could be fierce and very dogmatic in certain moods, but he was undoubtedly the finest critic we have had since James Agate.[37]

As it happened, Tynan declined to attend the execution himself, since he was sickened by the prospect.

After the excitement of Cuba, Tynan returned to New York to the fag end of what he chose to tell his British readers in the *Observer* was 'a dowdy Broadway season',[38] even if it had been the most lucrative ever, grossing $40 million.[39] Each spring, the members of the New York Critics' Circle gather together to choose their awards for that season, and in 1959, Tynan lobbied hard to ensure that the five daily critics were defeated by the remaining six weekly reviewers in their desire to bestow the accolade of Best Play to the reviled *J.B.* After much horse trading – a flair for which he would increasingly demonstrate in his negotiations with the board of the National Theatre – Tynan was successful, and Lorraine Hansberry, the first black woman to have a show on Broadway, received the award for her work, *A Raisin in the Sun*. Tynan was ecstatic, not simply because this was a significant breakthrough, but because it was the first time that the all-powerful daily critics had failed to have their way. *J.B.* had to be content with the Pulitzer Prize for Drama.

There were two more memorable moments before Tynan finished for the summer. The big summer show was *Gypsy*, but he initially had difficulty gaining entrance. Its producer, David Merrick, had been so incensed by Tynan's dismissal of the musical version of *Destry Rides Again*, which he had described as 'deficient' in early May,[40] that he gave instructions that the critic be denied first-night tickets. Recognising the foolishness of this – Tynan was now seen in the first rank of the Critics' Circle and would very likely exploit his barring in the way that he had exploited Donald Wolfit's clumsy attempts to exclude Tynan from his shows in England – Merrick's co-producer, Leland Hayward, offered him his own seats. The incident gained a small amount of publicity, but nothing compared to the response to Tynan's notice and the musical's reception. The production sent Broadway wild, and Tynan was moved to speak of the perfection of the first act and the brilliance of the second.[41] The other event that reminded him of New York's capacity for surprise and hope came in a concert by Judy Garland. Although beleaguered by tax worries, a disintegrating marriage and an, as yet undiagnosed, malfunctioning liver, which left her bloated with fluids,[42] she still exuded star quality:

> . . . where else, as they say, but in America would you find Miss Garland at the Metropolitan Opera House while the Bolshoi Ballet was appearing at Madison Square Garden? . . . a squat woman now, and it takes some effort of puckering and wrinkling for her face to achieve the hopeful, trusting smile that first transfixed us. But she can still do it . . . When the voice pours out, as rich and as pleading as ever, we know where, and how moved, we are – in the presence of a star, and embarrassed by tears.[43]

Shortly after Tynan saw her, Garland entered hospital suffering from acute hepatitis exacerbated by a lifetime of alcohol and drug abuse.

'In '59 we agreed to spend the summer safely, serenely and sanely apart',[44] Elaine records, but the summer months were anything but relaxing for the couple. Initially, Elaine took Tracy to Martha's Vineyard, whilst Tynan flew back to Europe to prepare articles on theatre in France and Germany, as well as holidaying in Spain. Having taken advice from his accountant, Tynan had decided to stay for a second season as the *New Yorker's* guest critic to avoid both Elaine and himself being liable for a large tax bill on his return to Britain. Such were the exigencies of the British tax laws that to visit London for anything longer than a fortnight would jeopardise their financial arrangements. So in May Tynan travelled to Paris to research an article on the contemporary French scene. Shortly after his arrival he went out for a drink with Thomas Quinn Curtiss, a reporter for the *Herald Tribune*, and was introduced by him to an American painter, Addie Herder. They immediately embarked on a month-long affair, which he described to her as coming about because he was undergoing a trial separation from his wife. But she was unconvinced – 'I didn't believe that. He was just in Europe, and his wife wasn't there.'[45] In early June they both moved on to Germany, a country at the centre of East–West tension, following the controversy surrounding the decision to site nuclear weapons on the soil of the western part. This produced no reining in of Tynan's enthusiasm for his visit to the Berliner Ensemble in East Berlin, though, and his report of the journey, published rather later than Shawn had hoped, in September, was his most detailed investigation of *Verfremdung* (Brecht's dramatic concept of making the familiar seem changed, to provoke reflection and action). His arrival at the theatre explains how even the very home of the Berliner Ensemble subverts expectations:

> . . . whenever I approach the place, I still feel a *frisson* of expectation, an anticipatory lift, that no other theatre evokes. Western taxis charge double to go to the East, since they are unlikely to pick up a returning fare, but the trip is worth it: the arrow-straight drive up to the grandiose, bullet-chipped pillars of the Brandenburg Gate, the perfunctory salutes of the guards on both sides of the frontier, the short sally past the skinny trees and bland neo-classical façades of Unter den Linden (surely the emptiest of the world's great streets), and the left turn that leads you across the meagre, oily stream of the Spree and into the square-*cum*-parking-lot where the theatre stands, with a circular neon sign – 'BERLINER ENSEMBLE' – revolving on its roof like a sluggish weather vane. You enter an unimposing foyer, present your ticket, buy a superbly designed program, and take your seat in an auditorium that is encrusted with gilt cupids and cushioned in plush. When the curtain, adorned with its Picasso dove, goes up, one is usually shocked, so abrupt is the contrast between the baroque prettiness of the house and the chaste, stripped beauty of what one sees on the expanses, relatively enormous, of the stage.[46]

Recognised as Epic theatre's chief supporter in the Western world, Tynan was welcomed by members of the Ensemble with great enthusiasm. He sat in on rehearsals, brought gifts for familiar friends and discussed with Helene Weigel the current state of the company. After Brecht's death, she had worried that the theatre would become like a museum, dedicated to the veneration of his memory, but his work was his testimony and the subsequent vibrant productions had allayed her fears. In this series of discussions about technique and the choice of plays, where he was treated as an equal by members of a theatre company, rather than as a potentially hostile force as a critic, Tynan was temporarily exploring a role that he would later permanently achieve at the National: the role of Dramaturg. This person worked with the Artistic Director or individual directors, acting as 'a researcher, adviser (usually textual), sounding board for ideas, and critic of process'.[47] S/he might also draw up lists of possible plays for production and help plan themed runs of shows. Tynan's visit to the Theater am Schiffbauerdamm confirmed for him not only that the tradition of Brecht was safe, but that here was a role that might be a natural progression from observer to active participant. Writing to Elaine of his experience, he commented that such was the warmth of his welcome that he almost 'defected', and they actually offered him this cherished role: '. . . they said that if I wanted to join them as a dramaturg (play-chooser and semi-director) I'd be welcome, and they weren't actually laughing'.[48] It was a hugely flattering offer, from the theatre company that Tynan idolised above all others, but he wanted to make his own history, and his eyes were still on the snail-paced developments regarding the British National Theatre in London.

From Berlin, Tynan flew back alone – his liaison with Herder over – to London for a brief stop-over. The theatre he was able to see demonstrated a variety that not even Berlin could match. Wesker's *Roots* and Hall's *The Long and the Short and the Tall* at the Royal Court; Behan's *The Hostage* transferred to the West End from Stratford East; and Olivier's definitive lead role in *Coriolanus* at the Shakespeare Memorial Theatre in Stratford all emphasised his distance from the action. London also made him maudlin about his marriage. His absence from Elaine, even when he was having an affair, had reminded him of their mutual, inexplicable attraction. Writing from the Hotel am Steinplatz on 13 June he told her that not only was he bereft without her but he now had temporary writer's block – 'I've discovered I absolutely can't do without you. It's now three days since I left Paris, and the desire to put it on paper is nil' – and he had attempted to analyse why they had flashpoints:

> In my solitudes I've been going over the moments – during this trip – when, had you been here, we might have had rows. They all turn out to be wildly trivial, and to fall under three headings:
> 1) My edginess on arriving in foreign cities, even when I've been there before. This makes me scared to use the language, and therefore reluctant to ask for directions and get into discussions. This edginess communicates itself to you – hence rows.
> 2) My chronic indecision, over such matters as: where to eat? Shall we meet X before or after the show? Shall we meet Y at all? This has remained as chronic as ever during this trip, but again it might have led us into rows, as it has often in the past. Honestly, these things are so peripheral and unimportant, beside the fact of your absence. Let's never let them divert us again.
> 3) Haste and hurry rows – including taxis (lack of).

Their essential problem was that they were too demanding of each other and he wanted to reassure her of his devotion:

The trouble is that all the time we're unconsciously saying to each other: 'Why aren't you perfect? Be perfect, damn you. Be decisive and unruffled and unafraid. Or: be patient and tender and understanding.' I've had time lately to realise that I don't want you perfect. I just want you. You are the only proof that I have that I exist. I am in love with you in the same way that the earth revolves around the sun . . .

He wrote a second time from London. Unable to return to their flat in Mount Street because it was still let to Melvin Lasky and his German wife (who thoroughly disapproved of Brecht), he stayed in the hotel they used to retire to for cocktails, the Connaught. It was an uncomfortable, pressurised stay – 'I'm not writing. It's hot, for one reason, and damp, for another, but that isn't all. Shawn cabled today, tactfully asking how I was, but really meaning where's the stuff' – and his discomfort was increased by a quick visit back to Mount Street on the pretext of borrowing a book. He found it 'clean and well, apart from my study, which Melvin has turned into a morass of manuscript' but his whole feeling was one of 'unreality'. He felt sexually frustrated – 'No sex, except occasional melancholy sessions of self-help to induce sleep' – and was desperate to see his wife again: 'If I could do anything to replenish your faith I would do it in print and now, but it can only happen by seeing you and holding you (try not to gag at the thought) and talking to you.'[49] This desperation was heightened by Elaine's adamant refusal to travel to Spain to meet him in Málaga, because she had become 'tired of the social game-hunting and the hanging around Big Personalities these *ferias* always involved'.[50] She had also commenced an affair with William Becker, a Rhodes Scholar whom she had first met in Paris. Following the receipt of the London letter, Elaine relented, and the family was reunited in Málaga. The dismal pattern of close contact continued, however – public rows, celebrity encounters and the bulls. Ernest Hemingway was at the Málaga *feria* and gave a classic demonstration of his unpredictability, according to Elaine:

Seated around a table of aficionados at the Miramar, listening to Hemingway praise the kill of the matador Jaime Ostos in the third bull, Ken was overheard to say that on the evidence of *his* eyes the kill was three inches off. Words were exchanged. 'I advise you Tynan,' said Papa at one point, 'to take your fucking eyes and stick them up your fucking ass'.

Fortunately, the next day the mood changed for the better:

. . . after the bull fight we were seated on the terrace of the Miramar. Papa approached and said to me, 'Did you like Jaime Ostos's kill this afternoon?' 'Yes, Papa', I said, acquiescing to him as I always did, 'very much.' 'Jaime Ostos *es numero tres,*' he pronounced solemnly. I concurred. He turned to Ken. 'Sorry about last night,' he said gruffly, 'too much vino.' Ken rose and faced him. 'Thank you, Papa,' he said. Papa extended his hand and Ken shook it. Hemingway moved on. Ken sank limply into his chair and said in tones of awe, *'I've been apologised to by a Nobel Prize Winner!'*[51]

At the end of September the *New Yorker* proudly announced that Tynan would be staying for a second season, but for the critic himself this now seemed to be for reasons other than the theatre. Broadway in 1959 bore uncanny similarities to the West End of 1954. The real drama was happening in the outside world. The tense Geneva conference about Berlin held in May defused the tension somewhat; the Soviets allowed their six-month ultimatum about access to the Western sectors of the city to pass without action; and then, sensationally, President Khrushchev invited himself to visit the US in September. Eisenhower, wary of the propaganda coup this could give the Soviet leader, reluctantly acquiesced, but although the two leaders were unable to resolve their differences at Camp David, Khrushchev stated that the Western powers could remain in Berlin for another eighteen months and agreement was reached for another summit the following year. Eisenhower's claim that this represented a climbdown on the Soviets' part was wishful thinking. Lighter moments of the visit included the Russian leader exchanging his watch for a cigar with a factory worker, visiting a corn farm in Iowa and feeling the maize cobs, and eating large amounts of hot dogs for the benefit of American television. For many Americans, he seemed to be less the incarnation of Satan that Foster Dulles (who had died of cancer the previous May) had worked so hard to depict, than a portly American politician pumping the flesh on a whistle-stop tour. Was this what the Cold War was really about?

It was during this tiniest sign of a melting of the Cold War freeze that Tynan accelerated the interviews of prominent American figures that he had been conducting for the previous twelve months. Commissioned by the British television company ATV to produce a 90-minute programme that interrogated the notion of American conformity, he had been seeking out the opinions of those who had taken an oppositional attitude to the American establishment. This was not a project likely to endear him to the American authorities dedicated to fighting alleged Communist infiltration. The FBI had begun to take an interest in his activities. An early entry on Tynan's now declassified file states that he was known for 'his eccentric behaviour' at Oxford. At the end of August 1959, one agent, A.H. Belmont, having got wind of Tynan's proposed programme and aware of his left-of-centre views, favourable review of *Desert Incident* and spring visit to Havana, sent a memo to the Director, F.J. Baumgardner. *We Dissent*, he wrote, 'appears to be an obvious effort by Tynan to discredit the American way of life and to put

the US in a bad light ... the possibility should be explored of putting the
spotlight of publicity on Tynan'.[52]

During the autumn of 1959, there was only sporadic evidence of enquiring minds
let alone dissenting views on Broadway itself. Dore Schary's *The Highest Tree* advocated the cessation of nuclear tests, but its excessively complicated structure brought
about the play's collapse: 'Seldom, perhaps, has a man more enthusiastically con-
nived at his own destruction,' Tynan lamented.[53] Jerome Lawrence and Robert E.
Lee's *The Gang's All Here*, too, chose the fruitful issue of corruption inside the American political system:

> ... but they do not indict the system itself or imply the existence of alternatives ...
> I longed for more debate, more polemical meat, more indications that the authors
> had a point of view and cared about drawing conclusions as well as characters.[54]

Plays of ideas were crowded out by works about individuals – 'whether or not it
denotes a waning of invention I am uncertain, but the American theatre seems to be
expending a large part of its energy on the life stories (or episodes therefrom) of
people still living or fairly recently dead'[55] – and he had in mind Moss Hart's *Act
One*, which he savagely and controversially dismissed, *The Diary of Anne Frank*, *The
Gang's All Here* and *Gypsy*. It was a preoccupation that was not associated with 'a
healthily creative theatre'. Insipid imports from Britain, such as John Gielgud's production of the loathed *Much Ado About Nothing* – 'this Benedick would hesitate
before swatting a fly'[56] – reinforced the sense of sterility; and there was a proliferation of ludicrous comedies that attempt to gain laughs through a tenuous link with
present day events. The epitome of this trend for Tynan was *Golden Fleecing*, which
corroborated a theory that he had 'cherished for some time: that no comedy in which
anybody is mistaken for a Russian spy is ever very good'.[57] (It followed the adventures of three employees of the navy who tried to break the bank at a Venice casino
by feeding the numbers from the roulette wheel into their warship's computers.) Not
even Rodgers and Hammerstein's new musical, *The Sound of Music*, could lighten the
gloom. It evoked for Tynan memories of the Ivor Novello type of musical theatre
('Romantic melodrama spiced with honey and bolstered by uplift') that critics had
'labored so hard, and so successfully to abolish'. He disliked the contrived love affair
between 'a Middle European nobleman and a winsome commoner', the 'sweetly
pubescent lyrics' and the familiar religious aspects. They were eerily reminiscent of
J.B. and were for him 'Broadway's spiritual response to the materialistic challenge of
Sputnik'. Evoking his closing sentences in his review of *Look Back in Anger*, he warns
that it 'is a show for all ages, from six to about eleven and a half'.[58]

The advent of the new decade brought an inevitable avalanche of retrospective
articles about the 1950s and hopeful predictions for the 1960s. Tynan took stock

for the *Observer* in December and created a significant route map for the evolution of British theatre to which he had contributed so much. His initial assessment provides a useful reminder that the so-called breakthrough of the mid-1950s bore its ripest fruit in the 1960s. His current prognosis was mixed:

> ... the patient's condition is still desperately enfeebled, but I do not think it deniable that at some point in the past ten years the English theatre regained its will to live, emerged from its coma, and started to show signs of interest in the world around it. Assuming that it gets the proper nourishment, it may walk again.

It is important not to get carried away, though:

> The face of the West End has not been lifted overnight, detective stories and inane light comedies are as prevalent today as they were ten years ago, and our musicals (apart from *The Boyfriend*, a deliberate exercise in nostalgia) sound archaically quaint besides such post-1950 Broadway products as *Wonderful Town, The Pajama Game, My Fair Lady, West Side Story* and *Gypsy* . . . The quality of the bad shows is as low as ever. It is the quality of the good ones that has risen.

The strongest influences on English drama of the 1950s have been transatlantic (even if the Broadway seasons he had witnessed had been so disappointing):

> For the first time in its history, the English theatre has been swayed and shaped by America, by which I mean Hollywood as well as Broadway. The young people who are moulding the shape of the London stage were all growing up at a time when the talking picture had established itself not merely as a viable medium but as a primary (perhaps *the* primary) form of art. They cut their teeth on the films of Welles, Wyler, Wilder and Kazan, and on the plays (later adapted for the screen) of Arthur Miller and Tennessee Williams. Some of them prefer Williams, others Miller, but you will find very few who dislike both.

Reinforcing his own personal aspiration, the future development of English drama, he said, now depended on supplying the country with an institution to match the Comédie Française and the Berliner Ensemble:

> My hope for the sixties is the same as my hope for the fifties, that before they are out I shall see the construction of the National Theatre. Or, rather, of two National Theatres, equal in size and technical facilities. One of them would focus its attention on old plays, the other on new ones. The talent is demonstrably there. All it needs is financial succour, official status, and a permanent address.[59]

With Brecht's legacy secure, Tynan now pledged himself on his return to a new crusade.

Tynan's final months in New York were dominated by the controversy generated in the US by the British showing of the TV series *We Dissent*. The impulse behind the programme was laudable: Tynan wished to demonstrate that the carefully constructed depiction of consensus that the American political classes had striven to create masked deep concerns about the nature of American society. Many people wished to debate issues without fear of being denounced as heretics – and worse, being summoned before a court – and the ability to dissent must be seen as the bedrock of any democratic society. Directed by Robert Heller and edited by Tynan himself, *We Dissent* gave a platform to twenty-five non-conformists, each of whom projected their own personal reaction to the notion of consensus. Their contributions were individual and often idiosyncratic – there was no attempt in the editing to project a coherent alternative political philosophy – and at times the result was slightly disjointed. James Thomas of the *Daily Express* was not alone in his scathing response, describing it as 'one of the most indigestible documentaries ever slipped into the network at the somnolent hour of 10.20pm . . . badly edited, poorly presented, scrappily produced',[60] but the more negative reviews tended to reflect the conservative, pro-American stance of their publications. 'Here are your hats, gentleman,'[61] the *New York Daily News* advised the contributors.

The eclectic nature of the contributions impressed more liberal journalists. For example, the economist J.K. Galbraith argued that a vibrant public sector would mitigate the excesses of capitalism; the leader of the American Socialist Party, Norman Thomas, highlighted the dominance and interdependence of the government, the military and big business; and the New York comic satirist Nipsey Russell spoke about segregation on lines of race. From the world of the arts and education, Allen Ginsberg discussed American speech in literature, Norman Mailer spoke about the implications of hipsterism and the Professor of Sociology at Columbia University, C. Wright Mills, lamented the lack of organised dissent. Other speakers included the comedian Mort Sahl; a member of the American Communist Party, Arnold Johnson; Clinton Jencks, a radical union leader; Harold Call, a campaigner for the reform of laws relating to homosexuality; and Reverend Maurice McCrackin, who had been imprisoned for refusing to pay that portion of his taxes which went towards military expansion.

The most inflammatory appearance was that of Alger Hiss, who had twice stood trial accused of being a Communist spy whilst working at the State Department. His rather restrained contention that the operation of law in the US had been strengthened by oppositional views drew the greatest attention. 'Why was this collective being offered the opportunity to dump on their own country via a television programme in Britain?' right-wing journalists screamed. The backlash was immediate. Norman Cousins, editor of the *Saturday Review* and chairman of the

Committee for a Sane Nuclear Policy, wrote to Tynan to complain that he had been duped into appearing in the programme. Tynan swiftly rebutted this and refused to pour oil on troubled water by replying: 'I distinctly recall explaining to you that our aim was to show as wide a spectrum as possible of non-conformist American thought . . . Your contribution was a powerful and timely one, and I am told it had great impact.'[62] Cousins was roused to even greater indignation: 'Your programme had the effect not only of slandering America but slandering the participants,'[63] he protested, but this was unlikely to concern the critic. The amused press coverage back home in Britain – 'American Blames ITV: Tape-Rigging in Programme' observed the *Daily Telegraph*[64] – was gratifying, in that it provided a welcome reminder that Tynan still possessed the ability to act as the *enfant terrible*. He was quoted by the *Daily Telegraph* as being 'deeply distressed' at the furore, since the programme simply set out to 'prove the vitality of American democracy'.

It was less easy to be nonchalant in the face of a letter he received from Benjamin Mandel, Research Director of the Senate Internal Security Sub-Committee (SISS), on 5 February, requesting a transcript of the programme. SISS was one part of the inquisitorial state apparatus that emerged in the 1950s to track down 'Communist subversives' who were allegedly working within the US to sap its strength. It was set up by the controversial Internal Security Act of 1950, sometimes called the McCarran Act after Nevada's Senator Pat McCarran, which argued for, amongst other things, the fingerprinting and registration of all 'subversives' and the creation of 'concentration camps' for 'emergency situations'. Understandably, this was seen as so draconian by President Truman that he vetoed it on the grounds that it 'would make a mockery of our Bill of Rights [and] would actually weaken our internal security measures'. But his veto was overridden by a humiliating 89 per cent majority vote, and McCarran's newly formed Senate Internal Security Sub-Committee worked closely with Hoover's FBI to ensure the upholding of its provisions requiring registration of members of the Communist Party with the Attorney General, and the outlawing of conspiracy to establish a totalitarian dictatorship. Because the Act also made it an offence to conceal membership of the Communist Party, SISS conducted Senate hearings for the next twenty-seven years to ensure that this was updated. It long outlived its sister – and more infamous – committee, the House Un-American Activities Committee, chaired by the notorious Senator McCarthy, but was motivated by a similar, if marginally less provocative, ethos.

Tynan initially proposed to the director of *We Dissent*, Robert Heller, that they deny that they possessed a transcript and that they should utilise delaying tactics. If SISS discovered that only ATV had evidence of the show back in Britain, that might cause them to lose interest.[65] But he was obviously aware that this was a rather vain hope. The rabid reaction of several southern newspapers was unnerving and

Cousins's history of litigation and persistent demands for a right of reply 'dismayed and shocked' him.[66] The shows that he was reviewing offered no distraction, whilst he waited for SISS's next move. In the middle of February his sense of foreboding was apparent when he wrote of the blood-letting as show after show closed:

> With the slow passage of the months, and the quick folding of the plays, it has become almost ghoulish to don a black tie for a Broadway opening; the wearer looks as if he had gone into premature mourning. Last week's candidate for oblivion was *Beg, Borrow or Steal*, an enthusiastic little musical nuisance that came swiftly to grief at the Martin Beck.[67]

He finally gave up on the season when halfway through Frank Loesser's *Greenwillow* a newborn calf was baptised. The 'imaginary pastoral paradise that even Sir James Barrie might have found a little on the quaint side'[68] was proof positive that little could be hoped for in 1960. 'Nymphs and Shepherds, Go Away' was the plaintive title of the review.

As Tynan waited for the next move from SISS, mock-lynchings in the southern states, counter-demonstrations by anti-racists and shameful filibustering in the Senate over a Civil Rights Bill underpinned the thesis that Tynan's modest programme had advanced: that the artificially constructed self-image of an affluent, comfortable, civilised country was a partial one. Unknown to Tynan, SISS's deliberations were now influenced by his rather benign attitude towards Cuba. The CBS journalist Robert Taber had written a pro-Cuba article for publication in the January edition of the *Nation*. From this emerged the idea to create a campaign dedicated to countering the anti-Castro material that was dominating much of the press, and in April 1960 an advertisement appeared in the *New York Times* proclaiming the aims of the 'Fair Play for Cuba Campaign'. The list of signatories was impressive, and Tynan joined Jean-Paul Sartre, Simone de Beauvoir, Truman Capote, Norman Mailer and James Baldwin in requesting more balanced reporting. This, if anything, interested the chairman of SISS, Senator Thomas J. Dodd, even more than *We Dissent*. Cuba was now viewed by conservatives as a rogue state and its status as an enemy of the US was axiomatic. Dodd was the perfect chair of SISS. A former agent of the FBI, he was a right-wing Democrat representing Connecticut, who enjoyed making lurid public speeches about the red threat and referred to them continuously during his SISS hearings. On 27 April Tynan became the first non-resident alien to have been Congressionally subpoenaed, but alarmingly the section explaining why he was being called was blank. On 5 May the committee convened at 10.55 a.m. and, declining to take the Fifth Amendment, Tynan took the stand. The chief counsel, J.G. Sourwine, first decided to investigate the Cuban connection. Had Tynan's signature to the advertisement in the *New York Times* been bought with 'Cuban gold'?

'My motive in adding my name was primarily as a journalist who has tremendous regard for complete and accurate reporting on any subject in any country. I approved of the attempt to – let us say to expand the American press repertory on the Cuban situation,' Tynan answered. 'I wasn't asking for your motives but specifically whether you had approved the content of the ad before it was printed,' Sourwine countered. Tynan agreed that he had. 'How did it happen that you took the action of signing the statement in support of Castro in defiance of the views of President Eisenhower?' Sourwine then enquired. Tynan informed the chief counsel that he was unsure whether his opinions should be formed by 'whether or not I am contradicting the opinions of the President of this country'. Five months later, recalling his interrogation by SISS for *Harper's Magazine*, Tynan wryly observed that he had 'been forming opinions all my life without worrying for a second whether or not they coincided with those of the President of the United States'.[69]

Rather put out by Tynan's attitude of calm defiance, Senator Dodd instructed, after a sycophantic request from Sourwine, that one of the recent speeches that he had made – 'How Not to Promote Anglo-American Understanding' – be entered into the record. The activities of certain campaigners were such, he claimed, that 'legitimate dissenters were maligned, while the pro-Communists were endowed with a respectability to which they are not entitled'. It was clear whom Dodd had in mind.

There then followed a brief discussion of *We Dissent*, with an unfruitful examination for SISS of how Tynan had contacted the various contributors. After some deliberation, it was decided reluctantly to allow Tynan to enter his own statement in the record. The 'governmental grilling of foreign newspapermen is not a practice that one instinctively associates with the workings of Western democracy',[70] he attested. Tynan's victory was complete, although his witness fee of $12 hardly offset his lawyer's bill of $1,500.

Tynan's performance must have stayed in Dodd's mind over the coming months, since he felt compelled to defend the workings of his committee in the light of Tynan's scathing description of the process in *Harper's Magazine* in October. In the November edition, making some play on the fact that he was an ex-FBI special agent, Dodd explained the legitimate and necessary purpose of SISS – to identify subversives and disseminate propaganda to counteract the Communist threat. That Tynan had rankled him so much illustrates how influential he had become by the end of his stay at the *New Yorker*. The theatre had been disappointing, but he had been able to maintain the quality of his writing in spite of months of monotony. His last review for the *New Yorker* encapsulated this:

A corpulent musical entitled *Christine*, as slow of tread as of wit, lumbered last week onto the stage of the Forty-sixth Street Theater. The task of throwing the book at it is not one that I particularly relish, mainly because the book – by Pearl Buck and Charles K. Peck, Jr. – is so leaden and elephantine as to be almost unthrowable.[71]

But the social life, celebrity shoulder rubbing and inadvertent political campaigning had been evanescent. In his last two months in New York he met Martin Luther King and Marilyn Monroe (whose 'bottom has gone to pot and whose pot has gone to bottom', he told Terence Kilmartin);[72] took part in the 17,000-strong rally of the Committee for a Sane Nuclear Policy on 19 May, having neutralised Norman Cousins's complaints, and threw a lavish farewell party in the Forum of the Twelve Caesars on 22 May to which 200 guests were invited. He had enjoyed a frenetic eighteen months and now decided to return to the *Observer*, from which he could launch himself into the National Theatre.

Chapter 6   *'We know what they are* against . . . *but what are they* for?'

The West End did not collapse as a result of the success of the Royal Court and Theatre Workshop. Far from it. Although transfers of ESC and Theatre Workshop productions to the West End; film adaptations of *Look Back in Anger*, *The Entertainer* and *A Taste of Honey*; the acerbic observations of the drama magazine *Encore*; and the establishment of television programmes such as ABC's *Armchair Theatre* and the BBC's *The Wednesday Play* and *Play for Today* further stimulated interest in the issue of working-class realism that many Royal Court productions were raising, there was still a considerable appetite for well-produced, lavishly presented light entertainment. Binkie Beaumont, the master purveyor of brilliant musicals, continued to earn profits for H.M. Tennent Ltd that exceeded those of the ESC by a hundredfold. For the financial year 1961/2, *My Fair Lady* made the astronomical profit of £138,381[1] and his shows retained the social cachet that many in the new movement so despised. After the first night of *West Side Story* (1958), for which there had been an overwhelming demand for tickets, the American ambassador to London wrote to Beaumont stating that

> All six of us enjoyed *West Side Story* to the utmost in our respective ways. Leaving our seats, I heard one lady say to another, 'I was watching the P.M. [Harold Macmillan] and the tears were running down his face.' I can't vouch for that, but I can that we all had a glorious time.[2]

Other pre-war features of the London theatre remained, including the penchant for productions with a star name, plays by successful dramatists with a recognisable and unthreatening brand and worthy revivals of European classics. For example, between 1958 and 1960 Rex Harrison, fresh from his triumph in *My Fair Lady*, starred in Chekhov's *Platonov* (1960); Vivien Leigh and Antony Quayle appeared in

Noël Coward's *Look After Lulu* (1959); and Ibsen's infrequently revived *Rosmersholm* (1959) was given an airing. All of these productions took place at the Royal Court, rather belying the misconception (first propagated by John Russell Taylor's book, *Anger and After*) that the ESC was simply a hotbed of radical drama.

On Tynan's return to Great Britain, things were slowly changing, but there had not been overnight improvement. May 8, 1956 had not created a big bang. The reorientation of British theatre was more evolutionary than revolutionary. The Lord Chamberlain continued to repress; Arts Council funding was meagre and erratic (in 1960 the ESC was awarded £8,000, whereas Theatre Workshop was given a meagre £2,000); the National Theatre was much talked about yet no nearer fruition; the Shakespeare Memorial Theatre had reformulated itself as the Royal Shakespeare Company, although uncertainty persisted about how the new director, Peter Hall, would manage to revitalise this monolith; and the audiences at the Royal Court and Stratford East constituted a tiny proportion of the London total.

On the positive side, there was at last a space for the new wave of playwrights and performers to occupy. It was not a very large space as yet, but the door was now open. The new generation of actors included Joan Plowright, Albert Finney, Peter O'Toole and Tom Courtenay and they were becoming more visible as they left their drama schools or everyday life for the stage. It was no longer essential for them to speak with a Home Counties accent, since formative experiences in working-class regions away from London were seen to give them a 'grittiness' that more conventional performers lacked (although the patronising nature of this claim is obvious). But, most of all, they were unshackled by earlier expectations of what drama entailed. Being so young, and having little experience of pre-war theatre, they were able to react in a fresh and open manner to the more contemporary drama that was beginning to be written. Courtenay, who describes his upbringing in the fishing city of Hull with gripping unsentimentality in *Dear Tom* (2001), came to prominence as Constantin in Chekhov's *The Seagull* at the Old Vic in September 1960. He had a very simple definition of this new theatrical movement that he was a part of:

> The New Wave, to me, is simply the product of writers of my generation who had benefited, unlike their parents, from the post-war Welfare State which gave them, through the eleven plus, the chance of being educated. Alan Sillitoe, Keith Waterhouse and Willis Hall, Shelagh Delaney, Arnold Wesker, David Storey . . . It is hardly surprising that young actors such as Albert [Finney] and myself should be the ones to benefit from the leading parts that suddenly appeared. With our lowly social backgrounds – especially mine, I have to say; Albert's Dad was a bookie and almost lower middle class – we were excellent casting for what was being written.[3]

Tynan's return to the *Observer* in May 1960 coincided with the need to ensure that such progress as had been made did not stall.

Things started well. Pinter's first commercial success, *The Caretaker*, Bernard Miles's performance as Galileo, Bolt's Brecht-influenced *A Man for All Seasons*, Wesker's monumental trilogy, *Chicken Soup with Barley*, *Roots* and *I'm Talking about Jerusalem*, and Dürrenmatt's *The Visit* were the blood transfusion Tynan had yearned for after the anaemic months on Broadway. Tynan was amongst good company when he willingly recanted – two weeks after he had returned from New York – his earlier indifference to the Pinteresque. 'With *The Caretaker* . . . Harold Pinter has begun to fulfil the promise that I signally failed to see in *The Birthday Party* two years ago,' he honestly began, but, immediately renewing his rivalry with Hobson, who had been the senior London critic during Tynan's sabbatical, he continued to be cautious about Pinter's allusiveness: 'symptoms of paranoia are still detectable . . . but their intensity is considerably abated; and the symbols have mostly retired into the background. What remains is a play about people.' It was the way that his characters conversed without communicating that most appealed, however:

> What holds one, theatrically, is Mr Pinter's bizarre use (some would call it abuse) of dramatic technique, his skill in evoking atmosphere, and his encyclopaedic command of contemporary idiom . . . Mr Pinter is a superb manipulator of language, which he sees not as a bridge that brings people together but as a barrier that keeps them apart. Ideas and emotions, in the larger sense, are not his province; he plays with words, and he plays on our nerves, and it is thus that he grips us.[4]

It also helped that 'three remarkable actors' – Donald Pleasance, Alan Bates and Peter Woodthorpe – helped embody the playwright's vision. Here was hope for the future – a new work by a contemporary writer in the West End with a young cast.

It now appeared that Brecht was seeping into the bloodstream, and Bernard Miles's production of *The Life of Galileo* in June 1960 was equally encouraging. Tynan felt that the performers coped commendably with the edicts of Epic theatre, emphasising that the playwright offers analysis instead of empathy, and in an extended metaphor impossible just two years previously, Tynan ushers in the 1960s by eliding sex and theatre:

> Most plays follow the pattern of the sexual act: they begin evenly, work up to a climax of emotion, and then subside; and the actor's job is to make the audience feel exactly what the characters on stage are feeling. Acting thus becomes a form of love-making, and is accounted successful when the spectator proclaims himself (or herself) ravished, overwhelmed or taken by storm. In costume pieces, the

wooing tends to be noisier and more importunate; and if the period is Renaissance, it is likely to border vociferously on rape.

To break up the clinch, along comes Brecht, bearing a bucket of cold water
in the shape of a play about the Italian Renaissance in which nobody rants, or
raves, or even raises his voice. The nearest approach to a climax – Galileo's recantation before the Inquisition – takes place offstage![5]

Peter Brook's production of Dürrenmatt's *The Visit* (June 1960), in which an embit-
tered multimillionaire bribes a whole town to buy their complicity in the murder
of a former lover, raised equally probing questions about the nature of capitalism.
Tynan had previously reviewed this 'play about money' for the *New Yorker* and now
doubted whether 'any theatrical text more wickedly subversive of the Western way
of life has ever been staged in London'.[6] He was bowled over by the production,
claiming that the noise Alfred Lunt emitted when terror made him vomit was 'as
naked an expression of anguish as anything we have heard since Olivier's Oedipus'.
Even when political plays went wrong, as he felt had Robert Bolt's study of Sir
Thomas More, *A Man for All Seasons*, which he saw as an 'essay in hagiography', it
was thrilling that playwrights were attempting to write in this genre. It was so very
different from New York, *We Dissent* and SISS.

For Tynan, the most significant event of the summer months was the staging of
the Wesker trilogy at the Royal Court, the three works which, above all, epitomised
the type of 'kitchen sink' drama that this theatre was producing. As with much of
the ESC's historiography, however, the true context of this production needs to be
examined. After he had completed *Chicken Soup with Barley* at the end of 1957, Wesker
sent the script to Lindsay Anderson, whom he had met while studying at the
London School of Film Technique. Anderson loved the three panoramic acts span-
ning three different decades, which depicted significant periods in the life of the
Kahn family. In the first act the family throbs with heady optimism for socialist
change. Their collective stand against the Mosley Fascists in the East End of 1936
inspires them to believe that a reorganisation of society is not only possible but
necessary. Sarah Kahn, the matriarch of the family, is the most fervent supporter of
the Communist Party. The hope is more tentative in the second act. The Labour
government has been elected in 1945, and there have even been two Members of
Parliament elected on the Party ticket, but there are now signs of disillusion. Ada
Kahn, the daughter, is weary of waiting for her husband Dave to return from the
war; his experience at the front suggests that the working man is motivated less
by socialist compassion than by competitive urges; and the glorious struggle of
the Spanish Civil War seems less romantic now in the light of the discovery of
atrocities on both sides. By the third act, set in December 1956 just after the Soviet

invasion of Hungary, disillusion has set in. Affluence has dulled people's appetite for change; the family has fragmented, jettisoning some of its former ideals; and Ronnie, the idealistic son of the second act, has been so shattered by the Soviet aggression that he has lost his faith in the Party. The play ends with Sarah urging her son not to give up now: 'Ronnie, if you don't care you'll die'.[7] Ronnie is unsure and the play ends on a deliberate note of irresolution.

Devine and Richardson were not as enthused by the work as Anderson – Devine, in particular, having a peculiar blind spot where Wesker was concerned and believing that *Chicken Soup with Barley* was suitable, at best, for their one-off Sunday productions[8] – but since the ESC was planning to run a week-long celebration of regional theatre to coincide with the fiftieth anniversary of British repertory, they passed it on to Brian Bailey, Artistic Director of the first newly built post-war theatre, the Belgrade at Coventry. The play was performed in July 1958, before being transferred to the Royal Court for a week, where it was praised by Tynan.

By August, Wesker had completed *Roots*, the second part of the trilogy. This time the play was set not in the urban East End of London but in rural Norfolk. Beatie Bryant returns to visit her family, full of talk about her boyfriend of three years, Ronnie. He is Ronnie Kahn of *Chicken Soup with Barley*. Against a background of quiet, domestic activity, Beatie continually quotes Ronnie's views on art, literature, music and politics, progressively irritating her relatives, who have no wish to countenance any disruption to their docility. The first two acts conform to the increasingly fashionable 'slice of life' template. Meals are eaten, plates are washed, Beatie takes a bath, gossip is exchanged and minor family tensions exposed. At one famous point a dinner of liver and onions is cooked. 'The front rows [in Coventry] gasped at the smell that wafted towards them as soon as the curtain went up,'[9] Wesker records, and this came to be seen as an iconic moment in the development of the Royal Court (even though it happened in the Midlands!). But the Royal Court was not initially keen on this work either. In the third act, the whole family gathers to greet Ronnie, who is meant to be travelling up from London. A real 'spread' is laid on, but a letter arrives confirming not only the audience's suspicions that Ronnie, like Godot, will never turn up, but that the political disillusion evident at the end of *Chicken Soup with Barley* has enveloped Beatie and Ronnie's relationship. 'My ideas about handing on a new kind of life are quite useless and romantic if I'm really honest,' he writes. 'If I were a healthy human being it might have been all right, but most of us intellectuals are pretty sick and neurotic – as you have often observed – and we couldn't build a world even if we were given the reins of government – not yet any-rate.'[10] The reading of the letter by Mrs Bryant provokes a furious exchange between Beatie and her mother. Beatie concedes that her earlier depiction of their relationship had been fraudulent – 'I *never* discussed things. He used to beg me to discuss things but I never saw the point of it'[11] – and Mrs Bryant's frustration at being depicted as bovine and uncultured bubbles over. In her attempt to counter her mother's criticism, Beatie discovers a new found and authentic eloquence. Ronnie's view of families like the Bryants and the Beales is that they live in 'mystic communion with nature', but Beatie recognises the utter banality of this statement. Communities like theirs are ignored because they have such low aspirations. The masses get the third rate because the masses only demand the third rate, she claims with increasing conviction. Then, with marvellous theatricality, she breaks off: 'D'you hear that? D'you hear it? Did you listen to me? I'm talking. Jenny, Frankie, Mother – I'm not quoting any more.'[12] It is a wonderful moment of the self-discovery of untapped potential.

Devine and Richardson were dissatisfied with the focus on rhetoric and elation rather than anticipation and action. Notwithstanding the success of *Chicken Soup with Barley*, they suggested that Wesker rewrite the third act and contrive it so that Ronnie puts in an appearance. Wesker was amazed: 'These brilliant men of the theatre had missed the point. Their suggestions had shocked me they were so banal. I rejected them and prepared to face the end of my career as a playwright.'[13] Fortunately, Peggy Ashcroft was on the board of the ESC and, having read the script, she suggested that Beatie was a role that Joan Plowright might play. The script went back to Coventry, Wesker waited for John Dexter, the original director, to leave prison (he had been sent to Wormwood Scrubs for six months in the autumn of 1958 for sex with a minor), and *Roots* was premièred in Coventry on 25 May 1959, with a set created by the up-and-coming designer Jocelyn Herbert. A quick London transfer to the Royal Court and the Duke of York's Theatre was negotiated, but the baking summer of 1959 depressed audience numbers and the play closed after a short run. Wesker's much-deserved triumph occurred the following year, when, at the third time of asking, the Royal Court agreed to stage the whole trilogy in June and July of 1960, with the final play, *I'm Talking About Jerusalem*, following the trusted path of Coventry première and Royal Court transfer.

To enjoy and champion works such as the Wesker trilogy was one of the reasons why Tynan was a theatre critic. His reception of these plays also demonstrated that he was developing a harder and more overt political edge to his wμriting in his second stint as the *Observer*'s critic. Having seen *Chicken Soup with Barley* for the second time – the first occasion being in 1958 – Tynan set the three plays in context:

> The theme is a vast one, and Mr Wesker is splendidly equipped to handle it. Like many Jewish writers, he thinks internationally, yet feels domestically; and it is this combination of attributes that enables him to bring gigantic events and ordinary people into the same sharp focus. The function of drama, in Mr Wesker's view, is not just to tell a story, but to interpret history.

Chicken Soup with Barley depicts the 'erosion of political certainties, and their replacement by apathy', and, although he disapproves of a partial political perspective, this is a work of true originality:

> Mr Wesker's socialism is more emotional than intellectual; he is concerned less with economic analysis than with moral imperatives. His rhetoric sometimes rings hollow, and what distinguishes his style is not so much its subtlety as its sturdiness. All the same, nobody else has ever attempted to put a real, live, English Communist family on to the stage; and the important thing about Mr Wesker's attempt is that they *are* real, and they *do* live . . . Although the Kahns bicker incessantly, they differ in one vital respect from the theatrical characters to which we are inured. They are not arguing about a way of earning, or a way of spending, or a way of making love. They are arguing about a way of life.[14]

The Wesker trilogy was the *Look Back in Anger* of Tynan's second stint at the *Observer*.

Eugène Ionesco's *Rhinoceros*, which was performed in the same week at the Strand, drew his mind back to his 1958 spat with this playwright. His view on the meaningless of Ionesco's work was unchanged. There was no life in this work, he felt, and it reminded him that there was 'nothing worse than a bad social play'.[15] *Roots* three weeks later provided the perfect antidote, primarily because of its implicit criticism of affluence – it 'draws our attention to the causes of mental apathy – among them television, the Light Programme and the popular press – as well as to its effects' – and its thrilling moment of self-awareness at the end:

> We expect capitulation. Instead, Mr Wesker gives us triumph. By losing Ronnie, Beatie finds herself, and proclaims, now with unassailable certainty, that she has been right all along. Her astonished cry of self-discovery brings down the curtain on the most affecting last act in contemporary English drama. It would be wrong to describe *Roots* as a Socialist play; but if anyone were to tell me that a Tory had written it, I should be mightily amazed.

Continuing his habit of finding it hard not to find something to criticise in Laurence Olivier's partners, Tynan felt that Joan Plowright was more 'urban Lancs' than rural Norfolk and that she was a 'touch too gawky' (something actually implied in the stage directions), but he had to concede that her performance 'grips one's attention throughout'. It was an astonishing evening.

The final part of the trilogy, *I'm Talking About Jerusalem*, provided the clearest expression of the new wave's consistent disappointment that the positive feeling engendered by the election of the Attlee government had been squandered. The unexpectedly heavy defeat of Hugh Gaitskell's Labour Party by Harold Macmillan was a bitter confirmation of this, and the culminating exchange between Sarah

Kahn and Dave Simmonds, as he finally admits that his rural experiment has failed, was rather too close to the bone for some left-wing intellectuals – Tynan included – at the beginning of the 1960s:

> SARAH. You were the God that fought in Spain, Dave, remember?
> DAVE (to RONNIE). Is that it? (*Pause.*) You can't really forgive me because I didn't speak heroically about Spain, can you?
> RONNIE (*reflectively*). The war that was every man's war.
> DAVE. A useless, useless bloody war because evil and Hitler still made it, didn't they, eh? And out went six million Jews in little puffs of smoke. Am I expected to live in the glory of the nineteen thirties all my life?
> SARAH. Sick! You're all sick or something! Who says evil ever finishes? Nothing finishes! A Rasputin comes, you oppose him; a Bismarck comes, you oppose him; a Hitler comes, you oppose him! They won't stop coming and you don't stop opposing. Stop opposing and more will come and the garden'll get covered in weeds and that's life you mad things, you. Everything must be measured. We won the last war didn't we? You forgotten that? We put a Labour Party in power and . . .
> RONNIE (*with irony*). Oh, yes, that's right! We put a Labour Party in power. Glory! Hallelujah! It wasn't such a bloody useless war after all, was it, Mother? But what did the bleeders do, eh? They sang the Red Flag in Parliament and then started building atom bombs. Lunatics! Raving lunatics! And a whole generation of us laid down our arms and retreated into ourselves, a whole generation! But you two. I don't understand what happened to you two. I used to watch you and boast about you [Ada and Dave]. Well, thank God, I thought, it works! But look at us now, now it's all of us.[16]

In the Kahns' disillusion, Tynan saw Wesker approaching the territory of another new playwright:

> The members of the Kahn family end up with their hopes baffled and their ideals defeated. The world outside has let them down; they feel alienated and rejected. No doubt they will 'carry on', but their passion for causes has abated, and they are no longer quite sure where they are going. One more disastrous adventure, you feel, and the path might well lead to Mr Pinter's room. Mr Wesker's conclusion, in short, is not very far from Mr Pinter's starting point: that there is something in our society that is irrevocably hostile to the idea of human brotherhood.

But the critic was eager to emphasise Wesker's distinctiveness. He was 'one of the few dramatists who can write about political idealists without mockery or condescension', even if 'the final outburst of affirmation comes across as an empty gesture, utterly devoid of intellectual substance'. His conclusion is both constructive and hopeful. Here was a writer whose finger was on the pulse of drama:

> Mr Wesker's view of his subject is blurred, at the end, by sentimentality and intellectual flabbiness, for which I have chided him. But he cannot legitimately be condemned for having tried to 'do us good'. I have been emotionally enlarged, and morally roused, by the experience of hearing Mr Wesker talk about Jerusalem. This is not, perhaps, what Mr Whiting means by art; but it is what most of us mean by theatre.[17]

How important it was to follow Wesker's example had been stressed by Tynan's column the previous week. Despite his enthusiasm for Wesker, he was not overly confident for the future – again challenging the orthodoxy of the 'big bang' theory which claims that everything was righted with the première of *Look Back in Anger*. The resilience of the old guard could not be underestimated, the public's appetite for the new wave needed further stimulation and the success of new musicals, such as Lionel Bart's *Oliver!*, threatened to create a school of similarly derivative works. He was also suspicious of the seductive appeal of Pinter, fearing that the elements of Absurdism in his work would suffocate the shades of social realism. For the first time since his return from New York, Tynan employed one of his most effective weapons, parody, in an article called 'What the Crystal Ball Foretells' that contained distinct echoes of his laments of 1954 and 1955:

> Today – there being no new West End shows to discuss – we improvise. The theme is prophecy. Basing our predictions on current and recent form, let us look ahead at next season, and at some of the plays that our more prominent contemporaries may have in store for us. (Any resemblance to the plays they actually write, living or dead, is purely uncanny.)
>
> As my imagination sees it, the season begins with a new comedy by T.S. Eliot, two years in the polishing and completed just too late for Edinburgh. Entitled *The Tradesmen's Entrance*, it represents Mr Eliot's first attempt to deal with the aspirations of the proletariat. Hard on its heels comes Graham Greene's *The Purifying Agent*, a thriller with mystical overtones, set in Hull, about a Middle-European spy who finds himself hounded by Heaven as well as M.I.5. Both are respectfully received, but neither rivals in popular acclaim the latest work of Lionel Bart, who follows up the success of *Oliver!* by turning *Bleak House* into a new cockney musical called *Bleak!* (In an interview Mr Bart discloses that his future plans, once he has finished *David!* and *Great!*, excitingly include an original cockney musical named *Jack's the Boy!*, loosely derived from the Whitechapel murders of half a century ago!)

From across the Channel we have *Cirque d'Automne*, a sour yet fragrant tragi-comedy in which M. Anouilh recaptures the creative mood, redolent of anguish and French railway stations, that moved him to write *La Sauvage* and *Eurydice*. *Cirque d'Automne* has to do with a travelling circus that is stranded in Perpignan on New Year's Eve; its central characters are a philosophic ring-master, a pretty trapeze *artiste* of all too pliable morality, and the latter's drunken catcher, who wants – as he puts it – 'to drop everything'. Translated as Autumn Circus, the play instantly runs into copyright trouble with the legal advisers of Miss Dodie Smith. Litigation of a similar kind also awaits the season's first transatlantic hit – a satirical farce adapted from episodes in the career of the inspired clown who founded the *New Yorker*. Mr Rattigan's lawyers immediately move into action against its title, *Ross*.

Meanwhile, Tennessee Williams enters the lists with a romantic dithyramb in one act, unearthed from some forgotten bottom drawer. Its hero is a sensitive cadet who runs away from West Point to become a hungover beachcomber in Ischia; and it is called *A Year of Dry Mornings*. It is described, even by the *Daily Telegraph*, as 'strangely compelling'. From Arthur Miller, no play emerges; although there is strenuous controversy in the pages of *Encore* about a lecture he delivers to the Yale Drama School on the theatrical implications of Bertrand Russell's latest book, *The Ethics of Catastrophe*, and Aldous Huxley's new collection of apocalyptic essays, *The Ending Revel*. In other quarters, pious attention is paid to Sir Michael Redgrave's autobiography, *Aloof in the Theatre*.

But when we have saluted *The Undertaker* (John Osborne's blistering attack on Martin Luther) and *Falling Over Backwards* (Arnold Wesker's biographical play about Ezra Pound), no doubt remains that the most vociferously debated theatrical offering of the season is Harold Pinter's smash hit, *The Area*. In accordance with the pattern set by Mr Pinter's previous plays, it begins as follows: –

Scene: A room. A camp-bed, unmade, centre. ALF, reading a telegram, wanders up and down. TAFF, wearing a cap and a Manchester United rosette, sits on the bed, dismantling a tin-opener. No doors, left, right or centre.

ALF: What you want to do, see, you want to watch out for that lot, or they'll have you round the twist, they will, and then where are you? Up the wall, that's where you are, that's where they'll have you, if you don't watch out for them. See, I know that lot. I've had my eye on the lot of them bellocking up and down Ladbroke Grove the minute the shops are shut. I know that sort inside out. They'll play Old Harry with you, that lot will. Not a spark of respect from top to bottom.
TAFF: You mean Old Nick.
ALF: What do you mean, I mean Old Nick?

TAFF: They'll play Old Nick with you. That's what you call the proper usage.

ALF: What's that got to do with it then?

Silence

You're a bit of what they call a live wire, aren't you? You don't want to come the idiomatic over me, if that's what you think you're doing. I've bought and sold better men than you with one hand held behind my back, any day of the week, right, left and centre, until it's coming out of my ears. You want to be bloody careful, mate, I'm warning you.

TAFF: You can whistle for your Heinz vegetable salad when that lot comes round after you. They'll give you Heinz vegetable salad all right, that lot will. What you want to do, see, you want to watch out for that lot . . . [18]

This was the Loamshire article for the second term.

Tynan spent his first stint at the *Observer* lacerating undemanding, parochial, class-bound drama. He quickly realised that, having put much of this drama to flight, his second stint would be dominated by a need to discover an audience for the new type of drama which could – if it was strong enough – move into the vacated territory. More attuned to exposure than reconstruction, this was not an easy task for him. It was made doubly difficult by the hellish nature of his relationship with Elaine. From the summer of 1960 they endured an 'open marriage'. This meant, according to Elaine, 'keeping our private lives and private thoughts closed from each other. It was the kind of marriage in which both partners openly seek and respond to the attractions of other people while rejecting those of their spouses.'[19] Inevitably the rows proliferated and they oscillated between a fortnight of silence and consolatory tenderness. It was around this point that Elaine began to suggest that they should divorce, and that the easiest way for this to happen was for one of them to go to Mexico and obtain one on the 'grounds of incompatibility'.[20] This option hung over them for the final three years of their marriage. No wonder Tynan's writing took a darker turn.

Two reviews in the autumn of the 1960/1 season epitomised his feeling that the theatrical glass was both half empty and half full. The first, 'Three for the Seesaw', was inspired by three works by playwrights from whom he had expected more. These were Keith Waterhouse's adaptation of *Billy Liar*, starring Albert Finney, which he found too farcical; Shelagh Delaney's disappointing follow-up play to *A Taste of Honey*, *The Lion in Love* ('a riot of loose ends, and no hint of an underlying philosophy'); and John Arden's *The Happy Haven* ('an elephantine comedy of humours'). It was a disturbing spectacle. Had the old guard been subdued for this, he wondered in September 1960?:

In quantity, the past week has been a bright one for supporters of the new movement in our theatre: three plays by gifted young authors cropped up on successive nights. Quality, however, is another matter; and it is here that my lips purse and the brooding begins.

We have irrevocably (and healthily) renounced the 'gentleman code' that cast its chilling blight on so much of twentieth century English drama. No longer are we asked to judge characters by the exquisiteness of their sensibilities, or by the degree in which, in moments of crisis, their behaviour is consonant with Bloomsbury standards of tact, good form and discreetly muted sentiment. Yet to these standards, rarefied and bloodless though they were, the audience assented, and in part aspired; they formed a shared territory of belief upon which communication of a sort was possible.

Now, dive-bombed by Mr Osborne and undermined by Miss Littlewood, they have been laid low. And the question arises: with what are they to be replaced? The old code, so to speak, has been cracked: where and what are the new assumptions which, jointly held by author and audience, will enable a new kind of communication to be achieved and sustained? For without some common ground, some area of truce wherein the playwright's convictions (moral, social or political) coincide with those of his spectators, drama quickly languishes; it may, in such circumstances, provoke a scandal, or bask in a fleeting *succès d'estime*, but it is very unlikely to take root.

The present state of the English theatre is one of deadlock. Its audience is still predominantly conservative, wedded by age and habit to the old standards; its younger playwrights, meanwhile, are predominantly anti-conservative, irretrievably divorced from the ideological *status quo*. Obviously, they need a new audience; but in order to attract it they will have to define and dramatise the new values for which they severally stand. We know what they are *against* – the human consequences of class privilege, the profit motive, organised religion and so forth – but what are they *for*?

Most of them are Socialists of one shade or another; but it is significant that Arnold Wesker, their foremost advocate of affirmation, concluded his trilogy with a play that affirmed nothing but the futility of Socialism. The only general assumption on which Mr Wesker, his colleagues and their audiences seem to be substantially agreed is that the lower strata of English society deserve a more central place on the English stage.

But this is an extremely tricky area of agreement; because English audiences (outside the Royal Court and Theatre Workshop) instinctively associate the lower strata of society with the lower strata of comedy. Give them half a chance, and they'll laugh their heads off; and this creates a great temptation to play into their hands – as, for all its merits, *Fings Ain't Wot They Used T'be* unquestionably does. The point is that it takes a stiff injection of social comment to persuade your average playgoer to accept shows of this genre on any level other than farce. *Roots*, which was thus inoculated, is Mr Wesker's best work. *Billy Liar* (Cambridge), adapted by Keith Waterhouse and Willis Hall from Mr Waterhouse's exuberant novel, lacks any such injection. The broader implications of the book are skirted or ignored; it is presented in terms of pure farce. The first-night audience accordingly treated it as such, and understandably found it wanting.[21]

That the old guard appeared reassuringly anachronistic, however, was confirmed by a brief appearance from once-mighty figures who had featured prominently during Tynan's first stint at the *Observer*, but had now been overtaken by events. Enid Bagnold's *The Last Joke* (September 1960) was a defining moment for British theatre, since it was such a star-laden disaster that it marked the demise of H.M Tennent's and the end of an era. Binkie Beaumont had tried to pull out all the stops by casting John Gielgud, Ralph Richardson, Anna Massey, Ernest Thesiger and Robert Flemyng to demonstrate that his old Shaftesbury Avenue empire could still compete with the encroaching new wave from Sloane Square and Stratford East. But it was a total catastrophe from the very beginning. Bagnold had problems with the script and wrote fourteen different versions of the third act right up to the first night. When presented with their parts at rehearsals, which were disrupted by Richardson's late arrival from filming in Cyprus, the cast could not make head nor tail of the laughable plot. It seemed to centre on a mathematician who wanted to commit suicide to confirm that he had discovered that God exists, but their collective incomprehension meant that the director, Glen Byam Shaw, had to hastily change some speeches to try and make it less bizarre.[22] Even the foolish, fate-provoking title seemed ominous to some. But not even the gloomy John Gielgud – who was now more mercilessly harried by Tynan than Vivien Leigh – was prepared for what Bagnold called 'the blackness of the disaster', which, in an unfortunate phrase, made her feel that she had been 'beaten about the head like a Negro being lynched'.[23] The Daily reviewers were united in their contempt. 'A meaningless jumble of pretentious whimsy' (*Sunday Despatch*), 'a perfectly dreadful charade' (*Daily Mail*) and 'a caravan of overblown nonsense (*Evening Standard*) were some of the more supportive comments, and it was left to Tynan to administer the last rites:

Alas for chivalry. Enid Bagnold has written a stinker. Yet of how strange a sort! *The Last Joke* (Phoenix) fails oddly, not as plays ordinarily fail, but in the way that house-parties fail – the guests don't mix, nobody knows quite why he has been asked, conversation degenerates into pointless tattle and incomprehensible reminiscence, and you get a strong feeling that somebody crucial has forgotten to turn up. (Possibly, in the present case, somebody like Edith Evans, who was the life and soul of Miss Bagnold's last house party, *The Chalk Garden*). The early arrivals include Anna Massey and Ernest Thesiger, who get the evening off to a standing start with a prolonged bout of gossip, so gnomically phrased as to be indecipherable to outsiders.

Only when it was over did I realise that this had been the exposition, and that thenceforth I was on my own. As a result, a good deal of what followed left me darkling. For example, I never fully understood why Sir John Gielgud found it necessary, at the end of the last act, to commit suicide. I saw him raise the toy gun to his temple, and suffered with him through the moment that elapsed between the click of the trigger and the imperfectly synchronised bang in the wings; but I cannot pretend to know why he did it.

'A suicide at a house-party?' you may ask; and, echoing a remark attributed to the late Queen Mary at the time of her son's abdication, you may even add: 'Really, one might be in Rumania.' In fact, one almost is. Sir John is cast as an *émigré* Rumanian prince, living in Chiswick Mall, where he pines for the wordy Balkan weekends of his youth. Pampered, potty, and something of an intellectual gymnast, he is obsessed with the idea that life has only two dimensions, whereas death has three.

Sir John plays the part in the special manner he reserves for characters who go mad in dressing gowns; it involves a lot of striding about the stage, interspersed by sudden turns on the heel, with an inscrutable smile and a defiantly out-thrust chin. The character's name is Ferdinand, which reminds one at once of Sir John's performances as that other Ferdinand in *The Duchess of Malfi* – the unhinged lycanthrope who goes hunting badgers by owl-light. By sheer neurotic energy, Sir John keeps the first act tingling with promise. The style, by turns baroque and elliptical, suggests that Miss Bagnold is attempting an audacious blend of Christopher Fry and Ronald Firbank. But the promise goes unfulfilled. It is as if an architect had planned a towering folly, and built instead a dilapidating ruin.

Ferdinand discovers that a self-made millionaire has acquired, by theft, a Vuillard portrait of his mother. Bent on reclaiming the loot, he disguises himself as a Levantine art dealer, and thus gains admission to the tycoon's mansion. What ensues is aimless and chaotic. The tycoon's daughter is in love with Ferdinand's brother (non-committally played by Robert Flemyng), but we can only guess what becomes of their affair, since Mr Flemyng inexplicably vanishes after the end of the second act. As the girl, Miss Massey pipes prettily. She does not get on with her father (in Bagnoldese: 'We share a sort of silence') and has never been told the identity of her mother, who turns out, unless I am mistaken, to be a Balkan prostitute. The dialogue is full of clues to mysteries that one has either solved already, or lost all interest in solving.

To compound the enigma, we have Sir Ralph Richardson as the larcenous magnate whose hoard Sir John is determined to raid. Though humbly born, he wears emerald rings, collects priceless paintings and takes baths with his ears under water. He is also a ferret-fancier. (That last piece of information refers to Sir Ralph himself, but it might equally well refer to the character he is playing). As always, his vocal eccentricities magnificently assert themselves. What other connoisseur would name, among his favourite painters, 'Soo Rat' and 'Oot Rillo'? And who else, urging a questioner to define his terms more precisely, would so far dislocate normal emphasis as to say: 'Spessy, Fie'?

Miss Bagnold's purpose may be to demonstrate that aristocratic patrons of art are spiritually preferable to bourgeois buyers who are motivated by spite and a desire to outbid their betters. A tenable conceit, had Firbank chosen to animate it; but in the modern world, it is little more than a *jeu d'espirit*, slim and soon exhausted. The walls are converging on us, as in Edgar Allan Poe's story; and although there is room still for diamonds, there is none for costume jewellery.[24]

The Tennent management never recovered from this fiasco, which saw the play withdrawn after two weeks, in spite of Bagnold's delusion that it merited a Broadway transfer. Gielgud was so wounded by the experience that he went into a period of semi-exile of performing his one-man show, *The Ages of Man*, but other once-mighty figures from the post-war period were not prepared to be shoved off the scene quite so easily. Noël Coward was the most rebarbative of these, having long continued a public campaign against the new movement of plays, and famously denouncing *Waiting for Godot*, which he first saw in August 1960, for being 'contrived in its madness, formless and incoherent'.[25] His most recent play, *Waiting in the Wings*, about a retirement home for actresses where the inhabitants concentrated on 'behaving beautifully', had received almost as brutal a response as *The Last Joke* – Bernard Levin of the *Daily Mail*, who many now saw as writing in the tradition of the earlier Tynan, calling it 'the most paralysingly tedious play I have ever seen' – but Coward chose to fight back in print.[26] In January 1961 he published three articles in the *Sunday Times* that purported to be a survey of the contemporary scene, but in reality were a diatribe against the new mood in theatre of which he so greatly disapproved. In the first one, 'These Old-Fashioned Revolutionaries', he condemned the new wave playwrights for being too political and propagandistic to be commercially acceptable. The most talented dramatist writes about 'the class he knows best', but the welfare state had removed the grounds for pessimism to the detriment of searching themes. He then turned to new wave actors in the provocatively titled 'The Scratch-and-Mumble School'. Actors should not just concentrate on performing as workers, he argued, because 'the Common Man . . . is not, dramatically, nearly so interesting as he is claimed to be'. These articles were now proving to be Coward's equivalent of Rattigan's Aunt Edna, and if the new movement had not quite got the point, the final article, 'A Warning to the Critics', alleged that the shift in theatrical fashion had been the result of a dismal conspiracy that stretched across the whole of the profession. Critics were all failed playwrights, he concluded, and their relationship with long-standing dramatists was one of the cobra and the mongoose. Their legacy was destructive, since future theatre in Britain was now being jeopardised by critical prejudice against traditional theatrical forms.[27]

One has to admire Coward's chutzpah. Although he claimed that his general attitude to drama was one of 'broad resignation', there is the sense of a fiery last stand in the face of impossible odds about these articles. His point concerning the commercial difficulties that the new wave faced was a shrewd one, however, and one which its supporters were slow to acknowledge. Many of the plays that are most readily associated with the breakthrough in social realism were produced in half-empty houses (the Wesker trilogy, *The Sport of My Mad Mother* and *Saved*, for example), but Coward was very obviously setting himself up for a fall. That he had spoken out so forcefully in Tynan's rival newspaper, the *Sunday Times*, heightened the joy of the arch-priest of the new movement in countering his denunciations the following week. Having seen the opening of *Three* (Arts), a cluster of plays by young playwrights, Tynan posed the ironic question, 'Where are the *old* playwrights?':

> Never, perhaps, in its history has our theatre been so thinly equipped with active, established dramatists past their thirties. We have Messrs Green and Rattigan, of course, but most of their co-evals and seniors are either inactive or under-performed, forced into silence by the swift, radical change in the theatrical climate. Shaw went on writing into his nineties, and Ibsen into his seventies; nowadays, 'too old at forty' is increasingly the rule. Where, for instance, is Mr Fry? And how is Mr Eliot? And who is N.C. Hunter?
>
> I see that I have omitted Mr Coward. We know where he is, all right; he is rebuking history in the pages of the *Sunday Times*, wagging his finger at the theatre's 'new wave', and daring it to drown him. Last week, in the first of three articles, he accused the younger playwrights of having failed in the cardinal task of attracting large audiences – an ambitious charge, coming at a time when *A Taste of Honey* and *The Hostage* are prospering on Broadway, when *The Caretaker* and *Billy Liar* are coining it in London, and when it has just been announced that Mr Coward's latest play will be shortly withdrawn after a run of less than six months.
>
> The bridge of a sinking ship, one feels, is scarcely the ideal place from which to deliver a lecture on the technique of keeping afloat. While flaying the new dramatists for boring their audiences with dirt, dustbins and Socialist dogma, Mr

Coward observed that 'political or social propaganda in the theatre, as a general rule, is a cracking bore'; the exceptions, presumably, include such of his own works as *Peace in Our Time*, wherein a 'progressive' English intellectual eagerly collaborates with the Nazis, and *Relative Values*, which ends with a climactic toast to 'The final inglorious disintegrating of the most unlikely dream that ever troubled the foolish heart of man – Social Equality.'

What Tynan found most reprehensible was Coward's opening claim that 'The first allegiance of a young playwright should be not to his political convictions, nor to his moral or social conscience, but to his talent.' The critic's response was stark: 'This wins my medal for the false antithesis of the month; for what if the author's "talent" is inseparable from his conscience and convictions, as in the best writers it is?'[28]

The third, and perhaps most unfairly maligned, member of this triumvirate of pre-1956 dramatists was Rattigan, but Tynan was equally unwilling to spare him the rod. If *The Last Joke* had been Bagnold's Waterloo, *Ross* (May 1960) was Rattigan's Stalingrad. In 'The Unravelling of Ross', Tynan used the replacement of Alec Guinness by Michael Bryant as an opportunity to write about the work nine months after its opening. Its commercial success was simply proof of Tynan's autumn assertion in 'Three for the Seesaw' that audiences needed better fare to raise their aspirations and he was brutal in his judgement:

> . . . my main objection to *Ross* is not that its view of history is petty and blink-ered; so, it might be urged, is Shakespeare in *Henry V*. What clinches my distaste is its verbal aridity, its flatness of phrase, and – above all – its pat reliance on the same antithetical device in moments of crisis. For examples, see below:–
> 1) 'I've an idea you don't care for authority, Ross.' 'I care for discipline, sir.'
> 2) 'There's nothing in the world worse than self-pity.' 'Oh yes there is. Self-knowledge.'
> 3) 'And so he will win his battles by not fighting them?' 'Yes. And his war too – by not waging it.'
> 4) 'And is this only the beginning?' 'It may be the ending, too.'
> 5) 'I think I must remind you that I have not yet offered you this appointment.' 'No. Nor have you. And I haven't accepted it, either.'
> 6) 'Your man must believe in them and their destiny.' 'What about your own country and *its* destiny?'
> 7) 'You're going to make it hard for me, are you?' 'I see no reason to make it easy.'
> 8) 'You sicken me.' 'I sicken myself.'

I will refrain from pressing the case, though it might be worth quoting, by way of conclusion, one spectator's comment on this most fashionable of chronicle plays. 'It was too episodic,' he said, 'to be really picaresque.' Non-commitment could hardly go further.[29]

Of course, there is an essential defensiveness about Tynan's writing here, because for all the difficulties of the most prominent members of the old guard, there was still a resilient appetite for commercial theatre. There were also a limited number of productions that Tynan could be truly passionate about in the first half of the 1960/1 season. Franco Zeffirelli's Old Vic version of *Romeo and Juliet* was a 'miracle' because the director allowed the characters to be neither 'larger nor smaller than life: they were precisely life-size'.[30] Tynan would remember this production when he moved to the National. But the familiar problem of life happening 'elsewhere' was beginning to haunt him. In his account of the *Lady Chatterley* trial in November 1960, Tynan recorded a crucial victory for literature in the battle against censorship, a battle that drama had decided to duck out of. A succession of expert witnesses, including Dame Rebecca West, E.M. Forster and the Bishop of Woolwich, had refuted the charge that the unexpurgated novel was a work of obscenity. By taking a collective stand at the Old Bailey, the forces of progression had compelled the forces of conservatism to make complete fools of themselves, most famously when the prosecuting counsel, Mr Mervyn Griffith-Jones, put the following series of questions to the jury: 'Would you approve of your young sons, young daughters – because girls can read as well as boys – reading this book? Is it a book you would have lying around your own house? Is it a book you would wish your wife or your servants to read?'[31] Why could not drama be as assertive in its battle against censorship? Tynan deliberately became the first person to write the word 'fuck' in a newspaper article, to demonstrate the latitude that was now rightly accorded the written word.[32]

Winter trips to Stockholm, Warsaw and Berlin reminded him how better funded continental European drama was. A spring visit to Broadway provoked a renewed sense of wanderlust, and he started to toy with the idea of leaving the *Observer* so soon after re-joining. He wrote to William Shawn, who was angling for him to return to the *New Yorker*, that he was only remaining with the 'groggy old newspaper' until the end of 1961 out of loyalty to Astor, who was facing a circulation battle after the launch of the *Sunday Telegraph*.[33] The question remained, though: for what would he be leaving?

Dan Rebellato, in his fascinating book *1956 and All That*, contends that one of the motivating factors behind the work of George Devine at the ESC was a dislike of the West End Tennent mafia that was partially inspired by homophobia. This controversial view has been challenged by those who point out the high proportion of gay men who worked at the Royal Court (Richardson, Dexter and Gaskill, for example), but a homophobic stance was one of many weapons that were used to denigrate the work of the Tennent empire. Rattigan and Gielgud were, after all, the mainstays of the organisation in the 1950s. Even Tynan, the critic of, in his words, 'the new movement', was not averse to implying that there was a depressingly effeminate uniformity to West End comedy that was the result of an excessive reliance on 'camp'. The appearance of Kenneth Williams, soon to achieve great fame with the *Carry On* films, in a series of comic sketches provoked a protest at the dullness of it all:

> The ability to camp (let us drop those misleading inverted commas) is a useful, even a vital, part of comic technique, but it is not the whole of it; and in recent years, I disrespectfully submit, we have had excess of it, our appetite has sickened, and English high comedy has very nearly died. Witness Kenneth Williams in *One Over the Eight*: The star, Kenneth Williams, seizes a handful of ripe opportunities; as a bowler-hatted cretin, unnerving strangers with a fund of misinformation ('You have five miles of tubing in your stomach'); as a shirt-sleeved illiterate whose hobby is dictating letters to the Prime Minister; and as a prancing *coiffeur*, stung by the slightest reflection on the virility of his male clients ('When anyone says to me "effeminate", I say "*pouf*!"'), Mr Williams has a matchless repertory of squirms, leers, ogles and severe, reproving glares, and must be accounted the *petit-maître* of contemporary camp. As such, I salute him; but I wish there were more to English comedy than this.[34]

Fresh from New York, where he had savoured the acerbic observations of Mort Sahl and Lenny Bruce, Tynan had quickly noticed that the big gap in English comedy was the practice of satire. 'Our theatre as a whole has been infected, and injured, by our weakness in the tiny, ancillary department of satirical cabaret,' he wrote in October 1960, and the main reason was that, unlike in New York or San Francisco, there were no specialist clubs where satirists could develop their skills: 'We lack a place in which intelligent, like-minded people can spend a cheap evening listening to forthright cabaret that is socially, sexually and politically pungent.'[35] How thrilled he was then in May 1961 by the appearance of Dudley Moore, Peter Cook, Alan Bennett and Jonathan Miller in *Beyond the Fringe* at the Fortune Theatre. English comedy had taken 'its first decisive step into the second half of the twentieth century'. The topicality of their material (targeting the H-bomb, Sunday night religious programmes and capital punishment); the decisive way that they lampooned contemporary politicians (such as Macmillan, the South African Prime Minister, Dr Verwoerd, and the Kenyan Nationalist leader, Tom Mboya); their liberating lack of timidity and the quality of their writing and delivery were the perfect antidote to Williams and effeminacy. Above all, Tynan celebrated their scoffing, in Michael

Frayn's words, at the 'unthinking attitudes of respect' that still existed in 1960s
Britain,[36] but the force of his enthusiasm was qualified by a desire to see them go
further still. The evening, he concluded,

> lacks a great deal. It has no slick coffee-bar scenery, no glib one-line blackouts,
> no twirling dancers in tight trousers, no sad ballets for fisherwomen clad in fish-
> net stockings, no saleable Kitsch. For these virtues of omission we must all be
> grateful; but it can be justly urged against the show that it is too parochial, too
> much obsessed with BBC voices and BBC attitudes, too exclusively concerned
> with taunting the accents and values of John Betjeman's suburbia. 'Beyond the
> Fringe' is anti-reactionary without being progressive. It goes less far than one
> could have hoped, but immeasurably farther than one had any right to expect.[37]

Whereas Harold Hobson was disconcerted by the birth of satirical revue, Tynan
pushed and prodded for more lacerating material.

This ambivalent response characterised his reception of two more premières by
the leading lights of the 'new movement', Arnold Wesker and John Osborne.
Wesker's *The Kitchen*, much admired for Dexter's direction and the single over-
hanging lamp that produced heat as well as light, was a financial lifeline for the
Royal Court, playing to 60 per cent houses (and ironically underlining the legitimacy of Coward's claims about commerciability).[38] Tynan hailed it as a 'metaphor
for the dehumanising world of commercialism and mass production', claiming that
it achieved 'something that few playwrights have ever attempted: it dramatises
work, the daily collision of man with economic necessity, the repetitive toil
that consumes the large portion of human life which is not devoted to living'. But
the pulsating didacticism was not matched by a convincing theatricality, in his
view: 'What mars the play is the fact that it gets nowhere; instead of ending it
stops.'[39] Wesker might legitimately respond that that is the very point: the play's
resistance to closure is the most powerful metaphor for the unending drudgery of
work that it contains.

Osborne's much-heralded *Luther*, which had its first outing in Paris, with the
rising star Albert Finney in the lead, was more disappointing for the expectant critic.
It seemed worthy but occasionally dull, and was suspiciously praised by Harold
Hobson. Structurally episodic, heavily influenced (despite the playwright's later
protestations) by Epic theatre and intellectually challenging, the work nevertheless
lacked dynamism. 'Always the play informs', Tynan reported; 'one's reservation
must be that it too seldom excites; the thrusting vigour of its style goes into exposition rather than action. Yet I count it (to burn a boat or two) the most eloquent
piece of dramatic writing to have dignified our theatre since *Look Back in Anger*.'[40]
It was not the ringing endorsement that it seemed on first reading.

At the end of the 1960/1 season it was announced that Joan Littlewood, tired and frustrated by her constant battles with funding authorities, was leaving Theatre Workshop. Tynan, too, spent the summer less engaged with the theatre, concentrating instead on producing 15 episodes of a 45-minute fortnightly arts programme for commercial television, called *Tempo*. Tynan enjoyed the work, which included interviews with Olivier, the stars of *Beyond the Fringe* and an elderly Gordon Craig, but, as with so many of his practical activities, it fizzled out at the end of its run. The Programme Controller for ABC, Brian Tesler, contacted Tynan after it was over, to give some feedback: 'Perhaps the programme wasn't always as successful as we both would have hoped . . . [but] at the very least you sowed the seeds of a new and valuable kind of ITV programme'.[41] But Tynan was becoming weary of preparing the ground for others. Particularly if they were slow to follow his suggestions.

On his return to reviewing in the autumn of 1961, therefore, he filed a sensational piece. The last six months of discontent bubbled over and the mouthpiece and bodyguard of the 'new movement' publicly questioned its very achievements. 'The Breakthrough That Broke Down' is a remarkable essay. Not only is it conveniently overlooked by those, such as John Russell Taylor, who argue that 8 May 1956 wrought an overnight revolution, but it reminds one of Tynan's perpetual need to be a crusading critic. The promise of the late 1950s was in danger of dissipating and he was unsure if he had the necessary interest (and energy) to mount a renewed campaign for the 'new movement'. But he still believed in the need to bang the drum for the National Theatre, even in the face of government knock-backs:

In a week void of London *premières*, I scan the list of available productions and am shocked. So little, in ten years, seems to have changed. The Royal Court has arrived and survived, a beach-head for our splashing new wave, but one beach-head, it becomes chillingly clear, doesn't make a breakthrough.

A decade ago, roughly two out of three London theatres were inhabited by detective stories, Pineroesque melodramas, quarter-witted farces, debutante comedies, overweight musicals and unreviewable revues; the same is true today. The accepted new playwrights then were Fry, Eliot and Anouilh; of this threesome Anouilh is still represented on the playbills of London, and the other two have been replaced by Arnold Wesker (*The Kitchen*) and John Osborne (*Luther*).

As for Theatre Workshop, it is almost as if it had never been. Unknown in London ten years ago, and recently decapitated by the loss of Joan Littlewood, it has no West End memorial except what must by now be a fairly apathetic production of *Fings Ain't Wot They Used T'Be*. Theatrically, though not otherwise, Brendan Behan has been silent since *The Hostage*; Shelagh Delaney has not yet fulfilled the glowing promise of *A Taste of Honey* and Alun Owen, all-conquering on television, failed to conquer Shaftesbury Avenue with *Progress to the Park*.

Signs of hope are actually signs of frustration. In spite of his potential, the West End 'shuns' Wesker; *Billy Liar* is the fruit of 'two working-class playwrights who owe their London success to a middle-class parlour farce'; and the 'new school of regional actors has two leaders, of whom one, Albert Finney, can be seen in *Luther*, but only for a limited season, while the other, Peter O'Toole, is busy filming in Arabia'. Perhaps expectations had been pitched too high: 'perhaps that is why the breakthrough broke down'. One of the main problems, he asserts, is that the new writers lack an overview of drama that can both take them back beyond the lumpen 1940s and 1930s, as well as show them the best overseas models:

> . . . nothing is more crucially stupid than to deride the artistic achievements of a social class because one deplores its historical record.
>
> Those achievements belong to the past. Between them and the work of people now living a link must be formed and maintained: between Strindberg and Osborne, Chekhov and Shelagh Delaney, Stanislavski and Joan Littlewood, Galsworthy and Wesker, Büchner and John Arden, and other such pairings. But these connections can rarely be made, since the opportunities for comparison so seldom arise. Lacking a National Theatre, London has no playhouse in which the best of world drama is constantly on tap, available for immediate ingestion by spectators of eclectic tastes. One function of such a theatre would be to bridge the gap between those elements of bourgeois theatre that lean towards the future and those elements of the new drama that extend a hand towards the past.
>
> That is the ideal, and at present it is impracticable. One resorts to statistics. Last night the London theatre was to all intents and purposes cut off from history. Of thirty-four playhouses, only three were staging plays that were written more than ten years ago – *Dr Faustus* at the Old Vic, *'Tis Pity She's a Whore* at the Mermaid and *The Rehearsal*, by Anouilh, at the Globe. This trio apart, the oldest play in London last night was Agatha Christie's *The Mousetrap*. I am all for modernity, but this is ridiculous.[42]

Lindsay Anderson, in the *Observer*'s letters page, was furious at what he saw as Tynan's betrayal,[43] but this article was less about pining for the past than maintaining a hope for the future. The prognosis at the end of 1961 was extremely poor, as far as Tynan was concerned. It was 'a thin season' but one which was, paradoxically 'dying from success . . . Whether in triumph (as now) or in failure (as more often), the commercial theatre tends irresistibly towards stagnation. From the spectator's point of view, the system is successful only when it is just managing to avoid breakdown.'[44]

There were other reasons for Tynan's low spirits in the autumn of 1961. In October his collection of theatre writing, *Curtains*, was published to warm acclaim. His old friend Harold Clurman in the *New York Times* hailed him as a literary 'phenomenon' who possessed the magnificent quality of commitment, and Clurman shrewdly explained how he had redefined the critic's role:

> . . . one must stress, apart from whatever reaction we may have to particular reviews, Tynan's *usefulness* to the theatre as a whole. This is a function of criticism usually overlooked by those who regard the theatre critic as still another entertainer on the scene. Tynan, apart from his other qualities, is a shrewd and witty journalist who knows how to play this role superbly. His cleverness at times stands out on the body of his work as a sort of decorative rash on a young man's face, but one of the most encouraging aspects of his work and his personality is that he constantly learns and grows.[45]

But he was attacked in print in his own paper by the American critic, Mary McCarthy, whose own collection of theatre reviews from the *Partisan Review, Sights and Spectacles*, he had rebuked in 1959 for being 'tethered to naturalistic minutiae' and spoiled by 'inconsistencies'. 'To quarrel with Miss McCarthy's pedantry,' he had concluded, somewhat uncharitably, was 'to quibble with a quibble'.[46] For someone who was often accused of being vituperative in his own writing, Tynan could be surprisingly sensitive to attack. The fact that this one occurred in the *Observer* (with echoes of his *Evening Standard* showdown eight years earlier) inevitably added to his sense of injury. McCarthy described the writing in *Curtains* as 'drawling and japish'. She objected to his overuse of parody, calling him a 'facile parodist', and protested that this was 'not criticism [but] a kind of quoting [that begins] where words, in the sense of rational discourse, fail the critic'. Her revenge went further. Tynan is 'most unconvincing when he is in earnest' and cannot possibly bear comparison with Shaw, because his writing is mere 'advertising copy'. Worst of all, she concluded, he is 'a somewhat adenoidal spokesman-for-those-under-thirty'.[47] Elaine felt that it was a 'very bitchy, personal and intemperate attack'[48] and Terence Kilmartin, Tynan's friend and ally, was so disconcerted by the force of McCarthy's piece that he commissioned a rebuttal from the critic Alan Pryce-Jones to be placed alongside the offending article. 'Here is a very clever lady writing about a very clever gentleman,' Pryce-Jones observed acidly, under the provocative title, 'Contrary Mary'. 'Adrenaline flows like the mill race at Rosmersholm. Anyone falling in will get drowned; and someone has fallen in; and it isn't Kenneth Tynan.' Upbraiding McCarthy for imprecision, inconsistency and a lack of knowledge of Tynan's work, Pryce-Jones expressed incredulity at her venom. 'It is not easy to see what Miss McCarthy really wants of Tynan. She dislikes him being both readable and quotable,' he complains, and ends by stating that Tynan's 'special art' is 'to convey the gusto of the [theatre] experience, and to relate it, with increasing care, to what is happening in the world'.[49] Although it was a piece of blatant puffery, Pryce-Jones's article was the more balanced assessment. Until the end of his full-time connection with the paper, Tynan was seen as a prize asset of the *Observer*, whose reputation must be upheld at all costs, particularly in the changed atmosphere post-1956. Frantic backstage efforts dissuaded him from serving another ill-conceived writ, and he was consoled by the support of fellow critics, not least Brooks Atkinson, who, writing in the *New York Times*, observed that the controversy had done little to shift his belief that 'Mr. Tynan consistently takes the theatre on a high level and writes about it with intelligence and vivacity'.[50]

One consequence of the new order after 1956 was, of course, an increasing lack of reverence for critics themselves. Tynan was not alone in being lacerated. Harold Hobson had been even more memorably lampooned in November 1959 by Penelope Gilliatt, Tynan's *Observer* colleague (and – briefly – girlfriend). Writing in *Encore* Gilliatt stated that 'It would be unfair to suggest that one of the most characteristic sounds of the English Sunday is the sound of Harold Hobson barking up the wrong tree'.[51] Accompanied by a caricature by James Bucknill of a canine Hobson straining at the leash and yapping at a tree-trunk, this formidable combination of witty cartoon and provocative comment quickly passed into theatrical folklore and dogged Hobson until his overdue retirement from the *Sunday Times* in 1976.

Quickly following on from this distressing professional event was a traumatic personal one. Rose Tynan had been suffering from dementia, possibly undiagnosed Alzheimer's disease, since before her son had left for New York, and he was contacted in early November 1961 by her doctor to say that she was now terminally ill. On 12 November Tynan travelled up to visit her and they sat singing hymns until she quietly passed away, tiny and thin. In the midst of his grief, Tynan blamed himself entirely for her isolation and neglect and he grew ever more depressed. The increasing commitments of his television programme, *Tempo*; the desperate deficiencies of his marriage; a growing intake of alcohol and the antidepressant Dexamyl; and even the competitive pressure engendered by Elaine writing her first play, *My Place*, which began casting for a production at the Cambridge on 23 November, all combined with the grief and guilt of his bereavement to cause a temporary breakdown. Having submitted an incomprehensible review to the *Observer* – evidence enough to his employers of the stress that he was under – he went to see a psychiatrist recommended to him by Jonathan Miller, Dr Paul Senft. Tynan justified this (as if justification was needed) by telling friends that he was undergoing analysis to rid him of the guilt that prevented him from leaving Elaine.[52] Tynan visited Senft up to three times a week until the following September, and he gradually began to feel more relaxed and at ease with himself. At the beginning of January, to both of their satisfaction, Tynan felt strong enough to leave Elaine and move out of Mount Street into a flat in Groom Street, Knightsbridge. This provided the necessary physical space for him to survive the attention that would greet the opening of Elaine's play on 29 January. Directed by the talented John Dexter, *My Place* started out at the Stratford Memorial Theatre before transferring to the West End. Tynan had warned his wife that any bad reviews would solely be on account of his colleagues wishing to get back at him (Philip Hope-Wallace in the *Guardian* loathed it).[53] This was a generous comment, particularly as the production lasted for only five weeks, and was matched by letters he wrote to both Elaine and her great friend, Gore Vidal, enquiring whether there was the slightest chance of them getting back together again. This emotional need was not matched by a physical one. Shortly after he moved to Groom Street Tynan began an affair with the painter Brenda Bury. Elaine sensed that this would give her grounds again for a divorce, and a new detective was employed to gather evidence. By March 1962, convinced that it was essential that they split up and armed with the evidence necessary for a Mexican divorce, Elaine had the relevant papers served. She demanded custody of Tracy and alimony. Tynan was devastated. Feeling that the death of his mother had left him abandoned and isolated (his daughter Tracy notwithstanding), he became hysterical and urged Elaine to visit Senft to discover just how unstable this had made him. Elaine agreed to this and Senft confirmed that at the present time he believed that Tynan was dangerously suicidal. Elaine agreed to hold off to allow his therapy to work, but was determined that this was a postponement of her action and not another cancellation.[54] The familiar pattern of devotion and desperation began again, but, in her own mind, needed to be resolved by the summer.

Given this personal turmoil, Tynan had to make a superhuman effort if he was to continue as a critic in the spring of 1962, but he responded well to the discipline of the deadline week after week. His columns were deflated and pessimistic, but it is difficult to ascertain whether this was a result of his continuing disappointment at the unfulfilment of the promise of the 'new movement' or of his own deep anxieties. In January he felt compelled to lament the dominance of Pinter-mania. He had no gripe with the playwright himself, but disapproved of the rash of sub-standard imitations that were cropping up in London.[55] This was also a warning that Absurdist writing, something he generally deplored, was threatening to displace social realism as the replacement for Loamshire drama. The publication of Martin Esslin's study, *The Theatre of the Absurd*, in June 1962 gave him the chance to man the barricades. Whilst prepared to concede that Absurdism had made an important contribution to 1950s drama, Tynan thought that the author's claims for the movement (which have deeply impressed subsequent generations of undergraduates) were exaggerated:

. . . when Mr Esslin ropes in Shakespeare, Goethe and Ibsen as harbingers of the Absurd, one begins to feel that the whole history of dramatic literature has been nothing more than a prelude to the triumphant emergence of Beckett and Ionesco. Overstatement and Mr Esslin are no strangers. He thinks N.F. Simpson 'a more powerful social critic than any of the social realists'; and I wish I had an extra month of life for every playwright in connection with whose work Mr Esslin refers to 'the human condition'.

Tynan restated his consistent view that these dramatists' work was an abnegation of life: 'My own response to the Absurdists, (apart from Beckett) is to enjoy their poetry while mistrusting their philosophy . . . What irks most about the Absurdists is their pervasive tone of privileged despair.'[56]

The type of play that best illustrated for Tynan the belief that the human condition was not one of despair but of the possibility of change for the better appeared in May 1962. Arnold Wesker's *Chips with Everything* – a real success for the Royal Court, in spite of Devine's continued reservations – was the one production about which he could be truly passionate since he had moved into Groom Street five months previously. Focusing on the hopelessness of National Service and conveying the monotony of it all through endless drilling (the director, John Dexter, recognising from his own experience the miserable futility of this),[57] it was 'a gauntlet of a play', Tynan felt,

> . . . furious, compassionate and unforgiving: taking as its microcosm a squad of R.A.F. conscripts, it reveals the class system in action – the process of unnatural selection that divides people into Lenin's categories of 'who: whom' – and although it invites us to rage at the rulers and to pity the ruled, it denies us the luxury of catharsis.
>
> Its purpose is not to purge us, but to prove that the body politic needs purging. We are studying a disease; and what matters is not so much the pain it inflicts as the extent to which it is curable.
>
> Men are not born obedient. Servility is a reflex brought about by a subtle and patient conditioning; and Mr Wesker explains how the habit is formed. To begin with, the airmen are sharply individualised: but after a sustained dose of indoctrination, they are barely distinguishable from the stereotypes of British war films and Whitehall farce. They have learned their place in the hierarchy, and may some day aspire to the ambiguous, compromised status of Corporal Hill, the N.C.O. in charge of their hut.

At this point, Tynan cites a long extract from the PT instructor, before adding: 'I wish I could quote more, if only to quell the prevalent rumour that Mr Wesker is a primitive who has no feeling for words. In fact, he uses them with a secure

adroitness that betokens not merely a good ear but a shaping mind and a remarkable flair for character-revealing rhythms.' The grit in the oyster was the desire of
the main character, the upper-class Pip, to be a 'messiah for the masses'. Tynan
found him too pat: 'I query the resolution; but the dramatic knot is magnificently
tied, and I shall not quickly forget the words in which the military Establishment
rebukes the man who defies it – "We listen but we do not hear, we befriend but do
not touch you, we applaud but we do not act. To tolerate is to ignore."' Overall,
though, the play affirmed a belief in humanity arising from moments of seeming
disappointment. It was the antithesis of Absurdism:

> Surveying Mr Wesker's working-class characters, one feels not only that this is
> how they were, but also that they could, in a better-ordered society, have turned
> out very differently. In what is, Mr Wesker implies what might have been; and
> there are few theatrical gifts more basic than that.[58]

The play raised his personal as well as his professional spirits.

The big theatrical event of the summer of 1962 was the opening of the Chichester Festival Theatre with a company under the direction of Laurence Olivier. A
local optician, Leslie Evershed Martin, was behind the plan to build an open-stage
theatre in the town, and in his desire for a suitable artistic director he had decided
– with little expectation – to go to the very top. The offer came at just the right time
for Olivier. He had finally married Joan Plowright in March 1961, while she was
appearing in the Broadway transfer of *A Taste of Honey*, and after she became pregnant in the summer of 1961, they decided to return to England. Evershed's offer was
gratefully received, and the newly married couple relocated to Brighton, a short
journey from the new theatre. In the twelve months prior to the first season, Olivier
began recruiting a high-calibre company. In hindsight, he was clearly serving an
apprenticeship for the position of Artistic Director of the National Theatre, but the
birth of this much-longed-for national institution was still very uncertain. Olivier's
company included Michael Redgrave, Alan Howard, Sybil Thorndike, Rosemary
Harris and Robin Phillips, not to mention Joan Plowright and Olivier himself. Only
the fledgling Royal Shakespeare Company could draw together such talent, and
expectations were high in the first week of July 1962, when the opening of
The Chances inaugurated the new venue. With exquisite timing it was also announced
that the government had finally consented to the building of a National Theatre.
There was everything to play for, for both the distinguished actor and the restless
critic.

Tynan described the announcement of the victory as a 'historic day'. He was less
enamoured by the minor Jacobean play that Olivier had decided to open with, but
decided to suspend judgement about the merits of the new stage space until he had

seen the second production, Ford's *The Broken Heart*, the following week. Typically, the announcement about the National simply spurred him on to a new demand. The RSC needed similar financial support, since 'we need not only a *comédie française* but a T.N.P. [Théâtre Nationale Populaire] to keep it up to scratch'.[59] The future of the Arts and Aldwych theatres was under financial threat, and it seemed perverse to see them disappear as the National was just over the horizon.

The following week, Tynan returned to Chichester for the Ford. He was completely underwhelmed and wrote his most surprising review ever, the famous 'Open Letter to an Open Stager'. *The Chances* had been a 'flimsy Jacobean prank', but *The Broken Heart* confirmed the 'general feeling that all is not well with you'. Olivier's direction was unconvincing – 'given a script so awkwardly split between nobility and banality, did you find a production style that might weld it together? I think not'; the acting faintly embarrassing – Joan Greenwood's Calantha was 'a stoical heroine reduced to the stature of a baritone Joyce Grenfell'; Olivier's own perform-ance was indifferent – 'Most remarkable of all, you were indistinct: one lost more than half of what you said'; and, recalling Tynan's earlier dislike of Stephen Joseph's innovations, the configuration of the theatre a step backwards:

> Chichester is a product of our gullibility: instead of letting the whole audience see the actors' faces (however distantly), we now prefer to bring them closer to the actors' backs. The Chichester stage is so vast that even the proximity argu-ment falls down: an actor on the opposite side of the apron is farther away from one's front-row seat than he would be from the twelfth row of a proscenium theatre – where in any case he would not deliver a crucial speech with his rear turned towards one's face.

It was a demolition job of the severest force – and the first time that Tynan had ever been even remotely negative about his idol. He concluded with a wag of the finger:

> Tomorrow *Uncle Vanya* opens. Within a fortnight you will have directed three plays and appeared in two leading parts. It is too much. Do you recall the tri-umvirate, made up of John Burrell, Ralph Richardson and yourself that ruled the Old Vic in those miraculous seasons between 1944 and 1946? Why not recruit a similar team to run the National Theatre – a joint directorship consisting of your-self, Peter Brook and Antony Quayle? I don't wish to be dogmatic; I am merely dropping names, and hints.[60]

Was this an unusual bid to put himself in the frame?

Joan Plowright hid this review from her husband, but secretly endorsed the critic's comments about his workload. For the last time, Donald Wolfit, who recog-nised that he had no chance of being part of the new project – partially because of

Tynan's antipathy – crossed swords with his nemesis. 'More than a few years ago I endeavoured to do a kindness by reviewing a production of yours in your amateur days,' he wrote in July.

> Ever since then you have left no stone unturned nor a phrase unwritten to do the utmost damage to my career in the theatre as both an actor and a manager . . . Your constant attacks have been vile and insidious. You know full well what you have done. Remorse could never touch your heart for your writing clearly shows that you have none. You delight in destruction, but I thank God that there are others who respect my life long service for the theatre.[61]

Unfortunately for Wolfit, his friends could not help him to the job he most cherished. As it happened, *Uncle Vanya* was a colossal success, crucial to salvaging Olivier's credibility, since on 9 August it was announced that he was, indeed, to be appointed the first Artistic Director of the National Theatre. Tynan spoke of the 'superlative'[62] performances of Olivier as Astrov and Redgrave as Vanya. It was a high point of post-war drama. For Tynan, Plowright's support would soon be of the greatest significance.

Immediately after reviewing *Uncle Vanya* Tynan flew off to Málaga for the bulls. Meanwhile in London, Elaine dined with Tennessee Williams who observed that, as far as he was concerned, the warring couple were 'both very much in love . . . I see it every time I'm with you two. You must go to him.'[63] Inexplicably, given that she had already initiated divorce proceedings, Elaine decided to fly over to Tynan's hotel, the Miramar. On her arrival, she discovered that Tynan was already involved in a holiday romance, so Elaine embarked on one too, with a public relations consultant. There was a brief reconciliation between the married couple, before Tynan gave her what she described as a 'position paper: pages of professions of love followed by pages of accusations mixed in with threats to kill himself'.[64] Elaine asked Orson Welles to intercede, but his response was that she had better divorce Tynan, because he was destroying her. This was confirmed when he came back to her room and attacked her, 'leaving me unconscious on the bathroom floor with two black eyes and a broken nose'. It was his lowest moment.

Back in London, Elaine had a restraining order placed on Tynan, but detected little remorse: 'On the whole he downplayed what he'd done – no apology, only an off-hand mention that his shrink had dismissed it, merely saying it was clear he'd kill me or I'd kill him if we stayed together. He was neither ashamed nor sorry for what he'd done. Nor did he seem embarrassed that I'd told people about it. There was always a part of him that gloried in his reputation as a lady-killer, the sinful, depraved Don Juan. The mad, bad, dangerous-to-know sadist.'[65]

A highly unexpected development followed this nadir. Tynan wrote – possibly on the suggestion of Senft – to Olivier stating that, in spite of his Chichester reviews, he would be applying for the post of dramaturg at the National Theatre – 'a brave and risky thing to do in the circumstances',[66] Plowright recalled. Olivier's response was understandably dismissive – 'How shall we slaughter the little bastard?' he asked his wife.[67] He had subsequently read the Chichester pieces and was outraged, but Plowright was an eloquent advocate. There were many reasons why it was actually a sensible idea. Tynan had a proven track record going back years as a significant supporter of the new project. He was the country's leading fan of Olivier himself, the Chichester reviews notwithstanding. He would be a persuasive spokesperson for the venture, not afraid of being provocative or unpopular. He was synonymous with the 'new movement' of theatre, which would tackle the charge that the NT was destined to be a museum and, in his devotion to Brecht, he was in touch with most important European drama. After Plowright pleaded Tynan's case, Olivier relented and sent him the letter that was to change Tynan's life, asking him to become the NT's dramaturg and jokingly adding the heartfelt handwritten comment beneath the typescript: '*God – anything* to get you off the *Observer!*'[68]

Further anxiety followed, while Olivier sought to persuade an unenthusiastic NT board of the necessity of Tynan's appointment. Olivier quickly came round to the wisdom of having Tynan beside him (it was hard for him to deny that his August letter had been the work of Plowright), writing in January 1963 to tell Tynan how pleased he was to have him on board,[69] but the discussions in committee seemed endless. Confirmation finally came through in February 1963 – to both the delight and regret of the *Observer*. Richard Findlater, a literary editor at the paper, informed Astor of the situation on 23 February:

> Lord Chandos and his fellow National Theatre Boarders have offered Ken Tynan a job as, in effect, literary advisor of the National Theatre and although this is not yet officially and contractually confirmed, he wants to take it and will take it unless there is some hitch next week. It will be for a year only at first; he wants to keep the door open back to the *Observer* – although he would be free to write generally about the theatre or about any other topic for us during that time, as long as he did not review current productions in London.
>
> This obviously raises several problems and I thought I would put them down on paper now:
>
> 1) We should surely keep him, if we can, on some sort of lien during the coming year. This might involve some sort of retainer figure.
> 2) The replacement would naturally have to be of top quality, and yet willing to take the job on the understanding that it would probably be only for a year.

The prestige of the post is so high that I don't feel that the time limit would be a deterrent to anybody with talent, although ideally the new boy would be somebody who would be willing to do a short notice every now and again if Ken was in the running for the general piece. I recommend that we try first Bamber Gascoigne . . .[70]

Of course, Tynan was irreplaceable and Findlater was asked to produce a long list of alternative successors. Possibilities included Siriol Hugh Jones, John Russell Taylor ('quite a good book on the new dramatists. Rather dull. Not quite good enough for us'), Lawrence Kitchin, Charles Marowitz ('too close in his moralising and left-wing attitude to Ken, to make this a good substitute'), Clancy Sigal, Roger Gellert, Wayland Young and Mervyn Jones.[71] Gascoigne was eventually confirmed as the successor.

With his longed-for position at the National confirmed, Tynan threw himself into an arduous round of preparations for its opening (scheduled for October with Peter O'Toole in *Hamlet*), whilst continuing his weekly *Observer* column and maintaining a complex series of affairs and liaisons. The most significant, which was to end in his second marriage, began in January after he met a young reporter in the offices of the Arts section of the *Observer*. Kathleen Halton had only been married to Oliver Gates for six months, but a strong attraction quickly developed between the two. They started to have secret weekly lunches, which continued despite a brief attempt at cohabitation with Elaine during Tracy's Easter holidays from Dartington Hall and a predictably unhappy gastronomic tour of France and subsequent visit to Pamplona. Professional engagements brought the pair together for a first extended period in late summer, when Tynan chaired a drama conference at the Edinburgh Festival and Kathleen was sent by her new employers, the *Sunday Times*, to prepare an article on the musical scene. The conference, organised by Tynan and the publisher John Calder, was a further testimony to his cachet. John Osborne, Joan Littlewood, Wole Soyinka, Max Frisch, Barry Reckford, Peter Brook, Eugène Ionesco, Bernard Kops, Jack Gelber and Joan Plowright (who passionately argued that subsidy was a 'recognition of the artist's right to fail')[72] all made contributions, and Tynan himself caused a sensation on the first afternoon when he attacked Western playwrights 'who use their influence and affluence to preach to the world the nihilistic doctrine that life is pointless and irrationally destructive, and that there is nothing we can do about it . . . Until everyone is fed, clothed, housed and taught . . . we should not indulge in the luxury of "privileged despair".' This stinging attack on Absurdist theatre caused great offence to some, and huge satisfaction to those who saw Epic theatre as the way forward. Harold Pinter tackled Tynan in the bar that evening by picking up a glass ashtray and saying that he could write a 'perfectly valid play about it without referring to social or economic conditions'. Tynan replied dogmatically that 'unless the play told me who made it and how much he was paid, I would feel cheated'.[73]

The conference was a huge success for Tynan. He had been the centre of attention at an event that he had organised. It had attracted the cream of modern playwrights, and delegates were eager to pick his brains about the imminent plans for the National Theatre. He felt that he was a player, at last. He also discovered that he and Kathleen had many things in common. They spent a blissful, if necessarily furtive, time together, smoothed, no doubt, by Kathleen's belief that Tynan's S&M needs were not shocking and 'masked a tender man'.[74] This alone suggested a promising compatibility – but not quite yet. Elaine was not completely out of his system, and his roving eye had briefly lit on Rita Moreno and the Chinese actress Tsai Chin, whom he took to the opening night of the National.

Tynan's tenure as the *Observer*'s theatre critic finally ended in August 1963. It had been a glorious association. As his day of departure approached, he found it difficult to motivate himself, in the face of the excitement of the National, to produce his weekly column. One of his final duties, however, was to review the first part of the Royal Shakespeare Company's *The Wars of the Roses*. Tynan was unusually diffident, and alone in withholding his admiration. 'What we have at Stratford,' he wrote, 'is gang warfare in armour, history seen as Lord Beaverbrook still sees it, in terms of the clashing greeds and temperamental incompatibilities of feudal potentates.'[75] More typical of the critical mood was Bernard Levin's description of the production as 'a landmark and a beacon in the post-war English theatre [and] a triumphant vindication of Mr Hall's policy, as well as his power, as a producer'.[76] The RSC had now set an impressively high standard – and the battle with Tynan and Olivier's National Theatre was about to begin.

Chapter 7   *Upsetting the Establishment*

One of the reasons why London came to be seen as the capital of world theatre in the 1960s was the existence of not just one, but two world-class state-subsidised companies. Yet the parallel existence of the companies was the subject of some doubt during the early years of the decade. Although the Royal Shakespeare Company (as it was called from March 1961) established its London base at the Aldwych in December 1960, its opening season was unspectacular and it suffered a monumental disaster with Franco Zeffirelli's *Othello* (1961), starring John Gielgud as the Moor. Gielgud's beard fell off, his body make-up blended into the dark set, the enormous pillars swayed when leant against, and Ian Bannen as Iago had great difficulties with his lines. It was 'a famous catastrophe',[1] in Peter Hall's view, and was only partly effaced by the appearance of a new young talent, Vanessa Redgrave as Rosalind in *As You Like It*. The uncertainty of the season's productions was equalled by continuing confusion about the company's relationship with the looming National Theatre. As early as 1959, Laurence Olivier had informed Peter Hall in a discussion in the restaurant at Stratford prior to *Coriolanus* that he was going to make a stab at the National Theatre and he invited Hall to join him as his potential number two, but in a response that typifies Hall's independent spirit, he politely declined the offer and stated that he was going to establish his own theatre – as 'number one'.[2]

It was the belief of Oliver Lyttelton, Lord Chandos, chairman of the Joint Council for the National Theatre, that a tripartite arrangement should be created binding together the Old Vic, Stratford and the new venture,[3] and initially Hall supported this notion. However, when the Chancellor of the Exchequer, Selwyn Lloyd, announced in March 1961 – to general astonishment – that the government would not support a new National Theatre and would award £400,000 to the Old Vic, regional theatre and Stratford, Hall rejoiced. Stratford's euphoria was short-lived, though. A concerted effort of political lobbying began. The Arts Council mounted a surprisingly effective public relations campaign; the Labour-controlled London County Council cleverly exploited the Conservative administration's discomfort by offering match funding of £1 million for a huge complex; and even the loyal establishment figure Lord Chandos himself pointed out that the decision insulted the Queen Mother, who had already laid several foundation stones.[4] Faced with such a constituency, Selwyn Lloyd relented and three months later asked the Joint Council to devise a plan to spend an annual subsidy of £400,000 a year on opera, ballet and theatre in a South Bank complex that would contain an opera house as well as a theatre.

Stratford's attitude now changed entirely, since it feared that what was being planned was less a partnership than a take-over. Fordham Flower, the chairman of the RSC board, was deeply suspicious of Olivier's intentions. He believed that he wanted to lessen the RSC's competitive edge, reduce its attraction for actors and have Peter Hall working with him rather than against him, as well as exploit Stratford's managerial practices and 'get his mitts' on their revenue.[5] Consequently, relations between Hall and Olivier began to cool in early 1962, with the actor making explicit his sense of insecurity: 'The trouble as I see it (and have from the beginning of your schemes),' he wrote in his characteristically convoluted manner,

> is that you have really set out to be the Nat Th yourself, or if you prefer it, for Stratford to develop a position for itself as heir to the throne, or else to make such a throne unnecessary. If this is *not* so (as I know you genuinely want a Nat Th) *it looks like it* (to observers I mean, not to me).[6]

In January 1962, Stratford seemed to confirm these suspicions when it withdrew from the Joint Council, thereby eliminating any prospect of a tripartite arrangement.

Fortunately 1962 was much more auspicious for the RSC on the stage. David Rudkin's *Afore Night Comes* (in which a tramp is ritually murdered on a rubbish dump) ensured that the company maintained a high public profile (an essential part of Hall's propaganda war with the putative National). Vanessa Redgrave continued to intrigue, this time as Katherina in *The Taming of the Shrew*. Harold Pinter, the flavour of the month, if not the year, co-directed *The Collection* with Hall, which boded well for future collaboration; and Peter Brook directed a much admired *King Lear*, with Paul Scofield as the King, Alec McCowen as the Fool and Diana Rigg as Cordelia. It was one of the first productions of the play that aimed to persuade the audience that Goneril and Regan had genuine grounds for dissatisfaction, and emphasised the RSC's intention to investigate new ways of interpreting old classics. Now that preparations were beginning for the commencement of the National's work at the Old Vic, the RSC seemed much better prepared to face the new competition. Its new robustness was confirmed in the summer of 1963 – three months before the NT opened its inaugural production – when the RSC mounted the mammoth enterprise that was to guarantee its existence.

Since his time as an undergraduate at Cambridge, Hall had been fascinated by the rarely performed three parts of *Henry VI*, and the linking play, *Richard III*. To round off the 1962/3 season, he planned in collaboration with John Barton and the designer John Bury (recently recruited from Theatre Workshop) a project based on these four works. It was to be named *The Wars of the Roses*. Adopting a policy that he was later to recant – 'I blush at our frenzy of adaptation in the light of the present fashion for authenticity,'[7] he commented in 1993 – Hall agreed that the plays needed to be compressed and Barton therefore prepared a script that reduced the three parts of *Henry VI* into two, renaming the second part *Edward IV* and concluding with *Richard III*. After constant revisions, 12,350 lines had been reduced to 7,450, of which 1,444 had been devised by Barton.[8] It was a breathtakingly liberating approach to text, at a time when the sanctity of Shakespeare's words approached that of the Bible's. Hall sought to justify the linking and rewritten sections by citing the guiding principle behind the whole project – the desire to stress the relevance of Shakespeare's work to a modern-day audience. It was a further extension of the Royal Court's approach to contemporary drama into the previously untouched (apart from the contribution of the tiny Theatre Workshop) realm of classic British drama. Reassured by the proof-copy of Jan Kott's soon to be influential *Shakespeare Our Contemporary*, which ventured that the depiction of the political process in the *Henry* trilogy foreshadowed the abuse of power in the client states of the Soviet Union, Hall argued that at any given moment there was 'only one way of expressing the intentions of that play. And those intentions must be expressed in contemporary terms. At any given moment it may mean that there is a slight refocusing of the dramatist's intentions.'[9] It was a wholly modern approach to theatre, and the hubris of this belief was emblematic of the growing confidence of the younger generation of the period. 'It was the very stuff of the sixties,' in Hall's view.[10]

This emphasis on the contemporary, with the memory of the Cuban missile crisis of November 1962 very much in people's minds, made an enormous impression on audiences. Its innovation was complemented by the stellar cast, including Peggy Ashcroft, Ian Holm and Janet Suzman, and John Bury's set design, which incorporated a monumental, tactile set of tarnished copper plates and a main floor of expanded steel, which echoed as actors walked across it. Hall was thrilled by this because it ensured 'that the inhuman tramp of authority was heard throughout the theatre'.[11] Shakespeare appeared reinvigorated, theatre once again seemed at the cutting edge of modern thought after the stalling of the 'new movement', and Hall's fierce battle for the independence of the RSC was viewed as necessary and complete. He was now delivering on his stated intention to create an unorthodox company of the 1960s that posed questions instead of offering answers, and, by juxtaposing new writing at the Aldwych with new approaches to Renaissance works at Stratford, he laid down a blueprint that persists until this day. The whole process was repeated in 1964, together with the complete cycle of history plays, to celebrate the 400th anniversary of Shakespeare's birth.

Effingham Wilson's original vision back in 1848 of a National Theatre had been that of a repository for Shakespearian performances, but this was no longer appropriate, given the success of the RSC, and many people started to question how the infant National Theatre would be able to establish its own identity. Supporters of the RSC, such as Harold Hobson, feared that a National Theatre would mount revivals of the classics at the expense of new drama, dissuade actors from experimentation, thwart the revival of drama in the provinces and act as a museum for 'culture-starved package tourists'.[12] Olivier's early appointments, aside from Tynan, gave a clue as to how he wanted to tackle these concerns. He recruited two practitioners recognised for their association with the new wave: William Gaskill, a devotee of Epic theatre, who had directed the plays of N.F. Simpson and Osborne's *Epitaph for George Dillon* at the Royal Court, and John Dexter, who had been closely associated with the plays of Arnold Wesker. Indeed, the first company demonstrated strong links with the ESC, in that Colin Blakely, Robert Stephens, Frank Finlay, Ian McKellen and Joan Plowright all appeared in the first season and Albert Finney was to join for the second. It would be misleading to claim, though, that the new NT was a Royal Court Mark 2, since Maggie Smith, Michael Gambon, Edith Evans, Derek Jacobi, Michael Redgrave and Max Adrian were all encouraged to join from the commercial sector as well. This was no mean feat, given the paltry salaries on offer in the subsidised sector. The basic wage was a mere £14 per week with an additional £1 per performance, Tynan received £46 per week for ten years' commitment and even Olivier only received £120 per week as the full-time Director.[13] The repertory theatre supplied Derek Jacobi and Anthony Hopkins, with Michael Gambon coming from amateur theatre. What bound the new company together was a spirit of adventure that meant that theatre professionals were prepared to work for wages infinitely lower than they might command in the West End. After the dominance of commercial theatre in the 1950s, the struggle to generate an audience for new types of work valiantly waged by the ESC and Theatre Workshop and the predictions that theatre would be made obsolete by television, there was now great optimism that this state-supported enterprise, led by one of the most charismatic actors the theatre had ever known, would change the face of British theatre. The detail of how this would be done was left in the main to Tynan.

Tynan's value to Olivier was that as the Literary Manager, and, in effect, dramaturg to the new institution, he would help set its priorities, plan the repertoire and act as a vocal public spokesperson. But he was also able to offer much more. Given his wide-ranging interest in European drama, he could keep the National in touch with the latest theatrical developments. His interest in the theory and practice of politics helped keep the company in the public eye. His fearsome intellect provided a natural foil to Olivier's instinctive brilliance, and his loyal devotion could compensate for Olivier's recurrent moments of insecurity and doubt. Tynan's close working relationship with Olivier caused consternation in some quarters – the increasingly irritable Osborne became a persistent sniper – but Olivier was generally indebted to his support and advice.

Throughout 1963, Tynan played a key role in laying the groundwork for the new institution. He sent a memo in May to Olivier suggesting a possible repertoire for 1964/5, which revealed his consistent aspiration for the National to stage the best of world drama with an ensemble quick-footed enough to respond to the requirements of each play without adopting a house style. Possible productions included Coward's *Hay Fever*, directed by Olivier; Miller's *The Crucible* with Paul Scofield directed by Gaskill; Arden's *Serjeant Musgrave's Dance* directed by either Gaskill or Olivier; *Much Ado About Nothing* directed by Zeffirelli; and a triple bill, which he saw as 'an ideal way of combining box-office with experiment', comprising Brecht's *Edward II* with Paul Scofield directed by Dexter, Congreve's *Love for Love* directed by Olivier and Chekhov's *The Three Sisters* to tour to Chichester.[14] Tynan's suggestions had a remarkable strike rate. Coward himself directed *Hay Fever* (October 1964); Olivier directed *The Crucible* (January 1965); Zeffirelli directed *Much Ado About Nothing* (February 1965); *Edward II* was eventually directed by Frank Dunlop (April 1968); Peter Wood directed *Love for Love* (October 1965); Olivier directed *The Three Sisters* (July 1967); and the company toured Chichester in the summers of 1963, 1964 and 1965. It was this broad, flexible ethos – shaped primarily by Tynan – which defined the work of the company for the next five years. It also set the NT apart from the RSC, which was primarily devoted to the work of one playwright, and the ESC, devoted to promoting the work of contemporary playwrights. Of the 98 productions performed at the Old Vic between 1963 and 1973, 47 had their origin outside Britain, in the nationality of the playwright or the director.

The degree to which Tynan was involved at the start in every aspect of the company was staggering. From the confirmation of his appointment in February 1963, he played a key role in helping to get the company up and running. The last performance of the Old Vic company took place in June 1963 and there then followed four months of 'frantic reconstruction and redecoration'.[15] The original lease was signed for five years – no one had any conception that it would take fourteen years for the NT to be fully installed at its permanent home on the South Bank – and during this period support staff, including Olivier, were based in temporary huts in

Aquinas Street, over half a mile from the theatre. From his cramped office in one of the huts, Tynan concerned himself with leaflets, bills, agents, programme designs and headed notepaper. He organised 'talkathons' with Dexter, Gaskill and Olivier, about the future repertoire and possible casting choices. He devoted a large amount of time to negotiating with playwrights' estates for performance rights, most tiringly with the Brecht estate over *Mother Courage*. Press enquiries were often directed to him for a scintillating response, and stroppy playwrights were sent his way as well, particularly if it was felt that he had a helpful relationship with them. The irascible John Osborne contacted him directly in November 1963 complaining that he had only received two tickets instead of three for the production of *Hamlet*. 'I do seem to be getting a whole lot of shit from the National Theatre,' he moaned. 'I know Brecht never answered letters but I could get into his theatre without having to ring bells.'[16] Tynan was deputed to calm him down.

The first production of the new National Theatre on 22 October 1963 was celebrated more for what it symbolised – the end of over a century of thwarted hopes and tenacious campaigning – than for what it achieved. Olivier's decision to cast Peter O'Toole, who had achieved stardom through the film *Lawrence of Arabia*, in the title role of *Hamlet* worried both Gaskill and Dexter, who were concerned that this might set an undesirable precedent of employing star actors. During rehearsal, Olivier, who was directing the play, clearly feared the worst – 'No one's going to like it – they never do'[17] – and after three weeks of the run he gloomily observed that it was the worst production of anything that he had ever seen.[18] Although it was rather slow and ponderous, such despondency was misplaced, however. O'Toole may have struggled, but his reputation as a film star was good box office, with tickets changing hands on the streets for the inflated sum of £60. The reviews were respectful if lukewarm in their enthusiasm. Committed to further film contracts, O'Toole was never going to become a permanent member of the company and, as it was, the play ran for just twenty-seven performances.

It was the third and fourth productions of the first season – *Uncle Vanya* (19 November, dir. Olivier) and *The Recruiting Officer* (10 December, dir. Gaskill) – that established the National as an institution worthy of the 1930s Old Vic seasons under Lilian Baylis and the glorious Richardson/Olivier years of the 1940s. *Uncle Vanya* had already been premièred at the Chichester Festival, but its revival at the Old Vic, with Olivier as Astrov, Michael Redgrave as Vanya and Joan Plowright as Sonya, was widely viewed as an equally spectacular achievement. Old foes were won over. Harold Hobson was sufficiently moved to describe it as 'the supreme achievement of the contemporary English stage'[19] and Robert Cushman commented that *Uncle Vanya* was simply 'the best Chekhov – maybe the best classic production and certainly the greatest feast of acting – ever. Michael Redgrave's

Vanya was an incomparable tragi-comic creation, a portrait of failure that made the spectator ache with recognition.'[20] The poignancy of the event is heightened in hindsight by the knowledge that the shaking that occasionally gripped Redgrave, and which many interpreted as a sign of alcoholism, actually marked the onset of Parkinson's disease.

The appeal of *The Recruiting Officer* was based on its blend of established talent with promising newcomers and directorial insight. It transformed the traditional approach to Restoration comedy by replacing stagy walks, affected voices and delicate fans with recognisably real situations. It was also the first production to reflect Tynan's commitment to Brecht and Epic theatre. In his memoirs, William Gaskill recalled that from the very beginning of the National 'the example of the Berliner Ensemble towered over us',[21] and his programme notes confirm his aim as a director to inculcate in the audience a desire to question the political basis of events as well as an emotional engagement with characters – fundamental elements of Epic theatre:

> *The Recruiting Officer* is based on Farquhar's first-hand experience while recruiting in Shrewsbury. Within the conventional framework of a Restoration comedy, he set down his detailed observation of the effect of a recruiting campaign on a small country town. There are no longer recruiting campaigns, conscription has been abolished, and war is now in the hands of scientists and politicians. What is the particular compulsion for us today of the image of a group of soldiers arriving in a country town? I think what we recognise from our own experience is the systematic deception of the ignorant to a pointless end by the use of heroic images of the past, a past no longer relevant. We may laugh at the recruits but we recognise our own plight.[22]

The influence of Brecht on the production was clear to all – Harold Hobson disapprovingly noting that 'It is inconceivable that *The Recruiting Officer* should not be a popular success. But I have one doubt about the National Theatre. Brecht looms over it.'[23] Most observers, however, were enthralled by the freshness of the approach, the comic genius of Olivier as Brazen (despite his having found Gaskill's improvisational exercises in rehearsal terrifying)[24] and the spirited, wilful performance of Maggie Smith as Silvia, a great success for the young actress.

The rest of the National's first season continued to demonstrate the link with key figures from the innovative theatre organisations of the 1950s. Sean Kenny from Theatre Workshop had already designed *Uncle Vanya*, Jocelyn Herbert of the Royal Court created the scenery and costumes for *Othello*, John Dexter revived the northern classic *Hobson's Choice*, Lindsay Anderson directed *Andorra* in January and George Devine himself was invited to direct Beckett's *Play*, as part of a double bill with Sophocles' *Philoctetes* for early April. The run-up to this production illustrated how the ill-defined nature of Tynan's role – he had no specific job description – could cause tension, but also how incredibly loyal Olivier would prove to his right-hand man over the next ten years.

Tynan's backstage role was many-faceted. He liaised with performers and com-panies which the sub-committee appointed by the board to design the repertory wished to appear in future seasons. A great deal of 1964, for example, was spent in correspondence with Helene Weigel negotiating about a possible guest visit (realised in 1965) by the Berliner Ensemble. He commissioned translations of plays and offered detailed observations about their potential to the associate directors.[25] He conceived projects that would be realised later on and took an active role in get-ting these off the ground. In August 1964, he approached the Professor of Poetry at Oxford, Robert Graves, about freshening up the Shakespearian work that he had always loathed the most, *Much Ado About Nothing*, with a view to 'replacing dead similes, archaisms and words of changed meaning with *living* Elizabethan words and images'.[26] This eventually formed the text that Zeffirelli used in 1965. He gave almost daily interviews to the press about every aspect of the company and, whilst prowling around the sprawling complex of Portakabins and rehearsal rooms, he would pop in to observe work in progress, write up his own rehearsal notes and fire them off to Olivier and other directors on bright yellow memoranda paper. Born of his lifelong yearning to be practically involved, this desire to be 'a resident early warning system'[27] was probably his most controversial internal activity and caused a significant spat in March 1964. Having observed the genesis of *Play* in March 1964 both before and after Beckett's arrival in the rehearsal room, he wrote to the guest director, George Devine, with some serious concerns:

> . . . before Sam B. arrived at rehearsals, *Play* was recognisably the work we all liked and were eager to do. The delivery of the lines was (rightly) puppet-like and mechanical, but not wholly dehumanised and stripped of all emphasis and inflections. On the strength of last weekend, it seems that Beckett's advice on the production has changed all that – the lines are chanted in breakneck monotone with no inflections, and I'm not alone in fearing that many of them will simply be inaudible . . . The point is that we are not putting on *Play* to satisfy Beckett alone. It may not matter to him that lines are lost in laughs; or that essential bits of exposition are blurred; but it surely matters to us. As we know, Beckett has never sat through any of his plays in the presence of an audience: but we have to live with that audience night after night!

Tynan was clearly anxious about the vulnerable nature of the embryonic National. One of the rising stars of the new generation of actors, Tom Courtenay, had starred in January in Max Frisch's *Andorra*, the first new piece of writing to be premièred at the National, but its impact had been less than Tynan had hoped. Was he overstepping the mark here out of an understandable anxiety to safeguard the company's reputation at a vulnerable time, or was he offering a constructive and necessary observation about the context in which *Play* would be performed? 'I wouldn't dream of writing in this way if it were just a question of difference of opinion between us,' he continued,

> you're the director and it's your production. But rather more than that is at stake. *Play* is the second new play the National Theatre has done. The first, *Andorra*, wasn't an unqualified success . . . If it fails to get over the maximum impact, it may jeopardise our future plans for experiment and put a weapon into the hands of those people (already quite numerous) who think the National Theatre, like the Proms, should stick to the popular classics and not cater for minority tastes. It may even provoke the more conservative members of the N.T. Board to start interfering in the choice of plays – which would be disastrous![28]

This would prove to be the case, with severe consequences for Tynan personally, with the proposed production of *Soldiers* four years later. Devine, however, inevitably saw this intervention as unwarranted and intrusive. Many theatre professionals viewed Tynan as a failed, frustrated actor/director who was, worse, an ex-critic, and they could not understand why Olivier valued him so highly. But insiders, such as Robert Stephens, offer an interesting counter-view:

> Ken only came in three afternoons a week, but he was at every board meeting and repertory meeting and really was Larry's right hand. There may have been a lot of bullshit with Ken, but none of it was to do with hierarchy or status among actors. He was a real breath of fresh air, and terribly amusing and stimulating. Although Larry may have appointed him for the wrong reason, and no one liked him very much, or even trusted him at all, he certainly made his mark and exerted an enormous influence, mostly, I think, for the good.[29]

Devine certainly did not see it that way. Tynan had a track record of animosity towards Beckett and Absurdist theatre in general, and the director chose to respond two days after the production had opened, on 9 April 1964, with an indignant riposte:

> I have purposely not answered your letter until now as I did not want to get involved during the last week of production . . . The presence of Beckett was a great help to me, and to the actors. Your snide comment about him I will ignore. If you don't agree with the interpretation I can't help it. I assume you read the stage directions 'voices toneless except where indicated. Rapid movement throughout.' It was always my intention to try and achieve this, as it is, in my

opinion, the only way to perform the play as written. Any other interpretation is a distortion . . . As for more than my production being at stake, I find your suggestion that a visiting director should be menaced with conservative members of the National Theatre Board quite preposterous. The simple truth appears to be that you got in a panic about *Play*, in case it did not 'come off'. I'm afraid you'll have to have a bit more guts if you really want to do experimental works, which nine times out of ten, only come off to a 'minority' to begin with . . . I am sorry that this incident occurred. My whole experience at work was excellent up to the last week, when your 'phone call and letter were most disturbing and unhelpful.[30]

It was a strong rebuke and a useful reminder of the difference between being a critic and a dramaturg. As a critic, Tynan need not necessarily take the feelings of his targets into account. It was, in many ways, an isolated pursuit. As a member of a large collective, and one who was viewed with some suspicion by many of his colleagues, he needed to be more mindful of the human impact of his observations. It was a difficult transition for him to make. This did not prevent Tynan from making a spirited reply, in which he offered his own vision of the type of theatre the National should aim to be, having first matched swipe with swipe:

You profess yourself 'shocked' by the idea that one's obligation to an author need not extend beyond a general loyalty to his script: there speaks the advocate of a *writer's* theatre. Like you, I would hate the NT to become a museum: but the best way to build theatrical museums is to regard every syllable of every stage direction as holy writ.

I believe in neither a director's nor a writer's theatre, but a theatre of intelligent *audiences*. I count myself as a member of an intelligent audience, and I wrote to you as such. That you should disagree with me I can understand, but that you should resent my expressing my opinions is something that frankly amazes me. I thought we had outgrown the idea of theatre as a mystic rite born of secret communion between author, director, actors and an empty auditorium. The 'dramatic purpose' you mention involves, for me, communication and contact with a live audience: and a live audience is something of which Beckett, by his own honest admission, has little personal knowledge. So far from wanting to 'turn the play into literature', I was proposing that we liberate it from the author's (to me) rather confined view of its dramatic possibilities.

He was only prepared to offer the slightest sign of contrition: 'Perhaps I was wrong, but I don't regret having worried.'[31] Called upon to arbitrate, Olivier appreciated both Devine's outrage at a heavy-handed and unjustifiable attempt to interfere in his artistic decisions and Tynan's understandable, but misplaced, concern for the health of the National Theatre. Replying to Devine on 12 April 1964 (in a letter dictated in his car on the way to a rehearsal), Olivier acknowledged Tynan's error but begged understanding, and tellingly referred to Devine's own difficulties in seeking to establish the ESC at the Royal Court.[32] Amongst his many attributes, Tynan was a useful lightning conductor for Olivier, deflecting criticism from his master, and the actor chose never to prune his dramaturg himself. Such hedging was to characterise Olivier's reign at the National and now seems less bumbling and more pragmatic than it did at the time. Through such smoothing of ruffled feathers, Olivier ensured that the National was successfully born.

Olivier's diplomatic administrative tasks were but one aspect of his function as director. He was very much *the* star actor of the company, its leader and figurehead, and nowhere was this more apparent than in his performance of *Othello*. Opening three weeks after *Play* on 23 April, this production, directed by Dexter and designed by Herbert, was the climax of the first season. Olivier's approach to the role illustrates how for him acting was a talent that was innate and instinctive. He discovered the character he was playing by focusing on an external feature and working from the outside in, rather than employing the Stanislavskian technique of identifying an inner emotion and working from the inside out, hence his discomfort with Lee Strasberg's 'Method' approach. Having cast the young Frank Finlay as Iago, thereby minimising the very real risk of Iago overshadowing Othello, given Finlay's age, Olivier embarked upon an intensive period of physical training in the gym, which he had had installed for the company at the Old Vic. He reduced the lower register of his voice by an octave (another early act had been to appoint a company voice coach, Kate Fleming) and decided that he would play the Moor as a Negro. Much effort was needed to achieve this metamorphosis. He shaved the hair from his chest, arms and legs; applied the black liquid, Max Factor 2,880, to his entire body, followed by a second coat of light brown and a third to give a mahogany sheen; had his skin polished by the dresser to make it shine; painted his nails with blue varnish and then coated his mouth with gentian violet. Such fastidious preparations took three hours to perform, and a further two hours were required to return him to his usual appearance.[33] This was in addition to the four hours of performance.

For many, the physical appearance, combined with the magnetism of Olivier, was simply breathtaking. Ronald Bryden in the *New Statesman* felt that he 'had seen history'[34] and Franco Zeffirelli went further, believing that Olivier's performance was 'an anthology of everything that has been discovered about acting in the last three centuries. It's grand and majestic, but it's also modern and realistic. I would call it a lesson for us all.'[35] Not everyone was as swept away, however. Many were disconcerted by Olivier's blacking up (something unacceptable in today's multiracial Britain) – Tony Richardson, for instance, spoke of the 'degrading image of a NEGRO in capital letters'.[36] Olivier was also criticised for selfishness, since his performances greatly overshadowed the role of Finlay's Iago. This harked back to his dominance of Ralph Richardson when he had played Othello in the Old Vic season of 1937/8. Despite such objections, the production was an enormous box-office success, with three performances a week in the first season, and two in the second, helping to ensure that a staggering 96 per cent of the National's seats were sold in 1964/5. A film version in 1965 was followed by a tour to Moscow – still an inaccessible place, hostile to the West – and the National Theatre was at last perceived as giving the RSC, fresh from *The Wars of the Roses* and Peter Brook's production of *Marat/Sade* (1964), a run for its money.

Othello was kept in the repertory for over two years. One down side to this great success, though, was the emergence of Olivier's stage fright, a problem first evident during a performance of *The Master Builder* (9 June, dir. Peter Wood) and a severe hindrance while playing the Moor. On one night Olivier was forced to whisper to Frank Finlay, 'Don't leave the stage, move downstage where I can see you – or I'll run – and whatever you do, don't look me in the eyes',[37] and these panic attacks were to haunt him intermittently until his retirement from the stage.

The National's first season ended in June 1964; the company had earned enormous prestige from *Uncle Vanya, The Recruiting Officer* and, above all, *Othello*, but financially had a loss of £70,000 over and above its subsidy of £130,000.[38] Tynan wrote down his reflections on its first year for Olivier's consideration in October[39] and in many ways these represented a surprising about-turn. The biggest difficulty he now saw in building the company was 'creating a permanent ensemble when the terms of reference are so wide' (this might equally apply to his own role). The success of the Moscow Art Company and the Berliner Ensemble was predicated on a 'small permanent nucleus of actors' staying from cradle to grave. But this was not the British tradition. Actors found it difficult – financially, emotionally, artistically – to commit to long-term contracts (a situation that would soon be exacerbated by the increasing lure of Hollywood). Even Peter Hall had taken several years to build his company and still had to 'cast outside it when he ventures outside Shakespeare'. Perhaps it was time to acknowledge, Tynan conceded, that 'the "guest performer" principle may have to be a permanent part of our policy'.

This was a recantation of Galilean proportions. Tynan's long-cherished ideal had been for a compact group of versatile and talented players learning and developing together and provoking each other. The pragmatic recognition of the difficulty of this, forged by the experience of the first season, must have been a disappointment to him. But it demonstrates his value to Olivier. Contrary to the view of his detractors, he was far from dogmatic, and the advice he gave Olivier, who had little willingness to devise this necessary overview of the company himself, was carefully thought through and usefully distanced from the complexities of rehearsal and production.

His other reflections were eclectic. They should recruit performers on the basis of 'character as well as talent . . . Talent alone is not enough to build a company.' More money was needed for the publications department. They should emulate the RSC magazine, *Flourish*. Seat prices should be reduced for experimental work. The quality of the supporting players needed improving, and gaps that required plugging included 'a really strong *jeune premier*, a good ingenue, a leading man between 35–50 and one or two solid character men'. Above all, the various guest directors had disappointed. With the memory of his spat with Devine firmly in mind – the direction of *Play* was included in his list of 'Errors of the season'[40] – he argued that 'our guest directors should be tactfully made to realise that every time we open a production, national prestige (not just *our* prestige) is at stake'.[41] This seemed a strange sentiment for the self-declared Marxist, but reflected how passionately he felt about the NT as a viable entity. The nettle had to be grasped as soon as problems began to show.

This applied to a certain extent to his personal life since the opening of the NT. Tynan had had numerous affairs during his marriage with Elaine, and had promised to marry several of his girlfriends, but with Kathleen Halton there seemed to be more than a grain of truth in his offer. One last attempt at reconciliation with Elaine was made in November 1963, when she flew over from the States, in part at the instigation of her mother. The visit was dominated by predictable acrimony between the pair and Elaine was yet again convinced of the need for a Mexican divorce. Having returned to Mount Street for one last time in March, to undertake a publicity tour for her new book, *The Old Man and Me*, she went with Tracy to see a matinée of *Othello*. Olivier covered Tracy in 'chocolate-coloured greasepaint' when he hugged and kissed her, but the façade of normality was simply designed to avoid compromising her book launch. After all the rows, the passionate reconciliations, the personal torment and the glittering trips, Elaine finally cut the cord that was threatening to strangle them both. 'I want you and you want me but we never give each other a chance,' she wrote in her final note before returning to the States in April. The divorce came through on 12 May. 'I understood that it was Ken's manipulative genius ever to pour oil on troubled water and then light it, that any contact with him whatsoever for any reason other than Tracy's affairs would be supping with the devil. We bumped into each other once, inadvertently. Other than that I never saw him again.'[42] This elegiac tone would come to dominate Tynan's life.

On the positive side, Tynan was now free to marry Kathleen, but she was still married to Oliver Gates. Such was the difficulty of her marriage break-up and the depth of his love that Tynan contacted her mother in August to justify his actions.

Having been informed by Kathleen that her mother had formed a rather dim view of him, his letter was one of emollience and bullishness. He regretted any distress that had been caused to others, but this would have to be balanced against 'the deep and permanent pain that Kathleen and I would have to feel if we had to give each other up'.[43] The summer holiday that they had shared in Spain, visiting the *feria* of San Jaime – Kathleen effortlessly slipping into the Tynan routine – had convinced them that they wanted to marry as soon as they were able. But Oliver Gates did not begin divorce proceedings until November 1965 and they were not finally married until June 1967.

The second season of the NT (1964/5) now needed to produce a new work by a British writer to counter the insistent charge that the enterprise would inevitably become a museum for the tried and trusted. Such a work arrived with Peter Shaffer's *The Royal Hunt of the Sun* (1964). After the success of *Five Finger Exercise* in 1958 Binkie Beaumont had been offered the first option on this new work, which focused on the attempt to conquer Peru for Spain by the conquistador Francisco Pizarro, and his encounter with the Inca King, Atahualpa. While staying at Beaumont's weekend retreat, Knotts Fosse, Shaffer overheard Beaumont's partner, John Perry, describe the play in the following way:

> You wouldn't believe it, Binkie, but it's set in the Andes mountains in South America and there's this Spanish army marching over them, and there's a big battle scene and they find this Inca king and all his Indians and there are blood sacrifices, and torture and mutilation and there's dozens of scene changes and a cast of hundreds . . .[44]

A horrified Beaumont, fearful of both the cost and any intimation of bad taste, rejected the script for H.M. Tennent, allegedly citing the difficulties implicit in the stage direction, 'The soldiers now climb the Andes',[45] but he did pass it on to the National Theatre, of which he was now one of Tynan's 'conservative board members'. Whilst the National might be unable to match the salaries on offer in the West End, it sought to outstrip the commercial sector in artistic ambition and *The Royal Hunt of the Sun* was to prove the perfect vehicle for this. John Dexter saw in the script the opportunity to demonstrate the National's versatility and its willingness to be experimental, and his decision to convey the panoramic nature of the work through a combination of tableaux vivants, Michael Annals's exotic costumes, Mark Wilkinson's haunting music inspired by Peruvian bird song, and the mime artist Claude Chagrin's movement sequences helped create a magical visual and emotional show that some chose to describe as 'total theatre'. Opening on 8 December, it was an unparalleled success. Bernard Levin of the *Daily Mail*, one of the new brand of acerbic 1960s theatre critics now visibly treading in Tynan's footsteps, was particularly struck by the aural and visual elements of the production – 'A second visit to Mr Shaffer's astonishing play confirms all my first impressions and provokes many more. And they all add up to the finest new play I have ever seen'[46] – whereas Herbert Kretzmer of the *Daily Express* spoke for those who felt the work touched upon fundamental issues:

> Woven deep into the glittering almost musical comedy fabric of the National Theatre extravaganza is the personal relationship between General Francisco Pizarro and Atahualpa, Sovereign Inca of Peru. In these two men is posed the eternal problem of conqueror and victim, Christianity and paganism, the new order and the barbaric simplicity of the old. No solution is offered, only pessimism and grief and pain at man's incapacity to live with his brother.[47]

Robert Stephens's performance as the sun god, Atahualpa, who offers to die and be reborn overnight to prove his divinity, was especially inspired. Influenced by the 'animal vitality and remarkable technical virtuosity'[48] of Olivier's Othello, Stephens employed a balletic dancing movement and developed a particular form of high-pitched articulation to convey a sense of the god's 'otherness'. Such was the charisma of his character that when, having been garrotted and surrounded by his followers awaiting his resurrection, the beam of morning light failed to stir him, the dismay on the part of the audience was palpable. Stephens's performance added to the growing belief that – stimulated by the example of Olivier – the actors, directors, designers and dramaturg at the National were coalescing into an accomplished and innovative collective.

One of Tynan's many roles was to negotiate with the Lord Chamberlain regarding licences for plays. In the autumn of 1964, he became involved in a spat over censorship that highlighted for the first time the uneasy relationship between the NT board and the company. One of the plays that Tynan wished to see in the repertory was Wedekind's *Spring Awakening*. Written in 1891, it sketched out the dangers of sexual repression and included two scenes where, in Tynan's words, 'two lonely boys tentatively and nervously kiss' and 'a group of boys in a reformatory engage in a game that can be interpreted as symbolising masturbation'.[49] The play had first been staged in England with a club performance at the Royal Court in April 1963. There had been no question of a public licence being granted, after the assistant examiner, Maurice Coles, had concluded that it was 'one of the most loathsome and depraved plays' he had ever read.[50] Tynan was prepared to be pragmatic, however. The scene with the boys kissing would be modified and an alternative to the masturbation scene found if a licence for an NT production could be granted. The Lord Chamberlain, Lord Cobbold, who had succeeded Lord Scarborough to the position in 1963 having been the Governor of the Bank of England for the previous fourteen years, reluctantly agreed, and all should have been well. At this point, however, Lord Chandos, the chairman of the National Theatre Board, intervened. A few weeks earlier, in August 1964, a brouhaha had occurred when the producer Emile Littler castigated the RSC for staging works such as *Marat/Sade* and *Afore Night Come*. They were unsuitable for public subsidy, he argued, besmirched the image of the Queen, who was the company's patron, and were simply 'dirty plays'. 'They do not belong, or should not, to the Royal Shakespeare Company,'[51] he believed. It did not pass unnoticed in the ensuing controversy that Littler was still smarting from Peter Hall's refusal of his Cambridge Theatre as the company's London base, but the main focus of contention quickly became the issue of public subsidy itself. Peter Cadbury, chairman of the ticket agency Keith Prowse Ltd, ludicrously stated that the RSC was in danger of killing off commercial theatre with its financial safety net and for a few weeks the issue of 'the right to fail' took centre stage.

Lord Chandos was unnerved by this debate and decided, to both Tynan and Olivier's incredulity, that in spite of the agreement of the Lord Chamberlain, *Spring Awakening* could not be staged. Worse still, the ten-man board (including Beaumont, Henry Moore and Sir Kenneth Clark) now intended to 'supervise all repertoire decisions'. Tynan cabled John Dexter with the news. Both he and Olivier felt that they had to insist on 'artistic control as [a] minimum requirement'[52] and Dexter replied that he would be happy to offer his own resignation, if that would be any help. Surprisingly, neither Tynan nor Olivier pushed things much further. A compromise was reached whereby if there was a disagreement between the Drama Advisory Panel and the board, the matter would be quietly resolved by a chat between Olivier and Chandos. It was a very British arrangement, but it was also a messy, unsatisfactory compromise, limiting Tynan's freedom of operation and storing up trouble for the future. Soon afterwards, Tynan tried to persuade the Lord Chamberlain to consider giving the National special treatment as far as the censoring of plays was concerned, to avoid such difficulties in the future. 'Whilst [the Lord Chamberlain] has the highest regard for the work being done by the National Theatre . . . he has no authority to give preferential treatment to one Management, whether State-supported or not,' was the reply.[53] For all the brilliance on stage, the lack of clarity of structures behind the scenes would prove the NT's Achilles' heel.

A year after the NT opened the company was working flat out – and no one more so than Tynan. In a plea to Olivier for more staff for his literary department (which comprised himself and his assistant, Rozina Adler), he set out in December 1964 the magnitude of his tasks. These involved collecting, distributing and returning the plays that the directors and assistant directors wished to read (90 books per week); acknowledging, distributing and returning scripts submitted for consideration (up to 20 per week); researching programme material, gathering photographs and compiling programme text;[54] 'travelling to see plays', meeting authors and directors, delivering speeches, and taking part in debates, both in London and abroad'; giving interviews for television and to critics and journalists (around five a week); 'acting as spokesman for the NT in answering appeals addressed to the Director, and sending messages on its behalf to other theatrical organisations'; 'working with playwrights and translators on scripts'; editing and contributing to NT publications (for example on *The Recruiting Officer* and *Othello*); attending board, Drama and Building Committee meetings; representing the company on other panels; writing newspaper and magazine articles; 'collating cast list material and supervising reprints'; and 'Preventing the *Wrong* plays from being chosen – as far as possible'.[55] It was a formidable and exhausting brief – but no help was immediately forthcoming. In the early days of the NT raw energy, commitment and dedication – fuelled by the excitement of being at the start of a thrilling journey – were deemed sufficient to overcome poverty wages, cramped working conditions and ill-defined internal systems.

In the spring of 1965, the company had another gilt-edged success – and this one demonstrated the significance of Tynan's role most visibly. Against the express wish of Dexter and Gaskill, Tynan had persuaded Olivier to engage foreign guest directors to mount productions. It would further develop the ethos of staging the best of world drama and, incidentally, might lessen the NT's dependence on the Royal Court. The first fruit of this policy was Franco Zeffirelli's *Much Ado About Nothing* (16 February). The freshness of Graves's script (commissioned by Tynan) was universally admired. The use of Italian accents for Dogberry's comic group demonstrated a commitment to experimentation that compared favourably with the RSC, and the innovation of the design, with a trellis of vivid coloured lights surrounded by human statues that would wink at key moments, startled the audience. But above all, the NT had drawn together (through Tynan's suggestions and Olivier's contacts) one of the finest ensembles of actors the British stage had ever witnessed. Maggie Smith and Robert Stephens played Beatrice and Benedick, Albert Finney and Derek Jacobi the two Princes, Ian McKellen and Lynn Redgrave Claudio and Margaret, and Frank Finlay was Dogberry. The quality of the minor roles can rarely have been surpassed: Edward Petherbridge, Ronald Pickup, Michael York, Christopher Timothy and Michael Byrne, for example, all played the obligatory 'attendant Lords'. Harold Hobson, no longer a curmudgeonly foe, continued his roll-call of superlatives. The production was the best in his 'memory that England had ever had',[56] and British theatre in the mid-1960s had entered, with the achievements of the three great subsidised companies, a second golden age after the Renaissance. There seemed no style that the NT would not tackle, be it the hedonism of *Much Ado About Nothing* or the stripped-down simplicity of Brecht's

Mother Courage and Her Children (12 May, dir. Gaskill). No wonder Tynan was to observe that in its eclecticism the NT were the Cavaliers to the RSC's Roundheads.[57]

Tynan was understandably thrilled to see his favourite play finally open at his longed-for theatre. It was ten years since he had first encountered Brecht and his consistent advocacy had now ensured that the playwright's work had gained a degree of acceptance in British theatre. The negotiations with Lord Cobbold over minor details of the script had been wearisome, but the significance of staging this seminal Marxist work at the National supported his contention that he was working from within the very heart of the establishment to question some of society's most obdurate values.

He adopted a similar guerrilla tactic the following November, in his ongoing battle against censorship. Invited on Saturday, 13 November to appear on the satirical programme *BBC 3* to debate the issue with his old adversary, Mary McCarthy, Tynan gave the following reply to a question from the host, Robert Robinson, about whether a play which featured sexual intercourse could be staged at the National Theatre. 'Oh I think so, certainly', he replied. 'I doubt if there are very many rational people in this world to whom the word "fuck" is particularly diabolical or revolting or totally forbidden.' No plug was pulled and the programme calmly proceeded with a discussion about the issue of live sex on stage (which he defended), Tynan concluding that a play should only be subject to the law of the land, and not to the whim of the censor.

Whilst the atmosphere in the studio was composed, the reaction to the first uttering of this particular four-letter word on British television was extraordinary. For several days, newspapers were in a froth of indignation. Tory MPs were quoted saying that they wanted Tynan prosecuted or sacked from his post and the BBC was forced to issue a press release expressing regret about the incident, but pointing out that the word had been used in the context of a serious discussion. Tynan's own postbag illustrated the nerve that he had hit. Many of the letters he received urged him to stand firm. 'Moral support in your splendid action against the self-righteous philistines,' a Manchester student, Bronwen Lee,[58] wrote. Other correspondents thanked him 'for helping the BBC and its listeners to grow up',[59] commended his 'honesty and intellectualism, a sentiment which I suspect is expressed by a thousand times as many people as have expressed their horror',[60] and urged him to ignore the 'narrow minded, disgusted people who I'm sure, are writing to abuse and vilify you'. There were certainly a large number of these. 'I think it my duty to let you know that in my opinion you are a dirty dog,'[61] stated A.E. Vine of Orpington. Mrs Shirley Harris of Kensington felt there was a darker reason behind his desire to use the word – 'I think your remarks show an obvious repression (even your film reviews are becoming smutty). Freud would probably have had an explanation. Perhaps this is why you stammer'[62] – and some of the anonymous letters were threatening: 'You are a disgrace to yourself and everyone associated with you. You will soon have the sack and my friends and I will be waiting for you to give you the best licking that you have ever had for your behaviour. So be careful and don't walk alone. We are waiting for you. It will be the last time you will have had a chance to show yourself off . . . You disgraceful blighter.'[63]

Having planned to launch this particular hand grenade all along, Tynan issued his own public statement: 'I used an old English word in a completely neutral way to illustrate a serious point, just as I would have used it in similar conversation with any group of grown-up people. To have censored myself would, in my view, have been rather an insult to the viewers' intelligence.' Ever since Oxford, Tynan had enjoyed stirring up controversy and then been slightly wounded by the backlash that it provoked. This was no different, but the real harm was caused to his later reputation. From now on, his huge contribution to the evolution of post-war British theatre would be overshadowed by his association with the word 'fuck', his involvement with *Oh, Calcutta!*, and the sad posthumous revelations, with the publication of the diaries (2001), of his graphic sexual delight in spanking women. Even Kathleen Tynan's account of her husband's life devotes barely 20 per cent of its pages to his work as a theatre critic – the singular achievement of his life.

George Devine's premature death in January 1966 robbed the post-war stage of one of its leading visionaries. His contribution to the rebirth of theatre, through the prioritising of the writer, had been acknowledged even during his own lifetime, and his departure had a knock-on effect for the NT, with Gaskill leaving to take up the reins at the Royal Court. This was a sad but not grievous loss. Gaskill's last production, which he co-directed with Dexter, had been John Arden's *Armstrong's Last Goodnight* (12 October 1965), another demonstration of the company's wide repertoire that incorporated new writing by cutting-edge playwrights, coexisting with fresh investigations of classic works (*Love for Love*, 20 October, dir. Peter Wood; *Trelawney of the Wells*, 17 November, dir. Desmond O'Donovan; *Miss Julie*, 8 March 1966, dir. Michael Elliott); the continuation of productions directed by foreign guest directors (*A Flea in Her Ear*, 8 February, dir. Jacques Charon); and star turns where Olivier himself either directed or appeared. But lacking a decisive rationale to match the RSC's mission to stage new takes on Shakespeare alongside new pieces of writing, the early NT was vulnerable to indifferent performances and productions. It would later be judged harshly when, inevitably, it fell below the stratospheric standards of the first four seasons.

To supplement his meagre income at the NT, Tynan wrote copious articles for a large number of publications. Up until May 1966, he served as the *Observer*'s film critic, earning approximately £4,000 per annum. Three articles a year for *Playboy*, one-off pieces on travel and theatres throughout the world and his frequent media appearances helped maintain his lifestyle, pay his alimony and contribute to Tracy's school fees, but he was never flush on around £10,000 per year.[64] He was rarely without lucrative offers, however. In November 1965 he agreed with William Shawn to contribute four articles a year for the *New Yorker* and told him that he had just turned down the lucrative position of drama critic for the *New York Times*.[65] Tynan's loyalty to the NT was unparalleled and often unacknowledged.

The NT's first stumble occurred in 1966. Shaffer's *Black Comedy* (8 March, dir. Dexter), conceived for a specific group of actors, had been another huge success and set up an unsustainable sense of expectation for John Osborne's adaptation of Lope de Vega's *A Bond Honoured* (6 June, dir. Dexter). In spite of Hobson's trilling that the production confirmed that Osborne was 'not only our most important dramatist; [but] our chief prophet',[66] the more widespread view was that this was a strange, uneven work. A similar sense of faltering overshadowed the opening production of the 1966/7 season, Ostrovsky's *The Storm* (18 October, dir. Dexter), so it was fortunate that Tynan's gamble on a play originally on the fringe of Edinburgh Festival, Stoppard's *Rosencrantz and Guildenstern Are Dead* (11 April, dir. Derek Goldby), and Olivier's definitive performance in *The Dance of Death* (21 February, dir. Glen Byam Shaw) infused the programme with a vibrancy palpably lacking elsewhere. But for how much longer could the company depend on the Herculean efforts of its leader? Similarly, there were some ominous signs for the chain-smoking Tynan. At a party thrown by William Styron, he received a chilling indication of his own mortality. 'The table was candle-lit,' he later recalled in his diary, 'and after dinner the male guests competed in blowing out the candles without pursing their lips (i.e. forming an open 'O') . . . Of the men, I alone couldn't perform the feat, even at a couple of inches' distance from the flame. "Aha," said someone (was it George?) "that means you have emphysema."'[67] It was the equivalent of the spot of blood on Keats's handkerchief.

Four years after he had accepted the post as Literary Manager at the NT, Tynan could justifiably be proud of his contribution to the successful creation of this artistic flagship. But many of his efforts had been subterranean. His need for attention had been partly assuaged by an exotic social life, but his yearning to play a more direct role in theatre now re-emerged. His disastrous experience as a director at Lichfield had gnawed away at him and his constant (only partially imagined) sense that members of the NT company would never value an ex-critic further encouraged him to seek an opportunity to strike out. Such an opportunity seemed to arise with Rolf Hochhuth's *Soldiers*.

The NT's partial decline in 1966 was matched by a galling demonstration of the courageous and far-sighted eclecticism of the RSC. Peter Brook's *US* was a searingly critical satire of American involvement in Vietnam, slightly before this cause was taken up across the world. Conceived as part of a 'Theatre of Fact' season, in succession to the astounding 'Theatre of Cruelty' two years earlier, it featured a scene calling for Hampstead (a fashionable district of London) to be napalmed to illustrate the horror to a docile British populace. Less successful artistically than *Marat/Sade* – audiences found the final descent by the cast into the audience with brown paper bags over their heads particularly embarrassing – the work was nevertheless significant in that it highlighted both the RSC's continuing ability to experiment and disconcert, as well as the increasingly anachronistic role of the Lord Chamberlain. Alarmed that the play might endanger the so-called special relationship between the two allies and that it would put the President of the RSC – the former Prime Minister, Anthony Eden – in a compromising position, Lord Cobbold attempted through quiet persuasion to have the whole venture dropped. After the difficulties of agreeing on an acceptable English version of *Mother Courage* at the National in 1965, Cobbold had asked Lord Chandos for 'a gossip about all this some time . . . I do not want your people and my people to get up against each other. It only complicates an already difficult state of affairs.'[68] It was this type of establishment chumminess that Tynan most loathed.

Cobbold's intervention over *US* was an extraordinary attempt at censorship on political grounds and far exceeded the Lord Chamberlain's admittedly vague brief. Unabashed, the RSC governors refused to accede to his wishes, backed the project and even quietly brought forward Eden's retirement, demonstrating the pragmatism of the chairman, Fordham Flower, whose support of Hall throughout his reign was as unswerving as it was vital. It contrasted strongly with the pusillanimous support of Olivier by Lord Chandos and his growing antipathy towards Tynan. Typically, Peter Brook put the incident to artistic use, reminding the actors that 'if this crisis had taken place in Vietnam, some of us would be dead by now'.[69]

Tynan had disliked what he felt to be a very lame investigation of such a serious issue. Hampstead, the home of liberal intellectuals, was hardly a suitable metaphor for the whole country, after all. At the end of the opening production, as the actors sonorously entered the audience and then stood perfectly still, to emphasise their collective complicity, he memorably broke the silence and the moment with a spectacular intervention from the stalls. 'Are we keeping you waiting or are you keeping us?' he boomed, but what really irked Tynan was that the RSC was stealing a march on the NT again. In spite of his best attempts to commission works that impacted directly on contemporary political events, neither a projected play on the General Strike nor a piece on the Cuban missile crisis came up to scratch. In the realm of docudrama – an increasingly popular dramatic form in the politically committed 1960s, and an area with which Tynan felt that he should be associated – the NT was lagging far behind.

In July 1966 Tynan was introduced to Rolf Hochhuth's new work, *Soldiers*, by Hochhuth's agent, Patricia Burke, and the playwright and translator David Macdonald. Tynan found the draft script of the first act, which promised an investigation of the issue of saturation bombing in the Second World War, electrifying. 'This is the kind of play that a company like ours exists to present,' he told Patricia Burke. 'It's also the kind of play that can help the theatre in general to fulfil its role as a public forum where history, art and morality are brought into focus. Please reassure Herr Hochhuth,' he added, rather too optimistically, 'that there are no political problems involved in the staging of such a play at the National Theatre. We are subject to no political pressures of any kind.'[70] As more of the play emerged, Tynan's enthusiasm grew. Having read the prologue and the early action in October, he told David Macdonald of his conviction that it was 'going to be absolutely marvellous', since, crucially, it was 'all that Peter Brook's *US* isn't – it is precise and specific instead of vague and general, it's informed and impassioned instead of ignorant and tepid and it's a blessedly fearless point of view'.[71] Worried that the RSC was now showing an interest – 'Both Peter Brook and Peter Hall have made direct approaches to Hochhuth about the play'[72] – Tynan warned Olivier that if they did not act quickly, they might lose the work for the National. In his view, the stakes were very high.

A month later, the whole play arrived. Its remit had broadened to include not only an investigation of the inevitability of wide-scale bombing (on this point Hochhuth was broadly in sympathy with Churchill), but a secondary strand implying that Britain's wartime leader had been complicit in the assassination of the leader of the Polish government-in-exile, General Sikorski, who had died in an air crash in July 1943. The reason for this, the play suggested, was that Churchill, desperate to maintain good relations with the Soviets, was aware that the post-war settlement would involve breaking his agreement with Sikorski by acquiescing in the incorporation of half of Poland into the USSR. Sikorski's presence also reminded him of his dishonourable decision to ignore historical 'fact' and accept the Soviets' dubious claim that they had not been responsible for the notorious massacre of Polish officers at Katyn in 1940.

Tynan was ecstatic. Here was the work of provocative analysis that the NT had been waiting for. Churchill's state funeral had been held only a year earlier and he was viewed as a national hero by many. What better figure to scrutinise, in the way that Brecht had scrutinised Galileo, in order to examine the forces of history and the creation of reputations? He immediately sent a memo to Olivier conveying his enthusiasm – 'I don't know whether this is a great *play*, but I think it's one of the most extraordinary things that has happened to British theatre in my lifetime. For once, the theatre will occupy its true place – at the very heart of public life'[73] – and both Olivier and Dexter were powerfully affected. But Tynan was the most inspired, and this strong reaction stemmed from several sources. These included personal frustration at his own role, anxiety at the success of analytical works at the RSC, envy of the enlightened board that Hall was able to work with and a misplaced conviction that the Sikorski sub-plot was certain historical truth that would provide sensational publicity. For a devoted Brechtian, always suspicious of the nature of historical 'fact', this was a strange position to take. Hochhuth had fantastically claimed that he had sworn statements from secret informants, witnessed by three eminent Swiss scholars, that proved the veracity of his claim. Unfortunately, these were deposited in a Swiss bank and could not be opened for fifty years. There was no evidence that led any prominent historian to state that this was a plausible thesis.

In spite of this, Tynan felt convinced of the need to produce the work, if for no other reason than that it would arrest the sense of drift that had recently beset the National. Early in the new year, Tynan explained his reasoning to Olivier:

> I'm worried. Nothing really specific: just a general feeling that we're losing our lead, that we are no longer making the running, that what the NT does has become a matter of public acceptance rather than public excitement . . . we are doing nothing to remind them that the theatre is an independent force at the heart of a country's life . . . We have had no *Marat-Sade*; we have no *US* . . . I think Hochhuth is the test of our maturity – the test of our willingness to take a central position in the limelight of public affairs. If the play goes on under our banner, we shall be a genuinely national theatre, and, even as the stink-bombs fly, I shall be very proud of us.[74]

Nevertheless, in preparation for the board meeting on 9 January 1967 that would decide on the repertoire for the following season, Tynan undertook a concerted campaign of research and lobbying. The NT's lawyers approved the script; Lord Goodman of the Arts Council was prevailed upon to say that whilst the script was a strange one to be staged at the National, the Council would not raise concerns; technical details were verified with the Ministry of Defence (although the Chief of Bomber Command, Sir Arthur Harris, felt it was a smear on Churchill, the war cabinet and himself); and Tynan persuaded Hochhuth, after a detailed correspondence, to make Churchill's personal knowledge of the plot slightly less apparent. Tynan also drew up a written submission for the board. Somewhat tendentiously he argued that since the assassination theory was a plausible one, the suppression of the work should not be undertaken lightly, since the 'Voltairean cliché – about disliking what a man says but defending to the death his right to say it – should surely be what distinguishes the conduct of affairs at the Old Vic from "state theatre" in a bad sense'. He also contentiously claimed that Lord Chandos would probably resign if the play were presented, having, as Oliver Lyttelton, been a member of the very war cabinet that was impugned; that the programme could be used to express dissenting opinions and that the RSC was waiting in the wings to step in should the National turn the play down.[75]

When the board finally met, it decided to buy time. Binkie Beaumont queried the historical claims, citing the opinions of Anthony Quayle, who, incredibly, had been in Gibraltar the day after Sikorski's crash. Chandos was explicit in his disgust, however: the play was a 'grotesque and grievous' libel.[77] Tynan kept up the pressure, though. Frustrated at the postponement, he wrote to Chandos to raise the general principles of the case – 'On the general question of whether we should give critics sticks to beat us with, I feel that from time to time this may be a very healthy thing to do. On the whole, I would rather be attacked by would-be censors than patted on the head'[77] – and, perhaps unwisely, contended that 'artistic policy should not be subject to interference on *political grounds*'.[78]

For a short period of time, the spotlight switched to matters on stage, when Strindberg's *The Dance of Death* opened on 21 February (dir. Glen Byam Shaw), with Olivier as the Captain. It was one of Olivier's finest roles. Once more he transformed his appearance, adopting a choleric red-face and close-cropped hair and moustache, and in its depiction of a traumatic marriage, the play evoked memories of his time with Vivien Leigh. Other members of the company, such as Robert Stephens, marvelled at the way the 'Master' painstakingly constructed his performance during rehearsal.[79] To produce it at a time of growing turmoil with the board seems remarkable, but Olivier recognised that, although he did not share Tynan's passion for *Soldiers*, the question of the very purpose of the National Theatre, never properly addressed before, was beginning to raise its head. Chandos saw its role as staging works that reflected the establishment face of British theatrical culture. Tynan saw it as staging works that occasionally scrutinised this establishment face. The board 'should administer the theatre's affairs, fix its budget, decide the broad outlines of its policy and appoint its artistic director,'[80] he argued. The Director then chooses the plays. It seemed strange that this issue was only being tackled now, four years after the NT opened and two years after the capitulation over *Spring Awakening*.

As the decisive meeting approached, Tynan began to speculate about what might happen if the board turned the play down. He approached the Lord Chamberlain to seek his opinion on the granting of a licence to a commercial production. Lord Cobbold refused to commit himself, but Tynan took his silence as an admission that he was part of a vast conspiracy: 'The reasons for your procrastination are, of course, perfectly obvious. The implication is that you propose to judge the play by one standard if it is presented at the National Theatre, and by another standard if the National Theatre decides against it and some other management undertakes the production.'[81] Privately, he indulged in some more ledge-standing, telling his

American father-figure, William Shawn, that 'if they decide against it, I shall very probably resign'.[82]

The board met on 24 April and its ten members, including Chandos, unanimously decided that the play was 'unsuitable for production at the National Theatre'. Their only concession was that Olivier could state his unhappiness at this verdict in the communiqué that they released. It was a significant defeat. Several issues now arose. What were the powers of the board to override the Artistic Director? What constituted a suitable play for this flagship organisation? Should the board be able to function as a *de facto* censor, and, above all, where did the bruising row leave Tynan? Despite his threat to resign in such a circumstance, both Olivier and he were soon galvanised by the possibility that the play could be staged elsewhere in the West End. In the heat of their indignation, they announced that they would be mounting the play with a company (the resurrected St James's Players) that would name Hall of the RSC and Gaskill of the Royal Court amongst its directors. The public symbolism of this was not lost on Chandos, who saw it as a declaration of war by Tynan against the NT, and said as much in the war of words that ensued: 'I think it's very odd that Mr Tynan should conduct a campaign against his chairman and board while retaining his salary,'[83] Chandos told the *Sunday Times*. 'My first loyalty is to the National Theatre, not to its Board,'[84] Tynan told the same paper the following week.

As the summer dragged on, the early enthusiasm for a non-National production began to wane. Dogged by his battle with prostate cancer, still suffering from the unwished-for departure of John Dexter earlier in the year – after Olivier had overruled his plans for a sexually provocative all-male *As You Like It* – exhausted by a long spell of touring, and deeply affected by the deaths of his former wife Vivien Leigh and his friend and agent, Cecil Tennent (who was killed in a car crash on the way home from her funeral), Olivier went back on his original desire to be involved with a separate production of *Soldiers*. Behind the scenes Olivier strove to protect Tynan from Chandos's wrath, after the latter wanted to instruct the Literary Manager not to publish any more attacks on the board, knowing that this would provoke his longed-for resignation. Joan Plowright acted as mediator, and an equally dispirited Tynan acceded to the request not to continue his public campaign against the board. In any event, now that he was on his own, he needed to devote all his energies to trying to get the play staged in Britain.

Soldiers had its world première in Berlin on 9 October 1967, where it was critically denounced. A production the following February in Toronto was more favourably received, but Tynan found it an uphill battle to get it staged in the country where it would provoke the greatest furore, Britain. One of the biggest obstacles was the Lord Chamberlain, who continued to prevaricate, making the bogus claim that he needed to obtain the permission of the living relatives of the historical characters before he could grant a licence. Lord Cobbold had other things on his mind, not least the battle for his own survival as censor.

By the early 1960s it was evident to all concerned with the theatre that the most influential arbiter of dramatic activity was an officer of the court. His dead hand, according to the innovative producer, Michael White, had overshadowed everything since the end of the Second World War: 'British theatrical life [had been] dominated not by great acting stars, mercurial playwrights or adventurous producers but by the far less well-known figure of the Lord Chamberlain.'[85] But his anonymity, legitimacy and the respect, no matter how disdainful, that had been accorded to his enormous power in the 1950s began to be challenged in the following decade. On the broadest level, people began to question whether the office of the censor was compatible with a healthy democracy. The expanding range of subject matter that the liberalising of social attitudes afforded dramatists (sexuality, violence, individual freedom) brought them into conflict with the rigidities of the censor's remit. The arbitrary way that the edicts were interpreted and the almost non-existent explanations as to why licences were refused provoked enormous frustration, as did the Lord Chamberlain's pretence that he was a licensing authority rather than a censoring one. The obvious anomaly that allowed identical scenes to be transmitted on television but banned in the theatre emphasised the farcical nature of the system. This was plainly illustrated in 1963 when a satirical revue, entitled *See You Inside*, had its licence withdrawn by the Lord Chamberlain shortly before curtain-up, because it contained a disrespectful sketch featuring Queen Elizabeth and Prince Philip setting out for Australia and being shipwrecked in a London dock.[86] The 450 audience members at the Duchess Theatre were deprived of seeing what 11 million viewers had witnessed earlier on BBC Television.

To the recognition of the ludicrousness of this situation was added a growing anger at the restriction of civil liberties and the Lord Chamberlain's lack of accountability. British society was slowing moving towards two pieces of social legislation that would give the individual more choice in matters of personal behaviour – ten years after the Wolfenden Report, the Sexual Offences Act of 1967 would decriminalise homosexuality for consenting adults over the age of twenty-one, and abortion was legalised in the same year. Not surprisingly, the theatre demanded a similarly mature treatment. The furore surrounding the 'dirty plays' controversy of 1964 underlined how important – and how enervating – matters such as good taste were for the British theatre. Tynan had continued to campaign against censorship whilst dramaturg at the NT and, in a witty article entitled 'The Royal Smut Hound' (written after the *Spring Awakening* dispute), he amusingly highlighted the futile and distracting nature of the Lord Chamberlain's scrutiny:

Since he is always recruited from the peerage, he naturally tends to forbid attacks on institutions like the Church and the Crown. He never permits plays about eminent British subjects, living or recently dead, no matter how harmless the content and despite the fact that Britain's libel laws are the strictest on earth. Above all, he feels a paternal need to protect his flock from exposure to words or gestures relating to bodily functions below the navel and above the upper thigh. This – the bedding-*cum*-liquid-and-solid-eliminating-area – is what pre-occupies him most, and involves the writers and the producers who have to deal with him in the largest amount of wasted time.[87]

Even the House of Commons timidly hinted at the possibility of loosening the noose. In December 1962, Dingle Foot, MP drew up a private member's bill concerning censorship, but his very intention was rather limited – he simply wished to make it optional to submit scripts to St James's Palace. In any event, he was refused permission to introduce the Bill.

By 1965, however, Lord Cobbold was beginning to feel the winds of change. In April of that year he granted an unprecedented interview to J.W. Lambert of the *Sunday Times*, in which he adopted an air of injured innocence in setting out his credo. Defining his personal view of the censor's function as the need 'to assess the norm of educated, adult opinion', he sought to stress both his reasonableness – he always employed 'a good deal of give and take' – and his refusal to interfere in the creative process: 'When we ask for a phrase to be altered we never, as is often alleged, ourselves suggest an alternative text.' Playwrights were often perplexing in their lack of good taste – 'You'd be surprised to see the number of four-letter words, and I think I can say obscenities, that are sometimes included in scripts by the most reputable people' – and they frequently caused him difficulties when wishing to deal with 'abortion ... farces about artificial insemination, physical contact between homosexuals and such like': all serious issues of the day. Intriguingly, Lord Cobbold concluded the interview with some observations on club theatres, which were a clear shot across the bows of the Royal Court. While (rather unconvincingly) claiming that he was very much in favour of venues where unlicensed plays could be produced – 'They give selective and interested audiences a chance to see experimental work' – he strongly disapproved of managements using them to put on works that had been refused a licence, and gravely commented: 'I very much hope myself that managements will have the good sense not to force the issue on this point, which might well involve difficulties for all theatre clubs and which would, in my view, be harmful to the general interests of the theatre.'[88]

Lord Cobbold's concerns were prophetic, since by forcing the issue with John Osborne's *A Patriot for Me* and Edward Bond's *Saved* later that year (1965), the Royal

Court was to strike a significant blow against his powers to censor and therefore hasten the emancipation of British theatre.

A Patriot for Me dealt with the career of the repressed homosexual and Austrian army officer Alfred Redl, and continued Osborne's shift away from the realism of *Look Back in Anger*. Although a work of tendentious claims (gays are always neurotic) and arguable quality, George Devine's tenacity in seeking to stage what he intended to be his last Royal Court production was admirable. The Lord Chamberlain's reader, Charles Heriot, was quite convinced that it was unsuitable for licensing, even though, in an ironically pertinent observation, he wrote that 'this is a serious but not a good play about homosexuality'. There were three principal and indefatigable objections: the first scene of the second act which contained a transvestite ball; Osborne's overall tone – 'Mr Osborne's overweening conceit and blatant authoritarianism causes him to write in a deliberately provocative manner. He never misses a chance to be offensive'; and the familiar fear that the play would influence an audience's sexual behaviour:

> If the company wish to try again then the whole of Acts II and III must be drastically revised with the ball left out and the inverted eroticism toned down. The present text seems to be a perfect example of a piece which might corrupt, since it reveals nearly all the details of the homosexual life usually left blank even in the newspaper reports.[89]

Seeing that there was no possibility of obtaining a licence, Devine decided to turn the Royal Court into a club theatre, requiring intending spectators to sign up in advance to join the English Stage Society, at a cost of 5 shillings. The public duly responded, and a month before the opening on 30 June 1965, membership had increased from 1,600 to almost 4,000,[90] but Devine was running a considerable risk. The decision to stage a club performance reduced the potential box-office take and the production costs were large; the possibility of a transfer was remote; British stars were still nervous of appearing as gay men (Maximilian Schell eventually played Redl); and the Lord Chamberlain had explicitly warned against the club loophole in his recent interview.

As it happened, the play opened to critical acclaim and played to 95 per cent capacity. The ball scene was deemed a *coup de théâtre*, the work received the 1965 *Evening Standard* award for Best Play, and the Lord Chamberlain was reduced to impotent fury. The Assistant Comptroller, Sir John Johnston, had written to the Director of Public Prosecutions, before the play opened, urging a pre-emptive legal strike 'to avoid a position where the law can be brought into disrepute by what is no more than a subterfuge',[91] but the incoming Labour government refused to sanction such a move, thereby signalling that although the Lord Chamberlain had prevented a public performance, the edifice of censorship was cracking. If Tynan and Olivier had stood up to the NT board over *Spring Awakening* in the same year, the momentum for dismantling censorship might have gathered pace even more quickly.

William Gaskill succeeded George Devine as Artistic Director of the ESC in July 1965. In a paper for the ESC's management company prior to his accession, he provided a neat summary of the three major changes that had occurred in the British theatre over the previous ten years:

1. The emergence of two large-scale permanent companies – The National Theatre and the Royal Shakespeare, playing in repertoire modern as well as classical plays
2. The decline of the West End theatre as a home for straight plays
3. The death of weekly rep, and the growth of two or three weekly rep. companies and the raising of the standard of plays (though not necessarily of performances) in the provinces.[92]

Given these events, Gaskill intended, as a direct result of his connection with the NT, to base the ethos of his ESC on the need to create a permanent company that played in repertoire. It would additionally focus on contemporary work, since this was 'the only structure in which one can nurse failures, support successes and give new writers the right conditions for their work to be seen'.[93] Gaskill would be given an early opportunity to demonstrate this principle. As with Devine, the third production of his opening season was to prove a defining moment.

Edward Bond's *Saved* was originally intended to open Gaskill's first season, but the objections of the Lord Chamberlain sabotaged this plan. That the play would prove controversial was well known to Gaskill. Heriot, in his confidential report to the Lord Chamberlain, had insisted on fifty-four changes, including the excision of the 'torture and death of the baby' (the harrowing scene 6) and the 'gratuitously salacious' mending of Mary's stocking. Heriot actually recommended ('reluctantly') that if these cuts were agreed to then a licence should be granted, but there was clearly no chance of the Royal Court acquiescing. In any case, his prefatory summary made it plain that he hoped that the work would never see the light of day, since it was a

revolting amateur play by one of those dramatists who write as it comes to them out of a heightened image of their experience. It is about a bunch of brainless, ape-like yobs with so little individuality that it is difficult to distinguish between them. They speak a kind of stylised Cockney, but behave in an unreal way, not because what they do is false, but that their motivation is not sufficiently indicated . . . They are all moral imbeciles . . . The writing is vile and the language and conception worse. Whether this could ever be considered a work of art is a matter of opinion; but it does seem that the taste of Messrs. Devine and Richardson has gone rancid – though with all the public money at their disposal, I don't suppose any one cares.[94]

There could be no repeat of the successfully evasive strategy used to stage *A Patriot for Me*. The Lord Chamberlain and his officers now knew that it was a fight to the death.

With a licence for an uncut version impossible to obtain, the Royal Court was again turned into a theatre club. The opening night took place on 3 November 1965 and whilst Penelope Gilliatt bravely championed the work in the *Observer*, Irving Wardle reflected the views of the majority of critics when he wrote that the work 'amounts to a systematic degradation of the human animal',[95] but there had been an even more hostile member of the first-night audience. Amongst the Lord Chamberlain's papers in the British Library lies a deposition from an anonymous reader about his previous night's visit to the Royal Court:

> As instructed I went last night to the Royal Court Theatre and witnessed a performance of a stage play entitled SAVED. I purchased a programme and a seat (K.17), programme and seat counterfoil are attached.
>
> At the box office I asked for a stall and was asked if I was a member, I said 'Yes' and was asked if I had a ticket: I again said 'Yes' and produced my wallet and started to produce the ticket at which the box office lady did not look, so I did not complete the manoeuvre. The box office lady said 'I'm sorry we have to ask you'.

The spy also recorded that the action included aspects specifically disallowed by the Lord Chamberlain. For example, in scene 3, 'when Colin says "What yer scratchin?", one of the actors is scratching his testicles through his trousers' and in scene 6 'the torture and murder of the baby was enacted in full', although intriguingly the spy later observes that it 'was quite horrible . . . [but] so badly played that one could not really believe there was a live baby in the perambulator'. He also conveys an interesting sense of this famous evening as a whole:

> The auditorium was two thirds full [overall the production played to 36.7 per cent capacity for its 24 performances[96]] and without exception, so far as I could see – in their various styles, the audience looked well dressed and affluent: far removed from the characters on stage . . . Only one woman walked out towards the end of the performance, which otherwise was received in dead silence except for a few sniggers at some of the more disgusting episodes, such as urinating in the parson's tea cup. There was quite warm applause at the curtain call, intended I thought, for the actors rather than for the play . . . During the interval I went to the bar and bought a bottle of light ale. There was only one lady there, working like a demon.

I was not asked to show my membership ticket and drinks were being bought quite indiscriminately, that is unless everyone present was a member, a most unlikely circumstance.

For this trivial violation of the licensing laws and for not completing the manoeuvre at the box office (in other words, for allowing a member of the audience who had not been a club member for over 24 hours to purchase a ticket), the Lord Chamberlain proceeded to mount a prosecution against Gaskill as Artistic Director, Greville Poke, the company secretary, and Alfred Esdaile, the licensee, for presenting an unlicensed play contrary to section 15 of the 1843 Theatres Act. Tynan had rushed to the barricades as early as 14 November, when he had chaired a 'teach-in' at the Royal Court about the implications of its censorship. Olivier, too, lent practical support when appearing as an expert witness at the second hearing of 7 March 1966 and making a passionate and eloquent defence of the Royal Court. Nevertheless, at the final hearing on 1 April, the magistrate, Leo Gradwell, upheld the case, giving the defendants a conditional discharge and levying a nominal fine of 50 guineas. This left nobody satisfied. The theatre was still at the mercy of the whims of the censor, and the Lord Chamberlain had received only half-hearted backing from the law, since Gradwell had made clear his dissatisfaction at the state of affairs: 'I am tied to the rock of the law waiting for Perseus to rescue me.'[97] It soon became apparent, though, that in reality the Royal Court had achieved an important moral victory.

Indignant and increasingly organised, the theatre profession redoubled its campaign to rescue drama from censorship, and in early 1967 the Joint Parliamentary Committee on Censorship – to which Tynan testified on 24 January 1967, arguing that the Attorney-General's office should handle the prosecution of productions, not the Lord Chamberlain – advocated the abolition of the 1843 Act. Although the Labour government dropped its support for new legislation in November 1967, pleading pressure of parliamentary time, George Strauss, MP pledged to take up the unfinished business with a private member's bill. The courage and tenacity of the Royal Court in staging what is now seen as a modern classic, coupled with the tenacious campaigning of eloquent activists such as Tynan, ensured that a new Theatres Act, removing the requirement of the Lord Chamberlain to license productions, was to reach the statute book on 26 September 1968. A new era had truly begun.

The most immediate benefit for Tynan of the demise of censorship was the removal of the last hurdle preventing the British opening of *Soldiers*. In partnership with the producer, Michael White, Tynan's long-held dream was realised when the work opened on 12 December 1968 at the New Theatre, but it had been hard going. Spiralling production costs, press antipathy, a row with one of the investors, the American jazz promoter Norman Granz, and an uneasy alliance with another, the right-wing historian David Irving, all increased stress levels – and then the threats started to flood in. White was forced to draw up a detailed list of security measures, including a minute search of the entire theatre before the doors were opened, but in spite of these difficulties the first performance was greeted with a cacophony of 'Bravos'. Tynan wept with joy and told reporters that the evening had proved 'the essential sanity of audiences in England'.[98] His elation was short-lived. Harold Hobson, whose daughter had married Lord Chandos's son, was unconvinced by Tynan's crusade – 'To say that this adds to Churchill's reputation is intellectual cowardice; it is like stabbing a man in the back, and then claiming you have improved his health.'[99] Winston Churchill's son called the play 'an infamous libel'[100] and, most disastrously, Sikorski's pilot, Edward Prchal, issued writs against Hochhuth, David Macdonald, White, Granz, Tynan, Clifford Williams (the director) and Donald and Ian Albery (the theatre owners). For all their meticulous efforts to get the play staged, Tynan and White had failed to notice that the Theatres Act of 1968, which they had so warmly welcomed, had made the laws of libel much stricter. Prchal, who was living in California, had barely been mentioned (and had seen the play in New York and Toronto with no visible sign of concern), but the association of his name with Hochhuth's hypotheses was enough for him to seek redress in law. It was, in White's words, 'the Lord Chamberlain's revenge, in a way'.[101]

The issuing of the writs reawakened public controversy and this, coupled with the reluctance of people to attend a play whose content had been so widely trailed in the media during the previous eighteen months, dealt a fatal blow to the London production. It closed after a short run in March, yet another aborted involvement for Tynan in a practical production. This hurt as much as any, since he had been the prime – often lone – instigator. Looking back on the draining battle the following autumn, Tynan told his friend, Tom Stoppard, how he now viewed his struggle with *Soldiers*: 'One of the hundreds of things that I've learned from the whole experience is that Establishment opinion can so penetrate the public mind that people feel ashamed to go against it. Another is that British audiences aren't ready for serious plays about politics, probably because the Lord Chamberlain has prevented people from writing them for more than two centuries.'[102]

It was undoubtedly another kick in the teeth, after a draining struggle that had been punctuated by progressive ill health (asthma, bronchitis and pneumonia). The libel case was eventually lost in May 1972, leaving him with an enormous bill for £20,000. It was to prove only too typical of the final decade of his life.

Chapter 8   *Private Demons — Centre Stage*

> I was quite aware that he was a spoiled darling of transatlantic liberal society, an archetypal left-wing trendy. But I believed — and still do — that he was totally sincere in his desire for a more just society even though most of our talk about revolution took place in high-priced restaurants. (Michael White)[1]

For all his posturing, Tynan was, above all, a writer at heart. Throughout his tenure as dramaturg at the NT, he maintained a prodigious output of articles, columns and asides. As the film critic of the *Observer* between 1964 and 1966 he traced the flourishing of continental European cinema, celebrating the work of Godard, Antonioni, Fellini, Truffaut and the burgeoning Czech film industry. He admired the political criticism of Czech institutions possible in the cinema of the Prague spring, as much as the dark prophecy of Peter Watkins's anti-nuclear work, *The War Game* (1966).

In late October 1967 his collection of writing since the 1950s, *Tynan Right and Left*, provided a salutary reminder of what he had given up to become associated with the NT. The first two chapters reprinted some of his finest reviews of plays and films, with further chapters on 'People', 'Places' and 'Comments and Causeries' bringing together similarly themed contributions that had initially appeared in a wide range of publications. All his favourite topics were covered — Orson Welles, bullfighting, Cordon Bleu cooking, high-class restaurants, cities in the US and Cuba — and the writing still seemed fresh and, with the benefit of hindsight, prescient. But the reviews reflected the changed attitude to the persona of Tynan. Whereas his eccentricity, striking looks, flamboyant dress sense and ready aphorisms had so lit up the 1950s, his flair for publicity, un-puritan socialism and dogged adherence to unpopular causes (such as *Soldiers*) were now deemed to be less acceptably provocative. Reviewers paid ritual tribute to the brilliance of his style and insight, but now started to suggest rather snidely that he was self-obsessed. Richard Boston, a writer for the *Times Literary Supplement*, wrote a review for the *New York Times* which epitomised this trend. 'The hero of *Tynan Right and Left* is, as the title suggests, Tynan,' he began:

> The ostensible subject matter is of course wider, for the book consists of Tynan's writing over the past 10 years, not only in his capacities as theater and cinema reviewer but also as the author of occasional pieces, interviews and essays on a wide variety of people . . . But whatever he is writing about Tynan never forgets the subject on which he is the leading world expert: namely Kenneth Tynan, cultural journalist, moralist, socialist. 'Occupation: opinion-monger, observer of artistic phenomena, amateur ideologue.' He has summarised the nature of good drama, he tells us in his foreword, as follows: 'If a play does anything either tragically or comically, satirically or farcically – to explain to me why I am alive it is a good play. If it seems unaware that such questions exist, I tend to suspect that it's a bad one.' This is an uncharacteristic statement in one way: Tynan is rarely so hesitant in his opinions as merely to 'tend to suspect.' But it is entirely characteristic in asking that a play should explain to Tynan why Tynan is alive – a problem, one would have supposed, that has worried few playwrights, major or minor, past or present.[2]

Amongst his adversaries in the establishment, Tynan could now count the press.

He returned to the safe house of the *Observer* in January 1968 to write a weekly column entitled 'Shouts and Murmurs', and was contracted until 30 March 1969 to produce forty articles a year for £4,000. If his earlier theatre columns had exploited the primness of the 1950s, this one now cherished the hedonism of the late 1960s and offered a handy public platform for his varied political causes. Throughout the spring and summer of 1968, he bemoaned the slow progress of the Theatres Act, condemned the Society of West End Managers for their last-ditch attempt to preserve censorship and criticised the Arts Council for devoting over a third of its £5.7 million budget to opera and ballet at Covent Garden and Sadler's Wells. He shared his enjoyment of American musicals, *The Tonight Show* ('the most highly evolved TV programme I have ever watched')[3] and cricket, and he celebrated the lyricism of the Beatles, the importance of the anti-Vietnam marches (which he joined) and, above all, the life-enhancing attributes of pornography. This was now becoming a significant preoccupation. His third column in January asserted that 'to oppose pornography, it is necessary to disapprove of masturbation'.[4] A recent visit to Hugh Hefner's *Playboy* mansion permitted a discussion on fellatio and, by April, with the letters of objection pouring in, Tynan formulated the rebuttal that he would increasingly use to defend his immersion in aspects of sex: 'An ungrateful reader complains that this column devotes too much attention to sex and politics. In fact, obedient mirror that it is, it merely reflects what the cultural scene sets before it.'⁵ Tynan may have felt that in being an obedient mirror he was reflecting a more mature and open attitude to sex that (arguably) existed beyond the closed world of Fleet Street, but he had now gifted an opportunity for envious journalistic critics to add the charge of smutty pornographer to that of champagne socialist, dilettante and publicity seeker.

All of this coincided with his preparations for *Oh, Calcutta!* and his association with *Playboy*, first as an occasional contributor and then as a token editor (he was listed as such, for circulation reasons, even though he never got near the editing process). Several of his *Playboy* articles became renowned works, not least his recollection of the Williams/Hemingway meeting in Cuba and his 'Open Letter to an American Liberal' (1968). This proposed a war crimes tribunal in the US to which the politicians responsible for the crime of Vietnam could be summoned.⁶ Even when the industry of the 1960s gave way to an illness-induced lethargy in the 1970s, he never lost the compulsion to prompt, urge and describe in prose, as evidenced by his private diary – possibly begun with half an eye on eventual publication to arrest his growing debts. The diaries, which cover the years from 1971 to 1980, were controversially published in 2001 by his daughter, Tracy. What disturbed most reviewers were their explicit descriptions of his spanking fetish with a new girlfriend, 'Nicole'. 'Mawkish celebrations of botty-whipping, encomiums to the anus' (Simon Callow);⁷ 'A blacker-than-black record of a boy wonder ceding to dirty old man' (Rosie Boycott);⁸ 'The only reply a reader can offer to the proposition "The full rectal presentation with the dear Scot's bum outstretched to bursting as the pink piston of prick slides up and down is something I shall never forget" is a heartfelt "No, indeedy"' (David Hare)⁹ were just some of the responses. But many of the entries retain the clarity, evocation and wit of his best theatre criticism. Witness his description of a gala dinner in aid of the United Nations Association, which he attended in 1971 in Dorchester:

> Bumper assembly of posh fascists. On my right Lady Rotherwick who says she can't read *The Times* since it became 'Communistic'. 'When was that?' I ask. 'When the Astors sold it.'[10] She says things are getting worse all over the world. 'We're Union Castle, you know. Ten years ago we had 150 ships. Now – how many d'you think?' I shake my head. '*Barely fifty*' – as if to say, '*Meat only once a week.*' Her opening sentence was uniquely calculated, in all its aspects, to start my adrenaline running. 'We've just been on a business trip to South Africa with the Rothermeres – it's a real paradise, isn't it?' She adds, 'That's the place to buy land – it's marvellous for spec' (i.e. speculative building). She confides that she and her husband own 'a lot of Rhodesia'. He is called Bunny and looks like a polished pink snooker

ball. They have estates in Oxfordshire, Scotland, and the Mediterranean and (of course) Rhodesia. She asks what I do. I say work at the National Theatre. 'Oh, where is that?' 'At the Old Vic,' I say. Hearing that I work for L.O., she observes, 'Vivien Leigh – oh yes, she died of cancer.' I quietly contradict her. '*I think you'll find she did*,' pipes this cheery, assured, empty-headed, infinitely tedious battener on thousands of lives. She looks about thirty-five but: 'Bunny and I have been married twenty years,' she says. The rich have the gift of elastic youth, which *can* be bought.

Laughingly, she tells me how a picture of her husband and herself at a night-club in Cape Town appeared with the caption: Lord and Lady *Rotherstein* – 'As if we were *Jewish*, my dear!'[11]

Tynan never forgot who the enemy was.

Two years of battling over a principle left Tynan in a very much weaker position at the National, now that he had crossed swords with Chandos, and this decline in his standing coincided with a series of uncertain shows. The downturn evident in 1967 continued with two uninspiring productions by a failing Tyrone Guthrie, *Tartuffe* (21 November 1967) and *Volpone* (16 January 1968). The Molière saw the NT début of John Gielgud, rescued from his self-imposed exile with *Ages of Man*, but the role of Orgon did not suit him, and the Jonson provided further support for the view that the ensemble principle was running out of steam. The young path-finders of the early years had melted away into film or commercial theatre and there was an enveloping sense of uncertainty. As always, an exception could be found. Peter Brook's version of Seneca's *Oedipus* (19 March 1968) was a disconcerting piece, praised for its vision and harrowing mood, but it again drew the observation that it had been transplanted from outside rather than evolving from within. Brook, after all, was a mainstay of the old rival, the RSC. The production was also scarred by an unnecessary spat between Brook and Olivier over the former's desire to replicate the switch to a lighter mood after the blinding of the protagonist that the Greeks would have expected. Brook wanted to achieve this by having an enormous golden phallus wheeled onto the stage and to have the National Anthem (still played at the end of each production) improvised by a jazz band, incorporating strands from 'Yes, We Have No Bananas'.[12] Wary of Chandos's reaction and motivated by a personal patriotism that was out of kilter with the time, Olivier refused to accede to Brook's request, but Tynan backed the renowned director. The only way around this impasse, given Brook's implacable insistence, was for Olivier to suspend the playing of the Anthem altogether and back down on the phallus, but his decision to stand his ground over this trivial issue (when he had been less proactive with the board elsewhere) inevitably damaged him in the eyes of the company.

The appointment of Frank Dunlop, a co-founding director of the Nottingham Playhouse, was designed to spread the administrative load and help make preparations for the company's eventual relocation to the South Bank, but it partially added to the sense of a declining regime, where no adequate succession had been planned. Dunlop's production of Brecht's *Edward II* (30 April 1968) was unfairly seen as faintly anachronistic, given Brecht's absorption into the mainstream, and the uneven triple bill, which linked Fielding's *The Covent Garden Tragedy* and Maddison Morton's *A Most Unwarrantable Intrusion* with John Lennon's *In His Own Write* (18 June 1968), appeared self-indulgent. Two members of the acting company, Robert Lang and Robert Stephens, directed the first two works, and Lennon's input (for which Tynan was responsible) was a classic example of celebrity bandwagoning. As always, Tynan articulated the unspoken thoughts of the company. Berating a lack of direction he told Olivier that 'the purpose of keeping the company together is [now] merely to keep the company together,'[13] and he was even more forthright at the end of 1968, when he delivered a damning status report: 'To sum up: no announced plans for Christmas, no spring productions fixed, no summer productions fixed, no autumn productions fixed, no film or tv plans discussed. I should add that I've been asked to go on television next week to talk about the future of the National Theatre.'[14] He also wondered whether his own sense of aimlessness might be arrested by offering to co-direct *King Lear* with Olivier, but, fearing rejection, he never seriously raised the idea. Eventually, he decided that he needed a sabbatical to write, recharge and reflect. It was just the opportunity Lord Chandos had been waiting for. Never a fan of Tynan and provoked to apoplexy by his campaign on behalf of *Soldiers*, he had been unmoved by Olivier's attempts to placate him. When the Artistic Director argued in October 1968 that if Tynan were to be sacked he would be quite stricken,[15] Chandos was given another reminder of Olivier's incredible loyalty, but he chose to see this as an impediment to his plans rather than a persuasive reason to view Tynan in a new light.

Chandos's response to the request, made in April 1969, for a six-month sabbatical, was to see this as a chance to remove Tynan once and for all. Sensing the trap that he was about to walk into, Tynan backtracked the following month. He would settle for a three-month break, and indicated that he would remain in his post only until the new building was open (at that stage, still an unknown prospect). For the first time, he raised the issue of his health –

Last year, an X-ray revealed that I was suffering from an incurable but not incapacitating lung disease called emphysema. The specialists who examined me have since urged me to take the first opportunity to spend some time in a better climate and a relatively unpolluted atmosphere . . .

– and he also used this opportunity to tackle the issue of his alleged 'disloyalty' directly with Chandos:

> I understand that exception was taken to my saying that my principal loyalty was to the National Theatre rather than to its Board. In my own defence, I can only say that this seems analogous to a Labour M.P. declaring complete loyalty to the Party while disagreeing with a specific Cabinet decision.[16]

As Chandos was an ex-Tory minister, this was perhaps not the most persuasive line to take with the chairman.

The next meeting of the board was due to take place on 9 June 1969, and Tynan was concerned about his prospects, particularly when he discovered that the question of his position could not be raised by either Olivier or himself. He sought to persuade one of the more sympathetic members, John Mortimer, that what he now wished for was 'peaceful co-existence' with Chandos, in the hope that he would speak on his behalf. The possibility of being fired would be 'a pretty big triumph for him, and a poor prospect for me', he reminded Mortimer. 'I gave up being the *Observer*'s drama critic to join the NT; the major critical posts are now all filled, and no other subsidised theatre needs a Literary Manager.'[17] A note of desperation was detectable.

The compromise, brought about by Olivier's urgings, was unsatisfactory to both parties. Tynan could take the full six months, but he would be demoted on his return to the position of Literary Consultant and would have to share the job with an, as yet, unidentified colleague. It was a *fait accompli* that Tynan had no choice but to accept, if he wanted to be a part of the company's move to its purpose-built home. Chandos sought to cover up this slight with warm words – 'no one has suggested that you are to be dismissed . . . What we have decided, as a matter of policy and in the interests of the National Theatre, is that in future the work which you now do should be done by a Consultant' – and attempted to sugar the pill with kind words about his health and a financial compromise – 'The Board was truly sorry to hear of your state of health . . . [and] are ready, as a gesture, to make three months of the period salaried'.[18] Tynan signalled his acquiescence on 18 June in a rather downbeat response – 'I should be glad if you could convey to the Board my thanks for their generous provision in the matter of my salary, and also for their sympathy in the matter of my health'[19] – for he had other things on his mind.

Tynan had written his acceptance letter the day after the world première of his erotic revue *Oh, Calcutta!* in New York. Having read the disastrous review from Clive Barnes of the *New York Times*, in which the pre-eminent critic had warned that there was 'no more innocent show in town – and certainly none more witless – than this silly little diversion' devised by the 'dirty-minded Kenneth Tynan',[20] he may have felt that he could not afford to leave the National, no matter how paltry the salary, but, for once, the butcher of Broadway's denunciation was to have little effect on the box office. *Oh, Calcutta!* was to earn its investors a phenomenal 600 per cent return over the next ten years,[21] although, typically, Tynan himself would barely see any of it. 'I share . . . the royalties with 13 other authors, 2 directors, 2 composers and a choreographer,'[22] he later told Olivier.

The original idea to 'use artistic means to achieve erotic stimulation' came to him three years earlier, in the summer of 1966. He contacted William Donaldson, the impresario responsible for *Beyond the Fringe*, to attempt to interest him in the concept. 'Nothing that is *merely* funny or *merely* beautiful should be admitted: it must be sexy. A certain intimacy is therefore necessary – i.e. a theatre seating not more than about 900.' To avoid difficulty with the Lord Chamberlain a variety licence would be needed, 'so that wordless items would not have to be submitted'. The show 'should be devised (or produced) by me, directed by some like-minded person (Jonathan Miller?) and choreographed by a non-queer'. He then went into the various possible titles of the show, before settling on his own favourite, *Oh, Calcutta!*, which was appropriately close to 'Quel cul t'as!', meaning 'What an arse you have!' Possible items included a 'pseudo-drag stripper . . . a pseudo-Lesbian singer . . . a sort of sexy *Batman*, preferably in colour . . . Vaudeville routines . . . a ballet based on the paintings (and the world) of Clovis Trouille' and, less palatably, 'Tableaux representing national erotic obsessions – such as a nun being raped by her confessor (Italy), a middle-aged bank manager bound hand and foot by a Superwoman (U.S.A.) and a St. Trinian's sixth-former being birched by John Gordon (Great Britain)', a puritanical Scots journalist, who had edited the *Sunday Express* until 1954.[23] Donaldson's initial interest waned, and Tynan quickly replaced him with the much more enthusiastic Michael White.

By December 1966, with Peter Brook having passed up the opportunity of directing, Harold Pinter was planning to direct and co-devise the show and Tynan busy soliciting contributions. He wrote to his old adversary, Mary McCarthy, explaining what he was looking for – 'Sketches can either be a) stage reproductions of a pet erotic fantasy or b) comments – ironic, satirical, what you will – on eroticism. Needless to say, they don't have to be funny. The tone can be as dark as you wish' – although there is no record of a reply. Undaunted, he fired off letters in all directions. Pinter's withdrawal, on the grounds of pressure of work, did not deter him. It was hoped that the show might be able to open the following July, but continuing delays in the abolition of the Lord Chamberlain's powers to censor meant that this date was unlikely – and *Oh, Calcutta!* was *the* definitive post-censorship work – so it was decided to open in New York in June 1969.

As so often with Tynan's association with the theatre, the practice turned out to be a great deal more stressful for him personally than the theory. The poor

financial arrangements meant that his final take was reduced to a minuscule per-
centage, a source of deep depression to him. Separated from rehearsals by the
Atlantic in the spring of 1969, he became increasingly frantic about the overall
quality of the show. The aggressive publicity campaign run by the New York producer, Levy's agent, Hillard Elkins, which included erecting a screen outside the
Eden Theatre that broadcast nude images of the cast, caused protests from religious
campaigners as well as car crashes by gawping drivers. When he eventually arrived
in New York in the middle of May, Tynan was now embroiled in the battle to save
his NT post, and was further distressed by the laconic pace of the rehearsals. 'Nancy
stroking Raina is by far the sexiest thing in the show so far,' he informed Hillard
Elkins, but too few of the acts seemed to cohere and it lacked the erotic thrill that
he had envisaged.[24] His concern turned to panic when he returned to London. 'I
came back to a pile of press clippings about *Calcutta* including two viciously contemporary reviews of the sketches at the press conference – *and* (which is much
more damaging) a full-length review of the Thursday preview, headlined: "Mr
Tynan! Your sex show is a total bore!",' he wrote to Elkins. 'This was in the *Evening
News*, which has 2 million readers.' In an action that evoked memories of his barring from the theatre by Donald Wolfit, he incredibly tried to get Elkins to prevent
reviewers from hostile British publications entering the theatre. Such negative coverage was unlikely to endear him to Chandos. 'Is there anything we can do to keep
[the English critics] out?' he pleaded. 'Could the box office be instructed to check
on ticket buyers with English accents by asking them if they are the press? The
effect all this is having in Britain is *devastating* . . .'[25]

After forty-one previews, the show finally opened on 17 June. If the critical reaction was dulled, the public's appetite was not. New Yorkers rushed to see a show
that seemed to have its finger on the very pulse of the city. The 'evening of elegant
erotica' contained a series of episodes related to sex. It began with Beckett's 30-
second *Breath*, the cast then entering in long white robes, before stripping completely naked. The sketches followed in rapid succession. They included 'Dick and
Jane', which featured a young couple engaging in rather mundane sex, before the
man tries to pep up the action with some S&M; 'Suite for Five Letters', which made
great play of the bizarre letters column of the now-closed magazine, *London Life*;
'Will Answer All Comers', the most explicit scene so far, which looked at the issue
of swingers, with one of the men being brought to a simulated orgasm; the more
morbid 'Jack and Jill', where the woman dies after having sex; 'Was It Good For
You Too', which saw a doctor conducting a medical experiment with a 'secre-
tiometer' while a young couple had sex; the only scene that Tynan wrote himself,
'Who: Whom', which gently explored his S&M fantasies ('Jean is now fully dis-
closed. From between her buttocks, the puckered rim of a virgin target tremulously

peeps');[26] and the final ensemble piece, called 'Coming Together, Going Together', which was meant to reflect the cast's journey from frigid embarrassment at the beginning of rehearsals to a less self-conscious physicality at the end. The very last stage direction illustrated how the show, for all its undergraduate humour, was liberated, carefree and sexually upfront:

> The group explodes joyously now, touching, holding, swinging each other around. Something has broken open. While they jump and shout a line is being formed upstage. Finally, all the actors join in a line – a 'daisy chain' – belly to belly, back to belly, back to back, humping in rhythm to the blues rock, yelling with the singer:
> I WANT IT!
> I WANT IT!
> I WANT IT!
> I WANT IT![27]

It was a long way from Rattigan.

Tynan spent much of his sabbatical planning for the London opening at the Roundhouse in July 1970 and contending with the increasingly aggressive publicity that was being generated by his opponents. There was a very real fear of prosecution, because of the repeated references to oral sex and S&M, and this was avoided only because the Attorney-General in the newly elected Conservative government wanted to avoid a fight with the liberal press.[28] After a panel of experts, set up to adjudicate on whether to prosecute or not, decided that there was no need to go to law – one panel member, Dame Margaret Miles believing that the revue 'recognised the greater honesty, openness and freedom with which sex is viewed at the present time'[29] – the Director of Public Prosecutions advised that a court case was just too risky. The London opening was preceded by the inevitable press hostility, but, as in New York, the production was sustained by the large numbers of curious people who flocked through the doors: £3 tickets quickly started to change hands for £50 and it became a must-see event. Tynan's show had become a cultural phenomenon and it is hard to disagree with Michael White when he argues that for all its immaturity, *Oh, Calcutta!* had 'a healthy effect on public consciousness'.[30] Nevertheless, Tynan himself was inevitably labelled a pornographer and did little to correct this misleading impression by embarking on a collection of (unpublished) masturbatory fantasies, 'For Myself Alone', and an 'erotic and anally sadistic'[31] film, with Andrew Braunschweig, the producer of Polanski's *Fearless Vampire Killers*. The first project foundered on an understandable lack of submissions from famous writers and the second because of a losing battle over financial backing which Tynan gave up, much to his distress, in 1975. The world-wide success of *Oh, Calcutta!* proved that there was a considerable market for less repressive depictions of sex and adult, erotic revue, but the cost to Tynan's health and reputation was immense. It was a pyrrhic victory against the forces of conservatism.

During Tynan's leave of absence, his thoughts were never very far from events at the Old Vic. In October 1969, Olivier had contacted him from the set in Shepperton where he was filming *The Three Sisters*, with the news of his new colleague, Derek Granger,[32] but the convivial tone was not reassuring. In particular, bruised by his constant drubbing in the press over *Oh, Calcutta!*, Tynan was concerned about possible press reaction to his effective demotion. 'I was perfectly content to let Lord C. get away with his little plan to downgrade me,' he replied, 'so long as it didn't look like a deliberate rebuff.'[33] In reality, though, he knew that his power to shape events was waning.

On his return to the National in January 1970 as one of two Literary Consultants, rather than as a single Literary Manager, his relationship with Olivier began to change. Feeling insecure in his new position, Tynan attempted to reassert his authority with a series of brusque memos advising on everything from future programmes to possible casting. This was no different from his early years as dramaturg, but Olivier now found the memos increasingly irritating. In February, he objected to these carping missives and requested that Tynan come to speak to him rather than fire off irritable letters.[34] The following month, he protested about a temperamental outburst over Tynan's conviction – and Oliver's (misplaced) uncertainty – that Olivier would make a great James Tyrone in *Long Days Journey Into Night*.[35] And in June, he made clear – prior to the British opening of *Oh, Calcutta!* – his reluctance to allow the National to be influenced by the permissiveness evident in Tynan's production, because it would simply look as if he was joining a rather tired-looking bandwagon.[36] Having throughout his career always craved Olivier's approval, this must have been a painful blow for Tynan.

On stage, events at the National were equally bumpy. From 1967 audiences had begun to dip, with the average attendance declining from 97 per cent to 67 per cent in 1971/2.[37] Peter Nichols's *The National Health* (16 October 1969, dir. Blakemore), a comic satire about the fear of pain and death set on a hospital ward stimulated by the playwright's own experience of having a collapsed lung, and Olivier's performance as Shylock in Jonathan Miller's production of *The Merchant of Venice* (28 April 1970) (for which Olivier had had his teeth altered and finally managed to conquer his stage fright) demonstrated that the company could still mount significant productions, but there was a continued lack of direction, coupled with a collective loss of confidence. The stupendous performances of John Gielgud and Ralph Richardson in David Storey's *Home* at the Royal Court in 1970 (before transfers to the West End and Broadway) raised the old suspicions that Olivier actively refused to employ actors of equal stature to himself out of competitive envy (it being widely felt that Olivier had never forgiven Gielgud for upstaging him in their alternating roles as Romeo and Mercutio in the 1935 production of *Romeo and Juliet* at the New Theatre). People also pointed to the continued absence of Alec Guinness, but such carping was temporarily silenced when real disaster struck in August 1970 with Olivier suffering a major thrombosis in his leg. This was a serious blow to the project which Tynan had seen as his way back into favour at the National, the much-discussed *Guys and Dolls*, with Olivier starring as Nathan Detroit. The board finally killed off the idea for financial reasons in June 1971.

Olivier's powers of recuperation were legendary – he had conquered pneumonia, appendicitis, cancer of the prostate and loss of memory over the previous decade – but his incapacity now compounded the feeling that the National was rudderless. Tynan was deeply affected. The year 1971 had started badly for him with a terrible row with Kathleen, precipitated by the need to come to a decision on the lease of their house, which had twelve years left to run. Kathleen, becoming increasingly concerned about their parlous financial affairs, wanted them to take up the option of extending it for a further fifty-five years at a cost of £19,000. She was now pregnant with their first child, Roxana, and was fully aware that financial salvation would not be coming from *Oh, Calcutta!* Tynan was more inclined to invest the money and put mobility over security. During the course of their row, he rejected her request for equal rights in this issue, denying that she was his equal partner and incredibly claiming that she was a 'kept' woman.[38] Shocked and distressed, Kathleen began to see her marriage in a new light.

In spite of having adapted *Macbeth* for Roman Polanski's film version, Tynan's familiar doubts about his creative input began to resurface. He became introspective about his own role. In February 1971 he made the following revealing entry in his increasingly confessional diary:

Around 1952 – when Clunes fired me from the Arts production – I had a choice between hanging back as an onlooker and plunging in as a participant – i.e. continuing as a director. I took the safer course and became a full-time critic. That is why, today, I am everyone's adviser – Roman's, Larry's, Michael White's – and nobody's boss, not even my own.[39]

He began to reflect on his perception of his own isolation, a theme that would come to dominate many sad entries over the next few years: 'Friendless virtually at forty-three: I have alienated my traditionalist friends by my left-wing politics, and my left-wing friends by my love of pleasure.'[40]

His spirits were hardly improved by a succession of production problems. The rehearsal process for Fernando Arrabal's *The Architect and the Emperor of Assyria* (3 February, dir. Victor Garcia) was fraught with tension and this was wittily captured by Tynan in his diary:

> The Garcia situation reaching a climax: L.O. disturbed by momentary Nudity of Anthony Hopkins at dress rehearsal. Garcia – five feet high, frizzed black hair, plaintive ochre face – has coped with L.O. with a nonchalant effrontery that fills us all with admiration. When he arrived for rehearsals in December, L.O. spent a night going over the Arrabal text, marking 200 passages that disturbed or offended him. On meeting Garcia he said: '*Cher maître* – there are just a few things I'd like to ask you about the play . . .' Garcia stepped forward and took the script from Larry's hand, between thumb and forefinger as if it were contaminated. With frigid distaste he dropped it into the wastepaper basket. 'Sir Laurence,' he said, smiling wanly, 'I detest literature. I abominate the theatre. I have a horror of culture. I am only interested in magic!' Collapse of L.O. who later recovers to ask nervously: 'There's a scene towards the end where the Architect *eats* the Emperor. How do you intend to stage that?' 'Sir Laurence,' says Garcia, sweetly as to a child, 'I *could* tell you; but it would scare the shit out of you; so I will *not* tell you.'[41]

The show, however, about two survivors of a plane crash who are marooned on a desert island and play fantasy games to pass the time, perplexed critics and public alike. 'Like marathon runners [the cast's] achievement is to last the course,' wrote Peter Lewis in the *Daily Mail*. 'If you last it yourself, you will actually have a unique experience.'[42]

Coriolanus (6 May, dir. Wekwerth and Tenscher) was most notable for its replacement of Christopher Plummer by Anthony Hopkins after a vote by the cast. Tynan saw this as 'a splendid vindication of the new collective leadership at the NT',[43] but for others it was further evidence of backstage disharmony. *Tyger* (20 July dir. Blakemore and Dexter), a project conceived and vigorously championed by Tynan, was an even greater disappointment. Two months before the first night, Olivier had raised objections to the swear words and sexual language of the script, and argued that he would need the approval of Lord Chandos before this celebration of William Blake's work could go ahead. Tynan was incandescent. It was as if the *Soldiers* episode had never happened. Arguing that Olivier had no need to obtain anybody's approval,[44] he ventured the hope that he might be able to mount another co-production with Michael White if Olivier withdrew the play. Olivier backed down, but continued to express his unhappiness with the script, most notably before the fourth preview show. He now demanded that the line 'God damn the Queen' be deleted, because it was unpatriotic. Tynan and Adrian Mitchell, the scriptwriter, refused out of hand, and Tynan pointed out that Mitchell had republican sympathies. 'Why don't you go and live in a republic then?' Olivier asked. Tynan expressed his frustration in his diary:

How one longs to reveal that if *Tyger* succeeds it will be in the teeth of panic-stricken opposition from this obtuse lick-spittle, L.O., who would rather insult and outrage a poet than cause a moment's dismay to Her Majesty. How ironic that the show, which deals with the efforts of snobbish and conservative officialdom to censor a revolutionary poet, should have a backstage plot that precisely echoes the one on stage![45]

To Tynan's bitter disappointment, *Tyger* was awarded 'the most venomous reviews' he could remember. His personal commitment to the show had been immense. Kathleen and he had called their son Matthew Blake Tynan, and he felt that it offered a 'radical vision of life and theatre'. He had even risked a row with Dexter about using a stage manager to help record Mitchell's song, 'The Child of William Blake', as a present to Kathleen on the birth of their son,[46] but all the main critics were now elderly, there was no one under forty of any significance and *Tyger* had 'outraged the new conformism of understatement, tact and compromise'.[47]

The National continued its stumbling progress through 1971. Olivier had already told Lord Goodman, the chairman of the Arts Council, in November 1970 that he could no longer work with the autocratic Chandos, who was now approaching eighty. In a messily handed *putsch*, he was asked to leave at the very next board meeting and succeeded as chairman by Sir Max Rayne. In hindsight, it was too little, too late. Confusion continued to surround the official role of Frank Dunlop, who administered the company for three years in Olivier's place, but who Olivier could never concede was his deputy; and the decision to expand by taking over the New Theatre (as a new West End showcase, to prepare for the logistical challenge of doubling the company in its new South Bank home) in addition to the Old Vic was at first a disaster.

Yet, it was in this climate that Olivier was to give one of his legendary performances. The last production at the New Theatre in 1971 (21 December, dir. Blakemore) was of Eugene O'Neill's *Long Day's Journey into Night*, and his phoenix-like role as James Tyrone was greeted with adulation – Michael Billington spoke of 'a massive performance . . . for a genuinely great actor to play a nearly-great actor is the hardest technical feat of all: Olivier does it to perfection'[48] – and enormous relief. Relief at his return to health and form, and relief that the National had arrested its decline. Olivier had worn Tyrone's suit every day for three weeks before the first night to think himself into the part, and during the four hours of the play managed to dominate the show without overshadowing his fellow actors. The respite from a critical press was temporary, however, since Max Rayne, keen to identify an eventual successor to Olivier, now began discreet negotiations with the man Olivier least wished to see don his mantle: his old rival at the RSC, Peter Hall. The obfuscation surrounding these soundings; the decision to keep Olivier in the dark; the demands of Hall (who had resigned from his current post as the director of Glyndebourne) for a much larger salary than Olivier and greater freedom to pursue outside work; Hall's tentative examination of the possibility of merging with the RSC; and the inevitable leaks to journalists caused a welter of bad feeling within the company, permanent distress to Tynan and Olivier and disastrous public relations outside.

Tynan was unaware of the negotiations in the spring of 1972, but was still unhappy about the weakness of the company and his own role and status.[49] He had contacted Olivier about this before the previous Christmas and Olivier's delayed reply indicated more than a passing glance at their place in history. Baulking slightly at Tynan's tone, Olivier enquired whether he was expected to put some sort of record straight. He then proceeded to do just that, by producing a list of productions which Tynan had conceived, those which had been the agreed choices of all concerned and those which had emerged without the blessing of Tynan's support. Thirteen works belonged to this last category – *The Royal Hunt of the Sun, Armstrong's Last Goodnight, Trelawney of the Wells, The Covent Garden Tragedy* ('I'm afraid' – LO*), Home and Beauty* ('strong resistance by KT'), *The Travails of Sancho Panza, The Merchant of Venice, Hedda Gabler, Cyrano de Bergerac, Mrs Warren's Profession, Captain of Köpenick, Amphitryon,* and *The Good-Natur'd Man*. The list of Tynan's sole suggestions was hugely impressive: *Othello, Much Ado About Nothing, Mother Courage, Black Comedy, A Flea in Her Ear* ('complete package deal/adapter/director/designer all Ken's'), *Andorra, The Dutch Courtesan, Rosencrantz and Guildenstern Are Dead, As You Like It, Oedipus, A Most Unwarrantable Intrusion, In His Own Write, The Advertisement, H, Back to Methuselah, The National Health, The Architect and the Emperor of Assyria, Tyger, Long Day's Journey into Night* and *Jumpers*.

Tynan protested that he had not requested a setting straight of the record in his December letter (though he proceeded to make some corrections to Olivier's list), but restated his need to know how he should operate. He was being asked to serve as the NT spokesman again, and wanted to clarify his role when Olivier was away for a week in March 1972 playing the Duke of Wellington in Robert Bolt's film, *Lady Caroline Lamb*. Poignantly, he added that 'my enemies attack me for holding a sinecure when the NT is doing well and blame the whole of our artistic policy on me when the NT is doing badly'. It was not a question of pay or status; what he wanted was 'simply . . . a recognition of the fact that whatever task I am performing at the moment, it is different from that which is being performed by Derek

[Granger]'.[50] Olivier's reply was brusque: there was absolutely nothing he could do until he spoke to the chairman and the prognosis was poor.[51] This tetchy correspondence was drawn to a close by the bombshell that now broke.

Tynan first heard the news of Hall's imminent appointment when his assistant, Rozina Adler, telephoned him on 10 April in France, where he was holidaying with Kathleen, with the news that both the *Observer* and the *Guardian* had run stories stating that Peter Hall had been appointed as Olivier's successor. Tynan telephoned Olivier immediately, who told him that Max Rayne had summoned him a fortnight earlier to tell him that the board had decided on Peter Hall.[52] This succession crisis had been long in the making. One of the reasons why Olivier had eventually fallen out with Chandos was that the former chairman had reacted so coolly to his suggestion that Joan Plowright be appointed as an Associate Director and that he groom her to be his replacement. Olivier was aware of his failing health but found it temperamentally impossible to contemplate life after the National. Chandos's successor, Max Rayne, a protégé of Lord Goodman, was not prepared for this to drag on. One of his first acts was to dine with Peter Hall and Goodman on 1 August 1971 and sound the director out about the possibility of taking over at the National. He emphasised the importance of total confidentiality, as he recognised the difficulty of broaching this with Olivier, but Hall left the meal convinced that he had been made a concrete job offer. Rayne began quietly consulting his fellow board members over the next few months, and although some doubts were raised about his propensity to empire-build – which were apt, given Hall's later aborted attempt to merge the RSC and the National – he was the only candidate with the track record of running a large, subsidised organisation successfully.

This quiet consultation proceeded unknown to Olivier, who during the winter of 1971/2 finally began to confront the issue of succession himself. After much prevarication, he settled on Michael Blakemore, whose star was ascending after *Long Day's Journey into Night*, but Rayne, who had already made his decision, was lukewarm. Olivier then returned with the idea of a triumvirate, consisting of Blakemore, Plowright and Tynan, which the chairman found even more preposterous. In any case, the die had already been cast.

Rayne justified his concealment from Olivier of the board's preference for Hall on the grounds that he wanted to wait until *Long Day's Journey into Night* had finished its run. A meeting was further postponed by Olivier's trip to Rome, and he was only able to reveal the bombshell on 24 March. Olivier was doubly shocked, both at Rayne's lack of consultation and Hall's willingness to accept the job. He had always believed in a very strict demarcation line between the RSC and the NT. Yet for all his dismay, he kept the information from his colleagues. On the very same day as the meeting with Rayne, Tynan had travelled to the Oliviers' Brighton home for drinks, but Olivier breathed not a word. He subsequently learned that Joan Plowright had been preparing to break her husband's confidence, but the arrival of Tracy Tynan and her boyfriend had thwarted that plan. During the next week, they had discussed 'future plans for the theatre which he knew were purely academic'.[53] It was an enormous breach of trust, in Tynan's eyes.

Tynan's opposition to Hall was complex. Like Olivier, he saw him as part of an enemy camp and feared his plans for the National. There was also a personal dislike, since he viewed Hall as a 'burnt-out conservative', and knew that there was little chance of them being able to work together. Above all, he hated the fact that they had all been out-manoeuvred and believed, unfairly, that this had all been Hall's doing. The conspiracy theory was fuelled the next day, when Tynan was informed by his ally on the board, John Mortimer, that he had been under the impression that Blakemore, Dexter and Tynan had all been consulted,[54] and by the discovery that Olivier and Hall shared the same agent, Laurie Evans.

Tynan saw treachery all around. The British establishment had secured the choice it had long desired. 'I hate the most important decision in the administrative history of the English theatre,' he told his diary, 'being taken by a property tycoon (Rayne) and a lawyer (Goodman), without any word from the people who planned, created and evolved the National Theatre.'[55] Goodman was particularly loathed: 'When it actually seems as if real democracy might be about to exert some genuine influence on the nation's life, the ruling class produces an antibody to counter it. The antibody in our time is Lord Goodman.'[56] When he confronted Rayne, the chairman simply replied that he regretted that Tynan had not approached him about the question of the succession six months earlier. But most distressing of all had been the behaviour of Olivier:

> What emerges from this is that Larry has behaved appallingly. He has sold us all down the river without a single pang – by refusing to nominate a possible successor from his own colleagues, he has passed a vote of no confidence in us all. He never wanted to work with anyone who might replace him, either as actor or director. He has hired us, stolen our kudos, and now shows no compunction about discarding us. I cannot recall his ever saying a word in public that gave credit to anyone connected with the NT except himself.[57]

The principle of the ensemble, where mutual respect led to collective decisions and artistic excellence, had finally been destroyed. Tynan's relationship with Olivier could never be the same again.

As an indefatigable lobbyist, Tynan continued the fight, privately aware that he was now part of a 'demoralised twilight regime'.[58] The board met on 18 April 1972 at a special session convened following the plethora of adverse press reports.

Rayne, in the face of Olivier's assertion that the morale of the company had been seriously damaged by the handling of the affair, was feeling defensive, but he acceded to Olivier's request that Blakemore, Tynan and Frank Dunlop should join the meeting and put their point of view. Characteristically, Tynan acted as spokesman, and he swiftly made his memorable comparison that pitched the RSC as the Roundheads against the National's Cavaliers, warning the board that under Peter Hall, the nation would have 'two Roundhead theatres'.[59] He also offered the following series of detailed proposals: that associate directors and the head of the Literary Department should attend board meetings, that Hall must give assurances that his connection with the RSC would be severed, that the present artistic policy be continued and the executives offered three-year contracts and that the executives should be consulted about the press release announcing Hall's appointment. Tynan learned the next day that, following the departure of the three of them, Olivier had asked that associate directors not be permitted to attend board meetings. It would be 'very embarrassing if artistic decisions should be taken at a meeting at which he could not be present',[60] but he completely failed to grasp that Tynan was setting down markers that might strengthen his position over the coming months of the interregnum. Tynan was incensed – 'What a traitor he has turned out to be,'[61] he observed – and the board unsurprisingly ignored Tynan's suggestions. It also ratified Hall's appointment, and issued a press release announcing its decision and providing the dubious sop that two of the new auditoria on the South Bank – still due to open on 1 January 1974 – would be called the Lyttelton (the family name of Lord Chandos, who died in 1972) and the Olivier. In the circumstances, it was an unfortunate coupling.

Although Blakemore, Tynan, Dunlop and Dexter had focused their ire on the secrecy behind Hall's appointment, and not on the merits of the appointment itself, Tynan was the only one who had clearly burnt his bridges. Two days after the board meeting he sent a characteristically frank letter to the director-designate, hoping that he had 'suffered no lasting wounds in the cross fire between the board and the executive':

> I told the Board on Tuesday (and you last week), none of us had anything against you personally. What we deplored about the whole exercise was the total lack of consultation. My own feeling was that within a year or two Michael Blakemore might have emerged as a candidate, and it shook me to learn that Max Rayne had never even met him; but if the appointment was to be made now, then it obviously had to be you.
>
> We also felt upset about the timing. It looked as if the Board had lost faith in the organisation at a moment when it just happened to be having one of its most successful seasons.[62]

It was true that *Long Day's Journey into Night* and Stoppard's new play, *Jumpers* (2 February, dir. Wood) had been welcome successes, to be followed by Ben Hecht and Charles MacArthur's *The Front Page* (6 July, dir. Blakemore) – 'a Tynan grand slam', in his view[63] – but this missed the point. The question of the succession could not be indefinitely postponed by the odd success, no matter how spectacular, and the emergence of a democratic artistic executive remained more an aspiration than a reality.

Hall and Tynan agreed to get together as soon as possible, but other commitments, including a brief trip to New York to undertake research for an article on Wilhelm Reich (the controversial psychoanalyst, follower of Freud and proponent of unorthodox theories on sex) that Tynan was undertaking for the *New Yorker*, prevented a meeting until early July. It was, Tynan recorded, 'a fairly definitive chat':

> He pays extravagant but (I think) sincere tribute to my part in creating the NT and adds (not '*but*' adds – he is too much of a diplomat even to *imply* 'but') that he hopes I don't envisage that I'm to be thrown out. Nevertheless, he's not entirely sure (and wants my views on) whether we shall get on, both being so good at politicking, both with such strong ideas. I disabuse him of the thought that I ever intended (even under Michael Blakemore) to stay on after the move to the new building, when I would like to be phased out. I sense he is privately relieved, though not surprised.[64]

This was no dissimulation on Tynan's part. Immediately acknowledging that the writing was on the wall, he had told his agent, Simon Michael Bessie, on 4 May that he intended to leave the National 'as soon as the job of piloting Larry into the new building is finished'[65] and now wanted to return to other projects, notably an autobiographical account of his time at the National, not to mention a biography of Reich. The meeting with Hall confirmed the wisdom of this, even if it was tinged with regret: 'I feel, of course, a slight pang now that all has been said and the end of the chapter settled. It *would* be exciting to plan a new NT with a new policy . . . But enough of this vicarious living. I must go back to taking responsibility for what I do, which is *write*.'[66] This need to return to writing was partly psychological – to fill the yawning gap that his departure from the Old Vic would create – and partly financial – he had just been stung with a bill for £6,000 for damages and £14,000 in costs,[67] having had, much against his wishes, to settle the Prchal case out of court. Worries over money and his inability to write, a new compatible girlfriend into S&M, and the acceleration of his emphysema would now dominate the remaining years of his life.

On his return from New York, Tynan saw the film of G.W. Pabst's *Pandora's Box*, starring Louise Brooks, whose face, he felt, was 'open to any sexual suggestion, candid and mischievous, full of delight and magnetism'.[68] He would come back to this image in his final days, but he was now more preoccupied with the other projects that he had turned his hand to. One was a proposed erotic film based on his own preferences and obsessions. The remorselessness with which he pursued this deeply disturbed Kathleen. She feared exposure and felt that such a public revelation would only open up the two of them to further ridicule. With great reluctance, he agreed to postpone the film in October, but was irritated that Kathleen did not recognise his self-sacrifice in this decision. 'Have I done right to deny myself a career to spare her feelings, since she seems so impervious to mine?',[69] he complained. He had hoped to direct the film himself, but another opportunity to make a direct contribution to the creative process had slipped away. Despite several abortive attempts to resurrect the idea, the film was never made.

A wedge had now been driven between Tynan and his second wife, and they both began affairs. In 1976, he listed her partners in his diary as 'Michael Blakemore, Christian Marquand, Bernardo Bertolucci, Warren Beatty, Gay Talese, [Dan Topolski], and others unadmitted'. His record was 'slimmer'[70] – 'Nicole' – but the meticulous detailing of their sexual activity in his diary caused as much damage to his posthumous reputation as his involvement with *Oh, Calcutta!* His first entry about 'Nicole' in February 1973 has an air of the confessional and began a series of revealing observations that were to recur in the next few years:

> Since last November I have been seeing (and spanking) a fellow spanking addict, a girl called 'Nicole'. Her fantasy – dormant until I met her – is precisely to be bent over with knickers taken down to be spanked, caned or otherwise punished, preferably with the buttocks parted to disclose the anus. She also enjoys exposing and spanking me. Meeting only for intensive and exhausting sexual purposes, we have delighted each other for months. Our fantasies exactly match: whereas I am conscious that Kathleen has had to *will* herself to fit my fantasy. But for all these months my sex life with K has languished, to her increasing distress. Two days ago, forced by real anguish on her part (blaming herself for my lack of physical interest) I told her about N – explaining, a trifle disingenuously, that there was no competition between them; that N represented the curry side of my life, whereas K represented French cooking; that I needed both, perhaps even at the same time (threesome situations are especially attractive to sado-masochists, who like an audience since they like humiliation); that it was only the guilt of concealment that kept me from fucking her.[71]

There were echoes here of the end of the 1950s, when Tynan's first marriage to Elaine had begun to founder over his sexual needs, and he drew an explicit link with his first wife, as his affair with 'Nicole' progressed:

'Nicole' is really a tremendous reaction to twenty-five years of feeling ashamed of my sexual preferences – being taunted and threatened and blackmailed with them by Elaine, who (except in moments of drunken reconciliation) spent fifteen years intimidating me by promising to tell my friends and employer all about my filthy desires unless I clove to her, and who actually *did* tell my daughter, then aged four, about them, in the small hours of one phantasmagoric night.[72]

Kathleen was alienated by his need for 'Nicole', but found the physical outlet of her affairs some form of compensation, and she remained willing to stay with Tynan as he became ever more irascible.

He had much to be irascible about. His annual Christmas trip to Paris with Kathleen in December 1972 had been ruined by a severe bronchial attack, which had exacerbated his emphysema and was a portent of the horrors to come. His description of the agony was chilling – 'The lungs burn and scald when coughing starts; breathing is like painfully clenching and unclenching two vast stiff fists – the lungs'[73] – but he was unable to dispense with his cigarettes. Olivier dropped another bombshell in January 1973, when he informed Tynan and Dexter that, bored with the administrative chores and no longer enthused by the creativity of the job, he was bringing forward his retirement to October 1973. Tynan had observed his declining interest in 'anything outside acting and gossip',[74] but had remained convinced that they would all depart together when the company had moved into the South Bank (put back yet again until 1975). Dexter and Tynan pointed out to Olivier that this left them all high and dry, as their plans had been formed on the basis of a departure with him in 1975, and it looked for a while as if they had persuaded him to rethink. But to their great surprise, a press conference was held on 13 March 1973 at which it was announced that Hall and Olivier would serve as co-directors from 1 April, before Olivier stepped down as Artistic Director in November. He would leave the National completely in December.

This was yet another 'breach of promise' in Tynan's eyes and he felt he had been completely left in the lurch. It added to the uncertainty of his life, graphically highlighted by the following diary entry in February: 'Youngish man approached me in the street in Soho and said: "Mr Tynan – I just wanted to tell you how much I approve of everything you are doing." I thanked him. There was a pause, after which he said: "Er – what – er – what *are* you doing?" Good question.'[75] He was also finding it increasingly difficult to concentrate on his proposed biography of Reich. Only two chapters were complete and although the analyst's belief, as expressed in *The Sexual Revolution* and *The Function of the Orgasm*, that orgasmic power was necessary for overall well-being was so attuned to Tynan's own philosophy, his ability to concentrate was beginning to wane. Reich maintained a lifelong conviction, which was derided by other psychoanalysts, in 'orgiastic potency'. Tynan, too, felt that the super-orgasm brought the mind and body into balance, but his waning health and gloomy spirits were affecting this quest as well as his career. In September, he reflected on the fragility of his confidence in his ability to write: 'There are writers who have written themselves out at forty; and there are writers who have written themselves *in*. There is no third kind.'[76]

With the dénouement of the succession crisis now being played, there now remained the question of Tynan's own departure. In spite of some surprisingly similar views about the future repertoire and a shared belief that Olivier might be directed in a production of *King Lear* (Tynan's own timid ambition),[77] it was evident that Hall wanted him to leave as soon as possible: he had actually asked for the National Theatre board to minute in July 1972 that it had been a condition of his accepting the post that Tynan must leave.[78] Concerned about his financial affairs, Tynan petitioned Olivier about the issue of severance pay. This was a legitimate point. Such was his dedication to the cause that he had not received a single pay increase over the past ten years, and his present salary was 'the official *minimum* wage for apprentice reporters in the newspaper world.'[79] The board had turned his request down, and his tenure at the National threatened to end in even greater bitterness. Could Olivier intervene? Olivier promised to look into it.

Meanwhile, the last of Tynan's suggestions for production, Trevor Griffiths's *The Party* (20 December, dir. Dexter), in which Olivier was to take the role of John Tagg, was in rehearsal. The pleasure of this project was severely compromised for Tynan, however, by Hall's decision to restrict it to thirty-four performances, because of his own impending production plans. The 'virulent' reviews – 'far worse than any of us expected'[80] – added to his depression, to say nothing of the unresolved issue of severance pay. After the second night, Olivier took him to the Savoy Grill to mark his retirement, and told him of the scroll of signatures that he was gathering to commemorate their decade together,[81] but it was a sad, downbeat end to a momentous period.

Olivier finally managed in February 1974 to secure £2,500 as a pay-off for Tynan, after pleading with Max Rayne. Tynan was overjoyed and contacted Olivier to express his thanks:

> On behalf of all my dependants, including my bank manager, my wine merchant, Kathleen's dress-maker, my Persian au pair, my honest accountant, my other accountant, the manager of La Mère Charles restaurant at Mionnet, near Lyon (trois étoiles, vaut le voyage), and the entire staff of Miss Floggy's Finishing School in Maida Vale, a thousand thanks for moving so many mountains to fix the not so little matter of the severance pay. It will come in handy. I'm open-mouthed with gratitude. Bless you and love to Joan.[82]

Such effusiveness would become rare as his health declined, and it was impossible to disguise his bitterness in the final years of his job at the National. Peter Hall's initial run of failures provoked the indisputable observation that 'Larry and I presided over a golden age'.[83] The proposed exhibition to mark the opening of the National Theatre at the South Bank in the spring of 1975 seemed to Tynan to have 'been designed to edit Larry [and, by implication, him] out of the listing of the NT'.[84] He heartily endorsed Olivier's observation that he had 'never known a man more dedicated to self-glorification' than Peter Hall,[85] and, when he met Olivier for one of the last times, to interview him for a television programme in September 1975, concurred with his belief that 'all sense of company solidarity has gone'.[86]

With his flair for publicity, his ability to coin a cutting aphorism and his sense of grievance, Tynan was one of several thorns in the side of Hall during the difficult years of transition from the Old Vic to the South Bank. Tynan so disliked the first new play that Hall presented there, Howard Brenton's *Weapons of Happiness*, that he was moved to boo for the 'first time in a decade'. The diary entry is revealing, though, for it evokes past glories as much as present unhappiness:

> This offensive piece purports to be an analysis of the possibility of a revolution in England . . . The whole history of the Left – the great movement which has made life tolerable and tenable for working people over the last two centuries – is reduced to a choice between despotic Stalinists and idiot children whose idea of revolution is to shit on the factory floor. The message, loudly and clearly proclaimed, is: how dare the working class complain about its lot, since the only alternative is tyranny? As if we hadn't heard again and again, ever since *Darkness at Noon*, that Stalinism was a bad thing. The mixture of arrogance and condescension was impossible to stomach: it almost made me long to be a critic again, since this rubbish has been praised by people as disparate as Billington of the *Guardian* and the berserk H. Hobson, now in the twilight of his loony reign on the *Sunday Times*.[87]

On 25 October 1976 the Queen officially opened the new National Theatre. It should have been an occasion of great joy for Tynan, but he recorded the event with a jaundiced eye for his diary. Olivier's speech did not praise one playwright, actor or director; the choice of play, Goldoni's *Il Campiello*, was 'perverse to the point of madness'; the company seemed panic stricken; the most significant performance was that given by the on-stage fountain; Olivier fell asleep in the second half, to the dismay of the Queen; and Ben Travers hit the nail on the head for the bitter ex-dramaturg when he observed that 'If they had to open the theatre with a thoroughly rotten play, why couldn't they choose a thoroughly rotten English play?' Tynan summed up what was felt by most people present. 'What a disaster! But will the press record it as such?'[88]

Tynan was now wounded, marginalised and sicker than ever. This was the last diary entry that he made as a resident of England. Three days later, in a desperate search for a kinder climate for his lungs, he flew to California – much to Peter Hall's undoubted delight.

The relocation to the States was the culmination of a two-and-a-half-year fight against worsening health, writer's block and bouts of depression. The immediate months after his departure from the National were a gloomy period. Two diary entries for 1974 testify to his dismal spirits and mounting debts:

> Outlook bleak on all my fronts – the film (out of which I *insanely* and *cravenly* let Kathleen talk me two years ago) seems to be a receding possibility – I can't find the remaining $150,000 necessary to complete the budget of $500,000. (The last time I remember feeling *confident* was two years ago when I returned from Egypt. Now, assurance corroded, energy depleted, would I be capable of directing the film even if the money was there?) The Reich book is hopelessly blocked: I'm stuck halfway through, and have lost control of my material (as well as interest in it). This carries with it debts to publishers and *The New Yorker* in excess of £25,000, and assurance of feminine approbation.[89]

This introspection continued the following month:

> What is my current profession? Drama critic: not since 1963. Impresario: not since *Oh! Calcutta!* four years ago. Nabob of National Theatre: not since last December. Journalist: virtually extinct. Film director: untested (at forty-seven). Author: blocked since January. Thus I have no active professional identity at all – a sepulchral prospect on which to wake up every morning. Were I to commit suicide, I would merely be killing someone who had already – to many intents and purposes – ceased to exist. These grim reflections have had a markedly depressing effect on my libido. Sex in such a context seems as trivial as reading comics in a cancer ward. (Have today decided to leave some money to 'Nicole': told K. as much, and was relieved when she received the news without resentment).[90]

What he most regretted was the loss of a '*stance*, an attitude, what Eliot called in a letter to Lytton Strachey, 'the core of it – the *tone*' in his writing. 'I used to have a sign by my desk: "Be light, stinging, insolent and melancholy." But I am no longer any of these things, except melancholy.'[91]

The publication of *The Sound of Two Hands Clapping* in 1975, a disparate collection of profiles of, amongst others, Lenny Bruce, Marlene Dietrich and Eric Morecambe (whom he termed High Definition Performers); accounts of National Theatre rehearsals (*The Recruiting Officer* and Olivier's great *Othello*); and essays on pornography ('One inalienable right binds all mankind together – the right of self-abuse')[92]

provided another reminder to the world of his talent as a writer, even if he continued to feel that his own country now viewed him as a useful punchbag. Lavishly
praised in the US – Jack Richardson called it a 'taut, intelligent, sharply written book
that should prove once and for all that critics can be just as delightful in their enthusiasms as they can be in their aversions'[93] – it was found less palatable in Britain.
Tynan was now a victim of his causes. John Osborne's play, *The End of Me Old Cigar*,
which opened in January 1975, was particularly wounding, because of its portrait of
a 'lilac-trousered Oxford trendy with a passion for inflicting dangerously painful
spankings'.[94] Osborne had always had an erratic attitude to Tynan, alternating
periods of deep friendship with cruel antipathy. Tynan had finally fallen out with
him in 1971, describing him as a 'friendless and mean-spirited man who feeds on
hostility and only feels fully alive when he is hating and hated',[95] after Osborne
had abused him and Olivier in the *Evening Standard*. Osborne had called Tynan 'the
archetypal Oxford clever dick'.[96] But these snide attacks still hurt, especially as the
symptoms of his emphysema were now flaring up with ever increasing frequency.
The summer of 1975 was a trial – 'In a way it is like living with Elaine in the bad
later years. After a week of furious activity (sleepless with coughing, every breath
during the day drawn in expectation of a cough) there will be a tapering off, enough
to fill me with thanksgiving: at which point another night of paroxysms will rack
me'[97] – and the climate of England seemed to make him more susceptible to colds
and infections. Kathleen might have been 'appalled'[98] to see him still smoking, but
there were few other consolations left to him.

In the autumn of 1975 Tynan was commissioned by the *New York Times* to write
about the current state of the Berliner Ensemble, and he travelled to Berlin to revisit
his favourite company. It was a sad reacquaintance. The theatre was like a 'haunted
house – part enslaved to, and part trying to break away from, his great ghost' and
nothing had taken Brecht's place in European theatre for nearly two decades.[99]
Despite the dispiriting discovery that the Ensemble had failed to follow Brecht's
maxim of the need for constant reinvention, and the debilitating emphysema, which
made 'walking a block in cold weather as exhausting as running half a mile used
to be, twenty years ago'(not that Tynan would have run anywhere),[100] the trip had
an invigorating effect. His stance had returned and he wanted to write. He also
received two tantalising offers from the US, a country that still seemed to respect
his achievements and potential. One was the offer of the post of drama critic of
New York magazine, and the other was a proposal from his much-loved former editor, William Shawn, to write six profiles a year for the *New Yorker* of between 4,000
and 10,000 words for $44,000.[101] On his return from Berlin, Tynan had begun to
think about the advisability of relocating to the US. It would be better for his
chances of earning contracts to help conquer his spiralling debts, might aid the

process of writing and would have a beneficial effect on his health. In early December he had contacted Shawn to inform him about the offer from the *New York* and say that he was giving serious thought to crossing the Atlantic again. He also tentatively enquired about the possibility of returning to the *New Yorker* as its drama critic.[102] Shawn replied that the post was likely to be filled by Brendan Gill for some time, but immediately made the suggestion of the profiles.

The two offers were received in December 1975 and Tynan spent the early New Year of 1976 weighing them up. There was only one real choice, however. Only Shawn could create the necessary mix of patience and prompting that would make the ailing Tynan produce the required work. Tynan communicated his acceptance on 19 January, thanking Shawn for such a generous offer and expressing delight that the plan allowed him 'a good deal of geographical mobility'. He would aim to arrive in the autumn.[103] In March he contacted Shawn with a list of possible subjects that included Harold Pinter, Tom Stoppard, Shirley MacLaine, Irving Lazar, Bob Kaufman, Peter Sellers, the ice-skater John Curry, Mel Brooks, George Burns, Johnny Carson (the number one choice), Robert de Niro and Ralph Richardson.[104] By the summer, he was having drinks with Richardson, and memorably captured the moment for his diary in a stylish manner that boded well for the project:

Drinks with Ralph Richardson, about whom I'm going to write a piece for *The New Yorker*. He gravely offers me his favourite drink – a large helping of gin, followed by a dash of Italian vermouth and a dash of French vermouth, topped off with a huge slug of vodka. He then sits down (in his stately Nash house overlooking Regent's Park) and says, 'I don't know what we're going to talk about. After all, where did we come from? Did you ever have visions of the place you came from before you were born? I did, when I was three years old, and I used to draw pictures of it. It looked like Mexico.' The man is a poet: who else would start a conversation like that? His voice reminds me of onion-skin, cf. The onion-skin image in *Peer Gynt*, R.R's great part, who peels himself down to what he hopes will be the kernel of himself, only to discover that the last onion-skin, when removed, leaves behind it nothing, or the transparent shell of prawns. I barely knew him before entering the room; when I left, after listening to an hour of his fantastic musings (and ingesting a steady flow of that murderous cocktail, which he replenished whenever the level fell more than an inch below the rim of the glass), I felt I had known him all my life.[105]

With his profiles, he was going back to the star-struck period of the late 1940s and early 1950s and his coruscating pen-portraits of *Persona Grata*. An unexpected offer in April to take over the repertory company in Leicester temporarily from

September during the eight-month sabbatical of Robin Midgley provoked further feelings of nostalgia:

> This is what I should be doing – what I always wanted to do until the dread morning in 1952 when I was fired by Fay Compton on the second day of direct-ing her at the Arts Theatre in *Les Parents Terribles*. Also the pay wouldn't be more than £125 a week. I shall turn the job down (having already accepted the job with *The New Yorker* for the same period), but I shan't congratulate myself on having done so.[106]

This debilitating sense that he had never achieved what he ought to have done would remain with him until his death.

There was one piece of unfinished business to which Tynan needed to devote himself before he finally cut his ties with England: the production of the successor to *Oh, Calcutta!*, *Carte Blanche*. By the mid-1970s the heady atmosphere of the post-censorship period had been replaced in the theatre by the feeling that more rigidly puritanical times lay ahead. The oil crisis had plunged several of the world's major economies into recession for the first time in ten years and the value of theatre to society was being questioned once again. The never-ending delays to the con-struction of the National Theatre, the succession of strikes that impeded progress and the ballooning cost of the whole project served as a metaphor for the indul-gence of theatre, in the eyes of its detractors. It was not a good time to mount another production of erotic sketches.

In January 1976, a jury acquitted Linda Lovelace's book, *Inside Linda Lovelace*, after the Director of Public Prosecutions had tried to prosecute the publishers for obscenity. Lovelace had been the star of *Deep Throat*, the smash-hit film about a woman whose clitoris is at the back of her throat, and who needs to perform oral sex to achieve sexual satisfaction. The news of the acquittal caused a furious back-lash in the press, and the *Times* ran a sulphurous leader headed 'The Pornography of Hatred' which shocked Tynan, since it 'singled me out as a writer who had him-self been "depraved and corrupted" by the pornography of cruelty, of the concen-tration camps, of rape and the rapist'. The offending section read as follows: 'Such pornography [as detailed in *Inside Linda Lovelace*] does deprave; indeed we can see that pornographers themselves have been depraved by such an exposure to the pornography of cruelty. (In last week's *Times Literary Supplement* Mr D.A.N. Jones analysed the development of Mr Kenneth Tynan's acceptance of cruelty [when reviewing *A View of the English Stage* and *The Sound of Two Hands Clapping*]; the process of corruption in a talented writer was precisely that of pornography.)[107]

Tynan expressed his dismay at this attack in his diary:

This flabbergasting charge has stunned me and inhibited all action since it appeared. I can hardly reply to it myself since it accuses me of having had my character perverted by exposure to pornography: independent witnesses are needed to attest that I'm not irreclaimably sunk in depravity. Letters from John Trevelyan and Eric Hobsbawm appear in my defence: but mud like this will stick.[108]

Although he finally secured a correction in May, when the paper stated that 'We did not intend to suggest, nor do we, that Mr Tynan condones rape and torture,'[109] it was another damaging attack on his reputation. But in his desire to avoid such publicity, Tynan was not always his own best friend. His decision to dress as Louise Brooks at a fancy-dress ball in May invited mockery and his ambitions for *Carte Blanche* took no account of the puritan backlash. Quite open in his desire for the audience to be 'sexually aroused without feeling either ashamed or manipulated', Tynan also had a more ambitious hope for this production than *Oh, Calcutta!* 'The audience should go out feeling freer, more relaxed, more intrigued, more informed, more tolerant and less guilty about sex than when it came in',[110] he argued, but this put an elevating patina on the show that it did not justify. Some of the proposed ideas were questionable – incest, flagellation, group sex – but the ultimate aim, to stage live sex on stage, would never survive a legal challenge. Michael White, the producer of *Oh, Calcutta!*, perhaps put off by the controversy generated by the *Times* leader, informed Tynan that he could not be involved until *Oh, Calcutta!* had finished its world-wide run,[111] so Tynan offered the script to another producer, Richard Pilbrow. Tynan, who had been thinking about possible sketches since the spring of 1975, was reinvigorated by this immersion in 'practical' creativity. In June, he tried – without success – to interest Pilbrow in reviving the idea of the erotic film script and he was moved to provide in his diary a positive justification for his interest in such projects:

> The millionaire hero of Terry Southern's *The Magic Christian* says that his life's ambition is to 'make things hot for people'. For my part, I enjoy *testing* people – exposing them to ideas/experiences that will for them reassess the values by which they live, either politically, theatrically or sexually. Hence *Oh, Calcutta!* and *Soldiers*: hence my penchant for disrupting suave dinner parties.[112]

The activity of his to which this description most keenly applies is the one that he leaves out – theatre criticism: his finest achievement.

The buzz that he gained from the preparations for the September opening of *Carte Blanche* and the planned move to the US was ended by a debilitating virus. He was so ill that on 4 July he had to enter Brompton Hospital, 'a ward full of ancient emphysema victims',[113] for a week. Things slightly improved in August, but he received a frightening reminder of his mortality when he met a fellow emphysema sufferer, Leonard Williams, while on holiday with Kathleen in Cornwall:

> Williams, at sixty-six, has had the disease for only two years: he is myself a few years hence. We exchange commiserations. He asks me whether I have trouble putting on weight, and speaks of a friend of his, dying of emphysema, who weighs barely six stone. This chills me. I thought my weight, steady at something like ten stone seven pounds, was a tribute to my diet (no sugar, no carbohydrates except in potatoes). I flattered myself that I was slender. I now see that I am simply wasting away. What I took as a source of pride has become a source of fear.[114]

He was now persuaded that it was essential that he move to a warmer climate.

The opening night of *Carte Blanche* took place on 30 September. Tynan had spent the previous weeks busying himself with the poster,[115] fighting to preserve one of his sketches, 'Triangle', which Pilbrow believed would 'drive people out of the theatre',[116] and battling against the constant coughing brought about by the strain and his emphysema. The reviews were, in his view, 'predictable', although several, having got wind of his imminent departure for the US, were particularly nasty. Under a quite dreadful picture of a haggard, heavy-lidded and painfully gaunt Tynan, in a crumpled suit and with two blondes on his arm, Jack Tinker of the *Daily Mail* sharpened his knife:

> I was vaguely saddened to witness an admired intellect like Mr Kenneth Tynan's going through its menopause crisis in public . . . Imagine him believing that this silly venture could raise the standards of eroticism (I paraphrase his previous statements) before he grabs the loot and beats a swift retreat from our shores. The only contribution it makes to erotica is that most of the sketches spell out in tediously witless detail the sort of four-letter fantasies one could not hope to read on a lavatory wall without getting arrested for loitering.[117]

Although Tynan made a half-hearted defence of the production – 'The reviews may be bad,' admitted a breathless Mr Tynan, 'but they are infinitely better than *Oh! Calcutta!*. I think we have made progress',[118] business was good and he was optimistic that the show would run well[119] – the level of vituperation merely confirmed the wisdom of going into exile. Having let their London home, Kathleen departed with the children for Los Angeles on 4 October, with Tynan intending to follow her at the end of the month after the opening of the National Theatre.

Recovering from jet lag in the Santa Monica house that Kathleen had rented, Tynan soaked up the sun in a temperature exceeding 90 degrees farenheit. 'What have I done – more ominously, what am I going to *have* to do to deserve this?',[120] he asked in his diary. Within a week of arriving in California, he had jetted off to New York to see Ralph Richardson appear with John Gielgud in *No Man's Land*. The sudden change in temperature was painful for his lungs, but he conducted a second helpful interview over lunch with Richardson, and garnered further material for his profile from Gielgud. The change of country appeared to have a beneficial effect not just on his health, but on his desire to write. It also revived his appetite for sado-masochistic sex. At the end of December, he visited an 'enema clinic' advertising 'spankable girls', which he turned into an amusing anecdote:

> The sweetheart assigned to me turned out to be a huge black girl built like a Watsui warrior with an Afro hairdo like a geodesic dome. She was under the impression that I wanted to wrestle with her, and opened the conversation menacingly informing me that she cycled twenty miles to work every day and twenty miles back home. I swallowed hard and went through the motions of putting her over my knee, but it was about as enticing as spanking Hong Kong. (Her buttocks were like black marble.) Apart from anything else, I have never derived any pleasure from spanking black girls: it conflicts with my belief in civil liberties.[121]

The frenetic burst of activity for his *New Yorker* profiles continued into 1977. A visit to the University of Santa Barbara, which was holding a Stoppard festival where Stoppard himself gave a lecture, was followed by the completion and publication of the Richardson piece in February. Of the five profiles that he was to finish – and which were to be published in book form as *Show People* in 1979 – this was the one that drew most closely on his personal immersion in English theatre since the 1940s. In his introduction to *Show People* Tynan explained that he had spent much of his life as 'a literary sprinter, writing thousand-word reviews of plays and movies', but he had also aspired to be 'a middle-distance man', and the pieces that followed were his 'latest efforts in the genre'.[122] This greater space permitted the profiles to be wide-ranging, witty and informative, as well as containing shafts of provocation that recalled his finest theatre criticism. 'At Three Minutes Past Eight You Must Dream' starts with a barb against Pinter's *No Man's Land* ('Whether the play is more than a cerebral game is a decision that will have to wait until we see it performed by second-rate actors')[123] and then, echoing his earlier diary entry, freewheels through Richardson's voice ('the vocal equivalent of onionskin writing paper – suave, crackling and resonant');[124] his regret at turning down *Waiting for Godot* in 1955; the differences between Olivier and Gielgud; the notion of Richardson as the 'Average Man'; Tynan's alcoholic interview the previous June ('Three things are known about Sir Ralph's relationship with alcohol. One: He enjoys it. Two: On working days he restricts himself, until the curtain falls, to a couple of glasses of wine, taken with luncheon. Three: He is never visibly drunk');[125] a survey of his life; a couple of hilarious anecdotes about Richardson's legendary clumsiness; Gielgud's reflections on his colleagues; Tynan's November luncheon at the Algonquin hotel; and a description of an interview with the chat show host, Russell Harty, of which the actor took complete control. This picaresque approach, interweaving personal anecdotes, interviews and stage incidents is immensely beguiling. Tynan even provides some contemporary venom by criticising Hall's (eventually aborted) plan to transfer plays from the National Theatre to the commercial sector, with the director and cast garnering a large cut of any profits. It was a 'profitable operation for all concerned – though there were purists who doubted whether the true function of a national theatre was to stage commercial productions for quick moneymaking transfers to the West End',[126] he laconically observed. Needless to say, Tynan was one of those purists. His dislike of Hall had not abated.

The Richardson profile was a triumph, but already the demons were beginning to close in on him again. Following a trip back to London to interview Olivier for another *New Yorker* article (never completed), Tynan travelled on to Madrid, where he met up again with 'Nicole'. What promised to be a pleasant interlude – no matter how distressing it must have been for Kathleen – turned into a nightmare, when he caught flu and was confined to bed for a week. He was already behind with his next *New Yorker* profile, had no income and was allowing debts to pile up back in Los Angeles. The Tynans had immediately joined the Hollywood set on their arrival in Santa Monica, and were regularly invited to the smartest parties (Gore Vidal's, at the end of January, included Paul Newman, Bianca Jagger, Johnny Carson, Billy Wilder, Tony Richardson and Christopher Isherwood).[127] He was prized as much for his repartee as for his contacts and store of scintillating and wicked anecdotes, but he was living beyond his means. He also went to see Dr Elsie Giorgi, who concluded that his lung tissue was being destroyed by a rare genetic deficiency and that this process was being accelerated by his addiction to nicotine.

Unsurprisingly, he found work on the subsequent profiles difficult. He optimistically reassured Shawn that he would receive the Stoppard piece by mid-March, the one on Johnny Carson at the end of April, Mel Brooks by June and the hoped-for Olivier and John Curry at some unspecified period.[128] The reality was a crippling writer's block, brought about by being 'cut off from audience reaction'[129] and the agonies of trying to give up smoking. A test at UCLA confirmed his enzyme deficiency and he was now confronted with an impossible dilemma:

> Now I can do almost anything without smoking, except write. Thus if I write as I have always written – cigarette in hand or mouth, it is likely that I shall die relatively soon. On the other hand, if I do not write, I shall be broke (at present I have $300 in the bank, an overdraft in excess of £5000 in London).[130]

Writing had never seemed such an obligation before. To add to his misery, he now wanted to return to England, having decided that Roxana and Matthew, who had been born in 1975, would be better educated there, but this conflicted with Kathleen's desire to remain in Los Angeles. As it was, the children remained in America, where they were sent to private school and had a succession of nannies. 'Matthew and I had a pretty ideal childhood,' Roxana recalls. 'Our experience of our parents' relationship was also pretty good, at least while we were very little. Things got rocky later on, but we were largely insulated from the worst of it. Unlike Tracy who had a very different experience.'[131] Kathleen was now becoming interested in scriptwriting as a career and would shortly begin the screenplay of her book on Agatha Christie, called *Agatha*. Later in the summer, when Dustin Hoffman agreed to star in the film, Tynan candidly confessed to 'a pang of chagrin about my own film and all those years of still unforgotten frustration'.[132] There was also the question of the tax bill he would be landed with, if he returned to England before April 1978.[133] He stayed put.

Several tactics were employed to break the blockage on the Stoppard article. In May 1977, he took a cruise with Kathleen from New Orleans to Cuba, briefly stopping off in Havana and reminiscing about Hemingway and his battles with SISS in 1963. He also became ever more preoccupied with pornography, a hobby graphically illustrated in his diaries.[134] Eventually in July, he completed a 28,000-word piece and sent it off to Shawn. The kind, generous, patient editor was so delighted that he sent Tynan, whom he knew to be ailing, a cheque for three times the agreed fee, $22,000. 'Stunned' and 'overwhelmed' was how Tynan recorded his reaction to this magnificent gesture,[135] yet Shawn was aware that his writer was producing his finest prose for fifteen years.

While the Stoppard profile was in press, Tynan began his third project, on Mel Brooks. A pattern was now emerging – a subject was chosen, research undertaken and then writer's block hit, painfully followed by the agonies of completion, a brief sense of satisfaction before the wheel began to turn again. Kathleen travelled to London in August, during which time Tynan was almost caught in a vice raid on a house where he was spanking a prostitute.[136] As always, he seemed quite able to separate his sexual escapades from his emotional attachment to Kathleen, declaring shortly after this incident that 'No matter what happens, we are the centre of each other's lives. In her absence, I am Saturn without its rings, a planet of leaden melancholy.'[137] She felt the marriage to be an increasing strain, however, and rows became the norm.[138]

The Stoppard profile was published in the *New Yorker* in December 1977. For all Tynan's worries that Stoppard had stolen his glory by writing about his meeting with Czech dissidents for the *New York Review* the previous July,[139] it was another literary high for him. By continuing the fragmentary approach of the Richardson profile, he managed to analyse Stoppard's work, contextualise his life and suggest a significant and highly relevant contemporaneous link with Václav Hável. Drawing on his unique vantage point as the pre-eminent observer of new wave drama, he divided playwrights into the hairy men who had been 'heated, embattled and socially committed' (Osborne, Arden and Wesker) and the smooth men, who were 'cool, apolitical stylists' (Pinter, Orton, Ayckbourn, Hampton, Gray and Stoppard).[140] An account of Stoppard keeping wicket for Pinter's cricket team, complete with an analysis of Pinter's facial expressions ('One of them, his serious mask, suggests a surgeon or a dentist on the brink of making a brilliant diagnosis')[141] elided with a persuasive thesis that Stoppard's world view was essentially conservative. The survey of his career was peppered with quotations from unperformed plays, to which Tynan had access; incisive analyses of his successes; and personal recollections from Tynan's period as the dramaturg at the National Theatre. His confession that Ronald Bryden's review of *Rosencrantz and Guildenstern are Dead* at the 1966 Edinburgh Festival had encouraged him to suggest a transfer of the play to the National provided a further rare example, to go with Hobson's review of *The Birthday Party*, of a lone critic helping to make a playwright's career.

The brilliance of the profile lies in the way that Tynan manages to conflate the life and careers of both Stoppard and Hável, the Czech dissident playwright, with whom Stoppard shared a country of birth. Hável had, in Tynan's view, given 'Absurdism a human face, together with a socially critical purpose',[142] but his career had been disrupted by the accession of the hard-line Communist regime that had replaced Dubček's more benign rule in 1968. As Stoppard became progressively more interested in exposing the totalitarian repression of Eastern Bloc regimes, which led to his play *Every Good Boy Deserves Favour*, Hável was being subjected to intimidation and persecution. In 1974, when Stoppard's third major work, *Travesties*, was premièred, Hável was reduced to stacking beer barrels as a way of sustaining his family, and worse was to follow in 1977, when he was imprisoned for being a spokesman for Charter 77, the Czech human rights movement. Both writers were fiercely committed to preserving free speech, but from very different perspectives. Tynan ended the profile with the claim that Stoppard had come to see Hável as his 'mirror image' and a description of the playwright's trip to Czechoslovakia, where he was eventually able to meet his counterpart for five or six hours. The article then deliberately peters out, for there had been no comfortable resolution to Hável's plight while Tynan was writing. The meeting of minds and dramatists was a brief flicker of hope in a totalitarian context.

Tynan felt far less optimistic about his own life. The gloom of Christmas 1977, when cheques began to bounce owing to an accounting error by his secretary, was temporarily alleviated by more approbation (and a cheque for $15,000) from Shawn for his profile of Johnny Carson. His overdraft in London had risen to £5,100 and he only had $600 in the bank in LA.[143] The more he tried to divert himself from this stark financial reality, with trips to Madrid to conduct research and team up with 'Nicole' or to see the bulls at the Mexican border town, Mexicali, with Kathleen, the more he exacerbated his monetary crisis. His favourite annual game, he now admitted, was 'planning the summer holidays'.[144]

Watching television in January, he came across another screening of *Pandora's Box*, the Louise Brooks film that had so intrigued him in June 1972. This actress, now in her seventies and living alone in Rochester, New York, seemed to him to be the most beautiful woman who had ever appeared on film. Shawn – also a fan – responded enthusiastically to the idea that he write a profile about her and Tynan contacted Brooks in February. After much hesitation, the reclusive actress agreed, provided that he write only a short tribute to her career in films, ask her nothing about her private life and give her the chance to vet the manuscript. They were to meet in May 1978.

That Tynan was entranced by her is evident in his delicate homage. Following his usual template, this profile is part career survey, part self-reflexive account of the interview process (she opens the door 'wearing a woollen bed jacket over a pink night-gown, and holding herself defiantly upright by means of a sturdy metal cane with four rubber-tipped prongs'),[145] and part attempt to draw subtle threads between interviewer and interviewee. This was easier with Louise Brooks than with his other subjects. Like him, she felt isolated and partly unfulfilled. Her attitude to sex was open and unselfconscious (although her account of her abuse as a child is suspiciously peremptory), and she was full of anecdotes and reminiscences about past glory days. Tynan compressed the three days he spent talking with her into one session, and the piece leaves one with the sense that it is a valediction forbidding mourning for both the interviewer and the interviewee. Her self-imposed exit from Hollywood had been a safety mechanism, as much as a deliberate choice, in the same way that his relocation to California had been essential for his personal well-being.

The Brooks profile was the last to be published in the *New Yorker* and in *Show People*, and represented Tynan's final published work. It was not intended to be that way at all. The summer holiday he had so looked forward to was an utter disaster. He had ambitiously (and naïvely) intended to spend some time with 'Nicole' in a villa in Mojácar and then have a family holiday, driving through Spain, but the fates disapproved. He lost his luggage, hired a faulty car, burst a blood vessel in his penis having energetic sex with 'Nicole', was robbed of his passport, credit cards and travellers' cheques, and then suffered a hernia after a prolonged bout of coughing. 'Nicole' was meant to depart before Kathleen arrived, but she was unable to get a seat on the plane, and had to stay with friends close by. No wonder the atmosphere was 'electric'.

Tynan, now 'immobilised by lung problems', was unable to drive, so the family set off with Kathleen behind the wheel. Throughout their trip, she felt he was talking 'gibberish', but he remembered nothing. As they waited to return to California, Tynan was mugged for a second time, and, to cap it all, the suitcase containing his *New Yorker* research and the 32,000-word manuscript of his profile of Mel Brooks was lost. He was eventually reunited with it, after it had made a detour via Rio de Janeiro.[146]

The gallows humour in his relation of this episode is amusing, but there is little doubt that it marked a significant staging post in his decline. The sexual injury he had sustained deprived him of one of his chief forms of pleasure, and he gloomily envisaged the headlines, if news of his inadequate erectile potential seeped out to the London press: 'MAN WHO SAID FUCK CAN'T FUCK'.[147] The degenerative symptoms of emphysema now meant that he required oxygen all night and he had a portable machine for use in the daytime, although none of this was as damaging to his morale as Olivier's attitude towards Tynan's proposed book. Seeking ever more lucrative projects to earn an income, Tynan had decided to write a 'belated act of thanksgiving' that focused on Olivier's post-war career. Enthused by the idea, he signed a contract with Simon and Schuster, but, concerned by the news that Olivier had reacted angrily to a piece in the *New York Times* which had published personal details about his marriage to Vivien Leigh, Tynan wrote to Olivier in April 1979, to beg him not to prevent '*all* attempts to capture you in print'.[148] The project was essential for his personal survival, as he doubted that he had more than one full-length book left within him.

Tynan's anxiety was justified. Olivier, planning to write his own autobiography, furious at the misrepresentation of his earlier life by intrusive interviewers and irritated by a mistaken report in the *Evening News* which implied that Kathleen had stated that Olivier had chosen her husband to write the definitive biography, forbade his friends from speaking to Tynan and refused to co-operate in any way. It was shattering news. The sacrifices that Tynan had undertaken for him had all been forgotten, but, worse, the personal breach seemed insurmountable. Tynan had no alternative but to return the advance, although he made several desperate efforts to get to the bottom of the problem. 'I cannot imagine,' he wrote 'why you seem so anxious to avoid being perpetuated in print by a colleague who has written about you with greater admiration than any other living critic.'[149] No satisfactory response was given to the dying man. It seemed an unforgivable betrayal.

Saddled with debts ($75,000 by January 1980); forced to move temporarily to Puerto Vallarta, Mexico, to avoid tax on the advance for the Olivier book; and with his hands now shaking so much that he could barely write,[150] Tynan made one last stupendous effort of will to sort out his affairs. Desperate to conceal the true nature of his health, he decided to write his autobiography. This was a project – oft mooted but never started – which at least he could control. He began to send out letters in early 1980 to friends and acquaintances requesting their memories and anecdotes about him. He told Adrian and Celia Mitchell that he was 'trying to walk the thin line that separates candour from self-pity', but there was an inevitable air of leave-taking about the whole project. *Show People* was published in the US in January to enormous acclaim, the *New York Times* hailing it as simply 'glittering',[151] but there was no possibility now of similar work being produced. The English press began to sniff around for information about his demise, and a report in the William Hickey column of the *Daily Express* made him send a desperate letter to his doctor, Elsie Giorgi, asking her to supply his lawyers with a statement that he was still 'physically capable of functioning as a writer',[152] since his publishers Lippincrott and Crowell and Weidenfeld and Nicolson felt that he was no longer an acceptable risk. Alerted to the fact that he was now seriously ill, Elaine re-established contact by sending him a copy of her biography of Peter Finch, *Finch, Bloody Finch*. It was their first direct communication for several years and Tynan was gratified that 'something like a normal relationship was being resumed', and by her reference to long-distant happiness. 'I know what you mean by Paris and always will,'[153] he wrote back. She also initiated a letter from another figure from his 1950s life, Harold Hobson. This kind man had always valued Tynan as a person, no matter how much Tynan had eclipsed him as a critic or shocked him with his very different set of moral values. Hobson generously observed that Tynan had almost always defeated him in battle and viewed their rivalry as 'part of some legendary Homeric past'. Tynan wrote back effusively: 'I certainly miss our duelling days – The trouble with our successors is that nothing seems *at stake* for them.'[154] The other key figure from that period was William Shawn. He alone in Tynan's professional life had stuck by him, and Tynan contacted him at the end of May to reassure him that his doctors had found a suitable rehabilitation programme and that he would be beginning his profile of Olivier when he could obtain 'a long period of peace in which to finish the writing'.[155] Peace came two months later on 26 July 1980, when he died in St John's Hospital, Santa Monica. He was fifty-three.

The paradox of Tynan's life is that he spent the greater part believing that the only way in which he could make a positive contribution to the development of theatre in Britain was by practical immersion in it. Humiliated by being fired as the director of *Les Parents terribles* by Alec Clunes, brusquely dispensed with as the Artistic Director at Lichfield and mocked for his brief appearance in Guinness's *Hamlet*, Tynan spent the rest of his life yearning to make up for these bitterly felt failures. His move into National Theatre bureaucracy and the production of *Soldiers, Oh, Calcutta!* and *Carte Blanche* were part of this cathartic process, and yet for all his frenetic and unsuccessful attempts to launch theatrical projects – so draining and depressing in the miserable last five years of his life – it was as an observer rather than as a participant that he shaped theatrical trends to a degree that has been surpassed by no other critic in Britain. This should come as little surprise, given the unique quality of his writing, the reverence with which his reviews were read between 1952 and 1963 and the copious testimony from theatre professionals active in that period that he helped usher in the decisive change from drawing-room drama to plays of social realism, but the fact that it does come as a surprise to many says as much about the relatively low status of the theatre critic in Britain (a status that is much higher in continental Europe), as it does about the after-life of Tynan in the twenty years since his death. For, quite simply, the focus on his life until now has – perhaps understandably – foregrounded the flagellation and the star worship at the expense of the analysis and crusading. When Kathleen Tynan's biography of her husband, *The Life of Kenneth Tynan*, first appeared in 1987, Tynanistas were mesmerised by the account of their exciting and turbulent marriage (it was also a skilful and compelling narrative). More recently, Elaine Dundy's autobiography, *Life Itself!* (2001), drew comment for its painful sections on their sexual incompatibility, and, most significantly, the publication of the *Diaries* (2001), revealing Tynan's profoundly depressing emphasis on his deteriorating health and sexual prowess during the last ten years of his life, has inevitably reinforced his image as the exemplum *par excellence* of 1960s permissiveness gone wrong.

In 2003 there is sufficient distance from his life for us to redress the balance. Tynan's enormous contribution to the evolution of post-war theatre far exceeded his abortive attempts to stage successful productions. The body of work he has left behind – a collection of 300- and 800-word reviews, which encapsulate an era and retain their ability to engage and provoke – more than matches Hazlitt's output or Shaw's obsessions. That they are still out of print is a scandal more telling than any production of *Soldiers* and their reissue is surely an urgent project. Bertolt Brecht wanted his audience to act on what they saw in the theatre: Tynan wanted his readership to act on what they read about it. The fact that they did – be they audience members, theatre professionals, playwrights, actors or fellow journalists eager to debate the points he had raised – is the true memorial to a man who could never quite grasp at his death the *true* achievement of his life.

Notes

Introduction

1 Michael Billington, 'Spanks for the Memory', *Guardian*, 11/11/2000.
2 Harold Hobson, 'Not Much Beyond Our Ken', *Guardian*, 29/7/80.

Chapter 1: A Gift for Performance

1 Elaine Dundy, *Life Itself!* (London, Virago Press, 2001), p.108.
2 Harold Clurman, *All People Are Famous* (New York, Harcourt, Brace, Jovanovich, 1974), p.174.
3 Kathleen Tynan, *The Life of Kenneth Tynan* (London, Methuen, 1988), p.23.
4 Ibid., p.25.
5 Tynan to Askey, 12/3/40, *Kenneth Tynan: Letters*, ed. Kathleen Tynan (London, Weidenfeld and Nicolson, 1994), pp.4–5.
6 Tynan to Holland, 27/12/43, ibid., pp.23–4.
7 Tynan to Holland, 19/2/44, ibid., p.37.
8 James Harding, *Agate* (London, Methuen, 1986), p.180.
9 James Agate, *The Contemporary Theatre, 1944 and 1945* (London, Harrap, 1946), p.54.
10 Tynan to Holland, 4/3/44, *Letters*, 1994, p.39.
11 Tynan to Holland, 13/3/44, ibid., pp.41–2.
12 Tynan to Holland, 9/12/44, ibid., pp.54–6.
13 Tynan to Holland, 9/1/45, ibid., p.59.
14 Tynan to Holland, 22/1/45, ibid., pp.60–1.
15 Tynan to Holland, 31/1/45, ibid., p.64.
16 Tynan to Holland, 3/3/45, ibid., p.69.
17 Tynan to Holland, 31/1/45, ibid., p.64.
18 Tynan to Holland, 17/2/45, ibid., p.66.
19 Ibid.
20 Tynan to Holland, 3/3/45, ibid., p.68.
21 Tynan to Holland, 19/3/45, ibid., p.71.
22 Tynan to Holland, 10/5/45, ibid., pp.71–4.

23   Tynan to Holland, 2/6/45, ibid., p.75.

24   Tynan to Holland, 5/6/45, ibid., p.77.

25   Tynan to Holland, 20/6/45, ibid., pp.80–1.

26   Tynan to Holland, 20/6/45, ibid., p.83.

27   James Agate, *Ego 8* (London, Harrap, 1946), p.71.

28   Godfrey Smith, 'Critic Kenneth Tynan Has Mellowed But Is Still England's Stingingest Gadfly', *New York Times*, 15/12/65.

29   Tynan to Agate, 25/7/45, *Letters*, 1994, p.84.

30   Tynan to Agate, 30/7/45, ibid., p.86.

31   Tynan to Holland, 8/10/45, ibid., p.89.

32   Tynan to Holland, 30/10/45, ibid., p.95.

33   Tynan to Holland, 21/11/45, ibid., p.97.

34   Tynan to Whittle, 15/12/45, ibid., p.100.

35   Tynan to Rowe-Dutton, September 1947, ibid., p.143.

36   30/5/47.

37   James Agate, *Ego 9* (London, Harrap, 1948), p.309.

38   *Isis*, 19/11/47.

39   Kathleen Tynan, 1988, p.70.

40   Ronald Harwood, *Sir Donald Wolfit CBE* (London, Secker and Warburg, 1971), p.227.

41   E-mail to the author, 19/11/02.

42   Kathleen Tynan, 1988, p.74.

43   Ibid., p.78.

44   "'First Quarto' Hamlet', *Christian Science Monitor*, 22/1/49.

45   Tynan to Harry James, 17/8/49, *Letters*, 1994, p.170.

46   Kathleen Tynan, 1988, p.82.

47   David Thomson, *Rosebud: The Story of Orson Welles* (London, Little, Brown, 1996), p.303.

48   Kenneth Tynan, *He That Plays the King* (London, Longmans, 1950), p.31.

49   Ibid., p.27.

50   Ibid., p.28.

51   Ibid., p.27.

52   Ibid., p.29.

53   Ibid., p.31.

54   Ibid., p.17.

55   Ibid., p.46.

56   Ibid., p.36.

57   Ibid., pp.42–3.

58   Ibid., p.143.

59   Ibid., p.244.

60   *Times Literary Supplement*, 27/6/51.

61   Dundy, 2001, p.20.

62   Ibid., pp.101–2.

63   Ibid., pp.104–5.

64   Ibid., p.106.

65   Ibid., p.109.

66   Ibid., p.112.

67   Ibid., p.111.

68   'Calypso for the Bride', *Daily Mail*, 26/1/51.

69   Dundy, 2001, p.113.

70   Ibid., p.114.

71 Wendy and J.C. Trewin, *The Arts Theatre London: 1927–1981* (London, Society for Theatre Research, 1986), p.12.
72 Tynan, *He That Plays the King*, 1950, p.141.
73 Wendy and J.C. Trewin, 1986, p.37.

Chapter 2: The Necessary Side

1   Tynan, *He That Plays the King*, 1950, p.23.
2   Ibid., p.17.
3   Roy Jenkins, *Churchill* (London, Macmillan, 2001), p.798.
4   Ibid., p.792.
5   Kenneth O. Morgan, *Britain since 1945*, (Oxford, Oxford University Press, 2001), p.29.
6   Ibid., p.49.
7   Peter Lewis, *The Fifties* (London, The Cupid Press, 1989), p.9.
8   Ibid., p.10.
9   Morgan, 2001, p.95.
10 Peter Clark, *Sixteen Million Readers: Evening Newspapers in the UK* (London, Holt, Rinehart and Winston, 1981), p.34.
11 Ben Pimlott, *The Queen* (London, HarperCollins, 1996), p.132.
12 Ibid., p.121.
13 Ibid., p.160.
14 Christopher Fry, *An Experience of Critics* (London, Perpetua, 1952), pp.38–40.
15 Irving Wardle, *Theatre Criticism* (London, Routledge, 1992), p.127.
16 Fry, 1952, p.42.
17 Ibid., p.53.
18 Ibid., pp.35–6.
19 *Daily Sketch*, 24/10/51.
20 Fry, 1952, p.47.
21 Ibid., pp.57–8.
22 Harold Hobson, *Indirect Journey* (London, Weidenfeld and Nicolson, 1978), p.49.
23 Ibid., p.44.
24 Ibid., p.71.
25 Ibid., p.73.
26 Ibid.
27 *Sunday Times*, 14/5/39.
28 Hobson, 1978, p.1.
29 See Harding, 1986, p.217.
30 'Film *Hamlet* Assayed', *Christian Science Monitor*, 24/5/48.
31 Interview with the author, 10/7/91.
32 Harold Hobson, Philip Knightley and Leonard Russell, *The Pearl of Days* (London, Hamish Hamilton, 1972), p.276.
33 Harding, 1986, p.217.
34 Interview with the author, 10/7/91.
35 Hobson, 1978, p.217.
36 Ibid., p.211.
37 Interview with the author, 10/7/91.
38 'Sartre Resartus', *Sunday Times*, 20/6/48.
39 'A Welcome Influence', *Sunday Times*, 14/3/48.
40 Tynan archive, British Library.

41 Harold Hobson, *Theatre in Britain* (Oxford, Oxford University Press, 1984), p.157.

42 'Miss Vivien Leigh', *Sunday Times*, 13/11/49.

43 'Black Magic', *Sunday Times*, 13/3/49.

44 Tynan archive, British Library.

45 Lewis, 1989, p.11.

46 Alec Guinness, *Blessings in Disguise* (London, Penguin, 1996), p.33.

47 Dundy, 2001, p.119.

48 'Disaster', *Sunday Times*, 20/5/51.

49 'Religious Drama', *New Statesman*, 26/5/51.

50 'Guinness and Scotch', *Observer*, 20/5/51.

51 'At the Theatre', *Tatler*, 30/5/51.

52 'Alec Guinness as Hamlet', *Daily Telegraph*, 18/5/51.

53 'The Worst *Hamlet* I Have Ever Seen', *Evening Standard*, 18/5/51.

54 'The Monstrous Regiment of Critics', *Panorama*, June/July 1951.

55 26/6/73, *Kenneth Tynan: Diaries*, ed. John Lahr (London, Bloomsbury, 2001), p.144.

56 Letters, *Evening Standard*, 22/5/51.

57 Kathleen Tynan, 1988, p.93.

58 '*Hamlet* Re-visited', *Sunday Times*, 17/6/51.

59 'Is He Great? I Say No', *Evening Standard*, 29/5/51.

60 *Evening Standard*, 31/5/51.

61 Ibid.

62 Ibid.

63 *Evening Standard*, 2/7/51.

64 'The Lass Unparalleled', *Observer*, 13/5/51.

65 *Drama*, October 1980.

66 *Evening Standard*, 9/7/51.

67 *Evening Standard*, 11/7/51.

68 Dundy, 2001, pp.125–6.

69 Ibid., p.122.

70 Tynan to Beaverbrook, 16/7/51, *Letters*, 1994, pp.180–1.

71 Dundy, 2001, p.121.

72 Tynan, *He That Plays the King*, 1950, p.241.

73 'Matador', *Evening Standard*, 7/8/51.

74 *Evening Standard*, 18/7/51 and 2/8/51.

75 *Evening Standard*, 19/10/51.

76 Thomson, 1996, p.313.

77 Dundy, 2001, p.117.

78 Ibid., p.132.

79 *New York Times*, 29/1/52.

80 *Spectator*, 1/2/52.

81 Tynan to Beaton, 22/3/52, *Letters*, 1994, p.184.

82 Dundy, 2001, p.131.

83 'London Warmly Welcomes Renowned French Players', *Christian Science Monitor*, 6/10/51.

84 *Sunday Times*, 2/12/51.

85 'All-talking Priestley', *Evening Standard*, 16/5/52.

86 'Miss Baddeley Prefers To Take It Neat', *Evening Standard*, 20/6/52.

87 Sheridan Morley, *John G* (London, Hodder and Stoughton, 2001), pp.217–18.

88 *Evening Standard*, 13/6/52.

89 Gary O'Connor, *Ralph Richardson* (London, Hodder and Stoughton, 1982), p.172.
90 Clurman, 1974, p.175.
91 Sherek to Tynan, 19/6/52, Tynan archive, British Library.
92 Littler to Tynan, 20/8/52, ibid.
93 Littler to Tynan, 13/9/52, ibid.
94 'Death with Father', *Evening Standard*, 26/9/52.
95 Rattigan to Tynan, 4/9/52, Tynan archive, British Library.
96 Dundy, 2001, p.132. Details of Tynan's creative routine are found on pp. 131–2.
97 Ibid., p.132.
98 Kenneth Tynan, *Bull Fever* (London, Longmans, 1955), p.vii.
99 Ibid., p.134.
100 Ibid., p.viii.
101 Ibid., p.5.
102 Ibid., p.11.
103 Ibid., p.32.
104 Ibid., p.24.
105 Ibid., p.71.
106 Ibid., p.175.
107 Ibid., p.102.
108 Ibid., pp.124–5.
109 Ibid, pp.127–8.
110 'Mr Scofield Comes to the Rescue of Mr Morgan', *Evening Standard*, 5/9/52.
111 'And Now Tybalt', *Sunday Times*, 12/10/47.
112 'Catfish Row Sets the Heart Pounding', *Evening Standard*, 10/10/52.
113 Quoted by Peter Brook in *Harper's Bazaar*, October 1954.
114 'Hardly the People for This Lordly Address', *Evening Standard*, 5/12/52.
115 'Arden and Cornwall', *Observer*, 7/12/52.
116 *Times*, 4/12/52.
117 Fry, 1952, p.63.
118 11/10/52, *Letters*, 1994, p.187.
119 15/10/52, ibid., p.188.
120 Dundy, 2001, p.138.
121 *Evening Standard*, 3/7/53.
122 'The Martyrs of Hammersmith', *Evening Standard*, 2/1/53.
123 Tynan to Beaton, 1/1/53, *Letters*, 1994, p.190.
124 'It's Too Soon to Call Her a Star', *Evening Standard*, 19/5/53.
125 'A Few Sore Throats Would Do These Romans Good', *Evening Standard*, 27/2/53.
126 'Redgrave Stokes the Furnace', *Evening Standard*, 20/3/53.
127 'Cleopatra from Sloane Square', *Evening Standard*, 1/5/53.
128 'To the Flames! – and No Wonder', *Evening Standard*, 10/4/53.
129 Guinness to Tynan, 17/3/53, Tynan archive, British Library.
130 Kenneth Tynan, *Alec Guinness* (London, Rockliff, 1953), p.12.
131 Ibid., p.27.
132 Ibid.
133 Ibid., p.68.
134 Ibid., p.77.
135 Ibid., p.79.
136 Ibid., p.42.
137 Ibid., p.94.

138   Guinness to Tynan, 29/10/53, Tynan archive, British Library.
139   Kenneth Tynan, *Persona Grata* (London, Alan Wingate, 1953), p. iv.
140   'Greene Has Written the Best Play of its Generation', *Evening Standard*, 17/4/53.
141   Tutin to Tynan, 4/3/53, Tynan archive, British Library.
142   Scofield to Tynan, June 1953, ibid.
143   Komisarjevsky to Tynan, 10/7/53, ibid.
144   'Sir Ralph – the 4-D Character in a 3-D World', *Evening Standard*, 27/3/53.
145   'Defeat – for a Guy in the Critical Dodge', *Evening Standard*, 29/5/53.
146   'New York Musical', *Sunday Times*, 31/5/53.
147   *New Statesman*, 6/6/53.
148   *Evening Standard*, 15/5/53.
149   *Evening Standard*, 19/5/53.
150   *Evening Standard*, 25/5/53.
151   *Evening Standard*, 3/7/53.
152   *Evening Standard*, 7/7/53.
153   Curran to Tynan, 26/7/53, Tynan archive, British Library.
154   Clurman, 1974, p.175.
155   Dundy, 2001, p.144.
156   Anthony Sampson, 'Observing David Astor', *Observer*, 9/12/2001.
157   Ibid.
158   Tynan to Astor, 30/7/53, *Letters*, 1994, pp.197–8.
159   Dundy, 2001, p.144.
160   Franklin to Tynan, 11/1/80, Tynan archive, British Library.
161   'Introducing Kenneth Tynan . . .', *Daily Sketch*, 2/10/53.
162   'A Crown for the Master', *Daily Sketch*, 30/10/53.
163   'Commonsense and Cucumber', *Daily Sketch*, 11/12/53.
164   'A Vehicle Made for Two', *Daily Sketch*, 11/12/53.
165   'Commonsense and Cucumber', *Daily Sketch*, 11/12/53.
166   'King Lom Plays the Ace', *Daily Sketch*, 9/10/53.
167   'Three Nights by the Sea', *Daily Sketch*, 27/11/53.
168   'Panic in the Theatre', *Daily Sketch*, 18/12/53.
169   Anonymous, 19/3/54, Tynan archive, British Library.
170   'But Oh What a <u>Wicked</u> Fairy', *Daily Sketch*, 6/11/53.
171   Tynan, *Persona Grata*, 1953, p.15.
172   Ibid., pp.50–1.
173   Ibid., pp.44–5.
174   Ibid., p.75.
175   Dundy, 2001, p.124.
176   '100 Friends', *New York Times*, 18/7/54.
177   Cooke to Tynan, 15/2/54, Tynan archive, British Library.
178   Chevalier to Tynan, 13/11/53, ibid.
179   Dundy, 2001, p.145.
180   Darlington to Tynan, 30/12/54, Tynan archive, British Library.
181   Curran to Tynan, 2/1/54, ibid.
182   'What Happened to Love?', *Daily Sketch*, 1/1/54.
183   Dundy, 2001, p.150.
184   Ibid., p.149.
185   Ibid., pp.148–51.

Chapter 3: 1954–56: Loamshire

1 Morgan, 2001, p.111.

2 Jenkins, 2001, p.845.

3 Ibid., p.852.

4 Peter Clarke, *Hope and Glory* (London, Penguin, 1999), p.243.

5 *Times*, 29/6/53.

6 Jenkins, 2001, p.862.

7 Ibid., p.863.

8 R.A. Butler, *The Art of the Possible* (London, Penguin, 1971), p.173.

9 All 6/4/54.

10 *Punch*, April 1954.

11 Evelyn Shuckburgh, *Descent to Suez: Diaries 1951–6* (London, Weidenfeld and Nicolson, 1986), p.157.

12 *Observer*, 29/8/54.

13 'London Theaters Face Post-War Challenges', *Christian Science Monitor*, 28/5/55.

14 Dundy, p.151.

15 Tynan archive, British Library.

16 Kathleen Tynan, 1988, p.115.

17 *Observer*, 5/9/54.

18 Alan Brien, 'The Boy Wonder', *Truth*, 1/10/54.

19 Tynan to the Editor, *Truth*, 8/10/54.

20 *Observer*, 19/9/54.

21 'West End Apathy', *Observer*, 31/10/54.

22 'Resurrections', *Observer*, 3/10/54.

23 'A Welcome Influence', *Sunday Times*, 14/3/48.

24 'Dead Language', *Observer*, 21/11/54.

25 'Another Joan', *Observer*, 24/10/54.

26 'Winter Fuel', *Observer*, 26/12/54.

27 Reader's Report on *Our Ladies Meet*, 1952, Lord Chamberlain's Papers, British Library.

28 *Evening Standard*, 6/11/53.

29 See Michael Darlow, *Terence Rattigan* (London, Quartet Books, 2000), p.310.

30 The 1955 Samuel French Acting Edition of *Separate Tables* renamed the two plays *Table No. 1* and *Table No. 2*, 'according to the Author's wishes', p.iv. I have retained the unamended titles of the 3rd Hamish Hamilton edition of the play, since this was published two years later, in 1957.

31 13/1/55, Tynan archive, British Library.

32 'Versatility', *Observer*, 20/2/55.

33 'In Camera', *Observer*, 7/11/54.

34 Dundy, 2001, pp.159–60.

35 Ibid., p.160.

36 'Indirections', *Observer*, 12/12/54.

37 'Big Three', *Observer*, 9/1/55.

38 Dundy, 2001, p.171.

39 Ibid., p.172.

40 'Some Stars from the East', *Observer*, 26/6/55.

41 'A Pair of Kings', *Observer*, 23/1/55.

42 'Dimmed Debut', *Observer*, 3/7/55.

43 'Try Again', *Sunday Times*, 3/7/55.

44 'Brecht Drama in Britain', *Christian Science Monitor*, 23/7/55.

45 Jenkins, 2001, p.889.

46 Lord Moran, *Winston Churchill: The Struggle for Survival: 1945–60* (London, Constable, 1966), p.617.

47 Butler, 1971, p.176.

48 'Convalesence', *Observer*, 30/3/55.

49 'Prose on Top', *Observer*, 5/6/55.

50 'Versatility', *Observer*, 20/2/55.

51 *Observer*, 23/3/55.

52 Williams to Tynan, 23/11/54, Tynan archive, British Library.

53 Ronald Hayman, *Tennessee Williams* (New Haven, Yale University Press, 1993), p.154.

54 Dundy, 2001, p.162.

55 'Reassessment', *Observer*, 14/8/55.

56 Williams to Tynan, 19/6/55, Tynan archive, British Library.

57 Williams to Tynan, 2/7/55, ibid.

58 Williams to Tynan, 26/7/55, ibid.

59 Tynan, *Diaries*, 2001, 9/6/71, p.52.

60 Morley, 2001, p.267.

61 Donald Spoto, *Laurence Olivier* (London, HarperCollins, 1991), p.219.

62 Morley, 2001, p.269.

63 Butler, 1971, p.177.

64 'Arrivals and Departures', *Observer*, 24/4/55.

65 'Old Vic Revived', *Observer*, 1/5/55.

66 'Nonpareil', *Sunday Times*, 12/6/55.

67 'Fates and Furies', *Observer*, 12/6/55.

68 'Sea-Change', *Observer*, 19/6/55.

69 Welles to Tynan, Tynan archive, British Library.

70 Joan Plowright, *And That's Not All* (London, Weidenfeld and Nicolson, 2001), pp.28–9.

71 'Diminution', *Observer*, 29/5/55.

72 J.B. Priestley to Tynan, 9/6/55, Tynan archive, British Library.

73 'A Ring Full of Grace, Valor, Poise and Pride', *New York Times*, 3/6/55.

74 Alec Guinness to Tynan, 16/5/55, Tynan archive, British Library.

75 Kathleen Tynan, 1988, p.121.

76 Jack Reading, letter to the author, 10/10/97.

77 'Duet for Two Symbols', *Evening Standard*, 4/8/55.

78 *Daily Express*, 4/8/55.

79 'An Evening of Funny Obscurity', 4/8/55.

80 'Making a Name', 2/1/55.

81 'Something New', *Sunday Times*, 13/3/55.

82 'Tomorrow', *Sunday Times*, 7/8/55.

83 Samuel Beckett, letter to H.O. White, 10/10/1955, referred to in Deirdre Bahr, *Samuel Beckett: A Biography* (London, Jonathan Cape, 1990), p.480.

84 Harold Clurman to Tynan, 19/8/55, Tynan archive, British Library.

85 *Observer*, 13/3/55.

86 'Hindsight View', *Observer*, 15/7/58.

87 A.P. Herbert, *No Fine on Fun* (London, Arts Council, 1957), p.16.

88 Simon Trussler, *The Cambridge Illustrated History of British Theatre* (Cambridge, Cambridge University Press, 1994), p.303.

89   Kitty Black, *Upper Circle* (London, Methuen, 1984), p.154.

90   'Cash and Colour', *Observer*, 2/11/47.

91   Richard Huggett, *Binkie Beaumont: Éminence Grise of the West End 1933–1973* (London, Hodder and Stoughton, 1989), p.418.

92   'Papers relating to H.M. Tennent', RP 95/2363, Theatre Museum, London.

93   'Aldwych Theatre', *Times*, 13/10/49.

94   Quoted in Huggett, 1989, p.420.

95   'State Patronage of the Theater', *Christian Science Monitor*, 7/1/50.

96   *Southwark Cathedral Magazine*, 1949.

97   *Hansard* (London, HMSO, 1949), p.2086.

98   'Hindsight View', *Observer*, 2/11/47.

99   A. Moody, letter to the *Observer*, 4/9/55.

100   'Chamber of Horrors', *Observer*, 21/8/55.

101   'The Actor as Artist', *Christian Science Monitor*, 20/3/33.

102   'A Modern Play', *Sunday Times*, 21/8/55.

103   John Osborne, *Look Back in Anger* (London, Faber and Faber, 1986), p.15.

104   'Mme Feuillère', *Sunday Times*, 11/9/55.

105   Letter to the Editor: 'Edwige Feuillère', *Sunday Times*, 18/9/55.

106   'Passion's Slave', *Observer*, 18/9/55.

107   'Francomania', *Sunday Times*, 25/9/55.

108   'Post Mortem', *Observer*, 25/9/55.

109   Dundy, 2001, p.174.

110   Kathleen Tynan, 1988, p.127.

111   Neville Cardus to Tynan, 20/9/55, Tynan archive, British Library.

112   Dundy, 2001, p.175.

113   'Hindsight View', *Observer*, 15/7/56.

114   See *Observer*, 5/12/54 – 'This brilliant play [*The Lark*] lacks the body of a great Anouilh vintage, but only because it is a *pièce rosé*, the thrill of which lies in its bouquet, a wry chateau-bottled (ditto) fragrance ... Mr Paul Scofield's sulky elegance would have delighted Stendhal. The part is short and somewhat boorish; yet by his inner electricity Mr Scofield not only dominates the evening but also achieves pathos. Nothing in our theatre speaks more tellingly of grief than the broken music of this actor's voice.'

115   'King's Rhapsody', *Observer*, 11/12/55.

116   'The Russian Way', *Observer*, 27/11/55.

117   Tim Goodwin, *Britain's Royal National Theatre* (London, NT/Nick Hern Books, 1988), p.5.

118   Ibid., p.6.

119   Ibid., p.9.

120   'The Old Vic and the National Theatre', *Sunday Times*, 16/10/49.

121   'Payment Deferred', *Observer*, 1/1/56.

122   Gordon Craig to Tynan, April 1956, Tynan archive, British Library.

123   Dundy, 2001, pp.123–4.

124   'Art for Our Sake', *Observer*, 22/1/56.

125   'The Vice of Versing', *Observer*, 5/2/56.

126   Ibid.

127   'The Way Ahead', *Observer*, 12/2/56.

128   'Young Lions' Den', *Observer*, 18/3/56.

129   'The Gentle Art of Padding', *Observer*, 11/3/56.

130   16/3/56, Tynan archive, British Library.

131   'Vista and Vision', *Observer*, 1/4/56.

132   'The Gentle Art of Padding', *Observer*, 11/3/56.

133   In my account of the early genesis of the ESC, I am indebted to Irving Wardle's *The Theatres of George Devine* (London, Eyre Methuen, 1979), pp.161–74.

134   Philip Roberts, *The Royal Court Theatre and the Modern Stage* (Cambridge, Cambridge University Press, 1999), pp.8–9.

135   See Robert Hewison, *Culture and Consensus* (London, Methuen, 1995), pp.89–90.

136   A. Alvarez, *The New Poetry* (London, Penguin, 1962), p.21.

137   Ibid.

138   Ibid., p.25.

139   George Devine, letter to Tony Richardson, 14/4/54, quoted in Philip Roberts, 'George Devine, Tony Richardson and Stratford', *Studies in Theatre Production*, No. 12, Dec. 1995, p.126.

140   George Devine, 'Thoughts on the Construction of a New Theatre', 7/1/55, quoted in Roberts, 1999, p.24.

141   Wardle, 1979, p.169.

142   Ibid., p.170.

143   Ibid., p.171.

144   Analysis of the production costs by Gillespie Brothers and Co. (Accountants), 17/1/59, in 'Papers relating to H.M. Tennent', RP 95/2363, Theatre Museum, London.

145   4/4/56, quoted in Wardle, 1979, p.67.

146   21/4/56, ibid.

147   'Novelists and Greasepaint', *Observer*, 8/4/56.

148   15/4/56, quoted in Wardle, 1979, p.171.

149   'Glorious Sunset', *Observer*, 15/4/56.

150   Dundy, 2001, p.175.

151   Ibid.

152   Morgan, 2001, pp.146–7.

153   'Glorious Sunset', *Observer*, 15/4/56.

154   Bagnold to Tynan, 26/4/56, Tynan archive, British Library.

155   Anderson to Tynan, undated (April), ibid.

156   'Broadway Abundance', *Observer*, 22/4/56.

157   'Manhattan and the Musical', *Observer*, 29/4/56.

158   These putative titles all appear on the Autograph MS Notebook for *Look Back in Anger*, held at the Harry Ransome Humanities Research Center, Austin, Texas.

159   John Osborne, *A Better Class of Person* (London, Penguin, 1982), p.274.

160   Ibid.

161   'Carry On Up the Zeitgeist – *Look Back in Anger*', BBC Radio 4, 3/4/92.

162   Osborne, 1986, p.15.

163   Ibid., p.20.

164   Ibid., p.17.

165   Ibid., p.35.

166   Ibid., p.84.

167   'Carry On Up the Zeitgeist – *Look Back in Anger*', BBC Radio 4, 3/4/92.

168   Rattigan, quoted in Geoffrey Wansall, *Terence Rattigan* (London, Fourth Estate, 1995), p.270.

169   Rattigan to Devine, 9/5/56, in Roberts, 1999, p.48.

170   'A Study of an Exhibitionist', *Daily Telegraph*, 9/5/56.

171   'This Bitter Young Man – Like Thousands', *Daily Express*, 9/9/56.

172   'This Actor is a Great Writer', *Daily Mail*, 9/9/56.

173   'Mr Osborne Builds a Wailing Wall', *Evening Standard*, 9/9/56.

174   John Osborne, *Almost a Gentleman* (London, Faber and Faber, 1991), p.22.

175   Ibid., p.11.

176   Ibid., p.22.

177   'The Voice of the Young', *Observer*, 13/5/56.

178   'A Critic of the Critics', *Observer*, 24/6/56.

179   John Osborne, 'They Call it Cricket', in *Declaration*, ed. Tom Maschler (London, Macgibbon and Kee, 1959), p.74.

180   Stephen Lacey, *British Realist Theatre* (London, Routledge, 1995) p.21.

181   Osborne, 1991, p.23. Parts of this section on *Look Back in Anger* have appeared in Shellard, *British Theatre Since the War* (New Haven, Yale University Press, 1999), pp.51–7.

182   *Observer*, 6/5/56.

183   Tynan to David Astor, 16/1/56, *Letters*, 1994, pp.207–8.

184   Kathleen Tynan, 1988, pp.129–30.

185   20/5/76, Tynan, *Diaries*, 2001, p.328.

186   'The End of the Noose', *Observer*, 27/5/56.

187   'The Iceman Slippeth', *Observer*, 10/6/56.

188   'Hindsight View', *Observer*, 15/7/56.

Chapter 4: 1956–58: Writing for Posterity

1   Kathleen Tynan, 1988, p.130.

2   Dundy, 2001, p.177.

3   Ibid.

4   Kathleen Tynan, 1988, p.131.

5   Morgan, 2001, p.147.

6   Devine to Bentley, 17/8/56, in Roberts, 1999, p.52.

7   'Welsh Wizardry', *Observer*, 26/8/56.

8   'Braw and Brecht', *Observer*, 2/9/56.

9   Astor to Tynan, August 1956, Tynan archive, British Library.

10   William Gaskill, *A Sense of Direction* (London, Faber and Faber, 1988), p.43.

11   'Berlin Postscript', *Observer*, 7/10/56.

12   'Dramatic Capital of Europe', *Observer*, 30/9/56.

13   Tony Richardson, *Long Distance Runner: A Memoir* (London, Faber and Faber, 1993), p.83.

14   'The Good Woman of Sezuan', *Times*, 1/11/56.

15   'Simple and Complicated', *Observer*, 4/11/56.

16   'A Doubt about Brecht', *Sunday Times*, 2/9/56.

17   'Bertolt Brecht', *Sunday Times*, 4/11/56.

18   'Edinburgh and London', *Observer*, 9/9/56.

19   'Dodging the Ban', *Observer*, 16/9/56.

20   'The Tragic Sense', *Observer*, 14/10/56.

21   'The Dismal Dilemma', *Observer*, 23/9/56.

22   See Arthur Miller, *Timebends* (London, Methuen, 1988), pp.474–5.

23   Dundy, 2001, p.178.

24   Miller to Tynan, 17/9/56, Tynan archive, British Library.

25   Dundy, 2001, p.181.

26   'The Fallacy', *Observer*, 4/11/56.

27   Morgan, 2001, p.152.

28   'Patriotism', *Observer*, 11/11/56.

29   'A World Crisis', *Observer*, 11/11/56.

30 Clive Fisher, *Noël Coward* (London, Weidenfeld and Nicolson, 1992), p.221.
31 'The Rake's Regress', *Observer*, 11/11/56.
32 'A World of Artifice', *Observer*, 25/11/56.
33 'The Unforgotten', *Observer*, 2/12/56.
34 Quoted in Plowright, 2001, p.42.
35 'Past and Present', *Observer*, 16/12/56.
36 'Backwards and Forwards', *Observer*, 30/12/56.
37 Dundy, 2001, p.182.
38 Ibid., p.183.
39 'The Way Ahead', *Observer*, 13/2/57.
40 'In All Directions', *Observer*, 17/2/57.
41 'German Measles', *Observer*, 20/1/57.
42 Actor and dramatist. Born 1855, died 1934.
43 Poet and dramatist from the turn of the century. Born 1864, died 1915.
44 'A Matter of Life', *Observer*, 3/2/57.
45 'For Heaven's Sake', *Observer*, 24/2/57.
46 'Drama in Doubt', *Observer*, 31/3/57.
47 'Restraint Run Riot', *Observer*, 24/3/57.
48 Biographical details from New Globe website, www.shakespeares-globe.org
49 'Too Many Means', *Observer*, 17/3/57.
50 Wanamaker to Tynan, 12/3/57, Tynan archive, British Library.
51 Wanamaker to Tynan, 21/3/57, ibid.
52 'Home and Colonial', *Observer*, 17/3/57.
53 'A Philosophy of Despair', *Observer*, 7/4/57.
54 Olivier, quoted in Spoto, 1991, p.226.
55 Miller, 1988, p.227.
56 Olivier, quoted in Richard Findlater, *At the Royal Court* (London, Amber Lane Press, 1981), p.40.
57 John Osborne, *The Entertainer* (London, Faber and Faber, 1990), 'Number 7', p.59.
58 Ibid., 'Number 5', p.42.
59 'A Magnificent Week', *Sunday Times*, 14/4/57.
60 'A Whale of a Week', *Observer*, 14/4/57.
61 'Dandy with a Machine Gun', *Observer*, 15/9/57.
62 Roberts, 1999, p.62.
63 'Beyond the Outsider', in *Declaration*, p.41.
64 'Along the Tightrope', ibid., p.69.
65 Ibid., p.100.
66 'They Call It Cricket', ibid., pp.58–9.
67 'Message from Manhattan', *Observer*, 26/5/57.
68 'From O'Neill to Capp', *Observer*, 2/6/57.
69 Dundy, 2001, p.184.
70 Ibid., p.185.
71 Ibid., p.188
72 'Hall and Brook, Ltd.', *Observer*, 7/7/57.
73 Astor to Tynan, 24/8/57, *Letters*, 1994, p.211.
74 Tynan to Astor, 28/8/57, ibid.
75 'The Play Competition', *Observer*, 18/8/57.
76 Eric Salmon, *The Dark Journey: John Whiting as Dramatist* (London, Barrie and Jenkins, 1979), p.29.
77 'Out of Touch', *Observer*, 6/10/57.

78   'Debit Account', *Observer*, 13/10/57.

79   'Back to Reality', *Observer*, 24/11/57.

80   'A World Elsewhere', *Observer*, 3/11/57.

81   'Three for the Gods', *Observer*, 15/12/57.

82   'The Hard Way', *Observer*, 8/12/57.

83   'Closing the Gaps', *Observer*, 22/12/57.

84   Quayle to Tynan, 23/12/57, Tynan archive, British Library.

85   'France in Shadow', *Observer*, 5/1/58.

86   Kathleen Tynan, 1988, p.141.

87   Thorndike to Tynan, 9/1/58, Tynan archive, British Library.

88   Barr to Tynan, 18/10/57, ibid.

89   'Hazards of Playgoing', *Observer*, 19/1/59.

90   *Sunday Times*, 19/1/58.

91   Osborne to Tynan, 7/2/58, Tynan archive, British Library.

92   Dundy, 2001, p.194.

93   17/6/74, Tynan, *Diaries*, 2001, p.182.

94   *Daily Mail*, 3/1/02.

95   'The Heights & the Depths', *Observer*, 2/2/58.

96   'Whisky Galore', *Observer*, 9/2/58.

97   See Dundy, 2001, pp.197–204.

98   See 10/4/73, Tynan, *Diaries*, 2001, pp.133–4.

99   *Tribune*, March 1958.

100   'Good Sportsmanship', *Observer*, 2/3/58.

101   Roberts, 1999, p.63.

102   'The Court Revolution', *Observer*, 6/4/58.

103   'Collector's Item', *Observer*, 16/3/58.

104   Logue to Tynan, 3/4/80, Tynan archive, British Library.

105   Colin Wilson, *Autobiographical Reflections* (Nottingham, Paupers Press, 1988), p.26.

106   'The Tenth Chance', *Observer*, 23/3/58.

107   Wilson to Tynan, 15/4/58, Tynan archive, British Library.

108   'Musing Out Loud', *Observer*, 11/5/58.

109   Rattigan to Tynan, *c.* May 1958, Tynan archive, British Library.

110   'Eastern Approaches', *Observer*, 25/5/58.

111   'Larger than Life at the Festival', *Sunday Times*, 5/1/58.

112   'The Screw Turns Again', *Sunday Times*, 25/5/58.

113   Peter Wildeblood, *Against the Law* (London, Weidenfeld and Nicolson, 1999), p.55.

114   28/3/54.

115   10/4/54.

116   'Vice: The Storm Breaks', *Daily Express*, 5/9/57.

117   I am deeply indebted to the following website for the background material to the Wolfenden Report: www.sbu.ac.uk/stafflag/wolfenden.html

118   Lord Chamberlain's Papers, British Library.

119   'Lennie Laughton', *Observer*, 1/6/58.

120   'Ionesco: Man of Destiny?', *Observer*, 22/6/58.

121   'The Playwright's Role', *Observer*, 29/6/58.

122   'Ionesco and the Phantom', *Observer*, 6/7/58.

123   8/5/76, Tynan, *Diaries*, 2001, p.325.

124   'Fathers and Sons', *Observer*, 20/7/58.

125   'The Elder Staggers', *Observer*, 31/8/58.

126   Tynan to Astor, 11/9/58, *Letters*, 1994, p.219.

127 Kathleen Tynan, 1988, p.146.

128 20/1/75, Tynan, *Diaries*, 2001, pp.217–18.

129 *Christian Science Monitor*, 15/10/58.

130 'New Amalgam', *Observer*, 19/10/58.

Chapter 5: Dissent

1 Quoted in Eric Pace, 'Obituary: William Shawn', *New York Times*, 9/12/92.

2 Ibid.

3 Dundy, 2001, p.207.

4 Ibid., pp.208–9.

5 Ibid., p.211.

6 Ben Yagoda, *About Town – The New Yorker and the World it Made* (New York, Duckworth, 2000), p.310.

7 Kathleen Tynan, 1988, p.151.

8 Ibid., pp.150–1.

9 Dundy, 2001, p.206.

10 Ibid., p.151.

11 'The Troubles in the Studio', *New Yorker*, 6/12/58.

12 Ibid.

13 'Portrait of the Artist as a Young Camera', *New Yorker*, 20/12/58.

14 'Singles and Doubles', *New Yorker*, 10/1/59.

15 'New Vics for Old', *New Yorker*, 27/12/58.

16 'Portrait of the Artist as a Young Camera', *New Yorker*, 20/12/58.

17 'Tiny Chinese Minds', *New Yorker*, 13/12/58.

18 Dundy, 2001, p.209.

19 Kathleen Tynan, 1988, p.154.

20 Elaine Dundy, 'The Sound of a Marriage', *Queen*, 13/4/60.

21 Dundy, 2001, p.210.

22 'The Matriarchal Principle', *New Yorker*, 28/2/59.

23 'Kate the Curst', *New Yorker*, 7/3/59.

24 'Matters of Fact', *New Yorker*, 21/2/59

25 Ibid.

26 'The Bright Side of Homicide', *New Yorker*, 7/2/59.

27 'Ireland and Points West', *New Yorker*, 21/3/59.

28 11/3/59.

29 Astor to Tynan, 18/2/59, Tynan archive, British Library.

30 Astor to Tynan, 3/3/59, ibid.

31 Ronald Powaski, *The Cold War* (Oxford, Oxford University Press, 1998), pp.122–7.

32 'The Biggest Question', *New Yorker*, 4/4/59.

33 Dan Wakefield to Tynan, 6/4/59, Tynan archive, British Library.

34 Powaski, 1998, p.131.

35 The accidental meeting is described by Tynan in 'Papa and the Playwright', *Tynan Right and Left* (London, Longmans, Green, 1967), pp.331–6.

36 Tynan to Kilmartin, 11/4/59, *Letters*, 1994, pp.231–2.

37 Guinness, pp.203–4.

38 'Pomp v. Circumstance', *Observer*, 26/4/59.

39 Gene Brown, *Show Time* (New York, Macmillan, 1997), pp.158–9.

40 'Empty Saddles', *New Yorker*, 2/5/59.

41 'Cornucopia', *New Yorker*, 30/5/59.

42 Gerald Clarke, *Get Happy: The Life of Judy Garland* (London, Little, Brown, 2000), p.347.

43 'The Losing Generation', *New Yorker*, 23/5/59.

44 Dundy, 2001, p.246.

45 Kathleen Tynan, 1988, p.162.

46 'The Theatre Abroad: Germany', *New Yorker*, 12/9/59.

47 John Lennard and Mary Luckhurst, *The Drama Handbook* (Oxford, Oxford University Press, 2002), p.354.

48 Tynan to Elaine, 26/6/59, Tynan archive, British Library.

49 Ibid.

50 Dundy, 2001, p.246.

51 Ibid., pp.221–2

52 FBI file, 28/8/59, copy in Tynan archive, British Library.

53 'Mr Schary's Bomb', *New Yorker*, 14/11/59.

54 'Thunder on Pennsylvania Avenue', *New Yorker*, 10/10/59.

55 'Ireland Vanquished', *New Yorker*, 3/10/59.

56 'Nothing Doing', *New Yorker*, 26/9/59.

57 'Eros Misconstrued', *New Yorker*, 24/10/59.

58 'The Case for Trappism', *New Yorker*, 28/11/59.

59 'Look Behind the Anger', *Observer*, 27/12/59.

60 'Why Do We Get 90 Minutes of Doubt?', *Daily Express*, 28/1/60.

61 Tynan, *Tynan Right and Left*, 1967, p.414.

62 Tynan to Cousins, 3/2/50, *Letters*, 1994, p.250.

63 Cousins to Tynan, 5/2/60, Tynan archive, British Library.

64 1/2/60.

65 Tynan to Heller, 8/2/60, *Letters*, 1994, p.251.

66 Tynan to Heller, 15/2/60, ibid., pp.251–3.

67 'Beat Attitudes', *New Yorker*, 20/2/60.

68 'Nymphs and Shepherds, Go Away', *New Yorker*, 19/3/60.

69 *Harper's Magazine*, October 1960.

70 Transcript of the SISS 'Fair Play on Cuba Hearing', 5/5/60, a copy of which is in the Tynan archive, British Library.

71 'Ship me Nowheres East of Suez', *New Yorker*, 7/5/60.

72 Tynan to Kilmartin, 7/4/60, *Letters*, 1994, p.255.

Chapter 6: 'We know what they are *against* . . . but what are they *for*?'

1 Balance Sheet of *My Fair Lady* in H.M. Tennent archive, RP 95/2363, Theatre Museum, London.

2 J.H. Whitney to B. Beaumont, 16/12/58, ibid.

3 Tom Courtenay, *Dear Tom: Letters from Home* (London, Doubleday, 2001), p.335.

4 'A Verbal Wizard in the Suburbs', *Observer*, 5/6/60.

5 'Brecht at the Mermaid', *Observer*, 19/6/60.

6 'The Economics of Murder', *Observer*, 26/6/60.

7 Arnold Wesker, *Chicken Soup With Barley: The Wesker Trilogy* (London, Methuen, 2001), p.79.

8 Roberts, 1999, p.59.

9 Ibid., Introduction, p.xxiii.

10 Arnold Wesker, *Roots: The Wesker Trilogy* (London, Methuen, 2001), p.150.

11 Ibid., p.151.

12 Ibid., pp.156–7.

13　Ibid., Introduction, p.xxii.

14　'The Drama as History', *Observer*, 12/6/60.

15　Ibid.

16　Arnold Wesker, *I'm Talking About Jerusalem: The Wesker Trilogy* (London, Methuen, 2001), pp.228–9.

17　'Finale without Finality', *Observer*, 31/7/60.

18　'What the Crystal Ball Foretells, *Observer*, 24/7/60.

19　Dundy, 2001, p.247.

20　Ibid.

21　'Three for the Seesaw', *Observer*, 18/9/60.

22　Morley, 2001, p.304.

23　Anne Sebba, *Enid Bagnold* (London, Weidenfeld and Nicolson, 1988), p.211.

24　'Madness in Great Ones', *Observer*, 2/10/60.

25　Fisher, 1992, p.231.

26　Ibid., p.230.

27　Ibid., pp.233–5.

28　'Let Coward Flinch', *Observer*, 22/1/61.

29　'The Unravelling of Ross', *Observer*, 5/2/61.

30　'The Straight Answer', *Observer*, 9/10/60.

31　H. Montgomery Hyde, *The Lady Chatterley's Lover Trial* (London, Bodley Head, 1990), p.22.

32　*Observer*, 6/11/60.

33　Tynan to Shawn, 8/1/61, *Letters*, 1994, pp.258–9.

34　'The Camp Followers', *Observer*, 9/4/61.

35　'Dead Spot in Drama', *Observer*, 23/10/60.

36　Humphrey Carpenter, *That Was Satire That Was* (London, Victor Gollancz, 2000), p.119.

37　'English Satire Advances into the Sixties', *Observer*, 14/5/61.

38　Roberts, 1999, p.86.

39　'The Genealogy of Arnold Wesker', *Observer*, 2/7/61.

40　'Rebel Writer on a Rebel Priest', *Observer*, 9/7/61.

41　Tesler to Tynan, 18/4/62, Tynan archive, British Library.

42　'The Breakthrough That Broke Down', *Observer*, 1/10/61.

43　'Letters', *Observer*, 8/10/61.

44　*Observer*, 17/12/61.

45　'A Critic's Performance', *New York Times*, 7/12/61.

46　'Above the Crowd', *Observer*, 10/5/59.

47　'Curtains for Tynan', *Observer*, 22/10/61.

48　Dundy, 2001, p.252.

49　'Contrary Mary', *Observer*, 22/10/61.

50　'Adverse Review of Tynan's Book by Mary McCarthy Creates Literary Tempest', *New York Times*, 27/10/61.

51　*Encore*, November/December 1959.

52　Dundy, 2001, p.254.

53　Ibid., p.258.

54　Ibid., p.261.

55　*Observer*, 21/1/62.

56　'Mortal Fools Without a Lord', *Observer*, 3/6/62.

57　John Dexter, *The Honourable Beast* (London, Nick Hern Books, 1993), p.13.

58　'The Chip and the Shoulder', *Observer*, 6/5/62.

59 'Dusting off the Minor Jacobeans', *Observer*, 20/5/62.

60 'Open Letter to an Open Stager', *Observer*, 15/7/62.

61 Wolfit to Tynan, 30/7/62, Tynan archive, British Library.

62 'In Defence of the Unmentionable', *Observer*, 22/7/62.

63 Dundy, 2001, p.263.

64 Ibid., p.265.

65 Ibid., p.268.

66 Plowright, 2001, p.97.

67 Peter Lewis, *The National: A Dream Made Concrete* (London, Methuen, 1990), p.4.

68 Olivier to Tynan, 21/8/62, Tynan archive, British Library.

69 Olivier to Tynan, 31/1/62, ibid.

70 Memo to the Editor from Richard Findlater, 23/2/63, *Observer* archive, University of Sheffield.

71 Memo to the Editor from Richard Findlater, 13/3/63, ibid.

72 Tynan, *Tynan Right and Left*, p.146.

73 Ibid., pp.146–7.

74 Kathleen Tynan, 1988, p.205.

75 'Gang War in Armour', *Observer*, 21/7/63.

76 See Sally Beauman, *The Royal Shakespeare Company* (Oxford, Oxford University Press, 1982), p.271.

Chapter 7: Upsetting the Establishment

1 Peter Hall, *Making an Exhibition of Myself* (London, Sinclair-Stevenson, 1993), p.167.

2 See David Addenbrooke, *The Royal Shakespeare Company: The Peter Hall Years* (London, William Kimber, 1974), p.231.

3 See Stephen Fay, *Power Play: The Life and Times of Peter Hall* (London, Hodder and Stoughton, 1995), p.129.

4 Ibid., p.133.

5 Ibid., p.135.

6 Ibid, p.129.

7 Hall, 1993, p.174.

8 Fay, 1995, p.155.

9 Ibid., p.156.

10 Hall, 1993, p.176.

11 Ibid., p.177.

12 'Danger Threatens the Theatre', *Sunday Times*, 6/7/58.

13 See Lewis, 1990, p.7.

14 Tynan memo to Olivier, 21/5/63, Tynan archive, British Library.

15 George Rowell, *The Old Vic Theatre* (Cambridge, Cambridge University Press, 1993), p.152.

16 Osborne to Tynan, 4/11/63, Tynan archive, British Library.

17 Olivier, quoted in Lewis, 1990, p.8.

18 Robert Stephens, *Knight Errant* (London, Hodder and Stoughton, 1995), pp.27–8.

19 'The Peerless Uncle Vanya', *Sunday Times*, 3/11/63.

20 Quoted in Goodwin, 1988, p.5.

21 Gaskill, 1988, p.55.

22 Quoted in Goodwin, 1988, p.31.

23 'Farquhar for All Souls', *Sunday Times*, 15/12/63.

24 See Stephens, 1995, p.70.

25 For example, see his detailed memo to William Gaskill about Keith Johnstone's adaptation of Sophocles' *Philoctetes*, January 1964, Tynan archive, British Library.

26 Tynan to Graves, 25/8/64, Tynan archive, British Library.

27 Tynan in Godfrey Smith, 'Critic Kenneth Tynan Has Mellowed But Is Still England's Stingingest Gadfly', *New York Times*, 15/12/65.

28 Tynan to Devine, 31/3/64, Tynan archive, British Library.

29 Stephens, 1995, p.65.

30 Devine to Tynan, 9/4/64, Tynan archive, British Library.

31 Tynan to Devine, 10/4/64, ibid.

32 Olivier to Devine, 12/4/64, ibid.

33 Spoto, 1991, p.283.

34 Goodwin, 1988, p.32.

35 Ibid., p.26.

36 Quoted in Lewis, 1990, p.17.

37 Spoto, 1991, p.289

38 Tynan to Graves, 30/9/64, Tynan archive, British Library.

39 *Letters*, 1994, pp.306–8.

40 Others included the casting of Colin Blakely in *Philoctetes* and Maggie Smith in *The Master Builder*; and the direction and casting of *Andorra* and *The Dutch Courtesan*.

41 'National Theatre Memorandum', 22/10/64, Tynan archive, British Library.

42 Dundy, 2001, pp.307–13.

43 Tynan to Jean Halton, *Letters*, 1994, p.302.

44 Quoted in Huggett, 1989, p.339.

45 See Lewis, 1990, p.20.

46 Levin, quoted in Goodwin, 1988, p.33.

47 Kretzmer, quoted ibid., p.35.

48 Stephens, 1995, p.74.

49 Tynan to Lord Cobbold, 29/10/64, Tynan archive, British Library.

50 Lord Chamberlain's Correspondence, 21/5/63, British Library.

51 *Evening News*, 24/8/64.

52 Tynan to Dexter, ?11/11/64, Tynan archive, British Library.

53 Lord Chamberlain, 5/5/65, ibid.

54 He also responded to correspondence about the programmes. On 10 March 1965 he sent a memo to George Rowbottom, the general manager of the NT, stating that George Devine had protested about an ad from the South African government in the programme for *Othello*. Tynan enquired whether it might be 'discreetly discontinued when the contract expires – if necessary on the simple and accurate grounds that it is giving offence to some of our customers.'

55 Tynan to Olivier and others, 1/12/64, Tynan archive, British Library.

56 'It's Great after the Fiesta', *Sunday Times*, 21/2/65.

57 National Theatre, Board Minutes, 18/4/72, National Theatre archive, National Theatre, London.

58 Lee to Tynan, 15/11/65, Tynan archive, British Library.

59 Bruno Vogel to Tynan, 16/11/65, ibid.

61 15/11/65, ibid.

62 16/11/65, ibid.

63 Undated, ibid.

64 Kathleen Tynan, 1988, p.270.

65 Tynan to Shawn, 10/11/65, Tynan archive, British Library.

66 'Passion and Exaltation', *Sunday Times*, 10/6/66.

67 Tynan, *Diaries*, 2001, 7/3/75, p.230.

68 John Johnston, *The Lord Chamberlain's Blue Pencil* (London, Hodder and Stoughton, 1990), p.184.

69 Quoted in Fay, 1995, p.186.

70 Tynan to Burke, 6/7/66, *Letters*, 1994, p.360.

71 Tynan to Macdonald, 2/11/66, ibid., p.366.

72 Tynan to Olivier, 9/11/66, Tynan archive, British Library.

73 Tynan to Olivier, 23/12/66, ibid.

74 Tynan to Olivier, 3/1/67, Tynan archive, British Library.

75 Tynan to National Theatre Board, 7/1/67, ibid.

76 National Theatre, Board Minutes, 9/1/67, National Theatre archive, National Theatre, London.

77 Tynan to Chandos, 13/1/67, Tynan archive, British Library.

78 Tynan to Chandos, 23/1/67, ibid.

79 Lewis, 1990, p.26.

80 'Three Aspects of the Hochhuth Situation', March 1967, Tynan archive, British Library.

81 Tynan to Assistant Comptroller, 10/4/67, ibid.

82 Tynan to Shawn, 14/4/67, ibid.

83 *Sunday Times*, 30/4/67.

84 Tynan, letter to the *Sunday Times*, 7/5/67.

85 Michael White, *Empty Seats* (London, Hamish Hamilton, 1984), p.88.

86 See Dominic Shellard, *Harold Hobson: Witness and Judge* (Keele, Keele University Press, 1995), p.196.

87 Kenneth Tynan, *A View of the English Stage, 1944–65*, (London, Methuen, 1984), pp.366–7.

88 'The Censorship', *Sunday Times*, 11/4/65.

89 Reader's Report for *A Patriot for Me*, 30/8/64, Lord Chamberlain's Papers, British Library.

90 See Wardle, 1979, p.275.

91 Correspondence on *A Patriot for Me*, Lord Chamberlain's Papers, British Library.

92 See Philip Roberts, *The Royal Court Theatre 1965–72* (London, Routledge, 1986), p.16.

93 Ibid., p.17.

94 Reader's Report on *Saved*, 30/6/65, Lord Chamberlain's Papers, British Library.

95 Wardle, 'Saved', *The Times*, 4/11/65.

96 Roberts, 1986, p.24.

97 Gaskill, 1988, p.69.

98 White, 1984, pp.112–13.

99 'Whose Crime?', *Sunday Times*, 15/12/68.

100 White, 1984, p.113.

101 Ibid., p.110.

102 Tynan to Stoppard, 1/4/69, *Letters*, 1994, pp.439–40.

Chapter 8: Private Demons – Centre Stage

1 White, 1984, p.107.

2 'Tynan Right and Wrong', *New York Times*, 10/12/67.

3 'Shouts and Murmurs', *Observer*, 19/5/68.

4 'Shouts and Murmurs', *Observer*, 28/1/68.

5 'Shouts and Murmurs', *Observer*, 7/4/68.

6 *Playboy*, March 1968.
7 *Guardian*, 8/12/2001.
8 'Randy, Spankable', *Guardian*, 27/10/2001.
9 'All Passion Spent', *Observer*, 7/10/2001.
10 The Astors owned the *Observer*.
11 Tynan, *Diaries*, 2001, 22/3/71, p.36.
12 Lewis, 1990, p.40.
13 Tynan to Olivier, ?August 1968, Tynan archive, British Library.
14 Tynan to Olivier, 13/11/68, ibid.
15 Tynan to Chandos, 24/10/68, ibid.
16 Tynan to Chandos, 28/5/69, ibid.
17 Tynan to Mortimer, 28/5/69, ibid.
18 Chandos to Tynan, 10/6/69, ibid.
19 Tynan to Chandos, 18/6/69, ibid.
20 '*Oh, Calcutta!* a Most Innocent Dirty Show', *New York Times*, 18/6/69.
21 White, 1984, p.132.
22 Tynan to Olivier, 1/10/73, Tynan archive, British Library.
23 Tynan to Donaldson, 28/6/66, ibid.
24 Tynan to Elkins, ?14/5/69, ibid.
25 Tynan to Elkins, 20/5/69, ibid.
26 *Oh, Calcutta!* (New York, The Grove Press, 1969), p.107.
27 Ibid., p.125.
28 White, 1984, p.129.
29 'How Two Dames Saved Oh, Calcutta!', *Guardian*, 23/12/2000.
30 Ibid., p.132.
31 Tynan, *Diaries*, 2001, 4/4/71, p.37.
32 Olivier to Tynan, 13/10/69, Tynan archive, British Library.
33 Tynan to Olivier, 21/10/69, ibid.
34 Olivier to Tynan, 24/2/70, ibid.
35 Olivier to Tynan, 10/3/70, ibid.
36 Tynan to Olivier, 12/6/70, ibid.
37 Lewis, 1990, p.40.
38 Tynan, *Diaries*, 2001, 24/1/71, p.23.
39 Ibid., 5/2/71, p.26.
40 Ibid., 13/3/71, p.34.
41 Ibid., 20/1/71, p.21.
42 'I Don't Wish to Know That', *Daily Mail*, 4/9/71.
43 Tynan, *Diaries*, 2001, 20/3/71, p.35.
44 Ibid., 3/5/71, p.45.
45 Ibid.,13/7/71, p.55.
46 Dexter, 1993, p.31.
47 Tynan, *Diaries*, 2001, 25/7/71, p.56.
48 '*Long Day's Journey Into Night*', *Guardian*, 1/9/72.
49 Tynan to Olivier, 9/12/71, Tynan archive, British Library.
50 Tynan to Olivier, 9/3/72, ibid.
51 Olivier to Tynan, 10/3/72, ibid.
52 Tynan, *Diaries*, 2001, 10/4/72, p.88.
53 Ibid., 14/4/72, p.89.
54 Ibid., 11/4/72, p.88.

55   Ibid., 12/4/72, p.90.

56   Ibid., 21/4/72, p.93.

57   Ibid., 12/4/72, p.90.

58   Ibid., 11/4/72, p.88.

59   Kathleen Tynan, 1988, p.314.

60   National Theatre, Board Minutes, 18/4/72, National Theatre archive, National Theatre, London.

61   Tynan, *Diaries*, 2001, 20/4/72, p.92.

62   Tynan to Hall, 20/4/72, Tynan archive, British Library.

63   Tynan, *Diaries*, 2001, 8/7/72, p.99.

64   Ibid., 5/7/72, p.98.

65   Tynan to Simon Michael Bessie, 4/5/72, Tynan archive, British Library.

66   Tynan, *Diaries*, 2001, 5/7/72, p.99.

67   Ibid., 12/5/72, p.84.

68   Ibid., 30/6/72, p.97.

69   Ibid., 1/10/72, p.102.

70   Ibid., 17/9/76, p.341.

71   Ibid., 20/2/73, p.121.

72   Ibid., 20/6/73, p.142.

73   Ibid., 8/12/72, p.113.

74   Ibid., 19/10/72, p.105.

75   Ibid., 18/2/73, p.120.

76   Ibid., 11/9/73, p.158.

77   Ibid., 5/4/73, p.131.

78   Peter Hall, *Peter Hall's Diaries*, ed. John Goodwin (London, Hamish Hamilton, 1983), p.11.

79   Tynan to Olivier, 1/10/73, Tynan archive, British Library.

80   Tynan, *Diaries*, 2001, 21/12/73, p.165.

81   Ibid., 21/12/73, p.166.

82   Tynan to Olivier, 5/2/74, Tynan archive, British Library.

83   Tynan, *Diaries*, 2001, 2/5/74, p.178.

84   Ibid., 17/9/74, p.191.

85   Ibid.

86   Tynan, *Diaries*, 2001, 12/8/75, p.267.

87   Ibid., 4/8/76, pp.336–7.

88   Ibid., 25/10/76, pp.343–4.

89   Ibid., 28/4/74, p.175.

90   Ibid., 7/5/74, p.177.

91   Ibid., 6/12/74, p.208.

92   Kenneth Tynan, *The Sound of Two Hands Clapping* (London, Jonathan Cape, 1975), p.191.

93   Jack Richardson, 'The Sound of Two Hands Clapping', *New York Times*, 11/4/76.

94   Tynan, *Diaries*, 2001, 29/1/75, p.223.

95   Ibid., 13/8/71, p.59.

96   John Osborne, 'The National', *Evening Standard*, 17/7/71.

97   Tynan, *Diaries*, 2001, 13/8/75, p.261.

98   Ibid., 19/10/75, p.283.

99   'Brecht Would Not Applaud His Theater Today', *New York Times*, 11/1/76.

100 Tynan, *Diaries*, 2001, 11/10/75, p.281.

101 Ibid., 31/12/75, p.292.

102   Tynan to Shawn, 2/12/75, Tynan archive, British Library.

103   Tynan to Shawn, 19/1/76, ibid.

104   Tynan, *Diaries*, 2001, 14/3/76, p.308.

105   Ibid., 14/6/73, pp.332–3.

106   Ibid., 3/4/76, p.311.

107   'The Pornography of Hatred', *Times*, 30/1/76.

108   Tynan, *Diaries*, 2001, 10/2/76, pp.301–2.

109   *Times*, 18/5/76.

110   Tynan to Clifford Williams and Hillard Elkins, January 1976, Tynan archive, British Library.

111   Tynan, *Diaries*, 2001, 10/2/76, p.302.

112   Ibid., 8/5/76, p.325.

113   Ibid., 4/7/76, p.314.

114   Ibid., 25/8/76, p.339.

115   Ibid., 25/8/76, p.338.

116   Ibid., 13/9/76, p.341.

117   'No, Madam, I Was Just Bored', *Daily Mail*, 1/10/76.

118   'Tynan Shrugs Off the Critics', *Daily Mail*, 1/10/76.

119   Tynan, *Diaries*, 2001, 7/10/76, p.341.

120   Ibid., 4/11/76, p.351.

121   Ibid., 28/12/76, p.360.

122   Kenneth Tynan, *Show People* (New York, Simon and Schuster, 1979), p.8.

123   Ibid., p.10.

124   Ibid., p.11.

125   Ibid., p.16.

126   Ibid., p.18.

127   Tynan, *Diaries*, 2001, 28/1/77, p.366.

128   Tynan to Shawn, 23/2/77, *Letters*, 1994, p.588.

129   Tynan, *Diaries*, 2001, 20/6/77, p.384.

130   Ibid., 30/5/77, p.379.

131   Email to author, 19/11/02.

132   Tynan, *Diaries*, 2001, 27/8/77, p.393.

133   Ibid., 22/5/77, p.378.

134   E.g. ibid., p.378.

135   Ibid., 18/7/77 and 21/7/77 respectively.

136   Ibid., 1/8/77, p.390.

137   Ibid., 13/8/77, p.392.

138   *Letters*, 1994, p.582.

139   Tynan, *Diaries*, 2001, 4/7/77, p.385.

140   Tynan, *Show People*, 1979, p.47.

141   Ibid., p.52.

142   Ibid., p.76.

143   Tynan, *Diaries*, 2001, 14/12/77, p.396.

144   Ibid., 18/3/78, p.404.

145   Tynan, *Show People*, 1979, p.297.

146   Tynan, *Diaries*, 2001, May–September 1978, pp.406–9.

147   Ibid., 1/10/78, p.411.

148   Tynan to Olivier, 2/4/79, Tynan archive, British Library.

149   Tynan to Olivier, draft, 15/6/79, ibid.

150   Tynan, *Diaries*, 2001, 11/1/80, p.419.

151   Christopher Lehmann-Haupt, 'Show People: Profiles in Entertainment', *New York Times*, 22/1/80.

152   Tynan to Elsie Giorgi, ?April 1980, Tynan archive, British Library.

153   Tynan to Dundy, 20/5/80, ibid.

154   Tynan to Hobson, ?May 1980, ibid.

155   Tynan to Shawn, 20/5/80, ibid.

Select Bibliography

Books

David Addenbrooke, *The Royal Shakespeare Company: The Peter Hall Years* (London, William Kimber, 1974)

James Agate, *The Contemporary Theatre, 1944 and 1945* (London, Harrap, 1946)

James Agate, *Ego 8* (London, Harrap, 1946)

James Agate, *Ego 9* (London, Harrap, 1948)

A. Alvarez, *The New Poetry* (London, Penguin, 1962)

Sally Beauman, *The Royal Shakespeare Company* (Oxford, Oxford University Press, 1982)

Deirdre Behr, *Samuel Beckett: A Biography* (London, Jonathan Cape, 1990)

Michael Billington, *One Night Stands* (London, Nick Hern Books, 1993)

Kitty Black, *Upper Circle* (London, Methuen, 1984)

George Brandt, *British Television Drama* (Cambridge, Cambridge University Press, 1981)

Gene Brown, *Show Time* (New York, Macmillan, 1997)

R.A. Butler, *The Art of the Possible* (London, Penguin, 1971)

Simon Callow, *The National: The Theatre and its Work 1963–1997* (London, Nick Hern Books, 1997)

Humphrey Carpenter, *That Was Satire That Was* (London, Victor Gollancz, 2000)

Peter Clark, *Sixteen Million Readers: Evening Newspapers in the UK* (London, Holt, Rinehart and Winston, 1981)

Gerald Clarke, *Get Happy: The Life of Judy Garland* (London, Little, Brown, 2000)

Peter Clarke, *Hope and Glory* (London, Penguin, 1999)

Harold Clurman, *All People Are Famous* (New York, Harcourt, Brace, Jovanovich, 1974)

Tom Courtenay, *Dear Tom: Letters from Home* (London, Doubleday, 2001)

Michael Darlow, *Terence Rattigan* (London, Quartet Books, 2000)

Peter Daubeny, *My World of Theatre* (London, Jonathan Cape, 1971)

Declaration, edited by Tom Maschler (London, Macgibbon and Kee, 1959)

Nicholas De Jongh, *Not in Front of the Audience* (London, Routledge, 1992)

John Dexter, *The Honourable Beast* (London, Nick Hern Books, 1993)

Charles Duff, *The Lost Summer – The Heyday of the West End Theatre* (London, Nick Hern Books, 1995)

Elaine Dundy, *Life Itself!* (London, Virago Press, 2001)

Stephen Fay, *Power Play: The Life and Times of Peter Hall* (London, Hodder and Stoughton, 1995)

Martin Esslin, *The Theatre of the Absurd* (1962; 3rd edition, Harmondsworth, Penguin, 1982)

Richard Findlater, *At the Royal Court* (London, Amber Lane Press, 1981)

Richard Findlater, *Banned* (London, Panther, 1967)

Clive Fisher, *Noël Coward* (London, Weidenfeld and Nicolson, 1992)

Christopher Fry, *An Experience of Critics* (London, Perpetua, 1952)

William Gaskill, *A Sense of Direction* (London, Faber and Faber, 1988)

Tim Goodwin, *Britain's Royal National Theatre* (London, NT/Nick Hern Books, 1988)

Howard Goorney, *The Theatre Workshop Story* (London, Methuen, 1981)

Alec Guinness, *Blessings in Disguise* (London, Penguin, 1996)

Peter Hall, *Making an Exhibition of Myself* (London, Sinclair-Stevenson, 1993)

Peter Hall, *Peter Hall's Diaries*, edited by John Goodwin (London, Hamish Hamilton, 1983)

Hansard (London, HMSO, 1949)

James Harding, *Agate* (London, Methuen, 1986)

Ronald Harwood, *Sir Donald Wolfit CBE* (London, Secker and Warburg, 1971)

Ronald Hayman, *Tennessee Williams* (New Haven, Yale University Press, 1993)

A.P. Herbert, *No Fine on Fun* (London, Arts Council, 1957)

Robert Hewison, *Culture and Consensus* (London, Methuen, 1995)

Harold Hobson, *Indirect Journey* (London, Weidenfeld and Nicolson, 1978)

Harold Hobson, *Theatre in Britain* (Oxford, Oxford University Press, 1984)

Harold Hobson, Philip Knightley and Leonard Russell, *The Pearl of Days* (London, Hamish Hamilton, 1972)

Richard Huggett, *Binkie Beaumont: Éminence Grise of the West End 1933–1973* (London, Hodder and Stoughton, 1989)

Roy Jenkins, *Churchill* (London, Macmillan, 2001)

John Johnston, *The Lord Chamberlain's Blue Pencil* (London, Hodder and Stoughton, 1990)

Jan Kott, *Shakespeare Our Contemporary* (London, Routledge, 1990)

Stephen Lacey, *British Realist Theatre* (London, Routledge, 1995)

John Lennard and Mary Luckhurst, *The Drama Handbook* (Oxford, Oxford University Press, 2002)

Peter Lewis, *The Fifties* (London, Cupid Press, 1989)

Peter Lewis, *The National: A Dream Made Concrete* (London, Methuen, 1990)

Joan Littlewood, *Joan's Book* (London, Methuen, 1990)

Arthur Miller, *Timebends* (London, Methuen, 1988)

H. Montgomery Hyde, *The Lady Chatterley's Lover Trial* (London, Bodley Head, 1990)

Lord Moran, *Winston Churchill: The Struggle for Survival: 1945–60* (London, Constable, 1966)

Kenneth O. Morgan, *Britain since 1945* (Oxford, Oxford University Press, 2001)

Sheridan Morley, *John G* (London, Hodder and Stoughton, 2001)

Gary O'Connor, *Ralph Richardson* (London, Hodder and Stoughton, 1982)

Oh, Calcutta! (New York, Grove Press, 1969)

John Osborne, *Almost a Gentleman* (London, Faber and Faber, 1991)

John Osborne, *A Better Class of Person* (London, Penguin, 1982)

John Osborne, *The Entertainer* (London, Faber and Faber, 1990)

John Osborne, *Look Back in Anger* (London, Faber and Faber, 1986)

Ben Pimlott, *The Queen* (London, HarperCollins, 1996)

Joan Plowright, *And That's Not All* (London, Weidenfeld and Nicolson, 2001)

Ronald Powaski, *The Cold War* (Oxford, Oxford University Press, 1998)

Anthony Quayle, *A Time to Speak* (London, Barrie and Jenkins, 1990)

Tony Richardson, *Long Distance Runner: A Memoir* (London, Faber and Faber, 1993)

Philip Roberts, *The Royal Court Theatre 1965–72* (London, Routledge, 1986)

Philip Roberts, *The Royal Court Theatre and the Modern Stage* (Cambridge, Cambridge University Press, 1999)

George Rowell, *The Old Vic Theatre* (Cambridge, Cambridge University Press, 1993)

George Rowell and Anthony Jackson, *The Repertory Movement: A History of Regional Theatre in Britain* (Cambridge, Cambridge University Press, 1984)

John Russell Taylor, *Anger and After* (London, Eyre Methuen, 1969)

Eric Salmon, *The Dark Journey: John Whiting as Dramatist* (London, Barrie and Jenkins, 1979)

Michael Sanderson, *From Irving to Olivier* (London, The Athlone Press, 1985)

Anne Sebba, *Enid Bagnold* (London, Weidenfeld and Nicolson, 1988)

Dominic Shellard, *British Theatre in the 1950s* (Sheffield, Sheffield Academic Press, 2000)

Dominic Shellard, *British Theatre since the War* (New Haven, Yale University Press, 2000)

Dominic Shellard, *Harold Hobson: The Complete Catalogue* (Keele, Keele University Press, 1995)

Dominic Shellard, *Harold Hobson: Witness and Judge* (Keele, Keele University Press, 1995)

Dominic Shellard, *The Lord Chamberlain Regrets . . .* (London, British Library Publications, 2004)

Evelyn Shuckburgh, *Descent to Suez: Diaries 1951–6* (London, Weidenfeld and Nicolson, 1986)

Donald Spoto, *Laurence Olivier* (London, HarperCollins, 1991)

Robert Stephens, *Knight Errant* (London, Hodder and Stoughton, 1995)

David Thomson, *Rosebud: The Story of Orson Welles* (London, Little, Brown, 1996)

Wendy and J.C. Trewin, *The Arts Theatre London: 1927–1981* (London, Society for Theatre Research, 1986)

Simon Trussler, *The Cambridge Illustrated History of British Theatre* (Cambridge, Cambridge University Press, 1994)

Kathleen Tynan, *The Life of Kenneth Tynan* (London, Methuen, 1988)

Kenneth Tynan, *Alec Guinness* (London, Rockliff, 1953)

Kenneth Tynan, *Bull Fever* (London, Longmans, 1955)

Kenneth Tynan, *He That Plays the King* (London, Longmans, 1950)

Kenneth Tynan: Diaries, ed. John Lahr (London, Bloomsbury, 2001)

Kenneth Tynan: Letters, ed. Kathleen Tynan (London, Weidenfeld and Nicolson, 1994)

Kenneth Tynan, *Persona Grata* (London, Alan Wingate, 1953)

Kenneth Tynan, *Show People* (New York, Simon and Schuster, 1979)

Kenneth Tynan, *The Sound of Two Hands Clapping* (London, Jonathan Cape, 1975)

Kenneth Tynan, *Tynan Right and Left* (London, Longmans, Green, 1967)

Kenneth Tynan, *A View of the English Stage, 1944–63* (London, Methuen, 1984)

Geoffrey Wansell, *Terence Rattigan* (London, Fourth Estate, 1995)

Irving Wardle, *Theatre Criticism* (London, Routledge, 1992)

Irving Wardle, *The Theatres of George Devine* (London, Eyre Methuen, 1979)

Arnold Wesker, *Chicken Soup With Barley: The Wesker Trilogy* (London, Methuen, 2001)

Arnold Wesker, *I'm Talking About Jerusalem: The Wesker Trilogy* (London, Methuen, 2001)

Arnold Wesker, *Roots: The Wesker Trilogy* (London, Methuen, 2001)

Michael White, *Empty Seats* (London, Hamish Hamilton, 1984)

Peter Wildeblood, *Against the Law* (London, Weidenfeld and Nicolson, 1999)

Colin Wilson, *Autobiographical Reflections* (Nottingham, Paupers Press, 1988)

Ben Yagoda, *About Town – The New Yorker and the World it Made* (New York, Duckworth, 2000)

Archives

The Lord Chamberlain's Papers, British Library, London

The Kenneth Tynan, Laurence Olivier, Peggy Ramsay, Harold Pinter and Ralph Richardson archives, British Library, London

National Theatre archive, National Theatre, London
The *Observer* archive, Farringdon Road, London
John Osborne archive, Harry Ransome Humanities Research Center, Austin, Texas
The Royal Court archives, The Theatre Museum, London

Index

Plays appear under authors' names, with cross-references from titles where helpful